COLLECTED PAPERS ON JAINA STUDIES

Other Publications by Padmanabh S. Jaini

1. *Silonmāṃ be Varsh,* Gujarat Vidyasabha, Ahmedabad, 1952 (in Gujarati).
2. *Abhidharmadīpa with Vibhāṣāprabhā-vṛtti,* K. P. Jayaswal Research Institute, Patna, 1959; reprinted 1977.
3. *Milinda-ṭīkā,* Pali Text Society, London, 1961.
4. *Laghutattvasphoṭa* by Amṛtacandra, Sanskrit text with English translation, L. D. Institute of Indology Series, No. 62, Ahmedabad, 1978.
5. *Sāratamā: A Pañjikā on the Aṣṭasāhasrikā-Prajñāpāramitā* by Ratnākaraśānti, K. P. Jayaswal Research Institute, Patna, 1979.
6. *The Jaina Path of Purification,* University of California Press, Berkeley, 1979. Reprinted by Motilal Banarsidass, Delhi, 1997.
7. *Paññāsa-Jātaka or Zimme Paṇṇāsa* (in Burmese Recension), vol. I (Jātakas 1-25), Pali Text Society, London, 1981.
8. *Jaina Sampradāya men Mokṣa, Avatāra aur Punarjanma,* B. J. Institute of Learning and Research, Ahmedabad, 1982 (in Hindi).
9. *Paññāsa-Jātaka or Zimme Paṇṇāsa* (in Burmese Recension), vol. II (Jātakas 30-50), Pali Text Society, London, 1983.
10. *Apocryphal Birth-Stories* (translation of the *Paññāsa-Jātaka*), vol. I (with I. B. Horner), Pali Text Society, London, 1985.
11. *Apocryphal Birth-Stories* (translation of the *Paññāsa-Jātaka*), vol. II, Pali Text Society, London, 1986.
12. *Lokaneyyappakaraṇaṃ,* Pali Text Society, London, 1986.
13. *Gender and Salvation: Jaina Debates on the Spiritual Liberation of Women,* University of California Press, Berkeley, 1991.

Collected Papers on Jaina Studies

Edited by
PADMANABH S. JAINI

With a Foreword by
PAUL DUNDAS

MOTILAL BANARSIDASS PUBLISHERS
PRIVATE LIMITED • DELHI

First Edition: Delhi, 2000

ISBN: 81-208-1691-9

Also available at:

MOTILAL BANARSIDASS

236, 9th Main III Block, Jayanagar, Bangalore 560 011
41 U.A. Bungalow Road, Jawahar Nagar, Delhi 110 007
8 Mahalaxmi Chamber, Warden Road, Mumbai 400 026
120 Royapettah High Road, Mylapore, Chennai 600 004
Sanas Plaza, 1302 Baji Rao Road, Pune 411 002
8 Camac Street, Calcutta 700 017
Ashok Rajpath, Patna 800 004
Chowk, Varanasi 221 001

Printed in India

BY JAINENDRA PRAKASH JAIN AT SHRI JAINENDRA PRESS,
A-45 NARAINA, PHASE-I, NEW DELHI 110 028
AND PUBLISHED BY NARENDRA PRAKASH JAIN FOR
MOTILAL BANARSIDASS PUBLISHERS PRIVATE LIMITED,
BUNGALOW ROAD, DELHI 110 007

Foreword

P. S. Jaini's career represents a fascinating scholarly journey. In introducing his *Collected Papers on Jaina Studies* to the interested academic and lay world, some words about his intellectual background might be felt to be of some value.*

Padmanabh Shrivarma Jaini was born into a devout Digambara Jain family residing in Nellikar, a small town near the famous Jain centre at Moodbidre in Tulunadu, that magical and culturally distinctive area in the southwest of the state of Karnataka. In similar manner to many Jains at the beginning of this century who were influenced by calls within the community to change their names in order to foster a greater sense of identity, Padmanabh's father had abandoned his caste name of Shetty and taken the surname of Jaini, in this case in imitation of J. L. Jaini, a noted translator of the *Tattvārthasūtra.* Although the local languages of Nellikar were Tulu and Kannada, Jaini's highly literate parents also encouraged the study of Hindi, and the household contained a large number of regularly consulted books from North India on Jain and other subjects.

When he was ten and had completed his elementary education, Padmanabh Jaini's parents sent him far from home to the north to board at a Digambara Jain *gurukula* at Karanja in Vidarbha (Maharashtra) in order to continue his schooling at secondary level. This establishment, Mahāvīra Brahmacharyāśrama Jaina Gurukula, had been founded by Brahmachari Devchand, who was later to become the celebrated monk Ācārya Samantabhadra. While the curriculum contained "modern" subjects such as English and the Sciences, the school was run firmly on traditional Jain principles

*I would like to acknowledge the assistance of Professor P. S. Jaini and Ms. Kristi Wiley in the preparation of this Foreword.

and carried out regular daily rituals in accordance with Digambara practice. It was here during a period of eight years that the young Jaini gained his first familiarity with many basic Jain texts and encountered some of the great Digambara lay scholars of the period, such as Devakinandan Siddhantashastri, Kailashchandra Siddhantashastri, Hiralal Jain, Nathuram Premi and A. N. Upadhye.

After completing his secondary education, Jaini entered the Arts College at Nasik, which was affiliated to the University of Bombay, to take a B.A. Hons. degree in Sanskrit with subsidiary Prakrit. During this time he supported himself by superintending a boarding house for Śvetāmbara Jain students who belonged to the Oswal caste. The duties of this post obliged Jaini to travel to various Śvetāmbara centres to collect donations, as a result of which he became aware for the first time of the social diversity of Jainism and the fact that there were other Jain sectarian groups, such as the Sthānakavāsīs, virtually unknown to the Digambaras of Tulunadu. For, while it is true that Jainism is in broad terms doctrinally unified, interaction between members of the two main sects, the Śvetāmbaras and Digambaras, was, and to a large extent still is, comparatively rare, apart from occasional ecumenical occasions.

This familiarity with Śvetāmbara Jainism was to stand in good stead when, on graduation in 1947, he was invited by the great Sthānakavāsī scholar Pandit Sukhlal Sanghavi to study with him in Ahmedabad. Although he died as recently as 1978, Sanghavi (born 1880) represents what now seems to be a virtually lost scholarly and intellectual world. Towards the end of the nineteenth century, leading members of the Śvetāmbara Jain community undertook to set up schools to train and develop academically promising youngsters as pandits who, as with the much stronger tradition of lay scholarship amongst the Digambaras, would master and edit Sanskrit and Prakrit scriptural and philosophical literature and thus serve the community's requirements for a learned understanding of the Jain religion. Sanghavi himself had been blind from the age of eleven (a victim of smallpox) but nonetheless became profoundly versed in Jain logic at such an institution, rising to be professor at Banaras Hindu University. Jaini's near-daily meetings with this scholar over this period involved not just formal instruction in *nyāya*, carried out in rigorous fashion through the medium of a close analysis of a portion of Hemacandra's *Pramāṇamīmāṃsā*, but also exposed the young Digambara to Sanghavi's views about the many controversies that had arisen in the Jain community at this time.

Jaini's intellectual formation within this traditional brand of Jain learning was a crucial factor in his scholarly development. It must also be regarded as virtually unique up to this time, because no one of Jaini's generation (nor, one suspects, anyone before it) could claim to have his familiarity with the culture and practice of the two main sects of Jainism. However, his interests were by no means confined to Jainism. Sanghavi had always insisted on the importance of the Pali canon for understanding the Jain scriptures, and Jaini was encouraged by him to utilise the library, housed at the Gujarat Vidyapith, of Dharmananda Kosambi, India's most distinguished scholar of Theravāda Buddhism. Eventually, Jaini resolved to continue his postgraduate work in Sri Lanka and, with the help of Muni Jinavijaya, the director of the Bharatiya Vidya Bhavan in Bombay, to which he had briefly moved from Ahmedabad, became in 1949 the first Dharmananda Kosambi Memorial scholar, studying as a layman in Colombo at the Vidyodaya Pirivena, a monastic training centre headed by the Venerable Baddegama Piyaratana Mahathero, a one-time fellow student of Kosambi.

During his two years there, Jaini thoroughly familiarised himself with the Abhidharma Piṭaka, later to become one of his main areas of scholarly expertise, and also studied widely in the commentary literature on the Sūtra and Vinaya Piṭakas of the Pali canon. Unwilling to restrict himself to the confines of libraries, he was able to witness the richness of Sinhalese Buddhist ritual and devotional life as he accompanied Mahathero on his travels round the island and also memorably met Dr. B. R. Ambedkar, who visited Sri Lanka prior to his momentous decision to convert to Buddhism along with vast numbers of his followers. This period was to provide the basis for Jaini's first publication, *Silonmāṃ Be Varṣa* ("Two Years in Ceylon"), which provides in Gujarati much information about the practicalities of Theravāda Buddhism and a discussion of the potential for a genuine Buddhist revival in India.

After being awarded the degree of Trīpiṭakācārya in 1951 at a special ceremony held at Prime Minister Senanayake's residence, Jaini returned to Ahmedabad to take up a lecturer's position. However, he was soon to be on the move again, being appointed in 1952 to a newly created lectureship in Pali at Banaras Hindu University. Paradoxically, there could have hardly been a course of action more likely to ensure that Jaini's academic interests in the religion of his birth remained undiminished, for during the 1950s Banaras and its many educational institutions were home to a large number of distinguished Jain scholars who carried on a lively intercourse on various aspects of Buddhism and Jainism.

However, Jaini's main research at this time remained firmly in Buddhist sphere. Professor A. S. Altekar, Director of the K. P. Jayaswal Institute in Patna, which housed the famous collection of manuscripts brought from Tibet in the 1930s by Rahula Sankrityayana, had succeeded in identifying one particular manuscript as the *Abhidharmadīpa* (along with its commentary, the *Vibhāṣāprabhāvṛtti*), a hitherto unknown work written on the model of Vasubandhu's Sautrāntika-leaning *Abhidharmakośa* and *Bhāṣya* but defending the position of the Vaibhāṣika sect. The editing of this manifestly important text, the only Vaibhāṣika work directed against the great Vasubandhu to have survived in Sanskrit, was entrusted to Jaini. While engaged in this task, he was visited in 1956 by John Brough, then Professor of Sanskrit at the School of Oriental and African Studies at the University of London, who was en route to Nepal. Brough was unquestionably impressed by Jaini's philological acumen, for the meeting quickly led to the offer and the subsequent acceptance of a lectureship at SOAS.

Jaini remained at SOAS from 1956 until 1967 as Lecturer in Pali and, subsequently, Reader in Pali and Buddhist Sanskrit. Under Brough's supervision, Jaini quickly finished his edition of the *Abhidharmadīpa,* for which he was awarded the degree of Ph.D. by the Univeristy of London, and then began to broaden his studies in Theravāda Buddhism by travelling in Burma, Thailand, Cambodia and Indonesia in order to collect manuscripts relating to the apocryphal Pali birth stories (*jātaka*) of the Buddha, which he later was to edit and translate for the Pali Text Society. Eventually, to British Indology's great loss, Jaini moved to the University of Michigan, Ann Arbor as Professor of Indic Languages and Literature and finally in 1972, the culmination of a long journey for the small-town Jain boy from Tulunadu, to California where he served until 1994 as Professor of Buddhist Studies in the Department of South and Southeast Asian Studies at the University of California, Berkeley and afterwards as Professor in the Graduate School at the same institution.

Commentators on the work of any significant scholar generally seek to draw attention to the unity and overall coherence, whether real or imaginary. In P. S. Jaini's case, the structuring feature of his writings can be easily defined. All his energies throughout his career have been devoted to the elucidation of the manifold facets of what Indian scholars call *śramaṇasaṃskṛti*, "the culture of the strivers", that is to say, the religious, philosophical and literary achievements of the Buddhists and the Jains. Jaini's intellectual control over this area has meant that he has been able to adopt various styles of investigation. Sometimes Buddhism and Jainism are approached by him as independent phenomena, or, as with the case of the Jaina Purāṇas, with reference to their engagement with the encircling Hindu world. More often, however, Jaini has been preoccupied with the interaction and overlapping of the two great renouncer religions, with evidence from the one tradition being deployed so as to throw light on the other.

To exemplify briefly the fruitfulness of this latter methodology. It is difficult to read far in Jain literature without encountering the terms *bhavya* and *abhavya*, expressions designating respectively those innately capable of advancing along the path of spiritual release and those innately destined to make no progress at all in this respect. This dichotomy, which implies acceptance of something akin to predestination, is highly problematic for a religion which argues for the supposedly essential equality of souls and their common ability to transform their status through effort, although Jaini seems to have been the first to draw serious attention to this. Jaini's explanation in his paper "*Bhavyatva* and *Abhavyatva*: A Jaina Doctrine of 'Predestination'" of the two categories by reference to the Buddhist Vasubandhu's *Abhdharmakośabhāṣya* and what can be reconstructed of the teachings of the Ājīvika leader Makkhali Gosāla is a masterly demonstration of the sectarian modifications of an old *śramaṇa* dcotrine of predestination. In similar fashion, Jaini's ability evinced in the paper "Jaina Monks from Mathurā: Literary Evidence for Their Identification on Kuṣāṇa Sculptures" to draw upon Pali sources, as well as a wide range of Jain literary evidence, enables him to confirm and amplify the validity of U. P. Shah's identification of Mathurā images of naked monks holding pieces of cloth as *ardhaphālakas*, possible forerunners of the influential medieval sect of the Yāpanīyas.

In the specifically Buddhist area, Jaini's earliest articles emerged from his work on the *Abhidharmadīpa*, being originally components of the voluminous introduction to his doctoral dissertation. They display at the outset two of the main virtues which have consistently characterised Jaini's work: close familiarity with the primary sources, which are carefully documented, and, above all, clarity. Jaini's travels in Southeast Asia led to the publication of a further body of work on the apocryphal Pali Jātakas. Only recently have scholars begun to approach Theravāda Buddhism as a trans-national phenomenon and it is likely that Jaini's publications in this area will prove an important point of reference in shifting the philological and ethnographic emphasis away from the canonical Pali literature of Sri Lanka.

Many scholars in this time of enforced specialisation would have been content to rest on their laurels purely on the basis of these Buddhological publications. Jain studies, however, had never been far from Jaini's thoughts even at the beginning of his career. During his stay in London, for example, he prevailed upon the leaders of the Mahavira Jain Vidyalaya in Bombay to produce editions of the Śvetāmbara Jain scriptures in the (still continuing) Jain Āgama Series on the critical model employed by the Pali Text Society. Having begun productive research on Jainism during the 1970s, most notably with his edition and translation of a unique Digambara philosophical stotra, the *Laghutattvasphoṭa* of Amṛtacandrasūri, for which he used photographs and a handwritten copy of the only manuscript given to him by Muni Puṇyavijaya, Jaini eventually came to realise that Jain studies had to be given a higher profile within undergraduate teaching of Indian religions and, specifically, to be more fully integrated into the South Asian Studies programme at Berkeley. Not finding any suitable textbook with which to effect this, he resolved to write one himself and so produced in 1979 the work for which he is probably best known, *The Jaina Path of Purification.* This book can be regarded, with only slight exaggeration, as having attained the authority of virtual primary source and its value in promoting and providing an entrée to its subject in the English-speaking world in recent years is inestimable, to the extent that the late Kendall Folkert felt able to talk of pre- and post-Jaini eras in recent Jain studies.*

It may be the case, as some friendly critics have suggested, that *The Jaina Path of Purification*, and some of Jaini's articles, do

*Kendall W. Folkert, *Scripture and Community: Collected Essays on the Jains* (edited by John E. Cort), Atlanta: Scholars Press, 1993 p. xv.

occasionally present the Digambara idiom of Jainism at the expense of the various Śvetāmbara sectarian traditions, although this increasingly strikes the present writer as a strength rather than a defect, since Digambara Jainism remains a woefully neglected subject. However, possible bias is certainly not a criticism that can be levelled at Jaini's most recent book, *Gender and Salvation: Jaina Debates on the Spiritual Liberation of Women*, whose Introduction is reprinted here (No. 9). In this remarkable and trailblazing work Jaini translates and analyses a range of Śvetāmbara, Digambara and Yāpanīya sources to provide a broad and yet detailed conspectus on what is, for South Asia, a unique debate on female religiosity, a subject growing in importance in Indian studies. As with Jaini's work on the apocryphal Pali *jātakas*, one feels that the full significance of *Gender and Salvation* will continue to emerge on further acquaintance.

If this were the foreword to a festschrift dedicated to Professor Jaini, then no doubt its writer would extol the honorand's many personal attributes, such as his affability, raconteurship and generosity with his copious knowledge. Such productions do, of course, have their place in academic life, but I would suggest that the publication of these two volumes represents something better. They will enable seasoned aficionados to refresh their familiarity with and appreciation of Jaini's work, provide those working exclusively in either Buddhism or Jainism with a sense of the mutual illumination these two traditions can cast upon each other, and, lastly reveal to a younger generation of scholars a corpus of writing at once inspiring, informative and provocative.

May Professor P. S. Jaini's Collected Papers be consulted and profited from for many years to come.

University of Edinburgh PAUL DUNDAS

Preface

Papers are written, for the most part, on a wide variety of topics for panels at conferences and for felicitation volumes in honour of distinguished colleagues in one's area of research. It never occurred to me when I was writing these papers that one day they would be brought together in some coherent form. Several of my colleagues suggested to me that a collection of them would be useful in focussing attention on two of the heterodox traditions of ancient India, namely Buddhism and Jainism. Notable among these is John Cort, a leading Jainologist at Denison University, who recommended the format of the volumes. It was also his suggestion that a senior scholar well-acquainted with both of these areas should write a Foreword, and he invited Paul Dundas, the celebrated author of *The Jains* (Routledge, 1992), to undertake this task. I am grateful to my esteemed friend Paul Dundas for his very generous Foreword, in which he reviews my career and evaluates my research.

Of the fifty papers collected here in two volumes, eleven were written as contributions to Festschrifts (Jaina Studies: 4, 5, 10, 14 and 16 and Buddhist Studies: 4, 5, 8, 16, 20, and 22) and fifteen were invited papers at conferences (Jaina Studies: 1, 5, 7, 12, 15, 17, and 21; Buddhist Studies: 1, 7, 9, 10, 17, 21, 24, and 26). There are a few texts and translations of small Ṣanskrit and Pali works, some in fragmentary form. A total of twelve papers, nine related to Buddhism (10, 11, 12, 13, 14, 18, 24, 25, 27) and three to Jaina Studies (17, 18, 19) were published in the *Bulletin of the School of Oriental and African Studies*, University of London, while others were published in India and elsewhere. This accounts for the variety of stylistic conventions for diacritical marks, spellings of words (Jaina/Jain) as well as bibliographical references, and so forth. Although the papers have not been revised, I have taken the opportunity where appropriate to recommend important works that have appeared since their initial publication.

The first paper of each volume ("Ahiṃsā: A Jaina Way of Spiritual Life" and "States of Happiness in Buddhist Heterodoxy") is presented as an introduction to the Jaina and Buddhist faiths, respectively. These are followed by articles on the state of Jaina Studies and Buddhist Studies at the time of their publication, 1976 for Jainism and 1956 for Buddhism. In the case of the Jaina volume, two rather lengthy Introductions reproduced from two of my earlier books (3 and 9) provide a detailed study of the doctrine of the bondage of the soul and the debate over salvation of women. Seven papers in the volume on Buddhist Studies are primarily based on Buddhist material but include also a number of Jaina sources. They demonstrate the interdependent nature of these two traditions and stress the need for exploring them together. Their titles are as follows: Śramaṇas: Their Conflict with Brāhmaṇical Society (1970); On the *Sarvajñatva* (Omniscience) of Mahāvīra and the Buddha (1974); The Jina as a Tathāgata: Amṛtacandra's Critique of Buddhist Doctrine (1976); Saṃskāra-duḥkhatā and the Jaina Concept of Suffering (1977); The Disappearance of Buddhism and the Survival of Jainism in India: A Study in Contrast (1980); Values in Comparative Perspective: *Svadharma* versus *Ahiṃsā* (1987); and On the Ignorance of the Arhat (1992).

I am deeply indebted to the original publishers of these papers for permission to reproduce them here. Special thanks are due to Kristi Wiley, a doctoral student in our programme, for efficiently organizing the material and preparing the copy for the Press. I also would like to commend Mr. N. P. Jain for his enthusiasm in publishing these volumes and thus promoting the study of Jainism and Buddhism.

University of California, PADMANABH S. JAINI
Berkeley

Contents

SECTION V
JAINA ETHICS AND PRAXIS

SECTION VI
JAINA PURĀṆAS

I

INTRODUCTION TO JAINA FAITH

CHAPTER 1

Ahiṃsā: A Jaina Way of Spiritual Discipline*

The Jainas, undoubtedly adherents of one of the most ancient religious traditions in the modern world, are also one of the smallest communities, being only slightly larger than Zoroastrians. According to the latest government census, Jainas number less than six or seven million people, or less than one percent of the entire Indian population. Even though the size of the Jaina community never compared at any time in its history with that of its religious rivals, it remained a largely urban population because of the heavy concentration of its adherents in commerce and industry; thus the Jainas were able to wield influence over the ruling powers—whether Indian, Mughal or British—out of all proportion to their numbers.

Traditionally, the Jainas have been grouped together with other non-Brahmanical communities, such as the Buddhists, and share many common features with those heterodoxies.[1] The Jainas, like the Buddhists, are distinguished by their belief in the attainment of enlightenment by their founding teachers and the possibility of their followers attaining the same goal. This is achieved not through the grace of a Deity, however, but via one's own exertion and personal dedication to the path of spiritual purification. This path involves the mental practices of meditation and the physical practices of self-

*Keynote address delivered at the International Symposium on Jainism: Religion, Ritual, and Art, in connection with the exhibition of Jaina Art from India, Victoria and Albert Museum, London, November 22, 1995.

denial and austerities engaged in by mendicants of both Buddhist and Jaina communities. Both religions have a bicameral community of laypeople and mendicants, the former living the household life raising families, the latter renouncing the world in total dedication to the path of salvation. Despite their real differences with such theistic creeds as Vaiṣṇavism and Śaivism, the atheistically oriented Jainas and Buddhists are unanimous with their Hindu brothers in upholding three pan-Indian doctrines: (1) the supremacy of a moral order (*karman*) (2) the concept of cyclical rebirth (*saṃsāra*) and (3) the innate capacity of human beings to escape that cycle (*mokṣa*).

Without going into too many details about the precise differences between Buddhism and Jainism, it may suffice to say at this juncture that the Jainas are distinguished from the Buddhists by their belief that each living being possesses an individual soul. This soul is characterized by consciousness, undergoes continuous changes between various grades of purity and impurity, ignorance and omniscience. The Jainas conceive that a soul takes up a new body after the death of its present body according to its volitional activities. This is accomplished by the soul drawing toward itself a subtle kind of matter (*karman*), which then envelopes it and defines for the soul the new kind of body it will receive. The volitional force driving the soul is what determines the state in which the soul finds itself. If the soul becomes subject to attachment and aversion, the soul becomes harmful (*hiṃsā*) to both itself and others; if instead it maintains detachment and compassion, the soul comes to be noninjurious (*ahiṃsā*) toward all beings. As a Sanskrit verse of the twelfth-century Jaina mendicant Amṛtacandra says:[2]

> aprādurbhāvaḥ khalu rāgādīnām bhavaty ahiṃseti/
> teṣām evotpattiḥ hiṃseti jināgamasya saṃkṣepaḥ//

Assuredly the nonappearance of attachment and other [passions] is ahiṃsā, and their appearance is hiṃsā. This is a brief summary of the Jaina doctrine.

The Jainas thus define hiṃsā as something that is ultimately linked to one's personal mental state and involves injury primarily to oneself. Ahiṃsā and the awareness of ahiṃsā becomes a constant concern for the individual, involving total mindfulness in mental, oral, and physical activities. The orientation of the Jaina discussion on ahiṃsā thus proceeds from the perspective of one's own soul and not so much from the standpoint of the protection of other beings or the welfare of humanity as a whole. Ahiṃsā therefore is a creed in its own right: identified with one's own spiritual impulses and informing all of one's activities, it may truly be called a way of personal discipline.

The social ramifications of what is fundamentally a personal salvific enterprise, however, is to be found in the basic organization of the Jaina community. When one speaks of a Jaina community—which, as I have mentioned, involves separate lay and mendicant orders—one is referring to a group of people who have consciously undertaken to lead a way of life in accordance with the basic tenet of non-violence by removing the volition toward attachment and aversion. Thus, to some extent, all members of the Jaina community, both lay and mendicant, may be said to practice non-violence. The outward expression of this practice is characterized by two explicit schemes of vows and restraints, called minor vows (*aṇuvrata*) and major vows (*mahāvrata*), which are applicable to laypeople and mendicants, respectively.[3] Historically, the mendicants of the Jaina community were governed by many of the same rules as those in the Buddhist and Brahmanical orders, though they were perhaps somewhat more austere in their observances. Jaina mendicants were particularly noted for their lifelong vow of refraining from taking food and water from sunset to sunrise as well as by the renunciation of all worldly possessions and all acts of violence in any form whatsoever toward both humans and animals. The ahiṃsā of Jaina mendicants was all but absolute since their mendicant laws demanded it; they had no social involvements that might entail the use of violence and they undertook no governmental or military obligations. The mendicants had no need of a livelihood as they could count on the voluntary support of the laypeople for their legitimate needs. It was therefore incumbent upon them to keep the precept of ahiṃsā in its totality. The mendicant was thus the embodiment of ahiṃsā and the exemplar of that ideal for the layperson.

In this context of a social order the Jainas developed a whole set of laws regulating the application of the ideal of ahiṃsā in day-to-day life. A great many grades of non-violence were thus accepted within the lay order, allowing the diligent layperson to progress toward the state achieved by the mendicant. This was accomplished through a series of vows called aṇuvratas, which outlined the progressive course to the renunciation of all violence. On the one hand, this course gradually widened the scope of the application of ahiṃsā on the part of the layperson and, on the other, progressively restricted opportunities for violence.

The Jainas discuss in detail three ways in which violence could be expressed. As we noted earlier, true ahiṃsā means not only refraining from inflicting injury on others but also renouncing the very will toward attachment and aversion that initiates such violence. The Jainas therefore examined in minute detail the intentions that lay behind the ordinary activities that constituted the daily life of a householder: earning a livelihood, raising a family, and supporting the mendicants. Not to entertain even the thought of injury would be a tall order for one who must deal every day with a world that is prone to violence. A householder's activities, however, could be examined to see whether they were free from what the Jainas called *saṃkalpaja-hiṃsā* (harm intentionally planned and carried out), as, for example, that intention with which a hunter might stalk his prey. Such willful violence had to be renounced in order for one to be considered a Jaina, and the Jaina texts are replete with sermons rejecting all violence perpetrated for sport or in sacrifices, whether sacerdotal or familial.

Adopting a proper means of livelihood thus becomes extremely important for a conscientious Jaina, since the chosen occupation determines the degree to which violence can be restricted. The Jaina lawgivers have drawn up a long list of professions that were unsuitable for a Jaina layperson.[4] Certain Jaina texts forbade, for example, animal husbandry and trade in alcohol or animal byproducts, leaving only such professions as commerce, arts and crafts, and clerical and administrative occupations. In all these activities, some violence to the lowest forms of life was inevitable, but Jainas could engage in them if they behaved with scrupulous honesty and utmost heedfulness. Injury done while engaged in such activities was considered *ārambhja-hiṃsā* (occupational violence), which could be minimized by choosing a profession like business that was reasonably free from causing harm, as indeed Jainas have traditionally done.

Given the Indian social structure, which reserved particular professions for specific castes, the Jainas, being predominantly members of the merchant community, were obliged to undertake commercial and industrial enterprises; military service, for example, was not generally expected of Jaina laymen, a fact that allowed them to observe their precept of ahiṃsā and follow it within the narrow sphere as laid down in their religious law. Larger questions facing modern society, such as national defence, weaponry of mass destruction, limiting populations of wild animals and insect-pests, the use of toxic chemicals, the morality of capital punishment, the use of animals in medical research, and other social concerns that perforce entail violence were beyond the pale of Jaina thought.[5] These were simply not vital issues for a tiny minority community that could rely on the surrounding society to legislate on these problems, and that was guarded by a caste structure that did not demand the direct participation of the merchant classes in any violent activities. Thus, the Jainas were able to continue down through the ages their practice of non-violence, this ideal influencing greater Hindu society in a very limited manner on the issues of animal welfare and vegetarianism.

For those of us, especially in the West, who are used to associating the practice of non-violence with such larger movements as anti-nuclear advocacy or civil rights, the Jaina preoccupation with eating vegetarian food and protecting domestic animals may seem rather trivial. But the privileged position accruing from being such a small minority appears to have given the Jaina community a unique niche in Indian society, so that it was able to concentrate all of its missionary zeal on reforming the dietary habits of other Indians. Here too, an argument similar to that used to justify non-violence in the first place was used to support vegetarianism: since meat cannot be procured without cruelty, partaking of the flesh of animals in fact harms oneself by creating a latent effect in the mind of the meat-eater. The acceptability of dairy products, however, did not involve a conflict with the Jaina logic on this point, but was justified because milking a cow, goat or buffalo did not involve any harm to the animal itself.

In their belief in the inviolability of all life, the Jainas extended their dietary restrictions to various types of vegetable life as well. In their attempts to categorize those types of plants that could be consumed with relatively less harm, the Jainas developed a whole science of botany that was rather unique in Indian religious history.[6] For example, eating fruits and vegetables that contains a large number of seeds (*bahubīja*), such as figs or eggplants, was not favoured: this was in distinction to fruits that had only a single stone, like mangoes, or vegetables that do not contain individual seeds, such as grains, legumes, and leafy vegetables, which the Jainas did not limit. At the same time, however, the Jainas recognized that plants were the lowest form of life—since they possess only a single sense, that of touch—and belong to a different category altogether from higher animals. Hence, plants could be eaten, provided that they were harvested and prepared with care.

We should reiterate, however, that for the Jaina, vegetarianism meant not only being kind to animals, but also being kind to oneself. In addition to whatever health benefits might accrue from a vegetarian diet, the fact that a person has undertaken such a regime shows that his soul has not fallen prey to the lusts of the palate. By thus refraining from causing harm to animals or lower forms of life, the vegetarian is accruing merit (*puṇya*) and developing positive mental states that will ultimately be to his own personal benefit.

Most religions have advocated kindness in some form or other to animals, either because they also are created by god, as some theistic religions might maintain, or because they were the embodiments of the same spirit as are human beings, as the Vedāntins might explain. But this has neither deterred the adherents of some of these religions from sacrificing animals for ritual purposes nor prevented the advocates of other religions where sacrifice has fallen into disuse to rationalize animal slaughter as necessary in order to sustain the higher life of humans. Notwithstanding the practical difficulties for all people to procure strictly vegetarian food, the Jainas have continued to argue that animal slaughter can never be tolerated under any circumstances. We may recall here the words of the Jina Mahāvīra:

> No being in the world is to be harmed by a spiritually inclined person, whether knowingly or unknowingly, for all beings desire to live and no being wishes to die. A true Jaina therefore, consciously refrains from harming any being, however small.[7]

The Jainas here share the pan-Indian belief that certain souls in their transmigration, that is from one birth to another, may be reborn as animals. For this reason, a being who today is an animal might once have been a human being or, by exercising moral powers, that same animal may be reborn in the future as a human being. In the course of transmigration, there is no spiritual progress possible during a lifetime spent in heaven or hell, states which the Jainas consider to be non-eternal but of long duration. Within the virtually infinite variety of animal life-forms; however, it is possible for a soul to progress from one animal rebirth to another until, through its developing moral force, it would be able to cut asunder its bonds to the animal realm and advance to a human existence. Jainas, thus, considered human existence to be the gravitational centre of the rebirth process and assumed that all other life forms had to be reborn in the human state in order to attain spiritual liberation. The Jainas seem to be unique in believing that all animals possessed of mind and the five sens—which would include all domestic animals as well as those wild animals that could be trained—were capable of such spiritual sensibilities and must therefore be allowed to naturally evolve toward their destinies without interruption by human violence.

A beautiful story about an elephant narrated in the Jaina scriptures illustrates the moral capacity ascribed to higher animals by the Jainas. This is the tale of an elephant who in his very next rebirth was born as Prince Megha and became an eminent Jaina monk under Mahāvīra.[8] This elephant was the leader of a large herd that was caught in a huge forest fire. All the animals of the forest ran from their haunts and gathered around a lake so that the entire area was jammed with beings, both large and small. After standing there for quite some time, the elephant lifted his leg to scratch himself, and immediately a small hare ran to occupy the spot vacated by his raised foot. Rather than trampling the helpless animal, however, the elephant's mind was filled with great compassion for the plight of his fellow creature; indeed, his concern for the hare's welfare was so intense that he is said to have cut off forever his associations with future animal destinies. The elephant stood with one leg raised for more than three days until the fire abated and the hare was able to leave. By then, however, the elephant's whole leg had gone numb and, unable to set down his foot, he toppled over. While maintaining his purity of mind, he finally died and was reborn as prince Megha, son of King Śreṇika, the ruler of Magadha.

This story is a perfect example of the choice that an animal may make in undertaking a good or evil act. The elephant had the option of simply trampling the hare but refused to do so, preferring to act as would a morally inclined human. Thus, he deserved not only to be reborn as a human in his next life, but also to proceed along the path to salvation by becoming a monk. This story has helped to mold the Jaina attitude toward animals through the ages.

In this story, one must distinguish between what the Jainas consider a superstitious belief (*loka-mūḍhatā*) in the holiness of certain animals, such as the proverbial sacred cow of the Hindus, and a respect for all animals engendered through the Jaina insistence that all life is inviolable. Indeed, no animal is regarded as sacred by the Jainas, and yet all life is considered inviolate. Jaina monks and nuns disseminated the message of the inviolability of animal life with great zeal and lobbied many non-Jaina kings, including the Mughal king Akbar (1570-1605), to forbid the slaughter of animals, called *amāri* (non-killing), on certain holy days.[9] The Jainas rightly claimed that compassion toward one's fellow living beings was not possible without realizing the value of the self—the source of all religious wisdom—and thus contended that by bringing about such a change of heart in alien kings, they had truly imparted the teachings of the Jina; for as the Jainas say, "First knowledge, then compassion." Thus they proved the truth of their own maxim: "Thus does one remain in full control. How can an ignorant person be compassionate when he cannot distinguish good from evil?"[10]

We have seen that the Jaina lawgivers defined the meaning of intentional himṃsā with great care and expressly forbade it to all Jaina believers but gave Jaina laymen dispensation with regard to certain types of violence associated with their legitimate occupations (*ārambhaja-himṃsā*). There remained, however, a certain grey area that could not be so explicitly characterized as either expressly evil or provisionally acceptable. This was the area known as the "just war," or violence in defence of one's property, honor, family, community, or nation. In this matter, the individual had to take into account not only the duties to himself but to society as a whole. The duty of a Jaina mendicant in this case was quite clear: he must not retaliate in any way and must be willing to lay down his own life in order to keep his vow of total non-violence. For a Jaina layman, however, appropriate conduct was not nearly so clearcut. There were always situations in which violence would be a last resort in guarding the interests of himself and his community. Unfortunately for the Jaina laymen, little comfort was to be found in the Jaina law books on this question, which generally avoided the problem entirely. The Jainas did not presume to legislate on violence that might be perpetrated by a member of society at large. After all, as members of a small minority community, Jainas would have only rarely been called upon to respond to such questions about social violence and would have deferred to the dictates of the worldly standards (*lokācāra*) current in the surrounding community. The Jaina lawgivers of medieval times accorded with customary Hindu law in these matters. Somadeva (c. tenth century), for example, stipulated only that: "A king should strike down those enemies of his kingdom who appear on the battlefield bearing arms, but never those people who are downtrodden, weak, or who are friends.[11]

For a religion that expected so much from its followers in terms of keeping the vows of ahiṃsā, such perfunctory advice on the legitimacy of Jaina participation in warfare must be considered a serious oversight. Nevertheless, there are indications both in canonical scriptures, some portions of which may go back to 500 B.C., and in the much later narrative literature that the Jaina lawgivers were concerned about this problem and recognized the contradictions inherent in the expression "just war".

One attempt to resolve this problem is indicated by the term *virodhi-hiṃsā*: that is, countering violence with violence. The Jainas allowed that such violence could be justified, albeit as a final resort, for a Jaina layman whose conscience demanded that he defend his rights or for one who was called upon to fight by his king. However, as the following narratives will show, the Jainas neither glorified the bravery involved in such violence nor held forth the prospect of birth in heaven to the protagonists, whether winner or loser.

The first story is the tale of Bāhubali,[12] who is placed by the Jainas at the beginning of the present time-cycle, which ushered in human civilization. During this golden age, Ṛṣabha, the first of the twenty-four supreme teachers of this age, had just appeared in the world and introduced both the secular laws legislating the conduct of society as well as the monastic laws governing the pursuit of salvation. When Ṛṣabha renounced the world to become the first Jaina mendicant of this civilization, his eldest son, Bharata, claimed kingship over his entire domain. But the younger son, Bāhubali, claimed title to a share of the kingdom and refused to submit to the rule of his elder brother. Disregarding the law of ahiṃsā, he challenged his brother to face him and his army on the battlefield. Bharata recognized that his duty as king compelled him to force the submission of his insubordinate brother, and war seemed unavoidable. The king's advisors, alarmed at the prospect of mass carnage, proposed single combat between the two brothers as means of settling the dispute. The brothers agreed to the duel, but Bāhubali got the better of his elder brother and defeated him decisively in a wrestling match. At this point, one would have expected that Bāhubali would cap his triumph by proclaiming himself king. But the Jaina texts maintain instead that he was overcome by great remorse for having humiliated his brother and suddenly awakened to both the futility of sovereignty and the bonds of possessions, which had blinded him to the true nature of the soul. To the great astonishment of the spectators and the defeated king, Bāhubali discarded his royal insignia and, inspired by his sudden spiritual impulse, renounced the world and declared himself a Jaina monk. The storytellers relate that Bāhubali stood steadfast in meditation at that very spot for so long that creepers grew over his body and anthills formed at his feet. Bāhubali thus became omniscient and continues to be revered by the Jaina community as the first man of this age to have attained emancipation (*mokṣa*) from the cycle of birth and death; colossal images of him in meditational posture are worshipped to this day.

The Jainas drew several morals from this story that are relevant in guiding Jaina laymen in determining their proper duty when confronted by an adversary in battle. First, it was maintained that valor was preferable to cowardice: Bāhubali was right in standing up for his familial rights to a share of the domain, but Bharata was also correct in attempting to maintain the territorial integrity of his realm. The king's ministers were also right to reduce the necessary violence to an absolute minimum by proposing single combat between the two brothers rather than involving both armies in the dispute. But the Jainas ultimately maintained that the victory of Bāhubali would not have truly settled anything for, had he succeeded to kingship as he was entitled, a new cycle of violence would certainly have ensued on the part of the loyalists of the vanquished monarch. This would have proved the truth of the Jaina maxim that all possessions are evil, for true non-violence cannot be practiced either by an individual or by a society that craves possessions and must therefore fight to acquire, augment, and protect its wealth. Total non-violence is possible only when possessions are relinquished, as was so admirably demonstrated by Bāhubali's renunciation of the world after his victory. Thus again is upheld the Jaina belief that only the valiant and the self-denying can pursue non-violence to its fullest extent, not the cowardly or the covetous. For the layman who was unable to forsake all possessions but was nevertheless keen to minimize his hiṃsā, the Jainas introduced a precept called *parigraha-parimāṇa* (voluntarily setting a limit on one's possessions) and included it as the last of the five *aṇuvratas* (minor vows). A Jaina layman wishing to take this vow was asked by a mendicant to set specific limits on his possession of such temporal items as gold and silver, real estate, grain, and furniture, and to vow not to acquire amounts in excess of this limit. He was further encouraged to lower these limits by a certain amount each year in emulation of the total non-possessiveness (*aparigraha*) of the mendicant. In demanding that an advocate of ahiṃsā should renounce all properties in excess of one's legitimate needs, the Jainas were showing great insight into the possibility of building a society that practiced minimal hiṃsā. It must still be said, however, that the Jainas lacked either the vision or the organization to translate this precept into a general social philosophy. It is much to the credit of Mahatma Gandhi, who was undoubtedly influenced by several devout Jainas,[13] that he espoused a philosophy founded upon ahiṃsā and aparigraha.

A second memorable story appears in the canonical *Bhagavatī-sūtra,* which purports to preserve the words of the last Jaina teacher Mahāvīra. There Mahāvīra is asked about a war between Koṇika, the Magadhan emperor contemporaneous with Mahāvīra, and a federation of eighteen independent kings that had reportedly left 840,000 men dead. Mahāvīra's disciple specifically wanted to know whether it was true that all those men would be reborn in heaven because they had perished on the battlefield. In answer to this question, Mahāvīra declared that only one man out of this large army was reborn in heaven, and only one reborn as a man; all the rest ended up either in hell or in the animal realms.

Contrary to the widely held belief that death on the battlefield is almost equal to holy martyrdom, the Jaina answer as put in the mouth of Mahāvīra shows extraordinary courage of their conviction that death accompanied by hatred and violence can never be salutary and must therefore lead to unwholesome rebirths. Mahāvīra's answer to this question is truly memorable and departs drastically from the traditional belief of the Hindus, as recorded in the *Bhagavad-Gītā,* where Kṛṣṇa, the incarnation of the God Viṣṇu, tells Arjuna, who was hesitant to participate in the war, that death in battle leads to heaven:

hato vā prāpsyasi svargaṃ,
jitvā vā bhokṣyase mahīm/

tasmād uttiṣṭha Kaunteya,
yuddhāya kṛtaniścayaḥ// (*BhG* ii.37)

(Slain, you will attain heaven,
Conquering you will enjoy the earth.
Therefore rise, O Arjuna,
Resolved to do battle.)

To return to our narrative, Mahāvīra then proceeds to tell the story of the two fortunate soldiers.[14] The man who ended up in heaven was a Jaina named Varuṇa, who had taken the aṇuvratas of the layman before he was drafted by his king and sent to the front. Prior to his departure, however, Varuṇa vowed that he would never be the first to strike anyone; he would always wait until he was struck first before attacking. Armed with bow and arrow, he took his chariot into battle and came face to face with his adversary. Varuṇa declared that he would not take the first shot and called on his opponent to shoot. Only after his opponent's arrow was already on its deadly flight did he let fly his own arrow. His enemy was killed instantly, but Varuṇa himself lay mortally wounded. Realizing that his death was imminent, Varuṇa took his chariot off the battlefield and sat on the ground. Holding his hands together in veneration to his teacher, Mahāvīra, he said:

> Salutations to Mahāvīra, wherever he may be, who administered to me the layman's precepts. Now the time has come for me to face my death. Making Jina Mahāvīra my witness, I undertake the total renunciation of all forms of violence, both gross and subtle. May I remain steadfast in maintaining absolute detachment from this body.[15]

Saying thus, he pulled out the arrow and, his mind at peace, died instantly and was reborn in heaven.

The second man, a friend of Varuṇa, was himself severely wounded in the battle. Even so, he followed after Varuṇa in order to help him in his resolve and witnessed his peaceful death. He died soon afterwards in the same fashion and was reborn as a human being.

Whatever the moral of this story, the Jainas are clear in their belief that a wholesome rebirth is assured only to those who die a peaceful death and who renounce all hostility and violence.[16] Without achieving these qualities, no amount of valour on the battlefield guarantees even true temporal victory, let alone improvement in one's spiritual life.

In upholding this imperative that one may have full control over one's own destiny through arranging the conditions that prevail at one's death, the Jainas have even gone so far as to proclaim the legitimacy of abandoning one's own life in a controlled manner. This is technically known as *sallekhanā*, literally "thinning one's own body and passions," a ritualized form of death allowed only to monks, nuns, and under special circumstances to advanced laypersons. The act of sallekhanā is governed by several conditions, the most important of which are that it can be undertaken only by a public declaration, never in private, and that death may only be induced through the gradual withdrawal from taking all forms of food and water. As a further limitation on who may undertake this act, one is expressly forbidden from beginning such a fast until death is imminent, a judgement that is made by the teachers and colleagues of the dying person. Terminal illness or total disability that would prevent a mendicant from keeping the mendicant vows are, thus, the only situation where a request by a mendicant to begin sallekhanā would be permitted by the superiors.[17] The basic justification for sallekhanā is that a person who has conscientiously led a holy life has earned the right to die in peace in full possession of his faculties, without any attachment to worldly bonds, including his own body. When undertaking this ritual, the person first confesses his transgressions of the moral vows he had taken earlier. Thus, while remaining in full possession of his faculties, the individual allows his life to ebb away at its own natural pace, neither desiring to prolong his life artificially nor anticipating unduly his demise.

The image of Jainas throughout their long history has been associated with the doctrine of ahiṃsā, and the Jainas themselves have ardently adhered to the observance of the practice in their day-to-day life. The fact that even in contemporary society where material culture is all-pervasive, Jaina mendicants, who scrupulously adhere to their vows of non-violence and non-possession, still number over 2000 monks and 5000 nuns—a large number indeed considering the very small size of the Jaina community—testifies to the continued dedication to the ideal of ahiṃsā. Without such total dedication, ahiṃsā itself would remain either a fond memory of a lost golden age or an unachievable future goal. Lay Jainas as well abjure all forms of intentional violence and reduce the necessary amount of violence associated with their occupations to the absolute minimum. This does not mean that the Jaina lay adherent is a total pacifist, however. A layperson, as we saw above, is given the option of countering an armed adversary in kind, with the reminder that it is proper for a Jaina not to be the first to strike. The combatant would also be asked to bear in mind the Jaina doctrine of *anekāntavāda* (multiple perspective), which allows the Jaina to recognize the validity of his adversary's point of view as well. By enabling him to recognize an area of common ground between himself and his opponent, a Jaina would therefore be able to avoid confrontation and try reconciliation, and resort to warfare only out of dire necessity. The Jainas thus appear to have outlined a path of non-violence that would allow the lay adherent to conduct his daily life with human dignity while permitting him to cope with the unavoidable reality of the world in which violence is all-pervasive.

The Jainas would be the first to admit in accordance with their own doctrine of *syādvāda* (qualified assertion) that other religions too might discuss some of these same issues. But what distinguishes the Jaina conception of non-violence from that found in other world religions is that it is a truly personal way of religious discipline. It forbids the taking of all life, however that might be justified or excused in other religions and warns that nothing short of hell or animal rebirth awaits those who kill or who die while entertaining thoughts of violence. This perspective, however, does allow the Jaina to sacrifice even his own life in order to guard and nurture his soul. In this way, the soul may remain unaffected by the injuries (hiṃsā) inflicted upon it by attachment and aversion and may meet its corporeal death in perfect peace with itself and the world. Indeed, the holy life is truly consummated when a Jaina dies reciting the words of the religion's most solemn prayer:

khāmemi savva-jīve, savvė jīve khamantu me/
metti me savva-bhūesu, veraṃ majjha na keṇavi//[18]
(I ask pardon of all creatures, may all of them pardon me.
May I have friendship with all beings and enmity with none.)

NOTES

1. Article 25 of the Constitution of India under Explanation II pertaining to Sub-clause (b) of Clause (2) says the following: "The reference to Hindus shall be construed as including a reference to persons professing the Sikh, Jaina, or Buddhist religion, and the reference to Hindu religious institutions shall be construed accordingly." While the Jainas accept this definition for legal purposes they are keen to point out that they are not Hindus in the traditional sense of those who follow Indian religions that trace their origins to the Vedas, e.g., various forms of Vaiṣṇavism. The Jainas reject the scriptural authority of the Vedas, Brāhmaṇas, and Upaniṣads, the *Mahābhārata* (including the *Bhagavad Gītā*) and *Rāmāyaṇa,* and the Dharmaśāstras. They deny the efficacy of sacrifice and refuse to accord any "divine" status to Brahmā, Viṣṇu, Śiva, or the great *avatāras* depicted in the eighteen traditional Purāṇas. They also reject many Hindu *saṃskāras,* notably the *upanayana* (the sacred thread ceremony with the Gāyatrī Mantra) and *śrāddha* (offering food to the spirits of the dead). For further details, see P. S. Jaini: *The Jaina Path of Purification,* pp. 291 ff., University of California Press, 1979.
2. *Puruṣārthasiddhyupāya* of Amṛtacandra Sūri, v. 44. Sanskrit Text and English tr. by Ajit Prasada, Lucknow, 1933.
3. For a detailed description of the Jaina vows, see P. S. Jaini: *The Jaina Path of Purification,* University of California Press, 1979, pp. 157-185.
4. For a list of occupations forbidden to a Jaina layman, see R. Williams: *Jaina Yoga: A Survey of the Mediaeval Śrāvakācāras.* London (Oxford University Press), 1963.
5. In this connection mention may be made of the historical presentation of *The Jaina Declaration on Nature* by Jaina delegates (Bhagavan Mahavira Memorial Samiti from India and the Institute of Jainology from London) in the presence of HRH Prince Philip at Buckingham Palace, London, on October 23, 1990. See also Padmanabh S. Jaini: "The Role of Economics and Development in Jainism." *World Faiths and Development: Papers from the World Bank—World Religions Meeting at Lambeth Palace,* London, February 1998. World Faiths Development Dialogue, 33-37 Stockmore St., Oxford, U.K. 1998. (Coordinator: Wendy Tyndale)
6. For a long list of plants and substances forbidden to a devout Jaina, see R. Williams: *Jaina Yoga: A Survey of the Mediaeval Śrāvakācāras.* London (Oxford University Press), 1963, pp. 110-116.
7. *Daśavaikālika-sūtra,* iv, #11. English tr. by K. C. Lalwani, Delhi,

1973.

8. *Jñātādharmakathāḥ*, Ch. 1, #180-187. Prakrit text ed. by S. Bharilla, Pathardi, 1964.
9. V. A. Smith: "The Jain Teacher of Akbar," in *Essays Presented to Sir R.G. Bhandarkar*, pp. 265-276, Poona, 1917. For policies towards the Jainas in the post-Akbar period, see "Jahāṅgīr's Vow of Non-violence" by Ellison B. Findly, *Journal of the American Oriental Society*, Vol. 107, No. 2, 1987, pp. 245-256.
10. paḍhamaṃ nāṇaṃ tao dayā, evaṃ ciṭṭhai savvasaṃjae/*Daśavaikālika-sūtra*, iv.
11. *Yaśastilaka-campū*, ii, 97, Nirnayasagara Press, Bombay, 1903.
12. For accounts of Bāhubali and Bharata, see *Ādipurāṇa* of Jinasena, Ch. xxxvi, ed. by Pannalal Jain, Varanasi, 1963; *Triṣaṣṭiśalākāpuruṣacaritra of Hemacandra*, I, iv-v, Tr: *The Lives of Sixty-three Illustrious Persons*, Vol. I, by Helen M. Johnson, Oriental Institute, Baroda, 1962.
13. See the correspondence between Mahatma Gandhi and a revered Jaina saint Śrīmad Rājacandra as given in *Collected Works of Mahatma Gandhi*, Vol. XXXII, pp. 601-602, Delhi (Government of India: Publications Division), 1958-1976.
14. See *Bhagavatī-sūtra* (*Viyāhapaṇṇatti*), VII, 9 (#302 ff.). Summary by Jozef Deleu, Tempelhof (Rijksuniversity of Gent), 1970.
15. namo'tthu ṇaṃ samaṇassa bhagavao Mahāvīrassa...mama dhammāyariyassa vaṃdāmi ṇaṃ bhagavaṃ tatthagayaṃ ihagae, pāsau me se bhagavaṃ tatthagae jāva vaṃdai namaṃsai. evaṃ vayāsī—pubbiṃ pi ṇaṃ mae samaṇassa bhagavao Mahāvīrassa antie thūlae pāṇāivāe paccakkhāe jāvajjīvāe evaṃ jāva thūlae pariggahe paccakkhāe jāvajjīvāe, iyāṇi pi ṇaṃ tasseva arihaṃtassa bhagavao Mahāvīrassa aṃtiyaṃ savvaṃ pāṇāivāyaṃ paccakkhāmi jāvajjīvāe...caramehiṃ ūsāsanīsāsehiṃ vosirāmi tti kaṭṭu....samāhipaḍikkante āṇupuvvīe kālagae. *Bhagavaī* VII, 9, #302 ff. (*Suttāgame*, ed. by Pupphabhikkhū, Gudgaon-Delhi, 1953.)
16. Just as death on the battlefield, regardless of one's bravery, was not considered conducive to a birth in heaven, neither was the practice known as "suttee," or that of a widow burning herself. In this connection we may note a story of the beautiful Vasantasenā, wife of King Śabara-Mayaṅka. His rival king, Vardhana of Jayapura, desiring Vasantasenā, leads an army against Śabara-Mayaṅka, who dies in the ensuing battle. Vasantasenā, unable to bear the pang of separation, enters the fire (*jalaṇa-pavesa*). She is instantly reborn in the sixth hell called Tamaḥprabhā: kāuṃ jalaṇa-pavesaṃ Vasantaseṇā vi piyavirahaduhiyā/mariuṃ Tamapuḍhavīe uvavaṇṇā nārayatteṇa// *Śrī Caityavandana-bhāṣyaṃ* (by Devendrasūri together with a Vṛtti by Dharmakīrti), p. 240, Jinaśāsana Ārādhanā Trust, Bombay, 1988.
17. For further details on *sallekhanā*, see P.S. Jaini: *The Jaina Path of Purification*, pp. 227-233.
18. Quoted in R. Williams: *Jaina Yoga* (from *Pratikramaṇa-sūtra*, 49), p. 207, Oxford University Press, 1963.

II

JAINA STUDIES

CHAPTER 2

The Jainas and the Western Scholar*

Anyone seeking to evaluate the Western contribution to Jaina studies cannot but be struck by the degree to which work on Jainism has lagged behind that devoted to both Hinduism and Buddhism. The history of Western scholarship in Buddhism in particular is a long and colourful one, covering a period of more than one hundred fifty years and including such interesting personalities as Csoma de Koros, Sarat Chandra Das, Sir Aurel Stien, Daisetz Teitaro Suzuki, and Giuseppe Tucci. In comparison the history of Jaina studies is brief and uninspired: the main portion of the Western scholarship in Jainism was completed during a period of about sixty years beginning toward the end of the last century; the scholars of Jainism during this period were interested less in the religion itself than in the linguistic peculiarities of the Prakrits and Apabhraṃśa in which Jaina works were written. Beyond this linguistic interest their religion was approached primarily as a tool for the comparative study of Buddhism.

What little work has been done exclusively on Jainism would seem to suffer from a lack of communication. The general impression that one receives when he looks into the relationship of Jainism and Western scholarship is that there is almost no interaction between the Western scholars and the object of their

---

*This paper was read before the Annual Meeting of the American Academy of Religion, Chicago, 1975. Reprinted from *Sambodhi*, pp. 121-131, L.D. Institute of Indology, Ahmedabad, July 1976.

study: with few notable exceptions, such as Jacobi and Stevenson, most Western scholars of Jainism have had no contact with the Jaina community in India. As for their contact with the indigenous Jaina scholarship, it has been restricted to what was available to them in the English writings of a few notable Jainologists like Jagmanderlal Jaini, Hiralal Jain and the late Professor A.N. Upadhye. Few Western scholars show any acquaintance with the vast amount of work published in Hindi (and/or Gujarati) during the last fifty years by such eminent Pandits as Jugal Kishor Mukhtar, Nathuram Premi, Mahendra Kumar Nyayacarya, Kamta Prasad Jain, Muni Punyavijaya, Muni Jinavijaya, Sukhalal Sanghavi, Bechardas Doshi, Kailash Chandra Shastri, Phoolchandra Siddhantashastri and Dalsukh Malvania.[1] The writing of these Pandits, although occasionally tinged with sectarian spirit, have had a tremendous influence on the Jaina community and continue to be a major factor in shaping its attitudes and ancient institutions in response to the needs of the present time.

The majority of Western works about Jainism were originally written in German, a much smaller number in English. The history of Jaina studies may be said to begin with the edition and translation of Hemacandra's *Yogaśāstra* by Windisch, published in Leipzig in 1874. This was followed by Weber's *Uber die heiligen Schriften der Jaina* in 1883, and the works of Hoernle (1885), and Schrader (1902). The notable successors of these pioneers were Buhler, Jacobi, Glasenapp and Schubring. Buhler's brief essay *Uber die Indiche Secte der Jaina* (1887)—translated into English by Burgess under the title *On the Indian Sect of the Jainas* (London, 1903)—remains even to this day the best introduction to the Jaina religion. It established the independence of Jainism from Buddhism and gave fresh hopes for finding what Buhler calls "the boundaries of originality between the different systems." Jacobi's major work, the *Jaina Sūtras* (SBE, 1882 and 1884), placed Jaina studies on a firm foundation, and established the antiquity of Jainism over Buddhism. His translation of the *Tattvārtha-sūtra* (1906) laid the basis for a systematic study of *Jaina Śāstras* and their vast non-canonical literature in Sanskrit. Glasenapp's *Doctrine of Karman in Jaina Philosophy* (Eng. tr. 1921) carried this study further, introducing a new set of technical literature known as the *karma-grantha*. Schubring's learned work, *Die Lehre der Jainas* (1938)—recently translated into English as *The Doctrine of the*

Jainas (Delhi 1962)—may be considered the culmination of this line of research; nothing more substantial has appeared subsequently on the Continent in the field of Jaina studies. Outside of Germany the frenchman Guérinot was the only major continental contributor to Jaina studies. His monumental *Essai de Bibliographie Jaina* (1906) is the only significant bibliographical work on Jainism, and served as a basis for Winternitz's section on Jaina literature in his *History of Indian Literature* (1933), still the only comprehensive history of Jaina literature.

In England the major emphasis in Indological studies was placed on the Vedas and Brahmanism on the one hand, and Pali and Buddhism on the other. The names of Max Müller, Arthur Macdonell and A. B. Keith are associated with the former; those of Mr. and Mrs. Rhys Davids and the Pali Text Society with the latter. It is of some interest to note here that one of the earliest publications of the Pali Text Society was the first critical edition of the *Āyāraṅga Sutta* by Jacobi in 1882.[2] One might have expected this to lead to the founding of a parallel Prakrit Text Society,[3] but the *Āyāraṅga* was destined to be the only Jaina text ever to be published in England. On the whole Jaina studies drew little attention, with several notable exceptions. Most early English references to Jainism were in accounts of travel in India during the period of the East India Company, such as those of Buchanan and Colonel Tod (*Travels in Western India,* 1839). The first British contribution to Jaina scholarship was probably James Ferguson's *History of Indian and Eastern Architecture* (1891) in which the author devoted two excellent chapters to the North and South Indian Jaina temples. J. Burgess' article on Jaina iconography (*IA* 1903) provided further information in English about Jaina mythology, particularly that of the Digambara sect. L. D. Barnett, in 1907, was responsible for the translation of two Jaina canonical texts, the *Antagaḍadasāo* and the *Aṇuttarovavāiyadasāo.* And credit for real scholarly work, including fieldwork, must go to Mrs. Stevenson of the Irish Mission in Gujarat, whose *Heart of Jainism* (1915) was the first Western work popularly read in both the East and the West by sociologists and students of religion.

In America there are only two names prominent in Jaina studies. Maurice Bloomfield published a translation of the *Pārśvanāthacarita* in 1919. And the Late Professor W. Norman Brown published a translation of the *Kālakācārya Kathā* in 1933, as well as

Miniature Paintings of the Jaina Kalpasūtra (1934) and *Manuscript Illustrations of the Uttarādhyayana Sūtra* (1941).

It would be accurate to say that by the beginning of World War II Western Jaina studies were at a standstill. On the Continent and in the English-speaking world, Jainism attracted little sustained study. Alsdorf, Frauwallner, and Renou all devoted sections of major works on Indian religions to Jainism, and some of their remarks are significant; but no independent works approaching Jainism from a religious point of view were forthcoming. Historians and sociologists, however, continued to devote some attention to Jainism. Max Weber (*The Religion of India*) touched upon Jaina society in order to compare it with that of Buddhism. The historian Vincent Smith in his *Jaina Stūpas and other Antiquities of Mathura* (1901) is to be credited with giving due attention to the ancientness of Jainism, and with placing the religion in its correct historical perspective, a perspective which is also apparent in his work on *Akbar the Great Moghul.* B. Lewis Rice, Director of Archaelogical Research in Mysore, in his voluminous publication of hundreds of Karnatic Jaina inscriptions (*Epigraphica Carnatica,* 1886-1904), helped to establish the value of Jaina sources for historical studies.

Among the more recent and contemporary scholars, one must mention Heinrich Zimmer, the only religious historian to turn his attention to Jainsim. Zimmer devoted a hundred pages of his Philosophies of India (1951) to Jainism drawing heavily upon Bloomfield's *The Life and Stories of the Jaina Saviour Pārśvanātha* (1919) and emphasizing the earlier period of the religion. Basham's book, *The History and Doctrine of the Ājīvikas* (1951) depends largely on Jaina sources for the life and career of Makkhali Gosāla. Basham takes Jaina history back past the life of Mahāvīra, and emphasizes the influence of the Ājīvikas on Jaina thought. Lastly R. Williams' *Jaina Yoga: A Survey of the Mediaeval Śrāvakācāras* (1963) is the most systematic western work on Jainism, which brings together a large corpus of medieval literature on the lay discipline.

Western scholars have been attracted to Jaina studies for various reasons, but almost none of them have been motivated by a passionate interest in Jainism as a whole and for its own sake. Consequently there have been great gaps in Western knowledge of Jainism, caused by the general superficiality of Western study as well as by the failure of most Western scholars even to recognize certain crucial areas in Jaina studies. For the remainder of this paper I shall criticize the lack of attention to three critical aspects of Jainism: first the sect of the Digambaras, who have been neglected almost completely in favour of the Śvetāmbaras; second, the question of determinism in Jainism and its relationship to the *niyativāda* of the Ājīvikas; and last, the sociology of Jainism, which, in comparison with even the most minor of the Indian religions and cults, has not been studied to any sufficient extent.

Ironically, it was Jacobi, one of the most dedicated Western scholars on Jainism, who was also largely responsible for the Western acceptance of Śvetāmbara claims to authenticity and for the consequent neglect of the Digambaras. Jacobi was the first to discover the importance of '*Keśi-Gautama saṃvāda*' of the *Uttarādhyayana Sūtra.*[4] As is well-known, this Śvetāmbara canonical text records the dialogue between Keśi, a disciple in the mendicant tradition of Pārśva, and Gautama, the chief disciple of Mahāvīra. It is alleged there that the mendicant disciples of Pārśva followed the *cāujjāma-dhamma*, translated by Jacobi as the "Law of the four vows," as opposed to the *pañca-mahāvratas*, the "Law of the five vows" laid down by Mahāvīra. The dialogue further claims that the mendicant disciples of Pārśva wore clothes, as do the present-day Śvetāmbara monks, whereas nudity was made obligatory by Mahāvīra for his ascetic disciples. Jacobi correctly showed the identity of the Jaina *cāujjāma-dhamma* with the Pali *cātuyāma-saṃvara* attributed to Nigaṇṭha Nātaputta (i.e. Mahāvīra) in the '*Sāmaññaphala sutta*' of the *Dīghanikāya*. Although the Pali term is obscure Jacobi was able to demonstrate that the Buddhist references must be to the school of Pārśva, thereby establishing the posteriority of Buddhism to Jainism. But in doing this he was guided by the Śvetāmbara meaning of the term *cāujjāma*, and appeared to be lending his support to the Śvetāmbara claims that the two Jinas abided by different sets of laws, and that, most importantly, the wearing of clothes is justified by a tradition going back to Pārśva's time. Thus Jacobi appeared to have granted external support for the authenticity of the Śvetāmbara canonical texts. Since the Digambaras do not accept the Śvetāmbara canonical texts and have no canonical texts of their own, Jacobi's findings focused attention on the Śvetāmbara tradition, and led to the almost complete neglect of the vast Digambara literature. The consequences of Jacobi's interpretation may be seen in works of Weber and Renou who follow his support of the Śvetāmbara view of the beginnings of ascetic nudity in the Jaina order.[5]

This provoked the Digambaras, who in due course were obliged to respond to the results of Jacobi's work in order to defend their own tradition.[6] They discovered that, although *caūjjāma-dhamma* was indeed a doctrine of Pārśva, Jacobi, depending exclusively on the later (8th century) Śvetāmbara commentaries, interpreted the doctrine incorrectly. Professor Prafulla Kumar Modi, for instance, has pointed out (in his Hindi Introduction to the *Pāsaṇāhacariu*, Prakrit Text Series, (1965) that the *cāujjāma-saṃvara* did not really consist of four vows (*vratas*) as alleged by the Śvetāmbara commentators and endorsed by Jacobi, but rather a single great restraint (*saṃyama*) called *sāmāyika.* In support of his contention Professor Modi quotes the *Ācārāṅga-sūtra,* where it is said that Mahāvīra himself accepted this "*sāmāyika cāritra*" (conduct) with the words, "I shall not perform any evil acts whatsoever".

He further maintains that the term "fourfold" must be seen in this context not as referring to four specific vows but rather as explained in the *Sthānāṅga-sūtra,* to the four modalities through which improper deeds may find expressions: viz., mind, speech, body and the senses (or, permissible possessions of a monk).[8] On the basis of his findings, Professor Modi has concluded that Mahāvīra simply elaborated the *sāmāyika* restraint, which had been taught by Pārśva as well. Whatever the merit of his findings, Professor Modi has succeeded in presenting a Digambara perspective on this controversial problem which remained untouched since the publication of Jacobi's thesis in 1884.

Western Jaina scholarship, then, has been essentially Śvetāmbara scholarship. Western scholars have favoured this school not only by translating canonical texts, which are by definition Śvetāmbara, but also by their translation of non-canonical works—e.g. Hemacandra's *Triṣaṣṭi-śalākā-puruṣacarita,* translated by Johnson in the *G.O.S.*; *Kumārapālapratibodha* translated by Alsdorf; and *Anyayoga-vyavacchedikā* (together with Malliṣeṇa's commentary *Syādvādamañjarī* translated by F. W. Thomas). In contrast, the Digambara authors like Kundakunda, Samantabhadra, Pūjyapāda, Jinasena, Akalaṅka, Vidyānandi, Somadeva, and Āśādhara, to mention only the most eminent, have been totally ignored. Virtually, none of the works of these *ācāryas* have been translated in the West,[9] and the few notices one gets of Kundakunda in the works of Frauwallner or Schubring cannot be considered adequate given the vast amount of commentarial material on his works. Renou was correct when he remarked that "the austerity of their [the Digambaras] habits matches their doctrine. In Europe (and in India too, I fear) little is known of the ancient Digambaras."[10]

A great deal of original research has been devoted to the connections of Jainism with Makkhali Gosāla and the Ājīvikas, but here again the Digambara tradition has been largely ignored. Basham has collected almost everything available in the Śvetāmbara canon and has given a creditable account of the sect and its connection with Mahāvīra. Hoernle claims that the Digambaras are actually the ancient Ājīvikas.[11] Basham rejects this view on the basis of the Digambara author Nemicandra's distinction between the Nirgranthas and the Ājīvikas.[12] He suggests rather that some of the Southern Ājīvikas may have been absorbed by the Digambaras, but this is the extent to which Basham considers the Digambaras at all.

No scholar has searched through the Digambara texts for mention of Makkhali Gosāla, assuming, no doubt, that since the Digambaras do not possess the canon, they have no recollection of Makkhali's encounter with Mahāvīra. There are, however, two texts,[13] *Bhāvasaṅgraha* and *Darśanasāra*, both by Devasena of the eleventh century, which seem to have been overlooked even by Basham. They preserve an ancient Digambara tradition that Makkhali [Gosāla] was a follower of (the tradition of) Pārśva and hoped to be chosen the chief disciple (*gaṇadhara*) of Mahāvīra. When he was not thus chosen, he walked out of Mahāvīra's assembly and established the creed of *ajñānavāda*. The Digambara sources seem to take "*ajñānavāda*" in this sense, "knowledge does not make any difference to the achievement of salvation," a belief which probably echoes the well-known Ājīvika doctrine that "both fools and wise (*bāle ca paṇḍite ca*) alike [wandering in transmigration exactly for the allotted time, shall then, and only then,] make an end of suffering (*dukkhassa'ntaṃ karissanti*)" (*Dīgha Nikāya*, I, p. 54). The Digambaras, it is true, make no reference to the contact between Makkhali and Mahāvīra prior to the latter's attaining Jinahood, nor to the subsequent episode of the violent confrontation which led to the death of Makkhali, as narrated in the Śvetāmbara canon. But a close scrutiny of the works of Devasena shows traces of some memory of a past dispute. For, whereas the Śvetāmbaras subsequently allow Makkhali to attain salvation, the Digambaras say that as a result of harbouring the doctrine of *ajñānavāda* he was born in the lowest existence possible, that of *nigoda*, a state from which may be difficult emergence into a higher birth.[14] Why the Digambaras would want to take such extraordinary punitive action against Makkhali must remain a mystery. In any case, the Digambara references to Makkhali Gosāla remain to be studied properly and evaluated for the light they may throw on the deterministic elements in Jainism. Among such elements there is, for example, their doctrine of *bhavyatva* and *abhavyatva* (a doctrine equally accepted by the Śvetāmbaras) according to which only certain souls are capable of attaining salvation while others, lacking that capacity, are condemned forever to life in *saṃsāra*.[15] Reference may also be made in this connection to a doctrine found in the works of Kundakunda, most importantly in his *Samayasāra*. Although rejected by the Śvetāmbaras as a heretical work, smacking of *ekāntavāda*, the *Samayasāra* has greatly influenced Digambara thinking for centuries, and has been acclaimed by them as the most profound exposition of the Jaina doctrine. It espouses what is styled "*śuddha-niścaya-naya*," a doctrine of "pure non-conventional view," according to which the infinite modifications (*paryāyas*) of any given substance (*dravya*), such as a soul, are fixed in a sequential order (*krama-baddha-paryāya*) which cannot be altered. In recent years this doctrine provoked a great deal of controversy within the community of the Digambaras, as a result of which a 'debate' (*tattva-carcā*) took place in Jaipur sponsored by prominent Digambara Jaina pandits. The proceedings of this debate have been published in two bulky volumes (a total of 846 pages) entitled Jaipur *Tattvacarcā*[16] (Jaipur, 1967). Needless to say this book has never been reviewed in the West, a fate it shares with most other works on Jainism written in Hindi.

The limitations of Western scholarship discussed above are evident as well in their work in the field of Jaina society. The research is superficial and an undue emphasis has been placed on the Śvetāmbaras. In examining Jaina society, Max Weber has commented upon the merchant ethics of the Jainas and upon similarities between the Jainas and the Protestants and Jews.[17] Drawing largely on Weber's work, an Indian scholar, Nevaskar, has also attempted to compare the Jainas with the Quakers.[18]

In *Jaina Yoga*[19] Williams goes beyond such facile observations to discuss the ritualistic and isolationistic nature of the traditional Jaina professions. Williams appears to be the only Western scholar who has seriously compared the Śvetāmbaras and the Digambaras. His work confirms the findings of previous studies of professional choices in Jain society and the resolution of the conflicting values of profit and *aparigraha.* Williams also confirms the theory of Hoernle, put forth in the 1880s, that Jainism survived where Buddhism did not because of the former's attention to the needs of the laity.

The works of these scholars, however, are textual studies; they are not based on fieldwork. It is very peculiar that the extremely ancient tradition of Jainism has not aroused the interest of sociologists and anthropologists to do such fieldwork. Even the opportunity to visit and study the celebrations and rituals connected with the recent 2500th anniversary of the *nirvāṇa* of Mahāvīra seems to have been neglected. Probably few people in the West are aware that during this Anniversary year for the first time in their long history the mendicants of the Śvetāmbara, Digambara and Sthānakavāsi sects assembled on the same platform, agreed upon a common flag (Jaina *dhvaja*) and emblem (*pratīka*); and resolved to bring about the unity of the community. For the duration of the year four *dharma cakras,* a wheel mounted on a chariot as an ancient symbol of the *samavasaraṇa* (Holy Assembly) of Tīrthaṅkara Mahāvīra traversed to all the major cities of India, winning legal sanctions from various state governments against the slaughter of animals for sacrifice or other religious purposes, a campaign which has been a major preoccupation of the Jainas throughout their history.

One of the areas to which sociologists have not paid sufficient attention is the possibility of influence on Jainism by a Kṛṣṇa cult. Renou has suggested such a possibility: "Kṛṣṇism seems to have left its mark on Jaina legend, a Kṛṣṇism which we must assume... to be an earlier form than that described in the Brahmanical texts."[20] There is no doubt that a large number of canonical stories (*kahāo*) are based on the legends of Kṛṣṇa and Nemi (the 22nd Tīrthaṅkara). In the post-canonical period, many Jaina monks composed *purāṇas* on the members of the Vṛṣṇi clan, and several lay poets (notably Pampa, Ranna and Janna) wrote Kannada *campu-kāvyas* with Kṛṣṇa as the central figure of Jaina adaptations of the Hindu *Mahābhārata*. Modern research on the cult of Kṛṣṇa, including the works by the Sanskritist Edgerton and the sociologist Milton Singer, has shown little or no acquaintance with this material in Prakrit, Sanskrit and Kannada. No one has attempted to investigate the depth or the extent of the influence of the figure of Kṛṣṇa on Jaina consciousness; few indeed are aware of the interesting fact that the Jainas have had no hesitation in sending Kṛṣṇa to hell for his deceitfulness and violence, a fate which, according to the Jaina account, also overtook Lakṣmaṇa for killing Rāvaṇa.

Many facile remarks have been made about the caste system and Jaina "self-brahmanisation" but no translations or serious studies have been made of the Jaina "law book", the *Mahāpurāṇa* of Jinasena (A.D. 840), which discusses the origin of the caste system from the Jaina point of view. Here too, Western scholars have remained content with the Śvetāmbara accounts found in the comparatively late works of Hemacandra (such as the *Triṣaṣṭi-śalākā-puruṣacarita*). In short, Jaina texts pertaining to the social order have not been fully investigated, Jaina-Hindu modern relations have gone unstudied,[21] and the Digambara society of Mysore, which shows a greater Brahmanisation than the Śvetāmbara society of Gujarat, has never been studied by Western scholars.

Only three or four scholars have ever visited the Jainas, and these only the Śvetāmbaras. Jacobi, through his search for Jaina manuscripts, came in close contact with a few ācāryas of the Śvetāmbara community. Renou, who visited a Sthānakavāsi community, admits that he knows nothing of the Digambaras (Renou, p. 123). As for Mrs. Stevenson, whose *Heart of Jainism* is written from a missionary's point of view, her several years with a Śvetāmbara community represents the most extensive fieldwork in Jaina studies, but her description of the heart of Jainism as being "empty" of divine power betrays her missionary malice.[22] Her last chapter is a plea to Jainas to accept Jesus; and she shows a total lack of understanding of Indian feelings, particularly Jaina feelings, regarding transmigration, vegetarianism, *ahiṃsā* and *karma*. Her book, probably the only of its kind to have come out of the Oxford University Press (1915) was never subjected to close scrutiny by Western scholars; and even Max Weber, turning a blind eye to her undisguised prejudices, found it possible to endorse and repeat that "the heart of Jainism is empty" (p. 201). Mrs. Stevenson certainly provoked much opposition in India and J. L. Jaini took her to task for her pretensions to preach to Jainas the value of love and brotherhood.[23] It is rather extraordinary that even after half a century her book has been reprinted in India (New Delhi 1970), without any revision or review.

Similar missionary sermonizing is evident in the Bombay Jesuit priest Zimmerman's preface to Glasenapp's *Doctrine of Karman in Jaina Philosophy*. The fact that the Jainas did not have their own "pagan" gods, yet still refused to accept Christianity, seems to have frustrated missionaries to the extreme. Champat Rai Jain, a Jaina apologist and the founder of a small Jaina Mission in London, responded to Christian criticisms of the Jaina doctrines in his *Jainism, Christianity and Science* (Allahabad 1930), probably the only Jaina work that was specifically addressed to the Christian world and read mainly by the educated Jainas in India.

The history of Western Jaina studies reflects the influence of scholars who looked to Jainism for that which was other than Jainism itself—for Buddhism, Ājīvikism, historical facts, art, linguistics, etc. Pertinent questions essential to an understanding of Jainism have been ignored, questions such as the presence of fatalism and the absence of Mahāyāna, bhakti, yoga or tantric movements in Jainism. Even the comparison of Buddhism and Jainism have been limited mainly to their practices of austerities, Jainism being described as "Buddhism's darker reflection" (Renou, p. 111). No attention has been paid to the comparative sociology of Jainas and Hindus. The influence of Jainas on general Indian political history has been ignored, as has been the Jaina claim to a share in the philosophy of Gandhi. Renou maintained that there is no dearth of scholars interested in Jaina studies, but that "the chief need of the Jainas is in fact for great spiritual leaders such as Hinduism has produced more than once" (Renou, p. 133). Yet the fact remains that no Western translation has appeared of the massive Gujarati writings of the Jaina saint Rājachandra (1863-1901),[24] whom Mahatma Gandhi described as one of his "gurus" (together with Tolstoy and Ruskin), and whose influence on the young Gandhi is well-known from the latter's autobiography. Thus, in conclusion, there would seem to be considerable justification for the Jaina contention that despite their antiquity, despite the richness of their religious literature, and despite the fact that they represent the sole surviving non-Vedic tradition in India, they have never received the serious attention of the Western scholar.

NOTES

1. It is ironical that Schubring should say: "For a long time research in Europe was known to the Jainas to but a certain degree, that is to say, as far as their knowledge of English allowed. Books and articles in German and other Western languages frequently remained beyond their reach." *The Doctrine of the Jainas,* p. 13 (Delhi, 1962).
2. Jacobi found it necessary to apologize for the inclusion of this text in the P.T.S. series: "The insertion of a Jaina text in the publication of the P.T.S. will require no justification in the eyes of European scholars...But it is possible that Buddhist subscribers...might take umbrage at the intrusion, as it were, of an heretical guest into the company of their sacred Suttas..." p. vii.
3. In fact this Society came into existence in India in 1953 and has published several volumes in its Prakrit Text Series.
4. *Jaina Sūtras,* part 2, pp. 119-29. See also his earlier article, 'On Mahāvīra and his Predecessors,' *Indian Antiquary* (*IA*), Vol. IX (June 1880), pp. 158-163.
5. "Mahāvīra seems to have developed the ethical aspect of Jainism by introducing a fifth axiom which brought a modification in the import of the fourth...Finally, it was he who required his monks to dispense with clothing, setting an example himself, whereas Pārśva's monks were clothed." Renou: *Religions of Ancient India,* p. 115 (London, 1953).
6. For the controversy generated by Jacobi's work among the Jainas, see articles by Puran Chand Nahar ('A note on the Śvetāmbara and Digambara sects,' *IA,* Vol. 58, pp. 167-8; 'Antiquity of the Jain sects,' *IA.* Vol. 61, pp. 121-126) and Kamta Prasad Jain ('A further note on the Śvetāmbara and Digambara sects,' *IA,* Vol. 59, pp. 151-154), who respectively represent the Śvetāmbara and Digambara traditions.
7. tao ṇaṃ...Mahāvīre...paṃcamuṭṭhiyaṃ loyaṃ karettā...savvaṃ akarṇijjaṃ pāvaṃ ti kaṭṭu sāmāyiyaṃ carittaṃ paḍivajjai...II, 15, 23. Jacobi's translation of this significant passage reads as follows: "After the Venerable Ascetic Mahāvīra had plucked out his hair...and vowing to do no sinful act, he adopted the holy conduct." (*Jaina Sūtras,* I, p. 198). It is remarkable that no one (including Professor Modi) has noted that Jacobi has here rendered "*sāmāyika*" merely as "holy," instead of giving the true technical meaning of this crucial term.
8. "cauvvihe saṃjame pannatte taṃ jahā: manasaṃjame, vai saṃjame, kāyasaṃjame, uvagaraṇasaṃjame." *Sthānāṅga* 385.
9. Faddegon's translation of the *Pravacanasāra* of Kundakunda (Jain Lit.

Society Series, Cambridge, 1935) would appear to be the sole exception.

10. *Religions of Ancient India*, p. 119. This observation made in 1956 is still valid today. A recent thirty minute videotape on Jainism by David Knipe (Department of South Asian Studies, University of Wisconsin, Madison) devotes less than three minutes to the Digambaras.
11. 'Ājīvikas' by A.F.R. Hoernle in *Encyclopaedia of Religion and Ethics*, Vol. I (New York, 1913) pp. 259-268.
12. *History and Doctrines of the Ājīvikas* (London, 1951), p. 181 ff.
13. Portions quoted from *Bhāvasaṅgraha* in Kamta Prasad Jain's *Bhagavān Mahāvīra aur Mahātmā Buddha* (Surat, 1929), p. 20. For *Darśanasāra*, see A. N. Upadhye's article '*Darśanasāra* of Devasena: Critical Text,' in the *Annals of B.O.R.I.*, Vol. XV, 3-4, pp. 198-206.
14. We quote below the relevant portions from the texts of Devasena:
    (a) Masayarī-Pūraṇa-risiṇo uppaṇṇo Pāsaṇāha-titthammi/
    siri-Vīra-samavasaraṇe agahiya-jhuṇiṇā ṇiyatteṇa//
    vahi-ṇiggaheṇa uttaṃ majjhaṃ eyārasaṅga-dhārissa/
    niggai jhuṇī ṇa aruho ṇiggaya vissāsa-sīsassa//
    ṇa muṇai jiṇa-kahiya-suyaṃ sampai dikkhāya gahiya Goyamao/
    vippo veyabbhāsī tamhā mokkhaṃ ṇa ṇānāo//
    Bhāvasaṅgraha, 76-8.
    (b) siri-Vīraṇāha-titthe bahussudo Pāsasaṁgha-gaṇi-sīso/
    Makkaḍa-Pūraṇa-sāhū aṇṇāṇaṃ bhāsae loe//
    aṇṇāṇādo mokkho ṇāṇaṃ ṇatthi tti mutta-jīvāṇaṃ/
    puṇarāgamaṇaṃ bhamaṇaṃ bhave bhave ṇatthi jīvassa//...
    jiṇa-magga-bāhiraṃ jaṃ taccaṃ samdarisiūṇa pāva-maṇo/
    ṇicca-ṇigoe patto satto majjesu vivihesu// *Darśanasāra*, 20-3.

    The Digambara version of Makkhali's fall into the *nitya-nigoda* seems to reflect an ancient and well-known tradition attested in Buddhaghosa's commentary to the *puggala-paññatti*: "sakiṃ nimuggo...nimuggo va hotīti"...etassa hi puna bhavato vuṭṭhānaṃ nāma natthīti vadanti. Makkhali-gosālādayo viya heṭṭhā heṭṭhā narakaggīnaṃ yeva āhārā honti (7.1). Also see my article 'On the Sautrāntika theory of *bīja*,' *BSOAS*, Vol. XXII, Part 2 (London 1959), p. 246, n. 2.
15. See my article ' 'Predestination' in Jainism and Buddhism: the Doctrines of *bhavyatva* and *abhavyatva*,' awaiting publication in the *Bhagavān Mahāvīra and his Teachings*, Bombay (Published in 1977).
16. Edited by Pandit Phoolchandra Siddhantashastri, Shri Todarmal Granthamala, Jaipur.
17. Max Weber: *The Religion of India* (Tr. and edited by Hans H. Gerth and Don Martindale). The Free Press, New York 1958, pp. 193-204.
18. Nevaskar: *Capitalists without Capitalism* (The Jains of India and the Quakers of the West), Connecticut, 1971.
19. R. Williams: *Jaina Yoga*, London, 1963.
20. *Religions of Ancient India*, p. 114.
21. A particularly noteworthy instance of such relations may be found in the Punjab, where, at the beginning of this century, the Jaina community was overwhelmed by the Ārya-Samāja in their drive for integration of the Hindu Society.
22. "The more one studies Jainism, the more one is struck with the pathos

of its empty heart. The Jainas believe strongly in the duty of forgiving others, and yet have no hope of forgiveness from a higher power for themselves" (p. 289).

23. Jagmanderlal Jaini: *A Review of the Heart of Jainism*, Ambala, 1925.
24. Śrīmad Rājachandra, Agas, 1951, p. 924.

ADDITIONAL NOTE

Since the publication of this article in 1976, there has been a great advancement in Jaina studies in the West. For a complete list of such works through 1993, see Klaus Bruhn, "Jainology in Western Publications I" and Colette Caillat, "Jainology in Western Publications II," both of which were published in *Jain Studies in Honor of Jozef Deleu*, edited by Rudy Smet and Kenji Watanabe, Tokyo, 1993. Among the works that have been published since these articles were written, we may note here the following: Paul Dundas, *The Jains*, Routledge, London, 1992; Phyllis Granoff and Koichi Shinohara, *Speaking of Monks: Religious Biography in India and China*, Mosai Press, London, 1992; Kendall W. Folkert, *Scripture and Community: Collected Essays on the Jains*, edited by John E. Cort, Scholars Press, Atlanta, 1993; N. N. Bhattacharyya, ed., *Jainism and Prakrit in Ancient and Medieval India: Essays for Professor Jagdhish Chandra Jain*, Manohar Publishers, New Delhi, 1994: Phyllis Granoff and Koichi Shinohara, eds., *Other Selves: Autobiography and Biography in Cross-Cultural Perspective*, Mosaic Press, Buffalo, 1994; Caroline Humphrey and James Laidlaw, *The Archetypal Actions of Ritual: A Theory of Ritual Illustrated by the Jain Rite of Worship*, Clarendon Press, Oxford, 1994; Nathmal Tatia, trans., *That which is: Tattvārtha Sūtra of Umāsvāti*, Sacred Literature Trust and Institute of Jainology, Harper Collins, London, 1994; Willem B. Bollee, *The Nijjuttis on the Seniors of the Śvetāmbara Siddhānta-Āyāraṅga, Dasaveyāliya, Uttarajjhāya, and Sūyagaḍa: Text and Selective glossary*, Franz Steiner Verlag, Stuttgrat, 1995; W. J. Johnson, *Harmless Souls*, Motilal Banarsidass, Delhi, 1995; James Laidlaw, *Riches and Renunciation: Religion, Economy, and Society among the Jains*, Claredon Press, Oxford, 1995; Moriichi Yamazaki and Yumi Ousaka, *A Pāda Index and Reverse Pāda Index to Early Jain Canons: Āyāraṅga, Sūyagaḍa, Uttarajjhāyā, Dasaveyāliya, and Isibhāsiyāiṃ*, Kosei Publishing Company, Tokyo, 1995; Lawrence A. Babb, *Absent Lord: Ascetics and Kings in a Jain Ritual Culture*, University of California Press, 1996; Moriichi Yamazaki and Yumi Ousaka, *Āyāraṅga: Word Index and Reverse Word Index*, Chuo Academic Research Institute, Tokyo, 1996; Moriichi Yamazaki and Yumi Ousaka, *Sūyagaḍa: Word Index and Reverse Word Index*, The Chuo Academic Research Institute, Tokyo, 1996; and J. W. de Jong and Royce Wiles, trans., *Nirayāvaliyāsuyakkhandha*: Uvaṅgas 8-12 of the Jain Canon (introduction, text-edition and notes by Josef Deleu), The Chuo Academic Research Institute, Tokyo, 1996; John E. Cort, Ed., *Open Boundaries: Jain Communities and Cultures in Indian History*, State University of New York Press, New York, 1998; Phyllis Thanoff, *The Forest of Thieves and the Magic Harden: An Anthology of Medieval Jain Stories*, Penguin Book, Delhi, 1998; Hemacandra: *The Lives of the Jain Elders*, Translation by R.C.C. Fynes, Oxford World's Classics, Oxford University Press, 1998; A. Shanta, *The Unknown Pilgrims: The Voice of the Sādhvīs: The History, Spirituality, and Life of the Jaina Women Ascetics*, Translated from French by Mary Rogers, Sri Sat Guru Publications, Delhi, 1997. (French title: La voice jaina, 1985)

III

SOME ASPECTS OF REALITY IN JAINA DOCTRINE

CHAPTER 3

Amṛtacandra Sūri's Exposition on Reality

(Abridged Version of the Introduction to Amṛtacandra Sūri's *Laghutattvasphoṭa*)*

Significant Discovery

The undated palm-leaf manuscript consisting of 53 folios of the *Laghutattvasphoṭa* was found in 1968 by Munishri Punyavijayaji in the Dela Bhaṇḍāra, Ahmedabad. The discovery of a manuscript of this totally unknown work by the celebrated Digambara Amṛtacandra Sūri was hailed as a great event by the entire Jaina community. Its being found in a Śvetāmbara Bhaṇḍāra by a Śvetāmbara Muni provided even greater significance, reminding the Jainas, on the eve of the 2500th anniversary of Lord Mahāvīra's nirvāṇa, of the essential unity underlying their sectarian traditions. When I heard the good news of this discovery I wrote to the Late Munishri begging him to allow me to work on this unpublished text; most magnanimously, he not only dispatched photographs of the original but even a copy which had been made under his supervision. In presenting this Sanskrit edition and English translation of the work, I hope to have at least partially fulfilled the task which he entrusted to me.

Authorship

The colophon states that the *Laghutattvasphoṭa* is the work of

*Originally published in Amṛtacandra Sūri's *Laghutattvasphoṭa* (text and translation), L.D. Series, no. 62 (Ahmedabad: L.D. Institute of Indology, 1978), pp. 1-40.

Amṛtacandra Sūri. Although the *Laghutattvasphoṭa* does not refer to any other work, two of its verses, Nos. 507 and 624, are identical with verses 270 and 141, respectively, of *Samayasāra-kalaśa*, which is part of Amṛtacandra Sūri's *Ātmakhyāti-ṭīkā*, a famous prose commentary on the *Samayasāra*[1] of Kundakunda. There are other similarities of both vocabulary and style between these two compositions; the *Laghutattvasphoṭa*, therefore, must be considered the work of this same Amṛtacandra Sūri. He is also the author of two more independent works, the *Tattvārthasāra*[2] and the *Puruṣārthasiddhyupāya*,[3] and of commentaries on Kundakunda's *Pañcāstikāya*[4] and *Pravacanasāra*;[5] these are called *Samayadīpikā* and *Tattvadīpikā*, respectively.

The present work does not add any new information regarding the time or life of Amṛtacandra Sūri. For this, we refer the reader to Dr. A. N. Upadhye's exhaustive introduction to his edition of the *Pravacanasāra* (pp. 93-96). The style of the *Laghutattvasphoṭa* and its preoccupation with problems pertaining to the omniscience of the Jina would seem to confirm Dr. Upadhye's suggestion that Amṛtacandra Sūri be assigned tentatively to the tenth century A.D.

Title

The colophon refers to the work by two titles: *Śakti-maṇita-kośa* and *Laghu-tattva-sphoṭa*. The former is not a later addition, as it is alluded to in the concluding verse (626): "hṛṣyan bahūni maṇitāni muhuḥ svaśakteḥ". The word maṇita, however, is obscure. It probably stands for maṇi (jewel), or could be a scribal error for 'bhaṇita';[6] in any case, this title appears less attractive than the second, *Laghutattvasphoṭa*, which we have thus adopted. This latter title is also alluded to in the second concluding verse (627), particularly by the words "parātmavicārasāre dig asau śiśūnām". It may be mentioned that Amṛtacandra's *Puruṣārthasiddhyupāya* also has a secondary title, *Jina-pravacana-rahasya-kośa*;[7] the fact that this too ends in kośa further confirms the identity of our author.

Although it has a rather austere title more befitting a philosophical manual than a poem, the *Laghutattvasphoṭa* belongs to the genre called 'stotra', a Sanskrit literary form that gained prominence under the influence of the bhakti movements of the early medieval period. A stotra is primarily a poem of praise addressed to the Deity, extolling his exploits and invoking his blessings for the devotee. As atheists, the Jainas had no use for either the Deity or his blessings, but their poets and mystics found the stotra an excellent medium to demonstrate their poetical talents (which they never applied to mundane objects)[8] and also to cater to the emotional needs of the faithful. Therefore, they cultivated this form of literature in praise of the Jina; and, lacking doctrinal basis for either a Deity or its worship, turned their stotras into philosophical 'poems', compositions which also propagated the Jina's doctrine.

The stotras could be addressed to any one or all of the Tīrthaṅkaras, human saints who had attained omniscience (*kevalajñāna*) and then preached the Law of the salvation of suffering humanity. The Jaina poets saw the Jina as a Perfected Yogin endowed with omniscience and bliss, totally free from all bonds of attachment and aversion (*vīta-rāga*). They saw him preaching his sermon in the holy assembly called samavasaraṇa, surrounded by the ascetic disciples who had chosen to follow his path, and devoutly attended by laymen and laywomen singing his glory. This glory consisted not in the royal insignia, i.e., the white umbrella raised high over him, nor in the presence of gods like Indra who descended from heaven to kneel before him; rather, it lay in his teachings.[9] These were characterized by the doctrines of anekānta, ahiṃsā and aparigraha, and thus to be distinguished from all other teachings. The stotras thus became songs not so much of the Jina but rather of the Dharma, the most glorious of all things, and came finally to be manuals of the Jaina 'darśana'.

Almost every major writer of the post-canonical period has a stotra to his name. Prominent among these are Siddhasena Divākara (5th century A.D.) and 'Svāmi' Samantabhadra (6th century A.D.), authors of the *Dvātriṃśikā*[10] and the *Svayambhū-stotra*[11] respectively. These works appear to have served as models for the *Laghutattvasphoṭa*. The *Dvātriṃśikā* is not really a single work devoted to a single topic, but rather a collection of 32 independent hymns in diverse meters each containing 32 verses. The *Laghutattvasphoṭa* has this same sort of uniformity: it is a collection of twenty-five independent chapters each having twenty-five verses in different meters. Each *Dvātriṃśikā* hymn is either a 'stuti' of the Jina or a critique of a specific 'ekānta'; in this respect the work compares well with the *Laghutattvasphoṭa*, which also aims at exposing the heretic systems, albeit in a less organized manner. But even a casual look at these two works shows a wide gap between them, both in style and the thrust of the subject matter. Siddhasena uses a classical Sanskrit style, closer to such contemporary poets as Kālidāsa; he demonstrates his erudition in Jaina siddhānta as well as in Vedic and Upaniṣadic literature and in the sciences of logic, disputation, etc. Amṛtacandra, on the other hand, displays a predilection of the alliterative Campū style of the late medieval period, and is content with expounding the niścaya-naya in the framework of syādvāda. In this respect his work shows greater affinity with Samantabhadra who also threads his subtle arguments in defense of the syādvāda through some of the most eloquent portions of his *Svayambhū-stotra*, a collection of twenty-four short hymns addressed to each of the twenty-four Tīrthaṅkaras. Both texts open with the word svayambhū, and the *Laghutattvasphoṭa* has a few lines which correspond to passages in the *Svayambhū-stotra.*[12] It is true that Amṛtacandra does not dedicate his chapters to the Tīrthaṅkaras but the first twenty-four verses of his initial chapter invoke the twenty-four individually, thus giving the *Laghutattvasphoṭa* the character of a stotra.

Contents of the Text with Critical Comments

As stated above, the *Laghutattvasphoṭa* is divided into twenty-five chapters with twenty-five verses to each. The chapters bear no titles; they are, however, well-marked by fresh salutations to the Jina, and often by a change of meter as well. The author seems to have intended for each chapter to deal with a specific topic, but he has allowed the various themes to become somewhat mixed; as a result, there are many repetitions and the chapters are a bit disconnected, failing to form finished parts of an integrated whole. Yet the work succeeds in conveying to the patient reader the bliss of the Jina's 'self experience' and the poet's overwhelming joy in describing it; further, it clearly elucidates the soul's essential independence in its transformation from bondage to freedom.

The first chapter has a hidden title of tis own, being appropriately called Jina-nāmāvalī, as the author invokes the names of different Tīrthaṅkaras in each verse. It is also unique in that the last verse bears the name of the author (Amṛtacandra-cid-ekapītām), giving that verse an appearance of a colophon. Amṛtacandra probably composed this chapter as an independent work to be used as a 'caturviṃśati-stava', an important part of an ancient Jaina liturgy.[13]

The first chapter is also the most formidable part of the entire work, as the poet turns quite a few of its verses into veritable riddles. The doctrine of syādvāda affords him unlimited opportunity to exploit the figure of speech called virodhābhāsa, whereby he can describe the Jina in such apparently contradictory terms as śūnya-aśūnyua, nitya-anitya, sat-asat, bhūta-bhaviṣyat, ātmaka-nirātmaka, eka-aneka, baddha-mukta, kartṛ-boddhṛ, etc. All Jaina poets employ these dual attributes for the soul in the spirit of anekānta, i.e. from the 'conventional' (*vyavahāra*) and 'non-conventional' (*niścaya*) points of view (*naya*). What distinguishes Amṛtacandra from the rest is his eloquent espousal for the niścaya-naya without departing from the anekānta doctrine. In the fourteenth verse, for example, he praises the infinitely variegated forms of the Lord's omniscient knowledge as it illuminates the infinite objects, but does not fail to emphasize that this omniscience is also non-dual (*advaita*) from the niścaya point of view. He proclaims that he worships that unitary great light (*advaitam eva mahayāmi mahan mahas te*); reminding us of his bold words in the *Samayasāra-kalaśa* (9): anubhavam upayāte bhāti na dvaitam eva.

The second chapter continues with the problem of the dichotomy created by the 'vaiśvarūpya' and 'ekarūpatā' which characterize the cognition of Jina. As if anticipating the Sāṃkhya objection that cognition of objects might destroy the unitary nature of consciousness, the poet asserts that the 'puruṣa', i.e. the pure soul, remains distinct from the world of objects even when he cognises them, undisturbed from the innate (*sahaja*) unity of his consciousness (*caitanya*). This is of course, possible only for the Jaina, who adheres to the doctrines of anekānta and syādvāda; the absolutist Sāṃkhya must deny any cognition by the puruṣa or soul, for this would imply contamination. The poet therefore calls the "ekāntavādin" a paśu, or ignorant person, literally an "animal".[14]

This term, although rather strong and of rare occurrence in other Jaina works,[15] occurs ten times in the *Laghutattvasphoṭa.*[16] It is invariably applied to an "ekāntavādin"; this could be an adherent of any of the classical darśanas, or even a Jaina who has strayed from the true path either by clinging to the 'external' (*vyavahāra*) discipline, at the cost of cultivating the niścaya, or by abandoning the 'vyavahāra' in the misguided belief that he has already attained the 'niścaya'. The poet characterizes the paśu as 'destroyer of the self' (*ātmaghātin*), 'devoid of insight' (*asta-bodha*), 'one of closed heart' (*mukulita-svāntaḥ*), etc. It should be mentioned that the term paśu comes to be used even more frequently in another of Amṛtacandra's works, the *Samayasāra-kalaśa.*[17] Its occurrences there are all in the chapter dealing with syādvāda, where the 'false' doctrines of the paśu are contrasted with the Jaina position, which is characterized by the tenet of syādvāda. A comparison of these passages confirms the identity of authorship of these two works.

The second chapter closes with a further affirmation of the varigated nature of the soul; this is expressed in a beautiful verse (50) which, as noted earlier, is identical with *Samayasāra-kalaśa* 270.

The third chapter provides one of the finest accounts of the spiritual career of a Jina found in the entire Jaina literature. This career consists of the gradual progress of the soul from its lowest state, that of nescience (*mithyātva*), to the highest state of spiritual growth, marked by omniscience. This path of purification has fourteen stages called guṇasthānas,[18] beyond which lies the total isolation (*kaivalya*) of the soul, the Jaina ideal of a Perfect Being (*siddha*). The turning point is the fourth stage, "samyaktva", which marks the entrance of the aspirant on to the Path. Amṛtacandra hails the moment of entering that path (*mārgāvatāra*) as one of great bliss (51). The samyaktva consists of insight into the true nature of the soul, which is defined as nothing but 'pure intuition and knowledge' (*dṛg-bodha-mātra*). The author equates this samyaktva with sāmāyika,[19] a Jain technical term for the tranquility of the soul which is gained only by such insight. Samyaktva leads to the relinquishing of all evil activities, activities which give rise to attachment and aversion and thus injure the soul. It has two stages, being first partially achieved while living as a layman (*śrāvaka*), and then totally while an ascetic (*muni*). These changes are indicated by the fifth and sixth stages, called deśa-virata and pramatta-virata, respectively. Through these stages the aspirant cultivates 'right-conduct' (*samyak-cāritra*), which to the nascent Jina comes so spontaneously that he is called the very embodiment of sāmāyika (*sāmāyikaṃ svayam abhūt*...52).

It might be argued by certain overzealous advocates of the 'niścaya-naya' that the noble aspirant endowed with such insight and equanimity, could dispense with the 'mere formalities' of becoming an ascetic (i.e. the *vyavahāra*).[20] As if to correct such a notion, the poet makes the pointed observation that external (*dravya*) and internal (*bhāva*) controls (*saṃyama*) are interdependent, and that the nascent Jina demonstrated this by first establishing himself in the discipline of the ascetic (*tvaṃ dravyasaṃyamapathe prathamaṃ nyayuṅkthāḥ*-53). The sixth stage, called pramatta-virata, is marked by numerous ascetic activities, particularly the practice of such austerities (*tapas*) as fasting and long hours of meditation. But these are all actions, albeit worldly wholesome ones (*śubha*), and must yield results according to the laws of karma. Further, the word 'pramatta' itself indicates more than simple carelessness in ascetic activities; it implies lack of mindfulness regarding the true nature of the self. Hence the true aspirant must turn 'completely inward', 'creating vast distance between the puruṣa and prakṛti'[21] (*dūrāntaraṃ racayataḥ puruṣa-prakṛtyoḥ*/61) i.e. between the soul and the karman, and attain the firm stage of pure consciousness (*śuddhopayoga*),[22] in which no new karma is generated. This stage is appropriately called apramatta-virata, the seventh guṇasthāna, which becomes the springboard for rapid advancement on the Path.

Up to this stage the aspirant had been engaged in controlling the avenues through which new influxes of kaṣāyas or passions (namely, anger, pride, deceit and greed) could enter (*āsrava*), hindering the realization of perfect conduct (*sakala-cāritra*). Secured in the firm stage of apramatta-virata, he exerts his energies to totally eradicate (*kṣaya*) the latent forces of these passions, passions which have been accumulated from time immemorial and present a potential threat to his purity.

The Jaina calls these latent forces "cāritra-mohanīya-karma", which he further divides into two categories: bhāva (psychological and internal) and dravya (physical and external). Attachment (*rāga*) and aversion (*dveṣa*), for instance, are bhāva-karmas, defiled (*vibhāva*) states of the quality (*guṇa*) called *cārita* (purity). In the beginningless stage of saṃsāra, this quality remains in its unnatural (*vaibhāvika*) mode (*pariṇāma*) and is perceived only as it undergoes fluctuations; in the state of mokṣa the same quality is brought to its natural (*svābhāvika*) mode and remains forever in that perfect state. Modification of the cāritra-guṇa is thought to be caused by an external force, also beginningless, called dravya-karma. The Jaina is unique in seeing this force as physical (*pudgala*) formed of a special kind of subtle 'karmic' matter; he designates it by function as "cāritra-mohanīya-prakṛti"—of the species which produce 'delusion' pertaining to conduct. It is believed that when a certain defilement (*vibhāva*), such as aversion, overpowers the soul, a fixed quantity (*pradeśa*) of this 'karmic' matter is absorbed by the soul just as a wet cloth absorbs dust. One may argue that there is no possibility of contact between material atoms and an immaterial substance (*amūrta-dravya*) like soul. The Jaina overcomes this difficulty by pointing to the phenomenon of perception, where such contact does occur, and maintains that the soul and the karmic matter do not actually 'mix' but merely occupy the same space (*ekakṣetra-avagāha*) without losing their own identity as soul and matter.[23] The example of milk and water mixture, seemingly homogenous but still separable, is often given to illustrate this point. The newly absorbed (*baddha*) dravya-karma is itself seen as an unnatural mode of the previously 'pure' atoms. This 'impure' matter remains for a fixed period (*sthiti*) within the same space as the soul, finally reaching maturity (*anubhāga*) and giving rise (*udaya*) to fresh occurrences of aversion. Having yielded its result, i.e. having served as the cause for a further transformation (*vibhāva-pariṇati*) of the soul, the dravya-karma reverts (*nirjarā*) to its 'pure' state, only to be absorbed once again upon the arising of new passions; thus the cycle is renewed forever.[24]

It should be noted here that unlike the Sāṃkhya, who allows change in the Prakṛti but does not admit any change in the soul (*puruṣa*), the Jaina believes that both soul and the matter undergo transformations without losing their own nature (*tadbhāva-avyayaṃ nityam*):[25] in other words, bondage is real, and not merely an 'illusion' as in the Sāṃkhya or the Vedānta systems. 'Freedom' in these systems is purely epistemic: ontologically there is no change, for the soul remains what it has always been, i.e. totally free, both before and after "gaining" knowledge of its true nature. For the Jaina, however, 'freedom' involves actual changes in the state of the soul as indicated by the doctrine of guṇasthānas, and also that of the karmic matter. He must explain how the soul is able to change something other than itself. If he admits the possibility of one substance (*dravya*) like *jīva* (soul) influencing the transformation of another substance like matter (*pudgala* or *dravya-karma*) or *vice versa,* then it might seem that soul and matter could never be free of each other.

The solution to this dilemma is to be found in the Jaina concepts of "existent" (*sat*) and "change" (*pariṇāma*). The Jaina defines the existent as that which is simultaneously permanent and changing. It endures as a substance (*dravya*) but also undergoes changes at each instant as an old mode (*paryāya*) perishes and a new mode arises within that substance (*utpāda-vyaya-dhrauvya-yuktaṃ sat*).[26] These modes belong to the qualities (*guṇas*) and the two together characterize a substance (guṇaparyayavad dravyam).[27] The innumerable souls (*jīvas*), for instance, are "substances" characterized by qualities like knowledge (*jñāna*), bliss (*sukha*), etc. which undergo constant change. These qualities are homogenous (*svābhāvika*) in the state of mokṣa and heterogenous (*vaibhāvika*), i.e. defiled and obscured by karmic matter, in the state of saṃsāra. In the case of matter (*pudgala*) also, each of the infinite atoms is a substance and has qualities of touch, taste, smell and colour (*sparśa, rasa, gandha, varṇa*) which change in a similar manner. Since change is as essential a feature of the existent as is permanence, and since it is found equally in both the pure and impure states, the Jaina declares that change is not adventitious but rather innate to reality; it must therefore take place regardless of an external agency. While the Jaina does admit a causal relationship between one substance and another, he nevertheless maintains that as far as change and permanence are concerned, the causality in no way affects the autonomous nature of either the substance or the qualities.

The inviolable individuality of each substance and quality is assured by a characteristic called agurulaghutva, found in all substances and hence called a sāmānya-guṇa. This is a characteristic by virtue of which one substance, while it may share a given space with others, does not assume the modes (*paryāyas*) of those. It also determines the fact that one quality does not, even in a defiled state, become other than itself, and the infinite qualities of a particular substance do not separate themselves from their locus i.e. that substance. Amṛtacandra puts this succinctly in the following words:

> sarve bhāvāḥ sahaja-niyatā 'nyonyasīmāna ete
> saṃśleṣe 'pi svayam apatitāḥ śaśvad eva svarūpāt/ (537)

It is because of this guṇa that knowledge does not take the nature of the objects known and that karmic matter does not assume the nature of the soul. The agurulaghutva, 'the state of being neither heavy nor light', is probably built into the existent (*sat*) in order to maintain its equilibrium in the face of the infinite modes necessitated by the very nature of reality. It preserves the exact identity of each substance and its innumerable qualities by denying any actual 'gain' (*guru*) or 'loss' (*laghu*) which might result from influence by the other members of the causal relationship.

The Jaina scriptures give a long list of 'assistance' (*upakāra*) rendered to one dravya by another. According to the *Tattvārthasūtra*,[28] the souls have as their function rendering assistance to each other. Matter (*pudgala*) renders 'service' to the jīva, first by transforming itself into this 'karmic' matter and then into body, vital life (*prāṇa*), sense organs, speech and the physical basis of mind (*dravya-manas*). The substances called 'dharma' and 'adharma' provide favourable conditions for the motion and rest, respectively of both jīva and pudgala. Ākāśa (space) provides location for the other four, as well as for time (*kāla*). And time functions as a common cause for the transformation of all the rest.

It should be noted, however, that this 'assistance' has strictly the nature of instrumentality (*nimitta-kāraṇa*); it is not nearly so vital as its counterpart, the operative or 'material' cause (*upādāna-kāraṇa*). Being a 'material' cause is the prerogative of the substance alone; that is, the substance (*dravya*) in one mode (*paryāya*) is the material "cause" of the substance in its subsequent mode, which is thus its "effect". There can be neither an addition to nor a subtraction from this innate power of the substance, the power to modify itself in accordance with its potential or 'upādāna', regardless of the presence or absence of instrumental (*nimitta*) causes. The Jaina therefore maintains that when the material cause (*upādāna-kāraṇa*) is present, instrumental causes (*nimitta-kāraṇas*) will automatically appear; in other words, whatever conditions are present will function as nimitta-kāraṇa at the appropriate time. The next mode of the substance will thus be achieved, in accordance with the upādāna, without any real interference from the outside.

Thus it appears that such statements as "bondage of the soul is caused by (*dravya-*) karma", or "the formation of the dravya-karma is brought about by the *kaṣāyas* (passions) of the soul" are purely conventional (*vyavahāra*) ones. These statements are based upon superficial observation of the proximity of the soul and the 'karmic' matter in the same space (*pradeśa*); they do not take into account the unique 'upādānas' or the mutual inviolability (deriving from their agurulaghutva) of these substances. From the non-conventional point of view, i.e. the niścaya-naya, the jīva is bound by its own upādāna; similarly the upādāna of the pudgala determines its formation into dravya-karma. The Jaina affirms that the change of the jīva from its defiled state to the state of purity is brought about essentially by its upādāna and not by the instrumentality of the 'karmic' matter (i.e. by its disappearance); such agencies as a superhuman being, an avatāra or a God are, of course, considered totally irrelevant. The uncompromising atheism of the Jaina, especially his rejection of the concept of 'grace', further underlines his total reliance on the upādāna for salvation and his call for adherence to the niścaya-naya which upholds it.

The Jaina contends that the chief cause of man's bondage is his mistaken belief that he can be the agent (*kartā*) of change in other things (*parapariṇati*), whether souls or the material world, and also that these can somehow effect change in his own destiny. Ignorant of the law of upādāna which governs both himself and others, he engages in manifold activities, morally wholesome or unwholesome, in the attempt to enforce such changes in others as would suit his egotistic wishes. These efforts, of course, invariably meet with frustration and sorrow. The path of salvation and peace lies in self-reliance and isolation, and these are gained only by realizing the law of upādāna. Having attained this realization, the aspirant will see that external supports and activities are both useless and undesirable; he will thus be led to relinquish them and to seek refuge only in the self.

But which self? The uninstructed person is aware only of that 'self' which he identifies with the body, the vital breath, and the sense faculties. These the Jaina includes in "bahirātman", the 'exterior' self; neither this nor the mind nor the psychological states which one experiences from moment to moment can be the true self. Mind, according to the Jaina, is twofold; it has a physical basis (*dravya-manas*), but also includes a non-physical 'organ' which cognises and coordinates the activities of the senses. This non-physical aspect is bhāva-manas; it is not different from the soul. But this cannot be the true nature of the soul either, for the obvious reason that it is invariably a defiled state from which the aspirant seeks dissociation. The mind is the seat of the *kaṣāyas* (passions), and although these are not material, they are nevertheless formed in the soul in association with karmic matter; the aspirant must understand them in this way and then reject them. In doing this it may be helpful to cultivate morally wholesome states, e.g. forgiveness (*kṣamā*), compassion (*karuṇā*) friendliness (*maitrī*), disinterestedness (*upekṣā*), etc., states which may lead to conditions favorable to the attaining of samyaktva (true knowledge of the self). This is called the "antarātman," the 'interior' self. But even this state is not the final goal of the aspirant. The true nature of the soul must be that which remains when one is totally isolated from both body and the mind. This is characterized by omniscience (*kevala-jñāna*), perfect energy (*vīrya*), perfect bliss (*sukha*) and perfect purity; once attained, this state can never be lost or defiled again. It is what the Jaina calls "paramātman" or the 'transcendent' self, the ultimate goal of the aspirant.[29]

The Jaina recognises that physical embodiment and psychological states are real and not imaginary, and also that they both belong to the soul and not to matter. But in order to transcend them he must deny their identification with the soul, reserving this identity only for the paramātman. Since the goal of the aspirant is isolation and salvation, the Jaina Ācāryas admonish him to regard every defiled state of the soul, (which technically includes all states of embodiment, i.e., the fourteen guṇasthānas),[30] as external to him; he must find no support, but 'pure consciousness', which transcends all activities, both wholesome (*śubha*) and unwholesome (*aśubha*). This is possible only by recourse to the śuddha-niścaya-naya, the transcendental viewpoint wherein all activities are denied to the self. From this perspective the self is seen as the 'knower' (*jñātṛ*), which it would of course be in the state of mokṣa. The aspirant has a glimpse of his transcendental viewpoint even in the fourth (*samyag-dṛṣṭi*) stage, but he is unable to retain it without the viratis. He comes to have the sustained pure consciousness (*śuddhajñāyaka-bhāva*) only when he becomes fully 'mindful' and thus attains the apramattavirata, the seventh guṇasthāna.

Such pure 'self-experience', called śuddha-upayoga, is repeatedly alluded to by Amṛtacandra in all his works. Rare and brief as it is, it ushers in unprecedented purity of the soul, preparing one for further conquest of the forces of karma. In the case of a less advanced aspirant, this may take the form of suppression (*upaśama*) of the kaṣāyas, affording only temporary relief. It is temporary as the aspirant must return to the defiled state having reached the eleventh stage called upaśānta-kaṣāya. But in the case of the nascent Jina, his insights are so consummate that he instantly climbs the ladder (*śreṇi*) of spiritual progress which leads unfailingly, in that very life time, to the total annihilaion (*kṣaya*) of all karmas. This is achieved in the eighth, ninth and the tenth guṇasthānas, called apūrva-karaṇa, anivṛtti-karaṇa[31] and sūkṣma-sāmparāya, respectively, during which the aspirant, by means of the 'dharma' and the 'śukla' dhyānas,[32] gradually destroys both gross and subtle forms of mohanīya-karma. He skips the eleventh stage as he has not suppressed the kaṣāyas and attains the twelfth stage called kṣīṇa-kaṣāya. Mohanīya-karma is the chief obstacle to releazing perfect purity; its elimination is followed immediately by the destruction of three more karmas called ghātiyā, those which obscure knowledge (*jñāna*), intuition (*darśana*) and energy (*vīrya*) respectively. Thus the aspirant becomes an omniscient (*sarvajña*) Jina; this state is indicated by the thirteenth guṇasthāna called sayoga-kevalin.

One who has thus reached his goal is called a Kevalin; endowed with kevala-jñāna, omniscient cognition; he is an Arhat, worthy of worship, an Āpta, a reliable guide and Teacher. It is to him that all stotras are addressed. And yet he is still a human being, as the descriptive term "sayoga" indicates. Yoga is a Jaina technical term for 'vibrations' of body, speech and mind. It is present in all human beings but prior to the twelfth guṇasthāna is associated with the kaṣāyas (passions). The Jaina cannot accept anyone's claim to be an Āpta until his kaṣāyas are totally destroyed, a prerequisite of truthfulness. Upon this destruction and the subsequent manifestation of omniscience, the 'yoga', now that of the Jina, turns into a perfect means of communicating the Law. Thus we have the omniscient teacher, the most venerable example of human existance; Amṛtacandra dwells at length upon the immeasurable glories of such a being, emphasizing time and again that his knowledge of objects neither contaminates his omniscience nor produces divisions in his unitary consciousness.

But even this stage is not yet perfect, for the soul must still overcome the 'secondary' (aghātiyā, literally, non-destructive as compared to the ghātiyā) karmas which produce the body (*nāma-karma*), social status (*gotra-karma*), feelings (*vedanīya-karma*) and the duration of life (*āyu-karma*). The Jaina maintains that the duration of one's present lifetime is invariably fixed in the immediately preceding one. Although premature death is conceivable for an ordinary person, it is ruled out in the case of the Jina, for he has totally destroyed all kaṣāyas, the only factor which could bring this about. The other three karmas, especially the vedanīya (which produces feelings of happiness and unhappiness), are always accumulated by the soul in quantities larger than can be brought to maturity in a single lifetime. The Jina too has surplus quantities of such karmic matter (*dravya-karma*); had he not attained to the twelfth guṇasthāna, it would have matured in subsequent births, but in the absence of a new birth it must be exhausted before his death. In other words, the quantity of the other three karmas must be reduced to a level corresponding to that of the remaining āyu-karma, which is unalterable. This is accomplished by an extremely curious yogic process called samudghāta (destruction by bursting forth); it is a sort of involuntary action which takes place but once, occupying only eight moments, a short time prior to the Jina's death.

The kevali-samudghāta is appropriately named since it is performed only by a kevalin. This doctrine is probably unique to Jainism; it casts light upon their theories of karma and jīva, demonstrating the absolute materiality of the dravya-karma and the inevitability of its effects on even the omniscient soul. The karmas must first be brought to maturity and their effects experienced by the soul; only then can they reach a state of exhaustion. There is no escape from these effects through any superhuman agency, nor is there a teleological possibility, such as that proposed by the Sāṃkhya, of the karmas themselves departing from the soul after "perceiving" its "disinterest".[33] The Jaina explains the samudghāta process with the example of a wet cloth which dries slowly when folded, but quickly when it is spread out. The karmic matter (*dravya-karma*) can be forced into maturity by the soul through a similar process. Without leaving the substratum of the body, the soul stretches self vertically and horizontally and fills up the whole universe (*loka-ākāśa*), 'mixing' as it were, its 'space-points' (*pradeśas*) with those of the karmic matter. Thus it forces matter out by a sort of thinning process.[34] The soul then contracts its space-points into the body, having reduced the level of the three karmas to that of the remaining āyu-karma.

As soon as this is accomplished, the soul stops all vibrations (*yoga-nirodha*) for the period required to utter five syllables. This stage is called ayoga-kevalin, the kevalin without vibrations, the fourteenth and last guṇasthāna. Then, just as a gourd held down by a coating of mud rises to the surface of water or as a flame by nature darts upwards, the soul moves instantaneously to the summit of the universe, beyond which there is no motion, and abides there forever.[35] This is the perfect state of isolation (*kaivalya*) called siddha-paryāya; it is declared to be sādi, "with beginning", but ananta, "without end". The only thing that remains from the mundane past is the size of the soul which is less than that of the immediately preceding body.

It is well known that the Jaina is unique among the ātmavādins in believing that the soul is neither all-pervasive (*vibhu*) as suggested by the Śaṅkara Vedānta, Nyāya-Vaiśeṣika, and Sāṃkhya, nor infinitesimal (*aṇu*), as in the theory of Rāmānuja; it takes the size of the body (*sva-deha-parimāṇa*), and is endowed with the ability to expand and contract its 'innumerable' (*asaṃkhyāta*) space-points (*pradeśas*).[36] This is considered a proper description on the grounds that such characteristics of the soul as consciousness are not found outside the body. One might expect that in the stage of mokṣa, where all signs of embodiment are eliminated, the soul would automatically become all-pervasive and maintain that condition forever. The kevali-samudghāta gives the soul a unique opportunity to overcome any karmically enforced 'shape', allowing it to become all-pervasive without actually leaving its substratum, the body. But its immediate contraction to the original shape just prior to death negates this unique experience and virtually fixes the liberated soul forever in the shape of its final body. It seems a bit strange that the kevali-samudghāta has not been made co-incidental with death, thus allowing the soul to be all-pervasive forever. Exactly why the Jaina wants to retain the size of the previous body for the siddha must remain a moot question, for the scriptures are rather uncomfortably silent on this point[37]. It is claimed only that there is no real gain or loss of ātma-pradeśas, whether the soul takes the size of its body or of the universe, and also that the kevalin is past the stage of wishing for anything anyway! Is it possible that the Jaina wants to maintain the individuality of the soul and furnish it with some differentiating mark where there would otherwise be no basis for distinction whatsoever? Does he wish to emphasize the fact that the exalted Jina, though he has overcome the modalities of worldly existence was himself a human being? If so, this theory could be construed as a further attempt to stay clear of merging into an Absolute, and also to distinguish the jīva, from the Sāṃkhya concept of an *ever*-free and all-pervading puruṣa.

The chapter ends with the author's devout wish that he too may become an omniscient being: bhavāmi kila sarvamayo 'ham eva (75).

The fourth and the fifth chapters continue with the theme of the omniscient Jina, seated in the holy assembly (*sado'nte*). He is described as a mass of knowledge (*vijñānaghana*), of which his cognition is a mere sport (*ātma-khelitam*—83). Although he has not transcended the mundane condition, the Jina has not abandoned that essential duality (*dvyātmakatā*) of permanence and change which characterizes all existents (89). His omniscience is larger than the totality of the objects which it knows. These objects do not produce knowledge, which exists by its own nature; they merely 'instigate' (*uttejana*) it. Even so it is held that there could be no 'inner knowables' in the absence of 'outer objects'; hence the Vijñānavādin doctrine of bahir-artha-nihnava stands condemned. Finally, the Jina's cognition, even when it illuminates an infinity of objects, is free from agitation (*anākula*); from the niścaya point of view, the Jina cognises the mere existence (*san-mātra*) which is one, partless, eternal and innate (anaṃśam ekaṃ sahajaṃ sanātanam—113).

The sixth chapter returns once more to the ascetic path of the nascent Jina, discussed in the third chapter. The aspirant turns all activities (*kriyā*) into śīla, i.e. perfect conduct. His heart is filled with profound disenchantment, and he offers his worldly life into the fire of austerities (*tapo'nale juhvad iha svajīvitam*—127). Moving all alone (*ekakam*) on the holy path (*brahma-patha*), he mounts the 'ladder' of the destruction of karmas (*kṣaya-śreṇi*—131) and arrives at the twelfth guṇasthāna; here arises "the omniscient knowledge which becomes a beautiful flame, kindled at the centre of the universe" (136). For the first time his soul realizes the true nature of reality, becoming totally indifferent towards the desire to act (*samasta-kartṛtva-nirutsuka*—137). Finally, the Jina becomes a siddha (138), shining forth in his peaceful light (*śānta-tejas*) and experiencing (*anubhava*) boundless bliss (*nirantarānanda*).

The seventh chapter opens with the declaration that the poet takes refuge only in the Jina, i.e. in Pure Consciousness (*śuddha-bodha*). It is pure in that all notions of action are absent when one sees this consciousness from the transcendental point of view: "All existents are naturally and eternally contained within the limits of their own being; they cannot be obstructed by others" (167). The state of omniscience is one of knowing and not of doing (*akartṛ-vijñātṛ*), for even when objects are cognized, the soul is merely manifesting its own nature by itself, for itself, and in itself. Thus it is devoid of instrumentalities (*kārakas*); there is no agent, object, instrument, receipient, point of departure, and location (*svabhāva evodayate nirākulam*—170).

The eighth chapter shows the Jina as supreme Teacher, the Āpta. The poet praises him for demonstrating to others, (i.e. the theists, whose teachers are super-human) the splendour of human endeavour (*pauruṣasya prabhāvam āvīṣkṛtavān*—181); by his valour he has destroyed the kaṣāyas and married Lakṣmī in the form of omniscient knowledge (*udvahan kevalabodhalakṣmīḥ*—181). Although he had achieved his goal, he used the remainder of his life for the benefit of the universe, showing the holy path by establishing a Tīrtha (182); thus the Jina is known as Tīrthaṅkara. This is strictly a Jaina term, one which the Buddha did not claim for himself and in fact used rather pejoratively to designate the śramaṇa teachers (*"titthiyā"*) of his time. One of these was the Nigaṇṭha Nātaputta, identical with Jñātṛputra Mahāvīra, last of the twenty-four Tīrthaṅkaras ("Ford-makers") of the present age. "Tīrtha" literally means a "ford", a way to cross the river. Metaphorically it is applied to the Doctrine which helps one to cross the ocean of transmigration, and to the fourfold Saṅgha of the Jainas: monks, nuns, laymen and laywomen. Each Tīrthaṅkara initiates a new Tīrtha and thus keeps the torch of the Law burning; only human beings can fill this role. Although at present there is no Tīrthaṅkara on earth, it is believed that they do exist in other parts of the universe, where they may be seen by earthly yogins.[38] The line of Tīrthaṅkaras has neither a beginning nor an end and it is open to all who seek to join it.

The Tīrtha appears to be the Jaina answer to the theistic conception of a single, eternally free (*nitya-mukta*) omniscient teacher, such as that propounded by the Yoga school. Patañjali calls this being Īśvara, the Teacher of even the most ancient sages; such an exalted being (*puruṣa-viśeṣa*) must be eternally free (*nitya-mukta*).[39] The Jaina finds this idea totally arbitrary, for if one 'person' can be nitya-mukta, why not all? In fact, the Sāṁkhya claims this very status for every puruṣa.[40] The Jaina thus replaces the Īśvara doctrine with an uninterrupted and endless succession of truly human teachers who rise in the course of time. Amṛtacandra admits the mutual dependence of the aspirant and the Tīrtha for the instruction of the former and the re-establishment of the latter. This mutual causality is like that of seed and sprout; the nascent Jina follows the "Ford" and the "Ford" proceeds from the Jina (*tīrthād bhavantaḥ kila tad bhavadbhyaḥ*—183). The Jaina believes that the periodical appearance of these Tīrthaṅkaras is part of the natural order, as are the changes of season or the transition from one era to the next. As to the number twenty-four, the Jaina seems to regard this, too, as a fixed part of the same inscrutable design.[41] Such a belief is paralleled by the doctrine of twenty-five Buddhas or that of the ten avatāras of Viṣṇu.

For the Jaina, all who attain mokṣa must also obtain omniscience (*sarvajñatva*); in this respect the Jaina arhat differs most fundamentally from his non-omniscient Buddhist counterpart.[42] Further, all Jaina arhats are not Tīrthaṅkaras; to be a Tīrthaṅkara one must have certain "abilities", albeit mundane, such as the "divine sound" (*divya-dhvani*), and the presence of apostles (*gaṇadhara*) who interpret that sound and propagate the teachings contained therein. These "abilities" are not gained through yogic powers, nor are they sought after by the Jina in his final mundane existence. Rather, they result from certain noble practices,[43] comparable to the praṇidhānas and pāramitās of the bodhisattva, undertaken by the Jina in his previous births; these acts come to fruition upon the attainment of omniscience (the thirteenth guṇasthāna). Thus, strictly speaking, the Tīrthaṅkara remains immersed in his omniscient cognition; there is no deliberation to preach a particular sermon or to teach a specific doctrine. And yet the teaching automatically comes forth; the "divine sound" emanates from him and the gaṇadharas make their dramatic appearance at the moment he attains to omniscient cognition. The Jaina thus avoids the apparent contradiction between activities of a teacher and the inactivity inherent to omniscient cognition.

The omniscient Jina perceives the whole of reality; yet there are no words adequate to express the universe in its totality. Therefore only an infinitesimal portion (*ananta-bhāga*) of the Jina's cognition is conveyed to gods and men, and only a few of these will have the purity of heart (*śuddhāśaya*—186) necessary to grasp it. Only through the Jina can one learn the true doctrine, that which asserts the dual (i.e. positive and negative) nature of reality (*dvyātmaka-vastu-vāda*—185). The preaching of the Jina is marked by the seal (*mudrā*) of syādvāda (187), the only means by which one can comprehend and fully express reality with its mutually opposed characteristics (anekānta). Thus he is called the supreme Teacher of all (*ko'nyo bhaved āptataro bhavattaḥ*—99).

The ninth chapter takes us once more to the spiritual career of the nascent Jina. The poet's description of this period in the Jina's life is strongly reminiscent of Mahāvīra's severe austerities as described in the *Ācārāṅgasūtra*[44] prior to his Enlightenment. The soul of the Jina is filled with tranquillity when he enters the holy path (*mārgāvatāra*—201). He fearlessly vows to remain isolated (*ekatva*), totally renouncing both internal and external attachments (*niḥśeṣitāntarbahiraṅgaḥ*—202). He fills his heart with compassion for all suffering beings (*dīnānukampī*—202). Living in accordance with the scriptures he protects the beings of all six classes (*saṃrakṣatas te...sūtreṇa ṣaḍjīvanikām*—203). Resolved to stay in meditation, he suffers the scorching rays of the sun by day and sits all night in the charnel ground, letting jackals crush his ematiated body (205). He fasts for two weeks, or even a month (*māsārdhamāsa-kṣapaṇāni kurvan*—206); thus he gradually attains to perfect conduct and omniscience. The Jina then preaches that path which he himself has practised, the path which is the very essence of the scriptures (*sūtrārtha*). Internally it consists in the destruction of passions (*antaḥkaṣāya-kṣapaṇaḥ*—209); externally, it demands a resolute pursuit of right conduct (*bahir yathāśakticaritrapākaḥ*—209). Both are necessary, for although insight is the most important factor in bringing about salvation, it loses efficacy in the case of one who lacks proper conduct (*ahetuvan niścaraṇasya bodhaḥ*—210).

The tenth chapter opens with a solemn declaration that the poet will praise the Jina from one standpoint, that of the purified view (*stoṣye jinaṃ śuddha-nayaika-dṛṣṭyā*—226). In this śuddha-dṛṣṭi, substance (*dravya*) is identified with only one of its qualities (*guṇas*) and with only the purest of its modes (*paryāyas*). The Jina's soul is endowed with innumerable qualities or powers (*śaktis*),[45] all manifest in their pure modes. Nevertheless, the śuddha-naya prefers to identify his soul with only one of these qualities, jñāna, and only its perfect mode, the omniscient cognition (*kevala-Jñāna*). Other modes are not unreal, but they are of no relevance to the path of salvation. The aspirant therefore fixes his attention only on this goal, using the śuddha-naya as a meditational device. In omniscient cognition, even knowledge of the infinity of objects is of no consequence; the śuddha-naya ignores this rather incidental aspect of kevala-jñāna and concentrates only on the aspect of 'self-experience' (*svānubhava*). This must be so, for from the transcendental (*niścaya*) point of view the soul knows only itself; it sees and experiences itself alone. The poet therefore describes the Jina as being a mass of pure consciousness (*viśuddha-vijñāna-ghana*) which seeks no end other than manifesting its own blissful nature. It is blissful (*anākula*) because there is no room in this cognition for the net of speculations (*vikalpa-jāla*) which produces such distinctions as 'existence' and 'non-existence'. These qualities have validity only in discussing the nature of reality; for the Jina, all vikalpas are at rest (*abhāvabhāvādi-vikalpajālaṃ samastam apy astamayaṃ naya*—232), and nothing shines forth but his manifest own-being (*svabhāva evollasati sphuṭas te*—232). Despite his cognition of the innumerable objects in their infinite modes, the Jina does not deviate from his innate and unified nature; he is compared to a piece of ice which appears wet on all sides but still retains its firmness (239). The unity of his character is like that of a piece of salt, having the same flavour (*ekarasa*) throughout (*vigāhase saindhavakhilyalīlām*—238). He has turned away from the cycle of kārakas and is free from distinctions of 'seer' and 'things seen'; he shines forth as pure intuition (*dṛg eva*—243); he is 'nothing but knowledge' (*bhāmātram*—247).

Chapter eleven and twelve, both in Ānuṣṭubh meter, continue the theme of the śuddha-naya initiated in the tenth chapter. According to this naya, the omniscient consciousness (*cit*) of the Jina remains unified even when a plurality of objects is cognized. This claim of unity needs further examination since the Jaina believes in the doctrine of two distinct operations (*upayoga*) of consciousness, called darśana and jñāna. These are enumerated in the scriptures as two separate qualities (*guṇas*) each having its own adversary ghātiyā karmas, called darśanāvaraṇīya and jñānāvaraṇīya, respectively. Darśana is described as 'indeterminate intuition' (*nirākāra upayoga*) and jñāna as 'determinate knowledge' (*sākāra upayoga*). The two operate always in succession (*krama*), with darśana first for all acts of cognition in the mundane state. There is no unanimous opinion, however, on the manner of operation of these two qualities during the state of arhatship, where both have reached perfection. Three views are prevalent and these have generally come to be associated with the three major sects of the Jainas, respectively.[46]

The Śvetāmbara tradition (represented by Jinabhadra)[47] takes its stand on the principle that two operations (*upayogas*) of one consciousness cannot take place simultaneously. It therefore maintains that darśana and jñāna must always operate in succession (*krama*) even in the state of omniscience. The Yāpanīya tradition (now extinct but represented in the *Sanmati-tarka*[48] of Siddhasena Divākara) maintains that the two stages of cognition, namely the 'indeterminate' and the 'determinate' have relevance only in the mundane state where the soul is dependent on the senses and the mind for its partial cognition. In the case of the Jina, there is no room for 'indeterminate' cognition. Therefore the Yāpanīya contends that in the state of omniscience there is 'non-distinction' (*abheda*) between darśana and jñāna. The Digambara tradition (represented by Kundakunda,[49] among others) disagrees with both these positions. The 'abheda' position is unacceptable because it violates the individuality of such guṇa, and such individuality is guaranteed by agurulaghutva. The soul attains to kevala-darśana, perfect intuition, at the same time that it realizes omniscience (kevala-jñāna); thus there can be no question of the former losing its identity in the latter. The Śvetāmbara contention that both retain their identity but operate in succession (*krama*) is also not acceptable for it renders the nature of the Jina imperfect. The Digambara argues that a perfect quality must always operate, as there are no hindrances to interrupt its function. In the krama theory the darśana and jñāna, though perfect, will operate only alternately thus depriving the Jina of one or the other of these two qualities at all times. The Digambara therefore maintains that whereas in the mundane state the darśana and jñāna operate in succession, they must operate simultaneously (*yugapat*) in the state of omniscience.

The Digambara is aware of the difficulty arising from the simultaneity of these two mutually exclusive (indeterminate and determinate) operations. He seeks to resolve their incompatibility by recourse to a new understanding of the term sākāra and nirākāra. The obscurity of these two canonical terms is probably responsible for the controversy that surrounds jñāna and darśana. During the post-canonial or scholastic period, when the Jaina logicians were defending theories of cognition against other systems, the terms darśana and jñāna seem to have gained their current meanings, namely, 'indeterminate' and 'determinate', respectively. Certain Jaina writers opined that darśana was 'indeterminate intuition' because it cognized the 'universal' (*sāmānya*), while jñāna was 'determinate knowledge' because it cognized the 'particular' (*viśeṣa*).[50] But this idea was found to be incompatible with the fundamental Jaina position that an existent is both 'universal' and 'particular', and that no act of cognition could be considered valid unless both these inseparable aspects were cognized. Darśana and jñāna therefore had to cognize both the 'universal' and the 'particular' aspects. This led such Jaina ācāryas as Vīrasena to redefine the two cognitions. Darśana was defined as the 'internal' cognition of the 'self', while jñāna cognized 'external' objects.[51] The two could thus operate together freely, each having its own sphere of actions within the same consciousness.

Amṛtacandra's affiliation with the Digambara tradition is well-known; it is further confirmed by his statement that, in the case of the Jina, darśana and jñāna operate 'non-successively' (*aparyāyeṇa*), since there is total destruction of all that might obscure his consciousness:

> eka evopayogas te sākāretarabhedataḥ/
> jñānadarśanarūpeṇa dvitayīṃ gāhate bhuvam//259//
> samastāvaraṇocchedān nityam eva nirargale/
> aparyāyeṇa vartete dṛgjñaptī viśade tvayi//260//

The poet's reasoning in the first part of verse 260 indicates his awareness of the controversy surrounding these two operations of the Jina's consciousness. But there is no clue here to his understanding of the terms sākāra and nirākāra.[52] In the twenty-third chapter, however, there is one passage which appears to allude to these terms. It speaks of the 'astonishing nature' of the Jina's consciousness, a consciousness which operates by way of 'contraction' and 'expansion' (*cit-saṅkoca-vikāsa-vismayakaraḥ svabhāvaḥ*—587). There is no doubt that the words saṅkoca and vikāsa here refer to the darśana and jñāna, respectively. Darśana is 'contraction' because it is focused on the self; jñāna is 'expansion' because it is turned towards the infinity of external objects. The same idea is conveyed by the expression 'bahir-antarmukha-bhāsa' (367) and the terms 'sāmānya' and 'viśeṣa' applied in the last chapter for the two operations of consciousness (*cit-sāmānya-viśeṣa-rūpam*—607). This interpretation agrees perfectly with the one attributed above to Jinasena. But the problem of 'unity' (*ekatva*) of the Jina's consciousness in the face of this 'dual nature' (*dvitaya*) remains unsolved. The oft-repeated 'unity' is probably to be understood as spoken from the śuddha-naya, leading the aspirant towards the 'nirvikalpa' stage. This is apparent from the opening portions of the twelfth chapter. The poet hails the Jina as "anekāntaśālin" and speaks of the infinite powers of his consciousness (*ananta-cit-kalā*). This is followed by the declaration that he will "ignore the manifold nature" and "regard him as undifferentiated knowledge" (*aneko'py atimanye tvaṃ jñānam ekam anākulam*—277). In this passage the word jñāna stands in the place of 'cit' and subsumes both darśana and jñāna. A little later, in verse 286, Amṛtacandra makes a similar statement, saying that Jina's "inner and outer light shines forth as nothing but intuition" (*dṛṅgmātrībhavad ābhāti bhavato'ntarbahiś ca yat*). This is very significant, for it appears that the poet here wishes to reduce even jñāna, knowledge of external objects, to darśana, 'intuition' of the self. This is a valid position, conforming to the doctrine of omniscience in which the Jina, from the niścaya viewpoint, knows only his self. One speaks of the knowledge of external objects from the vyavahāra ('conventional') point of view only, as Ācārya Kundakunda says in the *Niyamasāra*:

> jāṇadi passadi savvaṃ vavahāraṇayeṇa kevalī bhagavaṃ/
> kevalaṇāṇī jāṇadi passadi ṇiyameṇa appāṇaṃ//159//

The thirteenth chapter continues with the topic of the supremacy of darśana according to the śuddha-naya. The concepts of 'contraction' and 'expansion' of consciousness appear here under the terms 'saṃhṛta' and 'asaṃhṛta'. The poet characterizes darśana as being the quality which, lacking all other objects, has been contracted on all sides (*paravedanāstamaya-gāḍhasaṃhṛtā*—310) and shines forth with only one object, namely the self.

Having thus stressed the śuddha-naya and having impressed the aspirant with the true glory of the Jina, the poet returns to the task of achieving a balance between the niścaya and vyavahāra. For it must be remembered that even the śuddha-naya, however exalted, is but a naya (a single view point) and can apprehend only one of the many aspects of the existent. Moreover, the Jina too is subject to the law which regulates the role of external causes in producing effects (*bahiraṅga-hetu-niyata-vyavasthā*—322), and he cannot prevent the objects outside his knowledge from being illuminated by his omniscience. Kundakunda's use of the term vyavahāra in the verse quoted above does not render the knowledge of the objects unreal, nor does it suggest any deficiency in the omniscient cognition. It is the very nature of that cognition, like that of the sun, to illuminate the totality of objects, and the Jina has neither any desire to know these objects (*na parāvamarṣa-rasikaḥ*—314), nor any consciousness of agency (*kāraka*) pertaining to the act of their cognition (*na hi tat-prakāśana-dhiyā prakāśate*—314). While pursuing the niścaya-naya, the aspirant must also be aware of the dual nature of reality, comprising both vyavahāra and niścaya (*niścaya-vyavahāra-saṃhatimayī jagatsthitiḥ*—318). He should see both the unity and multiplicity of consciousness as forming the essential nature of the self (*dvitaya-svabhāvam iha tattvam ātmanaḥ*—325). The chapter ends with the poet's call for self-realization, the state in which these manifold aspects are effortlessly subsumed (*anubhūtir eva jayatād anaṅkuśā*—325).

In the fourteenth chapter the poet views the Jina both sequentially, i.e. considering each quality (*guṇa*) separately, and simultaneously, i.e. considering his substance (*dravya*) in its unity (*kramato 'kramataś ca numaḥ*—326). Looked at from the point of particulars, omniscience consists, for example, of both intuition and knowledge (*dṛg-bodhamayaṃ*), but from the unified standpoint it is seen as pure consciousness alone (*citimātram idaṃ*—326). The chapter fashions such contrasting viewpoints into a string of riddles; they are presented with heavy alliteration in the pleasant Toṭaka meter, as the poet skillfully harmonizes the conflicting claims of diverse aspects within the same existent. But the doctrines of anekānta and syādvāda have goals beyond merely describing the nature of reality. The Jina taught them in order to produce discrimination between self and other (*vivekakṛte niraṇāyi*—338). The method is one of asserting what belongs to the self and negating that which belongs to others; hence it is known as 'vidhi-pratiṣedha-vidhi' (338). "The objects of knowledge do not belong to the self and yet the knower is drawn by them; therefore an aspirant's soul should take itself as its object" (*svam ataḥ kurutāṃ viṣayaṃ viṣayī*—345). A person whose mind is endowed with such discrimination does not take delight in externally oriented actions (*na viviktamatiḥ kriyayā ramate*—346); he attains to the immovable fruition of consciousness (*citipākam akampam upaiti pumān*—347); for such one there is no rebirth (*apunarbhavatā*), for he has forcefully uprooted the seed of transmigration (*bhava-bīja-haṭhoddharaṇāt*—347).

The vidhi-pratiṣedha method mentioned earlier (338) receives further attention in the fifteenth chapter. The poet characterizes it as a weapon (*bodhāstra*) which has been sharpened innumerable times by the Jina during his mundane state (*niśāyitam anantaśaḥ svayam*—353). Vidhi and niṣedha, i.e. the positive and negative aspects, are mutually antithetical. But when properly balanced (*ubhayam samatām upetya*) through the doctrine of syādvāda, they work together for the accomplishment of the desired goal, namely discrimination between the self and the not-self (*yatate saṃhitam artha-siddhaye*—357). By vidhi is understood the own-nature (*svabhāva*) of an existent, defined by its own substance (*sva-dravya*), own space (*sva-kṣetra*), own time (*sva-kāla*) and own modes (*sva-bhāva*). All existents are at all times endowed with (*vidhi*) their own fourfold nature. They are at the same time devoid of (*pratiṣedha*) the fourfold nature of other existents (*para-bhāva*). Thus both the positive and the negative aspects abide equally and simultaneously in the same existent (*samakakṣatayā 'vatiṣṭhate pratiṣedho vidhinā samaṃ tataḥ*—358).

Although existents are well secured in their own nature and never partake of 'other nature', they do not thereby become entirely independent of each other; there also exists the law of causation (*kārya-kāraṇa-vidhi*), which demands mutual assistance. "Cause" is the designation for a complex situation; it involves self and other, i.e. of both material (*upādāna*) and efficient (*nimitta*) causes, which operate in mutual dependence (*na kila svam ihaikakāraṇaṃ... na para eva*—365). The Jina's being the embodiment of knowledge is not dependent upon any other substance; similarly, the innumerable distinctions (i.e. the reflections of the objects cognized) within the omniscience are not inherent to it; dual causality is thus clearly evident in the omniscient knowledge of the Jina:

na hi bodhamayatvam anyato na ca vijñānavibhaktayaḥ svataḥ/
prakaṭaṃ tava deva kevale dvitayaṃ kāraṇam abhyudīyate//366//

The interdependence of existents, or the law of "causation", and their independence, or the law of 'own-nature', should both be seen in proper perspective: the two laws are properly balanced when one applies to them the conventional and absolute points of view:

vyavahāradṛśā parāśrayaḥ paramārthena sadātmasaṃśrayaḥ/370.

In the sixteenth chapter the poet applies the twin laws of causation and being to the cognition of the Jina. Just as the movement of schools of fish leaves a wake in the sea (*timikulam iva sāgare*), this entire universe produces an infinitely great net of vikalpas in the omniscient cognition (*anantam etad yugapad udeti mahāvikalpajālam*—386), vikalpas with the form "this [objects] is thus" (*idam evam iti*). And yet, because the Jina possesses both positive and negative aspects (*vidhi-niyamādbhutasvabhāvāt*), the distinction between his self and others is never lost (*svaparavibhāgam atīva gāhamānaḥ*—387). This is because both objects and the knowledge of these objects have their own space-points (*sva-pradeśa*) as well as their own substance, time and modes; hence there is no possibility of any defiling mixture or confusion (*saṅkara*) between them.

As if to forestall the false conclusion that the vikalpas in the omniscient cognition are not part of its own nature (*svabhāva*), the poet hastens to add that the Jina undergoes these infinite transformations at every moment by his innate power (*anantabhāvaiḥ tava pariṇamataḥ svaśaktyā*—391). This process is always subject to the law of dependence upon both material (*sva-nimitta*) and efficient (*para-nimitta*) causes; the objects play their proper role as external and instrumental causes in the transformation of the cognition.

In the seventeenth chapter the poet discusses the relationship between words, the qualification 'syāt' ("maybe"), and the reality expressed by them. The positive aspect (*vidhi*) by itself proclaims the object as established in its own substance, space, time and modes. But this assertion is meaningless unless it simultaneously implies exclusion (*niṣedha*) of that object from the substance, space, time and modes of others. There is no single word which can ever succeed by itself in expressing both these aspects simultaneously. Qualifying one-dimensional assertions with 'syāt', however, renders them expressive of actual, multi-dimensional reality. The spoken word (such as asti, nāsti, nitya, anitya, śuddha, aśuddha, eka, aneka, etc.) itself expresses the 'primary' (*mukhya*) aspect, whether positive or negative, which is desired by the speaker (*mukhyatvam bhavati vivakṣitasya*). The qualification syāt implies the other aspects, which are 'subordinate' (*gauṇa*) insofar as they were not expressly mentioned (*gauṇatvaṃ vrajati vivakṣito nayaḥ syāt*—421). Thus the two positions abide in mutual compatibility and express the referent fully.

It could be asked whether this syāt produces a power that was not present in the words or merely brings out one that was already there (417). The Jaina answer to this question conforms to syādvāda. The dual power of words is innate to them; no external thing can produce a power in something else which does not already exist there. But the manifestation (*vyakti*) of that dual power never occurs without the accompaniment of the expression "maybe" (*na vyaktir bhavati syādvādamantareṇa*—418).

Chapters eighteen and nineteen continue further with the dual nature (*dvyātmakatva*) of the existent and the manner in which that nature is harmonized by the device of syādvāda. The Jina is seen, from different viewpoints, as both substance and modes, universal and particular, eternal and momentary, existing and non-existing, expressible and non-expressible. The poet returns once again to his favourite theme of the upādāna and nimitta causes (443). He accepts objects as the efficient cause of omniscient knowledge, but asserts that the subject-object relationship is similar to that which obtains between an indicator (*vācaka*) and the thing indicated (*artha*). There is no real interpenetration (*na anyonyagatau tau*), dependence (*na parāśrayaṇam*), or actual mixing of one substance with another (*na bhāvāntara-saṅkrāntiḥ*—452). Existents are always complete in their own-beings (*nijabhāvena sadiva tiṣṭhataḥ*—456) and are secured within the impregnable limits of their own space-points (*nijapradeśavihito vastuparigrahaḥ svayam*—452). All existents are endowed with mutually opposed aspects. They are "proportionately divided" into substance, modes, etc. through the doctrine of "maybe" (*syādvādena pravibhaktāmavibhūtiḥ*—450). Although divisions, i.e. the modes (*paryāyas*) are real, to dwell in them is to dwell in speculations of instrumentalities (*kāraka-cakra*), speculations which cast blemish on the splendour of the own-being (*bhavanaikavibhūtibhāriṇas tava bhedo hi kalaṅkakalpanā*—465). Therefore the aspirant takes note of them but abides only in that aspect which is enduring (*nirantara*), which affirms only 'beingness' (*bhāvamātratā*), which is the unbroken stream (*avimukta-dhārā*), the undifferentiated substance (*dravya*) itself; he becomes aware of the unified light of the Jina's consciousness, free from divisions of time and space (472).

The twentieth chapter is of special interest as it is a critique of Buddhist doctrine, a singular honour not accorded any other darśana by our author. We have seen how the Jaina stresses the importance of viewing reality in its multiple aspects (*aneka-anta*), and how the device of 'syāt' is employed to fully express that reality. The Jaina characterizes the other classical darśanas' as partial expositions of reality which claim to be speaking the whole truth. This he brands as "ekānta", one-sidedness, a term which also carries the stigma of blind dogmatism. The Vedāntic doctrine of monistic absolutism or the Buddhist doctrine of momentary dharmas are examples of such ekānta; the former apprehends only substance (*dravya*), declaring the modes (*paryāyas*) to be unreal, while the latter concerns itself only with the present moment and totally excludes the 'substance' (*dravya* or *ātman*) which is the underlying unity of past and future states. Both doctrines are mutually exclusive and must give a false (*mithyā*) description of reality.

The Jaina admits that there is an element of truth in both these points of view if they are qualified by an expression like 'maybe' (*syāt*), hence asserting one view while suggesting the existence of the remaining aspects of reality. Qualified in this manner, the Vedāntic doctrine can be accepted as a 'synthetic'[53] or saṅgraha-naya (477) and the Buddhist momentariness as a 'straight-thread'[54] or ṛju-sūtra-naya (478); both are valid insofar as they represent reality as it is successively perceived. By the use of syādvāda the Jaina can not only transform the false, i.e. the absolutist doctrines into instruments of valid knowledge (*naya*) but he can even play 'devil's advocate' with no apparent inconsistency:

atattvam eva praṇidhānasauṣṭhavāt
    taveśa tattvapratipattaye varam/
viṣaṃ vamantyo'py amṛtaṃ kṣaranti yat
    pade pade syātpadasaṃskṛtā giraḥ//476.

The twentieth chapter provides a fine example of a Jaina attempt to accord validity to the Buddhist tenet of momentariness by transforming it into the ṛju-sūtra-naya. The tenet can thus be accommodated with the rest of the Jaina doctrine and can even be presented as a teaching of the Omniscient Jina, who thus deserves to be called 'Sugata' or even 'Tathāgata', two time-honoured epithets of Śākyamuni Buddha! (*ato gatas tvaṃ sugatas tathāgato jinedra sākṣād agato'pi bhāsase*—495).

Although kṣaṇabhaṅgavāda is the main tenet for 'assimilation', the poet makes a broad sweep, bringing almost all shades of Buddhist doctrine under his purview in the brief span of twenty verses. The chapter abounds in Buddhist technical terms, e.g. *niraṃśa-tattvāṃśa* (478), *vibhajyamāna, viśīrṇa-sañcaya, bodhadhātavaḥ* (479), *kṣaṇa-kṣaya, niranvaya, nairātmya* (481), *nirvāṇa, antya-citkṣaṇa* (484), *pradīpa-nirvṛti, eka-śūnyatā* (485), *vijñānaghana* (486), *bahir-artha-nihnava* (490), *apoha* (491), *sugata, tathāgata* (495), *samastaśūnyatā* (496), etc.

It hardly needs to be stated that although such an 'assimilation' appears to be technically possible, the whole exercise is purely poetic. The poet's handling of the kṣaṇa-kṣaya (478-483) appears reasonably satisfactory, since that position is, with qualifications, acceptable to the Jaina. But his 'defense' of the bahir-artha-vāda is really not serious; lacking a metaphysical basis in the Jain system for the rejection of external objects, he is content with a metaphorical treatment as given in verse 490. Elsewhere, lacking even a metaphor, he resorts merely to a play on words, as in his approach to the concept of apoha (491-495). He chooses to understand apoha as simple 'exclusion'. This rendering serves well to describe the Jaina doctrine of 'reciprocal exclusion' (*parasparāpoha*—492), a doctrine leading to the establishment both of one's own nature (*svadravya-kṣetra-kāla-bhāva*) and that of others (*para-dravya,* etc.) essential to simultaneous affirmation and negation of one and the same object. In all this Amṛtacandra is not without precedent; even the Buddha is said to have resorted to a similar device to overcome the criticism of his opponents. When asked by a brahmin if he was an 'akiriyāvādi', a 'jegucchi', a 'venayika' or a 'tapassi', the Buddha is reported to have said that there was indeed a way in which he could be described by all these terms, i.e., by understanding each of them in a sense different from what the questioner had in mind.[55] We should probably look at these verses as a Jaina attempt to appreciate Buddhist doctrine in the spirit of anekānta, hindered in its effort at assimilation by the antipodal positions of the two schools. This is no more evident than in the last few verses (496-500) dealing with śūnyavāda, which correctly portray the Jaina objection yet betray a subtle fascination with that strange doctrine of nirvikalpa, as we hear our poet pray to his 'tathāgata': *praveśya śūnye kṛtinaṃ kuruṣva mām*—500.

The twenty-first chapter is probably a criticism of the Nyāya-Vaiśeṣika system, which regards the universal (*sāmānya*) and the particular (*viśeṣa*) as two separate entities related to the other padārthas by means of 'inherence' (*samavāya*). For the Jaina the sāmānya and the viśeṣa constitute reality itself and hence cannot be separated (*svayam eva tad dvayam*—512). What is called universal is the substance (*dravya*), which 'becomes by way of similarity', i.e., which is the continuity among the particulars, namely the modes (*parāyas*):

samaṃ samānair iha bhūyate hi yat
tad eva sāmānyam uṣanti netarat/513.

The same rule applies regarding non-existence (*abhāva*). In the Jaina system an existent is characterized by both bhāva and abhāva. It is bhāva from the point of view of its own being (namely, substance, space, time and modes) and is abhāva, from the point of views of the other (524).

Although of miscellaneous character, chapters twenty-two, twenty-three and twenty-four can be considered together as they touch repeatedly upon one of the author's favourite themes, omniscient cognition and its incorruptibility by the impact of the objects cognized. In the Jina all feelings have been eradicated because he has turned his face away from attachment to external objects (*bāhya-sparśapraṇayavimukhāt kṣīṇasaṃvedanasya*—526). A wondrous stream of bliss flows within him, carrying his 'concentrated insight' (*magnāṃ dṛśaṃ*) even more deeply into his soul (526). It is even possible to suggest that the objects are not perceived at all, that only the knowledge is; for is it not true that the 'internalized objects' are nothing but transformations within and of the knowledge? And yet the Jina's teaching does not consist in negating the reality of the objective universe (*yan netṛtvam kimapi na hi tal lokadṛṣṭaṃ pramārṣṭi*—536). He need not negate the objects, for there is no fear either of their entering into or making actual contact with the soul. This is because all existents have mutual boundaries which are innate and fixed; they never fall away from their nature (537). The Jina can in no way be contaminated by his cognitions (*viśvād bhinnaḥ snapaya bhagavan saṅkaras te kutaḥ syāt*—537). He abides forever deep in the boundless mass of innate knowledge. Because of the absence of delusion he will never again have the notion of agency (*kartṛbhāvo na bhūyaḥ*). Even if it is alleged that knowing involves agency, what can the Jina 'do' other than know (*jñānād anyat kim iha kuruṣe*—539)? Cognitions are not able to move the Jina away from the unified consciousness of his self (*śuddhajñāna-svarasamayatāṃ na kṣamante pramārṣṭum*—542). The aspirant should cast out all vitiated transformations of the soul until there shines the light of omniscience, the only thing which cannot be removed:

> pītaṃ pītaṃ vamatu sukṛtī nityam atyantam etat
> tāvad yāvaj jvalati vamanāgocaro jyotir antaḥ/549.

Only then is the firm knot of passions totally dissolved, (*granthir gāḍhas tadā pravilīyate*—558), and upon this dissolution cognition exists only as Knower; it is neither a 'doer' nor an 'enjoyer' (*tava param idaṃ jñātṛ jñānaṃ na kartṛ na bhoktṛ ca*), but merely Being itself (*tat tad eva*), and its apparent 'enjoyment' is nothing but self-realization (*anubhavaḥ svayaṃ*—560). Let the aspirant therefore think deeply upon the Lord Jina, who is nothing but that very substance of the consciousness (*citidravye jinendre majjāmaḥ*—576) which is on every side endowed with shining glory, touching the entire universe (*viśvaspṛśi*), glowing with the power of its innate light (*sahaja-prakāśa*).

The twenty-fifth and final chapter deals with karma-jñāna-samuccaya (615), the integration of action and knowledge, which would appear to be the heart of Jaina teaching. The poet, as usual, begins with the importance of knowledge. There is, he says, some subtle thing (i.e. the bond of attachment) that obscures the true nature of the Jina from the seeker (602). Ignorant persons indulge in ever more severe activities (*caṇḍaḥ kriyāḍambaraḥ*) but fail to perceive the truth. As to those who dissolve the knot of subtle attachment and devote themselves to restraints (*saṃyama*), they obtain the inner light (*antarmahaḥ*) and secure their own natural state (*te vindanti...sahajāvasthām*—603). Great effort should therefore be made to control the totality of desires, for there is no release for the yogin who undertakes merely the restraint of 'vibrations' (*yogas*) but remains bound by inner attachments (612). Activity pertaining to perfect conduct must, however, remain the sole refuge (*karmaiva tāvad gatiḥ*—613) until one has attained release from internal bonds; thereafter, as in the case of an arhat, these activities are involuntary and have no further goal (613). As to those who, deluded by the mere touch of an occasional glimpse of self-realization, think they can dispense with the actions pertaining to pure conduct and cease to be vigilant, they will surely fall away from their asceticism (*śrāmaṇyād*) and injure themselves again (*te yānti hiṃsāṃ punaḥ*—615). But those who are at all times firmly secure in "sharp awareness" of the self and behave with equanimity towards all (*sarvatra santaḥ samāḥ*), they will reside in their own selves (*svam adhyāsate*), which are filled with both intuition and knowledge (617). The aspirant, knowing the importance of both knowledge and action, applies himself to the entire field of scriptural knowledge (*śruta-jñāna*) with great resolution, grasps fully the nature of the soul, and remains secured in the restraints which lead to perfectly pure conduct. Dispelling darkness, he destroys the bondage of the karmas. Such a soul, touching his own reality (*svatattvaṃ spṛśan*), i.e. the self, attains to the domain of omniscient knowledge which illuminates the whole universe; only then does he come to rest:

viśvodbhāsiviśālakevalamahīm ākramya viśrāmyati/ 618

Laghutattvasphoṭa and the _Samayasāra-kalaśa_

The *Laghutattvasphoṭa* is thus a work dedicated to cultivation of the śuddha or the niścaya ("non-conventional") viewpoint in order to attain undifferentiated consciousness (*nirvikalpa-upayoga*), the goal for the Jaina aspirant. It can therefore be considered a continuation of the *Samayasāra-kalaśa,* to which it bears close resemblance in both vocabulary and spirit. Two of its verses (50 and 624) are identical with the *Samayasāra-kalaśa* (270 and 141) and numerous verses in both works have the word paśu for the absolutist (*ekāntavādin*). In addition, there are many passages of varying length in the *Laghutattvasphoṭa* which can be placed side by side with portions of the *Samayasāra-kalaśa.*[56] Both employ common similies, such as the mass of salt and its flavour (238) or the whitewash and the wall (378), to illustrate the relationship between internal and external divisions, respectively. What is even more remarkable is the frequency of occurrence in both works of such terms as anākula, anubhava, uddāma, uddhata, ghasmara, cakacakāyita, ṭaṅkotkīrṇa, dvitayatā, nirbhara, śāntamahas, śāntarasa, samarasa etc.; a certain amount of uniformity in style and expression is undeniable. These parallels and resemblances indicate the possibility that Amṛtacandra composed the *Laghutattvasphoṭa* after completing both the *Ātmakhyāti-ṭīkā* (of which the Samayasāra-kalaśa is only a part) and his other known works. Of these, the *Tattvārthasāra* is most certainly the earliest, being merely a summary in verse of the aphorisms of the *Tattvārthasūtra.* The *Puruṣārthasiddhyupāya,* a brief text of 226 verses, appears to be his next work. Although it is a śrāvakācāra (lawbook for the laity), in which the vyavahāra-naya is more relevant, this work foreshadows the author's predilection for the niścaya-naya.[57] His commentaries on the *Pañcāstikāya, Pravacanasāra* and *Samayasāra,* three authoritative works written by Kundakunda primarily for the ascetic order, probably followed. To the author of the *Puruṣārthasiddhyupāya,* these three works must have been a natural choice, especially since he was attracted by the mysteries of the śuddha-naya and its usefulness in meditative practices leading to instantaneous self-experience. The first two commentaries are mostly in prose and seek merely to elucidate the teaching in the vigorous and pedantic style characteristic of our author. There are 21 verses in the *Pravacanasāra-ṭīkā,* but Amṛtacandra's poetical eloquence finds real expression only in the commentary on the *Samayasāra.* This commentary has a total of 278 verses, appearing at the culmination of each section and hence called "pinnacle" (*kalaśa*)[58] verses. Since *kalaśa* also means "pitcher", its use here may imply the purificatory purpose of the verses. Being a part of the commentary the *kalaśa* verses must follow the scheme laid out by Kundakunda, and to that extent the poet's freedom in dealing with his subject-matter is inhibited. The *Laghutattvasphoṭa* may be considered Amṛtacandra's last work, independent and original, devised on an ambitiously large scale equal to his talents, an overflow of the spiritual vision and poetical expression seen in the *Samayasāra-kalaśa.*

As seen above in our brief summary of the contents, the author has carried over almost all the major topics of the *Ātmakhyāti-ṭīkā* into the *Laghutattvasphoṭa.* Śuddha-naya, jñāna-darśana, agurulaghutva, svabhāva-vibhāva-parabhāva-viveka, upādāna-nimitta-viveka, jñāyakabhāva, karma-jñāna-samuccaya and syādvāda are some of the favourite concepts of our author; he returns to them again and again in his quest for a solid basis upon which to erect the superstructure of realization (*anubhava*) of the undifferentiated cognition. Unfortunately, this is a structure liable to be shaken by the multitude of the nayas, a harsh legacy of the doctrine of syādvāda. Our author is keenly aware of the difficulty of a Jaina who, advocating the śuddha-naya, is liable to be mistaken for a monist Vedāntin or an eternalist Sāṃkhya.[59] But he realizes that the doctrines of anekānta and syādvāda are means to an end and must not be allowed to become an 'obsession' (*durāśā—ko' nekāntadurāśayā tava vibho bhindyāt svabhāvaṃ sudhīḥ*—581) which is detrimental to the true goal. They are taught primarily to instruct the ignorant, to correct his biases and help him grasp the multi-dimensional existent; in this way he may perceive for himself the distinction between the self and the non-self. Having achieved this discriminatory vision (*bheda-vijñāna*) the aspirant must free himself from the tangle of the nayas, not because they are no longer real but because they are not relevant and in fact hinder attainment of undifferentiated cognition. Transcendence of the nayas must of course be gradual, taking the aspirant step by step on, but at the same time away from, the 'prescribed' path. In this process the boundaries of what is generally called vyavahāra (the 'conventional') and niścaya (the 'non-conventional') must also change; "that which is to be followed" (*upādeya*) is constantly relegated to the status of "that which is to be abandoned" (*heya*) until all dualities in consciousness are transcended in omniscient cognition. The Jaina has no deity towards which he can gravitate for this purpose; he must therefore find within himself a support to which he can adhere, a support which is not abandoned even in the state of total isolation (*kaivalya*). The Jaina ācāryas, notably Kundakunda and Amṛtacandra, have found this support in what they style the śuddha-jñāyaka-bhāva, 'the state of pure awareness', a state which abides forever and endures through the vicissitudes of cognized objects (*vikalpa*) and karma-produced psychological states (*saṃkalpa*). The yogin must "watch" this state of awareness with extreme diligence and mindfulness; thus he will prevent its being affected by both vikalpas and saṃkalpas, for he will never lose sight of the fact that these are distinct and separate from awareness. The objects cognized (*jñeya*) and the psychological states experienced (*bhogya or vedya*) owe their existence, partially or wholly, to the non-soul. Their existence cannot be denied, but their identity with the soul is permissible only from the vyavahāra ('conventional') viewpoint. The aspirant is therefore asked to reject this vyavahāra and to remain secured in 'mere awareness' (*jñāyakamātra-bhāva*) by adhering to the niścaya ('non-conventional') naya, the standpoint which perceives the soul as totally isolated from these beginningless but adventitious accretions. Here even the considerations of the syādvāda, valid for discussing the nature of reality, are set aside; for as the poet states in the *Samayasāra-kalaśa,* "only those who abandon partiality for a naya and remain constantly secured in their own nature, whose hearts have been pacified through breaking free from the net of vikalpas, only they will drink this ambrosia of immortality":

> ya eva muktvā nayapakṣapātaṃ svarūpaguptā nivasanti nityam/
> vikalpajālacyutaśāntacittās ta eva sākṣād amṛtaṃ pibanti//69//

Amṛtacandra as a Devotee

We will conclude this survey with a brief note on Amṛtacandra as he reveals himself through the verses of the *Laghutattvasphoṭa.* Being a stotra and an independent composition, the work reflects the personality of our author to an extent not found in his other works. One might think of this learned Ācārya, so confident of his poetical talents and of his scholarship and so dedicated to the path of knowledge (*jñāna-mārga*), as being austere and cold. But the concluding verses of the chapters of the *Laghutattvasphoṭa* portray a devout soul constantly seeking the company of the Jina, reaffirming with deep humility his resolve to attain supreme enlightenment. In one place he says that he is "dried up by austerities"(*tapoviśoṣitaṃ*—125) and begs the Jina to kindle him with the overwhelming splendour of his light (*prabho māṃ jvalayasva tejasā*—125). Continuing the same metaphor, he implores the Jina to enter into him "like a blazing fire forcefully infusing an iron ball" (*viśann ayaḥpiṇḍam ivāgnir utkaṭaḥ*—150). He is intensely aware of his shortcomings and deplores his own dullness (*jaḍimā mamaiva saḥ*—150) blaming it for his failure. He is thirsty (*pipāsita*) for that bliss which dawned upon the nascent Jina when he had entered the path of liberation (*mārgāvatāra-rasa*), and begs the Jina to favour him also with that experience (*asmākam ekakalayāpi kuru prasādam*—51). He wants the Jina to throw open the hidden treasure of his heart and illuminate it in such a way that he too may become an omniscient being (*bhavāmi kila sarvamayo'ham eva*—75). Helpless, he has wandered countless times through the cycle to transmigration; but now, he ardently takes refuge "beneath the cloak of the consciousness of the Jina" (*lagāmy ayaṃ deva balāc cidañcale*), for the Jina "rests in his own abode" (*svadhāmni viśrāntividhāyinas tava*—151). He says fondly that the Lord, also full of affection (*ativatsalaḥ*) showered the ambrosia of wisdom upon him alone out of the whole world (*prahāya viśvaṃ...mama...prakṣaritaḥ*—154). But how much can he, a person of limited awareness (*abodhadurbalaḥ*), possibly drink of that ambrosia? (*kṣameta pātuṃ kiyad īśa mādṛśaḥ*—154). Still he does not despair: he is aware of the fact that by partaking of even a bit of wisdom his health has been restored; he must now fully encompass the entire teaching (*mamaiva peyaḥ sakalo bhavān api*—155). And of course this teaching consists of seeing the true nature of the Jina, which is also the true nature of the self and can be seen only through the śuddha-naya. He will therefore develop this vision (*stoṣye jinaṃ śuddhanayaika dṛṣṭyā*—226) and will perceive the Jina, who is nothing but a mass of pure consciousness on all sides (*viśuddha-vijñānaghanaṃ samantāt*—226). Like a lamp-wick pervaded by fire his entire self has been pervaded by meditation on the nature of the Jina; now there can be no doubt that he too will partake of this nature (275). His self is always fixed on the Jina (*nityaṃ yuktātmano mama*); "may ever-new experiences of you", he prays, "flash forth within me in an unbroken series" (*sphurantv aśrāntam ārdrārdrās tavāmūr anubhūtayaḥ*—300). Though progress is slow, even his small contact with the pure consciousness has rendered the passions ineffectual (*tava deva cidañala-lagnam api glapayanti kaṣāyamalāni na mām*—350). Like a child enjoying the flavour of sugarcane (*rasayan bāla ivekṣukarṇikām*) his inner heart is captivated by the sweetness of experiencing the Jina. He savours this ambrosia day and night but is still not satisfied (*na hi tṛptim upety ayaṃ jano bahu-mādhurya-hṛtāntarāśayaḥ*—350). He is immersed in an upwelling flood of the flavour of self-realization (*svarasaplava eṣa ucchalan parito māṃ vṛuḍito kariṣyati*—374). He has kept himself awake and is confident that, by virtue of taking refuge in the Jina, the night of his delusion has passed (*viratā mama mohayāminī tava pādābjagatasya jāgrataḥ*—375). He is subdued by his experience and confides that he is an ardent devotee: "May the Lord lift me upward and hold me in his lap" (*kṛpayā parivartya bhāktikaṃ bhagavan kroḍagataṃ vidhehi mām*—375).

These are the words of an Ācārya who is both a poet and an advocate of the niścaya-naya, and should be understood accordingly. The Jina is no Deity dispensing salvation by 'grace'; rather he is the embodiment of pure and undifferentiated consciousness (*citidravye jinendre majjāmaḥ*—576), the living example for an aspirant who can achieve the same state through insight and exertion. A Jaina has only one support and that is his own self. As our author says; 'Constantly drinking the ambrosia of your wisdom, and holding intact my internal and external controls, I shall certainly, by my own efforts (*svayaṃ*) become like you. For what is there that cannot be achieved by those who have accepted the vows of self-control?":

anāratam bodharasāyanaṃ pibann-
akhaṇḍitāntarbahiraṅgasaṃyamaḥ/
dhruvaṃ bhaviṣyāmi samaḥ svayaṃ tvayā
na sādhyate kiṃ hi gṛhītasaṃyamaiḥ//156//

NOTES

1. *Samayasāra,* Prakrit text with English translation by A. Chakravarti, Bharatiya Jnanapitha, Banaras, 1950; Prakrit text, and the *Ātmakhyāti-ṭīkā* of Amṛtacandra Sūri with a Marathi translation by D. H. Bhore, Shri Mahavira Jnanopasana Samiti, Karanja,1968. There also exists a separate edition of *Samayasāra kalaśa,* with Hindi translation, by Phoolchandra Siddhantashastri, Songadh, 1966.
2. *Tattvārthasāra,* text with Hindi translation by Pannalal Sahityacharya, Shri Ganeshprasad Varni Granthamala Banaras, 1970.
3. *Puruṣārthasiddhyupāya,* text with English translation by Ajita Prasad, The Sacred Books of the Jainas, Vol. IV, 1933.
4. *Pañcāstikāyasaṅgrahaḥ,* Prakrit text with the *Samayadīpikā-ṭīkā,* Digambara Jain Svadhyaya Mandir Trust, Songadh, 1953.
5. *Pravacanasāra,* Prakrit text with the *Tattvadīpikā* of Amṛtacandra and the *Tātparyavṛtti-ṭīkā* of Jayasena, edited by A. N. Upadhye, Rajacandra Jain Shastramala, Agas, 1964.
6. "śakti-bhaṇita" corresponds to "śakti-saṃsūcita", an expression appearing in the colophons of Amṛtacandra's commentaries on the *Pañcāstikāya* and the *Samayasāra*:
svaśaktisaṃsūcitavastutattvair vyākhyā kṛteyaṃ samayasya śabdaiḥ/
7. iti śrīmad Amṛtacandrasūrīṇāṃ kṛtiḥ *puruṣārthasiddhyupāyo*'para nāma *Jinapravacanarahasyakoṣaḥ* samāptaḥ/ (p. 85).
8. Dramas, for instance, are conspicuously absent in the vast Jaina literature, which consists mainly of Purāṇas and Kāvyas. This is also true of the Buddhists, who have contributed even less in the field of Purāṇas.
9. The following verse lists six miracles that attend a Jina:

aśokavṛkṣaḥ surapuṣpavṛṣṭir divyadhvaniś cāmarabhāsanaṃ ca/
bhāmaṇḍalaṃ dundubhir ātapatraṃ ṣaṭ prātihāryāṇi jineśvarāṇāṃ//
[*Nitya-naimittika-pāṭhāvalī*, Karanja]
But these are not considered the true marks of a Jina:
devāgamanabhoyānacāmarādivibhūtayaḥ/
māyāviṣv api dṛṣyante nātas tvam asi no mahān//1//
[*Āpta-mīmāṃsā* of Samantabhadra]

10. For the complete text of the *Dvātriṃśikā* (only 21 are extant) see Siddhasena's *Nyāyāvatāra and Other Works*, edited by A. N. Upadhye, Jaina Sahitya Vikasa Mandala, Bombay, 1971 (pp. 111-169).
11. For the text of the *Svayambhū-stotra* see *Nitya-naimittika-pāṭhāvalī*, pp. 19-44, Shri Kamkubai Pathya-pustakamala, Karanja, 1956.
12. Compare, for instance, the following lines from the *Svayambhū-stotra*: svayambhuvā bhūtahitena bhūtale (1), yataś ca śeṣeṣu mateṣu nāsti sarvakriyākārakatattvasiddhiḥ (21), bāhyaṃ tapoduścaram ācaraṃs tvam ādhyātmikasya tapasaḥ paribṛṃhaṇārtham (83), with these from the *Laghutattvasphoṭa*: svāyambhuvaṃ maha ihocchalad acchaṁ īḍe (1), so'yaṃ tavollasati kārakacakracarcā (5), tapobhir adhyātmaviśuddhivardhanaiḥ prasahya karmāṇi bhareṇa pāvayan (130).
13. See *Jaina Yoga* by R. Williams, London Oriental Series, Volume 14, p. 195.
14. Dharmakīrti uses the word 'paśu' for the Sāṃkhya in a similar context:
vijñānaśaktisambandhād iṣṭaṃ cet sarvavastunaḥ/
etat Sāṃkhyapaśoḥ ko'nyaḥ salajjo vaktum īhate//
[*Pramāṇavārttika*, I, 167]
15. For other references see Pandit Mahendrakumar Nyayacarya's Introduction to his edition of the *Nyāyakumudacandra*, p. 53.
16. See *Laghutattvasphoṭa* verses 28, 36, 37, 38, 44, 45, 80, 312, 611 and 612.
17. We quote the relevant passages for comparison with our text: parito jñānaṃ paśoḥ sīdati (248), paśur iva svacchandam ācaṣṭate (249) jñeyākāraviśīrṇaśaktir abhitas truṭyan paśur naśyati (250), ekākāracikīrṣayā sphuṭam api jñānaṃ paśur necchati (251), svadravyānavalokanena paritaḥ śūnyaḥ paśur naśyati (252), svadravyabhramataḥ paśuḥ kila paradravyeṣu viśrāmyati (253), sīdaty eva bahiḥ patantam abhitaḥ paśyan pumāṃsaṃ paśuḥ (254), tucchībhūya paśuḥ praṇaśyati cidākārān sahārthair vaman (255), sīdaty eva na kiñcanāpi kalayann atyantatucchaḥ paśuḥ (256), jñeyālambanamānasena manasā bhrāmyan paśur naśyati (257), naśyaty eva paśuḥ svabhāvamahimanyekāntaniścetanaḥ (258), sarvatrāpy anivārito gatabhayaḥ svairaṃ paśuḥ krīḍati (259), nirjñānāt kṣaṇabhaṅgasaṅgapatitaḥ prāyaḥ paśur naśyati (260), vāñcchaty ucchaladacchacitpariṇater bhinnaṃ paśuḥ kiñcana (261).
[Syādvādādhikāra, *Ātmakhyāti-ṭīkā*]
18. On the doctrine of guṇasthānas see *Ādhyātmika Vikāsakrama* (*guṇasthāna*) by Pandit Sukhlalji Sanghavi, Ahmedabad 1929; *Studies in Jaina Philosophy* by Nathmal Tatia, pp. 268-280, Jaina Cultural Research Society, Banaras, 1951.
19. On the ritual of sāmāyika see *Jaina Yoga* by R. Williams, pp. 131-139. Also my article 'Sāmāyika: A Jain path of purification' in the *Problems*

of Defilements in Oriental Religions, Tokyo, 1975.

20. The validity of 'niścaya' versus 'vyavahāra' has provoked a great deal of controversy within the community of Digambara Jainas from the time of Ācārya Kundakunda; a formal debate among prominent Jaina scholars aiming to settle this controversy took place as recently as 1967. The proceedings of this debate are given in two volumes entitled *Jaipur* (*Khāniyā*) *Tattvacarcā,* Shri Todarmal Granthamala, pushpa 2 and 3, Jaipur, 1967.
21. The use of the terms puruṣa and prakṛti for the jīva and karman indicates a certain Sāṃkhya influence on the Jaina writers. It must be pointed out, however, that the term 'prakṛti' is also a Jaina technical term used for 'types' of karmic matter. For details see Tatia: *Studies in Jaina Philosophy,* pp. 220-260.
22. Amṛtacandra applies the śuddhopayogaḥ in the following manner: yo hi nāmāyaṃ paradravyasaṃyogakāraṇatvenopanyasto 'śuddha upayogaḥ sa khalu mandatīvrodayadaśāviśrāntaparadravyānuvṛttitantratvād eva pravartate na punar anyasmāt/tato'ham eṣa sarvasminn eva paradravye madhyastho bhavāmi/evaṃ bhavaṃś cāhaṃ paradravyānuvṛttitantratvābhāvāt śubhenāśubhena vā śuddhopayogena nirmukto bhūtvā kevalasvadravyānuvṛttiparigrahāt prasiddhaśuddhopayoga upayogātmanātmany eva nityaṃ niścalam upayuñjaṃs tiṣṭhāmi/eṣa me paradravyasaṃyogakāraṇavināśābhyāsaḥ/ [*Pravacanasāra-ṭīkā,* ii, 67]
23. yena prakāreṇa rūpādirahito rūpīṇi dravyāṇi tadguṇāṃś ca paśyati jānāti ca, tenaiva prakāreṇa rūpādirahito rūpibhiḥ karmapudgalaiḥ kila badhyate/ anyathā katham amūrto paśyati jānāti cety atrāpi paryanuyogasyānivayatvāt/ ....ātmano nīrūpatvena sparśaśūnyatvān na karmapudgalaiḥ sahāsti sambandhaḥ, ekāvagāhabhāvasthita-karmapudgalanimittopayogādhirūḍharāgadveṣādibhāva-sambandhaḥ karmapudgalabandhavyavahārasādhakas tv asty eva/ [*ibid.,* ii, 82]
24. "savve vi puggalā khalu kamaso bhuttujjhiyā ya jīveṇa/ asaiṃ aṇaṃtakhutto puggalapariyaṭṭasaṃsāre//" Quoted in the *Sarvārthasiddhi,* ii, 10. (Bhāratīya Jñānapīṭha Prakashana, Banaras, 1971).
25. *Tattvārthasūtra,* v. 31.
26. *Tattvārthasūtra,* v. 30.
27. *Tattvārthasūtra,* v. 38.
28. gatisthityupagrahau dharmādharmayor upakāraḥ/ākāśasyāvagāhaḥ/ śarīravāṅmanaḥprāṇāpānāḥ pudalānām/sukhaduḥkhajīvitamaraṇopagrahāś ca/parasparopagraho jīvānām/vartanāpariṇāmakriyāḥ paratvāparatve ca kālasya/[*Tattvārthasūtra,* v, 17-22]. For a further elucidation on these 'upakāras' see Phoolchandra Siddhantashastri's *Jaina-tattva-mīmāṃsā,* (chapter iv), Benaras, 1960.
29. hahir-antaḥ-paraś ceti tridhātmā sarvadehiṣu/upeyāt tatra paramaṃ madhyopāyād bahis tyajet//4// *Samādhi-śataka* of Pūjyapāda, ed. R.N. Shah, 1938. Also see Tatia: *Studies in Jaina Philosophy,* p. 281.
30. jīvassa ṇatthi vaṇṇo ṇa vi gandho ṇavi raso ṇavi ya phāso/ṇavi rūvaṃ ṇa sarīraṃ ṇavi saṇṭhāṇaṃ ṇa saṃhaṇaṇaṃ//50//jīvassa ṇatthi rāgo

ṇavi doso ṇeva vijjade moho/ṇo paccayā ṇa kammaṃ ṇokammaṃ cāvi se ṇatthi//50// jīvassa ṇatthi vaggo ṇa vaggaṇā ṇeva phaḍḍayā keī/ ṇo ajjhappaṭṭhāṇā ṇeva ya aṇubhāyaṭhāṇāni//51//..... ṇo ṭhidibandhaṭṭhāṇā jīvassa ṇa saṃkilesaṭhāṇā vā/ ṇeva visohiṭṭhāṇā ṇo saṃjamaladdhiṭhāṇā vā//54// ṇeva ya jīvaṭṭhāṇā ṇa guṇaṭṭhāṇā ya atthi jīvassa/ jeṇa du ede savve puggaladavvassa pariṇāmā//55//

[*Samayasāra* of Kundakunda]

31. For details on the operation of these 'karaṇas' see Tatia: *Studies in Jaina Philosophy*, pp. 269 ff.
32. *Ibid.*, pp. 283-293.
33. raṅgasya darśayitvā nivartate nartakī yathā nṛtyāt/ puruṣasya tathātmānaṃ prakāśya vinivartate prakṛtiḥ//

[Īśvarakṛṣṇa's *Sāṃkhyakārikā*, 59]

34. For details see Tatia, p. 280.
35. tadanantaram ūrdhvaṃ gacchaty ā lokāntāt/ pūrvaprayogād asaṅgatvād bandhacchedāt tathāgatipariṇāmāc ca/ āviddhakulālacakravad vyapagatalepālābuvad eraṇḍabījavad agniśikhāvacca/

[*Tattvārthasūtra*, x, 5-7]

36. See *Syādvādamañjarī* of Malliṣeṇa, verse ix, and A. B. Dhruva's copious notes on the problem of 'vibhutva' in his edition, Bombay Sanskrit and Prakrit Series, No. LXXIII, 1933.
37. Amṛtacandra is aware of this problem and makes the following observations in the *Tattvārthasāra:*
alpakṣetre tu siddhānām anantānāṃ prasajyate/parasparāparodho'pi nāvagāhanaśaktitaḥ//nānādīpaprakāśeṣu mūrtimatsv api dṛṣyate/na virodhaḥ pradeśe'lpe hantāmūrteṣu kiṃ punaḥ//ākārābhāvato'bhāvo na ca tasya prasajyate/anantaraparityaktaśarīrākāradhāriṇaḥ// śarīrānuvidhāyitve tat tadabhāvād visarparṇam/lokākāśapramāṇasya tāvan nākāraṇatvataḥ// śarāvacandraśālādidravyāvaṣṭabhayogataḥ/alpo mahāṃś ca dīpasya prakāśo jāyate yathā//saṃhāre ca visarpe ca tathātmānātmayogataḥ/ tad abhāvāt tu muktasya na saṃhāravisarpaṇe// [*Tattvārthasāra*, VIII, 13-18]
38. There is a popular tradition that Ācārya Kundakunda had by his yogic powers paid a visit to the holy assembly (samavasaraṇa) of Tīrthaṅkara Sīmandhara in the Videha land. See Upadhye's Introduction to the *Pravacanasāra*, pp. 5-8.
39. kleśakarmavipākāśayair aparāmṛṣṭaḥ puruṣaviśeṣa īśvaraḥ/ tatra niratiśayaṃ sarvajñabījam/ pūrveṣām api guruḥ kālenānavacchedāt/

[*Pātañjalayogasūtra*, i, 24-26]

40. tasmān na badhyate 'sau na mucyate nāpi saṃsarati kaścit/ saṃsarati badhyate mucyate ca nānāśrayā prakṛtiḥ// [*Sāṃkhyakārikā*, 62]
41. Somadeva Sūri makes the following comments on the problem of the tīrtha and the Tīrthaṅkara:
bhavatāṃ samaye kila manujaḥ sann āpto bhavati tasya cāptatvātīva durghaṭā samprati saṃjātajanavad, bhavatu vā, tathāpi manuṣyasyābhilaṣitatattvāvabodho na svatas tathā darśanābhāvāt/paraś cet ko' sau paraḥ? tīrthakaro'nyo vā? tīrthakaraś cet tatrāpy evaṃ paryanuyoge prakṛtaṃ anubandhe/ tasmād anavasthā/....tathāptenaikena bhavitavyam/ na hy āptānām itaraprāṇivad gaṇaḥ samasti, saṃbhave vā caturviṃśatir iti niyamaḥ kautuskataḥ....

tattvabhāvanayodbhūtaṃ janmāntarasamutthayā//
hitāhitavivekāya yasya jñānatrayaṃ param//79//
dṛṣṭādṛṣṭam avaity arthaṃ rūpavantam athāvadheḥ/
śruteḥ śrutisamāśreyaṃ kvāsau param apekṣatām//80//
sargāvasthitisaṃhāragrīṣmavarṣātuṣāravat/
anādyanantabhāvo'yam āptaśrutasamāśrayaḥ//83//
niyataṃ na bahutvaṃ cet katham ete tathāvidhāḥ/
tithitārāgṛhāmbodhibhūbhṛtprabhṛtayo matāḥ//84//
[*Yaśastilakacampū*, chapter 6]

42. See my articles: 'The Concept of Arhat', *Ācārya Shri Vijayavallabha-sūri Smārakagrantha,* Bombay 1956; 'On the omniscience (*sarvajñatva*) of Mahāvīra and the Buddha', *Buddhist Studies in Honour* of *I.B. Horner,* pp. 72-90, (Reidel Pub. Co.) Holland, 1975.
43. Sixteen conditions are listed for the 'influx' of that karma by which the status of tīrthaṅkara is attained: darśanaviśuddhir vinayasampannatā śīlavrateṣv anaticāro 'bhīkṣṇajñānopayogasaṃvegau śaktitas tyāgatapasī sādhusamādhir vaiyāvṛtyakaraṇam arhadācāryabahuśrutapravacanabhaktir āvaśyakāparihāṇir mārgaprabhāvanā pravacanavatsalatvam iti tīrthakaratvasya/ [*Tattvārthasūtra,* vi, 24] tāny etāni ṣoḍaśakāraṇāni samyagbhāvitāni vyastāni ca tīrthakaranāmakarmāsravakāraṇāni pratyetavyāni/ [*Sarvārthasiddhi,* vi, 24]
44. See *Jaina Sūtras,* (tr., Hermann Jacobi) Part I, pp. 79-88, Sacred Books of the East, vol. XXII.
45. Amṛtacandra enumerates 47 śaktis in the Sarvaviśuddhajñāna chapter of the *Ātmakhyāti-ṭīkā.*
46. For a detailed study of this controversy see Tatia's *Studies in Jaina Philosophy,* pp. 70-80; Mohan Lal Mehta's *Outlines of Jaina Philosophy,* pp. 48-52; Paṇḍita Kailashcandra Shastri's *Jaina Nyāya* (in Hindi), pp. 147-152, Bhāratīya Jñānapīṭha, Banaras, 1966.
47. *Viśeṣāvaśyaka-bhāṣya,* vv. 3089-3135.
48. *Sanmati-tarka,* ii, 30-33. (*Nyāyāvatāra and Other Works,* p. 180). See Dr. Upadhye's Introduction to this work regarding the affiliation of Siddhasena Divākara with the Yāpanīya sect.
49. jugavaṃ vaṭṭai ṇāṇaṃ kevalaṇāṇissa daṃsaṇaṃ ca tahā/
diṇayarapayāsatāpaṃ jaha vaṭṭai taha muṇeyavvaṃ//
[Kundakunda's *Niyamasāra,* 160]
50. tarke mukhyavṛttyā parasamayavyākhyānam/tatra yadā ko'pi parasamayī pṛcchati Jaināgame darśanaṃ jñānaṃ ce'ti guṇadvayaṃ jīvasya kathyate tat kathaṃ ghaṭata iti....teṣāṃ pratītyarthaṃ sthūlavyākhyānena bahirviṣaye yat sāmānyaparīcchedanaṃ tasya sattāvalokana-darśana-saṃjñā....siddhānte punaḥ.. sūkṣmavyākhyāne...ātmagrāhakaṃ darśanaṃ vyākhyātam iti...
[Brahmadeva's *Vṛtti* on the *Dravyasaṅgraha,* p. 44. (See note 46)]
51. sāmānya-viśeṣātmaka-bāhyārthagrahaṇaṃ jñānaṃ tadātmakasvarūpagrahaṇaṃ darśanam iti siddham/
[*Dhavalā* on *Ṣaṭkhaṇḍāgama,* I.i.4. (See note 46)]
52. Cf. anākāropayogamayī dṛśiśaktiḥ/ sākāropayogamayī jñānaśaktiḥ/
[*Ātmakhyāti-ṭīkā,* (sarvaviśuddhajñānādhikāra)]
53. svajātyavirodhenaikadhyam upānīya paryāyan ākrāntabhedān aviśeṣeṇa samastagrahaṇāt saṅgrahaḥ/ [*Sarvārthasiddhi,* i, 33]

54. ṛjuṃ praguṇaṃ sūtrayati tantrayatīti ṛjusūtraḥ/ pūrvāparāṃs trikālaviṣayān atiśayya vartamānakālaviṣayān ādatte, atītānāgatayor vinaṣṭānutpannatvena vyavahārābhāvāt/ tac ca vartamānaṃ samayamātram/ tadviṣayaparyāyamātragrāhyam ṛjusūtraḥ/ nanu saṃvyavahāralopaprasaṅga iti cet, na; asya nayasya viṣayamātrapradarśanaṃ kriyate/ sarvanayasamūhasādhyo hi lokasaṃvyavahāraḥ/ [*Sarvārthasiddhi*, i, 33]

55. "arasarūpo...nibbhogo...akiriyavādo...ucchedavādo...jegucchī... venayiko...tapassī...appagabbho...bhavaṃ Gotamo" ti? "atthi khv'esa, brāhmaṇa, pariyāyo yena maṃ pariyāyena sammā vadamāno vadeyya—'arasarūpo...pe...apagabbho samaṇo Gotamo' ti...no ca kho yaṃ tvaṃ sandhāya vadesi". [(abridged) *Pārājika*, I, i]

56. The following passages may be compared:

Laghutattvasphoṭa	*Samayasāra-kalaśa*
(a) asy eva ciccakacakāyitacañcur uccaiḥ/2	(a) jīvaḥ svayaṃ tu caitanyam uccaiś cakacakāyate/41
(b) advaitam eva mahayāmi/14	(b) bhāti na dvaitam eva/9
(c) ekaṃ kramākramavivartivivartaguptaṃ/34	(c) evaṃ kramākramavivartivicitracitram/264
(d) tīvrais tapobhir abhitas ta ime ramantām/41	(d) kliśyantāṃ svayam eva duṣkarataraiḥ/142
(e) prauḍhaprakāśarabhasārpitasuprabhātam/47	(e) śuddhaprakāśabharanirbharasuprabhātaḥ/268
(f) nityoditaikamahimanyudite tvayīti/49	(f) śuddhasvabhāvamahimanyudite tvayīti/269
(g) sucaritaśitasaṃvidastrapātāt/379	(g) prajñācchetrī śiteyaṃ....pātitā sāvadhānaiḥ/181
(h) nirbhāgo'pi prasabham abhitaḥ khaṇḍyase tvaṃ nayoghaiḥ/529	(h) sadyaḥ praṇaśyati naye kṣaṇakhaṇḍyamānaḥ/270
(i) jñānād anyat kim iha kuruṣe nirviśaṅko ramasva/539	(i) jñānin bhuṅkṣva...nāstīha bandhas tava/150
(j) tyajasi na manāk ṭaṅkotkīrṇāṃ....cidekatām/566	(j) ṭaṅkotkīrṇaprakaṭamahimā spūrjati jñānapuñjaḥ/193
(k) vyaktiś cet parivartate kim anayā jñānasya nājñānatā/620	(k) ajñānaṃ na kadācanāpi hi bhavet jñānaṃ bhavat santatam/150

57. niścayam iha bhūtārthaṃ vyavahāraṃ varṇayanty abhūtārtham/ bhūtārthabodhavimukhaḥ prāyaḥ sarvo'pi saṃsāraḥ//5// abudhasya bodhanārthaṃ munīśvarā deśayanty abhūtārtham/ vyavahāram eva kevalam avaiti yas tasya deśanā nāsti//6//

58. None of Amṛtacandra's works refer directly to any other composition. Could the following verse be an allusion to his *Samayasāra-kalaśa*?:

śamarasa-kalaśāvalī-pravāhaiḥ
  kramavitataiḥ paritas tavaiṣa dhautaḥ/
niravadhi-bhava-santati-pravṛttaḥ
  katham api nirgalitaḥ kaṣāya-raṅgaḥ//378//

59. The warning in the following verse that the Jaina should not imitate the Sāṃkhya in treating the soul as "inactive" is a good illustration of this point:

mā kartāram amī spṛśantu puruṣaṃ Sāṃkhyā ivāpy Ārhatāḥ
kartāraṃ kalayantu taṃ kila sadā bhedāvabodhād adhaḥ/
ūrdhvaṃ tūddhatabodhadhāmaniyataṃ pratyakṣam enaṃ svayaṃ
paśyantu cyutakartṛbhāvam acalaṃ jñātāram ekaṃ param//

[*Samayasāra-kalaśa* 205]

CHAPTER 4

Svatantravacanāmṛta of Kanakasena*

The single manuscript of this unpublished short Jaina poem is to be found in the collection of the Bibliothèque Nationale of the University of Strasbourg.[1] A brief description of this manuscript (of two palm-leaves) appears in the *Catalogue of the Jaina Manuscripts at Strasbourg,*[2] p. 222 and p. 240. As can be seen from the text and the translation produced below, the work belongs to the genre of the dvātriṃśikās (<<philosophical compositions in thirty-two verses>>) popular among the Jainas from the time of Siddhasena Divākara (fourth century), the celebrated author of the *Ekaviṃśati-dvātriṃśikāḥ.*[3] The title of the present composition is not referred to elsewhere and although the name Kanakasena appears at the end of the poem we have no further information on his identity or his date. Since the name ends in -sena, the author may be said to belong to Senagaṇa,[4] a mendicant order of the Digambara sect.

The text can be divided into three parts. The first (vv. 1-9) puts forth views of several of the traditional *darśanas* on the nature of the soul. The second part (vv. 10-24) expounds the Jaina view of the soul, seeking to overcome the apparent contradictions by recourse to the device of *syādvāda.* The third part (vv. 25-31) speaks of the triple path of insight, knowledge and conduct culminating in the state of *mokṣa.* Despite its brevity, the

---

*This article was published originally in *Indologica Taurinensia,* Vol. VIII-IX, pp. 201-207, 1981. Reprinted with kind permission of the Editor, Indologica Taurinensia, Torino (Italy).

Svatantravacanāmṛta can be considered a complete exposition of the Jaina doctrine pertaining to the freedom of the soul from the bonds of *karma*.

***Svatantravacanāmṛta:* Text and Translation**

śrī vītarāgāya namaḥ/
jīvājīvaikabhāsāya prāṇair bhāva-tad anyakaiḥ/
kāryakāraṇamuktaṃ taṃ muktātmānam upāsmahe //1//

Salutations to the auspicious one who is free from passions!

We venerate that free soul who is emancipated from the cycle of cause and effect [namely the defiled state of bondage] and from the signs of embodiment and vital life and one who illuminates with his knowledge the entire range of the sentient and the insentient (1).

atha mokṣasvabhāvāptir ātmanaḥ karmaṇāṃ kṣayaḥ/
samyagdṛgjñānacāritrair avinābhāvalakṣaṇaih// 2 //

There is the attainment of the true nature of emancipation when there is the total destruction of the karmas accumulated by the soul. And such a state is not to be found without the simultaneous presence of true insight, right knowledge and pure conduct (2).

sati dharmiṇi tad dharmāś cintyante vibudhair iha/
moktrabhāve tataḥ kasya mokṣaḥ syād iti nāstikaḥ // 3 //

Here the nihilist [the *Cārvāka*] objects: << The wise consider the qualities *(dharmas)* only when there is a substance *(dharmin)* indicated; in the absence of a soul who attains emancipation (i.e. whose freedom can be talked about?) (3).

asty ātmā cetano draṣṭā pṛthivyāder ananvayāt/
piśācadarśanādibhyo 'nādiśuddhaḥ sanātanaḥ // 4 //

[The ātmavādin says:] There is a soul. He is sentient and being the perceiver cannot be subsumed under [such substances] as earth, etc. [He must be considered different from the body] on the analogy of perception of goblins, etc., [who do not have gross bodies.] This soul moreover is eternally and forever pure (4).

sa nirlepaḥ kathaṃ saukhyasmarakrodhādikāraṇāt/
dehād evādihetubhyaḥ kartā bhoktā ca neśvaraḥ // 5 //

<< The soul cannot however be [totally] free from blemishes because of the presence of such conditions as pleasure, sexual desire, anger etc., which arise with the body. For these reasons the soul is the agent [of his actions] as well as the enjoyer [of the results]; he certainly is not the lord of himself >> (5).

īśvarābhāvatas tasmin na tadvatvaṃ prasiddhyati/
sādhanāsambhavāt so 'pi brūte(?) Yogamati(ī)ṣṭikṛt // 6 //

<< In the absence of this lordship he cannot truly be established as endowed with thatness, [namely being the agent and the enjoyer] >>, so says a disciple of the Yoga school, the performer of sacrifices, [namely, a devotee of the Lord] (6).

sat[t]vāt kṣaṇika evāsau tat phalam kasya jāyate/
api durgṛhitam evaitat pratyabhijñādibādhakāt// 7 //

Here the Buddhist says: If the soul is an existent, then it must be momentary. Such being the case, to whom would the result accrue? [The Jaina replies:] Surely this is wrongly perceived since your position is invalidated by recognition, etc. (7).

śruta(i)prāmāṇyataḥ karma kriyate hiṃsādinā yutam/
vṛthety arpaiti(?) na xxxx sambhavāt // 8 //

Here the Mīmāṃsaka says: Actions are performed mixed with injury to beings as they are prescribed by the revealed scriptures (the Vedas). [The Jaina replies:] Surely that is futile [as injury cannot be the means of salvation] (8).

advaitasādhanaṃ nāsti dvaitāpattis tad anyathā/
nyūnād ity ācchabodhāder dehinām iti jainadhīḥ // 9 //

As for the Advaita-Vedānta, if there is only one reality, there can be no means to establish it. And if it is established, duality will result. [Moreover, there must be plurality] because of the deficiencies perceived in the pure (i.e. normal) consciousness of sentient beings. The Jaina view on the soul therefore is (9):

draṣṭā jñātā prabhuḥ kartā bhoktā ceti guṇī ca saḥ /
visrasordhvagatir dhrauvyavyayotpattiyugaṃgamaḥ // 10 //

The soul is the perceiver, the knower, the Lord, the agent, the enjoyer and possessor of qualities. [When freed from the karmas and the conditions of embodiment] the soul is of the nature to rise upwards spontaneously [reaching the summit of the Universe]. [As an existent] the soul is enjoined simultaneously with production [of a new state], loss [of an old state] and the endurance [as a substance with its own qualities] (10).

asti-nāsti-svabhāvo 'sau dharmaiḥ svaparasambhavaiḥ /
guṇāguṇasvarūpaś ca sva-vibhāvaguṇair bhavet // 11 //

The soul is characterized by positive and negative aspects which rise from the assertion of his own qualities and the denial of others' in him. In this way when we look at his innate nature he will be seen as endowed with [perfect] qualities. When his defilements [arising from the contact of karmas] are however perceived he would appear to be devoid of such [perfect] qualities (11).

vyapadeśādibhir bhinnaḥ sukhādibhyo 'paras tathā /
pradeśair bandhato mūrtir amūrtaḥ sa tad anyathā // 12 //

Although truly speaking, he must be distinct from the states where he is designated [as human, divine, animal, etc.,] he must nevertheless be identical with the [changing] states of happiness, etc. Similarly, he has a form when bound by karmic matter and is formless when he is free from bondage (12).

jātikśakteś ca caitanyād ekaḥ sa syād anekatām/
āpnoti vṛttisadbhāvair nānā jñānātmanā tataḥ// 13 //

The soul can truly be seen as << non-dual >> when one

perceives his consciousness in its universal aspect [that is when the objects reflected therein are seen as modifications of consciousness and not distinct from it]. But the same consciousness can be described as << manifold >> when one perceives its multiple operation in relation to particular souls (13).

kṣaṇikaḥ svaparyayair nityair guṇair akṣaṇikas tathā/
śūnyaḥ karmabhir ānandād aśūnyaḥ sa mataḥ satām// 14 //

The soul is momentary [if one looks only at its modifications]; it is not momentary however if one perceives its eternal qualities. It can be called empty (*śūnya*) since it is devoid of karmas but the wise would call it << non-empty >> also as it is filled with bliss (14).

cetanaḥ sopayogatvāt prameyatvād acetanaḥ/
vācyaḥ kramavivakṣāyām avācyo yugapadgiraḥ// 15 //

The soul is sentient because of its cognition but [in a way] it is insentient too since it becomes the object of knowledge. It can be called << describable >> if one were to speak of it in a sequential order [asserting certain properties and denying certain others] but it would become << inexpressible >> if one were to attempt to express both the positive and negative aspects simultaneously (15).

dravyādyaiḥ svagatair bhāvo 'bhāvaḥ paragataiḥ sadā/
nityaḥ sthiter anityo 'sau vyayotpattiprakārataḥ// 16 //

The soul is existent because of its own substance, etc. It can be called non-existent in as much as it lacks the substance (nature) of others. It is eternal [when one views] its durable substance; non-eternal, however, [when viewed purely] from the gain and loss of its modifications (16).

ākuñcanaprasārābhyām aghātebhyas tanupramaḥ/
samudghātaiḥ pradeśaiḥ syāt sa ca sarvagato mataḥ// 17 //

Because of expansion and contraction—which do not however

destroy it—the soul is said to be of the same measure as its body. However the same soul can be called << omni-present >> when it performs the act of << bursting forth >> *(samudghāta)* and extends itself throughout the universe [in order to thin out the Karmic matter of the << non-destructive >> type (i.e. the *Vedanīya karma*)] (17).

kartā svaparyayeṇa syāt akartā 'paraparyayaiḥ/
bhoktā pratyātmaṣamprīter abhoktā 'karaṇāśrayāt// 18 //

The soul is the agent only of its own modifications. It is not the agent of the states of other existents. It can be called << the enjoyer >> to the extent that it attaches itself to its own body and senses but it is not the enjoyer [if one perceives the fact that] it is not truly supported by the sense organs (18).

svasaṃvedanabodhena vyakto 'sau kathito jinaiḥ/
avyaktaḥ parabodhena grāhyo grāhako 'py ataḥ// 19 //

The Jinas have declared that the soul is << experienced >> only in reference to self-cognition but the same soul can be called << beyond experience >> when it becomes the object of others' cognition. For the very same reasons the soul is also described as the cognizer and the cognized (19).

ity anekāntarūpo 'sau dharmair evaṃvidhaiḥ padaiḥ/
jñātavyo 'nantaśaktibhyo svabhāvād api yogibhiḥ// 20 //

Thus the soul indeed is characterized by a manifold nature and it is to be known by [such apparently contradictory] expressions. By the yogins, however, the soul can be known in its own nature [endowed] with its infinite qualities (20).

nayapramāṇabhaṅgībhiḥ sustham etan mataṃ bhavet/
nayā syus tv aṃśagās tatra pramāṇe sakalārthage// 21 //

Through the method of applying the partial and comprehensive means of knowledge [the manifoldness of the soul] is well-established. The *nayas* apprehend only portions of realities whereas the two *pramāṇas*, [namely the direct and indirect perceptions] apprehend the totality of knowables (21).

bhūtābhūtanayo mukhyo dravyaparyāyayadeśanāt/
tad bhedā naigamādyāḥ syur antabhedās tathāpare// 22 //

The *nayas* are primarily twofold referring to the real and the relative, the substantial and the modificational aspects. These are further divided as *naigama-naya*, etc. and each of these is further subdivided (22).

pratyakṣaṃ spaṣṭanirbhāsaṃ parokṣaṃ viśadetaram/
tat parmāṇaṃ vidus tajñāḥ svaparārthaviniścayāt//23//

The direct perceptions (i.e. omniscient perception) is that which is clear and without blemish. The indirect perception [namely that which is mediated by mind and the senses] is partly clear and partly unclear. Both these are called valid means of knowledge by the wise since they determine the objects inclusive of the self and others (23).

syād asti-nāsti-yugaṃ syād avaktavyaṃ ca tat trayam/
saptabhaṅgīnayair vastu dravyārthikapurassaraiḥ // 24 //

The object of knowledge is approached by the sevenfold viewpoints expressed as exists, does not exist, both, inexpressible, and the three combinations thereof, all statements qualified by the term *syāt* (in some sense). These seven statements will proceed [with having] in view [either] the substance [or the modes] (24).

nirleśyaṃ nirguṇasthānaṃ sac-cij-jñānasukhātmakam /
ātyantikam avasthānaṃ sa mokṣo 'tra yad ātmanaḥ // 25 //

The emancipation of the soul is that state when the soul becomes free from karmic << colouration >>, transcends the [fourteen][5] stages of the progress towards perfection, becomes the embodiment of pure being, pure consciousness, infinite knowledge and bliss and endures there eternally (25).

dṛgjñānāvṛtimohākhyavighnāvidyodarānvayāḥ/
karmāṇi dravyamukhyāni kṣayaś caiṣām asau bhavet // 26 //

The emancipation takes place when there is the total annihilation of nescience *(avidyā)* which is also known as the major karmic matter, the obscurer of perception and knowledge and the producer of delusion and obstruction (26).

niṣkiṣṭakāḷakaṃ svarṇaṃ tat syād agniviśeṣataḥ/
tathā rāgakṣayād eṣa kramād bhavati nirmalaḥ // 27 //

Just as a piece of gold by coming into contact with a special kind of fire can become free from all dirt, similarly the soul gradually becomes free from [karmic] dirt by the destruction of attachment (27).

bāhyāntaraṅgasāmagrye paramātmani bhāvanām/
yo 'bhyudety ātmanaḥ samyak [tat] samyagdarśanaṃ matam //28//

The true insight is that which arises in the soul when there is the contemplation of the true self in the presence of the totality of the internal and the external efficient causes (28).

svaparicchittipūraṇaṃ yat tat praticchittikāraṇam/
jyotiḥ pradīpavad bhāti samyagjñānaṃ tad īritam // 29 //

The right knowledge is said to be that which shines like a flame and is the immediate cause of perceiving the objects as well as discriminating between the self and non-self (29).

tatparyāyasthiratvaṃ vā svāsthyaṃ vā cittavṛttiṣu /
sarvāvasthāsu mādhyasthyaṃ tad vṛttam atha vā smṛtam // 30 //

The pure conduct is described as that which is firmness in that state [of discrimination], the complete stillness of all operations of the mind and the equanimity in all states (30).

etat tritayam evāsya hetuḥ samuditaṃ bhavet/
nānyat kalpitam anyair yad vādibhir yuktibādhitam// 31 //

Only the combination of these three may be considered the proper means of [attaining] this [emancipation] and not those imagined by the disputants whose arguments are opposed to reasoning (31).

itthaṃ Svatantravacanāmṛtam āpibanti
svātmasthiteḥ Kanakasenamukhendusūtam/
ye jivhayā śrutipuṭe t[r]iyugena bhavyās
te cājarāmarapadaṃ sapadi śrayante// 32 //

These are the immortal words on the free soul coming from the moon-like mouth of Kanakasena [the poet], well-established in his own self. Those devout souls, who with body, speech and mind receive this ambrosia of words through their ears and taste it with their tongue [i.e. listen to it and repeat it] surely will instantly attain to the state free from decay and death (32).

iti Svatantravacanāmṛtaṁ samāptam//

Thus is completed the Immortal Sayings on the Free Soul.

NOTES

1. I am grateful to the authorities of the Bibliothèque Nationale et Universitaire de Strasbourg for their kind permission to publish this manuscript.
2. C. Tripathi, *Catalogue of the Jaina Manuscripts at Strasbourg,* Leiden, 1975.
3. A. N. Upadhye, *Siddhasena's Nyāyāvatāra and Other Works,* Bombay, 1971, pp. 111-69.
4. On the history of Senagaṇa see V. P. Johrapurkar, *Bhaṭṭāraka-Sampradāya,* Sholapur, 1958, pp. 1-38.
5. On the fourteen *guṇasthānas,* see P. S. Jaini, *The Jaina Path of Purification,* Berkeley, 1979, pp. 257-73.

IV

SOME ASPECTS OF *KARMA* THEORY

CHAPTER 5

Bhavyatva and *Abhavyatva*: A Jaina Doctrine of 'Predestination'*

One of the most fundamental doctrines of the Jains is their division of souls *(jīvas)* into two unalterable categories called *bhavya* and *abhavya*: those who are capable and those who are incapable of release from the bondage of transmigration (*saṃsāra*). Adherence to such a belief of 'predestination' is fraught with serious consequences and must be a liability to any religion, especially to Jainism, on account of its rejection of the theistic doctrines of a Creator and His Grace and its espousal of the efficacy of free-will of a striving soul. Yet one looks in vain for any satisfactory discussion of this topic among the works of the great *ācāryas*, whether of the Digambara or of the Śvetāmbara tradition, who seem to urge its acceptance solely on the authority of the Omniscient (*sarvajña*) Jina. An attempt will be made in this paper to summarize this doctrine and to discover a possible rationale underlying its institution.

Although the Jain *āgamas* abound in stray references to the terms *bhavya* and *abhavya*, the most familiar scriptural source for this doctrine is the *Tattvārtha-sūtra* of *ācārya* Umāsvāti. The terms *bhavyatva* and *abhavyatva* occur here in connection with the description of the distinctive characteristics of the soul (*jīva*) as opposed to the non-soul (*ajīva*). Umāsvāti enumerates five kinds of dispositions (*bhāva*), four of which arise in the soul respectively from subsidence (*upaśama*), destruction (*kṣaya*),

*This article was published originally in *Bhagavān Mahāvīra and His Teachings: 2,500 Nirvāṇa Anniversary Volume,* (Bombay, 1977), pp. 95-111.

destruction-cum-subsidence *(kṣayopaśama)*, and the rise (*udaya*) of *karmas.* The fifth, called the *pāriṇāmika* disposition, is inherent in the nature of the soul and exists independent of the operation of *karmas.*[1] *Jīvatva,* for instance, is a *pāriṇāmika-bhāva* of a soul, since 'soulness' is not dependent on the fluctuations of the *karmas*; whether a soul is bound or free, it will never cease to have the quality of 'soulness', i.e., consciousness. Umāsvāti includes *bhavyatva* and *abhavyatva* also under the same category, which confers on these two mutually exclusive dispositions as innate and inalienable a character as is accorded to *jīvatva.*[2] A soul thus must not only be a *jīva* at all times, but must also be a *bhavya* or an *abhavya.* A *bhavya,* by definition, means one who is capable (at some indefinite time) of either suppressing or destroying the *mohanīya-karma* to such an extent that he gains the corresponding 'self-realization' (*samyaktva=bheda-vijñāna*) which eventually must culminate in liberation (*mokṣa*). An *abhavya,* on the other hand, is one who totally lacks such ability and is never able to overcome his 'wrong-faith' (*mithyātva*), and thus remains forever chained to the wheel of transmigration. Capacity for liberation (*bhavyatva*), therefore, is not something to be acquired by any means whatsoever by any soul; rather it is something that is either built into a soul as inalienably as consciousness or is absent from a soul as eternally as is consciousness (*caitanya*) from matter (*pudgala*).

This incomprehensible theory of so radical a distinction between souls is rendered even more inscrutable when we realize that the system does not provide any clear signs by which a soul might be identified as a *bhavya* or an *abhavya.* The terms are not restricted to the 'faithful' (i.e. a Jain by birth) and the 'non-faithful' (i.e. a non-Jain), nor to a 'meritorious' (*puṇyavān*) and a 'sinful' *(pāpin)* person. According to *ācārya* Kundakunda (and his commentator *ācārya* Amṛtacandra) an *abhavya* may learn by heart all the twelve Aṅgas (the scriptures of the Jains), keep (outwardly of course) the precepts and the five great vows (*mahāvratas*) of a recluse (*muni*), and perform all the penances and austerities prescribed by the Jina, and yet not be able to overcome his *mithyātva.* In the course of his transmigration an *abhavya* may by dint of his mighty virtues be born in the heavens, even in the Graiveyakas, yet never attain the state of the liberated souls (*siddhas*).[3] Sobering as these thoughts may be for those who are given to overconfidence regarding their spiritual achievements, the doctrine cannot but have a most debilitating effect on the spiritual career of an aspirant who must always live with a terrible uncertainty regarding his status as a *bhavya* or an *abhavya.* *[See additional note at the end.]

It is unlikely that a doctrine of such blatant predestination could have become part of the tradition without giving rise to some controversy, however mild, about its validity and its compatibility with other Jain tenets of bondage and freedom. Unfortunately we know of only a single work, namely, the *Viśeṣāvaś yaka-bhāṣya* of *ācārya* Jinabhadra (6th cent. A.D.), which contains a rather meagre treatment of this topic. In a short but celebrated part of this work entitled the *Gaṇadharavāda*[4] (v.v. 1549-2094) there appear some seventeen verses (1820-1836) devoted to the controversy of *bhavya* and *abhavya.* The question is put by Maṇḍika, the sixth *gaṇadhara,* prior to his conversion to Jainism by Bhagavān Mahāvīra.

Their supposed dialogue, in the light of Maladhāri Hemacandra's *Vivaraṇa* (A.D. 1231),[5] brings out some salient points of the controversy:

Question: Is the union of *jīva* and *karma* eternal like that of *jīva* and *ākāśa* (space), or non-eternal (i.e. without a beginning but with an end) like that of gold and dirt?

Answer: Both these examples are correct and there is no contradiction in it. The former (eternal) refers to the *abhavya* souls whereas the latter (non-eternal) refers to the *bhavya* souls.[6]

Question: A distinction between souls exists on account of their *karma,* as for instance, between a human being and an animal or a being in hell. But you maintain that the distinction between a *bhavya* and an *abhavya* is not caused by *karma.* When the soulness (*jīvatva*) is common to all, why make any distinction (between a *bhavya* and an *abhavya*)?[7]

Answer: This is not a valid objection. The soul (*jīva*) and space (*ākāśa*), for instance, share several common properties, e.g., 'substanceness' (*dravyatva*), 'objectness' (*prameyatva*), etc., yet there are innate differences between the two. *Ākāśa,* for instance, is devoid of consciousness (*caitanya*), whereas the *jīva* has it as its very nature. The same is true of the *bhavya* and the *abhavya.* Soulness (*jīvatva*) is their common property, yet there is an innate difference between them.[8]

Question: According to you *bhavyatva* is an innate disposition like *jīvatva*. Being innate it must also be eternal. But unless the *bhavyatva* (capacity for release) is terminated there can be no emancipation, since the liberated soul (*siddha*) cannot be said to be a *bhavya* (capable of release) or an *abhavya*. How can you terminate that which is innate to a soul?[9]

Answer: This too is not a valid objection. Although beginningless, the antecedent non-existence (*prāg-abhāva*) of a jar comes to an end with the coming into existence of the jar. Similarly, *bhavyatva* is terminated by some proper means (such as faith, knowledge and conduct) together with the attainment of *mokṣa*.[10]

Question: If all *bhavyas* attain *mokṣa* won't there come a time when the world—like the decreasing hoard of a granary—is emptied of all *bhavyas* and will consist of only the *abhavya* souls?[11]

Answer: There is no fear of that happening, since the number of *bhavya* souls is infinite (*ananta*) like that of future time. Being infinite this number is inexhaustible even when an equal number is deducted from it. Moreover, past time and future time are equal in extent. Although the number of the *bhavyas* is infinite (*anata*), only an nth part of that number (which is also infinite) has attained liberation in the past and a similar number of them will become *siddhas* in the future.[12]

Question: How can it be established that the number of *bhavyas* is infinite and yet only an nth part of them will attain *mokṣa*?[13]

Answer: It is established on the analogy of time (i.e. the extent of time and *bhavyas* is inexhaustible). Or rather you should accept this as true because it is my word, the word of an omniscient (*sarvajña*) being, like the findings of an impartial arbiter who knows the facts.[14]

Question: If as you maintain, some *bhavya* souls will never attain salvation, what good is their *bhavyatva*? Surely, they are to be considered *abhavyas*?[15]

Answer: By the term *bhavya* is meant a soul who is capable (*yogya*) of attaining liberation; the term is not restricted only to souls who actually attain liberation. Having the potentiality alone does not guarantee its realization, as the latter depends upon the co-ordination of favourable conditions. Take, for instance, the example of impure metals. Not all impure metals have the capability of purification (=not all souls have the capability of liberation, e.g. the *abhavyas*). But in all cases of impure gold (comparable to the *bhavyas*) there is a potentiality of purification. Nevertheless, purification takes place only in those cases which have access to the purifying agents, such as fire and chemicals.[16] In the same manner, not all *bhavyas* realize their potentiality, but only those who obtain the co-ordination of favourable conditions.[17] The rule here is that when the favourable conditions do indeed become available, only the *bhavya* soul will be able to benefit from them, and not the *abhavya*, who is devoid of the potentiality for liberation.[18]

It is hardly necessary to point out the glaring flaws in the above arguments, weakened further by an unwarranted appeal for faith in the words of the omniscient Jina. The central problem, namely, the basis for the division of *bhavya* and *abhavya*, remains unanswered, or rather is deliberately evaded. An extraordinary admission has been made that despite its status as an innate *bhāva*, *bhavyatva* can somehow be terminated at the time of liberation. This is certainly a major concession, for no other *pāriṇāmika-bhāva* is allowed to lapse; granted doubtless more for expediency than out of the demands of logic.[19] This accords *bhavyatva* a unique status, although for all practical purposes it resembles the other three mundane dispositions, namely, the *aupaśamika*, *kṣāyopaśamika* and the *audayika*, which also are destroyed at the cessation of all *karmas*. Is it possible that at some stage of its development Jainism found it necessary to introduce *bhavyatva*, a unique property, innate and yet terminable, unlike any other *bhāvas*? The uniqueness of *bhavyatva* probably holds the key to unravelling the mystery that surrounds the problems of predestination in Jainism.

Certain theistic systems profess multiple categories of souls, as for instance Calvin's distinction between the salvable and the damned,[20] or, in the Indian context, Madhva's tripartite classification, namely, salvable (*mukti-yogya*), ever-transmigrating (*nitya-saṃsārin*) and damnable (*tamo-yogya*).[21] The doctrine of predestination in these systems is a corollary of the belief in the omnipotent power of the Creator God. The determining factor, here, namely, the Grace of the Almighty God, or His sovereign power of Election, lies outside and independent of the human soul. The Madhva doctrine of *mukti*, for instance, has as its foundation the famous *Kaṭha Upaniṣat* text in which Yama declares to the aspirant Naciketas:

> "By him alone can He be won whom He elects:
> To him this Self reveals His own true form."[22]

Salvation in these schools is not to be won by exertion, not even by devout faith, but is a divine gift flowing from the free choice of the Deity.

How does an atheistic system like Jainism (or Buddhism) account for salvation? Tīrthaṅkaras may be omniscient (*sarvajña*) human beings, able and willing to teach; but they are not omnipotent like the God of the theists who withholds or effects the salvation of His own creation, at His sweet and unimpeded will. Salvation for a Jain must come from within, and must therefore be inherent in the self. During the state of bondage, however, which has no beginning in time, the inherent qualities such as knowledge (*jñāna*) and bliss (*sukha*) are vitiated (*vibhāvapariṇata*) and suppressed "like a gourd tied to a heavy stone in water"[23] by the equally beginningless power of the *karmic* matter. With the inherent qualities perpetually held in check and without recourse to an outside agency like the Grace of a Deity, how can a soul be considered able to achieve freedom?

Bhavyatva would appear to provide an escape from this impasse confronting the Jain. It is innate to the soul and yet it is not affected in any way by the forces of *karma*. It is beginningless in time and yet it can be brought to an end (*anādi-sānta*). It exists in a parallel relationship to *karma* and terminates itself at the disappearance of the latter. *Bhavyatva* should be looked upon as a special force of dynamite, as it were, planted into the soul as an inherent force to demolish the oppressive mountains of *karma*.[24] This force could remain dormant forever, but it could also be ignited by an appropriate spark; then, having accomplished the destruction of the *karmas*, it would burn itself out. The recognition that *bhavyatva* is indispensable but not wholly competent by itself for the attainment of *mokṣa* is highly significant; it prevents *bhavyatva* from assuming the characteristic of mechanical infallibility. The doctrine thus is able to provide a good measure of scope for the free play of the human will, the timely presence of a teacher and such other factors (*kāla-labdhi*, etc.) deemed necessary for the emergence of *samyaktva*, which together act as the crucial spark activating the dormant force.

This interpretation of *bhavyatva* gains credibility when it is compared with the theory of *kuśala-dharma-bīja*, a device employed by Buddhists confronted with a similar problem.[25] This revolutionary doctrine was introduced by Vasubandhu, the Sautrāntika author of the *Abhidharma-kośa-Bhāṣya*,[26] to explain the following *sūtra* passage:

> "A person is endowed with *kuśala* (wholesome) as well as *akuśala* (unwholesome) *dharmas*. His *kuśala-dharmas* disappear. But there is in him the root (*mūla*) of *kuśala* not destroyed. Even this *kuśala-mūla* is in the course of time completely annihilated, whereupon he comes to be designated as a *samucchinna-kuśala-mūla*."[27]

Here arises a problem regarding the rise of a new wholesome thought (*kuśala-citta*) in the thought-series (*santati*) of such a person. An unwholesome *citta* cannot be followed by a *kuśala-citta*, or vice versa, as the law of causation demands a certain homogeneity between two succeeding (*samanantara*) moments. According to this theory a person who has exhausted all his *kuśala-mūlas* has no chance of conceiving a new *kuśala* thought (for good cannot immediately succeed bad). The Buddhist here must either modify the law of causation pertaining to immediate succession (*samanantara-pratyaya*), or must let such a person drift forever in *saṃsāra* for want of a new *kuśala-citta*. Vasubandhu solves this dilemma by postulating his innovative theory of *kuśala-dharma-bīja*.

This new theory is based on the admission of two kinds of *kuśala-dharmas*. The first consists of those *dharmas* which are acquired by exertion, like the practices of meditation, etc., and are therefore called *prāyogika*. The second variety, advocated by the Sautrāntika, consists of those *dharmas* which are described as subtle (*sūkṣma*), which do not presuppose any effort (*ayatna-bhāvī*), and which persist throughout the series of existences (*upapattilābhika*). The Sautrāntika maintains that when a person falls so low as to be called a *samucchinna-kuśala-mūla*, as in the *sūtra* passage quoted above, only the former, i.e., the acquired (*prāyogika*) *kuśala-dharmas* are totally lost. As for the innate *kuśala-dharmas*, these are never destroyed (*na samudghātaḥ*) and will remain intact in the *santati* of such a person; from these will arise new *kuśala-dharmas.*[28] We have shown elsewhere[29] that the innate and incorruptible *kuśala-dharmas* of the Sautrāntika must be supermundane (*lokottara* or *aṇāśrava*) elements capable of producing the states of Arhatship or Buddhahood. These are accordingly described in the Mahāyāna texts as "roots of the good that lead to liberation" (*mokṣa-bhāgīya-kuśala-mūla*), or simply the "seeds of salvation" (*mokṣa-bīja*).[30] The Yogācāra doctrine of innate (*dharmatā-pratilabdha*) *gotras,* particularly its distinction between a *śrāvaka* a *pratyeka-buddha* and a *bodhisattva,* is a further development of this Sautrāntika theory of *mokṣa-bīja.*[31]

It would be repetitious to enumerate the many points of resemblance between the Buddhist concept of *mokṣa-bīja* (or *gotra*) and the Jain concept of *bhavyatva.* Mention must be made, however, of the interesting fact that the Mahāyāna texts liken the *mokṣa-bīja* to a seam of gold hidden in metal-bearing rocks,[32] a comparison strongly reminiscent of the Jain metaphor to describe *bhavyatva* in the *Gaṇadharavāda.* The correspondence between the two concepts becomes even more striking when we realize that the Sautrāntika also looked upon the *mokṣa-bīja* merely as a potency (*cetasaḥ sāmarthyam*)[33] that did not automatically produce new *kuśala-cittas,* but like the Jain *bhavyatva* had to be activated by the presence of favourable circumstances (*pratyaya-sāmagrī-sannidhāne sati*).[34]

Assuming that we have found a logical basis for the concept of *bhavyatva,* we may now examine the nature of its opposite, the *abhavyatva. Abhavyatva* is declared to be an innate disposition (*pāriṇāmika-bhāva*) of those souls who are not *bhavyas.* Although the literal meaning of the term is 'absence of *bhavyatva*', it should probably be regarded as a positive force forestalling the presence of *bhavyatva.* In its function it resembles the *mohanīya-karma,* since both hold the soul down in the bondage of *mithyātva.* Yet, *abhavyatva* is not *karma* as it partakes of the nature of soul, resides in the soul, and prevents the soul's 'self-realization', the key to salvation. We will probably never know the precise reasons that led the Jains to institute such a category, which places an infinite (*ananta*) number of souls in perpetual bondage.[35] Even the Mahāyānists, with all their seeming idealism (expressed in the bodhisattva's vow of leading *all* beings to enlightenment) admit the existence of such 'incurable' (*acikitsya*) beings, albeit a small number, and indeed use the term *abhavya* as their appellation. The *Abhisamayālaṅkāra*, for instance, declares that an *abhavya* will not attain salvation even in the presence of a Buddha, as a dead seed does not grow even when there is ample rain.[36] The term *abhavya* in this passage is identical with the Yogācāra term *agotra-stha*, described by Asaṅga as referring to a person who is totally devoid of the 'condition' of salvation (*hetu-hīna*), and hence doomed forever to dwell in *saṃsāra*.[37] Such a person, says Asaṅga, should be matured by the Bodhisattva not for *pari-nirvāṇa* but only for wholesome states (*sugati*) within the mundane existence.[38]

The remarkable concurrence between the Jains and the Buddhists on the concepts of *bhavya* and *abhavya*, and the conspicuous absence of such a doctrine in any but the later theistic *darśanas*, such as of Rāmānuja[39] and Madhva, points to the possibility that belief in 'predestination' in some form or other originated with the ancient śramaṇas. It is even conceivable that these theories developed as plausible modifications to the absolute determinism or *Niyati-vāda* of the śramaṇa Makkhali Gosāla,[40] a contemporary of both the Buddha and Mahāvīra. This doctrine finds concise expression in the *Sāmañña-phala-sutta*,[41] a Buddhist text of great antiquity:

> "There is no cause, either ultimate or remote, for the depravity of beings; they become depraved without reason and without cause. There is no cause, either proximate or remote, for the rectitude of beings, they become pure without reason and without cause. The attainment of any given condition, of any character, does not depend on one's own acts or on the acts of another or on human effort. There is no such thing as power or energy, or human strength or human vigour. All animals, all creatures (with one, two or more senses), all beings (produced from eggs or in a womb), all souls (in plants) are without force and power and energy of their own. They are bent this way and that by their fate, by the necessary conditions of the class to which they belong, by the individual nature, and it is according to their position in one or other of the six classes that they experience ease or

pain.

"There are fourteen hundred thousands of the principal sorts of birth, and again six thousand other, and again six hundred.... There are eighty-four hundred thousand periods during which both fools and wise alike, wandering in trasmigration, shall at last make an end of pain (*dukkha*). Though the wise should hope: 'By this virtue or this performance of duty, or this penance, or this righteousness will I make the *karma* (I have inherited) mature that is not yet mature'—though the fool should hope, by the same means, gradually to get rid of *karma* that has matured—neither can do it. The ease and pain, measured as it were, with a measure, cannot be altered in the course of transmigration; there can be neither increase nor decrease thereof, neither excess nor deficiency. Just as when a ball of string is cast forth it will spread out just as far, and no farther, than it can unwind, just so both fools and wise alike, wandering in transmigration exactly for the allotted term, shall then, and only then, make an end of pain.'[42]

It is not surprising that the rigid fatalism of Makkhali Gosāla was severely condemned by the Jains and the Buddhists,[43] who found in it a total rejection of the efficacy of *karma*. The main thrust of their attack was no doubt directed against the doctrines it implied, namely (1) 'salvation through transmigration'—*saṃsāreṇa suddhi* as the Buddhist text aptly puts it—,[44] and (2) salvation for *all* beings, 'fools and wise alike'. The Jains (and also the Buddhists) evidently found both these claims repugnant and might have taken a counterposition (1) that salvation was not for 'fools', and (2) even for the 'wise' it was not automatic. It is impossible to be sure, given the present state of our knowledge of the Ājīvika scriptures, whether the terms '*bāla*' and '*paṇḍita*' (as reported by the *Sāmañña-phala-sutta*) had any special technical meaning in the system of Makkhali Gosāla; nor if these were two categories as fixed in character as *bhavya* and *abhavya*. The Buddhist texts would lead us to believe that the term '*bāla*' indicated a person given to the most gross forms of evil views (*micchā-diṭṭhi*), precisely those views which were held by their rivals, particularly by Makkhali Gosāla. As a matter of fact the Buddha considered Makkhali the most dangerous of all *tīrthikas* and is reported to have said: "I know not of any other single person fraught with such loss to many folk, such discomfort, such sorrow to *devas* and men, as Makkhali, the infatuate."[45] Buddhaghosa, in his Aṭṭhakathā on the *Puggalapaññatti* singles out Makkhali Gosāla as an illustration of a person that can be called a Buddhist '*abhavya*'. While commenting on a *sutta* passage that describes a person who is called 'once drowned, drowned forever',[46] Buddhaghosa states that such a person is possessed of totally evil views (such as nihilism, the theory that there is no cause, and no efficacy of *karma*) and is consequently 'drowned forever'. As if he was reporting an ancient belief, Buddhaghosa further adds: "For such a one they say that there is no rising from [the mire of] transmigration. Like Makkhali Gasāla and others they become the food for the fire of lower and lower hells."[47]

The choice of Makkhali Gosāla to illustrate an '*abhavya*' may not be purely accidental. It is quite likely that both the Buddhists and the Jains considered such *mithyā-dṛṣṭins* as totally 'incurable', the number of whom might have been very small, as the word *kaścit*[48] employed by Asaṅga to indicate the *hetu-hīna* (=*agotrastha*) beings would seem to indicate. In the course of time, the class of such beings who were doomed forever might have developed into the category of the *abhavya* in Jainism and the *agotrastha* in Mahāyāna Buddhism.

The early Buddhists, in keeping with their well-observed habit, seem to have refrained from theorising on these cetegories.[49] The Jains on the other hand, being more ancient and much more closer to the Ājīvikas, appear to have pushed the belief in the categories of *bhavya* and *abhavya* to its logical conclusion. The fact that the Buddhists were content to leave the number of the *abhavyas* undefined and that the Jains replaced this unspecified and arbitrary number with infinity (*ananta*) points to the thoroughness of the Jains in defining and modifying an ancient śramaṇa doctrine of 'predestination'.[50]

NOTES

1. *Sarvārthasiddhi* (with *Tattvārthasūtra*), edited by Phoolchandra Siddhanta Shastri, Bhāratīya Jñānapīṭha, Delhi, 1971.

2. *Ibid.*, II.7.
3. *Samayasāra* 273, 274. *Samayasāra* of Kundakunda (with Amṛtacandra's *Ātmakhyāti-ṭīkā*), Karanja, Mahāvīra Jñānopāsanā Samiti, 1968; *Viśeṣāvaśyakabhāṣya* 1219. *Viśeṣāvaśyakabhāṣya* of Jinabhadragaṇi (including *Vivaraṇa*), Divyadarshan Karyalaya, Ahmedabad, 1962, 3 parts.
4. *Gaṇadharavāda*, Translation and explanation, by E.A. Solomon, Gujarat Vidya Sabha, Ahmedabad, 1966.
5. I have used the text of the *Gaṇadharvāda* as given in Solomon's edition. She also gives a literal translation of the *Vivaraṇa*.
6. *Gaṇadharvāda* 1820-21 ab.
7. *Ibid.*, 1821 cd. 1822.
8. *Ibid.*, 1823.
9. *Ibid.*, 1824 with *Vivaraṇa* 1824.
10. *Ibid.*, 1825.
11. *Ibid.*, 1827 ab. *Vivaraṇa* 1827 ab.
12. yasmāc cātītānāgatakālau tulyāv eva, yataś cātītenāpi kālenaika eva nigodānantatamo bhāgo 'dyāpi bhavyānāṃ siddhaḥ, eṣyatāpi bhaviṣyatkālena tāvan mātra eva bhavyānantabhāgaḥ siddhiṃ gacchan yukto ghaṭamānakaḥ, na hīnādhikaḥ, bhaviṣyato 'pi kālasyātītatulyatvāt/ tata evam api sati na sarvabhavyānām ucchedo yuktaḥ, sarveṇāpi kālena tadanantabhāgasyaiva siddhigamanasambhavopadarśanāt/ [*Vivaraṇa* 1828]
13. *Vivaraṇa* 1829.
14. *Ibid.*, 1830 cd. 1831.
15. *Ibid.*, 1833.
16. *Ibid.*, 1834.
17. *Ibid.*, 1835 with *Vivaraṇa* 1835.
18. *Ibid.*, 1836.
19. aupaśamikādibhavyatvānāṃ ca/ [*Tattvārtha-sūtra* X, 3]
.... bhavyatvagrahaṇam anyapāriṇāmikanivṛtty artham tena pāriṇāmikeṣu bhavyatvasyaupaśamikādīnāṃ ca bhāvānām abhāvān mokṣo bhavatīty avagamyate/ [*Sarvārthasiddhi* X, 3]
20. See Emil Brunner: *The Christian Doctrine of God* (on the history of the doctrine of predestination, pp. 340 ff.), the Westminister Press, 1949.
21. B.N.K. Sharma: *Philosophy of Śrī Madhvācārya*, Bharatiya Vidya Bhavan, Bombay, 1962.
22. nāyam ātmā pravacanena labhyo na medhayā na bahunā śrutena/
yam evaiṣa vṛuṇute tena labhyaḥ tasyaiṣa ātmā vivṛṇute tanūṃ svām/
[*Kaṭhopaniṣat* II, 23]
23. *Sarvārthasiddhi* X, 7.
24. Cf. "*...bhettāraṃ karmabhūbhṛtām*". [*Sarvārthasiddhi* I, 1]
25. See my edition of the *Abhidharmaaīpa* with *Vibhāṣāprabhā-vṛtti*. Tibetan Sanskrit Works Series, Vol. IV, pp. 166-170. See my paper "The Sautrāntika theory of bīja" in the *BSOAS*, University of London, Vol. XXII, Part 2, 1959, pp. 236-249.
26. *Abhidharmakośa-Bhāṣya* II, 36 (Pradhan's edition, Patna, 1967).
27. "samanvāgato 'yaṃ puruṣaḥ kuṣalair api dharmaih" iti vistaraḥ.../ te 'sya pudgalasya kuśalā dharmā antardhāsyanti...asti cāsya kuśalamūlam anusahagatam anupacchinnam upapattilābhikam/ tad apy apareṇa samayeṇa sarveṇa sarvaṃ samucchetsyate/yasya samucchedāt samucchinna-kuśalamūla iti saṃkhyāṃ gamiṣyatīti / [*Abhidharmadīpa-Vṛtti, kā.* 199]

28. kuśalā api dharmā dviprakārā ayatnabhāvino yatnabhāvinaś ca ye ta ucyante utpattilambhikāḥ prāyogikāś ceti/ tatrāyatnabhāvibhir āśrayasya tadbījānupaghātāt samanvāgata upaghātād asamanvāgata ucyate samucchinnakuśalamūlaḥ/tasya tūpaghāto mithyādṛṣṭyā veditavyaḥ /na tu khalu kuśalānāṃ dharmāṇāṃ bījabhāvasyātyantaṃ santatau samudghātaḥ/ [*Abhidharmakośa-Bhāṣya,* II, 36]

This view comes under a severe criticism by the Vaibhāṣika author of the *Abhidharmadīpa-Vṛtti*:
"sūkṣmaṃ kuśaladharmabījam tasminn akuśale cetasy avasthitaṃ yataḥ punaḥ pratyayasāmagrīsannidhāne sati kuśalaṃ cittaṃ utpadyate" iti Kośakāraḥ/yuktyāgamavirodhāt tan neti Dīpakāraḥ/ [*kā.* 199]

29. See 'The Sautrāntika theory of bīja' (See fn. 25).

30. mokṣabījam ahaṃ hy asya susūkṣmam upalakṣaye/ dhātu-pāṣāṇa-vivare nilīnam iva kāñcanam//
Quoted by Yaśomitra in his *Sphuṭārthā Abhidharma-kośavyākhyā,* p. 644.

31. tatra prakṛtisthaṃ gotraṃ yad bodhisattvānāṃ ṣaḍāyatanaviśeṣaḥ/ sa tādṛśaḥ paramparāgato 'nādikāliko dharmatāpratilabdhaḥ/ tatra samudānītaṃ gotraṃ yat pūrva-kuśalamūlābhyāsāt pratilabdham/ ... tat punar gotraṃ bījam ity ucyate dhātuḥ prakṛtir ity api/... asati tu gotre sarveṇa sarvaṃ sarvathā bodher aprāptir eva veditavyā/ [*Bodhisattvabhūmi,* p. 1 (Dutt's edition, Patna 1966)]

32. See fn. 30.

33. Sautrāntikāḥ punar varṇayanti 'bījaṃ sāmarthyaṃ cetaso gotram' iti ... *Sphuṭārthā,* p. 583.

34. See fn. 29.

35. icceiyammi duvālasaṃge gaṇipiḍage... aṇaṃtā jīvā aṇaṃtā
ajīvā aṇaṃtā bhavasiddhiyā aṇaṃtā abhavasiddhiyā... paṇṇattā/
bhāvamabhāvā heumaheū kāraṇamakāraṇā ceva/
jīvājīvā bhaviyamabhaviyā siddhā asiddhā ya // 82 //
. . . bhavyāḥ anādipāriṇāmikabhāvayuktāḥ, ete anantā prajñaptāḥ I tathā abhavyāḥ anādipāriṇāmikābhavyabhāvayuktaḥ ete anantā prajñaptāḥ... *Haribhadrasūri-Vṛtti* on *Nandi-sūtragāthā* 82, Prakrit Text Series, Vol. X.

36. varṣaty api hi parjanye naivābījaṃ prarohati/
samutpāde 'pi buddhānāṃ nābhavyo bhadram aśnute/ VIII.10.

37. (a) agotrasthaḥ pudgalo gotre 'sati cittopāde 'pi yatna-samāśraye saty abhavyaś cānuttarāyāḥ samyaksambodheḥ paripūraye/
[*Bodhisattvabhūmi,* p. 1 (Dutt's edition, Patna, 1966)]
(b) agotrasthavibhāge ślokaḥ—
aikāntiko duścarito 'sti kaścit kaścit samudghātitaśukladharmā/
amokṣabhāgī yaśubho 'sti kaścin
nihīnaśuklo 'sty api hetuhīnaḥ//11//
aparinirvāṇadharmaka etasminn agotrastho 'bhipretaḥ/sa ca samāsato dvividhaḥ/ tatkālāparinirvāṇadharmā atyantaṃ ca/...atyantāparinirvāṇadharmā tu hetuhīno yasya parinirvāṇagotram eva nāsti/
[*Mahāyāna-Sūtrālaṅkāra,* III. 11 (Paris, 1907)]

38. tatra paripācyāḥ pudgalāḥ samāsataś catvāraḥ/śrāvakagotraḥ śrāvakayāne/ pratyekabuddhagotraḥ pratyekabuddhayāne/ buddhagotro mahāyāne paripācayitavyaḥ/ agotrastho'pi pudgalaḥ sugatigamanāya paripācayitavyo bhavati/ [*Bodhisattvabhūmi,* p. 55]

39. On the admission of a class of 'nitya-saṃsārins' in the system of Rāmānuja,

see Sharma: *Philosophy of Śrī Madhvācārya*, p. 209.

40. See A. L. Basham: *History and Doctrine of the Ājīvikas*, London, 1951.
41. *Dīgha-nikāya* I=*Dialogues of the Buddha*, Vol. I, translated by T. W. Rhys Davids, London, 1956, (pp. 65-95).
42. *Dīgha-nikāya* I, pp. 53-4.
43. For a complete bibliography and an exhaustive treatment of this doctrine, see Basham: *History and Doctrine of the Ājīvikas.* (See fn. 40).
44. (a) "itttham kho me, bhante, Makkhali Gosālo sandiṭṭhikaṃ sāmaññaphalaṃ puṭṭho samāno saṃsārasuddhiṃ byākāsi"/
[*Dīgha-nikāya* I, 54]
(b) n'atthi dvāraṃ sugatiyā/niyatiṃ kaṅkha, Bījaka/
sukhaṃ vā yadi vā dukkhaṃ, niyatiyā kira labbhati/
saṃsārasudhi sabbesaṃ, mā turittho anāgate/ [*Jātaka*, VI, p. 229]
45. nāhaṃ bhikkhave aññaṃ ekapuggalam 'pi samanupassāmi yo evaṃ bahujanāhitāya paṭipanno bahujanāsukhāya bahuno janassa anatthāya ahitāya dukkhāya devamanussānaṃ yathayidaṃ bhikkhave Makkhali moghapuriso/
[*Aṅguttara-nikāya*, I, p. 33]
46. idha bhikkhave ekacco puggalo samannāgato hoti ekanta-kāḷakehi akusalehi dhammehi, so sakiṃ nimuggo nimuggo va hoti/
[*Puggala-paññatti*, VII, 1]
47. 'sakiṃ nimuggo' ti ekavāraṃ nimuggo/ 'ekanta-kāḷakehī' ti ekanten' eva kāḷakehi natthikavāda-ahetukavāda-akiriyavāda-saṃkhātehi niyata-micchādiṭṭhi-dhammehi/ evaṃ puggalo...nimuggo va hoti/ etassa hi puna bhavato vuṭṭhānaṃ nāma natthī ti vadanti/ Makkhali Gosālādayo viya heṭṭhā heṭṭhā naraka'ggīnaṃ yeva āhārā honti/
[*Puggala-paññatti-Aṭṭhakathā*, VII, 1]
48. See fn. 37.
49. The *Kathāvatthu* contains many controversies allied to the topic of the *kuśala-mūla-samuccheda* and *sandhāna*. See *kappaṭṭha-kathā, niyatassa niyāma-kathā, accanta-niyāma-kathā*, etc. The Uttarāpathakas are accused of entertaining a belief somewhat similar to the Yogācāra doctrine of the *agotrastha*.
50. For a distinction between the *niyativāda* of the non-Jains, and a modified Jain version of this doctrine (in the light of the *anekāntavāda* of the Jains) entitled *'samyak-niyativāda'*, see *Jaina-tattva-mīmāṃsā* (in Hindi) by Paṇḍita Phoolcandra Siddhāntaśāstrī, Benares 1960. In this work the author examines the following Jain text which seems to support a doctrine of '*niyati*':
jaṃ jassa jammi dese jeṇa vihāṇeṇa jammi kālammi/
ṇādaṃ jīṇeṇa ṇiyadaṃ jammaṃ vā ahava maraṇaṃ vā//321//
taṃ tassa tammi dese teṇa vihāṇeṇa tammi kālammi/
ko sakkai cāleduṃ indo vā aha jiṇindo vā//322//
evaṃ jo ṇicchayado jāṇadi davvāṇi savvapajjāye/
so saddiṭṭhī suddho jo saṃkadi so hu kuddiṭṭhī/323//
(*Dvādaśānuprekṣā* of Svāmī Kārttikeya)
The conclusions presented in this remarkable work provoked a great deal of controversy among the community of the Digambara Jains as a result of which a 'debate' sponsored by prominent Jain scholars took place in Jaipur. The proceedings of this debate are given in two volumes entitled *Jaipur* (*Khāniyā*) *Tattvacarcā*, Shri Todarmal Granthamālā, pushpa

2 and 3, Jaipur, 1967. Paṇḍita Phoolcandra takes up the problem of 'niyati' once more in this debate and relates it to the Jain doctrine of 'kramabaddha-paryāya', according to which the infinite modifications of any given substance (*dravya*) such as a soul are fixed in a sequential order which cannot be altered, (See vol. 1, pp. 160-375). This interpretation of 'niyati' is of considerable significance for a historical study of 'predestination' and opens a new field of research for a comparative study of the Ājīvika and the Jain doctrines of bondage and salvation.

ADDITIONAL NOTE*

The seventeenth-century Svetāmbara logician Upādhyāya Yaśovijaya (1604-1687) has anticipated the problem facing an aspirant who might entertain such a doubt. In his *Adhyātmamataparīkṣā* (verse 172), Yaśovijaya expounds on this matter and concludes that a person who wonders whether he is *bhavya* or *abhavya* must be given the benefit of the doubt, for anyone who asks such a question of himself must truly be a *bhavya*. In support of this contention, he quotes the following passage from the Ācāra-ṭīkā (reference not traced): "*abhavyasya bhavyābhavyatvaśaṅkāyā abhāvāt* (because of the absence in an *abhavya* of a doubt regarding his being *bhavya* or *abhavya*)." (*Adhyātmamataparīkṣā*, with Sanskrit commentary and Gujarati translation, published by Shri Adishvara Jain Temple Trust, Valakeshvar, Bombay, no date.)

In his *Upadeśarahasya-svopajña-ṭīkā* (verse 188) Upādhyāya Yaśovijaya gives further details on the nature of *bhavyatva*. A question is raised as to why all beings who are characterized as *bhavya*, being equal in their capacity, do not attain *mokṣa* at the same time. In response he points out that *bhavyatva* must be considered different for each individual soul. This is called the doctrine of *tathābhavyatva*, which could account for the variation in time that different souls spend in *saṃsāra* before attaining the goal of *mokṣa*. The specific nature of each soul's *bhavyatva* could also explain, according to Yaśovijaya, why certain souls become Tīrthaṅkaras or Gaṇadharas while others attain *mokṣa* without any distinguishing features. (*Upadeśarahasya* with *Svopajña-ṭīkā* and Gujarati translation, published by Andheri Gujarati Jain Sangh, Ville Parle, Bombay, 1983.)

CHAPTER 6

Tīrthaṅkara-Prakṛti and the Bodhisattva Path*

Among the many technical terms which have similar meanings in Buddhism and Jainism, the terms 'Tīrthaṅkara' (Pali *titthakara*)[1] and 'Buddha' have a particularly large number of common connotations. The term 'tīrthika' (Pali *titthiya*)[2] although it has been used rather pejoratively by the Buddhists to denote the non-Brahmanical 'heretics', conveys to the Jainas the very same elements that one associates with the terms 'Buddha' or 'Samyaksambuddha'.[3] I shall mention briefly a number of points of similarity between the two terms.

Both 'Buddha' and 'Tīrthaṅkara' are applied only to the Teachers of the respective orders and not to the disciples, and at any given time only one Buddha or Tīrthaṅkara exists in any one *lokadhātu*.[4] Both Teachers have achieved omniscience (*sarvajñatva*), the Buddha by having removed all *kleśāvaraṇa* and *jñeyāvaraṇa*, and the Tīrthaṅkara by having destroyed the *mohanīya* and the *jñānāvaraṇa* karmas.[5] Although in each religion there is an eternal line of Teachers, each Buddha or Tīrthaṅkara lays the foundation for a new order (called *śāsana* or *tīrtha*), which lasts for a certain number of years and then ends, to be renewed by another teacher in the series. And in each kalpa there are exactly twenty-four Tīrthaṅkaras and twenty-five Buddhas.[6]

---

*This article was published originally in *Journal of the Pali Text Society*, IX (*Centenary Volume*), (London, 1981), pp. 96-104. Reprinted with kind permission of the Pali Text Society, London.

The first Buddha and the first Tīrthaṅkara of each age makes a prophecy concerning the identity of the last one. The first Buddha, Dīpaṅkara, prophesied that a Brahman named Sumedha would eventually become the last Buddha, Gautama. Likewise, the first Tīrthaṅkara of our kalpa, Ṛṣabha, prophesied that his grandson, Marīci, would become the last Tīrthaṅkara, Mahāvīra.[7] Similar comparisons can be drawn between major occasions in the lives of Gautama the Buddha and Mahāvīra the Tīrthaṅkara: the dreams preceding their conceptions, their births, with gods in attendance; their renunciation, enlightenment, and first sermons; and finally their nirvāṇas. Buddhist and Jaina communities celebrate these events in almost identical ways.[8]

The similarities between Buddhist and Jaina conceptions of their Teachers and Founders of orders would suggest that the path leading to Buddhahood and Tīrthaṅkarahood are equally similar; nevertheless, there must be doctrinal and temperamental differences between the two paths, inasmuch as Jainism adheres to the doctrine of noninvolvement in the affairs of other souls, while Buddhism lays great stress upon the need to cultivate *mahākaruṇā,* the great compassion, so as to help other beings attain nirvāṇa. Consequently there are some major differences between the careers of a follower of a Buddha and a disciple of a Tīrthaṅkara. It is of great interest to the students of religion to examine these similarities and differences.

The path of the Buddha is known as the Bodhisattva path, to distinguish it from the path of arhat. An arhat is said to be the follower of a lower path as he remains content with the role of the disciple and who, although free from all moral impurities (*kleśa*), continues to have a residual ignorance. This 'ignorance' is a deficiency which, according to certain Buddhist schools, prevents the arhat from being a Teacher;[9] the Buddha's omniscience, on the other hand, enables him, indeed compels him, to be a Teacher and the founder of a new Order. For the Jainas such a distinction between an arhat and a Tīrthaṅkara is impossible, since omniscience (*kevalajñāna* or *sarvajñatva*) is a prerequisite for the Jaina nirvāṇa.[10] In Jainism, therefore, the distinction between an arhat and a Tīrthaṅkara is based not upon the degree of knowledge attained, but on the presence or absence of certain miraculous powers, notably the *divya-dhvani* ('divine sound') which enables certain omniscient beings to be

Teachers.[11] Not all arhats need to be Teachers; only a few have practiced those virtues which are said to confer upon them the status of a Tīrthaṅkara (by endowing them with *divya-dhvani*) at the time of their first sermon after attaining the arhatship.

Bearing these conditions in mind one can now examine the significant features of these two paths. The prominent feature of the Bodhisattva path is the practice of the six *pāramitās*, viz. *dāna, śīla, vīrya, kṣānti, dhyāna,* and *prajñā*. The Bodhisattva traditionally produces the *bodhicitta,* the resolution to become a Buddha, in the presence of a Buddha, as for example, Sumedha, who made his resolution in the time of Dīpaṅkara Buddha. He then receives a prophecy from that Buddha, to the effect that he will become a Buddha at such and such a time. Thereafter he practices the *pāramitās* for four (to sixteen) *asaṁkhyeyas* and one hundred thousand *kalpas*, serving different Buddhas, until he finally reaches perfection and attains to Buddhahood.[12]

Three major elements stand out in this process. First, the Bodhisattva is fully aware that he wants to become a Buddha. Second, he practices the virtues repeatedly over the course of a number of births. Third, he undertakes each action with the resolution that it should accumulate such karmic forces that it finally will yield as its fruit the attainment of nirvāṇa on the part of all beings. Furthermore, the Bodhisattva is constantly aware of his future role as a Teacher.

The career of a would be Tīrthaṅkara basically resembles that of a Bodhisattva, in that he practises virtues which roughly correspond to the six *pāramitās*. The Jainas list sixteen practices (*bhāvanā*) which eventually result in Tīrthaṅkarahood: (1) Purity of insight (*darśana-viśuddhi*); (2) reverence of one's elders; (3) the observance of the vows; (4) the ceaseless pursuit of knowledge; (5) constant fear of saṃsāra; (6) charity (*tyāga*); (7) austerities (*tapas*); (8) removal of obstacles that threaten the equanimity of ascetics; (9) serving the meritorious by warding off evil; (10) devotion to arhats; (11) devotion to one's preceptors; (12) devotion to the learned in scriptures; (13) devotion to the scriptures; (14) the practice of the six essential duties (daily confession of transgressions, etc.); (15) propagation of the teachings of the Tīrthaṅkara; and (16) fervent affection for one's brother in faith.[13]

Although this list is longer than the Buddhist list of the

pāramitās, it can also be divided into the traditional Buddhist categories of *śīla, samādhi,* and *prajñā.* The Jainas emphasize *tyāga* and *darśana-viśuddhi,* just as the Buddhists emphasize *dāna* and *prajñā,* thus stressing the mundane and supermundane aspects of the path. The Jainas do not insist that all sixteen *bhāvanās* must be practised, or that they be practised to the same extent.[14] This would indicate that the list of sixteen is an elaboration of an earlier list, which probably corresponded more closely to the list of six *pāramitās.*

These sixteen *bhāvanās,* severally or collectively, are said to cause the influxes of karmic matter which must inevitably lead one to the state of being a Tīrthaṅkara, that is to say, an arhat who teaches. This karmic matter, therefore, is called *tīrthaṅkara-prakṛti,* karma which yields rebirth as a Tīrthaṅkara.[15]

One would expect the Jainas to map out their path in greater detail as did the Buddhists in the Jātakas or in such sūtras as the *Daśabhūmika* or treatises like the *Bodhisattvabhūmi.* Strangely enough, not a single Jaina work deals exclusively with the path of a Tīrthaṅkara. Although Jaina literature is full of didactic stories which extol the virtues comprising the sixteen *bhāvanās,* they are not set forth as stages of a career culminating in the birth as a Tīrthaṅkara. The Tīrthaṅkara-path seems here to have been subsumed under the path of an arhat, the *mokṣa-mārga* of the Jainas.

One can, however, follow the career of the Tīrthaṅkara by looking at the legendary biographies of various Tīrthaṅkaras in such works as the *Ādipurāṇa*[16] of Jinasena (9th century) or the *Triṣaṣṭiśalākāpuruṣacarita*[17] of Hemacandra (12th century). It is astonishing to find that in no case did the Tīrthaṅkara-to-be ever become aware of having initiated such a career. In other words, there is nothing in Jainism comparable to the idea of the *bodhicittotpāda,* the bedrock upon which the entire career of the Bodhisattva was founded. According to the Jainas the karmic forces called *tīrthaṅkara-prakṛti* become attracted to the soul of the Tīrthaṅkara-to-be at a specific time when one of the virtues, probably charity or protection of ascetics, reaches its perfection. There is no conscious effort or resolution on the part of this soul to become a Tīrthaṅkara, nor is there any awareness that such karmas have been attracted determining his future status as Tīrthaṅkara. This can probably be explained on the grounds that any such wish to become a Tīrthaṅkara would itself constitute an unwholesome act and would render his virtues impure. The Jainas have maintained that the bartering (called *nidāna*) of one's virtuous deeds for the attainment of supernatural powers or rebirths in heaven, not to speak of Tīrthaṅkarahood, is the greatest obstacle on the path of salvation.[18] It is, therefore, understandable that while a Jaina devotee, either lay or mendicant, might wish to lead a pure life and perfect his virtues, he would not entertain the thought that he might attain an exalted status, such as that of an arhat or a Tīrthaṅkara. One becomes a Tīrthaṅkara quite unawares, and that fact, in itself, is considered the perfect proof of one's saintliness.

This is a major departure from the Buddhist point of view, and it explains the absence of a Jaina-bodhisattva path, since there can be no starting point like the moment of *bodhicittotpāda*.[19] Another important distinguishing feature is the element of the time required to become a Tīrthaṅkara. While the Buddhists tend to lengthen the period into many kalpas and countless births, the Jaina legends concerning the Tīrthaṅkaras consistently mention no more than a single intermediate lifetime between the birth during which the *tīrthaṅkara-prakṛti* was attracted and the (final) incarnation as a Tīrthaṅkara.[20] This would be too short a time if the Tīrthaṅkara-to-be were required to practice the perfections in the Buddhist manner. The intervening birth is usually in a heaven[21] from where the soul descends into the womb of his human mother and is immediately endowed with a body suitable to a Tīrthaṅkara-to-be. He then becomes recipient of the various honours (e.g. the celebration of the *kalyāṇas*) eventually attaining to *kevalajñāna* at which time the *divya-dhvani* will emanate from his person and he will be recognized by all as a new Tīrthaṅkara, the founder of a new *tīrtha*.

NOTES

1. The original meaning of the term, 'the founder of a sect', is well preserved in the following passage of the *Sāmaññaphalasutta*: ayaṃ, deva, Pūraṇo Kassapo saṅghī c'eva gaṇī ca gaṇācariyo ca ñāto yassassī titthakaro

sādhusammato bahujanassa rattaññū cirapabbajito addhagato vayo anuppatto. *D I* 48 foll. It should be noted that Makkhali Gosāla, Ajita Kesakambali, Pakudha Kaccāyana, Sañjaya Belaṭṭhiputta, and Nigaṇṭha Nāṭaputta, the contemporary śramaṇa leaders of Gautama Buddha, are also described in an identical manner in that sutta.

The Jainas take the term *tīrtha* to mean the scriptures:
tīrthakṛtaḥ saṃsārottaraṇahetubhūtatvāt tīrtham iva tīrtham āgamaḥ tat kṛtavataḥ.
Quoted in Jinendra Varni, *Jainendra-siddhānta-kośa,* Delhi, 1971, II, p. 372.

2. Edgerton quotes the following use of *tīrthika* as an exception:
tīrthikā vā bhavanti bhavasūdanāḥ.
(*Mvu* I, 106, 8) where the term *tīrthika* is said to refer to the Bodhisattva in the eighth *bhūmi* (F. Edgerton, *BHSD,* p. 254).
3. Compare, for example, the *Śakrastava* addressed to the liberated souls:
namo 'tthu arihantāṇaṃ bhagavantāṇaṃ āigarāṇaṃ titthayarāṇaṃ sayaṃsambuddhāṇaṃ savvadarisīṇaṃ...namo jināṇaṃ jiyabhayāṇaṃ.
Quoted in R. Williams, *Jaina Yoga,* London 1963, p. 193.
4. The Jainas divide the abode of human beings into the realm of enjoyment (*bhogabhūmi*) and the realm of spiritual activity (*karmabhūmi*) and contend that the Tīrthaṅkaras are to be found only during the third and fourth (out of a total of six) stages of the temporal half-cylces known as *utsarpiṇī* (progressive) and *avasarpiṇī* (regressive). Only one Tīrthaṅkara may appear in a given *karmabhūmi* at one time. They also believe that there are certain *karmabhūmis* (known as *Videha-kṣetras*) which are free from such temporal changes and hence Tīrthaṅkaras are to be found there at all times. For details, see W. Schubring, *The Doctrine of the Jainas,* Delhi 1962, § 12-15; § 120. The Theravādins, on the other hand, believe that the Buddhas are born only in the Jambudīpa and hence discount the possibility of a Buddha currently living anywhere in the Universe. See G.P. Malalasekera, *DPPN,* II, 298. The Northern Buddhists seem to disagree on the precise meaning of the term *lokadhātu.* The Vaibhāṣikas seem to favour the view that only one Buddha can appear in the entire universe at one time, whereas the Mahāsāṅghikas maintain that many Buddhas can appear simultaneously in different world systems:
sūtra uktam—'asthānam anavakāśo yad apūrvācaramau dvau Tathāgatāv arhantau samyaksambuddhau loka utpadyeyātām. nedaṃ sthānaṃ vidyate. sthānam etad vidyate yad ekas Tathāgataḥ.' ...idam atra sampradhāryaṃ—kim atra trisāhasramahāsāhasro lokadhātur loka iṣṭaḥ, utāho sarvalokadhātava iti? nānyatra Buddhā utpadyanta ity eke. ...santy evānyalokadhātuṣu Buddhā iti nikāyāntarīyāḥ.
Abhidharmakośabhāṣya, (ed. P. Pradhan) Patna 1967, III, 96.
5. For a comparison between the Buddhist and the Jaina theories of omniscience, see P. S. Jaini, 'On the sarvajñatva (omniscience) of Mahāvīra and the Buddha,' in *Buddhist Studies in Honour of I.B. Horner,* Dordrecht 1974, pp. 71-90.
6. The following verses list the names of the twenty-four Tīrthaṅkaras of the present *avasarpiṇī* in the Bharata-kṣetra of the Jambudvīpa:
Usabham Ajiyaṃ ca vande Sambhavam Abhinandanaṃ ca Sumaiṃ ca Paumappahaṃ Supāsaṃ jinaṃ ca Candappahaṃ vande. Suvihiṃ ca

Pupphadantaṃ Sīyala-Sejjaṃsa-Vāsupujjaṃ ca Vimalam Anantam ca jinaṃ Dhammaṃ Santiṃ ca vandāmi. Kunthum Araṃ ca Malliṃ vande Muṇisuvvayaṃ Nami-jinaṃ ca vandāmi Riṭṭhanemiṃ Pāsaṃ taha Vaddhamāṇaṃ ca. evaṃ mae abhithuā vihūya-raja-mala pahīna-jara-maraṇā cauvīsaṃ pi jinavarā titthayarā me pasīyantu.
Quoted in R. Williams, *Jaina Yoga*, p. 195. For a list of the twenty-five Buddhas of the Theravāda tradition, see Ja I 44. The Northern tradition seems to have expanded on this list, as can be seen from the *Lalitavistara* which enumerates fifty-four Buddhas, and the *Mahāvastu* which lists more than a hundred Buddhas under whom the Bodhisattva is said to have attained the different *bhūmis* of his career.

7. It should be noted, however, that the prophecy regarding Marīci was made by Ṛṣabha in response to a question from Bharata (the first Cakravartin, the eldest son of Ṛṣabha) and also that Marīci became puffed up with pride and fell away from the true path; he is credited by the Jainas with founding the Sāṅkhya heresy:
atra kiṃ kaścid apy asti, bhagavān, bhagavān iva, tīrtham pravṛtya Bharatakṣetram yaḥ pāvayiṣyati. śaśaṃsa bhagavān evaṃ, ya eṣa tava nandanaḥ, Marīcir nāmadheyena, parivrājaka ādimaḥ...ciraṃ ca saṃsṛtya bhave, bhaviṣyaty atra Bhārate, ayaṃ nāmnā Mahāvīraś caturviṃśas tu tīrthakṛt.
Triṣaṣṭiśalākāpuruṣacarita (of Hemacandra), I, vi, 372-379 (Bhavanagar, 1933.

8. For a description of the ceremony attending these sacred events known as the *pañca-kalyāṇakas* (*garbha-janma-dīkṣā-kevalajñāna-mokṣa-kalyāṇa*), see P. S. Jaini, *The Jaina Path of Purification*, Berkeley, 1979, p. 195 foll.

9. This is a view of the Vaibhāṣika a school:
ajñānaṃ hi bhūtārthadarśanapratibandhād andhakāraṃ, tac ca bhagavato Buddhasya pratipakṣalābhenātyantaṃ sarvathā sarvatra jñeye punar anutpattidharmatvād hataṃ; ato 'sau sarvathā-sarvahatāndhakāraḥ. pratyekabuddhaśrāvakā api kāmaṃ sarvatra hatāndhakārāḥ. kliṣṭasammohātyantavigamāt, na tu sarvathā; tathā hy eṣāṃ buddhadharmeṣv ativiprakṛṣṭadeśakāleṣu cārtheṣu cānantaprabhedeṣu bhavaty evākliṣṭam ajñānaṃ. [*Abhidharmakośabhāṣya*, I, 1]

10. mokṣaprāptiḥ kevalajñānapūrviketi kevalajñānotpattikāraṇam ucyate:
mohakṣayāj jñānadarśanāvaraṇāntarāyakṣayāc ca kevalam/
bandhahetvabhāvanirjarābhyāṃ kṛtsnakarmavipramokṣo mokṣaḥ/
Sarvārthasiddhi (Bhāṣya on the *Tattvārthasūtra),* X, 1-2.

11. The Tīrthaṅkara is believed to speak in a human language that is 'divine' in the sense that men of all regions can understand it in their own languages:
Tīrthakarasya...samudbhūto divyadhvaniḥ...yojanāntaradūrasamīpasthā-ṣṭādaśa-bhāṣā-saptaśatakubhāṣāyutatiryagdevamanuṣyabhāṣākārāny-ūnādhikabhāvātīta-madhuramanoharagambhīraviśadavāgatiśayas-ampannaḥ...Mahāvīro 'rthakartā.
Quoted in Jinendra Varni, *Jainendra-siddhānta-kośa*, II, p. 430.

12. For details, see G. P. Malalasekera, *DPPN*, II, 324.

13. yad idaṃ tīrthakaranāmakarmānantānupamaprabhāvam acintyavibhūtiviśeṣa-kāraṇaṃ trailokyavijayakaraṃ tasyāsravavidhiviśeṣo 'stīti? yady evam ucyatām ke tasyāsravāḥ. ity ata idam ārabhyate—darśanaviśuddhir

vinayasampannatā śīlavrateṣv anaticāro 'bhīkṣṇajñānopayogasaṃvegau śaktitas tyāgatapasī sādhusamādhir vaiyāvṛtyakaraṇam arhadācāryabahuśrutapravacanabhaktir āvaśyakāparihāṇir mārgaprabhāvanā pravacanavatsalatvam iti tīrthakaratvasya/ [*Sarvārthasiddhi*, VI, 24]
For a longer list containing twenty items, see *Triṣaṣṭiśalākāpuruṣacarita*, I, i, 882-903.

14. apy ekaṃ tīrthakṛn-nāmakarmaṇo bandhakāraṇaṃ,
madhyād ebhyaḥ sa bhagavān, sarvair api babandha tat.
Ibid. I, i, 903. Compare also:
etāni ṣoḍaśakāraṇāni samyag bhāvyamānāni vyastāni ca tīrthakaranāmakarmāsravakāraṇāni pratyetavyāni. [*Sarvārthasiddhi*, VI, 24]

15. The *tīrthaṅkara-prakṛti* is included in a category of karmic matter known as *nāma-karma* (i.e. that by which a designation, e.g. man, animal, god, etc. is given to a being in a particular existence). By virtue of this *prakṛti* a Tīrthaṅkara-to-be is born with a body suitable for a Teacher, worthy of the *garbha* and the other *kalyāṇakas*, endowed with the power of *divyadhvani* which manifest at the moment of his first sermon:
jassa kammudayeṇa jīvo paṃcamahākallāṇāṇi pāvidūṇa titthaṃ duvāḷasaṅgaṃ kuṇadi taṃ titthayaranāmaṃ.
Quoted in Jinendra Varni, *Jainendra-siddhānta-kośa*, II, p. 373.

16. *Ādipurāṇa of Jinasena*, pts. 1-2, Sanskrit text with Hindi tr. Pannalal Jain, Varanasi, 1963-65.

17. *Triṣaṣṭiśalākāpuruṣacarita* of Hemacandra, tr. by Helen M. Johnson as *The Lives of Sixty-three Illustrious Persons*, 6 vols. Baroda (Oriental Institute), 1962.

18. *Nidāna* seems to be a Jaina technical term meaning an unbecoming wish on the part of an aspirant. When intense, such a wish is considered to be a form of *ārta-dhyāna* ('painful meditation'). Jainas assert that even a wish to be reborn as an ācārya (spiritual leader of the mendicant order) or as a Tīrthaṅkara (i.e. a Jina) in return for one's austerities, etc., is sinful, since such a wish demonstrates a residual lust for power and pride in oneself:
bhogakāṃkṣāturasyānāgataviṣayaprāptiṃ prati manaḥpraṇidhānaṃ saṃkalpaś cintāprabandhas turīyam ārtaṃ nidānam ucyate. *Sarvārthasiddhi*, IX, 33.
See also:
māṇeṇa jāikularūvamādi āiriya-gaṇadhara-jiṇattaṃ,
sobhaggāṇādeyaṃ patthanto appasatthaṃ tu.
Quoted in Jinendra Varni, *Jainendra-siddhānta-kośa*, II, p. 607.

19. The Jainas use the term 'bodhi' to indicate the initial attainments of the Right faith, Right knowledge, and Right conduct:
samyagdarśana-jñāna-cāritrāṇām aprāptaprāpaṇaṃ bodhiḥ. (Quoted in Jinendra Varni, *Jainendra-siddhānta-kośa*, III, p. 196). This places a Jaina aspirant on the stage called *samyag-dṛṣṭi*, functionally corresponding to the *darśana-mārgá* or the *sotāpatti-magga* of the Buddhists. The term 'bodhisattva', however, is conspicuously absent from the Jaina lexicon. The parallel between the Jaina and the Buddhist paths was however noticed by one Jaina author, namely the celebrated Haribhadrasūri, the eighth century author of the *Yogabindu*. Haribhadra, rather boldly, asserts that the Jaina *samyagdṛṣṭi* can be called a 'bodhisattva' as the former has 'all the char-

acteristics of the latter': Like the Bodhisattva (as held by the Buddhists), the *samyag-dṛṣṭi* also may never commit a volitionally inspired evil act, will aspire to do good to others, and will become endowed with the "supreme bodhi", or attain to the status of a Tīrthaṅkara.':
ayam asyām avasthāyāṃ bodhisattvo 'bhidhīyate, anyais tal lakṣaṇaṃ yasmāt sarvam asyopapadyate. kāyapātina eveha bodhisattvāḥ paroditaṃ, na cittapātinas tāvad etad atrāpi yuktimat. parārtharasiko dhīmān mārgagāmī mahāśayaḥ, guṇarāgī tathety ādi sarvaṃ tulyaṃ dvayor api. yat samyagdarśanam bodhis tat pradhāno mahodayaḥ, sattvo 'stu bodhisattvas tadd hantaiṣa 'nvarthato 'pi hi. varabodhisameto vā tīrthakṛd yo bhaviṣyati, tathā bhavyatvato 'sau vā bodhisattvaḥ satāṃ mataḥ.
The Yogabindu of Ācārya Haribhadrasūri, (ed. K.K. Dixit), Ahmedabad, 1968, 270-74. Notwithstanding the similarities noted above, Haribhadra's comments should not be taken literally. A bodhisattva is destined to be a Buddha whereas a *samyagdṛṣṭi* may or may not become a Tīrthaṅkara; the fact that most of the *samyagdṛṣṭis* end their careers as ordinary (i.e. non-Teacher) arhats, albeit with omniscience, underlines the basic difference between the two careers.

20. Compare, for example, the story of King Nandana (Mahāvīra's soul in a previous birth) who renounced his kingdom, became a Jaina monk, practised severe austerities, attracted the *tīrthaṅkara-prakṛti*, and was reborn in the Prāṇata heaven. From there he was reborn, in his final incarnation, as Vardhamāna Mahāvīra. See *Triṣaṣṭiśalākā-puruṣacarita*, X, i, 217-84. As a matter of fact, the Jainas have made a rule that one must become a Tīrthaṅkara in the second birth after being 'bound by' the *tīrthaṅkara-prakṛti:*
pāraddhatitthayarabandhabhavādo tadiyabhave
titthayarasantakammiyajīvāṇaṃ mokkha-gamaṇaṇiyamādo.
Quoted in Jinendra Varni, *Jainendra-siddhānta-kośa*, II, p. 371.

21. Although all the twenty-four Tīrthaṅkaras of the present cycle have descended from heaven (as did Gautama from the Tuṣita heaven), the Jainas believe that certain souls may come from purgatories (*naraka*) and be born as Tīrthaṅkaras. King Śreṇika Bimbisāra of Magadha is said to fall in this category. He was a great devotee of Mahāvīra and had by his devotion attracted the *tīrthaṅkara-prakṛti*, but he committed suicide and was born in the first *naraka*. It is believed that he will be reborn as the first Tīrthaṅkara of the next *kalpa*. See *ibid.*, IV, p. 71.

CHAPTER 7

Karma and the Problem of Rebirth in Jainism*

Although nearly every religious or philosophical tradition of India has accepted the idea of *karma* as valid, a wide divergence exists in the extent to which various schools have developed this idea into a coherent system of doctrine. In terms of the level of interest shown in such development—a level best measured by the amount of sacred and scholastic works devoted to it—one tradition, that of the Jainas, stands clearly apart from all others. In addition to the large number of *Karma-grantha* texts found among the Śvetāmbara scriptures, Digambaras possess some thirty-eight volumes of the *Ṣaṭkhaṇḍāgama*, the *Kaṣāya-prābhṛta*, and their commentaries.[1] Portions of the latter are said to represent the only surviving examples of the ancient *Pūrva* texts, which Digambaras suggest may even predate Mahāvīra himself. All of these materials deal in great detail with various problems relating to *karma* in its four aspects, namely, influx (*āsarva*), bondage (*bandha*), duration (*sthiti*), and fruition (*anubhāga*).[2]

Jainas seem to have been preoccupied with these problems from the earliest times; not only do their own scriptures pay a great deal of attention to such matters, but certain Buddhist writings in Pali attempt to discredit Jaina theories of *karma*, indicating that these theories were even then seen as

*This article was published originally in *Karma and Rebirth in Classical Indian Traditions,* ed. W. O'Flaherty, (University of California Press, 1980), pp. 217-238. Reprinted with kind permission of the University of California Press, Berkeley.

fundamental to the overall Jaina world-view.[3]

We are not yet in a position to explain definitively the earlier and more intense interest in karma shown by Jaina thinkers (and, to a lesser extent, by those of the Buddhists) relative to their Brāhmaṇical counterparts. Perhaps the entire concept that a person's situation and experiences are in fact the results of deeds committed in various lives may be not of Āryan origin at all, but rather may have developed as part of the indigenous Gangetic tradition from which the various Śramaṇa movements arose. In any case, as we shall see, Jaina views on the process and possibilities of rebirth are distinctively non-Hindu; the social ramifications of these views, moreover, have been profound.

A significant issue in Indian philosophy concerns the actual size of the soul. Virtually all the Vedic *darśanas* assert that the soul is *vibhu,* omnipresent; Rāmānuja's theory of an atomic, dimensionless soul stands as the only orthodox exception to this view. An all-pervasive soul would of course be free from spatial limitation by the body; indeed, the very idea of "dimensions" cannot be applied to such an entity at all. Jainas, however, have consistently rejected the *vibhu* theory, arguing that since a soul cannot experience the sorrow or happiness resulting from its karma except in the context of mind, senses, and body, any existence of the soul outside that context becomes incompatible with the function of the *karmic* mechanism. This line of thought leads directly to the basic Jaina doctrine that a soul is exactly coterminous with the body of its current state of bondage (*svadehaparimāṇa*).[4] Even a fully liberated soul (*siddha*), having completely transcended contact with the material realm, is said by the Jainas to retain the shape and size of that body which it occupied at the time *mokṣa* was attained.[5] This latter doctrine is certainly a rather unexpected one, since, even in Jaina terms, total freedom from *karmic* bonds eliminated the necessity for any limitation upon the extent of the soul. The liberated soul, in other words, could have been seen as *vibhu* without in any way contradicting the Jaina position of the interdependence of soul and body.[6] One can only conclude that the idea of this interdependence so dominated the minds of Jaina thinkers that they were somehow reluctant to dispense with the body completely even in the case of *mokṣa.* Hence we have a doctrine in which the emancipated soul, though said to be forever free of former influences, seems to display through its shape a sort of shadowy association with the embodied state.

The Hindu doctrine of *vibhu,* as we have noted above, has some difficulty in explaining the limitation of soul's experiences. That is, if the soul is in fact at all times everywhere, how does it come to undergo the experience of only one individual being at a time? This problem is dealt with by postulation of the so-called subtle body (*sūkṣma-śarīra*), an entity said generally to be composed of eighteen[7] subtle elements and to provide the link whereby a soul may—and must—be associated with a particular "gross" (i.e., manifest) state of embodiment. The subtle body is, in other words, a sort of "agent" for the soul; while the latter "stands still," as it were, the subtle body inhabits one life-matrix (human, animal, or whatever) after another, in each case associating the soul with the experiences of that matrix. Now, since the soul can experience nothing *except* in this limited way, it might be asked why the Brāhmaṇical thinkers bothered to introduce the notion of *vibhu* in the first place; it is an attribute which certainly seems to have no practical effect upon the experiences of the soul.

The answer to this question lies in what is perhaps the most fundamental point of disagreement separating Brāhmaṇical and Jaina philosophies. For the Brāhmaṇical schools, that which is eternal (e.g., soul) cannot change, whereas for the Jainas, *all* existents, whether sentient (*jīva*) or insentient (*ajīva*), are eternal (as *dravya,* "substance") and at the same time subject to change (as *paryāya,* "modes") at every moment.[8] Thus it is possible for a soul in the Jaina system to move, to expand or contract into various shapes, and so forth. How, then, can it be said to be eternal? Because, the Jainas suggest, every existent (*sat*) possesses a quality called *agurulaghutva* ("undergoing neither gain nor loss"), whereby its total number of space-points (*pradeśa*) remains unchanged regardless of the area into which these points must be accommodated. This is described as analogous to a piece of cloth, the total material of which is the same whether it is folded or spread out flat.

Bearing in mind the Brāhmaṇical and Jaina views on the nature of the soul, we are now ready to compare the actual mechanisms of rebirth that these traditions have proposed.

The most widely accepted Brāhmaṇical description of this mechanism is strongly biological in tone. We are told that after severing its connection with the human body, the soul dwells for some twelve days in a transitional ghostly form (*preta*). Thereafter, free from this limbo through ritual offerings (*śrāddha*) by the son of the deceased, it travels upward to the "realm of the father" (*pitṛ-loka*), there to remain for an indeterminate period. Eventually it is brought back to earth with the rain, enters the food chain through absorption by a plant, and finally becomes associated with the seed of a male who has eaten the fruit of that plant.[9] The act of intercourse thus "introduces" this soul into the womb where its new body will grow, and the entire process begins once more. The force of karma operates here in determining which potential father will eat which plant, thus guaranteeing the soul a set of circumstances appropriate to its prior experiences.

Given their emphasis on the role of the body, we might have expected the Jainas to provide an account even more heavily oriented towards the physiological than the one given above. For some reason, however, this was not the case. To the contrary, Jaina texts make absolutely no mention whatsoever of how a soul actually enters the body of the mother-to-be. It is said only that the soul moves into a new embryo within a single moment (*samaya*) after the death of the previous body.[10] Perhaps this doctrinal assertion of so brief a period between births precluded the detailed elaboration of what actually took place during that period. It is also possible that Jaina *ācāryas* may have simply been reluctant to include sexual references in their discussions. We are, however, only speculating here; all that can be said with certainty is that the issue of the soul's physical entry into the womb is simply ignored. Indeed, Jainas even seem to have been unaware of the theories put forth by their rivals; no mention, much less any attempt at refutation, is made with regard either to the Brāhmaṇical notions already discussed or to the Vaibhāṣika theory that the transmigratory consciousness (referred to as *gandharva*)[11] enters the vagina at the moment of intercourse and is thus trapped therein. Their silence here is unfortunate, since critical discussions of others' views would have forced both the parties criticized and the Jainas themselves to develop their positions in a more rigorous manner. Even in the absence of such discussions, however, it is by no means impossible to infer, on doctrinal grounds, the sorts of objections that Jainas would have voiced had they chosen to do so. This may well prove to be an instructive exercise, since it will bring into focus certain of the beliefs most central to the Jaina conception of life in the universe.

Consider, for example, the Brāhmaṇical schema in which first rain, then plants, act as "vehicles" whereby a soul makes its way to its ultimate destination. For the Jainas, the realm of sentient existence is far too wide and diverse for such a thing to be possible; in their view *even the raindrops,* not to mention plant life, constitute examples of embodied souls. In this context it is possible for a soul to be *reborn* as a "water-body" (*āp-kāyika*) or as a plant (*vanaspati-kāyika*), but not for these latter entities to function simply as insentient props in the life of a soul on its way to a human existence. The general Brāmaṇical explanation of the human rebirth process, therefore, would in Jaina terms entail at least two intermediate births in extremely low-level destinies (*gati*), a suggestion which violates Jaina rules pertaining to the operation of karma. To see how this is so, let us look in more detail at the various kinds of destinies in which the Jainas believe a soul may find itself.

In common with other Indian schools, Jainas affirm the birth-categories of gods, men, hell-beings, and *tiryañcas* ("those going horizontally," e.g., animals). Each of these categories is generally associated with a particular vertically ordered tier of the three-dimensional universe; men, for example, dwell in the centrally located *madhyaloka,* gods above them in the *devalokas,* and hell-beings below in the various infernal regions. (The case of the *tiryañcas* is somewhat more complex, as will be seen below.) The Jainas, however, have extended this system in two ways. On the one hand, they have postulated a class of emancipated souls, the "liberated ones" or *siddhas* referred to earlier, who are said to have gone beyond *saṃsāra* altogether and remain forever at the very apex of the universe.[12] On the other hand, they have broken down the *tiryañca* into numerous carefully defined subcategories. While this latter move may at first glance seem to be a mere scholastic exercise, closer examination reveals that what we have here is a doctrinally significant analysis of the lower reaches of existence. The addition of this analysis, together with that of the *siddha* theory referred to above, transforms the standard "four destinies" model from a rather simplistic description of the range of life into what is, for the Jainas, a truly comprehensive statement of the possibilities available to the soul. As we shall see, moreover, there may well be implicit in the Jaina system what can only be called a theory of evolution. While the Jainas themselves subscribe to the notion of a cyclic, beginningless universe and so do not accept any such theory, their own texts seem to provide justification for such an inference. To make this point clear, let us consider more closely the specific manner in which the various *tiryañcas* have been described.

It should first be noted that "levels of existence," in the Jaina view, reflect a scale of "awareness" (*upayoga*) on the part of the soul; hence the liberated soul is omniscient (*sarvajña*), gods have a wider range of knowledge than do men, and so on. The same system of ordering obtains within the *tiryañca* category itself. At the top of this group stand those animals, such as the lion,[13] which are said to possess five sense-faculties (*indriya*), plus a certain capacity for reflection (*saṃjñi*). Next are those which have five senses but *lack* the reflective capacity (*asaṃjñi*). Moving down the list, we are told of creatures with four, three, and two senses, respectively. Finally, and most important to the present discussion, are the *ekendriyas*, single-sense beings whose whole awareness is limited to the tactile mode. Whereas the higher *tiryañcas* are of a limited number and dwell in the *madhyaloka*, *ekendriyas* are too numerous to count and may be found in every part of the universe. They consist, moreover, of five distinct types: *pṛthvī-kāyika* ("earth-bodies"), *āp-kāyika* ("water-bodies"), *tejo-kāyika* ("fire-bodies"), *vāyu-kāyika* ("air-bodies"), and *vanaspati* ("vegetable life").[14] As the names suggest, the first four of these are little more than single "molecules" of the various fundamental elements, each one a rudimentary body for some soul. The *vanaspati* are, again, of two kinds: those called *pratyeka*, which have an entire plant-body "to themselves" (i.e., one plant/one soul), and finally, the *sādhāraṇa*, or *nigoda*, those which are at so low a level that they do not even possess an individual body, but rather exist as part of a cluster or "ball" (*golaka*) of organisms of the same type. Souls in such clusters, moreover, must live and die as a group, supposedly attaining rebirth in the same state eighteen times within the space of a single human breath.[15] Not only are the *nigodas* "colonial" (in the sense that this term is applied to algae, for example), but the clusters in which they dwell may in turn occupy the bodies of *other*, higher souls, thereby achieving an almost parasitic mode of existence. *Nigodas* are said to be found in virtually every corner of the universe; only the bodies of gods, hell-beings, and the "element bodies" referred to above do not harbour them. It is further believed that these tiny creatures tend to become especially concentrated in the flesh of human beings and animals as well as in certain roots and bulbs. Such likely "hosts" are therefore banned as food for the devout Jaina, since their consumption would involve the death of an unacceptably large number of souls.[16]

It may well be asked what sort of deeds (*karmas*) one must commit in order to deserve rebirth in a state so debased as that of the *nigodas*. In the only known reference to this problem we are told how Makkhali Gośāla, leader of the Ājīvika sect, doomed his soul to just such a fate by propounding what must have been for the Jainas the ultimate heresy, namely, that knowledge was in no way efficacious in terms of the possibility of attaining *mokṣa*.[17] (Buddhists seem to have been equally offended by Gośāla's views; their texts suggest that not only must he have gone to hell, but for such a person there could be no possibility of enlightenment even in the future.)[18] It is clear, then, that only some shockingly evil act could send a soul to the *nigoda* realm. This idea seems to present no difficulties until we consider one further—and little-known—aspect of Jaina doctrine concerning the *nigodas*. This states that there are in fact two distinct types of souls in *nigoda*: those which have at some time been in higher states but have fallen back, as Gośāla did, and those which have *never yet* been out of *nigoda* existence. The souls in question are referred to as *itara-nigoda* and *nitya-nigoda* respectively. *Nitya* here has the sense not of "forever" but of "always up to now"; *itara* means simply "those other than" the members of the *nitya* class. These are Digambara terms; those employed by the Śvetāmbaras are very similar in meaning. The *nitya-nigoda* are, for example, called by them *avyāvahārika*, "not susceptible of specific designation," that is, having no individual forms, while the *itara-nigoda* receive, along with all higher beings, the label of *vyāvahārika*, "specifiable". Members of the *itara* group are of course also without individual bodies, but they have, at some time, at least entered the system wherein such bodies are obtained.[19]

Now, what can it mean to say that there are certain souls which have *always* been *nigodas*? If such were indeed the case, then the whole notion of placement within a given destiny on the basis of previous deeds (*karmas*) would be undermined, since these beings would clearly have had no prior opportunity to perform any karmically meaningful actions whatsoever. The very term *avyāvahārika*, moreover, supports the suggestion that the *nitya-nigodas* are in some sense beyond the operation of karma, just as are the *siddhas* at the opposite extreme. In fact, this apparent connection between the *high* and *low* points of existence is by no means accidental. Given that for Jainas the number of beings in the realm of *vyavahāra* is finite (albeit "uncountable"), the question is raised as to how it is that the steady "departure" of souls through the attainment of *mokṣa* does not eventually deplete the universe of all sentient existence. The Jainas deal with this problem by means of the *nitya-nigoda*. These beings are, unlike those of any other category, said to be infinite (*anantānanta*) in number, and thus to provide an inexhaustible reservoir of souls; as we might suspect, the rate at which members of the *nitya-nigoda* class leave their dismal condition and enter higher states for the first time is either equal to or greater than that at which human beings in various parts of the universe attain *siddha*-hood. (Such an attainment is possible only from the human condition. At least one hundred and eight souls become emancipated in each period of six months and eight moments.)[20]

This makes a convenient system, but it leaves the Jaina position open to the kind of interpretation referred to earlier, namely, that there is in fact a definite beginning and end to *saṃsāra*, and that a soul's progress from the former to the latter seems in many respects to mirror the very evolution of consciousness itself. The key point here is that no reasonable explanation has been given, in karmic terms, for the situation of the *nitya-nigoda*. Furthermore, while the Jainas have asserted that there exists a class of souls, the *abhavya*,[21] that can never attain *mokṣa*, they have *not* suggested an analogous group whose members never dwelt within the *nitya-nigoda* realm. Given the Jaina admission that *some* souls begin their existence in this rather primordial and undifferentiated state, we may not be wrong in inferring that such could be the case for *all* souls. Adding to this the fact that every soul is said to exist along a virtual continuum of consciousness, from the minimal but ineradicable trace of awareness (*nitya-udghāṭita-jñāna*)[22] possessed by the *nigoda* to the omniscience (*ananta-*, i.e., *kevalajñāna*) of the *siddha*, we have here a model which is both linear and evolutionary in its conception.

Neither the Jainas' doctrine that souls frequently regress to lower states, nor their assertion that the *abhavyas* can proceed no higher than the *devalokas*, is incompatible with this model. Even under the restrictions noted, it is clear that souls are *in general* imagined to make slow but definite progress from minimal to maximal awareness, from what might be called "*proto-saṃsāra*" to a state beyond *saṃsāra* altogether. We may find in this kind of speculation, moreover, a rather ingenuous but interesting parallel to the modern view that the highest forms of life on our planet are, ultimately, descended from primitive micro-organisms which inhabited the ancient seas.

As we have indicated previously, Jainas will reject out of hand any suggestion that a soul's progress in the universe is either linear or evolutionary. The former notion, of course, flies in the face of their cherished belief in cyclic, beginningless operation of karma. As for the latter, it seems to have been anticipated as a potential problem; hence we find certain Jaina stories claiming that groups of souls sometimes leave *nigoda* existence and proceed directly to the human destiny, from which, with no further rebirths, they attain to *siddha*-hood.[23] (This sort of "example" is not really useful to the

Jaina argument here, since it denies only *gradual* evolution.) It should be asked, therefore, how it is that these very notions, which Jainas are at such pains to deny, are according to our analysis readily inferable from some of their oldest and most basic doctrinal materials. Is it possible that, for the Jainas, the doctrine of karma represents a relatively late (albeit prehistorical) accretion, a set of ideas imposed upon what was already a well-developed theoretical framework describing the operation of the universe? This framework, of course, would have been the linear-evolutionary one to which we have referred, remnants of which are discernible even now as certain seeming "inconsistencies" within Jaina doctrine (e.g., the case of the *nitya-nigoda*). Evidence that such an ancient framework did in fact exist is to be found through examination of a tradition closely associated with Jainism, that of the Ājīvikas. It is well-known that Gośāla, the most famous teacher of this school, was a contemporary of Mahāvīra. Basham and others have maintained, moreover, that these two *śramaṇa* sects interacted to a large extent; one scholar has even suggested (probably erroneously) that the Ājīvikas were ultimately absorbed into the Digambara Jaina community.[24] In any case, what few references to the Ājīvikas have survived indicate the school's belief in definite limits to *saṃsāra*, with each soul passing through exactly 8,400,000 *mahākalpas* ("great aeons") before reaching *mokṣa*.[25] That the Jainas may have originally subscribed to a similar doctrine is suggested not only by the evidence already set forth, but by the fact that the number 8,400,000 has been retained in their system to the present-day, although in a significantly altered context. This number is, for Jainas, the sum total of conceivable birth-situations (*yoni*) (i.e., the four destinies divided into all their sub-categories, sub-sub-categories, etc.) in which souls may find themselves, again and again, as they circle through *saṃsāra*.[26] Again, we seem to have a fragmentary holdover from an earlier doctrine. This issue need not be pursued further here; the point has been made that certain apparent anomalies in Jaina thought on karma can perhaps be best understood if we consider the possibility of a common background with the Ājīvika tradition. The important thing, for our purposes, is that in Jainism the model of a karmically ordered universe, in which the soul's position could be improved or worsened by action, did prevail over the kind of fatalistic determinism accepted by the Ājīvikas.

Our discussion of the *ekendriyas* has, it seems, led us rather far a field. The reader will recall the point that Jaina emphasis on the sentient nature of such simple beings makes it impossible for them to accept any notion of rebirth similar to that proposed by Brāhmaṇical schools. As for the Vaibhāṣika theory of the *gandharva* referred to above, this too stands in direct contradiction to a fundamental Jaina premise, namely, that the inter-birth period constitutes only a single moment in time. The fact that the *gandharva* state is said to persist for as long as seven weeks (see note 11) renders it, for Jainas, not a stage of transition at all but a whole separate destiny, in many ways reminiscent of the *preta-loka* (realm of spirits). Indeed, this same "too much time between births" objection could apply equally well to the idea of slow transmigration through rain and plants, even if this idea were not unacceptable for the quite different reasons that we have discussed. Why did the Jains place so much emphasis on the doctrine of a momentary transition?[27] To answer this question, we must now examine their discussion of rebirth in some detail.

By conceiving of the soul *vibhu*, Brāhmaṇical thinkers effectively avoided the question of a soul's movement from one body to another. Such a soul of course pervades the physical space of *all* bodies and therefore need not "go to" one or another of them; only the mechanism of its experiential association with a particular body needs to be explained. In Jainism, however, the movement of the soul itself is fundamental to the operation of the rebirth process. We might first ask how it is that a soul, momentarily separated from a gross body, is able to undergo any motion at all. To this the Jaina will reply that movement is an *inherent property* of every soul. In its purest form, this movement proceeds directly upwards, like that of a flame; hence the *siddha*, free of all restraints, shoots like an arrow to the very top of the inhabited universe (*lokākāśa*).[28] When still under *karmic* influence, the soul will dart in a similar manner to its next embodiment. In both cases, the speed involved is so great that according to the Jainas, the distance between any two points connectible by a straight line will be traversed in a single moment. (Given the multidimensional structure of the Jaina universe, certain circumstances of rebirth will require as many as two changes of direction before the appropriate *loka* and spot within it are reached. Motion along a curve is not admitted; therefore, as many as three moments may occasionally be necessary before the soul can enter its new state.)[29] It is important to recognize here that karma is not in any sense considered to *impel* the soul; it functions, rather, to channel or direct the motive force which is already present, much as a system of pipes might be used to "send" upwardly gushing water to a desired location.

Now, it should be clear that as a soul moves between two gross physical bodies, that is, during the state called *vigraha-gati*,[30] it cannot be accurately described as "totally free of embodiment"; if such were the case, it would simply fly upwards as the *siddha* does. For the system to work, in other words, the karmic "channel" must exist in some manifest, if subtle, form in which the soul is contained. This is in fact exactly what the Jainas have claimed; the transmigrating soul is said to be housed by a "karmic body" (*kārmaṇa-śarīra*), as well as by a so-called luminous body (*taijasa-śarīra*).[31] The former is composed of the sum total of one's karma at a given moment; the latter acts as a substratum for this karmic matter during the *vigraha-gati* and also functions to maintain body temperature during gross physical existence. Both of these invisible bodies are said to suffuse the gross and visible one during life; thus they not only "convey" the soul from one birth state to the next but constitute a real physical link between these states as well.

Committed as they were to the doctrine that the *vigraha-gati* typically occupies only a single moment, Jaina thinkers faced one major difficulty, namely, explaining how the "choice" of exactly appropriate circumstances for the next birth could possibly be made in so short a time. (Recall, in this connection, the *gandharva's* lengthy "search" for a proper birth-environment.) They have dealt with this problem by positing the existence of a unique factor, the so-called *āyuḥ-* ("longevity") *karma*. To understand the function of this factor, we must examine certain general points of Jaina doctrine concerning the types and modes of operation of karmic matter. In addition to the four major "vitiating" (*ghātiyā*) *karmas*,[32] which effectively keep a soul in bondage, Jainas have delineated four minor categories said to be responsible for the mechanism of rebirth and embodiment. Among this latter group, known as *aghātiyā*, we find the following: (1) *nāma-karma*, a cover term for the collection of karmic material whose fruition determines some ninety-eight different aspects of the future body, for example, its destiny or class of existence (human, animal, etc.), its sex, colour, number of senses, conformation of limbs, and the like;[33] (2) *gotra-karma*, controlling whether the environment into which one falls is or is not conducive to the leading of a spiritual life;[34] (3) *vedanīya-karma*, producing either pleasant or unpleasant feelings in response to the environment, hence the level of happiness or unhappiness which characterizes an individual; (4) *āyuḥ-karma*, whereby the exact duration of life (ostensibly measured, among human beings, by the number of breaths to be taken) is established.

While this classification appears at first to be in a simple one, it is complicated by the fact that *āyuḥ-karma*, as we have indicated above, functions in a most unusual manner. *Every other sort of karma* in the Jaina system is said to be in a constant bondage (*bandha*) and fruition (*anubhāga*) relationship with the soul; some *nāma-karma*, for example, is at every moment being bound, to come to fruition at some future time, while another is at every moment producing its result and falling away (*nirjarā*) from the soul. *Āyuḥ-karma*, however, is bound *only once* in a given lifetime, and its fruition will apply only to the very next life.[35] This specificity of application effectively places *āyuḥ-karma* in a position of primacy relative to the other *aghātiyā karmas*, since these must "fall into place" in conformity with the life-period that has been fixed. Given an *āyus* of seventy years, for example, only those *nāma-karmas* generating rebirth in a destiny where such a life span is appropriate could conceivably come into play. Thus it is that the "selection" of the particular *aghātiyā karmas* determinative of the next existence occurs *before the moment of death.* There need be no "search" during the *vigraha-gati*, since all "choices" have already been made.[36]

The peculiar characteristics attributed to *āyuḥ-karma* not only bring greater consistency to the Jaina theory of a momentary *vigraha-gati*, but have implications on the level of conduct as well. This second aspect relates particularly to prevailing ideas concerning when the *āyuḥ-karma* may be fixed. Jaina teachers have agreed that this event cannot take place until some moment during the final third of the present lifetime, and that indeed it will often not occur until death is very nearly at hand. The determination of one's *āyuḥ-karma*, moreover, is held to be extremely susceptible to the effects of one's recent volitional activities. Thus the devout Jaina is encouraged to pay ever more strict attention to his religious vows and duties as he grows older. Activities during the first two-thirds of life are not irrelevant in this context, however, since these will have created the habits which largely define a person's behavioural tendencies as the end of his life approaches. It must be emphasized here that one is not *aware* of the moment at which the *āyuḥ-karma* is fixed; thus it will behoove him to live until his last breath as if it were still possible to influence the specific outcome of this event. This orientation is most vividly expressed in the Jaina practice of *sallekhanā*,[37] in which a mendicant of advanced age may undertake a ritual fast ending only in death. It is hoped that he will thus be enabled to face his final moments in a state of absolute tranquillity, free of the fears, desires, or other strong volitions which characterize the consciousness of the average person at this time. The fixing of *āyuḥ-karma* under such controlled and peaceful conditions is held to be extremely auspicious; not only will rebirth in lower existences be effectively precluded in this way, but the individual in question is deemed likely to find himself in an environment conducive to rapid spiritual development.

Although emphasis on the religious significance of the last moments of life is by no means unique to the Jainas (similar notions prevail among Hindus, Buddhists, and certain non-Indian communities as well), it might be said that the idea of *āyuḥ-karma*, on the basis of which Jainas rationalize this emphasis, *is* unique. But this idea itself is not a fundamental one; it seems to function, as we have seen, mainly as an explanatory adjunct to *the* distinctive Jaina doctrine pertaining to rebirth, namely, the momentariness of *vigraha-gati.* The significance of this doctrine goes far beyond the context of mere scholastic dispute. Indeed, it is not unreasonable to say that the basic social distinction between Jainas and their Hindu neighbours derives mainly from the disagreement of these communities over the period of time required for transmigration to occur. Whereas Jainas have adopted many Hindu customs and ceremonies pertaining to such things as marriage, the coming of the new year, childbirth, and so forth, they have never taken up what is perhaps the most important of all rituals in Hindu society, namely, *śrāddha,* the offering of food by a son to the spirit of his dead parent. We have noted the belief that this offering is essential if the parent is to obtain a body suitable for entrance into the *pitṛ-loka,* and hence to gain the chance for eventual rebirth. It is further believed that failure of a son to perform this ritual will result in the loss of inheritance and in his wife's being rendered barren by the curse of the spirits thus stranded in the disembodied state. The *śrāddha* ritual not only represents a significant expression of the underlying parent-child tensions characteristic of the Indian family[38] but also provides perhaps the most important function of the Brāhmaṇical castes. The latter point is made in reference to the Brahmins' monopolization of the role of intermediary between the donor and the departed; only if Brahmins consume the offerings can these be "converted" into the material from which the new body of the spirit is built up.

It will be apparent that for Jainas the very idea of *śrāddha* is doctrinally invalid; a soul which goes to its next body in one moment cannot by fed, propitiated, or dealt with in any other way by those left behind. For this and other more "common sense" reasons, we find such writers as the thirteenth-century commentator Malliṣeṇa making light of the entire *śrāddha* ritual:

> Even through the performance of *śrāddha,* increase in posterity is in the case of most people not found; and...in the case of some, as in that of donkeys, pigs, goats, etc., even without performance thereof we see it still more....And...

> "If even to dead beings the *śrāddha* is
> the cause of satisfaction,
> Then oil might increase the flame of an
> extinguished lamp."

If it is said that "What is enjoyed by the Brahman accrues to them (i.e., the ancestors)," whoever is to agree to that? Since only in the Brahman do we see the fattened bellies; and transference of these into theirs (the ancestors') cannot be espied; and because only on the part of the Brahmans is satisfaction witnessed.[39]

There is one other tenet of the Jaina system pertaining to rebirth which must be mentioned here, as it provides a further basis for the unacceptability of the practice of *śrāddha*. Whereas this practice clearly assumes that the actions of one person can affect the destiny of another, Jaina tradition has always held that an individual soul can experience results accruing only to actions which it has *itself* performed. The tenth century *ācārya* Amitagati has provided us with a forceful statement of the adamant position taken by Jainas on this matter:

> Whatever karma a soul has acquired through its own prior deeds,
> it will obtain the good and bad results thereof.
> If one could obtain results from the deeds of others,
> then surely his own deeds would be meaningless.
>
> Except for karma earned for oneself by oneself,
> no one gives anything to anyone.
> Reflecting upon this fact, therefore,
> let every person, unwaveringly,
> abandon the perverse notion that
> another being can provide him with anything at all.[40]

This emphasis on reaping the fruits only of one's own *karma* was not restricted to the Jainas; both Hindu and Buddhist writers have produced doctrinal materials stressing the same point. Each of the latter traditions, however, developed practices in basic contradiction to such a belief. In addition to *śrāddha*, we find among the Hindus widespread adherence to the notion of divine intervention in one's fate, while Buddhists eventually came to propound such theories as the boon-grating *bodhisattvas*, transfer of merit, and the like. Only the Jainas have been absolutely unwilling to allow such ideas to penetrate their community, despite the fact that there must have been a tremendous amount of social pressure on them to do so.

In this discussion we have examined various aspects of the Jaina approach to rebirth. By way of conclusion, we might reiterate the important points raised thereby. The Jainas, first of all, show a remarkable tendency to associate the soul with some sort of bodily influence, whether during ordinary existence, transmigration, or even after the attainment of *siddha*-hood. In spite of this tendency, however, no biological explanation of the mechanism whereby a soul enters its new environment has been offered. The description of the possible states of rebirth includes one category, the *nitya-nigoda*, the nature of which suggests a more primitive and possibly linear concept of existence underlying the set of beliefs now taken as orthodox. Jaina views on rebirth are unique in their emphasis on the single moment involved in movement of a soul from one embodiment to the next. This emphasis, together with the less unusual but very strictly applied belief in non-transference of *karma*, has been reflected in the complete absence from the Jaina community of certain ritual forms typical of Brāhmaṇical society. The deeper ramifications of these issues, particularly the final one, definitely require further exploration; it is to be hoped that future researches will move in these directions.*

APPENDIX 1

The Jaina Universe (*Lokākāśa*)

The Jaina "universe" (*loka*) is a three-dimensional structure divided into five parts. (A) The Lower World consists of seven layers and is the abode of infernal beings (*nāraki*) as well as certain demi-gods (demons, titan, etc.). (B) The Middle, or Terrestrial, World consists of innumerable concentric island-continents with Jambudvīpa in the centre.

* I should like to acknowledge the assistance of Joseph Clack in the preparation of this paper.

This is the abode of humans and animals. Human beings are not found beyond the third "continent" from the centre. In (C), the Higher, or Celestial, World, are found the abodes of heavenly beings (*devas*). (D) Beyond the border of the Celestial World, marked by the crescent,

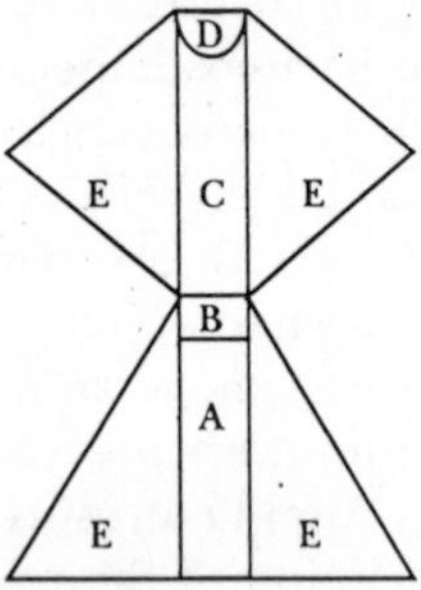

is the permanent abode of the Liberated Souls (*siddhas*). This region is the apex of "World-space" (*loka-ākāśa*). (E) Contains abodes restricted to inhabitation by *ekendriyas.* (While these single-sense organisms occupy all parts of the *lokākāśa, trasas* [beings having two or more senses] are restricted to areas A-C; hence we find only *ekendriyas* here.) The area surrounding this entire structure is known as "Space without Worlds" (*aloka-ākāśa*), which is devoid of souls, matter, and time. It should be noted that there is no provision for a *pitṛ-loka* (World of Ancestors) in the Jaina cosmology.

NOTES

1. For a complete bibliography of the Śvetāmbara *Karma-grantha* literature, see Glasenapp, *The Doctrine of Karman in Jain Philosophy* (Bombay, 1942), pp. xi-xx.
The *Ṣaṭkhaṇḍāgama* is said to have been composed by Puṣpadanta and Bhūtabali (circa A.D. 200). It comprises 6,000 aphorisms (*sūtras*) in Prakrit and is divided into six parts. The first five parts have a commentary called *Dhavalā* by Vīrasena (A.D. 816), which has been edited by Hiralal Jain and published in sixteen volumes by the Jaina Sāhityoddhāraka Fund, Amaravati, 1939-59. The sixth part of the *Ṣaṭkhaṇḍāgama*, called *Mahābandha,* is better known by the alternate title *Mahādhavalā*; it has been edited by Phool Chandra Sidhāntaśāstrī and published in seven volumes by the Bhāratīya Vidyāpīṭha (Benares, 1947-58). A second important scriptural work belonging to the same genre is the *Kaṣāyaprābhṛta* of Guṇabhadra (A.D. ca. 200). This text, together with its commentary

Jayadhavalā by Vīrasena and his disciple Jinasena (A.D. ca. 800-870), has been edited by Phool Chandra Siddhāntaśāstrī and published in fifteen volumes by the Bhāratīya Digambara Jaina Granthamālā (Mathura, 1942-75). All of these Digambara works, which are of epic proportions (comprising altogether some 172,000 "ślokas" [1 śloka = 32 syllables]), have been brought to light only in the last thirty years and have not been fully studied even in India outside a small circle of Jaina scholars. Umāsvāti's *Tattvārthasūtra* and Pūjyapāda's commentary thereon called *Sarvārthasiddhi* are the two most popular works studied in Jaina schools. For a translation of the latter work, see S. A. Jain, *Reality* (Calcutta, 1960).

2. The fact that Jainas regard karma as material (*paudgalika*), in contrast to such relatively abstract concepts as *saṃskāra* of the Brāmaṇical schools and *bīja* of the Buddhists, is too well-known to require discussion here. For a lucid presentation of the comprehensive Jaina teaching of the karmic process, see N. Tatia, *Studies in Jaina Philosophy* (Benares, 1951), pp. 220-260.

3. ...evaṃ vutte...te Nigaṇṭhā mam etad avocuṃ: "Nigaṇṭho, āvuso, Nātaputto sabbaññu sabbadassāvī aparisesaṃ ñāṇadassanaṃ paṭijānāti"...so evam āha: "atthi kho vo, Nigaṇṭhā, pubbe pāpakammaṃ kataṃ, taṃ imāya kaṭukāya dukkarakārikāya nijjīretha; yam pan' ettha etarahi kāyena saṃvutā vācāya saṃvutā manasā saṃvutā taṃ āyatiṃ pāpassa kammassa akaraṇaṃ; iti purāṇānaṃ kammānaṃ tapasā byantibhāvā, navānaṃ kammānaṃ akaraṇā, āyatiṃ anavassavo, āyatiṃ anavassavā kammakkhayo, kammakkhayā dukkhakkhayo, dukkhakkhayā vedanākkhayo, vedanākkhayā sabbaṃ dukkhaṃ nijjiṇṇaṃ bhavissatī ti..." (*Majjhimanikāya* I, p. 93 [PTS])

4. For a Jaina critique of the *vibhu* theory, see Malliṣeṇa's *Syādvādamañjarī* edited by J. C. Jain (Bombay, 1970), pp. 67-75 (henceforth referred to as *SM*).

5. *anākāratvān muktānām abhāva it cen na; atītānantaraśarīrākāratvāt. Sarvārthasiddhi* 9.4. Edited by Phool Chandra Siddhāntaśāstrī (Benares, 1971), (henceforth referred to as *SS*).

6. syān matam, yadi śarīrānuvidhāyī jīvaḥ, tad abhāvāt svābhāvikalokākāśaparimāṇatvāt tāvad visarpaṇaṃ prāpnotīti. naiṣa doṣaḥ. kutaḥ? kāraṇābhāvāt.
SS 9.4. The Jainas allow the possibility of a soul spreading throughout the *lokākāśa* (without abandoning its body) just prior to attaining *siddha*-hood. This is called *kevalisamudghāta*:
yat punar aṣṭasamayasādhyakevalisamudghātadaśāyām ārhatānām api ...lokavyāpitvenātmanaḥ sarvavyāpakatvam, tat kādācitkam. [*SM*, p. 75]

7. pūrvotpannaṃ asaktaṃ niyataṃ mahadādisūkṣmaparyantam/
saṃsarati nirupabhogaṃ bhāvair adhivāsitaṃ liṅgam//
[*Sāṅkhyakārikā* of Īśvarakṛṣṇa, 40]

8. sat dravyalakṣaṇam/ utpādavyayadhrauvyayuktaṃ sat/
tadbhāvāvyayaṃ nityam/ [*Tattvārthasūtra* 5.29-31]

9. For details, see Paul Deussen, *The System of the Vedānta*, New York, 1973, pp. 357-398.

10. *ekasamayā 'vigrahā/* [*Tattvārthasūtra* 2.29]
See also note 29.

11. "trayāṇāṃ sthānānāṃ sammukhībhāvāt mātuḥ kukṣau garbhasyāvakrāntir

bhavati. mātā kalyā pi bhavati, ṛtumatī ca. mātāpitarau raktau sannipatitau ca. gandharvaś ca pratyupasthito bhavati" iti. antarābhavaṃ hitvā ko'nyo gandharvaḥ...naiva cāntarābhavikaḥ kukṣiṃ bhitvā praviśate, api tu mātur yonidvāreṇa....taṃ deśaṃ āśliṣya...iti upapanno bhavati. *Abhidharmakośabhāṣya*, ed. P. Pradhan [Patna, 1967], 3.12-15.
As the following quote suggests, there was no unanimity of opinion among Vaibhāṣika teachers as to the precise amount of time spent in the *gandharva* state; the tradition of seven days' "search" for new parents has perhaps been most widely accepted:
kiyantaṃ kālam avatiṣṭhate? nāsti niyama iti Bhadantaḥ...saptāhaṃ tiṣṭhatīti Bhadanta Vasumitraḥ...saptāhānīty apare...alpaṃ kālam iti Vaibhāṣikāḥ. [*Ibid.* 3, 14]. For an example of the belief in a seven-week period, see *The Tibetan Book of the Dead*, edited by W. Y. Evans-Wentz (New York, 1960).

12. See Appendix 1 to this chapter for a diagrammatic representation of the Jaina universe.
13. It is believed that *saṃjñi* animals are capable of receiving religious instruction and also that Mahāvīra himself was awakened to the spiritual life while existing as a lion. See Guṇabhadra's *Uttarapurāṇa*, 74.167-220, (Benares, 1968).
14. *pṛthivyāptejovāyuvanaspatayaḥ sthāvarāḥ/* [*Tattvārthasūtra* 2.13]
15. sāhāraṇodayeṇa ṇigodasarīrā havanti sāmaṇṇā/
te puṇa duvihā jīvā bādarasuhumātti viṇṇeyā//
sāhāraṇamāhāro sāhāraṇamāṇapāṇagahaṇaṃ ca/
sāhāraṇajīvāṇāṃ sāhāraṇalakkhaṇaṃ bhaṇiyaṃ//
jatthekka marai jīvo tattha du maraṇaṃ have aṇaṃtāṇaṃ/
bakkamai jattha ekko bakkamaṇaṃ tattha 'ṇaṃtāṇaṃ//
Gommaṭasāra(Jīvakāṇḍa) 191-193 (Agas, 1959).
16. The following plants are among those forbidden as food for a Jaina: turmeric, ginger, cardamom, garlic, bamboo, carrot, radish, beetroot, tamarind, banyan, margosa. For details, see R. Williams, *Jaina Yoga* (London, 1963), pp. 110-116.
17. See A. N. Upadhye, "Darśanasāra of Devasena: Critical text," in the *Annals of the Bhandarkar Oriental Research Institute*, 15, nos. 3-4, 198-206. Also my article, "The Jainas and the Western Scholar," in *Sambodhi* (Prof. A. N. Upadhye Commemoration Volume), L. D. Institute of Indology (Ahmedabad, July, 1976), pp. 121-131.
18. "sakiṃ nimuggo nimuggo va hotī ti"... etassa hi puna bhavato vuṭṭhānaṃ nama natthī ti vadanti. Makkhali-gosālādayo viya heṭṭhā narakaggīnaṃ yeva āhārā hontī ti.
Puggalapaññati-Aṭṭhakathā 7.1. See my article. "On the Sautrāntika Theory of Bīja," *Bulletin of the School of Oriental and African Studies*, vol. 22, part 2, (London, 1959), p. 246, n. 2.
19. atthi aṇaṃtā jīvā jehiṃ ṇa patto tasāṇa pariṇāmo/
bhāvakalaṃkasupaurā nigodavāsaṃ ṇa muñcanti//
[*Gommaṭasāra* (*Jivakāṇḍa*), 197]
dvividhā jīvā sāṃvyāvahārikā asāṃvyāvahārikāś ceti. tatra ye nigodāvasthāta udvṛtya pṛthivīkāyikādibhedeṣu vartante te lokeṣu dṛṣṭipathamāgatāḥ santaḥ...vyāvahārikā ucyante. te ca yady api bhūyo 'pi nigodāvasthām upayānti tathāpi te sāṃvyāvahārikā eva, saṃvyavahāre patitatvāt. ye punar anādikālād ārabhya nigodāvasthām upagatā evāvatiṣṭhante te

vyavahārapathātītatvād asāṃvyāvaharikāḥ.
Quoted from the *Prajñāpanāṭīkā* in *SM*, p. 259.

20. sijjhanti jattiyā khalu iha saṃvavahārajīvarāsīo/
enti aṇāivaṇassai rāsīo tattio tammi//
iti vacanād yāvantaś ca yato muktiṃ gacchanti jīvās tāvanto 'nādinigoda-vanaspatirāśes tatrāgacchanti. na ca tāvatā tasya kācit parihāṇir nigoda-jīvānantyasyākṣayatvāt [*SM*, p. 259]
Cf. nanu aṣṭasamayādhikaṣaṇmāsābhyantare aṣṭottaraśatajīveṣu karmakṣayaṃ kṛtvā siddheṣu satsu...
Quoted from the *Gommaṭsāra (Jīvakāṇḍa) Keśava-varṇiṭīkā* (196) in *SM*, p. 302.
21. See my article, "Bhavyatva and Abhavyatva: A Jaina Doctrine of 'Predestination'," in *Bhavavān Mahāvīra and His Teachings* (*2500 Nirvāṇa Anniversary Volume*), Bombay, 1977, pp. 95-111.
22. For several scriptural passages on this point, see N. Tatia, *Studies in Jaina Philosophy*, p. 240.
23. anādimithyādṛśo 'pi trayoviṃśatyadhikanavaśataparimāṇās te ca nityanigodavāsinaḥ... Bharataputrā jātās te...tapo gṛhītvā... stokakālena mokṣaṃ gatāḥ.
Quoted in Jinendra Varni's *Jainendra-siddhānta-kośa*, II, p. 318, Bhāratīya Jñānapīṭha Publications, Varanasi, 1971.* See addition to note at the end.
24. A. F. R. Hoernle, "Ajīvakas," in *Encyclopedia of Religion and Ethics*, vol. 1, pp. 259-268; A. L. Basham's *History and Doctrines of the Ājīvikas* (London, 1951).
25. ...cullāsīti mahākappuno satasahassāni, yāni bāle ca paṇḍite ca sandhāvitvā saṃsāritvā dukkhass' antaṃ karissanti
Dīghanikāya, 1.53-54 [PTS]. See Basham *ibid*., p. 14.
26. *sacittaśītasaṃvṛtāḥ setarā miśrāś caikaśas tad yonayaḥ/* [*Tattvārthasūtra* 2.32]
tadbhedāś caturaśītiśatasahasrasaṃkhyā āgamato veditavyāḥ. uktaṃ ca:
ṇiccidaradhādu satta ya taru dasa viyaliṃdiyesu chacceva/
suraṇirayatiriya cauro coddasa maṇue sadasahassā// [*SS* 2.32]
27. While Theravādin and Sautrāntika writings have set forth a doctrine of instantaneous rebirth analogous to the appearance of an image in a mirror (*bimba-pratibimba*), this doctrine seems never to have gained so wide an acceptance among Buddhists as did the *gandharva* theory. Even if it had become the standard Buddhist view, Jainas would have rejected it on the grounds that a thing which arises and perishes within the same moment cannot undergo motion. (Recall that in the Jaina system three moments are actually involved: those of death, movement of the soul, and rebirth, respectively.) Indeed, the Vaibhāṣikas' awareness of this problem very likely led them to the notion of an extended transition-state in the first place.

Certain Sāṅkhya and Yoga thinkers also proposed a rebirth process occurring instantaneously or in a very short period. It must be asked, however, whether such views ever had any meaningful impact on Hindu society; even in those cases where they might have been accepted in theory, we have no evidence that the practice of *śrāddha* (rendered meaningless within such a framework) was actually abandoned. Because only one instant (*samaya*) intervenes between death and the following rebirth, it is possible for a person dying in the act of copulation to be born as his own child. The idea that a man is in some sense identical with his son is well-known to Hindu literature. Thus, for example, *Manusmṛti* defines a wife as follows: "The husband, entering into the wife, becoming an embryo, is born here. For that is why the wife is called wife (*jāyā*), because he is born (*jāyate*) again in her" (9.8). On the other hand, it is only in the Jaina literature that this belief is made literal. In fact, such an occurrence is attested to in a Jaina Purāṇa, the source of which I have unfortunately lost. (See *Jainendra-siddhānta-kośa*, vol. 2, p. 313 for a reference to such a birth.)

28. tad anantaram ūrdhvaṃ gacchaty ā lokāntāt/pūrvaprayogād asaṅgatvād bandhacchedāt tathāgatipriṇāmāc ca/ [*Tattvārthasūtra* 10.5-6] ...tathāgatipariṇāmāt. yathā...pradīpaśikhā svabhāvād utpatati tathā muktātmā 'pi nānāgativikārakāraṇakarmanivāraṇe saty ūrdhvagatisvabhāvād ūrdhvam evārohati. [*SS* 10.7]
Beyond this point there is said to be only empty space (*alokākāśa*), where matter and even the principles of motion, rest, and time are absent. See *Tattvārthasūtra* 10.8.
29. This takes place only when there is movement to or from those realms inhabited exclusively by *ekendriyas*. See S.A. Jain, *Reality*, p. 70, n. 1.
30. vigraho dehaḥ. vigrahārthā gatir vigrahagatiḥ. [*SS* 2.25]
31. yat tejonimittaṃ tejasi vā bhavaṃ tat taijasam. karmaṇāṃ kāryam kārmaṇam...ayaḥpiṇḍe tejo 'nupraveśavat taijasakārmaṇayor vajrapaṭalādiṣu...lokāntāt sarvatra nāsti pratīghātaḥ...nityasambandhinī hi te ā samsārakṣayāt niraveśaṣasya saṃsāriṇo jīvasya te dve api śarīre bhavata ity arthaḥ. [*SS* 2.36-42]
32. The four *ghātiyā* karmas are (1) *mohanīya* (engendering "false views" and preventing "pure conduct"; (2) *jñānāvaraṇīya* ("knowledge-obscuring"); (3) *darśanāvaraṇīya* ("perception-obscuring"); (4) *antarāya* ("restrictor of the quality of energy (*vīrya*)").
33. gatijātiśarīrāṅgopāṅganirmāṇabandhanasaṃsthānasaṃhanana-sparśarasagandhavarṇānupūrvyāgurulaghūpaghātātapodyotocch-vāsavihāyogatayaḥ pratyekaśarīratrasasubhagasusvaraśubhasūkṣmaparyā-ptisthirādeyayaśaḥkīrttisetarāṇi tīrthakaratvaṃ ca/ [*Tattvārthasūtra* 8.11]
34. This interpretation (supported by scripture) runs contrary to the popular Jaina understanding of *gotra* as "caste," etc. Jaina doctrine, of course, does not accept the notion of a caste status fixed by birth.
35. See *Jaina Jñānakośa* (in Marathi), Part 1, by Ajñāta (Aurangabad, 1972), p. 233 (*āyu*).
36. Śvetāmbara texts (Jacobi, *Jaina Sūtras*, Part 2, p. 225) contain the well-known story that the embryonic Mahāvīra underwent a transference from the womb of a Brāhmaṇa woman to that of a Kṣatriya one, the latter becoming his actual "mother." Does this suggest some breakdown in the determinative process begun by the fixing of *āyuḥ karma*? If so, it may explain the Digambara refusal to accept any such tale as valid. Śvetāmbaras, for their part, have simply labelled this event as one of the inexplicable miracles which may occur in a given aeon of time (*aṇaṃteṇa kāleṇa*). See *Sthānāṅgasūtra*, #1074.
37. See Williams, *Jaina Yoga*, pp. 166-172.

38. It is tempting to read Freudian symbolism into this belief system: the son, though perhaps desiring to "kill" his father (by preventing his rebirth), nevertheless performs his filial duty out of fear of "castration" (the loss of property and offspring). Perhaps more to the point, however, is the fact that in Indian society the parent seems fundamentally unwilling to relinquish his control over the son, to recognize the latter's adult status; through the institution of *śrāddha,* some semblance of parental control is maintained even in death. It would be interesting to investigate whether Jainas, lacking the institutionalization of filial responsibility that *śrāddha* represents, have created some substitute ritual or social form which functions in an analogous manner.
39. *SM* XI (tr. F.W. Thomas, pp. 69-70).
40. svayaṃ kṛtaṃ karma yad ātmanā purā phalaṃ tadīyaṃ labhate śuhhāśubham/
parena dattaṃ yadi labhyate sphuṭaṃ svayaṃ kṛtaṃ karma nirarthakaṃ tadā//
nijārjitaṃ karma vihāya dehino na ko 'pi kasyāpi dadāti kiñcana/
vicārayann evam ananyamānasaḥ paro dadātīti vimuñcya śemuṣīm//
(*Dvātriṃśikā*) *Nitya-naimittika-pāṭhāvalī,* Karanja, 1956, p. 22.

ADDITIONAL TO NOTE*

The abridged version of the citation quoted here needs to be read in full since it contains some information relevant to the problem of *nitya-nigodas* proceeding directly to the human destiny and attaining siddhahood in that very life. The original version of the story appears in a commentary on verse 17 of the Digambara text *Bhagavatī Ārādhanā* (by Ācārya Śivārya, c. 2nd century). The text itself simply says that even those who hold wrong views from beginningless times (*anādi-mithyādṛṣṭis*) can attain siddhahood in a matter of moments through the practice of spiritual discipline (*cāritra*). Commenting on this verse, Aparājitasūri (probably a Yāpanīya mendicant) in his *Vijayodayā Ṭīkā* states that several princes Bhaddaṇa (i.e. Vardhana), etc., *mithyādṛṣṭis* from beginningless time, had attained to the state of a *trasa* (a being with more than one sense, in this case a human being) for the first time. These princes heard the law from the first Jina, Ṛṣabha, and having practiced right conduct, etc., attained *mokṣa* in that very life. It should be noted that Aparājita does not specifically use the word *nitya-nigoda* to describe their former state, which therefore could have included other one-sensed beings like earth-beings, etc.

However, this story is developed further by another Digambara author by the name of Brahmadeva (c. 1292-1323), who wrote a Sanskrit commentary on the *Bṛhad-Dravyasaṃgraha* of Nemicandra (c. 1018-1068). In his commentary, in the context of a discourse on the nature of transmigration, Brahmadeva says that a group of 923 dwellers of the *nitya-nigoda* state had been born for the first time ever as *trasa* beings called *indragopas* (a three-sensed being, according to the Śvetāmbara *Uttarādhyayana Sūtra,* chapter 36, verse 139; translated as cochineal by Jacobi, *Jaina Sūtras,* part 2, page 220). They were all trampled upon simultaneously by the elephant of the *cakravartin* Bharata and died together and were immediately reborn as the sons of Bharata, called Vardhana, etc. They never spoke to anyone. Therefore, Bharata asked about them in the preaching-hall of his father, the first Tīrthaṅkara Ṛṣabha, who narrated this past of theirs. Upon hearing this story, they accepted the Jaina ascetic practice (*tapas*), and in a short time they died and attained *mokṣa*. Brahmadeva says that this story is unique and without comparison and refers to a sub-commentary, now extinct, to the *Bhagavatī Ārādhanā* as the source of this narrative. (anupamam advitīyam...*Ācārārādhanā-ṭippaṇe* kathitam āste).

While the significance of the number 923 remains a mystery, Brahmadeva's version of the story, introducing an intermediate birth between *nigoda* and human existence, is probably meant to conform to the law of *karma* as detailed in the *Dhavalā* commentary (c. 8th century), which stipulates that beings who come out of the *sūkṣma* (subtle) variety of *nigodas* and immediately become human beings are not able to assume the mendicant vows (i.e., they will not attain *mokṣa* in that life).

Brahmadeva's version of this story thus seems to imply (which was not clarified in the earlier *Vijayodayā Ṭīkā*) that these souls had indeed come from *sūkṣma-nigoda*. (For references, see *Jainendra-siddhānta-kośa*, II, p. 318.) Assuming this to be the case, it still remains to be ascertained if a three-sensed being fulfils the condition of being reborn as a human and attaining *mokṣa* in that very life.

The Śvetāmbaras also have preserved a story that compares well in principle with the narrative in the *Vijayodayā Ṭīkā* version. Haribhadra (c. 9th century) in his *Pañcavastusaṃgraha-svopajñabhāṣya* discusses a very famous event in the life of Marudevī, the mother of the first Jina, Ṛṣabha. It is claimed (in post-canonical literature) that in previous lives the soul of Marudevī had always been a *nigoda* from beginningless times and from that existence had suddenly attained human birth. The story tells us that Marudevī, riding on an elephant, accompanied by her grandson Bharata, came to the hall where her son, Ṛṣabha, had just attained enlightenment (*kevalajñāna*). It is said that at the sight of her son's omniscient glory she destroyed all of her karmas thereby attaining omniscience, and she immediately died, thus becoming the first human being to attain *mokṣa* in our present time-cycle, even without the benefit of hearing a sermon of a Jina. Haribhadra is aware that this is an incredible story and hastens to declare that it must be considered as one of those astonishing (*āścarya*) events that happen only once in an infinite time-cycle (*accheragabhūyaṃ*) and should be treated like the other ten such events described in the canon (including the removal of the embryo of Mahāvīra, etc.):

> Marudevisāmiṇīe ṇa evaṃ ti suvvae jeṇaṃ/sā khalu kila vaṃdaṇijjā, accantaṃ thāvarā siddhā//924//
>
> saccamiṇaṃ accheragabhūyaṃ puṇa bhāsiaṃ imaṃ sutte/ aṇṇe vi evamāyī bhaṇiyā iha puvvasūrīhiṃ//925//
>
> kim uktaṃ bhavati? yad uta āsaṃsārebhyaḥ uddhṛtya siddhyatī ti gātārthaḥ.

Śrī Pañcavastukaḥ Jinashasana Aradhana Trust, Bombay, 1988.

These stories, found both in the Śvetāmbara and Digambara traditions, lend support to our assumption that there might have been a belief, surviving albeit in a fossilized form, in a linear progression of a sudden nature from *nigoda* to *siddha*-hood, with a brief birth as a human being in between, without the necessity of undergoing the long and arduous process of progressing through the innumerable varities of life-forms before attaining *mokṣa*.

See Padmanabh S. Jaini, forthcoming article: "From Nigoda to Mokṣa: The Story of Marudevī." Paper presented at the International Conference on Jainism and Early Buddhism in the Indian Cultural Context, Lund University (Sweden), June 4-7, 1998. (Coordinator: Olle Qvarnstrom)

CHAPTER 8

Muktivicāra of Bhāvasena: Text and Translation (Abridged Version)*

Introduction

Of the many doctrinal disputes that separate the two ancient Jaina sects of the Digambaras and Śvetāmbaras, two stand out as the most controversial: *Kevalibhukti* and *Strīmukti.*

The ninth-century Jaina author Śākaṭāyana—who belonged to the now-extinct Yāpanīya sect, which favoured the Śvetāmbara positions on the above questions—appears to have been the first exegete to write an independent treatise on both of these central controversies. His works, entitled *Kevalibhukti-prakaraṇa* and *Strīnirvāṇa-prakaraṇa,*[1] put forth the basic arguments of both schools using appropriate syllogistic formulae as supported by appropriate scriptural testimony. In subsequent centuries, a large body of literature developed in the logical works of both sects concerning these two controversies. I am at present editing a volume which will bring together selections bearing upon the issue of the salvation of women, and have identified more than a dozen texts representing both the Digambara and Śvetāmbara positions. Almost all of these texts had earlier been edited by eminent Jaina scholars, with the exception of one text, the *Bhukti-mukti-vicāra,* by the fourteenth-century Digambara author, Bhāvasena. The

*This article was published originally in *Indologica Taurinensia,* Vol. XIII, pp. 203-219, 1985-1986. Reprinted with kind permission of the editor, *Indologica Taurinensia,* Torino, Italy.

date of Bhāvasena, who was distinguished by the title of Traividyadeva, has been discussed by Dr. V.P. Johrapurkar, who places him in the fourteenth century.[2] Only a single manuscript of this unpublished work has survived, and is part of Professor Ernst Leumann's library, which is now preserved at the Bibliothèque Nationale, Strasbourg. A description of this manuscript appears in Chandrabhal Tripathi, ed., *Catalogue of the Jaina Manuscripts at Strasbourg*,[3] no. 164. Although it carries only a single title, it consists of two separate works: *Bhukti-vicāra*, pertaining to the problem of *Kevalibhukti*, and *Mukti-vicāra*, dealing with the controversy over *Strīmokṣa*. In the summer of 1980, thanks to a grant from the Social Sciences Research Council, Washington, D.C., I was able to examine the *Bhukti-mukti-vicāra* and obtain a copy of it through the kind permission of the Bibliothèque Nationale.

The text treated in this article is only the *Mukti-vicāra*, which begins on folio 132 and ends at folio 135 of the manuscript. It is thus a short text that, in spite of its erudite demonstration of knowledge concerning logical fallacies, does not add significantly to the arguments given in earlier works by scholars of the two sects. As a matter of fact, our author, Bhāvasena, has devoted only two paragraphs (nos. 23-24) to a discussion of the central Śvetāmbara and Digambara position: i.e., the former claim that a woman is able to attain *mokṣa* because, like a man, she is free from the conditions that prevent her from attaining perfection in conduct and understanding; and the latter position that, unlike a man, a woman is incapable of attaining <<perfection>> in any sense, whether it be the extreme demeritoriousness that causes one to fall into the lowest hell, or the extreme purity that results in *mokṣa*. Apparently our author decided not to enlarge on this topic as he himself says that the matter was discussed in full detail by his predecessors, Ācāraya Siddhasena, Dharasena, and Āryanandi in their treatises on this topic. The works he mentions still need to be identified, but there is no doubt that Bhāvasena has drawn heavily upon the *Prameyakamalamārttaṇḍa* by Prabhācandra, which he acknowledges as being his main source in expounding on this controversy.

The importance of Bhāvasena's work, however, lies in a new argument put forth by him: namely, that if Malli, the nineteenth Tīrthaṅkara, was a woman, as alleged by the Śvetāmbaras, there would be no reason for the images of that particular Jina to be always depicted as male, as they are even today in Śvetāmbara temples. This argument is not found in works earlier than the *Bhukti-mukti-vicāra* and point out a new direction for research on this controversy concerning the salvation of women: i.e., using iconographic evidence to ascertain contemporary forms of worship that will serve to support or disprove rival doctrinal perspectives. The Śvetāmbara reply to the position of the *Mukti-vicāra* appears in such later works as Meghavijaya's *Yuktiprabodha,*[4] written in the eighteenth century, but the credit for first raising this controversial topic must go to Bhāvasena's minor work.

Bhāvasenaviracito Muktivicāraḥ

§ 1 atha evaitad yathākathanaprathitapṛthumatisvayūthyais tathyatayā vacanaṃ kathyate, strīnirvāṇe ko 'yaṃ doṣo viduṣāṃ dūṣaṇāyate, strīpuruṣayoḥ strītvasyaiva mukhyatvāt /

§ 2 strīliṅgādhikaraṇe strītvam ādyam, ādhāryādhārabhūtasya jagato jananadarśanāt / strītvaṃ vinā jagadutpatter abhāvāt / striyo hy asārasaṃsārasukhakāraṇabhūtāḥ pūtāś cākhilanarāmararājasamājā saha suśobhante Lakṣmī-Sarasvatī-kīrti-vanitāstrītvena saundaryās toṣyatāṃ gatāḥ, sarvatra strīṇāṃ ādhikyaṃ saṃkhyayā buddhyā ca budhair bambhaṇyate / strītve hi vaśaṃgato lokaḥ / tasmāt tādṛgbhūtasya vasudhāpradhānastrīrūpasya nirvāṇaṃ nāstīti vacanaṃ kathaṃ śobheta yato dānapūjādidharmānuṣṭhāne strī jananī pravartate / strīnirvāṇaṃ na bhavatīti vadan vidvān vādī svamātur vyāghātakārī babhūva /

§ 3 iti cet, na / na tāvan mukhyāmukhyatvam atra gaṇyam / jñānavairāgyaviśiṣṭadhyānaviśeṣād upalabhayamānamuktipadasyādhāryādhārabhāvaḥ strītve na sambhavati / kutaḥ?

§ 4 caturbhir mahābhūtaparamāṇubhiḥ kāryakāraṇadarśanāt strītvaṃ vinā jagadutpatter abhāvo vaktuṃ na yuktaḥ, parasparaṃ kāryakāraṇabhāvābhāvaḥ strītvaṃ vinā pṛthivyādipadārthapradarśanāt /

§ 5 strītve vaśaṃgato loka ity api phalguvalganam / svātmani dattacittavṛttayo mahābhāgā puṇyādhikā maharṣayo vanitāvasuvasundharās tṛṇāyo manyante, nispṛhasya tṛṇaṃ jagad iti nyāyāt / yasmād āsannabhavyatāyāṃ vidyamānāyāṃ tatprabhāveṇa dānapūjādikarmaṇi pravartanā pratibhāsate / tato na mātur vyāghātakāritā /

§ 6 kiñca, etāvatā strīkṛtopakārasmaraṇapariṇatastrīlolupānāṃ vacanād ābāliśaṃ(?) gatā anvarthasaṃjñāsampannatāṃ gatā / tatas tāsāṃ muktikathanaṃ bhavatām eva doṣāya, nāsmākam /

§ 7 tathā coktaṃ ślokaḥ / karmabhūdravyanārīṇāṃ nādyaṃ saṃhananatrayam / vastrādānād acāritraṃ tat tāsāṃ muktikathā vṛthā // tasmāt strīmuktir na yuktiyuktā tadukter vicārāsahatvāt /

§ 8 katham? strītvaṃ hi mahāpāpasya phalam / kutaḥ? <<samyagdarśanaśuddhā nārakatiryaṅnapuṃsakastrītvāni>> iti strītvasya niṣedhāt /

§ 9 strīṇāṃ mahāvratārhajātarūpatvābhāvāt / bahulaṃ dīkṣāgrahaṇe 'pi strīṇāṃ nirgranthatā tāvat pūrvapuruṣaiḥ [na] śrutā na cedānīntanair dṛśyate / nirgrantho mokṣamārga iti siddher na prasiddhir vṛddhasammatā / yadi sagranthena mokṣas tadā sarvasaṃganirvṛttirūpasya yatidharmasya vaiyarthyaṃ samarthitaṃ bhavati /

§ 10 kiñca, jñānadhyānavairāgyaviśiṣṭanirgranthalakṣaṇopalakṣitamumukṣubhiḥ pakṣīkriyamāṇo mokṣaḥ / tallakṣaṇātiriktasyaiva tasya kathaṃ kāraṇaṃ kathyate? tasmād yauktikajanasūktyā strīnirvāṇaṃ sarvātmanā gīrvāṇasaridaparatīraṃ [na] tetīryate /

§ 11 napuṃsakasya nirvāṇaṃ nāstīti svayam evābhidhānāt tatrāsmākaṃ na prayāsaḥ, ahituṣāriśiṣyanyāyāt / mahīyasaḥ yogyasya puṃsaḥ sarvato nirvāṇaṃ sukhena jāghaṭyate / tasmāt tasminn arthe pramāṇaṃ samarthayāmaḥ /

§ 12 na strīsvarūpaṃ sākṣān mokṣabhāg bhavati, nairgranthyāyogyarūpatvāt / yad yad nairgranthyāyogyarūpaṃ tat tat sākṣān mokṣabhāg na bhavati/ yathā napuṃsakasvarūpam / nairgranthyāyogyarūpaṃ ca vivādāpannaṃ strīsvarūpam / tasmān na sākṣān mokṣabhāg bhavati / nairgranthyāyogyarūpatvād eva napuṃsakasya nirvāṇaṃ na bobhhavīti yathā tathā strīrūpasyāpi /

§ 13 tathā strītvaṃ dharmī mokṣahetur na bhavatīti sādhyo dharmaḥ, durantaduritodayatvāt / yad durantaduritodayaṃ tat tat muktihetur na bhavati / durantaduritodayañ ca vivādāpannaṃ strītvam, tasmān muktihetur na bhavati /

§ 14 tathā mokṣo dharmī strītve na sambhavati, prakṛṣṭaduṣṭāṣṭakarmakṣayarūpatvāt / yo yaḥ prakṛṣṭaduṣṭāṣṭakarmakṣayarūpaḥ sa sarvo 'pi strītve na sambhavati, yathā prasiddhasiddhasvarūpam / prakṛṣṭaduṣṭāṣṭakarmakṣayarūpaś cāyaṃ mokṣaḥ / tasmāt strītve na sambhavati /

§ 15 tathāpagatākhiladoṣaduḥkhapakṣa mokṣaḥ strītve na prāpnoti, praṇaṣṭaduṣṭāṣṭakarmarūpatvāt / vyatireke strīvedodayavat / ity anvayavyatirekābhyām upalabhya nirvāṇasvarūpaṃ strītve na sambhavatīti syādvādavidyāvinodibhir niścīyate / sarvatra syādvādavidyāvikramaḥ saṃkrāmati, ākramati ca parākramaṃ pareṣāṃ viduṣām /

§ 16 vivādāpannā strīnirvāṇaṃ na labhate, strīvedodayatvāt / yathedānīntanī kācit kāntā / tasmāt tathā / strīvedodayatvād ity asya hetoḥ pakṣe sadbhāvān na svarūpāsiddhatvam / na vyadhikaraṇāsiddhatvaṃ ca, ubhayavādibhiḥ hetor niścitatvāt / nājñātāsiddhatvaṃ na saṃdigdhāsiddhatvañ ca / sādhyaviparīte niścitāvinābhāvābhāvān na viruddhatvam / vipakṣe vṛttirahitatvāt nā naikāntikatvam / prativādyasiddhasādhyasādhanatvān nākiñcitkaratvam / sapakṣasattvaniścayān nānadhyavasitatvam / pakṣe sādhyābhāvāvedakapratyakṣānumānāgamalokasvavacanānām abhavān na kālātyayāpadiṣṭatvam / parapakṣe 'strīrūpatvān na prakaraṇasamatvam [iti] hetudoṣābhāvo vibhāvyate bhāvaiḥ vidvajjanaiḥ /

§ 17 kācit kāntā nirvāṇaṃ na prāpnotīti sādhyasya sadbhāvān na sādhyavikalo dṛṣṭāntaḥ / strīvedodayatvād iti sādhanasya sadbhāvān na sādhanavikalo dṛṣṭāntaḥ / ubhayasadbhāvān nobhayavikalo dṛṣṭāntaḥ / idānīntanakāntādṛṣṭāntāvaṣṭambhenokto nāśrayahīno dṛṣṭāntaḥ / vyāptidarśanapūrvakatvāt nāpradarśitavyāptikaḥ / anvayadṛṣṭānte sādhanasadbhāvapradarśanena sādhyasadbhāvasya darśitatvāt na viparītavyāptiko 'pi / iti nirdiṣṭānumānāt śiṣṭānuśiṣṭāviśiṣṭānāṃ dṛṣṭeṣṭasiddhir bhavaty eva /

§ 18 nanv etāvatā katham iṣṭasiddhir buddhimatāṃ hetor anaikāntikadoṣaduṣṭatvāt? bhagavati Mallibhaṭṭārake strīvedodayatvād iti sādhanasya sadbhāve nirvāṇaṃ na prāpnotīti sādhyābhāvāt, tena hetor vyabhicāras sutarāṃ sañcarati /

§ 19 maivaṃ kathayantu bhavantaḥ / tat katham iti cet / tasya bhagavataḥ parameśvarasya puṃstvasādhakapratyakṣānumānāgamapramāṇānāṃ bahūnāṃ bahuśo darśanāt /

§ 20 tathā hi loke na kvāpi pratyakṣeṇa bhagavatpratikṛtau strītvaṃ darīdṛṣyāmahe, puruṣākāratvenopalabhyamānatvāt / tathā 'numānapramāṇaprayogo 'pi yuktiparipāṭikoṭim āṭīkate / vivādādhyāsito bhagavān pumān eva bhavati, pratikṛtau strītvenādṛśyamānatvāt / yathā ubhayoḥ siddhānte prasiddho Vardhamānasvāmī, tathā cāyaṃ tatas tathā /

§ 21 punaś ca / vivādāpannaḥ strī na bhavati, jinapratibimbe strīrūpeṇāvidyamānatvāt, strīliṅgatvenānupapannatvāt, puruṣatvenopapannatvāt, tadvad ity ādibhir bahubhir hetubhis tasya puruṣatvasamarthanena na vyabhicāraḥ sañcaraty asmākīnahetoḥ /

§ 22 <<puṃvedaṃ vedaṃtā>> ityādy āgamo 'pi yuktighaṭām āṭāṭyate(?) / tathā ca stotraṃ

<<yasya maharṣeḥ sakalapadārthāh, pratyavabodhāt samajani sākṣāt>> / [iti] pūrvācāryastutirūpatvaṃ pulliṅgatvam eva sādhayati, strīrūpajinastuter adarśanāt / strītvajinastavanasyāvidyamānatvāt / loke na ke 'pi strīrūpajinābhāsam arcayanti /

§ 23 athāsti strīṇāṃ mokṣaḥ, avikalakāraṇatvāt, prasiddhapuruṣavat/

§ 24 maivam / mokṣahetujñānādiparamaprakarṣaḥ strīṣu nāsti, paramaprakarṣatvāt / saptamapṛthvīgamanakāraṇā puṇyaparamaprakarṣavat / tathā, yo mokṣahetuḥ saṃyamo dharmī strīṣu nastīti sādhyo dharmaḥ / sādhūnām eva vidyamānatvāt / vyatireke gṛhasthavat / nāsti strīṇāṃ mokṣaḥ, bāhyābhyantaraparigrahatvāt / gṛhasthavat /

§ 25 tasmāt bhagavatparameśvarasya strītvapratipādakaṃ Śvetāmbarādivākyaṃ vandhyāstanandhayadhanurvidyāvaiśāradyavad idānīṃ hṛdyatāṃ gatam, saṃkṣepeṇa bhuktimuktiyuktisūktyā vicāritā, tathā pramāṇaprameyaprasiddhaSiddhasenācāryeṇa Bhuktimuktiprajñaptigranthe grathitvā nirūpitā, tathā syādvādavidyādharaDharasenamuninā Bhuktivivaraṇe praṇītā, tathā Āryanandimunīndreṇa Bhuktimuktikathāyāṃ grathitvā kathitā vistarataḥ, Prameyakamalamārttaṇḍe pracaṇḍaPrabhācandrapaṇḍitadevair nānāpramāṇaiḥ prapañcitā, bhuktimuktiyuktijñair veditavyeti siddhaṃ naḥ samīhitam //

Translation

§ 1 There are those people (namely, the Śvetāmbaras) whose faculties have been dulled by virtue of hearing the words handed down in the tradition. They accept the words of the leader of their own <<herd>> and (boastfully) state the following: What kind of fault is it that attaches to the intelligent in accepting (the claim) that women attain *mokṣa*, since, between men and women, it is the female who is more prominent?

§ 2 In all matters pertaining to the feminine gender, the human female occupies the foremost position. This is because it is the female who is seen to be the begetter of the world, which is both the support (the earth) and the supported (living beings). Indeed without women, the very origin of the world would not take place.

Moreover, women are also the source of happiness in this joyless (*asāra*) world of transmigration. Women are also pure of heart, and they bring glory to men, gods, and royalty by virtue of being the embodiments of the Goddess of Wealth (Lakṣmī), the Goddess of Learning (Sarasvatī), and the Goddess of Fame (Kīrti). They also become praiseworthy because of their beauty. Thus, because of their number (i.e., population) and their intelligence, in all ways the superiority of women has been accepted by the wise.

Indeed, the whole world has come under the sway of women. Therefore, is it really proper to say that there is no *mokṣa* for women who are of such eminence and who are foremost on earth? Surely, why otherwise would the woman participate in the practice of the *dharma* through charity, worship, etc. (if she were not certain of attaining *mokṣa* thereby)? Surely, the learned opponent who maintains that women cannot attain *mokṣa* has set up an obstruction to his own mother's (salvation).

§ 3 We deny this claim. Here, (in the matter of *mokṣa*), the relative superiority or inferiority (of men or women) is not what should be considered. We maintain instead that a female body does not provide the kind of support that is required for the attainment of *mokṣa*, (since *mokṣa*) is obtainable only by an extraordinary kind of trance that is distinguished by (perfect) knowledge and detachment. How so?

§ 4 Since one can perceive the cause-and-effect relationship produced by the atoms of the four great material elements, it is therefore not proper to maintain that there would be no production in the world without a feminine principle. Neither is there any mutual cause/effect relationship between femininity and the world, since such elements as earth, etc. are seen (to be produced without the presence of a feminine principle).

§ 5 Equally futile is your statement that the world has come under the sway of womanhood. The great souls who have directed their mental activities toward their own selves, as well as the noble sages who have accumulated great merit, all consider women, wealth, and earth to be (as insignificant as) a blade of grass. As the gnome (rule) says, <<For a man without desire, the whole world is like a blade of grass>>. Neither is there any setting up of an obstacle to the salvation of mothers, since when the conditions conducive to the attainment of *mokṣa* are present, the force of that (totality of cause) will create in women a natural turning toward such activities as charity and worship.

§ 6 Moreover, those (who maintain that women attain *mokṣa*), say so because of their attachment to women, which is engendered by their memory of the many goods deeds done for them by women (such as giving birth and rearing them). Therefore, it is appropriate that you have come to receive the designation <<childish>>.

§ 7 For it has been said in the following verse:

Those who are physically women in the realm of action are not endowed with the first three kinds of configurations of joints in the body. (In the absence of these first three configurations), they must accept clothes and, hence, are not fit to assume (the highest) conduct.[5]

Therefore, the doctrine of the salvation of women is not reasonable, nor does it stand up to scrutiny.

§ 8 How so? Femininity is the result of great sinfulness. On what grounds? Because femininity is rejected (by those with right vision) as in the following phrase: <<Beings who are pure on account of right insight (are not reborn as) hell-beings, animals, hermaphrodites, or females>>.[6]

§ 9 (Femininity is also the result of great sinfulness) because women are unable to practice nudity, which is the prerequisite for assuming the great mendicant vows.

Moreover, even though women are ordained as nuns, no one in the past has ever admitted (lit., heard) that they attain freedom from all possessions (*nirgranthatā*), nor is this seen at present by any of us. It is admitted by all that the path of *mokṣa* involves the total freedom from all possessions. Therefore, your claim (that women may attain *mokṣa*) is not accepted by the elders (of the tradition). If *mokṣa* could indeed be attained while retaining possessions, then this would amount to supporting the futility of the mendicant discipline, which consists of forsaking all attachments.

§ 10 Moreover, *mokṣa* is that which is adhered to by those aspirants who are characterized by nonpossession and distinguished by (their perfection of) knowledge, meditation, and dispassion. How could you claim that keeping (possessions, such as the nuns' wearing of clothes), which is devoid of the characteristics of *mokṣa*, could act as the very cause of *mokṣa*? Therefore the doctrine that women may attain *mokṣa* must be considered entirely incapable of reaching the other shore of the river of the valid arguments put forth by the logicians.

§ 11 There is no need for us to strive to prove that hermaphrodites (congenitally) may not attain *mokṣa*, since our opponent has also accepted it. This (statement is made) according to the accepted law that when an eagle is present, a teacher does not need a disciple to get rid of a snake.[7] It can be proved with great ease in all cases that a man who is a great yogin may attain *mokṣa.* Therefore we will put forth valid arguments to prove that he (alone) attains *mokṣa.*

§ 12 (Proposition): A being in a woman's body cannot attain *mokṣa* in that very life.

(Reason): Because it is a body which is unsuitable for the relinquishment of all possessions (i.e., holy nudity is not allowed).

(Invariable concomitance): Whatever body is unsuitable for attaining the stage of holy nudity (*nairgranthya*) is unable to attain *mokṣa* in that very life.

(Example): As is the case with the body of a hermaphrodite.

(Application): The body of a woman, which is under debate here, is similarly unsuitable for hold nudity.

(Conclusion): Therefore, a being in a female body cannot attain *mokṣa.* Just as *mokṣa* is not admitted for a hermaphrodite because of its unsuitability for holy nudity, so it is also for a woman's body.

§ 13 (Proposition): Similarly, womanhood is the locus. It is not the cause of *mokṣa*—this is the proposition to be proved.

(Reason): This is because exceedingly miserable karmic results occur in her.

(Invariable concomitance): Whatever is (the result of) exceedingly miserable karmic actions cannot become a cause for *mokṣa* (as is the case for hell-beings or animals).

(Application): Womanhood, which is under debate here, is the result of the origination of the most miserable *karmas.*

(Conclusion): Therefore, womanhood is not a cause for *mokṣa.*

§ 14 Similarly, *mokṣa* is the locus; and it is incompatible with womanhood because of the nature of *mokṣa,* which involves the total destruction of the eight kinds of extremely evil *karmas.* Whatever has the nature of bringing about the destruction of these eight kinds of *karmas*[8]—as has, for example, the liberated soul, about which there is no dispute—cannot possibly occur in women. The *mokṣa* we talk of is precisely of that nature and, therefore, cannot possibly occur in women.

§ 15 Similarly, *mokṣa* has the nature of being totally free from all passions and suffering. It is impossible in woman, because that *mokṣa* has the nature of bringing about the total elimination of the eight kinds of evil *karmas.* The contrary example is the rise of the female libido in a woman, (which proves that she is not free from passions and suffering and the *karmas* that cause those). In this manner, by both supporting and contrary examples, it is determined by those who are trained in the application of the Jaina doctrine of conditional statements (*syādvāda*) that the nature of *mokṣa* is incompatible with womanhood. In all cases, the application of the tropology prevails, and it also overcomes the arguments of the learned opponents.

§ 16 The woman under dispute (i.e., the Jaina nun) does not attain *nirvāṇa,* because the female libido arises in her, as in any other woman. (The nun) is like (any other woman). The reasoning given by us (for not allowing her to attain *mokṣa*)—namely, the occurrence of the female libido (in her)—is valid, because (none of the following ten reasons by which a *hetu* can be proved invalid apply):

1. The reasoning given is not vitiated by the fallacy of *svarūpāsiddhatva,* because of the reasoning—namely, that the rise of the female libido is present in the locus of a woman's body.
2. The reasoning given is not vitiated by the fallacy of *vyadhikaraṇāsiddhatva,* because both parties to the dispute accept the fact that the female libido does exist in a woman's body.

3. & 4. It is not vitiated by either the fallacy of *ajñātāsiddhatva.* or
The fallacy of *saṃdigdhāsiddhatva,* since the opponent is neither ignorant about the presence of the female libido in a woman's body, nor does he entertain any doubts about that.

5. There is no fallacy of *viruddhatva,* because of the reasoning given by us—namely, that the rise of the female libido in a woman is not found elsewhere (with unfailing invariable concomitance).
6. There is no fallacy of *anaikāntikatva,* since the rise of the (female libido) cannot be proved to exist in either its locus or non-locus.
7. There is no fallacy of *akiñcitkaratva,* because it does not prove the opposite—namely, the salvation of women, which has not yet been established by the opponent.

8. There is no fallacy of *anadhyavasitatva*, because the reasoning (of the libido arising) is also found in similar cases (i.e., in other women).
9. There is no fallacy of *kālātyayāpadiṣṭatva*, because of the absence of any perception, inference, scriptural authority, or worldly convention by which one could assert the absence of that reason (the rise of the libido) in the locus (the nun).
10. There is no fallacy of *prakaraṇasamatva*, since there is no matching argument put forth by the opponent which would support his claim more than ours.

Thus, the learned have shown that our reason is free from all the fallacies (of logic).

§ 17 Our example is free from the fault of *sādhyavikala*, since there exists the locus of that which is to be proved, i.e., that no woman attains *mokṣa*.

Our example is free from the fault of *sādhanavikala*, because of the presence of the reason given by us.

Our example is free from the fault of *ubhayavikala*, because the example is applicable both to the nun as well as to the reason given.

Our example is free from the fault of *āśrayahīna*, since our example is valid for any woman at this present time.

Our example is free from the fault of *apradarśitavyāptika*, since the invariable concomitance between the reason and both the locus and the example has been demonstrated.

Our example is also free from the fault of *viparītavyāptika*, because we have demonstrated that *mokṣa* is not possible when there is the rise of the female libido.

Thus, by the aforementioned inferences, for those distinguished people who have been taught by the noble teachers, there would be the establishment of the desired object which is perceived by us to be true.

§ 18 Objection: But surely, how could you say that, for intelligent people, this is established, as you want it to be?, since the reason given by you is vitiated by the fault of *anaikāntika* (a fault arising by virtue of the reason not being universally applicable). Your thesis that *mokṣa* is not possible for women because of the rise of the female libido is not applicable in the case of the Lady

Malli (who was a female Tīrthaṅkara). The exception of Malli proves that your argument is fallacious.[9]

§ 19 You should not say this. This is because, we perceive many means of verification, such as perception, inference, and scriptural testimony which prove the masculinity of the exalted Lords, the Tīrthaṅkaras.

§ 20 For example, no one in the world has ever perceived the (alleged) femininity of the images of the Lord Malli; on the contrary, those images are always depicted in masculine gender. Similarly, the syllogistic application of the inference also shows that it has reached the perfection of reasoning(?). The Lord under debate must be a man, because he is never portrayed as female in his images. This is like the images of Vardhamāna (Mahāvīra), which are well-known to be male in the traditions of both parties. The same is the case here (with Malli), so it must be like that (i.e., since her image is male, Malli must actually have been male).

§ 21 Moreover, the person under debate (Malli) cannot be a woman, because that Lord is not to be found in female form in the images of the Jinas. This is because the images of that particular Lord are not found to be endowed with feminine characteristics, but only with male qualities, etc. This and many other reasons support (our claim) that the Lord was male, and no reasons (of the opponent) vitiate the reasoning which we have put forth.

§ 22 As far as scriptural testimony is concerned, the following statement, "experiencing the male libido, etc." also supports the same argument.[10]

Moreover, there is also this panegyric (in praise of the Lord Malli): <<That great sage (Maharṣi), in whose omniscience appeared the direct cognition of all existing knowables>>.[11] Thus, the panegyric uttered by the ancient teachers supports only the masculinity of the Lord Malli (for the word *maharṣi* in the above verse is in the masculine gender); nowhere is there found any praise of a Jina's femininity. There also does not exist any panegyric which praises the Jina as possessing a female form, nor does anyone in the world worship the image of a Jina in a female form.

§ 23 But surely women may attain *mokṣa*, because the conditions required for *mokṣa* are not absent in them, as is also the case with men (who are accepted by both sects as being able to attain *mokṣa*).[12]

§ 24 Do not say this! The condition for *mokṣa* is the extreme perfection of knowledge, etc. That perfection is not found in women, because it is a perfection (that a woman can never achieve), as is the case with her not being able to attain the extreme form of demerit which alone can lead to seventh (and lowest) hell. Thus, the cause of salvation, which is perfect conduct, is not found in the locus, namely women, but only in the male mendicants. The contrary example is that of the householders. (Thus we may conclude that) women do not attain *mokṣa,* because they have the internal (passions) and external (clothes, etc.), just as do householders.

§ 25 Thus, the words of the Śvetāmbaras purporting to show the femininity of the Lord, the Tīrthaṅkara Malli, are as enchanting as the expertise in archery of the son of a barren woman. This we have examined in brief in this work, which has given arguments against the *mokṣa* of women and the eating of food (*bhukti*) by the Kevalin. Similarly, the Ācārya Siddhasena, who is well-known for his treatment of the objects and theories of knowledge, has explained this matter properly in the work called *Bhuktimuktiprajñapti.*[13] It has also been set forth by the sage Dharasena, the great master of Syādvāda, in his work, *Bhuktivivaraṇa.*[14] So also has it been discussed in great detail by the great sage, Āryanandi, in his compilation, *Bhuktimuktikathā.*[15] Finally, the great learned one, Prabhācandra, who is the wisest of the learned, has examined this issue in great detail with many means of verification, in his work, *Prameyakamalamārttaṇḍa.*[16] These arguments should all be known from these sources by those who wish to know the arguments refuting the *mokṣa* of women, as well as the eating of food by the Kevalin. Thus is established our objective (in this work).

NOTES

1. Ed. Jambuvijaya, Bhavanagar, 1974.
2. *Viśvatattvaprakāśa* of Bhāvasena, Sholapur, Jīvaraja Jaina Granthamālā, 1964 (Introduction).
3. Leiden, E. J. Brill, 1975.
4. Ratlam, Rishabhdev Keshrimal, 1928.

5. The use of the world *karmabhū* (<<realm of action>>) is meant to exclude the realm of enjoyment (*bhogabhūmi*), from whence *mokṣa* cannot be achieved. The word *dravyanārī* (<<physically women>>) excludes from consideration people who are physically male but may entertain female libido and thus metaphorically be called female. The word *saṃhanana* (<<configurations of joints>>) refers to different types of joints. Jainas believe that there are six grades of such joints, from the perfect joint, noted for its adamantine quality, to the weakest joint. It is further believed that the highest trances can be entered into only by those who are endowed with one of the first three grades of joints. For details, see Jinendra Varṇī, *Jainendrasiddhāntakośa*, IV, New Delhi, Bhāratīya Jñānapīṭha, 1973, p. 156.
6. samyagdarśanaśuddhā nārakatiryaṅnapuṃsakastrītvāni /
   duṣkṛtavikṛtālpāyur daridratāṃ ca vrajanti nāpy avratikāḥ //
   Ratnakaraṇḍa-śrāvakācāra of Samantabhadra, Māṇikacandra Digambara Jaina Granthamālā, No. 24 Bombay, 1926, verse 35.
7. The rule given here is rather obscure. The purport seems to be that when an eagle is present, a teacher does not need to have anyone else, like a disciple, to remove a snake, as eagles are said to be invincible in capturing snakes. Since both the Śvetāmbaras and Digambaras agree that hermaphrodites may not attain *mokṣa*, the Digambara is under no obligation to provide new arguments to prove that point. It should be recalled here that the Digambaras use hermaphrodites as an example of a category of human beings who cannot attain *mokṣa*, and they seek to show that, unlike men, women belong to the same category.
8. For these eight kinds of *karmas* see P. S. Jaini, *The Jaina Path of Purification*, Berkeley and Los Angeles, University of California, 1979, Chapter 4, pp. 107-133.
9. The Jainas believe that, in each time-cycle, twenty-four Tīrthaṅkaras appear in the world. According to the Digambaras, all of these are male. In the Śvetāmbara canon (i.e., *Nāyādhammakahāo*, viii), however, one of the Tīrthaṅkaras of the current cycle was female, namely Malli. The images of Malli even in Śvetāmbara temples are, however, conventionally depicted as male. It may be noted in this connection that a stone-image of Jaina female mendicant seated in cross-legged posture was found recently in North India and is now in the Lucknow Museum. A plate of this image was reproduced in my *Jaina Path of Purification*, where scholarly speculation that it might have been a Śvetāmbara image of the Tīrthaṅkara Malli was discussed. Unfortunately, the image is decapitated, which compounds the difficulty of identifying the figure. Since the publication of my book, it has been brought to my attention that long, braided hair is found represented on the backside of the image, a feature quite inconsistent with the appearance of a female mendicant. Thus, the possibility of this image being that of Malli is no longer tenable.
10. The complete verse reads as follows:
    puṃvedaṃ vedaṃtā je purisā khavagaseḍhimārūḍhā /
    sesodayeṇa vi tahā jhāṇuvajuttā ya te du sijjhanti //
    Prakrit Siddha-bhakti, verse 6; quoted in *Prameyakamalamārtaṇḍa* of Prabhācandra, ed. Mahendra Kumar Shastri, Bombay, 1941, p. 333. The Digambaras quote this verse in support of their sectarian claim that only a person who has a

male body (*puruṣa*) may attain *mokṣa* even if he should entertain a female libido (*strī-veda*); the verse is also used to prove that a woman may not attain the same goal even if she should entertain male libido (*puṃ-veda*).

11. This verse is from the *Svayambhū-stotra* (verse 106), by the Digambara mendicant-poet Samantabhadra. See *Nityanaimittikapāṭhāvalī*, Karanja, 1956, pp. 29-44.
12. This is the central point of the argument used by all Śvetāmbara scholars in defence of their position. Our author's reply, given in the following paragraph (§ 24), that women are incapable of attaining perfection in conduct or knowledge, also sums up the Digambara position on this controversy.
13. Nothing is known about this work and it is not included in the extant works of Siddhasena (also known as Siddhasena Divākara). See *Siddhasena Divākara's Sanmati-tarka*, edited by Sukhalal Sanghavi and Bechardas Doshi, Bombay, Jain Shvetambar Education Board, 1939.
14. Ḍharasena in probably identical to the Digambara Ācārya Dharasena, the author of the *Ṣaṭkhaṇḍāgama-sūtra* (edited with its commentary *Dhavalā* by Hiralal Jain, Amaravati, Jaina Sāhityoddharaka Fund, 1939-59). The *Bhukti-vivaraṇa* is probably the name given by Bhāvasena to those *sūtras* which deal with the *guṇasthānas* attained by a woman, e.g. *Dhavalā*, I, p. 348, *sūtras* 107-108.
15. Nothing more is known at present about this work attributed to Āryanandi.
16. For the *Premeyakamalamārttaṇḍa*, see supra, note 7.

CHAPTER 9

Jaina Debates on the Spiritual Liberation of Women

(Introduction to *Gender and Salvation: Debates on the Spiritual Liberation of Women*)*

Background of the Jaina Sectarian Debate

#1 The salvation or spiritual liberation of women (called *strī-nirvāṇa, strī-mokṣa,* or *strī-mukti*) has been a matter of great controversy between the two major sects of Jainism, the Digambaras and the Śvetāmbaras. The former vehemently have insisted that one cannot attain *mokṣa,* emancipation of a soul from the cycles of birth and death (*saṃsāra*), as a female, while the latter have steadfastly refused to claim exclusively male access to the liberated state (*Arhat* or *Siddha*) of the soul. The beginning of the feud between the two sects—which eventually split Jaina society into two hostile camps—is itself shrouded in mystery; no one has yet been able to ascertain with any precision either the direct cause of the division or the dates of the initial controversy. Both traditions agree, however, that the final breach took place around 300 B.C. during the time of the Venerable Bhadrabāhu, a contemporary of Emperor Candragupta, the

*This introduction was published originally in *Gender and Salvation: Debates on the Spiritual Liberation of Women,* (Berkeley: University of California Press, 1991), pp. 1-30. Reprinted with kind permission of the University of California Press, Berkeley. For chapter numbers and bibliographic references in the notes below, please refer to the book itself. The abbreviation *JPP = Jaina Path of Purification,* University of California Press, 1979.

founder of the Mauryan dynasty. Since that time, the two sects have refused to accept the validity of each other's scriptures; indeed, the Digambaras have even claimed that the original words of Mahāvīra were irrevocably lost.[1] In addition, the adherents of both sects refuse to recognize their rival's religious as true mendicants (*muni* or *sādhu*), setting up a debate that tears at the very fabric of the entire Jaina community.

#2 One of the major issues dividing the two sects was the acceptability of ordained persons wearing clothes. While this might seem to us moderns a trivial issue on which to base what was to become a major sectarian dispute, the debate masked basic concerns in Jaina soteriology that were hardly frivolous. On one point there was unanimity: the last great teacher (known by the title of Jina, or a spiritual victor) of their religion, Vardhamāna Mahāvīra, who lived, according to the tradition, from 599 to 527 B.C., had been a naked ascetic (*acelaka śramaṇa*), and some of his early adherents had been similarly "sky-clad" (*digambara*) and hence came to be known as *jinakalpins* (i.e., similar to the Jina).[2] But this was the extent of the consensus. The Digambaras, who went naked (*nagna*) following Mahāvīra's example, claimed that a mendicant must renounce all property or possessions (*parigraha*), including clothes; the only exceptions they allowed were a small whisk broom (*rajoharaṇa*) for brushing insects away from one's seat and a water gourd (*kamaṇḍalu*) for toilet purposes. They therefore accepted only naked monks as the true mendicant adherents of the Jina and regarded the Śvetāmbara monks, who continued to wear white clothes (*śveta-ambara*) after ordination, as no better than celibate laymen (*brahmacārī-gṛhastha*). Nudity thus became for the Digambaras the fundamental identifying feature (*muni-liṅga*) of the mendicant life, and they maintained that without undertaking at least that modicum of practice, one could not hope to attain the most exalted of states, *mokṣa* or *nirvāṇa*.

The Śvetāmbaras, of course, conceded that Mahāvīra adopted the practice of nudity (*acelaka*), but they regarded the renunciation of clothes as optional for monks, somewhat similar to the practice of austerities such as fasting, which, although entirely commendable, was hardly mandatory. The Śvetāmbara position became increasingly intransigent, however, until the leaders of that sect came to claim that clothes were an integral part of the holy life and that they were the only true mendicants because they wore clothes. As the debate became even more inflammatory, the Śvetāmbaras even resorted to eschatological arguments to justify their claim: the practice of nudity, while commendable during the time of Mahāvīra himself, was no longer advisable in this degenerate age. Their scriptures related that soon after Mahāvīra's death the practice of nudity became extinct. Its revival was deemed inappropriate during the subsequent period, in a fashion reminiscent of the *kalivarjya* practices—or those practices once legitimate but now condemned—in the Hindu law books. Śvetāmbaras therefore considered the Digambaras heretics for rejecting the authenticity of their canon (*āgama*), especially for defying the canonical injunctions against nudity, and for showing disrespect to the large mendicant order of the white-clad Śvetāmbara monks who were following the prescribed practice of the *sthavirakalpa*, that is, being clothed and being a member of the ecclesiastical community.

#3 With the overriding importance that the Digambaras attached to nudity, it is no surprise that clothes came to occupy a central position in the debates on the possible salvation of women as well. For reasons that are never specifically stated, even the Digambaras did not grant women permission to practice nudity under any circumstances and insisted that women wear clothes. This injunction effectively barred women from ever renouncing *all* "possessions" and, accordingly, from attaining *mokṣa* in that life. Female mendicants, although called noble or venerable ladies (*āryikās* or *sādhvīs),* were technically not considered mendicants at all but simply celibate, albeit spiritually advanced, laywomen (*utkṛṣṭa-śrāvikā*)—a status similar to that which the Digambaras were willing to accord to the Śvetāmbara monks. The Śvetāmbaras, on the other hand, did not consider clothes a possession (*parigraha*) but rather an indispensable component of the religious life (*dharma-upakaraṇa*). Therefore, even though nuns wore clothes in strict accordance with the prohibition against nudity, they were on an equal footing with monks and were granted the full status of mendicancy. More important, however, women were thus considered eligible to attain *mokṣa* in that very female body—a prospect possible to any nun who was sufficiently adept spiritually. *Mokṣa* was therefore based not on biological condition but on spiritual development alone.

#4 The Digambaras, however, refused to accept any possibility of a person, whether male or female, attaining *mokṣa* without renouncing one's clothes, for the retention of clothes implied residual sex desire (expressed through *lajjā* or shame); when coupled with their prohibition against women ever renouncing their clothes, this refusal led to the formulation of the doctrine that a person could not attain *mokṣa* while having a female body. Strangely, this development is neither attested in the pre-Mauryan canon, the *Dvādaśāṅga-sūtra*—admittedly recognized only by the Śvetāmbaras—nor discussed in the earliest stratum of postcanonical literature of the Digambara sect (e.g., the *Ṣaṭkhaṇḍāgama-sūtra*, c. 150). The earliest indication that there was such a controversy in the Jaina community of mendicants (*saṅgha*) is to be found in the Prakrit *Suttapāhuḍa* of the Digambara mendicant Kundakunda (c. second century A.D.). While explaining the true nature of renunciation (*pravrajyā*), Kundakunda observes that one becomes a Jaina mendicant when one renounces not only internal attachments but also all forms of external possession, including one's clothes, and assumes the state of complete nudity (*nagnabhāva*). He then states, rather casually, that a woman's renunciation is not comparable to that of a man:

> There is also the emblem [*liṅga*, i.e., order] for women: a nun is called *āryikā* [a venerable lady]. . . . She wears a single piece of cloth and eats only one meal a day.
>
> In the teaching of the Jina a person does not attain *mokṣa* if one wears clothes. . . . Nudity is the path leading to *mokṣa*. All others are wrong paths.
>
> The genital organs of the woman, her naval, armpits, and the area between her breasts, are said [in the scriptures] to be breeding grounds of subtle forms of life. How can there be [full] renunciation for a woman?
>
> Their minds are not pure and by nature they are not firm in mind or in body. They have monthly menstruation. Therefore, for women there is no meditation free from fear.[3]

#5 Kundakunda does not identify the school which might have claimed that a nun's renunciation was as complete as that of a monk. One would expect his opponents to be the Śvetāmbaras, who have traditionally held that view. Yet the earliest extant work dedicated to a systematic refutation of the Digambara position does not originate in the Śvetāmbara camp. Rather, this honour belongs to an obscure Jaina sect known as the Yāpanīya, which probably came into existence around the second century and was extinct by the twelfth.[4] Śākaṭāyana, a ninth-century mendicant of this order, is credited with a work called the *Strīnirvāṇaprakaraṇa*, a short treatise in some fifty verses, together with a commentary (the *Svopajñavṛtti*), that establishes him as the first known Indian expounder of a woman's (i.e., a nun's) ability to attain *mokṣa.*

#6 The Yāpanīya sect seems to have combined in its practices elements drawn from both of the two major Jaina sects. Following the Digambaras, their male mendicants went naked; but, like the Śvetāmbaras, the Yāpanīyas acknowledged the authority of the Śvetāmbara canon and professed that nudity was prohibited for women because in their case that practice was not necessary to achieve *mokṣa.* For the Yāpanīyas, a modicum of clothing was not a hindrance to the attainment of *mokṣa* in the present life for a woman or even for a man who, after becoming a monk, developed inflammations such as fistulas that needed to be covered by clothing. The Śvetāmbaras, who had close affinities with the Yāpanīya sect, appear to have subsequently adopted the Yāpanīya arguments in favour of the possibility of women attaining *mokṣa* and challenged the Digambaras on this issue. The controversy spanned a thousand years and was carried forth in the works of such Śvetāmbara mendicant writers as Haribhadra (c. 750), Abhayadeva (c. 1000), Śāntisūri (c. 1120), Malayagiri (c. 1150), Hemacandra (c. 1160), Vādideva (c. 1170), Ratnaprabha (c. 1250), Guṇaratna (c. 1400), Yaśovijaya (c. 1660), and Meghavijaya (c. 1700).[5] The Digambara responses probably begin with Vīrasena (c. 800), and continue in the works of Devasena (c. 950), Nemicandra (c. 1050), Prabhācandra (c. 980-1065), Jayasena (c. 1150), and Bhāvasena (c. 1275). Notwithstanding the continued attempts made by scholars of both schools to refute their rival's position, the lines of argument remained fundamentally the same and the sectarian battles became increasingly acrimonious.

#7 As is well-known to students of Indian philosophy, the basic texts of the six philosophical schools (*darśanas*) have one common goal: establishing the validity of their conception of *mokṣa* or *nirvāṇa*—synonymous in Jainism—the classical ideas of salvation in India, which bring an end to the cycle of rebirth (*saṃsāra*). It is extraordinary indeed that no other school except the Jaina ever questioned the inherent capacity of a woman to attain *mokṣa* in her present body, in her present life. The Jainas are conspicuous, therefore, in introducing what is basically a sectarian dispute into their philosophical texts. It should be remembered that both Digambaras and Śvetāmbaras are almost unanimous in their approach to refuting the doctrines of the non-Jaina philosophical schools (*darśanas*). However, once authors affiliated with either of the two main Jaina schools finish their discourse on the true nature of *mokṣa*, there inevitably appears a dispute over the physical prerequisites necessary to attain that state: the Digambaras claim that *mokṣa* is attainable only by males, while the Śvetāmbaras maintain that having a female body is no obstacle to salvation. One might expect the Jainas to settle this matter through recourse to their scriptures; but, as noted above, the sects do not always share the same body of texts. They do, however, share a common belief system and in many cases their positions are identical regarding the status of women vis-à-vis men within the ecclesiastical order or with reference to the laws of *karma* that apply to male and female rebirth processes.

The syllogistic formulas (of the traditional Indian type called *prayogas*) employed by both schools, when examined from the standpoint of the significance of their shared beliefs and doctrines, thus provide interesting examples of the sectarian disputes that racked the medieval Jaina church in particular, as well as the attitude of Indians in general toward women, both in the religious and social spheres. I propose here to compile briefly some of the major arguments used by the Jainas in their treatments of the possibility of women attaining *mokṣa* and will focus in particular on those inferences that are presented in syllogistic form. This examination will also enable us to draw out the implications of that controversy for the wider problem of religious salvation for women.

Format and Substance of the Debate

#8 The general format of the initial series of argumentation is the Digambara's denial of *mokṣa* for women, the Śvetāmbara's affirmation of women's capacity to achieve salvation, and the Digambara's rebuttal. The Digambara makes the opening statement:

> There is *mokṣa* for men only, not for women;
> because of the absence of valid evidence to support that claim;
> as is the case with congenital hermaphrodites (*napuṃsaka*) [who are considered unfit to attain *mokṣa* in both sects].[6]

#9 The Śvetāmbara answers:

> There is *mokṣa* for women;
> because there is no deficiency in the causes [called *ratnatraya*, or the "Three Jewels"] that lead to *mokṣa* for them;
> as is the case for men.

In their refutation of the Digambara claim, the Śvetāmbaras retort that the Digambaras must cite an adequate piece of evidence that would prove the absence in women of the conditions that lead to *mokṣa.* Surely, say the Śvetāmbaras, such insufficiency in women cannot be proved by perception (*pratyakṣa*); nor can it be established via a valid inference (*anumāna*), since such an inferential mark (*liṅga*) that has invariable concomitance (*vyāpti* or *avinābhāva*) with what is inferred (*sādhya*) cannot be found. Nor is there any scope for resorting to scripture (*āgama*) in this case, for they find no passage in the texts which would conclusively prove that one cannot attain *mokṣa* in a female body. On the other hand, they can prove that a woman is free from those deficiencies which prevent her from attaining *mokṣa.* For what is the primary condition for attaining *mokṣa*? As described in a treatise accepted as authoritative by both schools, the *Tattavārthasūtra,* the path to *mokṣa* consists of Three Jewels (*ratnatraya*)—right view (*samyak-darśana*), right knowledge (*samyak-jñāna*), and right conduct (*samyak-cāritra*)—and all three of These Jewels are to be found together in women. Women therefore have no deficiency in regard to the attainment of *mokṣa.*

#10 The Digambara rebuttal to the Śvetāmbara position may be paraphrased as follows. We of course admit that the Three Jewels are to be found in women, as you mentioned, but only in an inchoate form. Merely possessing the rudiments of the Three Jewels, however, does not qualify them to attain *mokṣa,* for otherwise all religious persons in the moment immediately following their initiation into mendicancy would necessarily attain *mokṣa.* But this, of course, is not the case. *Mokṣa* is possible only when the aspirant attains to the absolute perfection of the Three Jewels, especially of right conduct, and that perfection, we maintain, is impossible for a woman.

#11 The Śvetāmbara objects to this stand by challenging the Digambara to show how one would ever perceive this perfection of the Three Jewels. Surely, the Śvetāmbara maintains, the point at which such perfection occurs is the penultimate moment of one's life, immediately preceding the attainment of *mokṣa,* and that moment is imperceptible. But is its imperceptibility sufficient cause to deny its existence? If you have any other logical means to prove your argument, then let us hear your arguments.

#12 The answers to this challenge given by the Digambara sum up the basic arguments of the debate. The Digambara says that, of course, there are valid proofs which support our own claim that women cannot attain *mokṣa,* because they are inherently inferior to men (*hīnatvāt*). This can be proved by the following reasons, all of which include appropriate syllogistic inferences (*prayoga*): (1) the inability of women to be reborn in the seventh and lowest hell, unlike men; (2) their inability to renounce all possessions, including clothes; (3) their inferiority in such skills as debating; (4) their inferior position in both general society and the ecclesiastical order.[7]

#13 Before turning to a consideration of the first reason, it is appropriate to explain initially a few cosmological details pertaining to the Jaina beliefs about an individual's rebirth in the lowest hell. The Jaina universe consists of three spheres: the upper heavenly abodes (*svargaloka*), the lower hellish abodes (*narakaloka*), and the tiny area in between called the middle abode (*madhyaloka,* the earth), wherein dwell human beings and animals.[8] There are a variety of heavens situated one above the other, abodes of ever increasing happiness. The highest heaven, called *Sarvārthasiddhi* (lit., Accomplishment of All Desires), was considered the highest point of worldly happiness and was achievable only by the highest kind of meritorious (*puṇya*) deeds. Similarly, there are seven successive hells, their misery increasing as one descends. The lowest hell, called *Mahātamaḥprabhā* (lit., Pitch Darkness), was attained only by those beings who commit the most inauspicious (*apuṇya* or *pāpa*) actions. Beyond the heavens but within the habitable universe (called *lokākāśa,* beyond which movement was not possible) was an area where the Jainas believed that emancipated souls called *Siddhas,* once freed from their karmic burden and all other forms of embodiment, rose automatically and abided forever in their omniscient glory. The summit of the universe was called the *Siddha-loka.*

The Jainas also had stringent restrictions on the process of rebirth between the three spheres. A being could born into one hell, for example, could not be reborn into another hell or into a heaven. By the same token, a heavenly being could not be reborn into a different heaven or into one of the hells. The destiny of both hell and heavenly beings was, therefore, in the *Madhya-loka* as a human being or an animal. The middle realm was thus the centre of gravity of the rebirth process and the springboard to rebirth in any other sphere. In agreement with general Indian beliefs, the Jainas also believed that *mokṣa* could be achieved only from a human existence.

#14 What is of particular interest for our controversy is the fact that the Digambaras and the Śvetāmbaras, who both accept this cosmology and the rules pertaining to rebirth, agree further that women, unlike men, are incapable of experiencing the most extreme form of unwholesome volitions; consequently, they are incapable of being reborn in the lowest, the seventh, hell. However, while the Śvetāmbaras did allow women to experience extreme purity of moral consciousness and therefore attain rebirth in the Sarvārthasiddhi, this possibility was denied by the Digambaras. The Digambaras used their belief in the disparity between the moral consciousness of men and women as justification for their dogma that women—who cannot fall into the lowest hell or rise to the highest heaven—are inherently incapable of achieving the Siddha-loka, a realm beyond the highest heaven at the summit of the Jaina universe.

#15 The rationale behind this argument was the mutually accepted doctrine that the intensity of a given volition determined the character of the action it catalyzed. The Jainas used the word "*dhyāna*" (concentration) to refer to both evil and good volitional impulses. Evil concentration was twofold: *ārta* (sorrowful) and *raudra* (cruel), of which the most extreme forms of the latter led to rebirth in the seventh hell. Wholesome concentration was similarly twofold: *dharma* (righteous) and *śukla* (pure). The cultivation of the former led to wholesome destinies, culminating in the highest heavens. Only by pure concentration (*śukladhyāna*), however, could one attain *mokṣa* after having completely eliminated all karmic bonds. They Digambaras maintained that only those who were capable of enteraining the most impure forms of concentration were similarly fit to entertain the purest types of concentration. They therefore argued that the inability of a woman to be born in the seventh hell was a sure indication of her incapacity ever to be born in the highest heaven. Even if, for the sake of argument, the Digambaras were to regard the attainment of the Sarvārthasiddhi heaven as immaterial to the debate about *mokṣa,* they still would have argued that the abode of the Siddhas—which represented cosmologically the highest extreme of the universe, in contradistinction to the seventh hell—could be attained only by those who were able to perfect that *śukladhyāna.*[9] Should the Śvetāmbara, however, insist that the female body was no obstruction to attaining not only Sarvārthasiddhi but even the Siddha-loka, then they perforce would also have to admit that women could be reborn in the seventh hell—a position that was against their own scripture and therefore false. The Digambara syllogism used to prove this point is as follows:

> The excellence of knowledge and so forth, required for *mokṣa,* is not found in women;
> because such excellence and so forth must have absolute perfection;
> just as women lack the ultimate extreme of demerit, which is the immediate cause of rebirth in the seventh hell. [They therefore also lack the absolute perfection required for attaining *mokṣa.*][10]

16 The Digambara position, based as it is on the alleged mediocrity of women and especially on their inability to experience the most evil forms of action, is countered by the Śvetāmbaras in the following argument, which recognized the fallacy of absence of invariable concomitance (*vyāpti*) in the Digambara syllogism. The Śvetāmbaras maintain that there is no invariable concomitance between the fact that women cannot fall into the seventh hell and their presumed inability to attain *mokṣa.* The Śvetāmbaras advocate that when there is invariable concomitance between two things, the presence or absence of one thing would always be accompanied by the presence or absence of the companion item. Fire and smoke are so related, so that whenever there is smoke there is fire; this is because there is a causal relationship between smoke and fire. The species of tree *śiṃśapā* is also invariably associated with trees, so that whenever there is an absence of tree, there would always be an absence of the *śiṃśapā*: thus there is a relationship of (noncausal) pervasion (based on identity) between tree and *śiṃśapā.* But, the Śvetāmbaras advocate, the fall into the seventh hell and the inability to attain *mokṣa* are neither causally related—as were fire and smoke or the Three Jewels and *mokṣa*—nor noncausally pervasive, as were tree and *śiṃśapā.* Hence to propose an invariable concomitance between the fall into the seventh hell and the inability to achieve *mokṣa* is fallacious. Because of this lack of causal connection, the Digambara argument remains inconclusive.

#17 On the face of it, the Śvetāmbara argument seems conclusive enough. But the Digambara response, which I have found in only a single text, the *Nyāyakumudacandra* of Prabhācandra (c. eleventh century), is worth noting.[11] Prabhācandra rejects the Śvetāmbara indictment of the Digambara claim, based as it is on the inherent problems involved in establishing a cause-and-effect relationship between falling into the seventh hell and going to *mokṣa.* He instead advocates a different type of relationship: that of indicator (*gamaka*) and indicated (*gamya*). Prabhācandra rejects the fault shown by the Śvetāmbara of the absence of invariable concomitance between going to the seventh hell and going to *mokṣa,* because the law of concomitance does not necessarily depend on a cause-and-effect relationship or on a relationship of pervasion based on identity. Invariable concomitance is possible even if the relationship pertaining between those things is merely that of a single cognition invariably linking two disparate things (*gamya-gamaka-bhāva*). In the cognition of the rise of the asterism Kṛttikā (the Pleiades), for example, the following rise of the constellation Śakaṭa ("the Cart," the five stars forming the next asterism Rohiṇī) can invariably be inferred, even though there is no causal relationship (or identity relationship) between the two asterisms. A similar relationship of indicator/ indicated exists between falling into the seventh hell and attaining *mokṣa*; thus the mutually accepted fact that women do not fall into the seventh hell is a valid condition for inferring that women do not attain *mokṣa*. Any attempt to claim otherwise would yield the undesirable consequence of denying the valid relationship pertaining between the rise of Kṛttikā and the rise of Śakaṭa.

Prabhācandra is careful to point out here that the two capacities of going to the seventh hell and going to *mokṣa* are in no way directly related. However, he proposes a certain inherence (*samavāya*) of these two capacities in a single whole, the soul of the individual person. Hence if a single soul has the capacity to fall into the seventh hell through extremely demeritorious action, that same soul must have the similar capacity to attain *mokṣa* through extremely pure actions. Thus the Digambaras are merely claiming that the inability of women to perform such extremely impure actions as would result in falling into the seventh hell allows one to infer that women are equally incapable of performing those perfectly pure actions—that is, to achieve the absolute perfection of the Three Jewels—which allow one to attain *mokṣa*. Without the absolute perfection of the Three Jewels, *mokṣa* will be impossible, for the law does not allow a result to follow without an initial cause. Therefore, the Digambaras reject the Śvetāmbara claim that there is no association between falling into the seventh hell and attaining *mokṣa*.

#18 The Siddha-loka—the abode of the emancipated soul, wherein the soul remains eternally at the summit of the universe in all its omniscient glory—provides the next occasion for investigating a relevant scriptural passage that seems to allude to the possibility of a woman's attaining *mokṣa*. In an aphorism appearing in the tenth chapter of the *Tattvārthasūtra*—the only Jaina treatise accepted by both the Digambaras and Śvetāmbaras (including the Yāpanīyas)—the author, Umāsvāti, lists the types of liberated souls from the standpoint of their worldly status prior to becoming Siddhas.[12] Some Siddhas, for example, attained *mokṣa* from the continent of Jambudvīpa, while others attained it from elsewhere; some attained Siddhahood at the time of a Tīrthaṅkara's appearance in the world, whereas others attained it in their absence. The controversial point in this aphorism is that the category of *liṅga*, literally "sign" but ordinarily referring to biological gender, is also listed.

The Jaina texts refer to three biological genders: male (*puṃliṅga*); female (*strīliṅga*); and indeterminate (*napuṃsaka-liṅga*), which roughly corresponds to a hermaphrodite in that its gender sign is not strictly male or female. By the last gender, Jainas understood only those who were born with features not explicitly male or female and not such beings as eunuchs, who might be neutered after birth. Both sects believed that these three gender signs were the results of *nāma-karma*, that is, a *karma* which projects the appropriate bodies whereby one can distinguish a being as heavenly, infernal, animal, or human and recognize its sex within this destiny. It was also further believed by both sects that a hermaphrodite may not receive ordination, as its physical condition produced an incurable restlessness of mind that prevented it from the kind of concentration required for spiritual exercises. Its physical gender thus created mental indecision as to the objects of its sexual desire, which produced in turn an eternal insatiability of mind.

Corresponding to these three *liṅgas*, which were permanent physical features of one's given life, the Jainas also proposed there psychological sexual inclinations. Called *vedas*, these were the products of deluding (*mohanīya*) karma, which was responsible for the arousal of sexual desires (veda, i.e., libido). A male's desire for a female would thus be known as *puṃveda*, or male libido; a female's desire for a male as *strīveda*, or female libido; and a hermaphrodite's desire for both male and female as *napuṃsakaveda*, or the hermaphrodite libido.[13] Regardless of their biological gender (*liṅga*), all human beings were believed capable of experiencing any of the three vedas. These libidos, however, must be totally annihilated by means of righteous meditation (*dharmadhyāna*) before a person could practice the purest meditation (*śukladhyāna*), a precondition for the attainment of Arhatship. The Siddha—a designation the Jainas applied exclusively to the totally disembodied soul of an Arhat after his death—was thus evidently free from both physical *liṅga* and psychological veda; yet, in a conventional manner, he could still be described as a Siddha who was formerly male or female (by gender) or a Siddha who experienced formerly, as he climbed to the summit of the spiritual path, any of the three libidos. The word "*liṅga*" that appears in this *sūtra* of Umāsvāti is used by the Śvetāmbara to corroborate his contention that the scriptures allow *mokṣa* not only for males but also for females and even certain hermaphrodites (the noncongenital type).

#19 The Digambaras, who admit the appearance of the word "*liṅga*" in this *sūtra*, contend, however, that the word should be interpreted instead as the psychological veda, whether of the male, the female, or the hermaphrodite. They cling to their belief that only a person who is physically male (i.e., a monk) is intended by the *sūtra*. According to them the terms "*strī*" and "*napuṃsaka*" are used there (i.e., in the terms "*strīliṅga-Siddha*" and "*napuṃsakaliṅga-Siddha*") to refer not to a former woman or a former hermaphrodite but to the past state of that kind of a monk who had started to climb the spiritual ladder (*guṇasthāna*, culminating in his Arhatship) with either a female libido (*strīveda*) or a hermaphrodite libido (*napuṃsakaveda*). Such a monk may be called metaphorically female or hermaphrodite in view of this strange orientation, giving rise to such expressions as *strīliṅga*-Siddha or *napuṃsakaliṅga*-Siddha. Physically, however, he is male and had to destroy all forms of veda long before he could arrive at the stage of the Arhat (the thirteenth *guṇasthāna*) and finally become a Siddha (who is even beyond the *guṇasthāna* ladder).

#20 Although the Yāpanīya author Śākaṭāyana rejected the very idea of distinguished libido along the lines of biological gender, arguing that sex desire, like anger or pride, is the same in man, woman, or hermaphrodite, this seems to be his personal view, for the scriptures of both the Śvetāmbara and the Digambara sects accept the theory of three libidos. The Śvetāmbaras therefore reject the Digambara interpretation of the Scriptural passage on a different ground. They retort that if a man may be allowed to attain *mokṣa* even when he had previously experienced *strīveda* (which was unnatural to him), then there are no grounds for denying *mokṣa* to a woman when she also similarly experienced *strīveda* (which was, of course, natural to her). Moreover, if indulging in a sexual inclination that is contrary to his nature does not prevent a man from attaining *mokṣa*, then surely that option should be available to a woman also, and thus she too should be able to attain *mokṣa* if she has experienced *puṃveda*.

#21 The Digambara reply to this objection appears in the following syllogism:

> A being who is unable to attain *mokṣa* because of its physical body must necessarily be unable to attain it mentally also;
> as, for example, animals and other nonhuman beings [who are barred from attaining *mokṣa*];
> a woman is unable to attain *mokṣa* because of her female body; therefore she is unable to attain *mokṣa* even by experiencing the male libido.[14]

The Digambaras thus propose that, regardless of the type of sexuality a person may entertain internally, only a person who is physically male has the ability to destroy all karmas through the perfection of *śukladhyāna*. The Digambaras' contention therefore follows from their fundamental idea that a female body is somehow inferior to a male body, as is expressed in the following syllogism:

> Woman are not worthy of attaining *mokṣa*;
> because they are inferior to men (*hīnatvāt*);
> as are hermaphrodites.[15]

#22 This fundamental inferiority of females is enunciated in the following argument used by the Digambaras:

> A female body is not able to destroy the hosts of karmas;
> because it is produced in association with that evil karma called wrong view (*mithyātva*);
> as is the case with the bodies of hell beings and so forth.[16]

The significance of this syllogism is very grave. The Digambaras have maintained that a person who generates the Jaina view of reality (*samyaktva* or *samyak-darśana*) may never again be reborn a female, regardless of whether at that time the person was male or female.[17] Although being born a man does not invariably mean that the person is endowed with *samyaktva*, birth as a woman is a sure indication that the soul inhabiting that body was endowed with *mityātva* at the moment of birth. This rule applies invariably to all women, according to the Digambaras, including even the mothers of the Tīrthaṅkaras. Of course, there is nothing to prevent a woman from generating *samyaktva* at a subsequent moment in her life but, unlike men, she is considered incapable of perfecting it in her present body.

This lack of perfection proceeds as a direct result of her female body. As Kundakunda pointed out, her genital organs and the area between her breasts are a breeding ground of minute forms of life. (This lead the Śvetāmbara author Meghavijaya to conclude: "For this reason, women suffer from constant itching caused by these beings, which does not allow them ever to have any cessation of sexual desire;" see chapter VI, #12.) Menstruation is seen as a source of injury (*hiṃsā*) to infinite numbers of submicroscopic lives, the demise of which inevitably disturbs the woman. Her body in general and menstruation in particular cause in her extreme forms of anxiety and mental restlessness (from which males by the very nature of their bodies are always free), thus preventing her from focusing her mind firmly on the holy path. It is even believed that the flow of menstrual blood is not an involuntary (i.e., natural) function of a woman's body but the result of a sexual volition (veda, a variety of *mohanīya-karma* responsible for the emergence of sexual passion), a phenomenon comparable to a man's emission of semen (*vīrya*) during a dream.[18] Her menstrual cycles are thus constant reminders to her as well as others that she is sexually desirable. This awareness begets shame (*lajjā*), which in turn leads to dependency on wearing clothes in order to shield herself from the lurid glances of men. It also makes her subject to the constant fear of being sexually assaulted by males thus making her dependent on society at large for protection. These two constant factors of shame and fear, which the Digambaras believe men may overcome, render a woman unfit to undertake the higher vows (*mahāvratas*) of a mendicant or to pursue the upper reaches of the meditational states through which alone one may extirpate the libido (i.e., the veda) and thereby climb to the summit of the purest meditation (*śukladhyāna*), which must terminate in *mokṣa*. For all these reasons, the Digambaras believe that the body of a woman is itself enough to render a woman incapable of attaining *mokṣa*.

#23 Strange as it may seem the Śvetāmbaras concur with the Digambara view that a person who has *samyaktva* at the time of his (or her) death may never again be reborn as a female. All the same, the Śvetāmabaras have claimed there is one exception to this rule. This exception is described as an *āścarya*, or an extraordinary event, indeed a miracle; it applies to the person of Malli, the nineteenth Jina, the only female of the twenty-four Jinas of our time, of whom Mahāvīra was the last.[19] It may be of some interest for us to look into the legend of this female Jina, as it provides a rare insight into the factors thought to lead to rebirth as a woman.

#24 According to Śvetāmbara legend, the soul that later became the female Malli was in a former (third from the last) life a king named Mahābala.[20] King Mahābala renounced the world together with seven friends, and they all became Jaina mendicants. It is customary for Jaina monks to engage in special austerities, such as fasting. All eight monks made a solemn agreement to undertake an identical number of fasts as part of their austerities. Now, Mahābala was by nature deceitful and constantly found excuses (such as ill health) to skip meals and thus broke the agreement by deviously accumulating a larger number of fasts than his friends. His conduct was otherwise faultless, and as a consequence of his great exertions in leading a holy life he generated such karmic forces as would yield him rebirth as a would-be Jina—that is, one whose conception (*garbha*), birth (*janma*), renunciation (*dīkṣā*), enlightenment (*kevalajñāna*), and death (*nirvāṇa*) would be celebrated as auspicious events (*kalyāṇa*) by gods and men. Even according to the Śvetāmbara canon a Jina must possess a male body, but because of the cunning of the monk Mahābala he was, after completing a long period in a heaven, reborn among the humans not as a male Jina but as Malli, a female. Since it is inconceivable that a would-be Jina could be devoid of *samyaktva* at birth, the Śvetāmbaras conclude that Malli was an exception to both karmic rules of rebirth—that a Jina must not be a female and that a woman may not be endowed with *samyaktva* at birth.

The legend tells us that whereas the monk Mahābala was born as a princess named Malli (lit., jasmine flower—because of her great beauty), the other seven monks were reborn as men, members of the warrior caste, rulers of neighbouring kingdoms. They all sought Malli's hand in marriage and even went to war over her. Disgusted to be regarded as a sexual object and to be the cause of violence, she renounced the world while still young and, having gained *kevalajñāna* or omniscience on the very day of her renunciation, became a Jainas, thus attaining the status equal to that of Mahāvīra. The Yāpanīyas appear to be unaware of this legend; the Digambaras vehemently reject it as blasphemy and consider it a Śvetāmbara fabrication to support their theory that a nun can attain *mokṣa.* According to them Malli (or rather Mallinātha as he is called) was male, a member of a royal family and pursued the career of a would-be Jina in the same manner as did the other Jinas, that is, by strictly observing the vows of a Digambara monk. Notwithstanding these two versions of the story, we may note that all Jainas share in the belief that such vices as cheating and crookedness (called *māyā* in Jaina texts) are the fundamental causes of rebirth as a woman.[21]

#25 Returning to the Digambara argument that a person with *samyaktva* may not be reborn as a woman, the Śvetāmbara contends that this karmic rule in itself should not hinder a woman's attaining *mokṣa,* since, as even the Digambaras admit, *samyaktva* can be generated at a subsequent time in a woman's life; thus an initial presence of *mithyātva* need not prevent a woman from later attaining the same goal as a male. With respect to the oft-repeated Digambara objection concerning a woman's dependence on wearing clothes—which allegedly stands in the way of her perfecting right conduct (*samyak-cāritra*) to the same level as a naked male mendicant—the Śvetāmbaras say that clothes are not to be considered possessions (*parigraha*) for a nun but rather aids to leading the holy life; they therefore are comparable to the small whisk broom (*rajoharṇa* or *piñchī,* a bunch of peacock feathers), allowed even for a Digambara monk.

#26 This brings us to what is probably the worst stumbling block in reconciling the Digambara and Śvetāmbara positions: the dispute over the permissibility of a monk's wearing clothes, on the one hand, and the prohibition against nudity for women, on the other, which virtually precluded women from *mokṣa*. The following syllogism is proposed by the Digambaras:

> The holy conduct of women is insufficient to attain *mokṣa*;
> because that conduct is dependent upon possessions [i.e., clothes];
> as in the case of householders [who are also barred from attaining *mokṣa* because of their property and other possessions].[22]

#27 The Śvetāmbara answer to this argument is, as pointed out earlier, that clothes should be considered an aid to the attainment of *mokṣa*, as are such requisites as the whisk broom, and should not be called property (*parigraha*). The Śvetāmbaras accept the Digambaras' assertion that a householder may not attain *mokṣa*, but the cause they cite is his attachment to possessions, which nuns are presumed to have overcome. The *Tattvārthasūtra* (vii, 12) declares that "Possession means attachment" (*mūrcchā*); for the Śvetāmbaras, therefore, attachment, not possession, is the issue. In the absence of such attachment, a nun's wearing clothes should be considered conducive to her keeping the percepts as well as indicative of her obedience to the injunction against nudity. The Digambaras might still insist that, despite her lack of attachment, a nun remains infatuated with clothes simply because she is compelled to continue wearing them. But the Śvetāmbaras reject this claim, raising the comparison of a Digambara mendicant seated in meditation on whom clothes are forced: if the Digambaras believe that that monk, because of the continued presence of nonattachment in his mind, has not broken the vow of nonpossession (*aparigraha*) even though he is "wearing" clothes at the time, they would also have to admit that a nun is similarly not rendered unfit for *mokṣa* just because she too is compelled to wear clothes.

#28 The Digambara counters this apparently unassailable argument by demonstrating the crucial difference between the nun and the monk in the example. In the case of the Digambara monk on whom clothes are forced, the Digambara maintains that the monk will certainly discard those clothes once he rises from his meditation. Even more important, once those clothes fall from his body, he will not entertain the thought of picking them up—certain proof of his being truly unattached to clothes. In the case of a nun, however, if clothes fall off her, she will deliberately pick them up—a sure sign of her continued attachment to those clothes. This point can be proved in the following manner:

> If something that has fallen is deliberately picked up, this proves there is no absence of attachment in the person who so picks it up;
> as in the case of gold and so forth [being picked up].
> Women do deliberately pick up clothes [when fallen];
> therefore, there is no absence of attachment for nuns, since they deliberately pick up [thing that have fallen].[23]

#29 The Śvetāmbara rejoinder is simply that a nun is merely obeying the injunction to remain clothed. But the dilemma over whether attachment is present in her remains unresolved. The Śvetāmbara reply to this argument is that a nun's picking up clothes is comparable to a naked monk's picking up his whisk broom when he rises from his meditation, an act that is also deliberate and yet considered blameless.

#30 The Digambaras' answer leads us back to their original premise that clothes are not appropriate requisites for keeping the precepts. They maintain that the monk uses the whisk broom to protect the lives of small insects that might alight on his seat; it is, therefore, a legitimate requisite for keeping his precept of *ahiṃsā*. Clothes, on the contrary, are a breeding ground for lice and their eggs; they also give rise to many anxieties and further one's dependence on the lay people who produce them. Precisely for these reasons the Tīrthaṅkaras have declared that clothes are possessions which should be renounced by an aspirant, in the same way that he should renounce such internal possessions as wrong views and passions. The following syllogism is offered in defence of this position:

Clothes are not conducive to *mokṣa*;
because their renunciation is enjoined;
as [is the renunciation of] wrong views.[24]

The Digambara position in this regard does not allow any compromise. The Digambara therefore insists that a woman wears clothes not so much to guard her precepts as to hide her shame (*lajjā*, a form of passion born of *mohanīya*-karma) and to protect herself from possible attack.

#31 The Śvetāmbara admits that washing and wearing clothes may entail some superficial harm. But he maintains that the great spiritual benefits that accrue to women from wearing clothes—without which they would be unable to lead the holy life—more than outweigh the slight amount of injury (*hiṃsā*) that those clothes engender. Clothes, therefore, should not be considered an impediment to *mokṣa* for women.

#32 The Digambara answer to this rejoinder is that they too prefer, indeed require, that nuns wear clothes; they too are not blind to the spiritual advantages that accrue to women who try to follow in the footsteps of the mendicant monks. But they insist that the paths of those male mendicants who go without clothes (*acelaka*) and those female religious who wear clothes (*sacelaka*) are fundamentally different and do not lead to the same goal. By logic, paths that begin separately cannot end in the same goal; therefore the Digambara rejects the equivalence of these two paths. The holy life of a nun falls a great deal short of complete renunciation and thus is ultimately comparable to the religious life of a layperson. Therefore, like the householder, she may be admitted to heaven, but she will be unable to attain mokṣa in her present life. If the Śvetāmbaras nonetheless continue to insist that a man's wearing clothes does not violate the precepts concerning nonpossession (*aparigraha*) or noninjury (*ahiṃsā*), then they must also admit that one of these two kinds of *mokṣa* is inferior to the other—a position their own scripture does not support.

#33 The significance of the scriptural passages cited above by the Digambaras and Śvetāmbaras concerning the inability of women either to fall into the seventh hell or to renounce clothes completely is debatable. But the adherents of the two sects have not relied entirely on scriptural testimony in advocating their beliefs. The Digambaras in particular have sought to strengthen their arguments by taking recourse to the inferior position of women both within Indian society as a whole as well as within the ecclesiastical order.

Although the Upaniṣads attest to the debating abilities of Brāhmaṇical women like Gārgī Vācaknavī (Zaehner, 1966, pp. 55-57), it is a lamentable fact of Indian monastic life that although technically women were not denied the study of the scriptures, it was certainly not their forte. There must, of course, have been learned women both in the Jaina and Buddhist orders of nuns, and they would probably have been allowed at one time to take part in the debates commonly held between adherents of rival schools, as witnessed by such texts as the Jaina *Uttarādhyayana-sūtra* and the Buddhist *Therīgāthā*. But in the postcanonical period of both religions, the role of women gradually receded until ultimately they were allowed to study only the most rudimentary texts pertaining to conduct, not the rival philosophical doctrines that men publicly debated. Participation in such debates was not merely a matter of scholarship; it also demanded demonstrable occult powers, whereby the guardian deities (*śāsana-devatā*) of one's own school—for example, the goddesses Cakareśvarī for the Jainas and Tārā for the Buddhists—could be summoned to help defeat one's rival.[25] Such powers, called *labdhis*, were deemed the prerogative of males only, who generated them through the impetus of their austerities and yogic powers. The laity, of course, was considered incapable of developing such powers, but society at large regarded nuns equally powerless, barred by their sex from invoking these deities or from indulging in any form of Tantric practices to call up these "guardians". For the Digambaras, the incompetence of nuns in such mundane matters as the ability to engage in debates or to generate occult powers indicated that they were equally incapable in such supramundane concerns as attaining that omniscience which is produced through extraordinary moral purity.

#34 The Śvetāmbaras' rejoinder is to the point: women may not participate in debate or develop occult powers; but there is no proof that such things are invariably linked with *mokṣa*. Even the Digambaras must admit that countless souls, known as *mūka-kevalins* (or silent Omniscient Beings) have attained *mokṣa* without uttering even a single word. Therefore, unless the Digambaras are able to prove an invariable concomitance between engaging in debate and attaining *mokṣa*, their point is moot and actually reflects social prejudice, which is totally out of place in serious discussion.

#35 While the Digambaras cannot demonstrate any invariable concomitance between the two factors, their rebuttal falls back on their central thesis: women cannot achieve the perfection of holy conduct and hence are unable to attain *mokṣa*. Their inference is again based on the indicator/indicated relationship: this imperfection is proved, they say, by women's inability to participate in debate or generate psychic powers, which allegedly result not so much from learning as from the rigours of austerities (*tapas*) and the purity of conduct. According to them, the latter are possible only to a Digambara monk, not to a nun, who fails to achieve purity of conduct.

#36 The disparity between the status of nuns and monks within the Śvetāmbara order provides the Digambara with still another point on which to reassert their original claim that women are inherently inferior to men and thus may not attain *mokṣa*. As was observed above, in the Digambara sect a woman may rise no higher than to the status of an advanced laywoman (*uttama-śrāvikā*), even though she is given the title "nun" (*āryikā*) out of courtesy. Her position, therefore, both technically and in practice, is inferior to that of a monk, though superior to that of laypeople. But this is not so in the Śvetāmbara sect. There women are considered the equals of men in leading the holy life, since both assume the same mendicant precepts and may possess the same degree of perfection in conduct. Technically, therefore, there is no disparity between them, although in practical terms a Śvetāmbara nun fares little better than her Digambara counterpart. This is manifest from the Śvetambara mendicant law, which stipulates that:

> Even if a nun is ordained for a hundred years she must pay homage to a young monk, even if that monk has been ordained that very day, by going forth to meet him and by greeting him in reverence.[26]

She may, moreover, confess to monks and be admonished by

them but is prohibited from assuming those duties herself. The Digambaras seized on this discrepancy between the technical and practical status of Śvetāmbara nuns and asserted that the nuns' inferior status in the rival ecclesiastical order proves their inherent inferiority in reaching the required perfection without which *mokṣa* would be impossible.

#37 The Śvetāmbaras' reply to this challenge is virtually identical to the previous one: there is no logical connection, let alone any invariable concomitance, between having one's greetings returned and attaining *mokṣa.* They use the example of a teacher and his disciple to illustrate this point: the teacher may not greet the disciple, but the disciple can still attain *mokṣa.* The Digambaras' rebuttal is also a restatement of their earlier position. Agreed, there is no concomitance between being greeted and going to *mokṣa*; however, the Śvetāmbaras must not forget that only those disciples who first attain perfection will attain *mokṣa,* and attaining perfection is not a universal occurrence. Otherwise, the Śvetāmbara would have to admit that all disciples, regardless of their preparation, may attain *mokṣa.*

In support of their claim, the Digambaras offer a counter example of the sons and daughters of a king. According to Indian laws of primogeniture only the eldest son may inherit the throne; however, the disenfranchised princes do not then become equal in status to the princesses. Princes may be considered for kingship under different circumstances; princesses, however, are never entitled to inherit the throne. In the same way, whether a disciple is greeted by a teacher or not, he may attain *mokṣa* only if he achieves the required moral perfection; it is therefore invalid to compare him to women, who are inherently ineligible for that achievement.

#38 In continuation of the same argument, the Digambara shows the inferiority of women with regard to worldly status as well. The inference is syllogistically framed:

> There is no attainment of the higher status [i.e., *mokṣa*] by women;
> because they are unworthy of the higher status desired by yogins, householders, or gods;
> as is the case with hermaphrodites.[27]

The Digambaras assert that the highest status attainable by a layman is that of the *cakravartin* (universal) king, while the highest status attainable by a heavenly being is that of Śakra (Indra), the king of the gods. No female is ever known to have attained either of these two most exalted states. Since even these worldly statuses are denied to women, it follows that they would certainly not be able to attain the supramundane status of Siddhahood. In every household as well, the man, not the woman, is master of the house. This situation also indicates to the Digambaras the inherent inferiority of women.

#39 The sectarian dispute between the Digambaras and Śvetāmbaras concerning the salvation of women might never have taken place if the Śvetāmbara scriptures had not affirmed that Mahāvīra himself (unlike Gautama the Buddha, for example) had practiced nudity and that women could not be reborn in the lowest hell (a matter on which all other Indian schools are also silent). The debate between the two sects, as outlined above, hinges on the significance of these two factors for understanding the Jaina attitude toward the position of woman as mendicant and her ability to attain that perfection (allegedly attained by men) without which *mokṣa* is not possible. For the Digambaras, it is a woman's anatomy that prevents her from observing the highest precepts of mendicancy (inclusive of nakedness), which in turn accounts for her lack of moral perfection. For the Śvetāmbara, possession denotes not the material things themselves but mental attachment to them. The crucial point of the controversy would thus appear to be the definitions of the words "*parigraha*" and "*vītarāga*"—that is, what constitutes a possession and what is its relationship to the absence of passion? Given the entirely literal interpretation of the term "*parigraha*" by the Digambaras, and the Śvetāmbara claim that clothes per se do not constitute possession whether for a man or a woman, it is not surprising that the Jainas could not resolve the problem of a nun's *mokṣa*. Furthermore, to non-Jainas the whole argument would appear to be fallacious, since it is not possible to prove a person's freedom from passions from his lack of possessions. This was in fact pointed out by the great Buddhist logician Dharmakīrti, who used the Digambara argument to illustrate a logical fallacy called "uncertainty" (*sandigdha*). To quote Dharmakīrti, the following Digambara statements are wrong:

> Kapila [the Sāṃkhya teacher] and others are not free from passions;
> because they are subject to the acquisition of property.

and

> One who is free form passions is not subject to acquisition;
> for example, Ṛṣabha, the Jaina teacher.[28]

The Jaina argument, says Dharmakīrti, is fallacious because the relationship between the lack of freedom from passions and acquisitions, as well as their absence in Ṛṣabha, is dubious. Hence this is a case of the negative example being defective inasmuch as one can doubt the absence of both the thing to be proved (*sādhya*) and the reason thereof (*hetu*).[29] This dubious relationship itself is the only thing that allows the contrary claims of the two Jaina sects to stand—the Digambara view that a woman cannot achieve the perfection of pure conduct (*samyak-cāritra*) and the Śvetāmbara contention that clothes do not constitute *parigraha* and therefore do not prevent a woman from attaining perfection equivalent to that of a male.

Non-Jaina Traditions of Mendicancy and Salvation for Women

#40 The Jaina debates on the salvation of women summarized above are indeed unique in the history of the religious literature of India. There is nothing even remotely parallel to this discussion in the whole Brāhmaṇical tradition, whether in the Vedic scriptures, the epics, or the law books (the *Dharmaśāstras*). Traditional Brāhmaṇical society certainly does uphold the fourfold system of *āśramas* culminating in *sannyāsa*, or renunciation, but unlike the Jainas, it never claimed that to be the exclusive path to *mokṣa*. Even when asceticism was the preferred path, Brāhmaṇical society never approved of mendicancy for women and made marriage mandatory for all women. After the death of her husband, a woman of the Brahman caste might to all appearances lead the life of a nun by observing chastity, shaving her head, and sleeping on the floor, yet she was not free to leave the household and join a mendicant order composed of other women like her. However pure the life of a widow, the lawbooks promise her nothing more than a rebirth in heaven, implying that that is the highest goal a woman can reach.[30] Probably the *Bhagavad-Gītā* is the first sacred text that even mentions a *parā-gati* (highest goal, i.e., *mokṣa*) in connection with women. Here too the author of the *Gītā* shows his disdain for women by bracketing them with members of the two lower castes, namely the Vaiśyas and the Śūdras, all described as baseborn (*pāpa-yonayaḥ*, lit., born from the very womb of sin) and declares that they too may attain *parā-gati* through devotion to the Lord.[31] It is not absolutely clear, however, whether such a woman will attain the "highest goal" in her present body and present life, a matter of contention in the Jaina debates discussed above.

#41 A comparison with Buddhism on this point is far more instructive. It is well known that Gautama, the Buddha, agreed only reluctantly, and only toward the end of his lifetime, to the establishment of an order of nuns (*bhikṣuṇīsaṅgha*). The Buddha is noted for his refusal to answer a great many philosophical questions, but fortunately he was quite specific on the question of a woman's ability to attain *nirvāṇa* in her present life. It is told that the Buddha thrice rejected his aged aunt's implorings to become a nun. At this point the venerable Ānanda intervened to ask the Buddha if women were capable of attaining *nirvāṇa*. The Buddha's answer was unhesitatingly affirmative and led immediately to the ordination of Mahāprajāpatī Gautamī, his aunt, as the first member of the Buddhist order of nuns.[32] Had the Jainas also asked a similar question of Mahāvīra, himself a contemporary of the Buddha, the Jaina debates discussed above might not have taken place. But then the Buddha categorically condemned nudity, whereas Mahāvīra practiced it himself and even advocated it for his disciples. The Jainas were thus left with a legacy of debating the status of a "sky-clad" versus a "cloth-clad" mendicant (who claimed clothing as an option) and especially the status of a nun who was left with no choice but to remain clad like a householder and thereby was liable to forfeit her right to attain *mokṣa*.

#42 Notwithstanding the Buddha's categorical admission that

a Buddhist nun can attain the same goal of Arhatship attainable by a monk, the Buddhists were not able to grant equal status to a nun within the mendicant order. In fact, the first of the Eight Major Rules (*gurudharma*) that applied only to a nun as a condition of her entering the saṅgha reads:

> A nun, even if a hundred years old [by ordination] must pay respect to a monk even if he has been ordained just the day before.[33]

The rule, as seen above, is almost identically applied to the nuns in the Śvetāmbara order. The Śvetāmbara position on the status of a woman appears very similar to that of the early Buddhists. Both believed that a woman was capable of attaining Arhatship, yet was inferior to a man in the matter of ecclesiastical organization. Both saw no contradiction in this dual standard, since a woman's status in the saṅgha only reflected her standing in lay society.

#43 The Digambara position, by contrast, appears to correspond to another Buddhist view according to which a woman may attain Arhatship but may not become a Buddha. Being born male (*puṃliṅga-sampatti*) was a precondition of being a Buddha.[34] No female Buddhas have ever been mentioned in the Buddhist texts, either in Pali or in Sanskrit. The prejudice against the female sex must have been deep-rooted in the popular mind. In the Pali *Jātaka*, for example, which narrates the stories of five hundred and forty-seven past lives of the Bodhisattva Gautama, there is not a single instance of his birth as a female, not even in his animal rebirths.[35] The Mahāyāna texts also are not exempt from the belief that a Buddha must be male. Witness, for example the story in the *Saddharmapuṇḍarīka-sūtra* of the eight-year-old Bodhisattva maiden Sāgara-Nāgarāja-duhitā, whose sex changes when a prophecy is made that she will become a Buddha.[36] Notwithstanding the *Prajñāpāramitā-sūtra* proclamations that matters of sex and physicality fall in the realm of convention, or similar grand utterances in such texts as the *Vimalakīrtinirdeśa*,[37] there has been no change in the belief that only males can become Buddhas. Add to this belief the singular doctrine of the *Saddharmapuṇḍarīka-sūtra* that *nirvāṇa* was attainable only by becoming a Buddha, and that the Hīnayāna Arhats were wrong in presuming that they had attained *nirvāṇa*, and we are led to the stark conclusion that only a male (i.e., a Buddha) was capable of attaining *nirvāṇa*.[38] This doctrine of the *Saddharmapuṇḍarīka-sūtra*, designated sometimes as Ekayāna, affords a certain parallel with the Digambara position. For both, being male is a necessary but not sufficient condition for attaining *nirvāṇa*. In the Ekayāna, the female Bodhisattva in transformed into a male Bodhisattva prior to attaining Buddhahood; is the Digambara view, the nun's deficiency in assuming the great vow (*mahāvrata*) of total *aparigraha* (inclusive of nudity) must result in her eventual rebirth as a man to qualify for the attainment of *mokṣa*.

Contemporary Relevance of the Debate Among the Jainas

#44 It would be appropriate to ask if these debates, interesting as they are for understanding the sectarian differences within Jainism, have any relevance for those men and women who are actually engaged in practicing the Jaina mendicant discipline. For unlike Ājīvikism, which became extinct, and Buddhism, which disappeared from India a long time ago, the Jaina *śramaṇa* (ascetic) tradition has not only survived but continues to flourish in its motherland. And although the present-day Jaina community consists of no more than some six million people (of which the Digambaras probably constitute a third), the total membership of the Jaina mendicant order can still be counted in the thousands. The precise number of monks and nuns within the two Jaina sects is not known. Modern attempts to tabulate their number—by counting the groups of mendicants in their various residences for the duration of the rainy season—has yielded a figure of some twenty-five hundred monks and as many as six thousand nuns. The percentage of Digambara mendicants is quite small: no more than a hundred naked monks (*munis*) and probably even fewer nuns (*āryikās*). The remainder are all within the Śvetāmbara community, including their reformist (i.e., nonidol-worshiping) subsects, namely, the Sthānakavāsī and the Terāpanthī. If the figure of six thousand for the modern-day community of nuns (for the entire Jaina community of only six million adherents) sounds staggering, consider the canonical claim that at the death of Mahāvīra his saṅgha consisted of fourteen thousand monks and thirty-six thousand nuns.[39] If this belief is based on fact (and there is no basis to doubt this since both sects agree with this figure), then even if the number of nuns has decreased since the time of Mahāvīra, their ratio to the *munis* has not changed significantly. The inferior status of the nuns in the Śvetāmbara mendicant community notwithstanding, the numerical superiority they have enjoyed through the ages must have contributed tremendously in shaping the Jaina community. Their impact is especially evident in their ability to promote the individual asceticism of the Jaina laywomen who routinely undertake severe dietary restrictions and long periods of fasting and chastity. No sociological research of any depth has been done on these women to tell us about their family backgrounds or their personal reasons for renouncing the household life. A casual inquiry I conducted a few years ago among small groups of these nuns in the areas of Kathiavad in Gujarat and the Marwad in Rajasthan revealed that a great majority of them came from the affluent merchant castes, such as the Śrīmālīs or the Oswāls. Almost half of them were unmarried and had entered the mendicant life at a very young age (some even at the age of nine), and in many cases they were recruited into the order by a female member of their own family, such as an aunt or sister, who had been ordained earlier in a similar manner.[40]

#45 It is a moot question whether the Śvetāmbara approval of *mokṣa* for women has contributed in any way to the survival of Jaina nuns as a saṅgha, especially in a country like India, where no other religious community claims a similar group of women freed from the bondage of the household life. Apparently approval of *strīnirvāṇa* and the survival of a saṅgha of nuns are not connected, since the Theravādin Buddhists of the Union of Myanmar (formerly Burma), Laos, Thailand, and Sri Lanka, who also grant Arhatship to nuns and count thousands of Buddhist monks in their present mendicant ranks, cannot claim even a single nun. The reasons for the demise of the Bhikṣuṇīsaṅgha, even in the Buddhist kingdoms of Southeast Asia, are shrouded in mystery. The Buddha's own dire prediction that because of the admission of women to the saṅgha the "true dharma" would last only five hundred years (instead of a thousand) could not but have contributed to the indifference of Buddhists to the survival of the order of nuns.[41] All attempts on the part of Sri Lankan Buddhist laywomen called Dasasilamattawa to revive the Bhikṣuṇī order in modern times have failed because of lack of support from the community of monks.[42]

The Buddhists' ambivalence to their own sisters aspiring for mendicancy has no place in Jainism, which has in recent years reported great increase in the membership of their orders of nuns. Significant gains have been made, for example, by the relatively modern reformist Jaina sect known as the Terāpanthī (a subsect of the Sthānakavāsī sect, founded in Marwad in 1760), which has five hundred fully ordained nuns—more than three times the number of monks in that order. This sect has even introduced an organizational innovation of female novices called *śramaṇīs,* currently under training to join the order of nuns. The number of such *śramaṇīs* who have taken the vows of poverty and celibacy runs to the hundreds, and almost all are unmarried and well-educated women of the affluent Oswāl community of Rajasthan.[43] Enthusiasm to lead a religious life at so young an age is probably fostered by the self-esteem that the enhanced status of the nun in the family and in the Jaina community at large bolsters. One ventures to think that a sense of self-esteem, so conspicuous among these young women, probably derives from their being treated as equal to men in the spiritual realm, a possible consequence of the Śvetāmbara doctrine of *strīmokṣa.* By contrast one can see the extremely small and declining number of nuns in the Digambara community. Most of them were widows before entering the order and with a few notable exceptions are less effective as guides and teachers in their lay communities than their Śvetāmbara sisters. One cannot fail to conclude that the rejection of *strīmokṣa* might in some way have led to a lack of enthusiasm for asceticism among the Digambara women, discouraging them from actively pursuing the vocation of nuns.[44]

These notions are purely speculative, however, since all Jainas, regardless of their sectarian affiliations, believe that neither a man nor a woman can attain *mokṣa* during our degenerate times of the so-called *kaliyuga* (the age of vice), the fifth stage of time (*pañcamakāla*) in Jaina cosmology, which will last at least for another twenty thousand years. *Mokṣa* will be possible only when the next Jina, called Mahāpadma (who will be a contemporary of the future Buddha Maitreya),[45] will appear—and that will be millions of years hence, at the beginning of a new era. In the meantime the Jainas, whether male or female, are instructed to lead a righteous life, one that will prepare them for renunciation under the new Jina. Here the Śvetāmbara nun has a lead over her Digambara sister, since she may realize *mokṣa* in her female body. But the Digambara woman's priority will be to overcome her femininity, since according to the doctrine of that sect *mokṣa* is a male prerogative, attainable only by the "sky-clad" monk.

NOTES

1. On the canonical literature of the two Jaina sects, see *JPP*, Chapter II.
2. The word used for the Jaina monks in ancient times is *nirgrantha* and not "Digambara" or "Śvetāmbara"; see Chapter II (n. 12). For a discussion on the nature of the *jinakalpa* in the two tradition, see Chapter II (n. 35).
3. See Chapter 1 (#1-18) and a commentary on these verses in Chapter IV (#6-8).
4. For various traditions concerning the origin of the Yāpanīyas, see Chapter II (#3).
5. Selections from the Sanskrit texts on *strīmokṣa* from some of these Śvetāmbara works appear in the *Strīnirvāṇa-Kevalibhuktiprakaraṇe* (App. II.).
6. For this argument and its counterargument at #9, see Chapters III (#1) and V (#1 and n. 1).
7. For a longer list of arguments against *strīmokṣa*, see Chapter VI (#25-41).
8. For a diagrammatic representation of the Jaina universe and a description of the abode of the liberated souls, see *JPP*, pp. 128 and 270.
9. On the *śukladhyānas* that are gained only toward the very end of the Jaina spiritual path, see *JPP*, pp. 257-270.
10. See Chapter III (#34).
11. See Chapter III (#36-45).
12. "The perfected souls can be differentiated with reference to the region, the time, the basis of birth, the gender, the mendicant conduct, and so forth."
    kṣetrakālagatiliṅgatīrthacāritrapratyekabuddhabodhitajñānāvagāhanā 'ntarasaṃkhyā'lpabahutvena sādhyāḥ. [*Tattvārthasūtra*, x, 7]
13. For details on these vedas or "libidos," see Chapter VI (#1-6).
14. See Chapter III (#84).
15. See Chapter V (#1 and n. 1).
16. See Chapter II (#89).
17. See Chapters II (n. 57) and IV (#13).
18. See Chapter VI (#89).
19. Birth of a female Tīrthaṅkara (*itthītittham*) is listed among the ten

extraordinary events that take place once in an "infinite" time cycle: uvasaggagabbhaharaṇaṃ itthītitthaṃ abhāviyā parisā, kaṇhassa Avarakaṃkā uttaraṇaṃ caṃdasuriyāṇaṃ. [1] Harivaṃsakuluppattī Camaruppāo ya aṭṭhasayasiddhā, asaṃjayesu pūā dasavi aṇaṃteṇa kāleṇa. [2] *Sthānāṅgasūtra*, #1074 (*Suttāgame*, p. 314).

20. For the Śvetāmbara account of Malli, see *Nāyādhammakahāo*, chap. viii; Roth (1983); *Triṣaṣṭiśalākāpuruṣacaritra*, vol. IV, chap. 6. For the Digambara version, see *Uttarapurāṇa*, chap. 46.
21. The Śvetāmbara account of Malli ends with an exhortation that cunning, even if employed in matters of piety, leads to the calamity of rebirth as a woman:
uggatavasaṃjamavao pagiṭṭhaphalasāhagassavi jiyasa, dhammavisaye iv suhumā vi hoi māyā aṇatthāya. [1] jaha Mallissa Mahābalabhavammi titthayaranāmabaṃdhe 'vi, tavavisayathevamāyā jāyā juvaittahetutti. [2]
[*Nāyādhammakahāo*, I, viii, 85]
22. See Chapter III (#60).
23. See Chapter III (#57).
24. See Chapter III (#70).
25. For the story of the Jaina logician Akalaṅka being helped by the goddess Cakreśvarī against the Buddhists who were being helped by their goddess Tārā in a debate, see *Nyāyakumudacandra*, Pt. 1. intro., p. 36.
26. See Chapter VI (#18).
27. See Chapter VI (#34).
28. Sandigdhobhayavyatirekaḥ, yathā: avītarāgāḥ Kapilādayaḥ, parigrahāgrahayogād iti, atra vaidharmyodāharaṇam...yo vītarāgo na tasya parigrahāgrahaḥ, yathā Ṛṣabhāder iti. Ṛṣabhāder avītarāgatva-parigrahāgrahayogayoḥ sādhyasādhanadharmayoḥ sandigdho vyatirekaḥ.
[*Nyāyabindu-ṭīkā*, #132]
29. Commenting on the above, Dharmottara says:
yathā Ṛṣabhāder iti dṛṣṭāntaḥ. etasmād Ṛṣabhāder dṛṣṭāntād avītarāgasya parigrahāgrahayogasya ca sādhanasya nivṛttiḥ sandigdhā. Ṛṣabhādīnāṃ hi parigrahāgrahayogo 'pi sandigdho vītarāgatvaṃ ca. yadi nāma tatsiddhānte vītarāgāś ca paṭhyante tathāpi sandeha eva.
[*Nyāyabindu-ṭīkā*, #132]
"Now, it is doubtful whether really in the case of this Ṛṣabha both the predicate and the reason, both the fact of being subject to passions and having the instinct of property are absent. Indeed, it is not certain whether Ṛṣabha and consorts are really free from the instinct of property and from passions. Although in their own school they are declared to be such, but this is nevertheless, very doubtful". Stcherbatsky's translation of the *Nyāyabindu* in *Buddhist Logic*, II, p. 246.
30. nāsti strīṇām pṛthag yajño na vrataṃ nāpy upoṣaṇam, patiṃ śuśrūṣate yena tena svarge mahīyate. [*Manusmṛti*, v, 155]
pitā rakṣati kaumāre bhartā rakṣati yauvane, rakṣanti sthāvire putrā na strī svātantryam arhati. [*ibid.*, ix, 3]
nāsti striṇāṃ kriyā mantrair iti dharmavyavasthitiḥ, nirindriyā hy amantrāś ca striyo 'nṛtam iti sthitiḥ. [*ibid.*, ix, 18]
The theme of *strīmokṣa* is conspicuous by its absence in P. V. Kane's voluminous *History of Dharmaśāstra* with the exception of a single reference to the possibility of women securing knowledge of *mokṣa* (in the

absence of their access to the Vedic scripture) on p. 921, n. 1468a (vol. V, p. II). Several ancient literary works (e.g., the *Kādambarī* of Bāṇabhaṭṭa, p. 80) refer to *parivrājikās* (female wandering religious mendicants of the Brāhmaṇical tradition). These seem to be individuals who practiced asceticism without forming a community, unlike the Jaina or Buddhist nuns who invariably were members of a saṅgha (community of mendicant orders).

31. māṃ hi Pārtha vyapāśritya ye 'pi syuḥ pāpayonayaḥ, striyo vaiśyās tathā śūdrās te 'pi yānti parāṃ gatim.
[*Bhagavad-Gītā*, ix, 32. See Chapter VI (#82, n. 43)]

32. alam Ānanda, mā te rucci mātugāmassa tathāgatappavedite dhammavinaye agārasmā anagāriyaṃ pabbajjā ...bhabbo, Ānanda, mātugāmo arahattaphalam 'pi sacchikātuṃ.... [*Vinaya Piṭakam, Cullavagga*, x, 1]

33. For these rules in the Pali *Vinaya Piṭakaṃ* and the Sanskrit *Bhikṣuṇī-vinaya*, see Chapter VI (n. 17).

34. manussattaṃ liṃgasampatti hetu satthāradassanaṃ, pabbajjā guṇasampatti adhikāro ca chandatā; aṭṭhadhammasamodhānā abhinīhāro samijjhati. [1] manussattabhavasmiṃ yeva hi ṭhatvā Buddhattaṃ patthentassa patthanā samijjhati, ...manussattabhave pi purisaliṃge ṭhitass' eva patthanā samijjhati, —itthiyā vā paṇḍakanapuṃsaka-ubhato byañjanakānaṃ vā no samijjhati.... [*Jātaka*, I, p. 14]

35. For an apocryphal story (called the *Padīpadānajātaka)* of Gautama's last female incarnation, see Jaini (1989).

36. pañcasthānāni strī adyāpi na prāpnoti. katamāni pañca? prathamaṃ brahmasthānam, dvitīyaṃ śakrasthānam, tṛtīyaṃ mahārājasthānam, caturthaṃ cakravartisthānam, pañcamam avaivartika-bodhisattvasthānam...atha tasyāṃ velāyāṃ Sāgara-Nāgarājaduhitā sarvalokapratyakṣam....tat strīndriyam antarhitam, puruṣendriyaṃ ca prādurbhūtam, bodhisattvabhūtaṃ cātmānaṃ saṃdarśayati.
[*Saddharmapuṇḍarīka-sūtra*, chap. xi]
Loss of a female rebirth is also considered to be one of the fruits of reading the *Saddharmapuṇḍarīka-sūtra*:
sacet mātṛgrāma imaṃ dharmaparyāyaṃ śrutvā...dhārayiṣyati, tasya sa eva paścimaḥ strībhāvo bhaviṣyati. [*ibid.*, chap. xxii]

37. Translated by Thurman, chap. 7. For a discussion on the significance of the sex change as described in the seventh chapter (The Goddess) of the *Vimalakīrti-sūtra*, see Paul (1979, chap. 6.)

38. *Saddharmapuṇḍarīka-sūtra*, chap. v, verses 59-83.

39. For the number of monks and nuns in the mendicant community of Mahāvīra and that of the two earlier Jinas, namely Pārśva and Nemi, see *Kalpasūtra* (Jacobi's trans. 1884 pp. 267-285). For a detailed survey of the mendicants of the Śvetāmbara sect, see John Cort's forthcoming article "The Śvetāmbar Mūrtipūjak Sādhu."

40. Of the thirty-four nuns interviewed in the area of Kutch, for example, fifteen (with ages varying from 16 to 45) were widows, three (ages 23, 32 and 36) were married but had been permitted by their husbands to become nuns, and the remaining sixteen (between the ages of 9 and 23) were unmarried at the time of their ordination (*dīkṣā*). For a brief account of the lives of a few leading Jaina nuns, see Shāntā (1985, pp. 437-518).

41. sace, Ānanda, nālabhissa mātugāmo...pabbajjam, ciraṭṭhitikam, Ānanda, brahmacariyam abhavissa, vassasahassam saddhammo tiṭṭhyeyya, ...pañc'eva dāni, Ānanda, vassasatāni saddhammo ṭhassati.

[*Vinaya Piṭakam*, *Cullavagga*, X, ii, 2]

42. On the state of nuns in the Theravāda tradition, see Falk and Gross (1980). For a history of the Dasasilamattawas seeking the status of nun, see Bloss (1987).
43. See Shāntā (1985, pp. 358-361).
44. It may be useful in this connection to draw attention to the legend of a sectarian debate on *strīmokṣa* reported by the Śvetāmbara author Merutuṅga in his *Prabandhacintāmaṇi*, pp. 66-69. According to this narrative, during the reign of Siddharāja (twelfth century) in Gujarat, a great Digambara mendicant named Kumudacandra from the Deccan arrived in his capital city Aṇahillapura and challenged the Śvetāmbara monks to engage in a debate on this question. The Śvetāmbara ācārya Deva (later to be known as Vādideva) accepted his challenge and defeated him in a public debate held at the court of Siddharāja. The Digambara Kumudacandra died of humiliation and shock, and the Digambaras in the city were made to leave the country in disgrace. It is said that Siddharāja's chief queen Mayaṇalladevī (probably because she also hailed from Karnataka) initially favoured the Digambara monk and even openly urged him on to victory. When she was told that the Digambaras opposed liberation for women while the Śvetāmbaras upheld it, however, she shifted her allegiance to the latter. This debate is not attested in the Digambara tradition, but it is not unlikely that it is based on historical fact. This is probably the only extant literary evidence that openly declares a prominent woman's conversion to the side which upheld the spiritual liberation of women in preference to the one which had denied this privilege to her. This supports my assumption that the great disparity in the number of nuns in the two sects is a reflection of women's response to the more supportive attitude taken by the Śvetāmbara tradition toward them.
45. On Maitreya and the future Jina, see Jaini (1988).

ADDITIONAL NOTES

Additional reading: Leonard Zwilling and Michael J. Sweet, " 'Like a City Ablaze': The Third Sex and the Creation of Sexuality in Jain Religious Literature." *Journal of the History of Sexuality*, Vol. 6, no. 3, January 1996, University of Chicago Press, pp. 359-384.

CHAPTER 10

[*Kevali*]*Bhuktivicāra* of Bhāvasena: Text and Translation*

Introduction

In my article on the *Muktivicāra* of the thirteenth century Digambara author Bhāvasena, a brief reference was made to its companion text, the *Bhuktivicāra*, by the same author.[1] Only a single palm-leaf manuscript of this work has survived and is part of Professor Ernst Leumann's library at the Bibliothèque Nationale, Strasbourg. As described by Chandrabhal Tripathi, the manuscript (no. 164) is complete and consists of no more than five folios inscribed in the Kannada script.[2] As I set out to transcribe the text, I found it to be in an extremely unsatisfactory condition, full of illegible words and repetitious sentences. Even so, the work seems to deserve attention as it deals with an ancient controversy over the nature of an Omniscient Being in the Jaina tradition. I therefore present here an abridged version (omission indicated by...) which preserves all of the major arguments appearing in the original text.

'*Bhuktivicāra*' is, of course, the author's own abridgement for the full title, the *Kevali-bhuktivicāra*, an 'Investigation into the Eating of Food by a Kevalin'. The topic pertains to a controversy between the Digambaras and the Śvetāmbaras, the two ancient sects of Jainaism, over the ability of an Omniscient Being (called

*This article was published originally in *Researches in Indian and Buddhist Philosophy: Essays in Honour of Professor Alex Wayman*, ed. R. K. Sharma, (Delhi: Motilal Banarsidass, 1993), pp. 163-178. Reprinted with kind permission of Motilal Banarsidass, Delhi.

Kevalin or Arhat in the Jaina tradition) to survive a lifetime without partaking of any food or water (*kavala-āhāra*, lit. food made into morsels). Both sects agree that the attainment of kevalajñāna (lit. knowledge isolated from karmic bonds, i.e. omniscience) is preceded by the total destruction of all forms of the desire-producing karma (called *mohanīya*), and also that such a person, subsequent to his becoming a Kevalin, leads the normal life of a Jaina mendicant (e.g. moving from place to place, preaching sermons, and so forth) for the duration of his life. They agree further that the Kevalin is still subject to the karmic force called *vedanīya*, which must at all times produce the experience of either physical pain (*asātā*) or pleasure (*sātā*), feelings inseparable from the state of embodiment. The Śvetāmbaras accordingly believe that a Kevalin, regardless of the absence of desire for food, must still feel the pain of hunger, and hence, like any ordinary human being, will not subsist without eating food. The Digambaras find this unacceptable, for they believe that eating as well as bodily functions such as answering the calls of nature, are incompatible with total freedom from desires as well as omniscient cognition which characterize a Kevalin. They have therefore asserted that in the absence of *mohanīya-karma*, the *asātā-vedanīya* of the Kevalin is incapable of yielding its karmic fruit, thus removing the very reason for eating food, namely, hunger and thirst.[3] The Digambaras don't deny that some form of *āhāra* or food is essential for keeping the body alive. They maintain, however, that this is accomplished by an involuntary intake (*āhāra*) of a subtle material substance called *nokarma-vargaṇā*, a process common to all embodied beings. In the case of ordinary beings, this *nokarma-vargaṇā* must be supplemented by some other form of food for the sustenance of their bodies. But, according to the Digambaras, the Kevalin's body undergoes such a transformation that his *nokarma-vargaṇā* also provides him with all necessary nourishment.[4] The Digambaras therefore describe the Kevalin's body as *parama-audārika*, an extremely pure body, a miraculous body as it were, free from all impurities and sustained by no other 'food' than the *nokarma-vargaṇā*. The Śvetāmbaras find no scriptural support for this theory of the *parama-audārika* body, and believe that a Kevalin, and even as exalted a person as the Jina Mahāvīra himself, must partake of food to assuage his hunger and to sustain his body. The debate between these two rival sects is thus an attempt to define the true nature of a Kevalin, to resolve the apparent conflict that exists between his Desirelessness (*vītarāgatva*) and his need to eat (*bubhukṣā*), between his Infinite Bliss (*ananta-sukha*) and the pain of hunger and thirst.

The beginnings of this debate are shrouded in mystery and probably are as old as the sects themselves, as is demonstrated by Dundas in his brilliant discussion in an article aptly entitled 'Food and Freedom'.[5] There is ground to believe that it was initiated by a second-century Jaina mendicant sect called the Yāpanīya.[6] This sect is now extinct, but a major treatise (in 37 verses) entitled the *Kevalibhuktiprakaraṇa*, together with a prose *Svopajña-ṭīkā* by the ninth-century Yāpanīya author Śākaṭāyana has survived. A critical edition of this work, together with the *Strīnirvāṇa-prakaraṇa-Svopajñavṛtti* was published by Muni Jambūvijayajī in 1974.[7] This excellent edition also includes a most valuable appendix which reproduces discussions on this topic by later Śvetāmbara mendicant authors, notably, Śīlācārya's commentary on the *Sūtrakṛtāṅga*, Abhayadevasūri's *Sanmativṛtti*, and Vādi-Devasūri's *Syādvādaratnākara*. The appendix also contains the twelfth-century Digambara author Prabhācandra's presentation of the Śvetāmbara arguments (the *pūrvapakṣa*) as found in his *Nyāyakumudacandra*, but unfortunately not his refutation of the Śvetāmbara position.[8] The dispute between the sects continues well beyond Prabhācandra's time, as can be seen in such Śvetāmbara works as the *Tarkarahasya-ṭīkā* (on Haribhadra's *Ṣaḍdarśanasamuccaya*) of the fourteenth-century Guṇaratnasūri,[9] the *Yuktiprabodha-Svopanjñavṛtti* by the seventeenth-century Meghavijaya[10] and the *Adhyātmamataparīkṣā* by the eighteenth-century logician Yaśovijaya.[11] On the Digambara side, Prabhācandra probably has the last words on this debate, for no later work with the exception of the *Bhuktivicāra* of Bhāvasena (as produced here) has survived and the latter, as is clear from the text (#27), had access to it. The importance of this short work therefore lies not in any original contribution to the debate, for it makes none. Bhāvasena's work is nevertheless of significance for its display of open sectarian animosity toward the Śvetāmbaras, a hostility provoked by the dispute over the nature of the Kevalin, which leads him to regard his rival Jainas even lower than the heretic 'bhaktas' (see #29), evidently the devotees of Viṣṇu and Śiva.

Bhavasenaviracitaḥ [Kevali]bhuktivicāraḥ

#1 vīraṃ jineśvaraṃ natvā traividyaṃ vādivanditam /
Bhukti-Mukti-vicārārtham arthaśāstraṃ prakathyate //1//
anenaivārthaśāstreṇa svapakṣaḥ sādhyate 'dhunā /
vighaṭyate vipakṣo 'pi Śvetāṃbaramatāgatha. //2//...

#2 ...īha hi bhagavadarhatparameśvarasyotpanna-kevalajñānasya bhuktiyuktiṃ kaścit Śvetāmbaravādī darśayann āha—

#3 "śarīram ādyaṃ khalu dharmasādhanam"/ tac ca śarīraṃ pañcamahābhūtātmakama āhārapūrvakam / dehasthityar-tham āhāraḥ, āhārād ṛte dehasyāvasthānānupapatteḥ / sthūlakṛśatvaṃ hi dehasyāhārānvayavyatirekānuvidhāyī, sati śarīre āhāraparihāro du[ṣka]raḥ syāt / pakṣamāsaṣaṇ-māsābdāvasāne 'py ekavāram āhāreṇa bhavitavyam /...

#4 dehasahāyam vihāya sarvajñatvaṃ bhagavatah. kathaṃ kathayanti tathyavādinaḥ, dehādhārāhāraṃ na mukhyakāraṇam [iti] āhārāt suprasannamanasi buddher āvirbhāvo bhavati, indriyapāṭavaṃ prakaṭatām aṭaty aṅgaṃ puṣṭāṅga-tāṃ yāti / no cel locanayor malinatvaṃ rasanajñāyāṃ nīrasatvaṃ nāsikāyām avyaktatā śrotrayor aspaṣṭatvaṃ kāyasya kṛśatvaṃ mater māndyaṃ gater jāḍyaṃ janair dṛśyate / tasmād asmai dehaparigraham urarīkurvatā syādvādavādinā 'hāro py urarīkartavyaḥ / ...

#5 ...Kevalinaḥ kavalaṃ bhuktiṃ pramāṇapañcakair prapañcyate / kevalin dharmī bhutimān bhavatīti sādhyo dharmaḥ / dvividhavedanīyasya vidyamānatvāt / yo ya īdṛśas sa tādṛśaḥ, yathā rathyāpuruṣaḥ / dvividhavedanīyavidyamānaś cāyaṃ kevalī, tasmād bhuktimān bhavatīti /...

#6 tathā kevaḷ(l)ī bhuktimān, ṣaṭparyāptimatvāt, taijasā... bubhu-kṣāpakṣatvāt; dīrghāyuṣā vihāratvāt; sammatapuruṣavat /

#7 tat sarvaṃ krameṇa vicāryate / dehāmukhyatāyām etad ayuktam / nānāprakārāhāravaikalyadarśanāt / pañcakṛtvā bhuñjānasya yādṛśī dehasthitir evaṃ catus trir dvir bhuñjā-nasya tādṛśaivaikabhojino hi tathā dinānitaritabhojinām api / tathā Bāhubaliprabhṛtīnāṃ prakṛṣṭayatīnāṃ pakṣamāsaṣaṇmāsasaṃ-vatsarapramitāhāravatāṃ prakṛṣṭaṃ dṛṣṭaṃ kāye kāntibalam / tathā bahutarakleśāyāsaśīlavatī Sītā sattvasametā / anaśanāditaponuṣṭhānaprakṛṣṭānāṃ yatīnāṃ doṣāvaraṇa-kṣayaḥ jñānātiśayaś ca dṛśyate / tathā cāyaṃ ślokaḥ—

doṣāvaraṇayor hānir niḥśeṣāsty atiśāyanāt /
kvacid yathā svahetubhyo bahirantarmal(l)akṣayaḥ //
[*Āptamīmāṃsā, kārikā 4*]

asyānaṅgīkāre svavyāghātaprasaṅgāt /

#8 ...apramattād ūrdhvam āhāravyavahāravirahāt, sūkṣmasāmparāye kṣutpipāsādicaturdaśaparīṣahāṇāṃ vidyamānatvāt...

#9 ...āhārapūrvikety atra āhāramātraṃ svīkriyate kavalāhāro vā? ...prathamapakṣe siddhasādhyatā prasiddhā syāt / sayogakevalini nokarmakarmāhāro 'smābhir abhidhīyate, tatra kavalāhārābhāvāt //

#10 athāhāro 'nnādilakṣaṇo lakṣyate tatreti cet /

#11 na, ṣaḍvidhāhārapāṭhāt / gāthāyāṃ tathoktam—"āhāro chabbidho ṇeyo" / anyathaikendriyāṇḍajajīvānāṃ dehasthiter avakāśo na syāt / tatra kavalāhāro na sambhavati /...tathā dvitīyapakṣe nākanikāyenānekāntāt / teṣāṃ kavalāhārābhāve 'pi dehasthites sadbhāvāt /

#12 atha kavalāhārābhāve katipayadinair asmadādivad dehasthiter abhāvo vibhāvyate vidvadbhir bhāvaiḥ, tadvat kevalino 'py abhāva eva, iti cet /

#13 na, tatsādhakānām anumānādīnāṃ bahuśo darśanāt / "yaḥ sarvāṇi carācarāṇi [as quoted in the *Viśvatattvaprakāśa*, p. 68]" ityādi svasaṃvedanasya...niratyaya ity āgamād avagamyate /...

#14 atha vedanīye vidyamāne "ekādaśa jine" [*Tattvārthasūtra*, ix, 11] santīti vacanāt kṣuttṛṣābubhukṣā tasmād bhaved iti / tathā 'numānam—bhagavati vedanīyaṃ phaladāyi, karmatvāt, āyuḥkarmavat /

#15 naitat sādhvanumānam / mohanīyasahāyaṃ vihāyāsātam api sātāyaiva /...tadatiśayajñānaviśeṣatvān [yathā] nakhakeśādivṛddhirāhityaṃ yathā caturāsyatvaṃ bhavati, bhavaty eva tathā kavalavikalatvaṃ tasmād asmin / kavalāhāravyavahāraparihārāt parīṣaparihāraḥ prabhavati /

#16 ...anantajñānaviśeṣād anantadarśanam anataviryatvam anantasukhatvaṃ sukhena jāghaṭyate / tathā coktaṃ ślokaḥ—

aiśvaryam apratihataṃ sahajo virāgaḥ /
tṛptir nisargajanitā vaśītendriyeṣu //
ātyantikaṃ sukham anāvaraṇā ca śaktiḥ /
jñānaṃ ca sarvaviṣayaṃ bhagavaṃs tavaiva // [?]

#17 viśiṣṭavedanīyodayabhogād bubhukṣābhuktiyuktir na bobhavīti / tasminn arthe pramāṇaṃ pravartate / vītarāgo bhagavān na kiñcid ādhātuṃ hātuṃ pravartate, pravṛttinivṛttiviṣayavidūratvāt, nivṛttavyāmohatvāt / ya īdṛśas sa tādṛśaḥ, yathobhayasammataḥ paramayogī / tathā cāyaṃ tatas tathā /...

#18 api cālokasāmānyamanuṣyatvaṃ bhagavati parameśvare dṛśyate /

#19 manuṣyatvāviśeṣe'pi...dīptataponidhīnāṃ paramayatīnāṃ tāratamyabhāvenāhāradūratvam / ... ślokas tathā—

mānuṣīṃ prakṛtim abhyatītavān /
devatāsav api ca devatā yataḥ //
tena nātha paramāsi devatā /
śreyase jina Vṛṣa prasīda naḥ //

[*Bṛhatsvayambhūstotra, kārikā* 75]

ityāgamoktatvāt /...

#20 etena śarīratvavaktṛtvapuruṣatvādayo hetavo nirastā veditavyāḥ /

#21 kiñca dhyānaviśeṣād āvaraṇakṣayāt...svaparaprakāśa-jñānānandātmakasya nijaniranjananirupamasvarūpasya bhagavadar-hatparameśvarasya kṣudhābubhukṣābhuktyā dainyāpādakaṃ Śvetāmbarācāryavacanam...acārutāyāḥ prathamaṃ prakaraṇam / kṣudhātṛṣābhayadveṣetyādikarmā-rātijayān mārajij jina ity abhidhānāt, anekaviṣamabhavagahana-vyasana-prāpaṇahetūn karmārātin jayantīti jinā iti vyutpatteś ca kṣudhādyanekadoṣaviṣayo na bhavatīti suniścitaṃ vipaścitām /

#22 ...atha kevalāvasthāyāṃ kavalāhāraparihāre samavasaraṇaviharaṇaṃ nopadyate?

#23 maivaṃ vaktavyam / tatpuṇyaprabhāvāc caturā-syatvādiguṇānāṃ niratiśayasvarūpāṇāṃ samavasṛtiprabhṛtivi-bhūtīnāṃ darśanāt /

#24 ...nanu ba[lava]tā vedanīyakarmaṇā nirmitapīḍāto bhuktibhāktvaṃ bhavatīti cet /

#25 na, agnir māṇavakaḥ, siṃho māṇavakaḥ, ity upamānāt; na hy agnisiṃhayoḥ māṇavakatvaṃ sambhavati / vedanīyopamā saṃjñā vijñāyate tajjñaiḥ / asahāyavedanīyaṃ kiñcit kartuṃ śaknoti? sahāyam antareṇa sphurati kiṃ pratāpaḥ, tejaḥprabhāvātigatabhasmavat? taddhy ekaṃ api vedanīyaṃ vedanām utpādayitum akṣama, yathaiko 'pi naṭabaṭuḥ svakīyaṃ skandham āruhya nārhati nartituṃ niḥsakhatvāt; niḥsahāyaḥ samartho 'py asamartha eva /...

#26 naitad bhuktiyuktir yauktikamatam avagāhate / tat kathaṃ? kavalāhāratvāt kevalikāyasya malamūtrādyapavitratādoṣānu-ṣaṅgo...cāṅgīkartavyaḥ? tataś ca sarvavitvahānir ānīyate tasmai / tasmād ekaṃ sandhitsor anyat pracyavate, ekaṃ kartum ārabdhasyānyathāgatam ityādi nyāyaparipāṭikoṭim āṭīkate(?) teṣāṃ Dupṭavādināṃ vacanam /...

#27 etāvatā kim uktaṃ bhavati? ...ataḥ prakṣīṇamohe bhagavati na prabhavanti vedanīyaprabhāvāḥ / tasmād dagdharajjusvarūpavedanīyāt kṣutbubhukṣāpakṣaḥ kakṣīkriyate /

#28 parīkṣitam atra vicakṣaṇaiḥ—tarhi lalanālīḍhāliṅganacumbanariraṃsā 'pi kiṃ na syāt? tathā ca sarvaveditvaṃ samastavastuniḥspṛhavṛttivītarāgatvaṃ vaktuṃ na yuktaṃ yauktikavādibhir bhavadbhis tatra /...bhavaduktā yuktiḥ, sā ca parameśvarasya nidrātandrāvyādhi...bādhādurbodhatvam eva sandhāti / tathā ca bhagavato jñānam indriyajam, jñānatvāt; asmadādijñāvad[iti]aniṣṭāpatteḥ /

#29 kiñca, kecid bhaktā bhagāder bhoktṛtvaṃ bhuyo bhāvayanti, te 'pi ṣoḍaśopacāreṇopacaranti, na hi sāttvikavṛttyā vartante / tato mithyādṛṣṭibhyaḥ kaṣṭatarāḥ Pāṇḍupaṭāḥ /... kutaḥ? kṣudhādyaśeṣadoṣadūṣitaṃ devaṃ...kaṭhinamatiḥ smarati sutarāṃ vivekavikalatvāt / svayaṃ kṣudhāgniduḥ-khadaṃdahyamāno hi devo kathaṃ pareṣāṃ kṣudhāgniṃ vidhyāpayati? svayaṃ patan pumān patantaṃ katham uddharati? anyenānyasyānyakūpapatanam, na hy abhimatas-thānaprāptiḥ / tathā 'nekapātakapatitasya Śvetapaṭavādino nāsti paramā gatiḥ, yato 'tra kṣudhādidoṣaprakṣayo-palakṣitavītarāgakevalini kavalagrasanavikasanakathanāt / tathā pūrvācāryavacanam—"kevalikavalāhārābhyavahara-ṇād avarṇavādo doṣaḥ darśna-mohasya", saptatikoṭākoṭisā-garopamāyuṣasthiter bhājo bhavaṃ bhavaṃ virājante /...

#30 tasmād yato bhagavān bhuktiyukto na bhavati—anantacatuṣṭayasvarūpatvāt,...prakṣīṇamohavyaūhatvāt, catustriṃś-adatiśayasametatvāt, pañcamahākalyāṇavibhūtiviśiṣṭatvāt,... vyatireke rathyapuruṣavat / iti nirdiṣṭebhyo 'numānebhyo...iṣṭasiddhir abobhūyiṣṭa /...//

Translation

#1 Having paid obeisance to Mahāvīra, the omniscient (traividya, i.e. the knower of the three times)[12] Lord of the Jinas, and one who is reverentially greeted by logicians (i.e. disputants in a debate), this meaningful treatise is expounded in order to investigate *Eating of Food [by a Kevalin (i.e. an Omniscient Being)] and Attainment of Mokṣa [by a Female].*[13] [1]

By this meaningful treatise our own doctrine will be established, and the opposite view as held by the Śvetāmbaras will also be refuted. [2]...

#2 [Digambara:] Here a certain Śvetāmbara holds the view that the Lord Arhat, the highest Lord who has attained omniscience (kevala-jñāna)[14] eats food. In support of this view he says:

#3 "The body is indeed the foremost means of achieving dharma"; and that body consists of the five great material elements supported by food. Food is for the sake of maintaining the body since without food the body cannot be sustained. This is proved by the fact that the thickness or thinness of the body invariably corresponds to the presence or absence of food. Hence as long as there is a body, the avoidance of food must be considered extremely difficult. [Even one who fasts] must eat at least once at the end of a fortnight, a month, six months, or a year....

#4 [Śvetāmbara:] How do those (i.e. the Digambaras) who claim to speak the truth assert even the endurance of omniscience in the Lord, without the assistance of his body? How can they maintain that the food that support the body is not the chief cause [of sustaining his life]? Because of food the mind is at peace, intelligence appears, clarity of sense organs is produced, and the body is well nourished. Otherwise, the eyes become weak, the tongue ceases to taste flavour, the nose does not experience smell, the ears do not hear clearly, the body becomes thin, the mind becomes dull, and one's gait becomes laboured; all this is evident to everyone. Therefore, a follower of the doctrine of Syādvāda (i.e. a Jaina), if he believes that the sustenance of the body is necessary for a Kevalin, must also admit food for such a person...

#5 [Śvetāmbara:]...Our view that a Kevalin takes food by morsels will be established by all five means of verification. [Here we present the following syllogism:] The point we seek to prove is that the Kevalin eats food. This is because there is in him the presence of the twofold *vedanīya-karma* [which produces pleasure (*sātā*) and pain (*asātā*)]. Whosoever is like that must eat food, for example, a person on the street. The Kevalin has the twofold *vedanīya-karma*. Therefore he must eat food.

#6 [Śvetāmbara:] Similarly, the Kevalin eats food because he has six *paryāptis* (a process by which a soul brings about the 'completion' of a new life).[15] He must have hunger (*bubhukṣā*, lit. "desire to eat") because of the 'heat body' (*taijasa-śarīra*, a body possessed by all embodied beings), and also because [even after attaining omniscience] he does move about for the duration of his long life, like any other human being...

#7 [Digambara:] All this will be examined in proper order...Your statement is not correct, since the body is not the most important factor here. This is because the stage of a body does not necessarily correspond to the number of days during which it remains devoid of food. For example, the condition of the body of one who takes food after skipping five meals, and of one who takes food after skipping four, three, or two meals, does not differ [proportionately]. Similarly, an extreme form of radiant energy is observed in the bodies of ascetics like Bāhubali who practice the highest form of control, and also in those who eat only once in a fortnight, a month, six months, or a year.[16] So was Sītā full of vigour, even after a great deal of suffering and exhaustion, while she kept her precepts.[17] In those mendicants who engage in austerities of fasting and so forth, there is also seen excellence of cognition as well as destruction of obscurations and passions, as has been said:

> The total destruction of defects (i.e. passions) and obscurations (of knowledge) must be possible in some person. Because these two admit of degrees [of absence in ordinary people]. For example, the internal and external dirt [in a piece of gold] which can be completely cleansed by proper means. [*Āptamīmāṃsā*, verse 4][18]

If you do not accept this, then you will be contradicting yourself.

#8 [Digambara:]...Moreover, all activities of eating cease beyond the [seventh spiritual] stage (*guṇasthāna*) called *apramatta-virata* (i.e. total renunciation free from all forms of carelessness).[19] As for the fourteen afflictions (*parīṣaha*, see below #14) beginning with hunger and thirst, these may exist only up to the [eleventh stage called] *sūkṣma-sāmparāya* (i.e. subtle desire) [and not beyond, in the thirteenth stage of the Kevalin].

#9 [Digambara:] Are you merely claiming some form of '*āhāra*' (food), or only that '*āhāra*' which is eaten by morsels (*kavala-āhāra*)? In the first alternative there is no need for argumentation, because in the Kevalin with Activities (i.e. the thirteenth stage), we also admit the intake of *āhāra* in the form of the quasi-karmic molecules (called *nokarma-vargaṇā*) that a soul automatically takes in during the state of embodiment. The second alternative is not [applicable to this stage] since eating in the form of food made into morsels is not found there.

#10 (Śvetāmbara:] But '*āhāra*' characterized as 'edible' is indicated [in the scriptures] for that stage.

#11 [Digambara:] No, because six kinds of *āhāra* are mentioned in the scripture, as is said in the verse: '*āhāra* should be known as sixfold'.[20] Otherwise there would be no possibility of the sustenance of the bodies of beings with one sense (e.g. plants), or beings in eggs; for food by way of eating morsels is not possible for them.... In the second alternative (of considering only the *kavala-āhāra* as food) there is the fault of inapplicability to those who live in the heavenly abodes. Their bodies are maintained even in the absence of food taken by morsels.

#12 [Śvetāmbara:] In the absence of food by morsels, within a few days the sustenance of the body is in peril. The wise (i.e. the physicians) can figure from signs that our bodies may cease to exist. The same would be the case of a Kevalin who is like us.

#13 [Digambara:] No, [the case is not similar] because of the many inferences that support our contention. It is also known from the scriptures, as for example 'One who [knows] all sentient and insentient beings[21] ....', and so forth, that the omniscient cognition [of the Kevalin] is free from all obstructions (i.e. it is not affected by the absence of *kavala-āhāra*)....

#14 [Śvetāmbara:] But surely as long as *vedanīya-karma* exists, the scriptural rule namely, 'Eleven [afflictions are possible] in a Jina' (*Tattvārthasūtra*, ix 11) would apply, and hence there would be thirst and hunger even for a Kevalin.[22] [We therefore offer the following] syllogism: The *vedanīya-karma* [even of a Kevalin] yields its fruit [in the form of hunger, etc.]. Because it is the nature of karma [to yield its fruit]. Similar to the *āyu-karma* [i.e. the karma which determines the duration of individual life) [which you admit, yields its fruit even for a Kevalin].

#15 [Digambara:] This is not a proper argument, because,

unassisted by *mohanīya-karma* (which produces passions such as desire and aversion), the pain-yielding (*asātā*) variety of *vedanīya* yields instead pleasure (*sātā*) only....[you admit that] due to the excellence of omniscient knowledge, the body of the Kevalin gains such translucence that he can be seen as having four faces (i.e. can be seen from all four directions), and also that his nails and hair cease to grow.[23] For the same reason there is also the absence of eating food by morsels. The [argument based on the] scripture pertaining to the number of afflictions [considered possible for a Jina] is thus overcome.

#16 [Digambara:]...By the excellence of infinite knowledge, the presence also of infinite perception, infinite energy, and infinite bliss (*ananta-sukha*) [which would not be compatible with hunger and thirst] is easily established, as is said in the verse:

> Your glory is unobstructed and your freedom from passion is natural. So is your contentment, and the innate control over the senses. Oh Lord, only in you is to be found complete happiness, the totally unobstructed energy and the cognition extending to all objects.[?]

#17 [Digambara:] The argument that the Kevalin is subject to the desire to eat (*bubhukṣā*) on account of the presence of the *asātā-vedanīya-karma* is rendered invalid by the following syllogism: The Lord, being free from attachment, does not engage in receiving or forsaking something. Because of being free from delusion, he has departed from actions to be performed or to be given up. One who is like this must be of such a nature, as is the highest yogin acceptable to both [sides of the debate]. This person under discussion [i.e. the Kevalin] is like that and, therefore, he must conform to this description....

#18 [Śvetāmbara:] But the Lord, the Highest Jina is [still a human being and is] seen to share conditions common to all human beings.

#19 [Digambara:] Notwithstanding his human condition [it can still be maintained that he does not eat]. [There is no single rule that uniformly applies to all human beings because] the periods of abstention from food can vary a great deal from one person to another, as is known from the examples of great mendicants, the veritable treasures of severe asceticism....As is said:

> You have indeed transcended the human nature;
> and are a divine being even to the heavenly beings;
> Therefore, Oh Lord, you are the highest divinity.
> Oh Jina Vṛṣabha, therefore, be gracious to us for our welfare.
> [*Bṛhatsvayambhū-stotra,* verse 75][24]

#20 [Digambara:] By the same [text] one should understand the refutation of arguments [for *kavala-āhāra*] based upon the Kevlin's corporeality, or his ability to speak, or upon his maleness, and so forth.

#21 [Digambara:] Moreover, by his pure meditation he has destroyed all obstructions to knowledge.... He is endowed with that bliss which accompanies his omniscience. He has gained his own nature, which is immaculate and incomparable. Therefore, the words of the Śvetāmbara teachers implicating hunger and thirst in the Lord Arhat, the Highest Lord...are extremely disagreeable. He is called Jina precisely because he has overcome evil (*māra*) in the form of hunger, thirst, fear, hostility, and other similar karmic enemies. Moreover the word *jina* etymologically means one who has won a victory over enemies in the form of karmas that are instrumental in leading [beings] into a great many terrible calamities of rebirths. Thus it becomes well-established for the learned that the Lord Jina is not subject to the defects of hunger and thirst, and so forth.

#22 [Śvetāmbara:] But in the absence of partaking of food, would it not be improper to say that the Kevalin moves about in the assembly hall [where he preaches]?

#23 [Digambara:] This should not be said. His moving about [even without food] is possible on account of his former meritorious acts, and is comparable to the various miraculous signs appearing in the assembly hall, such as his [being seen as having] four faces (i.e. his visibility from all four sides), an so forth.

#24 [Śvetāmbara:]...[We still submit that the Kevalin] may become an eater of food on account of the affliction [of hunger] produced by the powerful [pain-yielding] *vedanīya-karma.*

#25 [Digambara:] Not so, because the learned speak of the presence of the pain-yielding *vedanīya-karma* in the state of a Kevalin in a [technical] sense comparable to the metaphorical usage such as 'This boy is fire (i.e. haughty)', or 'This boy is a lion (i.e. brave)'; surely, the fire and the lion do not become that boy. The *asātā-vedanīya-karma* [in a Kevalin] is incapable of producing its effect without the assistance [of the passion-producing *mohanīya-karma*]. Its existence there is comparable to a heap of ashes devoid of heat. Does fire blaze forth without the assistance [of fuel and wind]? The *vedanīya-karma* alone is incapable of producing any pain. It would be as absurd as a young juggler without an assistant climbing on his own shoulder and dancing; this is because truly even a capable person without help is incapable....

#26 [Digambara:] Moreover, your argument is not valid for the following reason also. If you admit that the Kevalin eats food, then you may have to accept that his body is subject to the impurities of faeces and urine, etc. This would certainly lead to the loss of his omniscience. Thus, in joining at one spot you have broken at another. You started with one objective but it resulted in something quite different. Thus the words of the Śvetāmbara (*Dupaṭavādins*, lit. those who wear clothes) cross the limits of logic.

#27 [Digambara:] What is the purport of all this? In the Lord, who has destroyed the *mohanīya-karma*, the painful effects arising from the presence of the *asātā-vedanīya-karma* do not prevail. The latter is comparable to a burnt piece of rope, from which you seek in vain to prove the presence of thirst and hunger [in a Kevalin].

#28 [Digambara:] This matter [namely, the presence of the desire to eat in the Kevalin] has been examined further by the learned [Ācārya Prabhācandra:] 'Why should not there also be the [presence of the] desire for such carnal pleasures as embracing a woman and kissing [and so forth]?[25] [Given your view of the presence in a Kevalin of the desire to eat] it is not proper for you, who profess to speak reasonably, to speak also of his omniscience and his total freedom from desire. Instead, your reasoning only links the defects of sleep, sluggishness, and disease (all proceeding from eating food) in the Highest Lord, the Kevalin. This will lead to the unwanted situation of admitting that the knowledge of the Lord is dependent on the senses, and therefore an ordinary knowledge, like the knowledge of people like us.

#29 [Digambara:] Certain [non-Jaina] devotees [of Viṣṇu or Śiva] believe [that their Deity] enjoys the pleasures of sex and so forth. They even worship [their Deity] with sixteen kinds of services, and also they do not behave in a wholesome manner. The Śvetāmbaras (called *Pāṇḍupaṭāḥ*, lit. wearers of white clothes) are worse than even these people who hold such wrong views.....How? Totally devoid of discrimination, this unintelligent person thinks incessantly of the Deity who is afflicted by the defects of hunger, and so forth. How can one who is himself burning with the pain of hunger, and so forth, be able to extinguish the fire of hunger in others? How can a falling man lift another falling person?...There is no arriving at the desired goal by this means. There is no attainment of the highest goal, namely *mokṣa*, for one who holds the view of the Śvetāmbara: the latter has fallen in manifold sins, since he speaks [blasphemously] of the eating of morsel food by a Kevalin who is free from desire and is characterized by the complete destruction of the defects of hunger, and so forth. This [is confirmed] by the words of ancient teachers: 'The sinful act of attributing faults [to the Kevalin] by saying that the omniscient eats morsels of food...[leads to the influx] of the faith-deluding variety of the *mohanīya-karma*'.[26] Such beings inherit karma that keeps them in transmigration for the long duration of seventy crores multiplied by seventy crores of the 'oceans' of time.[27]

#30 [Digambara:] In conclusion, the Lord Kevalin does not eat food because he is of the nature of four infinities (of knowledge, perception, bliss and energy), because he has completely destroyed the mass of passion-producing karma, because he is endowed with thirty-four miracles,[28] because he is distinguished by the majesty of five great auspicious events (viz. conception, birth, renunciation, enlightenment and *nirvāṇa*], all of which are not to be found in an ordinary person [lit. person on the street, i.e. one who eats food]. By these arguments well set forth, we have achieved our desired objective.

NOTES

1. Padmanabh S. Jaini "*Muktivicāra* of Bhāvasena: Text and Translation", *Indological Taurinensia*, pp. 168-82, Vol. XIII, Torino, 1985-86. For a discus-

sion on the date and works of Bhāvasena, known also as Bhāvasena Traividya, see the *Viśvatattvaprakāśa of Bhāvasena*, ed. V. P. Johrapurkar. Sholapur (Jīvarāja Jaina Granthamālā), 1964.

2. Chandrabhal Tripathi, *Catalogue of the Jaina Manuscripts at Strasbourg*, Leiden (E. J. Brill), 1975.
3. On the *sātā* and the *asātā* varieties of the *vedanīya*-karma see Helmuth von Glasenapp, *The Doctrine of Karman in Jain Philosophy*, p. 80. Bombay (The Trustees, Bai Vijibhai J. P. Charity Fund), 1942. For rules pertaining to the transformation of one karman into another, see Nathmal Tatia, *Studies in Jaina Philosophy* (p. 255). Varanasi (Jaina Cultural Research Society), 1951.
4. For the functions of the *nokarma-vargaṇā*, see Balachandra Siddhānta-śāstrī, *Jaina Lakṣaṇāvalī*, Vol. II, p. 651. Delhi (Vīra Sevā Mandir), 1973.
5. Paul Dundas, "Food and Freedom: The Jaina sectarian debate on the nature of the Kevalin", *Religion*, XV, pp. 161-98. London (Academic Press Inc.), 1985.
6. For the history and literature of the Yāpanīya sect, see Padmanabh S. Jaini, *Gender and Salvation: Jaina Debates on the Spiritual Liberation of Women*, pp. 42-48. Berkeley (University of California Press), 1991.
7. *Strīnirvāṇa-Kevalibhuktiprakaraṇe* of Śākaṭāyana (with two *Svopajña-vṛttis*), Sanskrit text ed. Muni Jambūvijaya. Bhavanagar (Jaina Ātmānanda Sabhā), 1974.
8. *Nyāyakumudacandra* of Prabhācandra [Kevalikavalāhārāvicāraḥ, vol. II, pp. 852-65] ed. Mahendra Kumar Jain. Bombay (Māṇikcandra Digambara Jaina Granthamālā), 1941. This topic is also discussed in the *Prameyakamalamārttaṇḍa* of Prabhācandra [pp. 299-307], ed. Mahendra Kumar Śāstrī. Bombay (Nirṇayasāgara Press), 1941.
9. *Ṣaḍdarśanasamuccaya* of Haribhadra with Guṇaratna's *Tarkarahasya-dīpikā-vṛtti* [see pp. 203-10), Sanskrit text with Hindi tr. by Mahendra Kumar Jain. Varanasi (Bhāratīya Jñānapīṭha), 1969.
10. *Yuktiprabodha* of Meghavijaya with *Svopajñavṛtti* [see pp. 126-63], ed. Muni Ānandasāgara, Ratlam (Ṛṣabhadevajī Keśarīmalajī Śvetāmbara Saṃsthā), 1928.
11. *Adhyātmamataparikṣā* [see pp. 300-47] of Yaśovijaya, Sanskrit text with Gujarati tr. by Muni Bhuvanabhānusūri. Bombay (Divyadarśana Kāryālaya), 1986.
12. The ordinary meaning of the term *traividya* (proficient in three branches of classical learning, viz., Logic, Grammar and Philosophy) is not applicable here. A reference to the title of the author (see n. 1) is probably intended.
13. See P. S. Jaini (1985-86) in n. 1 and P. S. Jaini (1991) in n. 6.
14. For a discussion on the nature of omniscience in Jainism and Buddhism, see Padmanabh S. Jaini, "On the Sarvajñatva (Omniscience) of Mahāvīra and the Buddha", *Buddhist Studies in Honour of I. B. Horner*, ed. L. Cousins. Dordrecht (D. Reidel Pub. Co.), 1974.
15. The Jaina texts speak of six possible stages of completion of a new life (*paryāpti*) in the following order: food (*āhāra*), body (*śarīra*), breath (*prāṇa*), sense organs (*indriya*), speech (*bhāṣā*), and mind (*manas*). For full details, see Jinendra Varṇī, *Jainendra Siddhānta Kośa*, III, pp. 39-44. Varanasi (Bhāratīya Jñānapīṭha), 1972.
16. For the legendary austerities of the Jaina mendicant hero Bāhubali, see

Padmanabh S. Jaini, *The Jaina Path of Purification* [p. 205]. Berkeley (University of California Press), 1979.

17. In the Jaina version of the *Rāmāyaṇa*, Sītā, the wife of Rāma, eventually becomes a Jaina nun. See the *Triṣaṣṭiśalākā-puruṣacaritra* of Hemacandra, iv, 10, translated by Helen M. Johnson, *The Lives of Sixty-three Illustrious Persons*. 6 vols. Baroda (Oriental Institute), 1962.
18. *Āptamīmāṃsā of Samantabhadra*, Sanskrit text (with a Hindu commentary) in the *Āptamīmāṃsā-Tattvadīpikā*, ed. Udayachandra Jain. Varanasi (Shri Ganeśa Varṇī Digambara Jain Saṃsthān), 1974.
19. For a description of the fourteen guṇasthānas, see Jaini: *The Jaina Path of Purification*, pp. 272-73.
20. Cf. ṣaḍvidho hy āhāraḥ:
    ṇokamma kammahāro kavalāhāro ya leppam āhāro;
    oja maṇo vi ya kamaso āhāro chavviho ṇeyo.
    Quoted in the *Prameyakamalamārttaṇḍa*, p. 300, see n. 8 above.
21. Verse quoted in the *Viśvatattvaprakāśa*, p. 68 (see n. 1 above).
22. The *Tattvārthasūtra* of Umāsvāti (albeit with several variant readings and sectarian commentaries) is probably the only scripture that is acceptable to both the Digambaras and the Śvetāmbaras. It describes (in *sūtra* ix, 9) twenty-two afflictions (*parīṣahas*), caused by various karmic forces, that a Jaina mendicant should patiently suffer as he progresses toward the goal of attaining the state of Kevalin. A question is raised about the number of afflictions that a Kevalin might suffer and the *sūtra* (ix, 11) answers that eleven afflictions—beginning with hunger, thirst, cold, heat (*kṣut-pipāsā-śīta-uṣṇa*)—which are produced by the *vedanīya*-karma are possible at this stage. This statement supports the Śvetāmbara position that the Kevalin eats food. The sixth-century Digambara commentator Pūjyapāda in his *Sarvārthasiddhi* commentary, however, interprets this *sūtra* differently. He maintains that hunger and thirst at this stage are spoken of only conventionally (*upacāra*) since *vedanīya*-karma is unable to produce such pain in the absence of the *mohanīya*. Alternatively, he suggests that the *sūtra* should be supplemented with the words 'do not arise in the jina':
    ...vedanīyasadbhāvāt tadāśrayā ekādaśaparīṣahāḥ santi...vedanābhāve 'pi dravyakarmasadbhāvāpekṣayā parīṣahopacāraḥ krīyate...athavā..., mohodayasahāyīkṛtakṣudhādi-vedanābhāvāt "na santi" iti vākyaśeṣaḥ. *Sarvārthasiddhi* [see ix, 11], ed. Phoolchandra Siddhāntaśāstrī. Varanasi (Bhāratīya Jñānapītha, 1971; translated by S. A. Jain, *Reality*. Calcutta (Vīra Śāsana Saṅgha), 1960. For the Śvetāmbara commentary (attributed to Umāsvāti), see *Sabhāṣyatattvārthādhigamasūtra*, ed. Khubchandra Siddhāntaśāstrī. Agas (Śrīmad Rājacandra Āśrama), 1932.
23. These are included in the thirty-four superhuman qualities (*atiśayas*) attributed to a Tīrthaṅkara Kevalin. For a full list, see Jinendra Varṇī, *Jainendra Siddhānta Kośa*, I, (*arhanta*, pp. 140-42).
24. *Bṛhatsvayambhū-stotra of Samantabhadra*, Sanskrit text included in the *Nityanaimittika-pāṭhāvalī*, Sanskrit and Prakrit Texts. Karanja (Kanakubai Pāṭhyapustakamālā), 1956.
25. Cf. tathāhi—bubhukṣā mohanīyānapekṣasyā vedanīyasya kāryaṃ na bhavati, icchātvāt, riraṃsāvat. bhoktum icchā hi bubhukṣā, sā kathaṃ vedanīyasyaiva kāryam? anyathā yonyādiṣu rantum icchā riraṃsāpi tatkāryaṃ syāt, tathā ca kavalāhāravat stryādāv api tatprasaṅgāt neśvarād asya viśeṣaḥ.

Nyāyakumudacandra, II, p. 860; also *Prameyakamalamārttaṇḍa*, p. 304 (see n. 8 above).

26. This refers to the Digambara interpretation of the following *sūtra:* kevaliśrutasaṃghadharmadevāvarṇavādo darśanamohasya.

[*Tattvārthasūtra*, vi, 13]

Commenting on the *avarṇa-vāda* of the kevalin, Pūjyapāda says: nirāvaraṇajñānāḥ kevalinaḥ...kavalābhyavahārajīvinaḥ kevalina ity evam ādi vacanaṃ kevalinām avarṇavādaḥ. [*Sarvārthasiddhi*, vi, 13]

Examples of the *avarṇavādas* are not provided in the *Sabhāṣyatattvārthādhigamasūtra* (see n. 22 above).

27. This is the maximum period of duration of this variety karma: ....mohanīyakarmaprakṛteḥ saptatiḥ sāgaropamakoṭī-koṭyaḥ parā sthitiḥ.

[*Sabhāṣyatattvārthādhigamasūtra*, viii, 16]

28. See n. 23 above.

ADDITIONAL NOTES

For an eighteenth-century Digambara compilation of eighty-four points of controversy between the two sects, see Padmanabh S. Jaini, forthcoming article:

"Hemaraj Pande's *Caurāsī Bol.*" *Shri Muni Jambuvijay Felicitation Volume,* Sharadaben Chimanbhai Educational Research Centre, ed. J.B. Shah, Ahmedabad, 1999.

See also "Umāsvāti on the Quality of Sukha." Paper presented at the International Seminar on Umāsvāti and His Works, Bhogilal Leherchand Institute of Indology, Delhi, January 4-6, 1999. (Coordinator: Vimal Prakash Jain)

V

JAINA ETHICS AND PRAXIS

CHAPTER 11

*Sāmāyika**

"One should forgive and help others forgive;
One should pacify oneself and help others to pacify themselves.
There is spiritual life for one who pacifies himself;
There is no spiritual life for one who does not pacify himself."
"Why is this said, Sir?"
"Because the essence of recluseship is pacification."

[khamiyabbaṃ khamāyiyabbaṃ;
uvasamiyabbaṃ uvasamāyiyabbaṃ.
jo uvasamai tassa atthi ārāhaṇā;
jo na uvasamai tassa n'atthi ārāhaṇā.
taṃ keṇ'aṭṭhenaṃ bhante?
uvasamasāraṃ khu sāmaṇṇaṃ. *Kalpasūtra,* 286.]

In these memorable words an ancient Jain text sets forth, for the benefit of all aspiring souls, the quintessence of salvation.

The Jains, probably the oldest of the *śramaṇas,*[1] have left a very rich spiritual legacy concerning bondage (*bandha*) and salvation (*mokṣa*)—the chief preoccupations of ancient India. Their community, most notably the laity, has preserved to this day an ancient method of purification called *sāmāyika,* which plays as significant a rôle as does *satipaṭṭhāna* (Mindfulness) in Buddhism.

The word Jaina means a follower of a Jina or 'spiritual victor';

*This article was published originally as "*Sāmāyika*: A Jain Path of Purification" in *A Study of Kleśa,* ed. G. H. Sasaki (Shimizukobundo Ltd., 2-4 Sarugaki-cho Chiyoda-ku, Tokyo, 1975), pp. 1-8.

this latter title was originally used both for Mahāvīra, the 24th Tīrthaṅkara,[2] and for Gautama the Buddha. In historical times, the Jain ascetics were known as Nigaṇṭhas (Skt. Nirgrantha), the 'Unattached' ones, because of their renunciation of all possessions. In the case of the Digambara ('sky-clad') sect of the Nigaṇṭhas, this renunciation extended even to clothing. But external renunciation was not an end in itself; rather it was symbolic of the detachment from internal "possessions", namely the *kleśas* or elements of moral defilement, which kept a soul in the bondage of transmigration (*saṃsāra*). The Buddhists—chief rivals of the Jains—were aware of this significance of the term *nigaṇṭha*, as can be seen from Buddhaghosa's gloss: "He is called '*nigaṇṭha*' because of his claim: 'We possess neither the *kilesa* of bondage nor the *kilesa* of obstruction; we are free from the knots (*ganṭhi*) of kilesa'".[3]

Although the term *kleśa* is not unknown to the Jains, they most often employ the equivalent expression "*kaṣāya*", indicating a kind of concoction or dye which leaves a lasting stain. The Jains maintain that the soul (*jīva*) which is bound to the wheel of transmigration from beginningless time, carries as it were this stain and remains in the state of impurity as long as the stain is not totally eradicated. The *kaṣāyas* are basically aversion (*dveṣa*) and attachment (*rāga*), which are elaborated as anger (*krodha*), pride (*māna*), deceit (*māyā*) and greed (*lobha*). Each of these is further divided into four, depending upon degree of intensity. The most durable of these is called *anantānubandhī*, the 'lifelong' passions, which have accompanied the soul from beginningless time. They are responsible for prevention of the soul's progress in the path of pure conduct (*samyak-cāritra*), and also act as accessories to the karmic forces of *darśana-moha*, which block the soul's realization of its own true nature. This realization (called *samyak-darśana*) consists in the awareness that the soul is characterized by pure consciousness (*caitanya*), infinite samyak knowledge (*ananta-jñāna*), and bliss (*ananta-sukha*), and further that it is totally distinct from the body, the senses, the mind, and all their activities, whether morally wholesome (*puṇya*) or unwholesome (*pāpa*). It is only when the soul, by means of great exertion, overcomes these two forces—one blocking 'true insight' and the other preventing even rudimentary 'right conduct'—that it is able to climb the 'ladder of purity' (*guṇa-sthāna*)[4] and attain its innate and perfect state of omniscience (*sarvajñatva*).

The attainment of *samyak-darśana* is a turning point in the life of an aspirant. He experiences for the first time a tremendous surge of internal purity, and a state of tranquillity hitherto unknown to his soul. However, this experience can last only a short period, for although the soul will never again fall to the same depth of spiritual delusion from which it has emerged, and to that extent can be said to have entered an irreversible course, the initial state of purity is nevertheless not a permanent one. The Jains maintain that this state must be temporary, as it is gained by only the suppression (*upaśama*) and not by the total destruction (*kṣaya*), of the relevant forces of karma, i.e., the *darśanamoha* and the *kaṣāyas* of the first degree of intensity. But suppression or temporary pacification (*upaśama-samyaktva*) does afford the aspirant a first glimpse, as it were, of the true nature of reality, and it gives him a taste of that bliss to which he will ever seek to return.

Once the suppressed karmic forces have asserted themselves, the individual falls away from his *upaśama-samyaktva*. Thereafter, he faces three alternatives: to grow sluggish and remain indefinitely in the state of *mithyātva* ('wrong belief'); to exert himself and, by repeatedly suppressing the relevant karmic forces, to attain time and again to (the temporary) *upaśama-samyaktva*; to undertake with increasing energy, a final struggle against the karmic adversaries, until he destroys (*kṣaya*) the *darśana-mohanīya* karma and the *anantānubandhī kaṣāyas* forever. If he carries out the last alternative, he comes to posses *kṣāyika-samyaktva*, a state comparable to the *darśana-mārga* of the Buddhists. A person who has reached this state is, like the Buddhist *sotāpanna*, destined to perfect his conduct (*sakala-cāritra*) and attain Arhatship within a few births, if not in the very same lifetime. For this reason, it is believed that the attainment of the *kṣāyika-samyaktva* is possible only under the most favourable circumstances, as for example the presence of a Tīrthaṅkara or his immediate disciples.

But such favourable circumstances are extremely rare, for although there are at present omniscient Jinas in other 'Worldsystems' no Tīrthaṅkara currently resides in our location (Bharata-kṣetra in the Jambudvīpa). Indeed, Mahāvīra was the last Tīrthaṅkara of the present 'time-cycle', and no other such

Teacher will arise here until, after numerous aeons, a new 'time-cycle' begins. It is therefore reasonable to assume that this is a time and place in which one can hope to attain only the state of *upaśama-samyaktva* (or to re-attain this state if, as is likely, he has experienced it in previous briths). Hence the Jain scriptures call upon human beings to utilize this lifetime to strengthen their 'self-realization' through various vows and rituals, so that the opportunity to attain the *kṣāyika-samyaktva* will not be missed for lack of proper preparation when the new Tīrthaṅkara once again appears on this earth.

The vows (*vratas*) consist of resolutions by which an aspirant voluntarily undertakes to refrain from unwholesome activities of body, speech and mind. These unwholesome activities are: violence (*hiṃsā*), untruthfulness (*anṛta*), stealing (*steya*), unchastity (*abrahma*) and possession of worldly goods (*parigraha*). To the Jains, however, all of these may be subsumed under the first, for every kind of evil act is seen as a form of violence. This follows from their position that any such act must proceed from attachment (*rāga*) or aversion (*dveṣa*); and the presence of either of these injures one's own soul. Hence, violence to self takes place even in the absence of injury to another being.[5] Refraining from such 'self-injury' is not easy for one who is constantly occupied with mundane existence. The Jain scriptures therefore prescribe a partial refraining from worldly activities (*deśa-virati* or *aṇu-vratas*) for the laity and total refraining (*sakala-virati* or *mahā-vratas*) for the ascetic or Nirgrantha. They further prescribe a set of rituals called 'necessary duties' (*āvaśyakas*)[6] for both; these are temporary for the layman and life-long for the ascetic. The rituals are six in number: *sāmāyika* (attainment of equanimity), *caturviṃśati-satva* (praise of the 24 Jinas), *vandanaka* (worship of monks), *pratikramaṇa* (confession of past faults), *pratyākhyāna* (forefending of future faults) and *kāyotsarga* ('the abandonment of the body' = standing still for a limited time). Although stated and performed separately, these six have in fact been generally integrated with the single practice called *sāmāyika*. This is the most important of Jain rituals; it has been performed continually since the earliest historical times, as the Pali literature attests, and it functions as the primary link between lay and ascetic practice.

The term *sāmāyika* is of uncertain etymology. Some take it as *aya* (attainment) of *sama* (equanimity), while others suggest the basic idea is *samaya*, 'fusion with the self'. The following verse gives us perhaps the most complete idea of what *sāmāyika* is:

> "Equanimity towards all beings.
> Self-control and pure aspirations.
> Abandonment of every thought
> afflicted by desire and hatred.
> That, truly, is considered *sāmāyika*."[7]

The Jain scriptures do not fix a definite time or require a given frequency for the performance of *sāmāyika*; even so, most Jain laymen regard that time of evening when work and meal are completed as most appropriate, with daily practice not uncommon and holy-day practice obligatory.

A lay aspirant who undertakes *sāmāyika* first withdraws to some solitary place, perhaps a temple, a monk's residence, or even a quiet room of his own dwelling. He lays aside all superfluous clothing, retaining only those garments required for a modicum of modesty.[8] Having paid obeisance to the Jinas and to the monks, he seats himself in the cross-legged position on a mat and utters the following formula:

> "I engage, Sir, in the *sāmāyika*, renouncing harmful activities, whether I have done them or caused them to be done by others; with neither mind, speech nor body shall I do them or cause others to do them. O Sir, I confess (these harmful acts); I reprehend and repent of them; I cast aside my former self."[9]

Next, in order to increase the tranquillity of his mind, he begs forgiveness of the entire world of beings:

> "I ask forgiveness of all beings,
> may all beings forgive me.
> I have friendship with all beings,
> and I have hostility with none."[10]

His mind thus put at case, the aspirant further pacifies himself by reaching toward all beings through the four 'boundless states'. These correspond exactly to the '*brahmavihāras*' in Buddhism and to the 'cultivations for mental pacification' in the Yoga system:

> "Friendship towards all beings
> Delight in the qualities of virtuous ones,
> Utmost compassion for affected beings,
> Equanimity towards those who are not well-disposed towards me,
> May my soul have such dispositions (as these) forever!"[11]

In this atmosphere, the first purpose of the *sāmāyika* is attained, for the aspirant is now ready to contemplate the nature of his true self. The Jain teachers have composed several recitations to be used in such contemplation; we will here reproduce a short version of one such '*sāmāyika-pāṭha*':[12]

> "I have equanimity towards all beings.
> I have no enmity towards anyone
> abandoning all attachments
> I take refuge in meditation.
> If, alas, any beings have been hurt by my desire,
> My hatred or my infatuation,
> May those beings forgive me
> Again and again I beg for their pardon."[13]

> "As long as I am seated in this meditation,
> I shall patiently suffer all calamities
> that may befall me, be they caused
> by an animal, a human being, or a god.
> I renounce, for the duration (of this meditation)
> my body, all food, and all passions."[14]

> "Attachment, aversion, fear, sorrow, joy,
> anxiety , self-pity... all these
> I abandon with body, mind, and speech.
> I also renounce all delight and all aversion
> with regard to sexuality."[15]

> "Whether it is life or death, whether gain or loss,
> Whether defeat or victory, whether meeting or separation,

Whether friends or enemies, whether pleasure or pain,
I have equanimity towards all."[16]

"For in all of these I am (nothing but) my own self.
Forever endowed with right knowledge, true insight
and pure conduct.
And it is my own soul which renounces
all associations formed in this world."[17]

"One and eternal is my soul,
Characterized by intuition and knowledge;
All other states that I undergo are external to me,
for they are formed by associations."[18]

"Because of these associations
my soul has suffered the chains of misery;
Therefore I renounce with body, mind and speech,
all relationships based on such associations."[19]

"Thus have I attained to equanimity
and to the nature of my own self.
May this state of equanimity be with me
until I attain to my salvation."[20]

Utterance of these verses will carry the aspirant to deep levels of meditation on the inner self. In that state, he tastes the bliss which comes from purification of the *kleśas*; thus he is confirmed in spiritual experience, albeit for a brief period, and he moves closer to eventual pursuit of the ascetic path.

The *sāmāyika* ritual is concluded with the universal prayer of the Jains:

"Cessation of sorrow,
Cessation of karmas,
Death while in meditation,
Attainment of enlightenment.
O holy Jina! friend of the entire universe, let these be mine, for
I have taken refuge at your feet."[21]

NOTES

1. On the antiquity of the *śramaṇas* and their non-Vedic doctrines, see my article 'Śramaṇas: Their conflict with Brāhmaṇical society' in *Chapters in Indian Civilization*, Vol. I, pp. 39-81 (Kendall/Hunt, Dubuque, Iowa, U.S.A., 1970).
2. On the life of Mahāvīra (whose 2500th *nirvāṇa* anniversary will be celebrated in 1974) and the history of the Jain Order of monks, see Hermann Jacobi (tr.): *Jaina Sūtras*, Part 1, Sacred Books of the East, xxii.
3. amhākaṃ gaṇṭhanakileso palibujjhanakileso natthi, kilesaganthirahitā mayan ti evam vāditāya laddhanāmavasena Nigaṇṭho.
   MA i, 423 (See *Dictionary of Pāli Proper Names*, vol. II, p. 64).
4. On the doctrine of *guṇa-sthāna*, see N. Tatia: *Studies in Jaina Philosophy*, pp. 268-280, Jain Cultural Research Society, Benaras, 1951.
5. aprādurbhāvaḥ khalu rāgādīnāṃ bhavaty ahiṃseti/
   teṣām evotpattir hiṃseti jināgamasya saṃkṣepaḥ//
   Puruṣārthasiddhyupāya of Amṛtacandra, 44 (The Sacred Books of the Jainas, vol. iv; Lucknow, (India), 1933).
6. For a detailed description of these rituals and also for the various *vratas* of the laity, see R. Williams: *Jaina Yoga*, London Oriental Series, Volume 14, 1963.
7. samatā sarvabhūteṣu saṃyamaḥ śubhabhāvanāḥ/
   ārtaraudrapartyāgas taddhi sāmāyikaṃ matam// [*Varāṅgacarita*, XV, 122]
8. Indeed, very advanced laymen of the Digambara sect may even become 'sky-clad' if they perform this ritual in their own quarters. It is probably this practice of temporary nudity among Jain laymen to which the Buddhists have alluded in a passage which is the most ancient reference to the *sāmāyika* ritual:
   atthi Visākhe Nigaṇṭhā nāma samaṇajātikā, te ...tadah' uposathe sāvakaṃ evaṃ samādapenti: ehi tvam ambho purisa sabbacelāni nikkhipitvā evaṃ vadehi—nāhaṃ kvaci kassaci kiñcanaṃ tasamiṃ na ca mama kvaci kassaci kiñcanaṃ n'atthīti.
   Aṅguttaranikāya, Part I, p. 206 (PTS edition).
9. "karemi bhante sāmāiyaṃ sāvjjaṃ jogaṃ paccakkhāmi jāva sahu pajjuvāsāmi duvihaṃ tiviheṇaṃ maṇeṇaṃ vāyāe kāyeṇaṃ na karemi karāvemi tassa bhante paḍikkamāmi nindāmi garihāmi appāṇaṃ vosirāmi."
   Quoted in Williams' *Jaina Yoga*, p. 132.
10. khāmemi savvajīve savve jīvā khamantu me/
    metti me savvabhūyesu veraṃ majjha na keṇavi//
    Āvaśyaka-sūtra, as quoted in R. Williams' *Jaina Yoga*, p. 207.
11. sattveṣu matrīṃ guṇisu pramodaṃ/
    kliṣṭeṣu jīveṣu kṛpāparatvam//
    mādhyasthabhāvaṃ viparītavṛttau/
    sadā mamātmā vidadhātu deva// [*Amitagati's Dvātriṃśikā*, 1]
12. Quoted from the *Nityapāṭhasaṅgraha*, Karanja.
13. sāmyaṃ me sarvabhūteṣu vairaṃ mama na kenacit/
    āśāḥ sarvāḥ parityajya samādhim aham āśraye//
    rāgād dveṣāt mamatvād vā hā mayā ye virādhitāḥ/
    kṣāmyantu jantavas te me tebhyo mṛṣyāmy ahaṃ punaḥ//

14. tiraścaṃ mānavaṃ daivaṃ upasargaṃ sahe 'dhunā/
kāyāhārakaṣāyādīn pratyākhyāmi triśuddhitaḥ//
15. rāgaṃ dveṣaṃ bhayaṃ śokaṃ praharṣautsukyadīnatāḥ/
vyutsṛjāmi tridhā sarvān aratiṃ ratim eva ca//
16. jīvite maraṇe lābhe 'lābhe yoge viparyaye/
bandhāvarau sukhe duḥkhe sarvadā samatā mama//
17. ātmaiva me sadā jñāne darśane caraṇe tathā/
pratyākhyāne mamātmaiva yathā saṃsārayogayoḥ//
18. eko me śāśvataś cātmā jñānadarśanalakṣaṇaḥ/
śeṣā bahirbhāvā bhāvāḥ sarve saṃyogalakṣaṇāḥ//
19. saṃyogamūlāḥ jīvena prāptāḥ duḥkhaparamparāḥ/
tasmāt saṃyogasambandhaṃ tridhā sarvaṃ tyajāmy aham//
20. evaṃ sāmāyikāt samyak sāmāyikam akhaṇḍitaṃ, vartatām.../
21. dukkhakkhao kammakkhao samāhimaraṇaṃ ca bohilāho ya/
mama hou jagadabandhava jinavara! tava caraṇasaraṇena//

CHAPTER 12

The Pure and the Auspicious in the Jaina Tradition*

According to Louis Dumont's well-known thesis concerning the Indian caste structure, the Varṇa system is based upon the fundamental opposition between the respective purity and impurity of the highest Brahman caste and the lowest untouchable, and the relative purity of the two intermediate castes.[1] As valuable as this thesis is for understanding traditional Indian society, however, it is valid only on the presumption that the Brahmans are indeed at the apex of the social structure. His interpretation would not apply to Indian social groups which uphold the major provisions of the Varṇa scheme, while rejecting the traditional hierarchy by degrading the Brahman one step, and similarly upgrading the Kṣatriya, and thus placing the latter at the apex of the social system.

The disjunction between sacredness and temporal power is supposed to account for the superiority of the Brahman and the subordination of the Kṣatriya. While this interpretation is certainly correct within the traditional Vedic Varṇa system, when the Kṣatriya is elevated to the highest position, the Brahman can no longer claim superiority on the basis of a purity which he is presumed to embody. The case of the Jainas, who claim to be not only non-Vedic, but even anti-Vedic, in their cosmological view, is of special significance for the study of such social groups as the Śramaṇas.[2]

---

*This article was published originally in *Journal of Developing Societies*, Vol. I, pp. 84-93, E. J. Brill, 1985. Reprinted with kind permission of E. J. Brill, Leiden.

To illustrate the radical reinterpretation of Dumont's thesis which is necessary when examining such non-Vedic groups, the legend relating the conception of Mahāvīra, the highest spiritual master of the Jainas, is particularly illuminating. We are told that he was originally conceived in the womb of Devānandā, a Brahman woman, the wife of a certain Ṛṣabhadatta. However, Indra, king of the gods, who had come to pay his respects to the foetus, became greatly agitated, and the following thought occurred to him:

> It has never happened nor does it happen nor will it happen that arhats, cakravartins...in the past, present or future should be born in low families, mean families, degraded families, poor families, indigent families, beggar families or Brahman families. For indeed, arhats, cakravartins ... in the past, present and future are born in high families, noble families, royal families, warrior families, families belonging to the race of Ikṣvāku or of Hari or in other such like families of pure descent on both sides. Surely this is an extraordinary event in the world: In the evermoving and endless progressive and regressive time cylces, it is possible that a prodigious exception might occur and an arhat, a cakravartin ... might enter the womb of a woman from an undeserving clan owing to the potency of the karma pertaining to the formation of their bodies and clans. But they have never been born from the womb of such a woman; they are never thus born, nor will they ever be born. Hence it is the established custom that the embryo of an arhat so conceived is taken from the womb of a woman and is transferred to the womb of a nobly-bred clan. I should therefore have the embryo of the last Tīrthaṅkara transferred from the womb of the Brahman woman Devānandā to that of Triśalā, a Kṣatriya woman of the Kāśyapa gotra, belonging to the Nāṭa clan, living in the Kṣatriya sector (the queen of King Siddhārtha) in the town of Kuṇḍagrāma.[3]

The Jainas believe that Indra ordered his commander of the army, a demigod named Harinegameśi, to conduct the transfer. The scene of the change of embryo (*garbhāpaharaṇa*) is depicted on the Jaina reliefs found at Mathura datable to the first century B.C.,[4] and the event itself constitutes the first of the *kalyāṇakas*, or auspicious events, together with the birth (*janma*), renunciation (*dīkṣā*), enlightenment (*kevalajñāna*) and death (*nirvāṇa*), which are celebrated by the Jainas even today in connection with the career of Mahāvīra.

The most startling feature of the Jaina legend is its strong rejection of the supremacy of the Brahman caste, and its proclamation of the superiority of the Kṣatriya. In the case of Mahāvīra the opportunity to be born as a Brahman was available, and yet rejected. For the other Tīrthaṅkaras as well, the Jainas have ordained that they be conceived only in a Kṣatriya womb;[5] the Jaina position appears to be totally uncompromising in this regard. The Buddhists too maintain that the Kṣatriyas are superior to the Brahmans, but do not prohibit the birth of a Buddha in a Brahman family. A passage in the *Jātaka* states unambiguously: "the Buddhas are not born in a family of Vaiśyas or of Śudras, but only in the two families of Kṣatriyas and Brahmans."[6] When we compare these two Śramaṇa attitudes, it becomes evident that for the Buddhists, as well as for the Jainas, both the Vaiśyas and Śūdras occupied the same low status as in the Brāhmaṇical system. However, the Buddhist ranking of the Brahman and the Kṣatriya was not fixed. It could be changed according to the will of the people (*lokasammuti*). The Jainas seem to have rejected any such option. For them, the Brahman was forever inferior to the Kṣatriya, although he remained higher than the two lowest castes. The Jaina reasons for maintaining the supremacy of the Kṣatriya must therefore be examined.

One of the reasons for placing the Kṣatriya at the pinnacle of the social order can be traced to the Jaina legend concerning the establishment of human civilization at the beginning of the present aeon (*kalpa*). The Jainas believe that Ṛṣabha, the first Tīrthaṅkara, was the creator of this civilization which began after the Golden Age,[7] when all people were equal and had no rulers. They obtained all of their needs from wish-fulfilling trees and, hence, had no necessity for human institutions of government, or defence, or administration. At the end of this period, however, the magic trees disappeared and new means of survival were required. With the need for food production and the just distribution of resources, the legend says that Ṛṣabha assumed the powers of king and appointed several men as armed defenders (*ugra*) and administrators (*bhoga*). The king as well as these officers assumed the title Kṣatriya. Thus, according to the Jaina mythology, at the beginning of civilization there were only two classes of people, the Kṣatriya and the non-Kṣatriya. Gradually, as Ṛṣabha invented the various occupations of agriculture, animal husbandry, and so forth, the Vaiśya and Śūdra castes (*jāti*) came into existence. There was still no Brahman caste at all.

According to the Jainas, the formation of the Brahman caste is attributed not to Ṛṣabha, but to his son Bharata, the first Universal Monarch or Cakravartin of India.[8] It is said that Ṛṣabha ultimately renounced the throne and became the first mendicant of our era, eventually achieving enlightenment and founding the first Jaina monastic order. Under his tutelage, a large number of people assumed the lay vows (*aṇuvratas*), which lead the layman progessively towards greater renunciation of worldly goods and family ties and culminate in the life of a recluse. It is said that Bharata honoured these lay disciples with gifts of wealth and marked them with special signs such as the sacred thread, and so forth, by virtue of which they were called *dvija* (twice-born). Their spiritual rebirth apparently released them from the incumbent duties of the other castes. The Ardha-Māgadhī form of the Sanskrit word *brāhmaṇa* is *māhaṇa.* The Jaina texts explain the derivation of this word as *mā haṇa* (don't kill); which was the advice given by *dvijas* to Bharata and other kings in conformity with their vows.[9] However ad hoc this etymology may be, it does attest to the Jaina belief that in the secular world there are only three castes and thus no place for Brahmans. Only a person who renounces the world sufficiently to be called a lay disciple may be called a Brahman. This lay disciple has no functions to perform for the material benefit of the society and does not fill any office either at court or the temple; his real associations are more with the ascetic who has totally renounced the world and who comes to be known as the "true" Brahman. The fact that Mahāvīra was not allowed to be born of Brahman parents and yet was given the title *māhaṇa* when he became a mendicant is sufficient to illustrate the Jaina refusal to accommodate the Brahman caste; the secular world consisted of only three castes and was not organized according to divine ordinance such as found in the Vedic *Puruṣasūkta.* While castes eventually became hereditary and may indeed have a hierachy of their own, this structure lacked any divine sanction and consequently remained entirely secular.

The legend of Mahāvīra's change of womb leads one to question why the Jainas thought it was unworthy of a Tīrthaṅkara to be born into a Brahman family. The story of course presupposes that the Brahman parents were not Jainas, whereas the new parents were followers of Pārśva,[10] the twenty-third Tīrthaṅkara and predecessor of Mahāvīra. But this alone is not sufficient to explain the rejection of the Brahman family. The word *bhikkhāya-kule* (beggar families), immediately preceding the word *māhaṇa*, in the quotation above, is very significant: it seems to allude disparagingly to the fact that the Brahmans subsisted on the favours bestowed by others, technically making them beggars. The Jainas have traditionally believed that only a mendicant may beg for his alms; a householder's position is to give, not receive, charity. The Brahman, by remaining a householder, violates the law when he accepts the gifts given by others, and is thus looked down upon by the Jainas in the same way as they might regard an apostate monk. It should be stated here that, by and large, the Jaina community, as it is constituted now, has no community of Brahmans. The Śvetāmbaras, as well as the Digambaras of the North, do not have a class of priests who perform rituals in their temples, nor do they employ any members of the Hindu Brahman caste to carry out these functions. While they show the incumbent respect to Brahmans, as Hindus would, they do not consider Brahmans superior to themselves. The one exception to this rule is found among Digambaras of Karnataka, who do in fact have a group of priests known as Indra (or Upādhye), sometimes euphemistically known as "Jaina-Brahmans."[11] The Indras are probably Hindu Brahmans converted to Jainism at some time during the early medieval period, who were entrusted with the task of attending to the temple rituals and catering to the needs of the Jaina laity on the occasions of various *saṃskāras*, such as marriage, child-birth, and funerals. Their main source of income is the offerings of food made regularly at the altar by households of a given village and the produce of the land attached to the temples, the proceeds of which they enjoy hereditarily. They are thus comparable to the traditional Brahmans of the traditional Hindu society. There is no intermarriage between the Indras and ordinary Jainas, nor, of course, with the members of the Hindu

Brahman community, who treat these Brahmans as non-Hindus.

There is a subtle distinction apparent here which is not without significance for our discussion on purity in Indian society. A Hindu Brahman is considered intrinsically pure and, for that reason, other castes do not hesitate to receive food from him. In the case of the "Jaina Brahman," however, orthodox Jainas who have formally taken the lay vows will not accept food from him even though he may take food from them. The inferiority of the Jaina-Brahman derives not only from the fact that he receives gifts (*dakṣiṇā*) from others for the ritual services performed, but also because he subsists upon the grains and fruits which have been offered by the devotees at the altar of a Jina. These offerings are called *devadravya* (goods intended for the worship of the Lord) and are considered *nirmālya*, fit to be discarded, either by burying them in the ground or by throwing them in water. In traditional Hindu temples such substances would be regarded as *prasāda*, food blessed by the Lord, and thus the purest of substances, which is eagerly consumed by the devotee. For the Jaina devotee, the worship of the Jina is a meditational act, despite its apparent similarity to the Brāhmaṇical *pūjā*. Strictly speaking, there is no deity in the Jaina temple: the Jina, unlike the Brāhmaṇical gods, transcends all pretense of "descending" into an image.[12] The visit to a temple is a meritorious act simply because it reminds the devotee of the Jina's preaching. The Jaina layman regards the temple as the holy assembly (*samavasaraṇa*) of the Jina and imagines the Jina's presence in that image. It would be socially unacceptable to approach such an august assembly empty-handed. The offerings therefore are neither received by the Lord nor blessed by any ritual act on the part of the priest. The "Jaina-Brahman," by eating the offered food, demeans himself and for that reason is considered lower in status than the *śrāvaka*, the initiated Jaina layman. These observations should show that, for a Jaina, neither the image, the offerings, nor the priest are holy or pure. Rather, the idea of renunciation, as symbolized by the image of the Jina,[13] is the source of purity. By extension, only the emancipated soul or his follower, the mendicant, may be regarded as the embodiment of purity. In Jainism, the Śramaṇa replaces the Brahman in the caste hierarchy, leaving no truly defined station for the latter. The Jina or his mendicant disciple may be called a *māhaṇa* metaphorically, but he is certainly not a Brahman in the sense of a member of the classical Brāhmaṇa *varṇa.*

Certain objects of veneration, which are also considered agents of purification are usually associated with the Brahman. One noteworthy example is fire *(agni)* which is thought to be sacred by all Hindus. Being both a divinity *(devatā)* as well as the priest of the gods, fire is believed to have an innate sacredness of its own. The importance of fire, around which almost all the *saṃskāras* revolve, including those associated with the funeral ceremony, is well documented. Given this pan-Indian belief concerning fire, one would expect the Jainas also to retain some modicum of veneration of fire. But such is not the case if one observes Jaina attitudes both as revealed in their scriptures and in their social customs. The Jainas do indeed include *agni* or fire in their list of astral beings *(jyotiṣka devas)* together with the sun and moon. But *agni* is not considered any more sacred than the other astral beings.

The ancient Jaina texts, on the other hand, repudiating the efficacy of the fire sacrifice, appear to be silent on the role of fire itself. In the post-canonical period, Jainas, especially in the South, undertook the task of integrating themselves into Brāhmaṇical society. It is to Jinasena, a ninth century Digambara *ācārya,* that credit is due for achieving this assimilation at a social level, without compromising the basic Jaina doctrines.[14] He introduced, apparently for the first time, a large number of *saṃskāras* for initiating a Jaina layman into the fourfold *āśrama* scheme, and laid down a variety of ceremonies involving the kindling of the sacred fire and the offering of food in Jaina temples. Explaining the worship of fire, however, Jinasena proclaims:

> Fire has no inherent sacredness and no divinity. But because of its contact with the body of the Tīrthaṅkara [at the time of his cremation], it can be considered pure. Such worship of fire, in the same way that the worship of holy places is made sacred by the Tīrthaṅkara's having attained *nirvāṇa* there, is not in any way blameworthy. For the Jainas, fire is regarded as suitable for worship only on a conventional level. It is in this way that Jainas worship fire as part of their veneration of the Jinas.[15]

The inauspiciousness of the funeral pyre notwithstanding, the Jainas have thus claimed that whatever sanctity fire has is solely derived from its contact with the dead body of the Jaina ascetic.

What is true of fire is probably true likewise of the other material elements *(mahābhūtas)*: earth, water and wind. It is well-known that the Hindus also regard these elements as sacred and worship them in various forms, considering them to be agents of purity. However, no hymn to earth, such as found in the *Atharvaveda,*[16] is attested to in Jaina texts. Jainas have decried all forms of respect shown to inanimate objects such as fields, stones, mounds or mountains. The Hindu custom of expiatory bathing in rivers and oceans, and worship of the Ganges and other rivers as holy objects, are totally unknown to the Jainas.[17] In fact, the Jainas prefer to use boiled water even for bathing and Jaina monks are not allowed even to touch cold water. All these material substances, including the wind element, are believed by the Jainas to be the bodies of one-sensed *(ekendriya)* beings, who constitute a form of life.

Vegetable life has also been treated by the Jainas in a manner similar to the *mahābhūtas.* The Hindus regard certain leaves, flowers and trees as more sacred than others, and make definite associations between these and certain gods and goddesses. The Jainas, however, have shown a totally different attitude toward vegetable life. The vegetable kingdom for the Jainas constitutes one of the lowest forms of life, called *nigoda,* and they are warned against destroying these beings. The Jainas are forbidden to eat a large number of fruits and vegetables, especially those with many seeds, like figs, or those which grow underground like potatoes. The Jaina spares their lives not because he considers them sacred or inhabited by divinities, but because they are the abodes of an infinite number of souls clustered together. The Jaina mendicant has even stricter dietary restrictions and is advised to avoid all forms of greens, since they are still alive; hence he subsists mainly on cereals and dried fruits which have no seeds.[18] He may neither kindle a fire nor extinguish one; he may neither draw water from a well nor fan himself. He thus protects the minute life present in these material elements. Even in modern Jaina monastic residences *(upāśraya)* the monks or nuns still live without lights or fans.

These observations should be adequate to show that the Jainas have not regarded as sacred those objects which are universally accepted as pure and auspicious by the Hindus. By repudiating the sanctity of these material objects, as well as of the "sacred cow" and the Brahman caste, the Jainas would seem to have divorced worldly life from the notion of purity. They see sacredness instead in renunciation, which is attributed not to any particular caste but to a group of people: the ascetics who embody renunciation and render other things sacred and pure only by their association with these people.

The Jaina rejection of the inherent purity of the material elements does not imply, however, that the Jainas refuse to accept any object as being auspicious and symbolic of wealth, fame and prosperity. A Tīrthaṅkara's mother, for example, is said to witness certain dreams at the moment of the conception of the child.[19] These dreams include such animals as a white elephant, a white bull and a lion; divinities like the sun, the moon, and the goddess Śrī; and objects like garlands of flowers, vases filled with water, an ocean of milk, a heap of jewels, and a pair of fish. All these are no doubt considered auspicious by the Hindus as well. The Jaina households and their temples are not devoid of some form of these representations. But what is significant is the Jaina insistence that these are not true *maṅgalas* (auspicious objects). They receive such status solely because of local custom (*deśācāra* or *lokācāra*) and, hence, are not sanctioned by the sacred texts.

The Jainas explain the term *maṅgala* as: (1) that which removes *(gālayadi)* impurities *(malāiṃ)*; or (2) that which brings *(lādi)* happiness *(maṅgaṃ sokkhaṃ)*. The *Pañcāstikāya-Tātparyavṛtti-ṭīkā*[20] enumerates several objects considered auspicious *(maṅgala)* by worldly people and seeks to prove that they are *maṅgala* only because of their similarity to particular qualities of the liberated soul. Sesame seeds (*siddhārtha*) are *maṅgala*, for example, only because their name reminds us of the *siddhas* (the perfected beings). A full pitcher (*pūrṇa-kumbha*) is *maṅgala* only because it reminds us of that *arhat* who is endowed with perfect bliss. Similarly a mirror (*mukura*) is to be considered an auspicious object only because it resembles the omniscient cognition of the Jina.

The Jainas are emphatic in their assertion that only ascetics—namely those who follow the Jaina mendicant laws—are truly auspicious (*maṅgala*). These are considered to be four holy objects (*cattāri maṅgalaṃ*)[21] in which a layman takes refuge for his spiritual salvation. They are: (1) the *arhat* or Jina, i.e. one who is worthy of worship; (2) the *siddha*: one who has accomplished his goal, by becoming free from embodiment; (3) the *sādhu*, or Jaina mendicant; and, finally, *dharma*, the sacred law taught by the *kevalin*: i.e. one who is isolated from the karmic bonds. The formula is also called *māṅgalika* and is chanted regularly by the Jaina laity and mendicants together with another sacred formula, the *pañca namaskāra mantra*, or salutations to the five holy beings: namely, the *arhat*, the *siddha*, the *ācārya*, the *upādhyāya* (mendicant teacher), and the *sādhu*. At the end of this ancient formula they finally recite a verse (of unknown date) in which it is asserted that this fivefold salutation which destroys all evils is pre-eminent (*prathama-maṅgala*) among all auspicious things.[22]

The Indian tradition has unreservedly accepted the holiness of the ascetic, because of his renunciation of worldly possessions. But it is doubtful that he was ever considered to be an auspicious (*śubha*) sight, especially in the context of such festive occasions as the celebration of a marriage, or the beginning of a new business venture. While the ascetic might have represented *śuddha*—the purity associated with the transcendental practices which led to *mokṣa*—*maṅgala* was reserved originally only for those worldly, meritorious activities (*puṇya*) which led to the three *puruṣārthas* of *dharma*, *artha*, and *kāma*. The Buddhists and Jainas attempted to assimilate the ascetic ideal into *maṅgala*, not by degrading the *śuddha*, but instead by raising *maṅgala* to a new status which incorporated both the worldly *śubha* and the supramundane *śuddha*.

In this new scheme, anything which was not *śuddha* was considered to be *aśuddha*: activities which were not productive of salvation. However, this *aśuddha* was subsequently subdivided into the mundane pure (*śubha*) and the mundane impure (*aśubha*), i.e., the dichotomies of good and evil, wholesome and unwholesome, which were only conducive to worldly happiness and unhappiness. Thus, for the Jainas, *maṅgala* came to refer both to the transcendental (*śuddha*), as well as to that portion of the mundane sphere which was pure (*śubha*). A similar pattern seems to be operating in the Theravādin Buddhist division of the meditational heavens into the Suddhāvāsa and Śubhakiṇha.[23] The former is "the pure abodes," inhabited by the *anāgāmins* who attain to arhatship from that abode in that very life, whereas the latter is the abode of Brahmās: beings who, however exalted, will return to the cycle of transmigration.

Accordingly, the Jainas begin with the repudiation of the innate sacredness of material objects but allow that an association with the "truly" holy (*maṅgala*) might render them auspicious (*śubha*). The Jaina refusal to allow the integration of the Brahman in their caste system seems consistent with their rejection of a category called "the auspicious" (*maṅgala*) independent of the worldly pure (*śubha*) and the transcendentally pure (*śuddha*).

NOTES

1. Louis Dumont, *Homo Hierarchicus* (Chicago: The University of Chicago Press, 1970).
2. See P. S. Jaini, "Śramaṇas: Their Conflict with Brāhmaṇical Society," in J. W. Elder, ed. *Chapters in Indian Civilization*, I, (Dubuque, Iowa: Kendall Hunt, 1970), pp. 39-81.
3. ...na eyaṃ bhūyaṃ'na eyaṃ bhavvaṃ, na eyaṃ bhavissaṃ, jaṃ ṇaṃ arahaṃtā vā cakkavaṭṭi vā...bhikkhāyakulesu vā māhaṇakulesu vā āyāiṃsu. [*Kalpasūtra* 21]

   See H. Jacobi, tr., *Jaina Sūtras*, Sacred Books of the East, Vol. XXII, Pt. 1, p. 225. It should be noted that the Digambara Jainas reject the authenticity of this Śvetāmbara scripture and also do not admit the legend pertaining to Mahāvīra's change of womb.
4. Vincent A. Smith, *The Jaina Stūpa and Other Antiquities of Mathurā* (1901; reprint ed., Varanasi: Indological Book House, 1969).
5. According to the Jaina tradition all the twenty-four Tīrthaṅkaras of the present age were born into the Kṣatriya families (17 in the Ikṣvākuvaṃśa, 2 in the Harivaṃśa, 1 (Pārśva) in the Ugravaṃśa and 1(Mahāvīra) in the Nāthavaṃśa). For details see Jinendra Varni, *Jainendra-Siddhānta-Kośa*, 4 vols (Delhi: Bhāratīya Jñānapīṭha, 1970-73).
6. ...Buddhā nāma Vessakule vā Suddakule vā na nibbattanti. lokasammute pana Khattiyakule vā Brāhmaṇakule vā dvīsu yeva kulesu nibbattanti, idāni ca Khattiyakulaṃ lokasammutaṃ, tattha nibbattissāmīti....*Jātakatthavaṇṇanā* ed. V. Fausboll, Vol. I, Pali Text Society, (reprint ed., 1963), p. 40. In conformity with this belief the Buddhists have stated that of the twenty-five Buddhas of the present period, twenty-two Buddhas were born into the Kṣatriya families and three (Koṇāgamana, Kakusandha and Kassapa, Nos. 22, 23 and 24) were born into the Brahman families. See *Buddhavaṃsa* and *Cariyāpiṭaka*, ed. N. A. Jayawickrama, Pali Text Society, 1974.
7. For the Jaina speculations on the origin of the castes, see P. S. Jaini, 1974, "Jina Ṛṣabha as an *avatāra* of Viṣṇu," in *Bulletin of the School of Oriental and African Studies*, XL, Pt. 2 (University of London, 1974), pp. 321-337.
8. For the Digambara account, see *Ādipurāṇa* (of Jinasena), Part I, chs. 38-40 (Varanasi: Bhāratīya Jñānapīṭha, 1963). For the Śvetāmbara account, see

Triṣaṣṭi-śalākāpuruṣacaritra (of Hemacandra), Vol. I., in *The Lives of Sixty-three Illustrious Persons*, tr. Helen M. Johnson, Vol. I (Baroda: Oriental Institute, 1962).

9. Bharato 'tha samāhūya śrāvakān abhyadhād idam/
gṛhe madīye bhoktavyaṃ yuṣmābhiḥ prativāsaram//
kṛṣyādi na vidhātavyaṃ kintu svādhyāyatatparaiḥ/
apūrvajñānagrahaṇaṃ kurvāṇaiḥ sthyeyam anvayam//
bhuktvā ca me 'ntikagataiḥ paṭhanīyam idaṃ sadā/
jito bhavān vardhate bhīs tasmān mā hana mā hana//
...krameṇa māhanās te tu brāhmaṇā iti viśrutāḥ..../
[*Triṣaṣṭiśalākāpuruṣacaritra*, I, 8, 227-248]

10. On the 23rd Tīrthaṅkara Pārśva, see M. Bloomfield, *The Life and Stories of the Jaina Saviour Pārśvanātha* (Baltimore: University of Maryland Press, 1919).

11. For further details on the Jaina priestly castes, see V. A. Sangave, *Jaina Community: A Social Survey* (Bombay: Popular Book Depot, 1959).

12. For a detailed description of the Jaina forms of worship see P.S. Jaini, *The Jaina Path of Purification* (Berkeley: California Press, 1979). It should be noted that many Jaina temples have images of *yakṣas* or "guardian spirits" who are worshipped by the laity. These are invoked by mantras and are believed to manifest themselves in their images. However, the Jaina layman is admonished to refrain from treating them as equal to the Jina and the mendicant is of course barred from even saluting them, since they are inferior to him. See *ibid.*, p. 194, notes 13-14.

13. The reformist Jaina sect known as the Sthānakavāsī rejects even this symbolic representation and regards idol-worship (*mūrtipūjā*) as a form of *mithyātva* (wrong behaviour) even when performed by a layman. See Jaini, 1979, ch. IX.

14. See R. Williams, *Jaina Yoga: A Survey of the Mediaeval Śrāvakācāras* (London: Oxford University Press, 1963).

15. na svato 'gneḥ pavitratvaṃ devatārūpam eva vā/
kintv arhaddivyamūrtījyāsambandhāt pāvano 'nalaḥ//
tataḥ pūjyāṅgatām asya matvā 'rcanti dvijottamāḥ/
nirvāṇakṣetrapūjāvat tatpūjā 'to na duṣyati//
vyavahāranayāpekṣā tasyeṣṭā pūjyatā dvijaiḥ/
[*Ādipurāṇa of Jinasena*, xl, 88-90]
The Buddhist texts go even further and reject all popular beliefs regarding the divinity of fire and water:
sikhiṃ hi devesu vadanti h'eke, āpaṃ milakkhā pana devam āhu/
sabbe va ete vitathaṃ vadanti, aggī na devaññataro na cāpo//
nirindriyaṃ santam asaññakāyaṃ, vessānaraṃ kammakaraṃ pajānaṃ/
paricāriya-m-aggiṃ sugatiṃ kathaṃ vaje, pāpāni kammāni pakubbamāno// [*Jātakatthavaṇṇanā*, VI, 892-3]

16. *Atharvaveda*, XII, 1 (63 verses).

17. Somadevasūri, a tenth-century Jaina author gives a long list of such practices forbidden to a Jaina layman:
sūryārgho grahaṇasnānaṃ saṃkrāntau draviṇavyayaḥ/
sandhyā sevāgnisatkāro gehadehārcano vidhiḥ//
nadīnadasamudreṣu majjanaṃ dharmacetasā...

varārthaṃ lokayātrārtham uparodhārtham eva vā/
upāsanam amīṣāṃ syāt samyagdarśanahānaye//
Upāsakādhyayana, vv. 136-140 (ed. K. Shastri, Varanasi: Bhāratīya Jñānapīṭha, 1964).

18. No less than thirty-two kinds of plants are forbidden for a Jaina layman. See R. Williams, *Jaina Yoga*, pp. 110-116.
19. For a canonical description of these dreams see H. Jacobi, *The Jaina Sūtras*, Part I, pp. 231-238.
20. For this text as well as for a detailed discussion on the *maṅgala* objects, see Jinendra Varṇi, *Jainendra-Siddhānta-Kośa*, Vol. III., pp. 251-255.
21. [*maṅglasuttāṇi:*] cattāri maṅgalaṃ:
arahantā maṅgalaṃ, siddhā maṅgalaṃ, sāhū maṅgalaṃ, kevalipannatto dhammo maṅgalaṃ/
cattāri loguttamā: arahantā...siddhā...sāhū...dhammo loguttamo/
cattāri saraṇaṃ pavajjāmi:
arahante...siddhe...sāhū...dhammaṃ saraṇaṃ pavajjāmi//
[pañcanamokkāramaṅgalasuttaṃ:]
ṇamo arahantāṇaṃ, ṇamo siddhāṇaṃ, ṇamo āyariyāṇaṃ, ṇamo uvajjhāyāṇaṃ, ṇamo loe savvasāhūṇaṃ//
Āvassayasuttam., 1-4, Jaina-āgama-series, no. 15, (Bombay: Śrī Mahāvīra Jaina Vidyālaya, 1977).
22. eso pañca-namokkāro savva-pāva-ppanāsano/
maṅgalāṇaṃ ca savvesiṃ paḍhamaṃ havai maṅgalaṃ//
Quoted in R. Williams, *Jaina Yoga*, p. 185.
This is comparable to the refrain "etaṃ maṅgalaṃ uttamaṃ" of the famous *Maṅgalasutta* of the Buddhists. This sutta also lists the perfect virtues of the enlightened person as the best of the *maṅgalas*:
tapo ca brahmacariyañ ca etaṃ maṅgalaṃ uttamaṃ//
Khuddakapāṭha, p. 3 (Pali Text Society, 1915).
23. For details on these abodes see G. P. Malalasekera, *Dictionary of Pali Proper Names*, Vol. II, Pali Text Society, 1960, pp. 1199 and 1229.

CHAPTER 13

Jaina Festivals*

Jainism

Jainism today is a religion whose followers are few in number, only about four million throughout India. Along with Buddhism it was one of the two most prominent Śramaṇa or non-Brāhmaṇical religions that originated in the Ganges valley during the sixth or seventh century BCE, but its history differs from that of Buddhism in two striking respects: Buddhism was destined to spread throughout South-east and East Asia, while Jainism never left the subcontinent; secondly, Buddhism declined and almost disappeared from India, while Jainism survives in almost all parts of India, especially in the Western states (Punjab, Rajasthan, Gujarat) and the Deccan (Maharashtra and Karnataka).

Jainism is recognisable as an Indian religion, espousing the doctrine of *saṃsāra* (the cycle of birth and death). This doctrine holds that all living beings are bound by their *karma* (effect of past deeds), which leads to their successive re-births in different bodies, but that there is a possibility of salvation in the form of freedom from the cycle of birth and death. Nevertheless, it rejects the authority of the Vedas and related texts, the efficacy of sacrifice, the existence of a creator-god, and the underlying rationale of the caste system. The human model emulated by the Jainas is that of the perfected ascetic, whom they call *Jina* (Vic-

---

*This article was published originally in *Festivals in World Religions*, ed. A. Brown, (London: The SHAP Working Party on World Religions in Education, Longman, 1986), pp. 140-149. Reprinted with kind permission of the SHAP Working Party on World Religions in Education.

torious), whence the name Jaina is derived, or *Tīrthaṅkara* (Maker of a bridge across the river of *saṃsāra*).

The Jainas, who hold to a variation of the typically Indian scheme of beginningless, cyclical time, believe that in each of an infinite number of cosmic cycles there is an ascending and descending phase, and in each phase twenty-four Tīrthaṅkaras teach the Jaina path. We are currently near the end of the descending phase, the first teacher of which was named Ṛṣabha, and the last Vardhamāna Mahāvīra. Only legendary accounts of the first twenty-two Jinas exist, while the twenty-third Jina, Pārśva, is considered an historical figure, since his followers, known as *Niganthas,* are mentioned in the Buddhist Tripīṭaka. Mahāvīra, the last Tīrthaṅkara and the supreme teacher of the present-day Jainas (599-527) BCE, flourished in the tradition of Pārśva and was a contemporary of Gautama the Buddha.

According to the canonical texts of the Jainas, their community at the time of Mahāvīra was comprised of lay votaries and mendicants, with as many as 14,000 monks (*sādhus*) and 36,000 nuns (*sādhvis*). Around 300 BCE the once unified Jaina monastic community was split into two major sects known as *Digambara* and *Śvetāmbara.* The Digambara (Sky-clad) monks claimed that total renunciation of clothing—as practised by Mahāvīra himself—was a prerequisite for being a Jaina monk and therefore adhered to the practice of nudity. The Śvetāmbaras (White-clad) maintained that nudity was forbidden to the members of the ecclesiastical community and adopted the practice of wearing white (cotton) garments. The two mendicant sects eventually rejected each other as being apostates from the true path, compiled their own scriptures, and ceased to perform their common rituals, such as confession, together. The lay followers, called *śrāvakas* (hearers of the law), of these two sects also formed their own social groups. They are distinguished mainly by the images of the Tīrthaṅkaras that they worship; the Digambara images are naked, while the Śvetāmbara images are decorated with ornaments of gold and silver. In the sixteenth century, moreover, there arose within the Śvetāmbara community a reformist movement (*Sthānakavāsī*) that condemned the worship of images. Thus, in spite of a basic agreement about the fundamental teachings of the Jina, there have been sectarian differences regarding the manner in which the Jaina festivals are celebrated.

Notwithstanding these sectarian differences the Jainas have been able to preserve their separateness from the Hindus, primarily because of their sizeable monastic community. According to the most recent count it includes about two thousand monks and five thousand nuns, who form the most important element in supervising the major Jaina festivals. During the course of more than two thousand years of close contact with the Hindus, especially the merchant castes, the Jaina laypeople have adopted many of the Hindu social customs, such as the caste system; and participate in Hindu festivals such as Vijayādaśamī (Dassehrā) and Divālī, which have become Indian national holidays. But the major Jaina festivals are observed exclusively by the Jainas, since they are celebrations of the holy careers of the Tīrthaṅkaras and of ascetic practices that emphasise non-possession (*aparigraha*) and non-violence (*ahiṃsā*), the two most important features of the Jaina teachings.

The Jaina Era and Calendar

The Jainas have traditionally reckoned the era of Mahāvīra (*Vīra-samvat*) to have begun in 528 BCE, the year after Mahāvīra's death. This era, also known as the *Vīra-nirvāṇa* era is, however, employed by Jaina authors only to indicate the dates of major events in the history of the Jainas (major schisms, councils, compilation of texts, and so on). For all other purposes the Jainas have used the *Vikrama-samvat* (beginning in 58 BCE), prevalent among the Hindus of Western India. Thus the holidays described below follow the traditional Hindu calendar (*pañcāṅga*).

New Year's Day has no special religious significance for the Jainas, since it is not associated with the holy career of the Jina. The birthday of Mahāvīra (Mahāvīra-jayantī), the only Jaina holiday recognized by the Government of India, therefore functions as the first of the annual cycle of Jaina festivals.

The Festivals

Mahāvīra-jayantī (April)

Mahāvīra-jayantī, or the celebration of Mahāvīra's birth, takes place on the thirteenth day of the waxing moon of Caitra. Although the annual festival of confession, the last day of the Paryūśana-parva is the holiest, Mahāvīra-jayaṇtī is the most important festival in social terms. All Jainas, regardless, of sectarian affiliations, come together to celebrate this occasion publicly, taking leave from work and school to participate in the activities.

According to tradition Mahāvīra was born in 599 BCE in Kundagrama, a large city in the kingdom of Vaiśālī (near modern Patna in the state of Bihar). His father, named Siddhārtha, is said to have been a warrior chieftain of the Jnatri clan. His mother, Triśalā, was the sister of the ruler of Vaiśālī. The Jaina myths say that five events in the life of a Jina are the most auspicious occasions (*kalyāṇas*), on which the gods come down to earth and attend upon him. His descent from heaven into his mother's womb (*garbha*) is the first occasion. At this time his mother has sixteen dreams, in which she sees sixteen auspicious objects, such as a white elephant, a lion, the full moon, the rising sun, an ocean of milk, and so on. The second auspicious event is his birth (*janma*). Indra, the king of gods, and his consort, Indrāṇi, come down to the royal palace and transport the baby to Mount Meru, the centre of the Jaina universe, and sprinkle him with water from all the oceans. Thus they declare the advent of a new Tīrthaṅkara.

During the Mahāvīra-jayantī, these two auspicious events are celebrated with great pomp by the Jaina laity in the form of a ritual which may strike an outsider as a dramatic re-enactment. The festival begins in the early part of the morning with the arrival of the Jainas at their local temple. On this day gold and silver images, which represent the objects in Triśalā's dreams, are prominently displayed in order to suggest the conception of Mahāvīra. A newly married or a wealthy couple will volunteer to assume the roles of Indra and Indrāṇi, and will worship a small image of the Jina by placing it on a pedestal (serving as Mount Meru) and pouring perfumed water on it, and anointing it with sandalwood paste. Those who play these roles distribute large amounts of money for charitable purposes as well as for the upkeep of the shrine. The other members of the community join in this ritual by chanting the holy litany while showering flowers on the image and waving lamps (*āratī*) in front of it.

If a monk or a nun happens to be in residence at that time, he or she will add to the occasion by reading the *Kalpasūtra*, the biography of Mahāvīra, and describe the three remaining *kalyāṇas* of his spiritual career: Mahāvīra's renunciation of household life (*dīkṣā-kalyāṇa*) at the age of 30, his severe austerities for a period of twelve and a half years culminating in his enlightenment (*kevalajñāna-kalyāṇa*), and finally his death (*nirvāṇa-kalyāṇa*) at the age of 72. The ceremony concludes with the chanting of the holy Jaina hymns in the praise of Mahāvīra and the laypeople returning to their homes to enjoy a feast in honour of Mahāvīra's birth.

Akṣaya-tṛtīyā (April/May)

The holiday of Akṣaya-tṛtīyā (Immortal Third) falls on the third day of the waxing moon of Vaiśākh. Akṣaya-tṛtīyā celebrates the first instance of alms being given to a mendicant, in this case the first Tīrthaṅkara of this cycle, Ṛṣabha. After his renunciation, Ṛṣabha went without food for six months, since none of his contemporaries knew the proper foods acceptable to a mendicant. A Jaina mendicant, who by law must be a vegetarian, observes a great many other dietary restrictions. He may not eat raw vegetables nor fruits like figs, which contain many seeds. Tradition has it that a prince named Śreyāṃsa dreamed that in a past life he had offered alms to a Jaina monk. This dream led him to recognize the kind of food acceptable to a Jaina mendicant. He then offered a pitcherful of sugarcane juice to Ṛṣabha, who, by drinking it, broke his six-month fast. The gods celebrated this event by showering jewels on Śreyāṃsa's household, and that day thus became known as the Immortal Third.

The present-day Jainas celebrate the first gift of alms to a Jaina mendicant by publicly honouring laymen and laywomen who undertake fasts similar to that of Ṛṣabha. In almost all major centres of Jaina population several elderly Jainas of both sexes vow to fast on alternate days for periods of six months or a year. The last day of these fasts (*varṣī-tapa*) falls on the Akṣaya-tṛtīyā, when the elders of the Jaina community, under the supervision of a monk or a nun, honour these devout Jaina laypeople by feeding them spoonfuls of sugarcane juice, thus helping them to break their fasts. This action recalls Śreyāṃsa's giving alms to Ṛṣabha and emulates the examples of the first Jaina ascetic in undergoing austerities on the path of salvation.

Śruta-pañcamī (May/June)

Śruta-pañcamī (Scripture-Fifth) is celebrated on the fifth day of the waxing moon of Jyeṣṭha. It commemorates the day on which the Jaina scriptures (*śruta*) were first committed to writing. At first the teachings of Mahāvīra were handed down orally; since they were sacred, Jaina teachers were not willing to commit them to writing. It was, however, not easy to maintain this oral tradition, since those monks who had committed the teachings to memory gradually died off, and, because of adverse conditions few new monks were trained.

The Digambara tradition maintains that around 150 CE two Jaina monks, Bhūtabali and Puṣpadanta, compiled those teachings that were available and wrote them down on palm leaves. The 'Scripture-Fifth' is said to be the day on which this scripture, entitled *Ṣatkhaṇḍa-āgama* (Scripture in Six Parts), was completed. The Śvetāmbaras, however, have a different set of scriptures called *Dvādaśa-aṅga-sūtra* (Scripture in Twelve Parts). These were compiled under the supervision of their pontiff (*ācārya*) Devārddhigaṇi Kṣamāśramaṇa, c. 450 CE. This event occurred at a different time of the year, and hence it is celebrated on the fifth day of the waxing moon of Kārttika (October/November). The actual celebrations, nevertheless, are almost identical.

On this day elaborately decorated copies of the scripture are displayed in Jaina temples, and devotees sit in front of the pedestal on which they are placed. They then sing hymns in praise of the Jinas who preached the teachings and the mendicants who faithfully preserve them. On such occasions it is customary for rich laypeople to commission new, illustrated copies of certain texts, especially the biographies of the Jinas such as the *Kalpasūtra*, and distribute them to the general public. Jaina children participate in this festival by copying the Jaina litanies and by giving gifts of paper and pens. The ceremony concludes with as sermon by a monk or a nun about the importance of reading scriptures in the search for knowledge. The public then recites a formula in veneration of the teachers. For this reason this day is also known as Jñāna-pañcamī (Knowledge-Fifth) or Guru-pañcamī (Teacher-Fifth).

Paryuṣaṇa-parva/Daśa-lakṣaṇa-parva (August)

The festivals described above last only a day and are associated with some historical event. On the other hand Paryuṣaṇa, which means 'passing the rainy season', is dedicated to the cultivation of certain religious practices of a longer duration. The Jaina monks and nuns, unlike their counterparts in other religions, do not have permanent abodes in the form of monasteries and nunneries; they are obliged by law to stay only a few days or weeks at a time in any one place. During the four months of the rainy season (*cāturmāsa*), however, they are required to choose a fixed place of residence and spend their time within the boundary of that village or town. The presence of nuns and monks (who must always live separately and in groups of a minimum of three persons) during the rainy season thus affords great opportunities for the lay devotees to undertake a variety of religious practices. The elders in the Jaina community plan for this occasion a year in advance by inviting a particular group of monks or nuns to come to their town for the rainy season. Since the Jaina mendicants must travel by foot, they set out on their journey early enough that they may arrive before the onset of the rainy season, which officially begins on the fourteenth day of the waxing moon of Āṣāḍha (June/July). On that day laypeople visit the mendicant teachers and resolve to lead temporarily a life of restraint which may include dietary restrictions (such as not eating certain kinds of foods or not eating at night time), sitting in meditation in a regular manner every day, or the study of a particular scripture.

Participation in these religious observances becomes more intense during the week-long celebration of the Paryuṣaṇaparva. For the Śvetāmbaras this begins on the twelfth day of the waning moon of Śrāvaṇa (August) and ends on the fourth day of the waxing moon of Bhādrapada. The Digambaras celebrate the same festival a week later, for ten days.

During these eight or ten days many members, young or old, of the Jaina community observe some form of restraint regarding food. Some may eat only once a day, or fast completely on the first and the last days; others refrain from eating and drinking (except for boiled water) for the entire week. These latter spend most of their time in temples or monasteries, in the company of monks. All participants attempt in these various ways to emulate the life of a mendicant for however short a time, detaching themselves from worldly affairs and leading a meditative life. Each day monks and nuns give sermons, placing special emphasis on the life and teachings of Mahāvīra. For a second time the Śvetāmbaras celebrate the birth of Mahāvīra by reading the

Kalpasūtra in public, thus rededicating themselves to his ideals.

The Digambaras refer to the festival of Paryuṣaṇa-parva also by the name Daśa-lakṣaṇa-parva, or the Festival of Ten Virtues: forgiveness, humility, honesty, purity, truthfulness, self-restraint, asceticism, study, detachment, and celibacy. They dedicate each day of the festival to one of the virtues.

The celebration of Paryuṣaṇa-parva comes to a climax on the last day, when Jainas of all sects perform the annual ceremony of confession, *Saṃvatsarī-pratikramaṇa.* This is the holiest day of the year for the Jainas, who take leave from work or school on this occasion to participate in the activities. On the evening of this day (on which almost all participants have fasted) Jainas assemble in their local temples, and, in the presence of their mendicant teachers, they confess their transgressions by uttering the words *micchā me dukkaḍam* (may all my transgressions be forgiven). They then exchange pleas for forgiveness with their relatives and friends. Finally they extend their friendship and goodwill to all beings in the following words:

> 'I ask pardon of all living creatures;
> May all of them pardon me.
> May I have a friendly relationship with all beings,
> And unfriendly with none.'

Vīra-nirvāṇa (November)

The festival of Vīra-nirvāṇa, or the anniversary of the death of Mahāvīra, occurs on the fifteenth day of the waning moon of Āśvina. On this night in the year 527 BCE Mahāvīra, at the age of 72, entered *nirvāṇa* (the state of immortality that is freedom forever from the cycle of birth and death) in a place called Pavapuri, near modern Patna. Towards the dawn, his chief apostle (*gaṇadhara*) Indrabhūti Gautama, a monk of long-standing, is said to have attained to enlightenment (*kevalajñāna*), the supreme goal of a Jaina mendicant. Tradition has it that Mahāvīra's eighteen contemporary kings celebrated both these auspicious events by lighting rows of lamps. This act of 'illumination' is claimed by the Jainas as the true origin of Divālī, the Hindu Festival of Lights, which falls on the same day. The Hindus, of course, have a different legend associated with Divālī, and their festival probably antedates Mahāvīra's *nirvāṇa.*

Devout Jaina laypeople observe Vīra-nirvāṇa by undertaking a twenty-four-hour fast, and spend this time in meditation. It is considered highly meritorious to keep vigil throughout this holy night, especially at the actual site of Mahāvīra's *nirvāṇa.* Those who cannot make the pilgrimage perform a memorial worship in their local temple by lighting lamps in front of an image of Mahāvīra. This solemn service takes place early in the morning of the next day, the first day of the waxing moon of Kārttika, prior to the breaking of the day-long fast. The ceremony concludes with a pubic recitation of an ancient hymn addressed to all 'liberated beings' (*siddhas*), including Mahāvīra:

> 'Praise to the holy, the blessed ones, who provide the path across, ... those who are endowed with unobstructed knowledge and insight...the Jinas, who have crossed over, who help others cross, the liberated and the liberators, the omniscient, the all-seeing, those who have reached the destiny of the *siddha,* from which there is no return and which is bliss immutable, inviolable, imperishable, and undisturbed; praise to the Jinas who have overcome fear. I worship all the *siddhas,* those who have been, and those who in future will be.'

***Kārttika-pūrṇimā/Ratha-yātrā* (December)**

The festival of the Kārttika-pūrṇimā, or the Jaina Car Festival (Ratha-yātrā), occurs within a fortnight of Divālī, on the full moon day of Kārttika. This marks the end of the rainy season. On the following day the monks and nuns, who have stayed in retreat for four months, must resume their wanderings. At the same time the laypeople are released from the various vows which they had undertaken for the duration of the season. The festival of Kārttika-pūrṇimā provides them with an opportunity to thank the monks and nuns for their sermons and counsel.

The laypeople celebrate this day by putting an image of the Jina into an immense, beautifully decorated wooden vehicle (*ratha*) and pulling it by hand through the streets of the city. The procession, headed by monks and nuns, begins at the local temple and winds its way through the city to a park within the city limits. Here a prominent monk gives a sermon, and the leading laypeople call for generous donations in support of the various social and religious projects (such as building temples, libraries, or hospitals) that have been inspired by the presence of the mendicants. The procession then returns to the temple, and the people go home in a festive mood.

Bāhubali-mastaka-abhiṣeka (Every Twelve Years, February)

Finally, we may mention a special ceremony, which, although not part of the annual cycle, is the most famous and by far the most spectacular of all Jaina festivals. This is called Mastaka-abhiṣeka (Head-anointing), and is held every twelfth year at Śravaṇabelgola, in Karnataka, in honour of the Jaina saint and hero, Bāhubali. The most recent performance of this very popular ceremony took place in February, 1981 CE, and was especially dramatic, since it fell on the thousandth anniversary of the consecration of Bāhubali's statue, which was installed by the Jaina general, Cāmuṇḍarāya. Hundreds of thousands of Jainas from all over India came to the small town of Śravaṇabelgola, in order to anoint and to meditate before this monumental statue of Bāhubali, which stands fifty-seven feet tall and was carved out of granite on a hill-top just outside of the town. The statue depicts Bāhubali, the first man to attain to *nirvāṇa* in our present time cycle, as standing erect, completely naked, immersed in deep meditation. Bāhubali is believed to have held this posture, oblivious to the vines and snakes gathering around him, for twelve months, in a heroic effort to root out the last vestiges of impurity. In order to honour his achievement and to gain great merit for themselves, the faithful come to Śravaṇabelgola every twelve years, and erect a temporary scaffolding behind the statue, with a platform at the top. From this platform they anoint Bāhubali with pitcherfuls of various ointments consisting of yellow and red powder, sandalwood paste, milk, and clear water; the colours of these materials symbolically represent the stages of purification of Bāhubali's soul as it progresses towards enlightenment.

Table of Jaina Festivals

February	Bāhubali-mastaka-abhiṣeka (every twelve years)
April	Mahāvīra-jayantī
April/May	Akṣaya-tṛtīyā
May/June	Śruta-pañcamī
August	Paryuṣaṇa-parva/Daśa-lakṣaṇa-parva
November	Vīra-nirvāṇa
December	Kārttika-pūrṇimā/Ratha-yātrā

CHAPTER 14

Indian Perspectives on the Spirituality of Animals*

Introduction

Casual visitors to Indian cities are often struck by the Indian habit of venerating such animals as the cow, as well as by the excessive preoccupation with vegetarian food and the apparently "misplaced" compassion toward pests like rodents or monkeys. Because of this obsessive concern with animal welfare and their relative indifference toward human suffering, Indians are often accused of lacking a sense of discrimination between the conflicting needs of higher and lower forms of life. To be sure there is an element of truth in this criticism: Indians do indeed consider animals to be akin to humans in a number of important ways. A widely known aphorism (*subhāṣita*) succinctly summarized the traditionally held belief in the close affinities between humans and animals:

> Human beings are equal to animals
> As far as food, sleep, fear, and sex are concerned;
> They are distinguished only because of *dharma*.
> [A person who] lacks *dharma* is the same as the animals.[1]

Indeed, Indians believe that only the *dharma*—the moral conscience which allows the individual to distinguish the whole-

---

*This is a revised version of an article published originally in *Buddhist Philosophy and Culture: Essays in Honour of N. A. Jayawickrema*, eds. D. Kalupahana and W. G. Weeraratne (Colombo, 1987), pp. 169-178.

some from the unwholesome—differentiates humanity from animals.

Animal Spirituality in Hindu Literature

The treatment of animals in Brāhmaṇical, Buddhist and Jaina fables, however, belies this distinction between men and animals purely on moral grounds. Indeed anyone familiar with Indian bestiaries like *Pañcatantra* or *Hitopadeśa* will be aware of the frequent references to the capacity of animals for moral and spiritual development. Virtually every Indian household, for example, knows the feats accomplished by the monkey-god Hanumān, the exemplary servant of Lord Rāma, in securing the release of Rāma's wife, Sītā, from the clutches of the demon Rāvaṇa. Equally well-known in India is the story of the bird Jaṭāyū, the giant vulture who gave its life while attempting to prevent Rāvaṇa's abduction of Sītā: in this epic tale, Lord Rāma himself lauds the bird's devotion and performs a funeral service for him on a par even with that performed for one's departed father. (*Rāmāyaṇa* 3.64.23-36)

Perhaps the most celebrated story concerning an animal, however, which involves neither service nor sacrifice but instead total devotion to the Lord, is a late story, *Gaja-mokṣa* ("Liberation of the Elephant"), appearing in the late tenth-century *Bhāgavatapurāṇa*. According to this tale, a certain elephant arrives at the bank of a lake to quench his thirst, only to be caught by a crocodile and dragged down into the mire. The elephant, realizing his hopeless position, happened to recall a hymn that he had learned in a previous life and uttered it with utmost surrender, begging Lord Viṣṇu to rescue him from his calamity.[2] The Lord appeared atop his mount, Garuḍa, killing the crocodile and saving the elephant. The narrator hastens to add that, at that very moment, the elephant lost his animal body and assumed the form of a four-armed Viṣṇu, suggesting thereby that he had attained a state of similarity (*sāmya*) with the Lord.[3] Although such a story is narrated in order to show both the extraordinary power accruing from devotion and the unlimited grace of the Lord, it is also probably intended to demonstrate the capacity of animals to attain salvation. Given this capability, and distinction between the various animal species and humans is purely conventional in nature and does not affect their innate spirits. One must, however, beware of taking this story too literally as implying that all animals are the equals of human beings. This is because the narrator, as if he were anticipating serious reservations about the ability of an animal to recollect a *stotra* learned lifetimes ago, adds that the elephant was the Pāṇḍya king Indradyumna in his previous life, who had improperly abandoned his royal duties and assumed the ascetic life without appropriate guidance. Because he thereby disregarded the duties to the sages incumbent on the householder, he was cursed by the sage Agastya and, as a result, was reborn as an elephant.[4] This disclaimer reduces the relevancy of the tale as referring to animals and places the focus instead on a human being who was temporarily shackled by a lower destiny; this, in fact, is a common feature of animal stories in the *Mahābhārata* and *Rāmāyaṇa.* It does not, therefore, allow us to universalize its claim that animals are capable of progressing toward salvation.

The Bodhisattva as an Animal in the *Jātakas*

There may not be any direct influence on this *Bhāgavatapurāṇa* story from the much earlier Buddhist *Jātakas,* but there are numerous points of convergence in the perspectives toward animals found in Buddhist texts. The spiritual capacity of animals is indicated by the fact that in almost all fables where the Bodhisattva appears as an animal-manifestation, he not only leads an exemplary life in practicing the perfections of charity and moral discipline, but even preaches the Dharma to human beings. The story of the hare in the *Sasa-jātaka* (see *J* 3.51-56) exemplifies the perfection of *dāna* (charity). In this tale, the Bodhisattva-hare not only keeps the *gihi-uposatha*—the twice monthly practice of taking the five precepts of a lay person[5]—but even offers his flesh to Śakra (the god Indra), who appears in the guise of a Brahmin, by jumping into a burning pyre. The *Hasti-jātaka* in the *Jātakamālā*[6] goes even one step further, by presenting the "anonymous Charity" (*gupta-dāna*) of an animal. In this story, the Bodhisattva-elephant attempted to save a thousand travellers who were lost and starving in the forest by providing his own body for their sustenance. Fearful that they would be physically incapable of attacking him, the Bodhisattva resorted to a subterfuge in order to rescue them. He told them that an animal has fallen to its death at a nearby cliff and that they should go there and consume its flesh; hurrying ahead, however, he beat them to the site and jumped, killing himself. Only later did they realize that the animal was the same one who had approached them before, and they praised the magnanimity of its deed. This leads the author of the *Jātakamālā* to remark: "Even though born as animals, there is seen the charitable activities of great beings, performed according to their capacities."[7]

Another relevant story is the *Nigrodhamiga-jātaka*, which relates the tale of a deer-king who offered magnanimously to exchange his own life for that of another deer. In brief, the tale relates that the king of Banaras was especially fond of venison and had built two corrals in a park outside of the city for two herds of five hundred deer. One herd was headed by the Bodhisattva-buck, Nigrodhamiga, the other by a buck named Sākha. In view of the great majesty of the leaders, the king had ordered the two of them protected, and the herds had worked out a deal whereby members of alternate groups would offer themselves for slaughter. One day, the turn of a pregnant doe in Sākha's herd arrived, and she begged her leader to postpone her death until after her fawn's birth. But Sākha contemptuously rejected her appeal, pontificating that never had there been anyone who wished to die a day early. Distraught, the doe approached the Bodhisattva, who consented to take her place and offered himself to the royal butchers. When the king learned of his self-sacrifice, he was deeply moved: "O Sir," he said, "even among men, I have never seen a person such as you who is so endowed with endurance, friendliness and kindness."[8] He then offered to extend his protection to the doe also, but the Bodhisattva appealed to the king's compassion and obtained from him guarantees for the protection of all the deer in that park, and ultimately for all animals, birds, and fish in the realm. The narrator concludes the story by relating that the buck then preached the Dharma to the king and established him in the five precepts. His instruction resonates with the words of the Aśokan inscriptions: "O Great King! Live righteously according to the conduct appropriate toward your parents, and toward

Brahmins, householders, and town and city dwellers. Thus living justly, after your death you will attain rebirth in heaven."[9] It is no wonder that the buck was immortalized by ancient Buddhist, who depicted the story of the noble deer in stone beside the *Dhammacakkappavattana* images at Sarnath.

Spiritual Capacity in Ordinary Animals

Magnificent as these stories are, they do not refer to the fate of ordinary animals, but only to the Bodhisattva in the guise of an animal, somewhat like the Brāhmaṇical story presented previously. There are, however, numerous other tales scattered throughout the Buddhist scriptures that relate how ordinary birds and beasts exhibit nobility and friendship comparable to that of human beings.

The first major type involves tales in which an animal personally serves the Buddha. These would be like the horse, Kaṇṭhaka, whom the Buddha rode at the time of his Great Renunciation: according to tradition the devoted horse died, heartbroken, after the historic ride and was immediately reborn in the Tāvatiṃsa heaven.[10] A similar story is told concerning a monkey who offered a honeycomb to the Buddha and was so overcome by Gautama's acceptance of his gift that he fell from the tree and died; at the time of his death, however, he was so moved with joy that he too was reborn in the Tāvatiṃsa heaven.[11] Perhaps the most memorable of such stories is the tale of the elephant, Pārileyyaka, who once served as attendant to the Buddha. During the Lord's voluntary retirement to the Pārileyyaka forest as a result of a bitter sectarian squabble that racked the Kośāmbī Saṅgha, this elephant had taken it upon himself to wait on the Lord by fetching him water and fruit and by warding off all intruders. After the Rains Retreat, when the monks had finally made peace, the Buddha consented to their pleas to return to Sāvatthi. The elephant wished to follow and continue in his role, but the Buddha bade him to remain in the forest with the words: "O elephant! There is no possibility of you, an animal, attaining the knowledge, insight, or the fruits of the supramundane path."[12] The elephant obeyed the Lord but died soon afterwards of a broken heart and was reborn in the Tāvatiṃsa heaven. In all these three stories, it is clear that animals are as capable as human lay followers (*upāsaka*) of great service and devotion to the Buddha and that such devotion, when accompanied by appropriate action, would lead even animals to heaven.

The second major type of animal story provides us with better insight into the specific features of the "religious" behaviour that was considered well within the scope of animals. We may take up two contrasting stories to illustrate this variety. The first is the story of a cow named Bahalā, who was accosted in a forest by a tiger (*PJ* 2, pp. 384-390). Before the predator could attack her, however, the cow pleaded with him to let her first go to the village to feed her young calf, who happened to be the Bodhisattva; she promised to come back to the forest and offer herself to the tiger later that evening. When the tiger asked for some guarantee that she would return, the cow declared that her cultivation of truthfulness (*satya*) obliged her to keep her word; succumbing to her sincerity, the tiger allowed her to leave. When she told her calf of her fate, however, the Bodhisattva was also so moved that he followed his mother and offered himself to the tiger in exchange for her life. Finally, overcome by the mother's truthfulness and the calf's filial devotion, the tiger spared them both. These events were so extraordinary that they shook the seat of Indra, king of the gods, and he appeared on earth to witness the miracle personally. Later, he took them all to heaven for a few days as guests of the palace before returning them to earth. Eventually all three animals were reborn in heaven as a result of their exemplary behaviour. While neither the Buddhists nor the Jainas regard any animals as sacred—not even a cow—still, by her truthfulness, the cow Bahalā may certainly be considered worthy of such an honour.

The second story is of quite a different bent. Here a wild buffalo was terrorizing the people of an outlying village, and the residents begged the Buddha to appease the beast. The Lord approached the animal and, touched by the Buddha's loving-kindness, the buffalo was subdued. Noticing the buffalo's seeds of previous learning, the Buddha then preached to him about impermanence, lack of substance, and the peace of Nirvāṇa.[13] He also reminded him of his past births in which he had been a teacher of Dharma himself. Overcome with remorse, the buffalo died and was reborn in Devaloka, the heaven of the gods. That even this subtle and profound dogma could be preached to an animal proves that Buddhists considered animals capable of insights that normally would be considered possible only for human beings.

A similar story is found in the tale of a cobra who had amassed substantial wealth as a greedy merchant in a previous life; now reborn as a snake, he was guarding the buried cache, frightening away anyone who might come near. The Buddha finally pacified him and had him recall his previous life, warning that if he persisted in his hostility, he would be reborn in hell.[14] The cobra repented and grieved over his past, but the Buddha consoled him with the verse:

> What shall I do now for you who has fallen into an animal birth?
> Why do you cry, you who have come upon the "wrong" time (for salvation)?
> It is good for you now to project your mind toward the Jina [the Buddha] with delight.
> Thereby, you will overcome your animal rebirth and be reborn in heaven.[15]

Accordingly, the snake, like the buffalo in the previous story, died thinking of the Buddha and was reborn in the Trāyastriṃśa heaven.

Animals Meriting Rebirth in Hell

The Buddha's warning to the cobra that by persisting in his greed and hostility he would be destined to be reborn in hell directly implies that it was possible for an animal to be reborn into the hellish abodes directly from the animal realm. Of course, by setting the cobra on the right path, the Buddha saved him from such a fate. It might come as something of a surprise that, like human beings, an animal could in fact engage in such extremely defiled volitional actions that hell would be the result. However, if we bear in mind that examples abound of animals being reborn in heaven, which requires similarly extreme wholesome actions, then this eventuality does not seem so unusual. Thus, while animals may retain some measure of moral conscience, this seemingly coexists with a certain amount of instinctive violence.

This conclusion is clarified by an extraordinary Jaina story concerning a tiny fish, who was called Śālisiktha (rice grain) after his small size (*BKK*, p. 341). The story relates that there was a giant whale inhabiting the outer ocean-ring encircling the world, who fed by keeping its jaws open for six straight months, devouring anything that entered. At the end of his feeding period, he would then close his jaws and hibernate for the remainder of the year. Śālisiktha, who had taken up residence in the whale's ear, was prone to extreme gluttony and became tormented at the sight of the whale allowing large numbers of small fish to escape through the spaces between his teeth. "Alas!" he thought. "How foolish and stupid this whale is. How can he so ignore what is good for him that he allows these beings to escape? If my body or mouth were as large as his, not a single fish would be able to escape from my mouth." Soon afterwards, both of the animals died, and the whale wound up in the lowest of the seven hells for having killed so many beings during his lifetime. But the narrator tells us that this tiny fish also was reborn in the lowest hell for having committed such brutal killings in his mind (*pariṇāmavadhena*).[16] That seemingly innocuous thoughts were met with such severe punishment might appear inappropriate to most Buddhists and many Jainas. Nevertheless, it confirms the Jaina belief that animals were on a par with human beings in being subject to the retribution accruing from evil actions.

We might note parenthetically that, according to Jaina doctrine, few beings indeed are capable of performing such heinous deeds as to merit rebirth in the seventh hell. The Jainas believe, for example, that birds can be born no lower than the third hell, quadrupeds not below the fourth, and snakes not below the fifth; only fish (and human males) are able to be born in the seventh hell.[17] While the texts do not tell us which animals other than fish can fall as far as the sixth hell, the Jaina tradition is unanimous in declaring that human females are unable to fall any lower than this penultimate destiny.[18] How and why fish are the equal of human males in being able to fall to the lowest hell—an exclusively Jaina belief—remains a mystery. At any rate, by declaring that animals are capable of such a fate, the Jainas are proclaiming that animals do have the capacity for wilful volitional actions, of both wholesome and unwholesome quality. However, compared to the tales of animals being reborn in the heavens for their skilful deeds, the stories of animals going to hell are rare indeed. In fact, the story narrated above was probably intended as much to warn human beings about the serious consequences of one's thoughts as to detail the possible destinies of animals.

Jaina Tales of Moral and Spiritual Capacity in Animals

The Jaina narrative literature, however, is replete with stories that discuss the wholesome aspirations of animals and their subsequent rebirth as human, or snakes and mongooses attending together a sermon of the Jina in perfect harmony. One such story concerns a frog who, while on his way to participate in Mahāvīra's holy assembly, was trampled by a royal elephant. The frog was immediately reborn in heaven because he had died with intense devotion in his heart for the Jina (*JDhKN* I.13). In this way, the frog story balances the fish story by demonstrating that animals, like humans, were also capable of wholesome rebirths.

The story of a pair of cobras named Dharaṇendra and Padmāvatī (*TPC*, vol. 5, p. 393) also indicates this same capacity. The story takes place in Varanasi during the time of Pārśvanātha, the immediate predecessor of Mahāvīra. There, Pārśva, the would-be Jina, is said to have saved from death a pair of cobras who were hiding within firewood being kindled by non-Jaina ascetics for their ritual practices. Pārśva put out the fire and had the firewood split open to free the two snakes, but it was too late to save them. While they died, Pārśva recited to them the holy Jina litany, the *Pañcanamaskāra-mantra.*[19] As a consequence of hearing this *mantra,* they were reborn in the abode of the *yakṣas* (demigods) and since then have been worshiped by the Jaina community as the guardian deities of their religion.

Another impressive Jaina story, however, concerns an elephant who, in his very next rebirth, was born as Prince Megha and became an eminent Jaina monk under Mahāvīra. The story of this elephant compares favourably with earlier stories we have noted above from Vaiṣṇava and Buddhist texts.

It relates that this elephant was the leader of a large herd caught in a huge forest fire. All the animals of the forest ran from their haunts and gathered around a lake, so that the entire area was jammed with beings large and small. After standing thus for quite some time, the elephant lifted his leg to scratch himself, and immediately a small hare ran to occupy the spot vacated by his raised foot. Rather than trampling the helpless animal, however, the elephant's mind was filled with great compassion for the plight of his fellow creature; indeed, his concern for the hare's welfare was so great that he is said thereby to have cut off forever his associations with future animal destinies.[20] The elephant stood with one leg raised for more than three days, until the fire abated and the hare was able to leave. By then, however, the elephant's whole leg had gone numb and, unable to set down his foot, he toppled over. While maintaining his purity of mind, he finally died and was reborn as Prince Megha, son of King Śreṇika, the ruler of Magadha. This story is a perfect example of the choice that an animal may make in undertaking a good or evil act. The elephant had the option of simply trampling the hare, but refused to do so, acting as a morally inclined human would. Thus he deserved not only to be reborn in his next life as a human, but also to proceed along the path to salvation by becoming a monk.

But the most remarkable Jaina tale must be that of Mahāvīra's own life as a lion and his awakening to enlightenment. We saw earlier in the Buddhist stories that hares could keep the *uposatha* and offer charity. But the story of Mahāvīra as a lion goes one step further. According to this story, once when Mahāvīra's soul was reborn as a lion, two Jaina *munis* (monks) happened to see him. They realized immediately via superknowledge that this was a soul who could benefit from religious discourse. They approached him and instructed him in the value of kindness and admonished him to refrain from killing. According to the story, the lion was deeply moved by their discourse and, receiving their words with great devotion, was immediately awakened to the true nature of his own self. He resolved then and there to take the minor vows (*aṇuvrata*) and desist from all injury to other beings. Thus refraining from all food, he died and, as a consequence of the virtue accruing from his fast, was reborn in heaven. This story is of great importance because, not only is the animal said to have been capable of understanding a discourse on the nature of the soul, but he was also able to exercise his will to assume religious vows.[21] This story suggests a belief that animals are on a par with Jaina laity, who advance on a spiritual course leading to mendicancy by adhering to such vows as nonviolence and nonpossession. Of course, animals would not be able to assume the precepts in the same way that humans do when they repeat verbally the vows of renunciation. It is, however, a commonly observed phenomenon that animals often refrain from food for some time before their deaths; this might have given support to the belief that such a fast was deliberate and motivated by spiritual impulses.

Concluding Reflections

Even discounting tales in which animals were the theriomorphoses of *bodhisattvas* or advanced sages, the above stories still include several illustrations of capacity of animals to lead a spiritual life. In such Buddhist tales as that of the wild buffalo, for instance, an animal displayed an almost human faculty for understanding such profound expressions of Dharma as *anitya* (impermanence), *anātman* (no-self), and *śānta* (tranquility). In the Jaina stories the sacred litany was imparted to a pair of serpents, thereby enabling them to achieve a superior rebirth. While in these stories the intervention of a great human being was necessary to catalyze understanding, this was not the case for all. The elephant, Pārileyyaka, for example, served the Buddha out of his own love and devotion, and the elephant in the Jaina story of Prince Megha refused to trample the hare because of his own inherent kindness.

The element innate in animals that allows such spiritual aspirations to develop is the subtle seed of liberation, termed variously *sūkṣma-kuśala-dharma-bīja* by the Buddhists or *nityodghāṭita-jñāna* by the Jainas (see Jaini 1959, 236-249; 1979, 135 ff.). This catalyst is clearly at work in such cases as the cow Bahalā's truthfulness or the elephant Megha's compassion. This belief in an innate capacity for salvation accords well with Jaina belief that humans share close affinities with animals. Animals and humans share the same cosmological region, the

Madhyaloka or "Middle Realm," and a being can move into the inferior hells or the superior heavens only from that realm. No movement between the different hells and heavens or directly from heaven to hell (or vice versa) is permitted. While the gods, the denizens of hell, and humans are each only a single species, animals number some 840,000 individual species.[22] They would thus be expected to continue passing interminably between different animal destinies before achieving rebirth elsewhere. Despite the overwhelming variety of animals, what most clearly distinguishes them from the denizens of hell and the gods is the fact that, like humans, they are able to assume the religious vows, as is exemplified in the Jaina story of the lion-Mahāvīra. This similarity with humans may partly explain the penchant of Indians—and particularly Jainas—to consider all life as inviolable. While this is not the same as exalting animal as holy beings, as some Hindus have done, it has prompted many Indians to renounce all violence toward lesser beings and recognize the sacredness of all forms of life.

NOTES

1. āhāra-nidrā-bhaya-maithunaṃ ca sāmānyam etat paśubhir narāṇām/ dharmo hi teṣām adhiko viśeṣo dharmeṇa hīnaḥ paśubhiḥ samānaḥ// [*Hitopadeśa*, vs. 25]
2. evaṃ vyavasthito buddhyā samādhāya mano hṛdi/ jajāpa paramaṃ jāpyam prāgjanmany anuśikṣitam// [*BHP* 7.3.1]
3. gajendro bhagavatsparśād vimukto jñānabandhanāt/ prāpto bhagavato rūpaṃ pītavāsā caturbhujaḥ// [*BHP* 8.4.6]
4. sa vai pūrvam abhūd rājā pāṇḍyo draviḍasattamaḥ/ indradyumna iti khyāto viṣṇuvrataparāyaṇaḥ// ...āpannaḥ kuñjarīṃ yonim ātmasmṛtivināśnīm/ haryarcānubhāvena yad gatatve 'py anusmṛtiḥ// [*BHP* 7.4.7-12]
5. A ceremony that includes offering *dāna* or meals to monks and spending the day on the monastic grounds in the company of monks.
6. See *Jātakamālā* 30, translated by J. S. Speyer, *Sacred Books of the Buddhists* (London: Oxford University Press, 1895), I:37-46.
7. tiryaggatānām api satāṃ mahātmanāṃ śaktyanurūpā dānapravṛttir dṛṣṭā. [*JmĀ*, p. 19]
8. rājā āha: sāmi suvaṇṇavaṇṇamigarāja, mayā tādiso khantimettānuddayasampanno manussesu pi na diṭṭhapubbo, tena te pasanno 'smi. [*J* I.151]
9. evaṃ mahāsatto rājānaṃ sabbasattānam abhyaṃ yācitvā uṭṭhayā rājānaṃ pañcasu sīlesu patiṭṭhāpetvā "dhammaṃ cara mahārāja, mātāpitūsu

puttadhītāsu brāhmaṇagahapatikesu negamajānapadesu dhammaṃ caranto samaṃ caranto kāyassa bhedā sugatiṃ saggaṃ lokaṃ gamissasī ti" rañño Buddhalīḷhāya dhammaṃ desetvā... araññaṃ pāvisi. [*J* 1.152]

10. kaṇṭhako pana...bodhisattassa vacanaṃ suṇanto ṭhatvā "n' atth' idāni mayhaṃ puna sāmino dassanan" ti... sokam adhivāsetum asakkonto hadayena phalitena kālaṃ katvā tāvatiṃsabhavane kaṇṭhako nāma devaputto hutvā nibbatti. [*J* 1.65]

11. ath'eko makkaṭo, madhupaṭalaṃ satthusantakam āharitvā... adāsi. satthā gaṇhi. so tuṭṭhamānaso taṃ taṃ sākhaṃ gahetvā naccanto aṭṭhāsi. ath'ssa gahitasākhā pi akkantasākhā pi bhijjiṃsu. so tasmiṃ khāṇe khāṇumatthake patitvā ... satthari pasannen'eva cittena kālaṃ katvā tāvatiṃsabhavane... nibbatti. [*DhpA* 1.60]

12. pārileyyaka idaṃ pana mama anibbattagamanaṃ. tava iminā attabhāvena jhānaṃ vā vipassanaṃ maggaphalaṃ vā n'atthi, tiṭṭha tvan ti āha. so rodamāno ṭhatvā satthari cakkhupathaṃ vijahante hadayena phalitena kālaṃ katvā satthari pasādena tāvatiṃsabhavane... nibbatti. [*DhpA* 1.63] See E. V. Burlingame, *Buddhist Legends* (Cambridge, Mass.: Harvard University Press, 1921), I:179-183.

13. bhagavatā tanmayyā gatyās tanmayyā yonyās tribhiḥ pādair dharmo deśitaḥ: iti hi bhadramukha, sarvasaṃskārā anityāḥ, sarvadharmā anātmānaḥ, śāntaṃ nirvāṇam iti. [*AŚ*, p. 148]

14. bhadramukha, tvayaivaitad dravyam upārjitaṃ, yena tvam aśīviṣagatim upapāditaḥ. sādhu mamāntike cittaṃ prasādaya, asmāc ca nidhānāc cittaṃ virāgaya. mā haiva itaḥ kālaṃ kṛtvā narakeṣūpapatsyasa iti. [*AŚ*, p. 129]

15. idānīṃ kiṃ kariṣyāmi tiryagyonigatasya te / akṣaṇapratipannasya kiṃ rodiṣi nirarthakam // sādhu prasādyatāṃ cittaṃ mahākāruṇike jine / tiryagyoniṃ virāgyeha tataḥ svargaṃ gamiṣyasi // [*AŚ*, p. 129]

16. śarīraṃ me mukhaṃ vāpi yadi tuṅgaṃ bhaved idam / tato naiko 'pi niryāti man mukhāddhi jhaṣādikaḥ // evaṃ cintayatas tasya śālisikthavisāriṇaḥ / mahato 'pi ca mīnasya yāti kālo śanaiḥ śanaiḥ // nānājīvavadhaṃ kṛtvā bṛhanmīno mṛtiṃ gataḥ/ trayastriṃśat samudrāyuḥ saptame narake 'bhavat//śālisiktho 'pi matsyo 'yaṃ mṛtiṃ kṛtvā sa duṣṭadhīḥ/ pariṇāmavadhenāpi saptamaṃ narakaṃ yayau// [*BKK*, p. 341]

17. prathamāyām asamjñina utpadyante, prathamadvitīyāyāḥ sarīsṛpāḥ, tisṛṣu pakṣiṇaḥ, catasṛṣūragāḥ, pañcasu siṃhāḥ, ṣaṭsu striyaḥ, saptasu matsyamanuṣyāḥ. *Tattvārthasūtra-Rājavārittikaṭīkā*, p. 118, quoted in *Nyāya-Kumudacandra*, edited by Mahendrakumar Jain [Bombay: Māṇikacandra Digambara Jain Granthamālā, 1941], p. 867, n. 2.

18. "asannirvāṇāstriyaḥ āsaptamapṛthivīgamanatvāt...ya evaṃvidhā na te nirvānti, yathā sammūrchimādayaḥ, tathāvidhāśca striyaḥ." iti (*Strīnirvāṇa-Kevalibhuktiprakaraṇe* [Bhavanagar: Jain Ātmānand Sabhā, 1974], p. 15). See Jaini 1991.

19. On this Jaina litany see Jaini 1979, 162.

20. tae ṇaṃ tumaṃ mehā! gāyaṃ kaṇḍuittā puṇaravi pāyaṃ paḍinikkhamissāmi tti kaṭṭu taṃ sasayaṃ aṇupaviṭṭhaṃ pāsasi pāsittā pāṇāṇukampayāe... se pāe aṃtarā ceva saṃdhārie no ceva ṇaṃ nikkhitte. tae ṇaṃ tumaṃ

mehā! tāe pāṇāṇukampayāe...saṃsāre parittīkae, māṇussāue nibaddhe. [*JDhKN* 1.1.33]

21. vidhāya hṛdi yogīndrayugmaṃ bhaktibharāhitaḥ/ muhuḥ pradakṣiṇīkṛtya prapraṇamya mṛgādhipaḥ// tattvaśraddhānam āsādya sadyaḥ kālādilabdhitaḥ/ praṇidhāya manaḥ śrāvakavratāni samādadhe// *Uttarapurāṇa* 86.207-208, edited by Pannalal Jain [Varanasi: Bhāratīya Jñānapīṭha, 1954].

22. On the significance of this number see Jaini 1980, 228.

REFERENCES

PRIMARY SOURCES WITH ABBREVIATION

AŚ — *Avadānaśatakam.* Edited by P. L. Vaidya. Darbhanga, 1958.

BKK — *Bṛhatkathākośa of Hariṣeṇa* (*Śālisiktha-kathānakam*). Edited by A. N. Upadhye. Singhi Jain Granthamālā, no. XVII. Bombay, 1943.

BHP — *Bhāgavatapurāṇa. Gorakhpur:* Gita Press, 1950.

Hitopadeśa. — *Hitopadeśa.* Varanasi: Hardāsa Saṃskṛta Granthamālā, 1946.

J — *Jātakatthavaṇṇanā.* Edited by V. Fausboll. 2nd ed. 6 vols. London: Pali Text Society, 1964.

JmĀ — *The Jātakamālā of Āryaśūra.* Edited by R. C. Dwivedi and M. R. Bhat. Delhi: Motilal Banarsidass, 1966.

JDhKN — *Jñātādharmakathāṅga* (*Nyāyādhammakahāo*). Edited by Pupphabhikkhu. In *Suttāgame,* Pt. 9. Gudgaon: Sūtrāgamaprakāshaka Samiti, 1952.

DhpA — *Dhammapadaṭṭhakathā.* Edited by H. C. Norman. 4 Vols. London: Pali Text Society, 1914.

PJ — *Paññāsa-Jātaka* (*Bahalaputtajātaka*). Edited by P. S. Jaini. London: Pali Text Society, 1983.

Rāmāyaṇa — *The Vālmīki Rāmāyaṇa.* Critical Edition. Baroda: Oriental Institute, 1960-1975.

TPC — *Triṣaṣtiśalākāpuruṣacarita.* Translated by Helen M. Johnson. Gaekwad Oriental Series, No. 139. Baroda: Oriental Institute, 1962.

SECONDARY SOURCES

Jaini, Padmanabh S. 1959. "The Sautrāntika Theory of *Bīja.*" *Bulletin of the School of Oriental and African Studies* 22 (no. 2): 236-249.

——. 1979. *The Jaina Path of Purification.* Berkeley: University of California Press.

——. 1980. "Karma and the Problem of Rebirth in Jainism." In *Karma and Rebirth in Classical Indian Traditions,* ed. Wendy Doniger O'Flaherty, 217-238. Berkeley: University of California Press.

——. 1991. *Gender and Salvation: Jaina Debates on the Spiritual Liberation of Women.* Berkeley: University of California Press, 1991.

CHAPTER 15

Is There a Popular Jainism?*

In asking the question, 'Is there a popular Jainism?', we are looking for practices within Jaina society that can be considered inconsistent with the main teachings of the religion, but so thoroughly assimilated with them now that they are no longer perceived as alien. In sociology, this study has taken the form of an examination of the 'great' and 'little' traditions within a culture, and we are familiar with the notable research done in this field by such pioneers as M. Srinivasan and Louis Dumont, which has dealt with various creeds within Hinduism. Considerable advance has been made in applying this method to the study of the Theravada Buddhists of Sri Lanka, and to a lesser extent of Burma, by such scholars as H. Bechert, G. Obeyesekere, M. E. Spiro, and R. F. Gombrich. In the latter's *Precept and Practice*,[1] a study of traditional Buddhism in the rural highlands of Sri Lanka, published nearly two decades ago, Gombrich has ably dealt with the kind of questions which we are asking here, with reference to Jainism. There is certainly a great deal of similarity between the Theravadins and Jainas, both due to the large number of mendicants within their respective communities as well as to the many practices engaged in by lay people that can be traced to Brāhmaṇical elements introduced in ancient times. A critical study of Jaina society following the leads of Gombrich's study of the Theravadins would yield very similar results, but the gap between Jaina

*This article was published originally in *The Assembly of Listeners: Jains in Society*, eds. Carrithers and Humphrey, (Cambridge: Cambridge University Press, 1991), pp. 187-199. Reprinted with kind permission of Cambridge University Press.

'precepts' and 'practices' would probably be much smaller.

Jainism, like Theravada Buddhism, is a *Śramaṇa* religion, and its primary teachings concern the path to *nirvāṇa* that is to be followed by those who are able to renounce the world. However, it also claims to teach a lesser but nevertheless honourable path of 'merit-making' for those who choose to remain in the household life. While the two paths are not truly complementary, they must still accommodate each other, if only because the mendicants are dependent upon the beneficence of the lay community for their support. The Jaina mendicants have opted for the exclusively 'supermundane' (*lokottara*) path, which is flexible enough to allow a certain amount of pastoral activity through which to guide the laity. The latter lead a sort of amphibious life, with one foot on the worldly path of making money and merit, and the other, rather hesitantly, on the path of *nirvāṇa*. As a result, they are constantly forced to seek a balance between the two paths. The mendicant Jaina lawgivers, unlike their Brahman counterparts, did not claim the prerogative of laying down laws for the laypeople, yet they hoped to persuade them by a process of education to adopt only those worldly ways which were conducive to the path of *nirvāṇa*. This is clear from the declaration of a tenth-century Jaina mendicant, Somadeva:[2]

> There are only two duties of the layman:
> The mundane (*laukika*) and the supermundane (*pāralaukika*).
> The former depends on the world and the customs thereof (*lokāśraya*);
> The latter is what one learns from the words of the Jina.

Somadeva was not, however, permitting the Jaina laymen to follow 'worldly custom' indiscriminately: this had to be judged by the one standard that invariably applied:

> All worldly practices are valid (*pramāṇa*) for the Jainas,
> As long as there is no loss of 'pure insight',
> No violation of the 'precepts'.

A wide variety of Hindu religious practices came under the scrutiny of Somadeva, who proposed to determine which of these 'worldly practices' were permissible to the Jaina layman.[3] The

Jaina list of proscribed practices included almost all rituals of the Hindus, most of which would be regarded today as belonging to the 'little tradition'. Somadeva declared that a Jaina must not indulge in the worship of the sun or fire, of trees or mounds of earth, since there was nothing sacred about these objects (*mahābhūtas*).[4] Nor should he bathe in the river or the ocean in hopes of gaining merit, nor spend money in connection with an eclipse (*grahaṇa*) or the passage of the sun into the summer and winter solstices (*saṃkrānti*). As for the 'holy' cow, no more inherent sacredness was attached to it than to other animals; hence the practice of touching its tail or drinking its urine was nothing but superstition (*loka-mūḍhatā*). He even considered the performance of *sandhyā* (a Vedic ritual) as wrong, since it involved sipping water at twilight hours, a practice not worthy of a devout Jaina. But the strongest words of condemnation were aimed at the practice of offering *śrāddha*, the funeral service to the manes.[5] *Śrāddha* presupposes the existence of a world of manes (*pitṛloka*). Since the Jainas maintain that the soul must be reborn instantaneously in either heaven, hell, human or animal/ vegetable existence, they therefore deny any *pitṛ-loka*, and hence adoption of this practice would undermine their very cosmology. Moreover, feeding the Brahmans in order to help the deceased to pass from a ghost-life into the *pitṛ-loka* would make mockery of the doctrine of karma, the efficacy of individual action, a cardial tenet of all Śramaṇa religions. It should be observed in this connection that the Theravadins also held views similar to these of the Jainas, but were unable to prevent their laity from falling prey to these customs. On the contrary, Buddhist monks in Sri Lanka participated in ceremonies like *matak-bhoj* (meal for the dead), and developed new doctrines like *patti-dāna* (merit transference) and *patti-anumodana* (rejoicing in the transference of merit), in their attempt to incorporate a clearly heterodox practice into Buddhism, giving rise in the process to what may be termed 'popular' Buddhism.

The second area in which the Jaina laity needed education was with reference to the nature of the deity. One became a Jaina by taking refuge in a Jina (spiritual victor), a mendicant who had completely overcome all forms of attachment (*rāga*), aversion (*dveṣa*), and delusion (*moha*), and was therefore worthy of worship. But the Jainas were surrounded by a vast majority of people whose deities, although armed with weapons and surrounded by spouses, nevertheless promised their devotees both salvation as well as daily bread and butter (*yogakṣemaṃ vahāmy aham*, as Kṛṣṇa says in the *Gītā*). Combating the influence of these Vedic and Purāṇic deities became an urgent preoccupation with the Jaina mendicant of medieval times. Somadeva typifies the missionary zeal with which Jaina teachers undertook the task of exposing the alleged divinity of the Hindu trinity:[6]

> Brahmā has his mind obsessed with Tilottamā, the nymph,
> And Hari, the Lord of Lakṣmī, is attached to her;
> Śambhu is half-man an half-woman,
> Look at these authorities on salvation!
> Vasudeva is his father, and Devakī his mother,
> He himself engaged in royal duties;
> Yet Hari is called a god!
> He dances naked and kills Brahmans at will,
> Destruction of the three worlds is his sport!
> Yet Śiva is said to be a god!
> One whose conduct is no better than that of a householder,
> One whose conduct is inferior even to that of an ordinary mendicant,
> If such a one be a god,
> Surely, there would be no dearth of gods!

Somadeva's comparison between Hindu gods and Jaina mendicants must have had a telling effect upon the Jaina psyche. Despite the tremendous social and emotional pressures that the medieval *bhakti* movements must have exerted, no cult of Śiva or Viṣṇu ever developed within Jainism. Nevertheless, Jaina teachers rejected only Śiva's ability to lead people to salvation; they accepted his existence as a minor god, and, according to one account even used him to promote their own religion. Ācārya Hemacandra is reported by his Jaina biographers to have converted the Śaivite King Kumārapāla (1143-72) by showing him a vision of Lord Śiva and obtaining from the latter a declaration that the religion of the Jina was superior to all. The king is said to have assumed at that very moment a life-long vow of vegetarianism, the hallmark of Jainism.[7] As for Rāma and Kṛṣṇa, the two most prominent *avatāras* of Viṣṇu, it is well-known that the Jainas composed new *Rāmāyaṇas* and *Harivaṃśapurāṇas* in which they elevated Rāma to the status of a Jaina saint by attributing the murder of Rāvaṇa to Rāma's brother, Lakṣmaṇa, and punished Kṛṣṇa for his war-mongering by consigning him to purgatory.[8]

The Jaina success in resisting the intrusion of Brāhmaṇical gods into their faith can be contrasted with the Sinhalese Theravadin attempt to maintain the purity of the Buddhist tradition. The two most powerful gods in the modern Sinhalese pantheon are not Buddhist but Hindu, one being Viṣṇu, and the other being Kataragama, a local variant of Kumāra Kārttikeya, a son of Śiva. It is true that neither was allowed to usurp the paramount position of the Buddha; nevertheless, without any valid reason Viṣṇu has been elevated to the status of a Bodhisattva, and Kataragama, although not a Buddhist either, has been accorded the position of protector of both Buddhism and the island. By making such concessions to the popular belief that Hindu gods were efficacious in worldly affairs, the Buddhist Saṅgha allowed a form of popular Buddhism to arise. The fact that shrines to these gods were erected on temple grounds proves that the Saṅgha officially supported 'Buddhist' cults that worshipped Hindu gods.

In this context, mention may be made of a purely Buddhist divinity of Sri Lanka, known by the name of Nātha. He is identified with the Bodhisattva Avalokiteśvara, a remnant of the Mahāyāna cult that has survived from ancient times. The popular Buddhism of modern times, probably influenced by western-educated Theravadins, has sought to identify Nātha with the Bodhisattva Maitreya, the future Buddha. Jainism also believes in a future line of twenty-four Jinas, and it is assumed that King Śreṇika, a contemporary of Mahāvīra (and the father of the Buddhist King Ajātaśatru) will be the first Jina of the new era. But the Jainas have never permitted the cult of a future Jina to develop, as it would be inconsistent with their doctrine that one may worship only a *tīrthaṅkara* in order to obtain salvation. Maitreya, enjoying heavenly pleasures while he awaits his descent to earth, might be holy to the Buddhists, but to the Jainas he would still be unworthy of the same honour that one accords to a mendicant. The fact that King Śreṇika's soul is consigned not to heaven but to hell, possibly as a consequence of committing suicide, is an additional indication that the Jainas have adhered to their doctrine far more scrupulously than the Buddhists. By not allowing an opening for excessive worship of the future Jina, the Jainas have eliminated one more possible source for the formation of a 'popular cult'. Similarly, Jainas have never worshipped the remains of the Jinas, and consequently have never developed anything parallel to the worship of the relics of the Buddha, the most popular practice in Sri Lanka.

I am not suggesting that the Jainas were impervious to every form of outside influence. The conspicuous presence of *yakṣa* images in almost all major medieval Jaina temples must belie any such claim; moreover, their continued worship by Jaina laymen even to this day parallels the Theravadin cults of *devas* and *yakkhas*. Even so, a look at the Jaina *yakṣa* cult, particularly as it was legitimised within the original tradition, would show that the Jainas were probably less supportive of these cults than the Theravadins, and hence more successful in arresting the growth of a 'popular' form of Jainism based on them.

It is well known that supernatural beings, variously referred to as *devas, nāgas, gandharvas* and *yakṣas*, were worshipped by the pre-Buddhistic people the Gangetic valley as 'guardian deities' who had specific protective functions. Buddhist and Jaina canonical texts abound in descriptions of their abodes, called *caitya* or *devāyatana*, which were situated outside major cities like Campā, Rājagraha and Vārāṇasī. The *caityas* were inhabited by *yakṣa* chiefs, such as Pūrṇabhadra and Maṇibhadra, who were also the tutelary gods of certain tribes and clans. Festivities were held in their honour on days sacred to them, and offerings of various kinds were made. Such *caityas* became the resting-places of many ascetics, including the Buddha and Mahāvīra, during their visit to these cities. Unlike ordinary people, the Buddha and Mahāvīra were not afraid to challenge the *yakṣas*' occupation of these grounds; hence they were able to subdue and convert them to their respective faiths, and enlist them as protectors of their lay followers. Several Buddhist *suttas*, notably the Maṅgalasutta, the Ratanasutta and the Āṭānāṭiyasutta, mention by name these converted demigods, who were promised a share in the merit earned by the laity in exchange for their protection.

One would expect the Jainas to have followed the example of the Buddhists and grant a similar status to their *yakṣas*. But the ancient Jaina texts are conspicuously silent on the status of the *yakṣas* within their religious fraternity; no Jaina *sutta* similar to the Buddhist *suttas* just mentioned has been found, nor have I come across statements that advocate the desirability of pleasing the *yakṣas*. Even the early Jaina images at Patna and Mathura are devoid of their company, except for those of the Jina Pārśva which are hooded by a cobra in a fashion similar to that of the Mucalindanāga Buddha. The subsequent development of a Jaina *yakṣa* cult can probably be traced to this hooded image of Pārśva.

By contrast, in the post-Gupta period, we begin to find images of the Jainas flanked by figures of guardian deities. No one knows for certain when this innovation took place. It is unlikely, however, that during their migration from Bihar in the Śunga period, the Jainas would not have taken with them cults of their own city-guardian deities, including those of Maṇibhadra and Pūrṇabhadra, which are repeatedly referred to in their sacred texts. It would seem probable that they would have even picked up a few more such deities on their way to Mathura, and thence, via Rajasthan and Gujarat, to the Deccan. A migrant community can be expected to adopt the deities of host communities as a means of integrating themselves with the local inhabitants. These new gods, being non-Jaina by nature, would inevitably have been looked upon by the Jaina teachers as unwelcome accretions to the original faith. It appears quite certain that the Jaina teachers of the early medieval period undertook the task of purging these non-Jaina admixtures from the lives of the Jaina laymen. It is possible that they could have devised a new set of guardian deities to replace the local, non-Jaina ones, thus giving the Jaina laymen the kind of protection that they had come to expect from the local gods. Only a stray reference in the work of Jinasena, an eighth-century Digambara teacher, has survived to show that the Jaina *ācāryas* had been active in educating their laity in this manner. Jinasena, who is credited with formulating a large number of Jaina house-holder rites, stipulates that a person upholding the true Jaina faith should remove images of the 'false gods' (*mithyā-devatā*) from his residence. 'He should in a public manner (*prakāśaṃ*) take them away somewhere else', says Jinasena, 'and abandon them, saying "Until now, out of ignorance, you have been worshipped by us with respect. However, now the time has come for us to worship our own guardian deities (*asmat samaya-devatāḥ*). Pray, do not be angry. You may go wherever you please."'[9]

Such a statement would seem to indicate that the laity of Jinasena's time were prone to worship non-Jaina gods, and that a movement to re-convert these Jainas gained strength under the leadership of the Jaina monks.

The reference to Jaina guardian deities in Jinasena's quotation above also suggests that it was during this time that Jaina teachers decided to institute a cult of guardian deities closely associated with that of the Jinas. Although there is no formal concept of an *iṣṭa-devatā* (favourite deity) among the Jainas, because the Jinas are above granting boons, for some reason or other, certain Jinas have enjoyed greater popularity among the Jaina laity than others. One would expect that Mahāvīra, being the last Jina and the closest historically to the Jaina community, would be most worshipped. But such is not the case. The shrines dedicated to his predecessor Pārśva, who preceded him by 250 years, are far more numerous in fact. The next two Jinas, in order of popularity, are Ṛṣabha, the first Jina, and Nemi, the twenty-second Jina and a cousin of Vāsudeva Kṛṣṇa. As for the rest of the Jinas, few independent images of them have been found, apart from their portrayal in a stereotyped row of twenty-four Jinas.

Pārśva's popularity over the other Jinas is probably due to his association with his guardian deities, the snake god Dharaṇendra with his consort Padmāvatī. The Jaina Purāṇas maintain that Pārśva, while still a young prince of Vārāṇasī, had saved a pair of snakes hidden in a piece of firewood, which was being kindled by a non-Jaina ascetic for a sacrifice. Pārśva stopped him from burning the log and showed him the dying pair of snakes. He uttered the holy Jaina litany (*pañca-namaskāra-mantra*) in the presence of the snakes, and as a consequence they were immediately reborn as the *yakṣas* Dharaṇendra and Padmāvatī. The haughty ascetic fiercely hated Pārśva, and was reborn as a demon (*vyantara*) named Śambara. When Pārśva subsequently renouned the world and sat in meditation, Śambara, remembering his past enmity, showered a hailstorm over him. And it was at this time that the pair of *yakṣas*, Dharaṇendra and Padmāvatī, remembering the good deed done to them, came down to protect their saviour Pārśva. Dharaṇendra spread his hood over the seated Pārśva, while his consort, who could not be permitted to touch an ascetic since she was female, stood by his side raising a parasol over him. This scene appears in the Ellora caves (c. ninth century) and is probably the earliest iconographic representation of the cult of these two *yakṣas* in association with Pārśva.[10] The primary purpose of the legend was no doubt to stress the great potency of the Jaina *mantra* and the power it had to lead a dying person to heaven. But the fact that these two 'snake gods' helped Pārśva in his time of calamity also contributed to the establishment of a cult in which they were worshipped as intercessors by the laity. Since Jaina doctrine does not allow worship of the laity, the category to which *yakṣas* belong, these two 'snake gods' could be invoked as guardian deities only in connection with the worship of the Jina Pārśva, whose attendants they had chosen to become.

Once the worship of such exalted householders had been legitimised, the establishment of a popular cult of guardian deities opened the way for further assimilation of non-Jaina elements. Thus, certain well-known Hindu gods and goddesses, who were already associated with sacred places adjacent to the sites of Jaina temples, could be incorporated into the Jaina fold.

The Girnar Hills in Saurashtra, famous for the inscriptions of Aśoka and Rudradāman, are sacred to Jainas and non-Jainas alike. The highest peak of this mount is dedicated to a Hindu mother-goddess named Ambikā, and a nearby peak is sacred to the Jainas who believe it was the site at which Nemi, the twenty-second Jina, attained *nirvāṇa.* Although there is no story connecting Ambikā with Nemi in the way that Padmāvatī was linked with Pārśva, it was only natural for the Jainas to associate them by making Ambikā (also called Kūṣmāṇḍinī) into Nemi's guardian deity. Similarly, other *yakṣas,* especially Kālī, Jvālāmālinī, Mahākālī and Gaurī, whose names definitely suggest connections with the Śaivite deity, Durgā, may have been brought into the Jaina pantheon as guardian deities of the Jinas—Suvidhi, Śītala, Śreyāṃsa, and Vāsupūjya (nos. 9-12) respectively.[11] Jaina laymen could then worship them as their own deities, without abandoning the Jaina faith.

Such legitimisation of *yakṣa*-worship within the Jaina faith may have helped to prevent the influence of Vaiṣṇava and Śaiva *bhakti* movements on the Jaina laity. All doctrinal compromises have their price, and Jaina laypeople, who previously had only worshipped the Jinas, were increasingly attracted to the worldly benefits available from the *yakṣas,* while the mendicants busied themselves with the task of devising new rites, litanies, and tantric practices to placate the *yakṣas.* This resulted in a new class of clerics , called Yatis and Bhaṭṭārakas, hitherto unknown to Jaina society, who claimed for themselves a special status similar to that of the '*mahants*' of Hindu religious establishments. Several centres, called Maṭhas, of such administrative clerics, came into existence all over Western India, and from these the clerics conducted an extraordinary number of business transactions, such as building temples and erecting images, both of the Jinas and of *yakṣas.* They also instituted various new rites and rituals to be employed in their worship, and managed large endowments offered by devout laymen for the perpetuation of their cults. Initially, the *yakṣas* could not be worshipped independently of Jina images, but gradually special annexes housing them were built adjacent to the main shrines, thereby increasing the importance of *yakṣas* in the Jain ritual. Eventually they were granted a status nearly equal to that of the Jinas themselves.

Several admonitions of leading Jaina *ācāryas* of the twelfth and thirteenth centuries show that this must have caused a great deal of alarm to some monks. Once again we may quote Somadeva, who was cognizant of the fact that the *yakṣas* had ceased to be mere complements to the Jina, and had nearly usurped the Jina's role as objects of worship. He sternly warned the Jaina laity against such gross heresy: 'Whoever treats as equals to the Jina, the Lord of the three worlds, and these demi-gods of the lower worlds, and worships them equally, surely is heading downward (toward purgatory). These deities were conceived in the holy scripture purely for the sake of guarding the teachings of the Jina. Therefore, these demi-gods should not be honoured beyond their proper share in oblations by Jainas who hold the right view.'[12]

Another layman of the thirteenth century, Paṇḍita Āśādhara (the author of the *Sāgāradharmāmṛta*) did not proscribe the worship of the *yakṣas,* but did decry it. He proclaimed that while weak-minded and ignorant people might stoop to *yakṣa* worship, the person of true insight would never do so, even when beset by great calamities. Such weak-minded people, he said, should be instructed and reaffirmed in their devotion to the Jina. We do not know what impact, if any, these admonitions may have had on contemporary Jaina society. There is no doubt, however, that the corruptions produced by the excessive adoration of *yakṣas* engendered protests against those monks who had been branded as *caitya-vāsīs* (temple-dwellers), who were looked upon as apostates from the true mendicant path. The Jaina reform movement of the fifteenth century declared idol-worship (*mūrti-pūjā*) itself to be a form of heresy unsupported by the ancient scripture, and its leader, Lonka Shah (c. 1450), formed a school which called itself *Sthānaka-vāsīs* (i.e. 'dwellers-in-halls' in contrast to the "temple-dwellers'). This school sought to purge all temple-oriented rituals from Jaina practice, and to reintroduce the laity to the meditational practices which were exemplified by the images of the Jina. The emergence of this reformist sect within Jainism has no parallel in Theravāda Buddhism, and its success can only be compared to that of Lutheran Protestantism within Christianity. The Sthānakavāsīs have flourished in the Punjab and Rajasthan, and form a very important group today, claiming as many as 1,000 monks and 1,400 nuns within their community. They are the true forerunners of Indian iconoclastic movements, even preceding the beginnings of Sikhism, which was founded by Guru Nanak (1469-1538). They might also be considered to have been a significant force behind the creation in 1875 of the *Āryasamāja*, a socio-religious movement founded in the Punjab by Svāmī Dayānand Sarsvatī (1824-83), a Hindu ascetic who not only shunned all image worship, but even rejected the cults of the *purāṇic* gods.

I began this chapter by exploring the characteristics of a popular form of Jainism, by comparing them with certain practices prevalent in the Buddhism of Sri Lanka. The comparison showed that the Jainas, unlike the Theravādins, were able to preserve the purity of their tradition by preventing the rise of popular cults based on worship of relics and of a future teacher. This study showed also that, while Buddhist monks became willing participants in popular rituals associated with offerings to the dead, the Jaina mendicants vigorously condemned them and effectively educated their laity to shun all such forms of superstitious behaviour. Both *Śramaṇa* traditions were greatly successful in resisting the Hindu theistic devotionalism that threatened to assimilate them. But both succumbed to strong popular demands for the worship of demigods, and had finally to legitimise some form of a cult of 'guardian deities'. In this respect, popular Jainism paralleled popular Theravāda Buddhism, and both went through an identical phase in which Brāhmaṇical accretions to their original pantheon hastened the degeneration of their monastic institutions.

In subsequent periods, however, the Jainas, unlike the Theravādins, initiated strong reforms to check the corruption resulting from excessive *yakṣa* worship. But one should not exaggerate the impact of the reformists. After initial successes, the iconoclastic Sthānakavāsīs, like many other reformists in India, formed a sect of their own, effectively removing themselves from the mainstream of the religion. Moreover, lay devotees of the Sthānkavāsī sect did not cease to worship at all temples, but only at the Jaina shrines. Many of the Rajasthan and Gujarat adherents were converted from Śaivism centuries ago,[13] and they continued clandestinely to worship their 'family deities' (*kula-devatās*), such as Cāmuṇḍā and Durgā. As for the Digambaras and Śvetāmbaras, their reformed religiosity found expression in such ritualistic activities as building new temples and consecrating more and more Jina images, thus seeking to gain merit in a legitimate manner. Indeed, the popular Jainism of our time is little more than indulgence in the most expensive and spectacular forms of image-worship. This was illustrated in 1981 at the celebrations of the head-anointing (*mastakābhiṣeka*) ceremony of the 1,000-year-old monumental image of Lord Bāhubali at Śravaṇabelgola.[14] The devotional ecstasies aroused in the hearts of Jainas by the dramatic scenes of that ceremony affirm the enduring presence of a popular form of Jainism, markedly different from the rigorous asceticism of its great tradition.

NOTES

1. R. F. Gombrich, *Precept and Practice* (Oxford, 1971).
2. 'dvau hi dharmau gṛahsthānāṃ laukikaḥ pāralaukikaḥ/ lokāśrayo bhaved ādyaḥ paraḥ syād āgamāśrayaḥ / ... / sarva eva hi Jainānāṃ pramāṇaṃ laukiko vidhiḥ / yatra samyaktvahānir na yatra na vratadūṣaṇam. *Upāsakādhyayana, kārikā* 477, Bhāratīya Jñānapīṭha, 1964.
3. sūryārgho grahaṇasnānaṃ saṃkrāntau draviṇavyayaḥ / saṃdhyā sevāgnisatkāro gehadehārcano vidhiḥ // nadīnadasamudreṣu majjanaṃ dharmacetasā / tarustūpāgrabhaktānāṃ vandanaṃ bhṛgusaṃśrayayḥ // gopṛṣṭhāntakanamaskāras tanmūtrasya niṣevaṇam / ratnavāhanabhūyakṣaśastraśailādisevanam // samayāntarapākhaṇḍavedalokasamāśrayam / evam ādi vimūḍhānāṃ jñeyaṃ mūḍham anekadhā // varārthaṃ lokavārtārtham uparodhārtham eva vā / upāsanam amīṣāṃ syāt samyagdarśanahānaye // [*Upāsakādhyayana, kārikā* 136-140]

4. na svato 'gneḥ pavitratvaṃ devatārūpam eva vā/ ...vyavahāranāyapekṣā tasyeṣṭā pujyatā dvijaiḥ //
Jinasena's *Ādipurāṇa*, xl, 8, Bhāratīya Jñānapīṭha.
5. See P. S. Jaini, Karma and the problem of rebirth in Jainism, in *Karma and Rebirth in Classical Indian Traditions*, ed. W. D. O'Flaherty (California 1980).
6. Brahmā Tilottamācittaḥ Śrīpatiḥ Śrīhariḥ smṛtaḥ / ardhanārīśvaro Śambhus tathā 'py eṣāṃ kilāptatā // gehinā samavṛttasya yater apy adharasthiteḥ / yadi devasya devatvaṃ na devo durlabho bhavet //
[*Upāsakādhyayana, kārikā* 62-93]
7. ...śrīHemācāryaḥ kiñcid dhiyā nidhyāya nṛpam āha: alaṃ purāṇadarśanoktibhiḥ śrīSomeśvaram eva tava pratyakṣīkaromi, yathā tanmukhena muktimārgam avaiṣi iti.../ atha... garbhagṛhe... nṛpo... apratimarūpam asambhāvyasvarūpaṃ tapasvinam adrākṣīt/... divyā gīrāvirāsīt: 'rājan, ayaṃ maharṣiḥ sarvadevatāvatāraḥ / ...etadupadiṣṭa evāsaṃdigdho muktimārgaḥ' ity ādiśya tirobhūte .../ atha taraiva nṛpater yāvajjīvaṃ piśita-prasannayor niyamaṃ datvā tataḥ pratyāvṛttau kṣamāpatī śrīmadAṇahillapuraṃ prāpatuḥ /
Merutuṅga's *Prabandhacintāmaṇi*, p. 85. Singhi Jaina Granthamālā, vol. I, 1933. See also G. Bühler, *The Life of Hemacandrācārya* translated by M. Patel, Singhi Jaina Series 11 (1931).
8. See P. S. Jaini, *The Jaina Path of Purification*, Ch. 9 (California, 1979).
9. nirdiṣṭasthānalābhasya punar asya gaṇagrahaḥ / syān mithyādevatāḥ svasmād viniḥsārayato gṛhāt // iyantaṃ kālam ajñānāt pūjitāḥ sma kṛtādaram / pūjyās tv idānīm asmābhir asmatsamayadevatāḥ // tato 'paṃṛṣṭitenālaṃ anyatra svairam āsyatām / iti prakāśam evaitān nītvā 'nyatra kvacit tyajet // [*Ādipurāṇa*, xxxix, 45-47]
10. See U. P. Shah, Evolution of Jaina iconography and symbolism in *Aspects of Jaina Art and Architecture*, ed. U. P. Shah, M. A. Dhaky (Ahmedabad, 1975).
11. See 'Tīrthaṅkara' in Jinendra Varni, *Jainendra-siddhānta-kośa* (Bhāratīya Jñānapīṭha, Delhi, 1970-73). It should be noted that the names of the *yakṣa/yakṣis* are not mentioned by Jinasena and Guṇabhadra in their *Ādipurāṇa/ Uttarapurāṇa*, the main biography of the Jinas in the Digambara tradition.
12. devaṃ jagattrayinetraṃ vyantarādyāś ca devatāḥ / samaṃ pūjāvidhāneṣu paśyan dūraṃ vrajed adhaḥ // [*Upāsakādhyayana, kārikā*, 697]
13. For a list of the Rajasthani communities converted to Jainism, see A. C. and B. Nahta, *Kharatara gacchake pratibodhita gotra aur jātiyāṃ* (Hindi), (Calcutta no date).
14. See Saryu Doshi, *Homage to Shravana* Belgola (Marg Publications, Bombay, 1981).

CHAPTER 16

Fear of Food: Jaina Attitude on Eating*

One of the several ways of distinguishing the Vedic tradition from the heterodox religious systems is to characterize the former as oriented to sacrifice (*yajña*) and the latter as adhering to the path of asceticism (*tapas*). Since a *yajña* primarily consists of offering some kind of food as oblation, the Vedic tradition may be described as that which consumes food initially offered to the Deity and hence sanctified by its acceptance. The Vedic seers declare that they have imbibed *soma* and have attained immortality: *apāma somam amṛtā abhūma.*[1] The Upaniṣads even declare that food is Brahman (*annaṃ brahma*)[2] and recite a prayer which expresses a wish "Let us all eat together" (*saha nau bhunaktu*).[3] The age-old Brāhmaṇical practice of offering *śrāddha* or food to the manes (*pitṛ*) by feeding the Brahmans has given rise to the adage that a Brahman is fond of food: *brāhmaṇo bhojanapriyaḥ.*

In contrast, the heterodox tradition of the *śramaṇas* ignores *soma* altogether, decries oblations to gods as fruitless, prohibits the eating of the so-called *prasāda,*[4] and ridicules the offerings to the manes as futile; it thus may be said to reject any notion of sacredness attached to food. The preferred mode of spiritual

---

*Paper read at the 41st annual meeting of the Association for Asian Studies (Washington, D. C.: March 18, 1989), Session 56: "Edible Complexes: Attitude Toward Food and Eating in South Asian Tradition and Culture."

This article was published originally in *Jain Studies in Honour of Jozef Deleu,* eds. Smet and Watanabe, (Tokyo: Hon-No-Tomosha, 1993), pp. 339-354. Reprinted with kind permission of the Editor, Kenji Watanabe.

activity of the *śramaṇas* is *tapas*, which primarily consists of 'heating' oneself, i.e., drying or thinning by reducing the intake of food and water. *Tapas* is thus a form of self-sacrifice which is said to bring about magical powers (*ṛddhi*) as well as achieve the spiritual goal of *mokṣa*. The Ājīvikas, the most ancient among the *śramaṇas*, have claimed that their teacher Gośāla had accumulated such heat (*tejo-leśyā*) within himself by fasting and that he was able to scorch to death two Jaina mendicants by throwing that power in their direction.[5] He is also said to have died fasting without water with only a mango stone placed in his mouth for the purpose of salivating.[6] Such a death was considered an extremely holy one and assured the highest heaven, if not *mokṣa*, for the departing soul. The *Ācārāṅga-sūtra* of the Jainas narrates at length the severe asceticism of Mahāvīra, the last Jaina Tīrthaṅkara. It is said that during the twelve years of his wandering life prior to his Enlightenment, Mahāvīra had lived on only three kinds of rough food—rice, pounded jujube, and pulses: "Taking only these three, he sustained himself for eight months. . . . Sometimes he ate only every sixth day or every eighth or every tenth or every twelfth. Free of desires, he remained engrossed in meditation."[7] According to the later commentators, during these twelve years Mahāvīra took food on a total of 349 days only; at other times he fasted completely.[8]

The Buddhist texts, too, make similar claims on behalf of Siddhārtha Gautama who is said to have fasted for long periods of time during the six years of his strenuous search for Enlightenment. In the *Majjhimanikāya*, he describes the severity of his fasting in the following word: "Because I ate so little, all my limbs became like the knotted joints of withered creepers; because I ate so little, my protruding backbone became like a string of balls; because I ate so little, my buttocks became like a bullock's hoof; because I ate so little, my gaunt ribs became like the crazy rafters of a tumble-down shed; because I ate so little, the pupils of my eyes appeared lying low and deep in their sockets as sparkles of water in a deep well appear lying low and deep . . . ."[9] There is no doubt that the famous Gāndhāran skeleton image of the meditating Buddha, now in the Lahore Museum, is a vivid depiction of this passage. As we know, the Buddha abandoned this practice in preference for his Middle Path. Condemning such fasting as a painful mortification unworthy of a seeker of *nirvāṇa*, he started taking food and is not known ever to have prescribed fasting for anyone else. But the Jainas found this so-called Middle Path of the Buddha as nothing but faintheartedness, a weakness of the spirit unworthy of a true follower of a Jina. They not only employed fasting as the best atonement for transgressions of mendicant rules,[10] but also recommended it as a supreme spiritual practice to their mendicants as well as lay disciples.

The Jainas are thus distinguished from the Brāhmaṇical tradition by their rejection of the sacredness of food, of sacrificial meat, but also of ghee and, by extension, rejection of the cow as a sacred animal. They are distinguished from the Buddhists by their emphatic adherence to the practice of fasting as a primary component of their spiritual path. Refraining from food for a period of time is not altogether unknown to the Brāhmaṇical scriptures. The *Manusmṛti* prescribes fasting as a form of expiation for certain transgressions especially by members of the Brahman caste.[11] The Purāṇic literature is also full of stories like that of Viśvāmitra whose years of fasting were rendered futile by the caprices of gods, jealous of the sage's superior Yogic powers. But these are, for the most part, legends and are not narrated to persuade the Hindu laity to imitate the sage by similar fasting. In the case of the Jainas, however, fasting by their teacher Mahāvīra seems to have left an indelible mark on their consciousness, making it the most important feature of Jaina *tapas*. This is demonstrated by the fact that a great many Jaina laymen and women of all ages undertake fasting on a regular basis and consider it the singular mark by which their community can be distinguished from that of the Brāhmaṇical society. Remarkable still is the most holy Jaina practice of *sallekhanā* which permits certain advanced Jaina mendicants to adopt total fasting as a legitimate way—in fact the only permissible way—of choosing death in the face of terminal illness.[12]

The Jaina emphasis on fasting thus invites an examination of their attitude to food and the reasons for their belief in the efficacy of fasting as a means of attaining *mokṣa*. Probably the Jaina doctrine of the material (*paudgalika*) nature of *karma* capable of producing impure transformation (*vibhāva-pariṇāma*) of the soul (*jīva*) is at the root of this belief. It is well-known that in Jainism *karmic* bondage is seen as an accumulation of an extremely subtle form of floating 'dust' which clings to the soul when the latter is overcome, moistened, as it were, by desire and other passions. These desires (present in all souls from beginningless time) in their most subtle form are called *saṃjñās*, a term which may be tentatively translated as 'instincts'. The Jaina texts enumerate four such *saṃjñās* universally found in all forms of life including the vegetable kingdom. Craving for food (*āhāra-saṃjñā*) is the most primary of these instincts. No being other than the liberated soul is exempt from it. This desire for food sets up competition between one living being and another which gives rise to the second instinct, namely that of fear (*bhaya-saṃjñā*). The consumption of food sets in motion the third and probably the most virulent of the instincts, the desire for sex (*maithuna-saṃjñā*), gratification of which produces further desire for food. This, in turn, produces a craving to accumulate things for future use, the instinct called *parigraha-saṃjñā*, which invariably goads the soul towards volitional harmful acts (*hiṃsā*) inspired by attachment and aversion (*rāga* and *dveṣa*). The Jainas therefore see the craving for food as the very root of all bondage, the uprooting of which is essential for the elimination of the other passions.[13]

The Jaina texts dealing with the training of mendicants constantly encourage the cultivation of distaste for food and stipulate a variety of ways of overcoming the desire for flavor (*rasa-parityāga*). They begin with the characteristic Jaina declaration that the desire for food is the prime cause for all forms of *hiṃsā* since food cannot be consumed without destroying another life form. Because life cannot be maintained without consuming some amount of food, the Jaina teachers have devised various means of minimizing this *hiṃsā* for their mendicants who have assumed the vow of total non-violence (*ahiṃsā-mahāvrata*).[14] In the Jaina classification of beings, souls endowed with all five senses (*pañcendriya-jīva*) occupy the highest position, while the vegetable life, endowed with only one sense, namely that of touch, is placed at the bottom of the list. Beings with two or more senses must not be wilfully violated even by a layperson because their organisms (muscle, blood, bones, etc.) are similar to that of human beings. Thus all forms of animal flesh, including foul and fish, are totally unacceptable for a pious Jaina who must depend on a vegetarian diet, with only dairy products as an exception to the rule (since it is believed that removal of milk does not hurt the animal). The list of prohibited food (*abhakṣya*), however, even extends to certain fruits and vegetables, especially the five kinds of figs (*udumbara*), fruits with many seeds (*bahubīja*), and a variety of plants called *anantakāyas*, which are thought to be inhabited not by individual souls but by an infinite number of living organism. These *anantakāyas* include as many as thirty-two varieties of food including turmeric, ginger, garlic, bamboo, radishes, beetroots, and carrots.[15] The Jainas extend their scruples against destroying *ekendriyas* even to water used for drinking. No observant Jaina may drink unstrained water (*agālita-jala*) and a mendicant may drink only boiled water which has been rendered free of all forms of subtle life.

Further restrictions apply to the time when permitted food may be consumed. Advanced laypeople as well as mendicants as a rule observe the vow of not partaking of any food or water after sunset (*rātri-bhojana-tyāga-vrata*) and the Digambara mendicants are restricted to a single meal (including water) a day. On certain holy days, such as the eighth and the fifteenth of each lunar month, many laypeople undertake fasts (called *anaśana*, lit. 'not eating', or *upavāsa*) and at least once a year all Jainas observe a communal fast and dedicate that day for begging forgiveness (*kṣamāpanā*) of all begins, including those *ekendriyas* whose lives they destroyed in the act of eating.[16] As for mendicants, who must constantly engage in austerities, the Jaina texts prescribe a variety of *tapas*: giving up stimulating dishes (*rasa-parityāga*), reducing one's diet to a few morsels (*avamaudarya*), and fasting for an entire day (*anaśana*).[17] Jaina fasts, whether practiced by the mendicants or the laypeople, must be distinguished from the "fasts" kept by the followers of Judaism, Christianity, and Islam. Fasting in these communities is, for the most part, restricted to the daytime only; often food is freely consumed after sunset. Even the followers of various Brāhmaṇical religious sects allow eating fruits or some form of uncooked food—and preferably at night!—on their fasting days. The Jaina fast, however, lasts from sunrise to sunrise and is total; only boiled water in limited quantities may be consumed and that too only during the daytime. An extraordinary feature of the Jaina fast—not much discussed in the books but tacitly observed—is that all sexual contact between couples is forbidden for the duration of the fast, even if only the wife or the husband has refrained from food. Although the vow of celibacy (*brahma-carya*) does not demand the vow of fasting, the Jainas seem to perceive the latter incomplete without the former. This demonstrates the unique Jaina belief that the sex instinct (*maithuna-saṃjñā*) is inseparable from the craving for food and cannot be overcome without controlling the desire for the latter.

Fasting for a day only is considered child's play among the Jaina laity. A great many Jaina laypeople, especially women, during the sacred week called the *paryuṣaṇa-parva* in the rainy season (*cāturmāsa*), undertake longer periods of fastings for three to eight days. The formal conclusion of a fast is called *pāraṇā* and takes place long after the sunrise, with a sip of boiled water, usually after an offering of food is made to a Jaina monk or nun visiting the household for collecting alms. The *pāraṇās*, especially after longer periods of fasting, are occasions for joyous celebrations by the relatives and friends of the person who has completed the vow faultlessly and cheerfully. Along with fellow members of the community they gather to feed such a person—in the majority of cases the fasts are undertaken by women, often newly wedded brides taking the lead and proving their zeal to their new relatives—with spoonfuls of boiled water or fruit juice. The participating community shows in this manner its delight in the spiritual progress made by one of its own and also earns merit by the act of giving food to so worthy a person.

As for the mendicants, the Jaina books describe a variety of fasts lasting sometimes several days, weeks, and even months. These are said to result in the immediate rebirth in the highest of heavens (where only Jaina mendicants may be born) to be followed by rebirth even as illustrious human beings (*śalākāpuruṣa*), such as a Cakravartin, a Nārāyaṇa, or even as a Jina, before attaining the supreme goal of *mokṣa*. The ninth-century Punnāṭa Jinasena in his *Harivaṃśapurāṇa* devotes a whole chapter of 154 verses to the description of a variety of fasts known by such grand names as the Sarvatobhadra (19 fasts), Vasantabhadra (35 fasts), Mahāsarvatobhadra (196 fasts), Trilokasāravidhi, Vajramadhyavidhi, Ekāvalī, Muktāvalī, Ratnāvalī, and the Siṃhaniṣkrīḍita, to mention only a few major ones.[18] The last of these fasts consists of 496 fasts with only 61 meals in between and is completed in as many as 557 days. It is said that Kṛṣṇa, a cousin of the 22nd Jina Nemi according to the Jaina epics, was in a previous birth a Jaina mendicant by the name of Nirnāmaka Muni (lit. 'the Sage Anonymous'!) and had then performed the above-mentioned Siṃhaniṣkrīḍita fast. He had as a result been born during the time of the Jina Nemi as the last Nārāyaṇa, the Great Hero of our age.[19]

Fasting for the Jaina is thus a holy act to be undertaken by the pious solely for overcoming the *saṃjñās* in order to weaken the bonds of *karma*. But a holy act for a mendicant can justly become a source of merit for the laity seeking worldly fortune. The Jainas consider the offering of food (*āhāra-dāna*) to a fasting monk or a nun on the *pāraṇā* day an act of extraordinary merit, a privilege envied even by gods. The Jaina Purāṇas are replete with stories of a great many pious laypeople, remembered in the tradition with deep affection, who were fortunate enough to be the donors (*dātā*) of alms to such worthy mendicants, especially when the latter were on the verge of attaining enlightenment. It is said that Ṛṣabha, the first Jina of our time, wandered without food for a whole year and concluded his fast with a handful of sugarcane juice offered by King Śreyāṃsa, a momentous event which was greeted by gods with a shower of wealth. The Jainas still celebrate this day, the third day of the waxing moon of Vaiśākha (April-May), as the Immortal Third (*Akṣaya-tṛtīyā*),[20] and aspire to offer a similar gift to mendicants who conclude their fasts on that day. Mahāvīra, the last Jina, is also said to have wandered for six months without food and water and finally broke his fast with some lentils offered to him by a slave girl called Candanā who subsequently became the head nun of his community of 36,000 nuns.[21] In the Buddhist tradition this honour goes to Lady Sujātā who had offered a dish of milk pudding to Siddhārtha Gautama on the very day of his enlightenment. It is said that this dish provided nourishment for the enlightened Gautama for 49 days.[22]

Fasting is an act of *tapas* and is figuratively spoken of as a blazing fire in front of which mountains of snow of *karma* vanish, bringing the aspirant ever more close to the goal of *mokṣa*. The merit resulting from offering the proper food to such holy persons is therefore rightly unequalled by any other charitable activity of a householder. On the other hand, the perils of denying food to a fasting mendicant on his *pāraṇā* day are proportionately great and the lay community must remain vigilant lest the fire of his *tapas* engulf the society itself! The Jaina narrative of

Kaṃsa (the notorious king of Mathurā who was killed by Kṛṣṇa) serves as an excellent illustration of the dire consequences that follow upon a mendicant's long fast, the *pāraṇā* of which has been thwarted by carelessness on the part of the laymen. In his former life, the soul of the person who will be known in his next life as the villain Kaṃsa, was a mendicant called Vasiṣṭha. He practiced the Brāhmaṇical asceticism of *agnisādhana*, i.e. sitting in meditation surrounded by burning logs of wood, which the Jainas considered false *tapas* on account of the *hiṃsā* caused by the blazing fire. He was subsequently converted to Jainism and became a devout Jaina monk of the Digambara order. He lived on the mount Govardhana, and the reputation of his great *tapas* reached the court of King Ugrasena of Mathurā, himself an ardent lay follower of the Jina. The muni Vasiṣṭha once undertook a monthlong fast. The king, desirous of earning merit by offering him food on the day of his *pāraṇā*, issued a royal decree in which he claimed that privilege for himself and threatened to punish any one who should come forth to feed the monk when his fast was over. At the end of the thirty days, the muni Vasiṣṭha came out of seclusion and entered Mathurā, walking in silence in front of the houses, expecting a layperson to properly invite him in for a meal, as befits a Digambara monk. Unfortunately, the king had forgotten his resolve to feed the monk, and the people were afraid of breaking the king's command. As a result Vasiṣṭha returned to his abode without concluding the fast and as is customary in such cases, he underwent another month of fasting. He returned again to Mathurā, but the king was distracted by a raging fire in the palace and Vasiṣṭha had to leave the city without food for the second time. He returned for the third time after the lapse of another month's fast, but as fate would have it, the king again failed to honour his promise occupied as he was with an elephant which had gone on a rampage, and Vasiṣṭha returned without finishing his *pāraṇā*. An old woman saw the silent monk returning without alms and informed him of the unjust order of the King Ugrasena. The *āhāra-saṃjñā* is a deadly instinct, and as the wise frog Gaṅgadatta of the *Pañcatantra* observed: "What sin would not a hungry man commit, for indeed weak men become devoid of pity!" (*bubhukṣitaḥ kiṃ na karoti pāpam, kṣīṇā narā niṣkaruṇā bhavanti.*)[23] Infuriated by this callous treatment, Vasiṣṭha in a moment of hunger forgot his mendicant vows and resolved to avenge this insult and deprivation. He died in anguish and was immediately conceived in the womb of Padmāvatī, the chief queen of the same King Ugrasena. Soon after, the queen started having pregnancy cravings (*dohala*) of an extraordinary kind. She conceived a desire, prompted no doubt by the fetus, to cut the heart of her husband and to drink his blood in her folded hands. The king, using certain stratagems, fulfilled her desires and a son was born whom both parents thought it wise to abandon to avert any danger to the kingdom. They placed him in a copper container (*kāṃsya-mañjūṣā*) with a royal seal indicating his true origin and floated it in the river Yamunā. Thus was the origin of the villain Kaṃsa who would eventually imprison his father the King Ugrasena and would himself be killed by Kṛṣṇa, the son of Vasudeva and Devakī.[24]

This is not the occasion for examining the question whether the pregnant woman in the story was projecting on the fetus her own desire to kill her husband, or to debate the possibility of the presence of an oedipal desire in a fetus. We are here concerned rather with the "edible" complex and should therefore look for the message the story might convey to the members of the Jaina community concerning the instinct for food. Even a fetus is not free from the ravages of the *āhāra-saṃjñā*, especially the fetus of a soul that has died of starvation. Notwithstanding the grave provocation which filled the dying *muni* Vasiṣṭha with rage, one would still expect a Jaina mendicant to crave a morsel of vegetarian food rather than lust for a drink of blood. The author of the story is no doubt employing a conventionalized way to describe an acute form of hostility of the frustrated hungry man—and a holy man—toward those who let him die of hunger. Even so, it is possible to argue that the story also points to the great difficulty of maintaining the practice of vegetarianism in the face of deliberate deprivation of permitted food or in the event of a natural calamity like a famine. We will never know why certain animals (e.g. cows, deer, elephants, etc.) are born vegetarians while others are not, but it can be safely said that human beings are vegetarians not by birth but by choice only. Indeed vegetarianism in the Indian context must be considered to be a religious habit acquired over many years of the strictest possible cultural conditioning. It is therefore liable to be lost if favorable conditions—such as donors readily offering appropriate food—were not forthcoming, as in the case of *muni* Vasiṣṭha in our story, or social pressures were to be relaxed as is now the case for many second generation Jainas who have settled in the West. In either case, craving for food, ever present due to the *āhāra-saṃjñā*, especially for the forbidden variety—the taste (*rasa*) for which has only been suppressed but has never been totally destroyed—is likely to surface at any time. According to the Jaina texts, the memories of these tastes are so tenacious that they are preserved through countless rebirths and may suddenly overcome a soul even under the best of circumstances. This is illustrated by several Jaina stories one of which may be noted here.

We referred earlier to the great fast called the Siṃhaniṣkrīḍita which was practiced by Kṛṣṇa in one of his previous lives when he had become a Jaina monk. The same narrative tells us that a few lives prior to that period, the soul of Kṛṣṇa was born as a human being and he had entered the service of a king as a cook and had gained great reputation for preparing the most delicious meat dishes. This distinction earned for him not only the lordship of ten villages as a gift from the king, but also the title *Amṛta-rasāyana* ("Abode of the Ambrosia Flavor"). This king died and his son who succeeded to the throne came under the influence of a Jaina monk and gave up eating meat altogether. He fired the cook and took away the ten villages previously granted to him by the dead king. The cook realized that a Jaina mendicant had deprived him of his living and deliberately fed that monk a poisonous bitter gourd, as a result of which the monk died. Because of this evil deed, upon the cook's death his soul was born in hell. When eventually he was reborn as a human being and had progressed enough to become a Jaina monk, he performed the Siṃhaniṣkrīḍita fast and, as a result, was (in his last birth) born Kṛṣṇa the Great Hero, a cousin-brother of the twenty-second Jina called Nemi. One would expect Kṛṣṇa to have by now given up all desire for meat, but such was not the case. It is said that on the eve of Nemi's wedding, Kṛṣṇa deliberately caused a great many animals to be penned in for the purpose of feeding their meat to the guests and, as a result, Nemi, utterly overcome by his compassion to the animals, renounced the world to become a Jaina mendicant.[25] Now it is well-known that Jainas have always considered themselves to be vegetarians, especially at the time of Kṛṣṇa and Jina Nemi, when the degenerate days of the *pañcama-kāla* (the Jaina version of the Kali-yuga in which we now live) had not yet arrived. Nor are the Jainas ever known to feed non-vegetarian food even to their non-Jaina guests. The belief that Kṛṣṇa, the Great Jaina Hero, and himself a cousin of the Jina, could have succumbed to such a totally unwholesome and unacceptable practice can only be explained in one way. The relish of the forbidden food and the memories of meat eating were so ingrained on his soul that they surfaced unexpectedly—triggered no doubt by the impending wedding feast—and drove him to commit that reprehensible act on account of which he was, at the end of his glorious life as a Nārāyaṇa, reborn in the third hell. The Jaina epics tell us that Kṛṣṇa's soul is still languishing in that purgatory, but they also promise us that he will emerge from that hell to be reborn again as a human being—and one who remains a vegetarian to be sure!—becoming even a Jina himself and thus will finally attain the goal of *mokṣa*.[26]

A person who does not climb higher is in no danger of falling lower. But there is no telling how far and low an apostate, having slipped from the high ground, may fall. The story of Kṛṣṇa does not fully spell out what probably the Jaina authors fear actually may happen to a Jaina who has ceased to be a vegetarian. The alleged craving for blood by the *muni* Vasiṣṭha in his new incarnation as the fetus Kaṃsa must inescapably lead to the horrible conclusion that, for an apostate, cannibalism is just a step away from eating animal flesh. One such story, the subject-matter of a long Kannaḍa *kāvya* called *Jinadattarāyacarite*, widely known in the Digambara Jaina community of Karnataka, might illustrate this point. The story tells us about the migration of Jainas in ancient times under the leadership of Prince Jinadatta from Northern Mathurā—the same city once ruled by Kaṃsa and Kṛṣṇa—to the newly founded Humcā (near the modern city of Shimoggā), the medieval seat of the Sāntara dynasty of Southern Karnataka.[27] In brief, the story is that Mathurā was ruled by a devout Jaina King Sākāra and his Queen Sīyaladevī. They have a son called Jinadatta obtained through the grace of Padmāvatī, the protector goddess (*śāsana-devatā*) of the Jina Pārśvanātha. Like the King Śāntanu of the *Mahābhārata*, King Sākāra once lost his way in a forest and found himself in love with the daughter of a king of hunters (*vyādha*). He secretly promised her father that he would give his kingdom to her son, and established her separately from his chief queen in the outskirts of the capital where she soon gave birth to a son called Māridatta. For a long while the king remained a vegetarian but with the birth of the new son, he began frequenting her house and in no time became fond of eating meat dishes cooked in her kitchen. One day, we are told, the cook could not find any animal to slaughter and, fearing the king's wrath, procured from the cemetery the flesh of a dead man and prepared a novel dish. The king was extremely pleased with the new dish and was not deterred even when he came to know the source of the meat. Indeed, he even secretly contrived with the cook to obtain freshly killed human meat every day for his table and arranged to send a small child, who would become the victim of the day, to the cook with the ruse of delivering a lemon. Soon small children began disappearing without a trace from the city of Mathurā. The king's addiction to human meat had reached a point of no return, enabling the hunter queen to use it to her benefit to get rid of Jinadatta, the rival to her son, by sending him to the cook to deliver the lemon. But fate intervened and Māridatta intercepted him, snatching the lemon away from him, insisting that he would himself deliver it to the cook and was thus killed instead. Jinadatta was miraculously saved, and he, taking his mother and his loyal army, fled Mathurā, migrated to the South, and established a new Jaina kingdom at Huṃcā, dedicating that city to his saviour goddess Padmāvatī. A terrible fall awaited the King Sākāra who had allowed himself to slip from vegetarian habits and had wantonly indulged in eating meat, leading to cannibalism. He died a horrible death and was reborn in the seventh hell.

The stories of Vasiṣtha, Kṛṣṇa and Sākāra examined above, progressively illustrate the manner in which the Jainas view the tremendous power which the instinct for eating (*āhāra-saṃjñā*) exerts upon an aspirant soul, and the need for ever guarding oneself against the temptation for food. Since the *saṃjñās*, whether for food, fear, sex or acquisition, are a form of desire, they will persist until all forms of deluding or *mohanīya karmas* are destroyed, whereupon the soul having attained omniscience (*kevala-jñāna*) comes to be designated a kevalin. One would expect the Jainas to believe that such a kevalin—a person like Mahāvīra, for example, who became a kevalin at the age of forty and lived for another thirty-two years—would altogether cease eating food.

The Jainas would also be required to devise an alternative means of sustaining the life of such a kevalin, freed as he is forever from the shackles of the *āhāra-saṃjñā*. This brings us to a most important controversy between the Jaina sects of the Śvetāmbaras and the Digambaras, who have maintained radically different views on the problem of hunger and the sustenance of life of an omniscient person, whether he be a Tīrthaṅkara kevalin like Mahāvīra, and hence gifted with special bodily features, or thousands of ordinary mendicant disciples who also attained to *kaivalya* during his time.[28]

Both sects agree that the instincts of fear (*bhaya*), sex (*maithuna*) and acquisition (*parigraha*), have their origin solely in mind and therefore these can be overcome by meditation on their opposites (*pratipakṣa-bhāvanā*) and are terminated without a trace at the time of attaining *kaivalya*. The instinct for food, however, falls in a different category, since the need for nourishment of the body operates independent of a desire to eat and cannot be wished away merely by the contemplation of the opposite. In other words, the absence of the *āhāra-saṃjñā* in a kevalin does not result in the absence of the need for nourishment. The question is how to account for the sustenance of a kevalin's body when he is totally devoid of the desire for food? The Śvetāmbaras saw no conflict here and argued that a kevalin continues to eat 'morsels' of food (*kavala-āhāra*) deposited (*prakṣipta*) in the body as before, even in the absence of the *āhāra-saṃjñā*. A kevalin must take such food, they argued, in order to sustain himself, i.e. to satisfy the biological conditions of hunger (*kṣudhā*) and thirst (*tṛṣṇā*), the two painful feelings (*asātā-vedanīya*) which, being a primary condition of all embodiment, must rise voluntarily, even in one who has brought an end to all desires.[29] But the Śvetāmbaras probably did not foresee the perils in permitting a kevalin the morsels of food (*kavala-āhāra*), for once it was admitted that even a kevalin may eat, albeit without the urgings of the *āhāra-saṃjñā*, there was no way of preventing the possibility of his consuming the forbidden food. The Śvetāmbara canonical story of Mahāvīra's eating of *kukkuṭa-māṃsa*—decades after his attaining omniscience—apparently for curing himself of the dehydration caused by the magic heat thrown by the Ājīvika Gośāla is a case in point. Notwithstanding the opinion of the old Śvetāmbara commentators and of the consensus of the Jaina public in our times that what was eaten was not any kind of meat but a medicinal herb—probably *bījapūra-kaṭāha* or belphal—the fact still remains that Mahāvīra could have been accused of such an act only because the Śvetāmbara tradition did provide for the possibility of a kevalin eating any food at all.[30] This precisely seems to be the point of controversy seized upon by the Digaṃbaras who vehemently rejected the idea of a kevalin ever eating any food subsequent to the attainment of omniscience. They maintained that with the end of the desire for food (*āhāra-saṃjñā*) also came the end of all hunger and thirst for a kevalin, as well as the need for answering the calls of nature, and also of sleep. They declared that with the attainment of omniscience the body of a kevalin automatically undergoes a bio-chemical change, as it were, his blood being transformed to milk as in the case of heavenly beings (*deva*), freeing him totally from hunger and thirst and thus from the dependence on the 'kavala-āhāra' for ever. This transformed body needs no additional nourishment for its sustenance other than that which is automatically provided by the *nokarma-vargaṇā*, a kind of *karmic* matter responsible for maintaining the structure and mass of given body. This subtle *karmic* matter is involuntarily drawn to the soul in a continuous flow by the mechanisms of the *nāma* and the *āyu-karmas*, forces which, at the time of the present rebirth, had projected the human body of the kevalin and had also determined its longevity.[31] The Digambaras proclaimed that the transformed pure body of the kevalin, now called the *parama-audārika-śarīra*, will be maintained not by any fresh food deposited (*prakṣipta*) in the mouth or absorbed through the pores of the skin (*loma-āhāra*), but solely by the nourishment derived from the *nokarma-vargaṇā*. Accordingly, they maintained that the body of the kevalin will be sustained by this voluntary *karmic* process until the end of his present life. Then, like a chunk of camphor, this pure body at the moment of death, will suddenly evaporate and the kevalin's perfected soul will reach the abode of the liberated ones (*siddha*) at the summit of the universe. *Saṃsāra* and food would thus appear to be coterminous for a Jaina; there never was a time when he has not eaten in this beginningless cycle of birth and death. The path of *mokṣa*, therefore, consists in overcoming the desire for food in all its forms, for true liberation is freedom from hunger for ever.

NOTES

1. *Ṛgveda* VIII.48.
2. Taittarīya-Upaniṣat III.1-6.
3. *Ibid.*, II.1.
4. See P. S. Jaini, "The Pure and the Auspicious in the Jaina Tradition," *Journal of Asian Perspectives* (Leiden) I, 1 (1985).
5. *Bhagavatī-sūtra* XV. 552; A. L. Basham, *The History and Doctrines of the Ājīvikas*, London, 1951.
6. *Ibid.*
7. Hermann Jacobi, *Jaina Sūtras*, pt. 1, Sacred Books of the East, vol. 20, p. 86 (*Ācārāṅga-sūtra* I.8.4).
8. See P. S. Jaini, *The Jaina Path of Purification*, Berkeley, 1979, p. 27 n. 61.
9. *Majjhimanikāya* I.80.
10. See Colette Caillat, *Atonements in the Ancient Jaina Ritual of the Jaina Monks*, L. D. Institute of Indology, no. 49, Ahmedabad, 1975.
11. *Manusmṛti* VI.20.
12. See P. S. Jaini, *The Jaina Path of Purification*, pp. 227-233.
13. Jinendra Varṇi, *Jainendra Siddhānta Kośa* IV, Bhāratīya Jñānapīṭha, Varanasi, 1973, p. 121.
14. On the *mahāvratas*, see H. Jacobi, *Jaina Sūtras*, pt. 1, pp. 202-210.
15. For a list of the forbidden food, see R. Williams, *Jaina Yoga*, Oxford, 1963, pp. 110-116.
16. See P. S. Jaini, *The Jaina Path of Purification*, pp. 209-217.
17. See *Tattvārtha-sūtra* of Umāsvāti, IX.19.
18. *Harivaṃśapurāṇa* of Jinasena, ed. by Pannalal Jain, Bhāratīya Jñānapīṭha, 1962, sarga 34.
19. *Ibid.*, sarga 33, verse 166.
20. See P. S. Jaini, "Jaina Festivals," *Festivals in World Religions*, ed. Alan Brown, London, 1986.
21. For the story of Candanā, see M. L. Mehta and Rishabh Chandra, *Prakrit Proper Names*, pt. 1, L. D. Institute of Indology, Ahmedabad, 1970, p. 246.
22. For the story of Sujātā, see *The Jātaka*, pt. 1, ed. V. Fausboll, Pali Text Society, London 1962, pp. 68-70.
23. *Pañcatantra* IV.16.
24. *Harivaṃśapurāṇa, ibid.*, sarga 33, verses 47-92. See also *Bṛhatkathākośa* of *Hariṣeṇa* (no. 106: Ugrasena-Vasiṣṭha-kathānakam), ed. A. N. Upadhye, Singhi Jain Series, no. 17, Bombay, 1943, pp. 267-276.
25. See *Harivaṃśapurāṇa, ibid.*, sarga 55.
26. For further references on this point see P. S. Jaini, *The Jaina Path of Purification*, p. 305.
27. See the introduction to the *Padmāvatīmāhātmye athavā Jinadattarāyacarite* (in Kannaḍa, c. 1800), published by the Vivekābhyudaya Kāryālaya, Mangalore, 1956.
28. For a full discussion on the controversy, see Paul Dundas, "Food and Freedom: The Jaina sectarian debate on the nature of the Kevalin," *Religion* XV (1985), pp. 161-198.
29. Umāsvāti's *Tattvārthasūtra* IX.9 is said to provide the scriptural authority for both sects on this controversy. For the Digambara view, see *Sarvārthasiddhi*

IX.9, ed. Phoolchandra Siddhāntaśāstrī, Bhāratīya Jñānapīṭha, 1971.

30. For a discussion on the nature of the food eaten by Mahāvīra, see P. S. Jaini, *The Jaina Path of Purification*, pp. 23-24.

31. For the Yāpanīya and the Śvetāmbara positions on kevali-kavalāhāra, see *Strīnirvāṇa-Kevalibhukti-prakaraṇe*, ed. Muni Jambuvijaya, Jaina Ātmānanda Sabhā, Bhavanagar, 1974, pp. 39-52 and 85-100. For the Digambara refutation, see *Nyāyakumudacandra* of Prabhācandra, ed. Mahendrakumar Nyāyācārya, Māṇikacandra Jaina Granthamālā, Bombay, 1941, pp. 852-865.

CHAPTER 17

Jaina Monks from Mathurā: Literary Evidence for Their Identification on Kuṣāṇa Sculptures*

Among the thousands of Jaina images found throughout India, those from Mathura produced during the Kuṣāṇa period are unique, for they alone contain representations of unclothed Jaina ascetics holding a single small piece of cloth in such a way as to cover their nudity. These curious figures cannot be identified with monks of the present-day Jaina sects of the Digambaras, who practise total nudity, or of the Śvetāmbaras, who wear two long pieces of unstitched white cloth wrapped around their bodies and occasionally a white blanket over their left shoulders. The veteran art-historian, the late Dr. U. P. Shah, in *Aspects of Jain art and architecture* briefly mentions these figures, noting that nowhere in the above references from Śvetāmbara as well as Digambara texts do we come across a reference to those figures on the siṃhāsana of a Jina which we find in a number of sculptures of the Kuṣāṇa period from the Kaṅkāli Ṭīlā.[1] Subsequently, in *Jaina-Rūpa-Maṇḍana*, he calls these figures *ardhaphālakas* (monks with partial covering) and speculates that these figures might be Yāpanīya monks, another Jaina sect that is now extinct, and states that these figures need further investigation.[2] In addition to Shah, N.

*This article was published originally in *Bulletin of the School of Oriental and African Studies*, Vol. LVII, part 3, pp. 479-494, University of London, 1995. Reprinted with kind permission of Oxford University Press.

P. Joshi has also discussed these *ardhaphālaka* images. He states that 'all the monks seen in the bas-reliefs, except one known to me, seem to belong to the *Ardhaphālaka* sect....Besides the monks seen in the bas-reliefs, those hovering in the air (*vidyā cāraṇas*) or seen on some of the *śilāpaṭṭās* are all *Ardhaphālakas*. This suggests that during the pre-Christian and early Christian centuries a large number of Jainas at Mathura followed this sect.'[3]

The earliest appearance of the terms *ardhaphālaka* and *yāpana* together can be traced to the Digambara Jaina narrative called the *Bhadrabāhukathānaka* (§ 131) in the tenth-century *Bṛhatkathākośa* of Hariṣeṇa (C.A.D. 931). This story, composed in a place called Wadhawan in Kathiawar, is of the legendary account of a major schism in the hitherto undivided community of Jaina mendicants that purportedly took place during the time of a pontiff (*ācārya*) named Bhadrabāhu of uncertain date.[4] A Kannada version of this legend (with numerous variations) is found in the *Vaḍḍārādhane* of Śivakoṭi, probably of the second half of the tenth century.[5] Shah's use of the terms *ardhaphālaka* and *yāpanīya* along with his brief account of the story in the *Bṛhatkathākośa*[6] certainly shows an acquaintance with the researches on these obscure schools by Upadhye. Upadhye, on the other hand, gives no indication of being aware of the problems posed by the peculiar Mathura images of the Jaina monks under study by Shah. The following is the extent of Upadhye's comments on the *Bhadrabāhukathānaka*:

> Though it presents some difficulties for a clear understanding and consequently needs careful collation and comparative study with other sources, both earlier and later, the story of Bhadrabāhu (no. 131) is important in various respects: it refers to the migration of Jaina Saṅgha to Punnāṭa territory in the Deccan and to the division of twofold Kalpa, Jina- and Sthavira-kalpa, and outlines the circumstances under which Ardhaphālakasaṅgha, Kambala-tīrtha and Yāpanīya-saṅgha were started.[8]

A more recent study of the Sanskrit and the Kannada versions of the *Bhadrabāhu-kathānaka* by B. K. Khadabadi[9] and subsequent research on the history of the Jaina sects of the Gupta era by Suzuko Ohira[10] also show a complete lack of interest in the Jaina antiquities of Mathura. I believe that a detailed comparative study of the Mathura images with Jaina texts such as the *Bhadrabāhu-kathānaka* and Buddhist texts that mention their rival Jaina ascetics—a task not undertaken by Joshi, Shah, or Upadhye—will shed further light on the mystery of these obscure Jaina mendicants of the Kuṣāṇa period.

We may note here briefly the events leading to the formation of the Yāpana-saṅgha as narrated by Hariṣeṇa in the earliest version, the *Bhadrabāhu-kathānaka*:

(i) vv. 1—27: Once, the Jaina monk Govardhana, the fourth knower of the Fourteen Pūrvas in the tradition of Vardhamāna (Mahāvīra), arrived in the city of Devakoṭṭa of the Pauṇḍravardhana country ruled by King Padmaratha.

There he obtained a young boy (*baṭuṃ svānte cakāra*) named Bhadrabāhu from his Brahmin parents, Somaśarmā and Somaśrī. He taught him various sciences and eventually initiated him as a (Digambara) Jaina mendicant. After Govardhana's death, Muni Bhadrabāhu became the head of the Jaina *saṅgha* and travelled to the country of Avantī, which was ruled by a Jaina king called Candragupta[11] from the city of Ujjayinī on the banks of the Viprā river.

(ii) vv. 28—44: One day, while wandering for his alms in the city of Ujjayinī, Bhadrabāhu entered an empty house and heard a baby's voice saying, 'O Sir, please quickly go away from this place (*kṣipraṃ gaccha tvaṃ bhagavann itaḥ*).' Bhadrabāhu by his super-knowledge realized that this was a prophecy of a twelve-year drought. He then counselled his mendicant followers 'to go near the salt-ocean (*yāta lavaṇābdhisamīpatām*)', but considering his own old age, he stayed behind in Ujjayinī. King Candragupta also became a Jaina monk, and this group of monks (*saṅgha*), under the leadership of Viśākhācārya, travelled to Punnāṭa (modern Karnataka) in the Southern Country (*Dakṣiṇadeśa*). Three other groups of monks led respectively by the *ācāryas* Rāmilla, Sthūlavṛddha and Bhadrācārya went to the country of Sindhu (*svasaṃghasamudāyena Sindhvādiviṣayaṃ yayuḥ*). Eventually, the *ācārya* Bhadrabāhu, having fasted for many days, died in the Bhārdrapada-deśa of Avantī.

(iii) vv. 45—48: When the drought was over, Viśākhācārya and his disciples, who had gone to the Southern Country, having adhered to their mendicant vows [for they were able to obtain proper food], returned to the Middle Country (Madhya-deśa, i.e., Avantī). But the other three groups (led by Rāmilla and so forth), who had gone to the country of Sindhu, were unable to obtain food or water during that severe drought. Upon returning [to Avantī?] they reported the following [in Ujjayinī?]:[12]

(iv) vv. 49—53: At that time of terrible drought, when there was neither food nor water, people gathered at the doors of houses and made a lot of noise. Because of this, the householders could not eat their food. They remained hungry during the day and started eating only at night (to avoid the crowd outside). [There laypeople said to us]'You, sirs, for fear of the people [outside], please obtain begging bowls (*pātras*) from our houses [and collect food going from door to door] during the night and eat the gathered alms during the day inside the residence of your host layman (*sva-śrāvaka-gṛhe*). Thus abiding by the wishes of the people, our *ācāryas* and other mendicants fed themselves accordingly.[13]

(v) vv. 54—60: One night a certain emaciated monk visited a Jaina household with his bowl in hand, and the sight of that naked (*nirgrantha*) monk caused such a fright to a young pregnant woman that she aborted the fetus. Seeing that, the Jaina laymen approached the heads of the monks and said, 'O sages! This is a time of calamity. When the good times arrive, you may, having undertaken the appropriate expiations (*prāyaścitta*), abide again by the rules of mendicancy. Therefore, for the duration of this period, you should [visit the households] at night covering yourself with half-a-piece of cloth (*ardhaphālaka*) held on your left arm and holding the begging bowl in your right hand, and eat the food [thus collected] during the daytime.' Hearing these assuring words of the laypeople, the monks acted accordingly.[14]

(vi) vv. 61—68: Time passed and there soon arrived conditions of prosperity and people became happy, freed from the state of misery. Then the three *ācāryas* consulted with each other and addressed their communities of monks: 'O monks, with your minds happy, abandon now your half-a-piece of cloth (*ardhaphālaka*), and for the sake of emancipation (*mokṣa*), resort to the excellent vow of nudity (*nirgranthatā*).' Hearing those words, some monks resumed the vow of nudity. The three *ācāryas*, namely, Rāmilla, Sthavira and Sthūlabhadra, also approached the venerable

Viśākhācārya and abandoning the half-a-piece of cloth (*ardhakarpaṭa*) assumed anew the vow of nudity.[15] But certain others, the cowardly weaklings, ignorant of the highest good, who did not like the advice of the teachers, formed this order (*tīrtha*) called the Ardhaphālaka, and [thus] created a twofold mendicant order: the Jina-kalpa and the Sthavira-kalpa.[16]

(vii) vv. 69—79: In the country of Saurashtra, in the city of Valabhī, there ruled a heretic (i.e. a non-Jaina) king named Vapravāda (Vaprapāḷa in the *Vaḍḍārādhane*). But his chief queen Svāminī became a great devotee of these Ardhaphālaka ascetics. One day a group of these monks arrived at the palace of this king at midday to collect alms. Seeing them the king became curious and said to the queen, 'O Lady! Your group of Ardhaphālaka monks is no good; they are neither clad nor naked; it is ridiculous (*saviḍambana*).' On another day, when a group of Ardhaphālaka monks entered the city, the king said to them, 'You should abandon this half-a-piece of cloth and assume nudity [as is proper].' They did not desire that, and the king, even more astonished, said, 'O ascetics, if indeed you are unable to assume the form of nudity, then give up this half-a-piece of cloth, the cause of your ridicule, and attire yourselves in proper clothes and reside happily here in my kingdom.'

(viii) vv. 80—81: From that day onward, by the order of the king Vapravāda, in the country of Lāṭa (Gujarat), there came into being the Kambala-tīrtha (the sect of monks who use a blanket?) [*Vaḍḍārādhane*, 93: Those who were of the Kambaḷa-tīrtha came to be called Śveta-paṭa (=the Śvetāmbara)]. From that *Kambalika-tīrtha*, in the Sāvalipattana, was born the *Yāpana-saṅgha* in the Southern Country.[17] [*Vaḍḍārādhane*, 93: In the Dakṣiṇāpatha, King Sāmaliputta became the leader of the Śveta-bhikṣu Jāpuli-saṃgha, which descended from the Śveta-paṭas.]

Since this is a Digambara account of the origins of their opponents the Śvetāmbaras and since there is no Śvetāmbara counterpart to any of these stories, it may not serve as a totally reliable document.[18] However, after a careful examination of the *ardhaphālaka* monks as depicted in the Mathura sculptures, I believe that the *Bhadrabāhu-kathānaka* may indeed contain a kernel of truth. The narrative is primarily talking about what one may call an *apavāda-veśa*, a temporary measure appropriate to a calamity, i.e., an exception to the mendicant laws regularly observed. The story assumes that all Jaina monks were Digambaras to start with, who—as is the practice even to this day—adhered to the twin vows of nudity (*nāgnya*) and of eating food from joined palms (*pāṇi-tala-bhojana*) once a day during the daytime only. The Digambaras have traditionally held a belief—partly supported by the sixth-century inscriptions of Shravanabelgola[19]—that a migration of monks to the South took place under the leadership of Bhadrabāhu, a contemporary of the Mauryan emperor Candragupta, during a 12-year period of drought in Magadha. They also have claimed that those monks who did not migrate and chose to stay in Magadha relaxed the rules of mendicancy, began to wear clothes, and started to use wooden bowls for collecting alms. For the Digambaras, these are the apostate monks (*Jainābhāsa*)[20] who came to be labelled at a later time as Śvetāmbaras or 'white clad' monks.

However, a direct connexion (assumed by the Digambaras) between a shortage of food and the wearing of clothes by hitherto naked monks remained unexplained, rendering this traditional Digambara account (of the origin of 'clothed' Jaina monks) unsatisfactory to any neutral observer.[21] The *Bhadrabāhu-kathānaka* seems to provide the missing link in the story of the naked monk on his nocturnal begging rounds frightening a pregnant woman resulting in a miscarriage. This led to the lay people's request that the monks should henceforth visit the households covering themselves with half-a-piece of cloth held on their left arm. The correspondence between these words and the way in which the Mathura monks are shown covering their nudity—with a short piece of cloth held on their left forearm—is truly remarkable and may not be purely accidental. Since such depiction appears nowhere else in Jaina art before or after the Kuṣāṇa era, the sculptures described above may be recalling a period of crisis through which the community of the Digambara monks had passed in not too remote a past.

Our assumption that the Mathura depiction of the *ardhaphālaka* attire was in response to an exceptional situation may not be altogether fanciful. There is at least one recorded instance of the Digambaras making a similar concession (subject of course to expiations) under unfavourable political conditions. In late medieval times the Digambara monks could not move about freely in certain areas of northern India where public nudity was frowned upon by Muslim rulers. The Digambara cleric (*bhaṭṭāraka*) Śrutasāgara (c. sixteenth century) reports an incident where a Digambara monk Vasantakīrti (of unknown date) living in Maṇḍapadurga (Rajasthan?) allowed his monks an exceptional garb (*apavāda-veśa*), namely, to cover themselves with a mat (*taṭṭī*) or a piece of cloth (*sādara* or *cādara*) while on their outings for meals and so forth. While he admits that this was an exceptional practice, Śrutasāgara nevertheless has no hesitation in condemning it as heretical.[22] In view of such a tradition of uncompromising attitude on the part of the Digambaras, it would not be incorrect to surmise that the *ardhaphālaka* monks of the Kuṣāṇa period, after a brief spell of public adoration—as demonstrated by the Mathura images—for their heroic efforts to survive the drought, might have returned to the original fold soon after the crisis had ended. This could be one explanation for the total absence of the depiction of the *ardhaphālaka* images in the Jaina tradition in subsequent periods.

Furthermore, the meaning of the term *yāpanīya* itself lends credence to this particular account of the origin of this sect, which is, in fact, shrouded in mystery. It is referred to by that name (Yāpàni[ī]ya) in the Sanskrit inscriptions of the fifth-century Kadamba king Mṛgeśavarmā.[23] The eighth-century Śvetāmbara author Haribhadra quotes a long Prakrit passage from a text of that sect which he calls the *Yāpanīya-tantra.*[24] In the Kannada *Vaḍḍārādhane* it appear as Jāpuli.[25] Upadhye, who made an extensive study of the inscriptions of the sect (originating for the most part in the districts of Belgaum, Dharwar, and Gulburga of Karnataka), found the name Yāpanīya appearing under various spellings, e.g., Jāpanīya, Yāpulīya, Javaliya, Jāvaligeya, and so forth. This led him to believe that the term *yāpanīya* could be an incorrect Sanskritization of the canonical Prakrit *javanijje* (*yamanīya,* as in *iṃdiyajavaṇijje,* i.e., those who control their senses).[26]

Upadhye's search for a Prakrit origin of the name Yāpanīya—justified no doubt by the inscriptional evidence—must be considered unfortunate. It has the effect of ignoring the true significance of the term '*yāpana*' employed to describe the conduct of the apostate Jaina monks in Hariṣeṇa's narrative. This word reminds one of the Pali form *yāpanīya* (from *yā+āpe*) meaning 'sufficient, i.e. just enough for supporting one's life', an adjective commonly applied to provisions (such as food, clothing, and shelter) for a Buddhist monk.[27] The Jaina monks in Hariṣeṇa's narrative could be designated as *yāpana* or *yāpanīya* because, faced by the calamity of a long period of drought, they followed an 'exceptional' way of obtaining food 'just sufficient for supporting' their mendicant lives.

Whether the relaxation of the rules allowed during this period of crisis eventually became a permanent way of life for these *ardhaphālaka* monks or whether it led to the wearing of full clothes as is claimed by the *Bhadrabāhukathānaka* cannot be answered by the evidence available. The arrival of such *ardhaphālaka* monks in Valabhī need not be disputed; but King Vapravāda's intervention and the subsequent rise of the order of fully-clothed monks—the kambala-tīrtha (leading the author of the *Vaḍḍārādhane* to characterize these new monks as the Śvetapaṭas) appears highly suspicious. It is significant that the narrator of the story applies the designation Yāpana-saṃgha not to those who lived in Gujarat (Lāṭa) but to those who migrated still further into the Deccan. The *ardhaphālaka* monks may indeed have appeared in the South with the half-a-piece of cloth as their mendicant emblem. Groups of such monks could have been identified initially as Yāpana or Yāpanīya, 'only just sufficient for supporting a mendicant way of life', possibly even as a derogatory term. Eventually the word was rendered into Kannada under different spellings and the original meaning was lost. Gradually as its members merged with the Digambaras in the South by adopting nudity or becoming advanced lay-disciples called the *bhaṭṭārakas*,[28] and with the Śvetāmbaras in the North by wearing full-length clothes, the old Yāpana-saṅgha could have lost its independent identity.

Nevertheless, certain later pieces of literature give some clue about the manner in which the origin of the Yāpana-saṅgha was not altogether forgotten. Guṇaratna, the fifteenth-century Svetāmbara commentator on Haribhadra's *Ṣaḍdarśanasamuccaya*, counts the Yāpanīyas as a sect of the Digambaras and yields a bit

PLATE I

Lucknow Museum no. J. 25. Seated Jaina Tīrthaṅkara, headless. Mathura, red sandstone, 3rd century A.D. (Courtesy of American Institute of Indian Studies, Varanasi.)

PLATE II

Lucknow Museum, no. J. 10. Pedestal of Jaina image. Mathura, red sandstone, 2nd century A.D.
(Courtesy of American Institute of Indian Studies, Varanasi.)

PLATE III

Lucknow Museum, no. J. 105. Relief fragment showing a Kinnara and a Jaina monk. Mathura (Kaṅkāli Ṭīlā), red sandstone, 1st century B.C. (Courtesy of American Institute of Indian Studies, Varanasi.)

of additional information that 'they were also known as Gopyas' (Yāpanīyā Gopyā *ity apy ucyante*).[29] The word *gopya* like Yāpanīya is also rather obscure. Used as an adjective it can mean something to be hidden and normally would be understood as a reference to genital organs. Used as a noun it can, in the present context, mean a person who hides his nudity. If this interpretation is correct, then the word *gopya* reinforces the lines examined above from the *Bhadrabāhu-kathānaka* and in addition to Ardhaphālaka and Yāpanīya can serve as a designation for the monks depicted in the Mathura sculptures.

It would seem that even though the Yāpanīya monks had allegedly returned to the vows of nudity and were by appearance indistinguishable from Digambara monks, they continued to adhere to certain doctrines which were repugnant to the Digambaras but were in accordance with the Śvetāmbara scriptures. This is clear from comments of the sixteenth-century Digambara cleric Śrutasāgara who calls them 'pseudo-Jainas' (*Jainābhāsa*) and says, 'the Yāpanīyas are like a mixed breed (*vesarā iva*): they believe in both [sects] (*ubhayam api manyante*). They read the [*Bṛhat-*] *kalpa* (a text of the Śvetāmbara canon) and believe that women may attain *mokṣa* in that very life and also that the *kevalin* eats morsels of food.'[30] The Yāpanīya monks would thus seem to have never been completely integrated with either of the main Jaina groups. Their sect disappeared leaving for posterity only a fragment of their literature and, as will be shown below, possibly their obscure representations on the Mathura pieces of Jaina antiquity.

As the term *ardhaphālaka* is not attested in any ancient Jaina texts,[31] it is not altogether unlikely that a storyteller seeing the Mathura sculptures could have invented the story of the Yāpana-saṃgha to explain the rather peculiar manner in which the monks were depicted there. Assuming such to be the case, one must question whether Jaina monks were recognized by the emblem of 'half-a-piece of cloth' (the *ardhaphālaka* or the *ardhakarpaṭa*) at any time prior to the *Bhadrabāhu-kathānaka* of Hariṣeṇa. One would not expect to find such a designation applied to Śvetāmbara mendicants in their scriptures since their mendicant rules have traditionally allowed a plurality of clothes. However, it is reasonable to assume that even in that tradition, the wearing of white clothes to cover the entire body may have been preceded by a practice of using just a single piece of cloth. In this connexion, the Pali texts of the Thervāda Buddhists, because of their numerous references to the Nigaṇṭhas—their prime rivals in ancient times—might provide some missing links for the study of the attire (or lack there of) of ancient Jaina monks.

The term *ardhaphālaka* is not known to the Theravāda Buddhists, but they are familiar with a group of ascetics called Ekasāṭakas, literally, those who wear only one garment, i.e., a single piece of cloth. The *Saṃyuttanikāya*, I (in a passage identical with the *Udāna*, vi, 2) mentions five groups of ascetics from Sāvatthī named respectively Jaṭila, Nigaṇṭha, Acelaka, Ekasāṭaka, and Paribbājaka (mentioned in that order), who were visited by King Pasenadi of Kosala. The text describes them all as 'those with long hair and nails' but does not provide any of their distinguishing marks. Of these, the Jaṭilas and Paribbājakas were evidently Brahmanical mendicants. The term Acelaka (lit. 'without clothes') was probably used for various groups of naked monks, including those of the Ājīvika sect (of Makkhali Gosāla). The term Ekasāṭaka clearly means an ascetic with a single garment, but this is not enough to identify this group with any known religious sect. As for the Nigaṇṭhas, they are clearly the ascetic followers of Mahāvīra (the Nigaṇṭha Nātaputta of the Pali canon). Unfortunately, the *Saṃyuttanikāya* reveals nothing about the attire of this group, let alone any evidence of knowledge of their sects such as the Acelaka and the Sacelaka (amply attested in the Jaina canon), the forerunners of the Digambaras and the Śvetāmbaras of later times. The text also fails to give a clue as to how the Nigaṇṭhas were distinguished from the naked Acelakas or from the clothed Ekasāṭakas.

However, a much later reference in the *Dhammapada-Aṭṭhakathā* attributed to Buddhaghosa (c. fifth century A.D.) reveals that the Theravāda Buddhists (of Sri Lanka where that commentary was compiled) considered the Nigaṇṭha monks to be naked and yet not identical with the Acelakas. Commenting on *Dhammapada* XXII, 8 (beginning with *alajjitā ye lajjanti...*) the narrator gives the following introduction for the Buddha's sermon contained in that verse:

> For one day the monks, seeing naked ascetics of the Jain Order, began the following discussion: 'Brethren, these Nigaṇṭhas are to be preferred to the Acelakas, who go entirely naked, for these ascetics at least wear a covering in front. These ascetics evidently possess some sense of modesty.' Overhearing the discussion, the Nigaṇṭhas said, 'It is not for this reason at all that we wear a covering. On the contrary, even dust and dirt are actual individuals, endowed with the principle of life; and so—out of fear they may fall into our alms-dishes—for this reason we wear a covering.'[32]

Although presented in a casual manner and originating from a distant place at a considerably later time (almost a thousand years after the time of the Buddha and Mahāvīra) the above description of the Nigaṇṭha monks is highly valuable for our present study. The nakedness of the Nigaṇṭhas is affirmed: but it is also maintained that their practice of 'wearing a frontal cover' (*purimapassaṃ paṭicchādenti*) distinguished them from the totally naked Acelakas.[33] The explanation that the coverings was [not as much for hiding nudity as] for protecting the earth-beings may or may not be authentic, but it demonstrates that the Pali commentator was familiar with the Jaina doctrine of *ekendriya-jīvas* or 'one-sensed beings', the protection of which distinguished as ascetic from a layman. What the monks used for this purpose is not described, but from the words 'frontal cover', we can assume it was not tied around the body (as a loincloth) but rather held by hand. It must have been large enough to cover the mouth of a begging bowl and was probably made of cloth. One must credit the Buddhist commentator for his accuracy in describing this group of naked Nigaṇṭha monks and for even providing a doctrinally acceptable reason (namely, the practice of *ahiṃsā*) for their carrying the so-called 'frontal cover'.[34]

One important thing missing in this otherwise highly credible account is the complete omission—an oversight possibly?—of any reference to the Jaina monks with full [white] robes, historically known by the designation of Śvetāmbara, who have traditionally been (and are to this day) far more numerous than the members of any other Jaina mendicant sects. Fortunately, this deficiency is made up for by Dhammapāla (c. sixth century) in his *Udāna-Aṭṭhakathā* (on the passage identical with the one appearing in the *Saṃyuttanikāya*, as in section 13 above). It is strange that he does not gloss the words Acelaka and Paribbājaka since they were part of the five mendicant groups mentioned in the text; instead, he comments only on the remaining three, namely, the Jaṭila, the Nigaṇṭha, and the Ekasāṭaka. While Buddhaghosa is unaware of the Śvetāmbara monks, Dhammapāla appears (in spite of his being a native of Kāñcī) ignorant of the totally naked (i.e. the Digambara) Jaina monks, unless we were to assume that for him they were indistinguishable from the Acelakas (whoever they might have been). It appears from his commentary that he knows only two varieties of Nigaṇṭhas: (i) the Setapaṭa Nigaṇṭhas, those who wear white clothes (*setapaṭa-nigaṇṭha-rūpadhārino*) and (ii) the Ekasāṭaka Nigaṇṭhas, those who move about with a small piece of cloth tied on their hands with one end of which they cover the frontal portion of their body.[35] This is rather ambiguous since, if the Nigaṇṭhas are clothed in white (*setapaṭa-rūpadhārino*), then there would be no need for them to use a piece of cloth (*pilotika-khaṇḍa*) to cover their frontal side. One must assume therefore that the Ekasāṭakas described by Dhammapāla must have been naked (and thus similar in appearance to the Nigaṇṭhas described in the *Dhammapada-Aṭṭhakathā*).

The similarity found between the Ekasāṭaka monks in the *Udāna-Aṭṭhakathā* and the *ardhapālaka* monks carved on the Mathura sculpture is truly astonishing. Both are naked and both hold a 'frontal cover' in such a way as to suggest an attempt at hiding their nudity. The monks of the Mathura images are not shown with their begging bowls (instead they are shown holding a small whisk-broom called a *rajo-haraṇa*, an emblem of a Jaina mendicant, in their right hands), but this important detail is corroborated from the account of the *Bhadrabāhu-kathānaka*. Seldom is a literary description matched to such an extent by sculptural evidence. It is therefore also possible to identify the monks depicted in the Mathura sculptures not as a group of the so-called 'apostate' monks of the Digambara sect but as a group of Ekasāṭaka Nigaṇṭha monks in the lineage of the mendicant disciples of Mahāvīra.

But if such were the true attire of the Nigaṇṭhas of Mahāvīra's time, then how do we account for the fact that Jaina mendicants are never described in that manner in either the Śvetāmbara or the Digambara scriptures? Why is there no mention of a *pilotaka-khaṇḍa* or an *ardhaphālaka* as a requisite (like the *rajo-haraṇa*, for example) of a Jaina mendicant? The Śvetāmbara scriptures openly advocate the use of robes and bowls for the Nigaṇṭha monks. As for the Digambaras, they have not traditionally allowed any sort of covering nor the use of bowls for their monks, as is laid down in the most ancient works of Kundakunda[36] and as was amply demonstrated above by the *Bhadrabāhu-kathānaka.* Is there any missing link that will bridge the gap between the Buddhist account of the Ekasāṭaka Nigaṇṭhas on the one hand, and the Digambara account of the Ardhaphālaka (or the Yāpanīya), on the other, as given in the *Bhadrabāhu-kathānaka?*

In this connexion, evidence of Mahāvīra's own asceticism as described in the oldest Śvetāmbara canonical text, namely the *Ācārāṅga-sūtra,* is of great significance. This text states that Mahāvīra went forth from the household (*pavvaie*) with a single cloth (*vatthagaṃ*) but that he was resolved not to cover his body with it during that winter. It further states that he kept this piece of cloth for 13 months and thereafter he abandoned it (*cāī*) and thus became a totally nude (*acelage*) houseless sage (*aṇagāre*).[37] This story is repeated in the *Kalpa-sūtra* with further embellishments that this piece of cloth is called a *devadūṣya,* (a divine cloth), and that when he became naked, Mahāvīra accepted alms in the hollow of his hand (i.e. he did not use a bowl).[38] I believe that this single piece of cloth (the so-called *devadūṣya*), which according to Śvetāmbara accounts was worn by Mahāvīra prior to his assumption of total nudity, provides the key for understanding both the Buddhist description of at least certain Nigaṇṭha mendicants 'with frontal cover' and the peculiar attire of the *ardhaphālaka* monks of the Mathura sculptures.

Neither the *Ācārāṅga-sūtra* nor *Kalpa-sūtra* gives any details about the single piece of cloth that Mahāvīra took with him when he left his home. But later writers like Hemacandra describe the *devadūṣya* as a finely woven piece of white cloth, made as if of the rays of the moon (that is, shining and soft), so called because the king of the gods, Indra, placed it on the shoulder of the Lord.[39] From this it would appear that when Mahāvīra left home, he did not use this cloth as a loincloth. Hemacandra does not describe the length of this piece of cloth, but it must have been long enough to hang on his shoulder and reach the lower portions of his body. As a matter of fact, modern paintings produced by the Śvetāmbaras of Mahāvīra's life during this period of asceticism depict a piece of cloth draped over his left shoulder covering his lower left forearm, which is positioned to cover his nudity in a manner reminiscent of the monks in the Mathura sculptures.[40]

I venture to suggest that the author of the *Dhammapada-Aṭṭhakathā* in his description of a particular group of Nigaṇṭhas and the author of the *Udāna-Aṭṭhakathā* in his description of the Ekasāṭaka Nigaṇṭhas are probably alluding to such a piece of cloth, in a shortened form, worn by at least some if not all Nigaṇṭhas prior to their giving up even that piece of cloth and becoming 'acelakas' in the manner of Mahāvīra himself.

By the Śvetāmbara account given above, Mahāvīra himself retained the *cīvara* (i.e., the *devadūṣya*) for 13 months prior to becoming totally naked (*acelae*). Even the Digambaras, who do not admit such a transitional period for Mahāvīra's full ordination as a *digambara muni*, cannot reject it on any doctrinal grounds. As a matter of fact, they have provided such a transitional period for a layman who leaves his household (*pravrajyā*) by instituting a semi-mendicant status called *ailaka* (probably meaning junior), in a manner reminiscent of the Śvetāmbara account of Mahāvīra's own renunciation. There is, however, one major difference: the *ailaka* of our times does not leave home naked with a single piece of cloth on his shoulder, but girded by a loincloth (*kaupīna*). But this is not of cardinal significance, because according to the Digambaras, a person with any piece of cloth whatsoever, whether it be a *devadūṣya* or a loincloth (*kaupīna*), would technically be granted only the status of a highly advanced layman (*utkṛṣṭa-śrāvaka*) even if he were revered as a holy man.[41]

Given the variety of possibilities presented in various sources, a conclusive identification of the sect of these *ardhaphālaka* images on the Mathura sculptures cannot be made from the available literary evidence. There is a remote possibility that they could be a branch of a Jaina order long extinct identified by the Buddhist commentator Dharmapāla as Ekasāṭakas who do not appear to be identical with the monks wearing a single piece of cloth (*ekasāṭaka*) as described in the Śvetāmbara *Ācārāṅga-sūtra.* Returning to the Jaina sources alone, we have more options to consider. In the light of the account of the two, namely, the *sacelaka* and *acelaka* phases of Mahāvīra's renunciation preserved in such ancient Śvetāmbara canonical texts as the *Ācārāṅga-sūtra,* these monks could be the forerunners of what came to be known as the Śvetāmbara order. They, like their master Mahāvīra, retained a single piece of cloth when they renounced the household but did not choose the option of subsequently renouncing clothes entirely as did the Jina. The affiliation of what at a later time came to be designated as the Śvetāmbara sect with the region of Mathura is corroborated by the depiction on Mathura sculptures of their legend of the transfer of Mahāvīra's embryo by Harinegamesi[42] as well as inscriptional evidence of certain ecclesiastical groups (*gaṇa, gaccha*) traceable to the list of the Elders (*sthavirāvalī*)[43] in the Śvetāmbara texts. Assuming these figures to be Proto-Śvetāmbara, we still do not know the period when that sect made the transition from an *ardhaphālaka* to the standard garb of two or three pieces of clothes traditionally worn by the Śvetāmbara mendicant community.

Turning to the Digambara narratives, one cannot entirely discount the possibility that the *ardhaphālaka* figures with a piece of cloth held over their left arms are naked Jaina monks who might have taken up this covering in response to a brief calamity such as the drought as related in the *Bhadrabāhu-kathānaka* and the *Vaḍḍārādhane.* On the basis of the available evidence, it is not possible to answer such pertinent questions as why such a representation does not appear before the Kuṣāṇa period—since the event referred to above took place much earlier—or why only at Mathura. Even so, their conspicuous absence in the subsequent period at any place whatsoever certainly lends credibility to the suggestion of several scholars that these *ardhaphālaka* monks might have been the Yāpanīyas, who were eventually assimilated into the Digambara or Śvetāmbara orders and their origins entirely forgotten.

NOTES

1. Shah (1975), 61.
2. Shah (1987), 28. n. 45. The term *ardhaphālaka* is cited by M. Monier-Williams (*Sanskrit-English Dictionary*, 1316, col. b) as m. or n. 'name of a particular garment,' m. pl., 'a particular Jaina sect. (*-mata*. n. its doctrine).' Unfortunately, he gives the citation of *Bhadrabāhucarita* but no further reference regarding the publication of this book. But from the word *mata*, which does not appear in the earliest version of this story, namely, the *Bhadrabāhukathānakam* of Hariṣeṇa, it is possible to trace his reference to a work by Ratnanandin (Digambara, sixteenth-century) published as part of Hermann Jacobi's article entitled 'Ueber die Entstehung der Śvetāmbara und Digambara Sekten' in *ZDMG*, 1884. In this text, Ratnanandin identifies the *ardhaphālakas* with the Śvetāmbara sect and attributes to them the doctrines of *strīmokṣa, kevalibhukti*, etc. Jacobi does not translate the word *ardhaphālaka* but gives the following comment: 'The name of the sect gives difficulty because in our dictionaries the word *phālaka* is not found in any applicable meaning. The word seems to refer to rags or things that are torn apart, since *phālaka* appears to be an erroneous Sanskritization of Prakrit *phālaya*, from the stem *phāla*, "to tear apart" (p. 16).' In the Kannada version (*Vaḍḍārādhane*) called *Bhadrabāhu Bhaṭṭārara Kathe*, which is almost identical with Hariṣeṇa's version, the corresponding expression is *ardhakappaḍa* 'half a piece of cloth, a rag'; and therefore this word does refer to a piece of cloth and serves as a designation for the mendicants who were known by this sign. Mention may also be made here of three more texts bearing on this topic. The first is an Apabhraṃśa version called *Kahā-Kosu* composed by the eleventh-century (c. 1066) Digambara Muni Śrīcandra (from Aṇahillapura, Gujarat). In his narrative of Bhadrabāhu—which follows closely the *Bṛhatkathākośa* of Hariṣeṇa—Śrīcandra uses the term *addhaphālīya* (ed. Jain, H., 1969: 479). The second is a prose version in Sanskrit by the twelfth-century author Rāmacandra Mumukṣu (see Jain, Rajaram, 1982: 73-5). He however uses the expression *ardhakarpaṭa*, as in *Vaḍḍārādhane*, instead of *ardhaphālaka*. The third work is an Apabhraṃśa poem composed by the fifteenth-century poet Raidhū (from Gwaliar, Central India). Raidhū uses neither of these terms but states that the monks tied a loin-cloth (*kaḍi-padi bandhivi*). (Jain, Rajaram, 1982: 36.) Ratnanandin's *Bhadrabāhucarita*, being the latest, closely follows these three versions. Mention will be made of these later texts only where relevant to our investigation.
3. Although the total number of extant *ardhaphālaka* images depicted in Mathura is not known, Joshi in his article has counted at least 26 such figures (1989, 343 and 347). From the illustrations (pls. I and II) it is quite apparent that the *ardhaphālaka* was not used by these monks as a loincloth. This fact is confirmed by the '*vidyā cāraṇa*' image (pl. III), which conclusively proves that these monks were naked and that they held this cloth on their left arms as a frontal cover for their nudity.

4. *Bṛhatkathākośa* (*Bhadrabāhukathānakam*), ed. A. N. Upadhye, 317-19.
5. *Vaḍḍārādhane* (*Bhadrabāhu Bhaṭṭārara Kathe*), ed. D. L. Narasimhachar, 92-3.
6. Shah (1987: 6).
7. Upadhye (1933; 1973; 1974). See also Joshi (1989: 358, n. 19): 'During discussions at the Mathurā Seminar in Delhi [1980] Professor Shah made the following observations: These monks with the strips of cloth on their folded hands, have been named as Ardhaphālaka for the first time by Dr. A. N. Upadhye, but the word appears only in the later texts. Early works do not give this sort of title. We may, therefore, call them the members of the Yāpanīya sect.'
8. *Bṛhatkathākośa*, Upadhye's Introduction, 89.
9. Khadabadi (1979).
10. Ohira (1982: section iv). Schlingloff, in his article, 'Jainas and other "heretics" in Buddhist art' (1994), also fails to mention the material at Mathura.
11. The traditional Digambara account of the migration of the Jaina monks to the South under the leadership of *ācārya* Bhadrabāhu takes place not in Avantī as in this story but from Pāṭaliputra (modern Patna) in the country of Magadha. This Bhadrabāhu is believed to be a contemporary of Candragupta Maurya, the founder of the Mauryan dynasty, the grandfather of Aśoka (and as is known from Greek history, a contemporary of Alexander the Great). The Digambara tradition has claimed that this Candragupta became a mendicant disciple (*muni*) of Bhadrabāhu and that the two together migrated to the South. (See Rice, 1909, Introduction, 3-10.) The event of the split in the mendicant Jaina community can thus be dated around 300 B.C. The Kannada Vaḍḍārādhane (p. 93), however, calls this Candragupta (of the *Bhadrabāhu Bhaṭṭārara Kathe*) as Samprati Candragupta, who also became a Digambara *muni*. Notwithstanding the fact that neither the Sanskrit nor the Kannada versions are historical chronicles, this rather casual reference to Candragupta as Samprati might point to the possibility of two *Bhadrabāhus*, the second a contemporary of Samprati, during whose time the events described in the *Bhadrabāhu-kathānaka* might have taken place. If this be the case, then the time of this event would have been about 100 years later, around 200 B.C. This would conform to another Jaina tradition that one Samprati (son of Kuṇāla), a grandson of Aśoka, succeeded to the throne and was greatly instrumental in spreading Jainism in such Southern countries as Āndhra and Damila, the lands of the Telugu- and Tamil-speaking people. We find reference to this king's services to Jainism in the *Pariśiṣṭaparva* (xi, 89-90) of the twelfth-century Śvetāmbara author Hemacandra. (For a comparison of the accounts of King Samprati Candragupta in the *Vaḍḍārādhane* and the *Pariśiṣṭaparva*, see Khadabadi, 1979: 128-30). Assuming that this Samprati, who ruled not from Magadha but from the West, is indeed the Candragupta of our present narratives, then the migration of the Jaina mendicants from Avantī to the South during the time of [the second] Bhadrabāhu would lend greater credibility to this story and its proposed connexion with the *ardhaphālaka* monks of the Kuṣāṇa period in the Mathura sculptures.
12. Rāmillaḥ Sthaviro yogī Bhadrācāryo 'py amī, trayaḥ/
ye Sindhuviṣaye yātāḥ kāle durbhikṣanāmani//47//

pānānnabhojanair hīne kāle lokasya bhīṣaṇe/
āgatya sahasā procur idaṃ te janasaṃnidhau//48//
13. vaideśikajanair dvāsthaiḥ kṛtakolāhalasvanaiḥ/
pitāputrādayo lokā bhoktum annaṃ na lebhire//49//
loko nijakutumbena bubhukṣāgrastacetasaḥ/
sādhayitvānnam ābālaṃ tadbhayān niśi valbhate//50//
bhavanto 'pi samādāya niśi pātrāṇi madgṛhāt/
nūnaṃ kṛtvā 'nnam eteṣu gatvā deśikato bhayāt//51//
svaśrāvakagṛhe pūte bhūyo viśrabdhamānasāḥ/
sādhavo hi dine jāte kurudhvaṃ bhojanaṃ punaḥ//52//
tallokavacanair iṣṭair bhojanaṃ prītamānasaiḥ/
anena vidhinā "cāryaiḥ pratipannam aśeṣataḥ//53//
14. anyadaiko muniḥ ko 'pi nirgranthaḥ kṣīṇavigrahaḥ//
bhikṣāpātraṃ kare kṛtvā viveśa śrāvakagṛham//54//
tatraikā śrāvikā mugdhā 'bhinavā gurviṇī tadā/
andhakāre muniṃ dṛṣṭvā tatra sā garbham āgatam//55//
taddarśanabhayāt tasyāḥ sa garbhaḥ patito drutam/
dṛṣṭvā 'muṃ śrāvakāḥ prāpya yatīśān idam ūcire//56//
vinaṣṭaḥ sādhavaḥ kālaḥ prāyaścittaṃ vidhāya ca/
kāle hi susthatāṃ prāpte bhūyas tapasi tiṣṭhata//57//
yāvan na śobhano kālo jāyate sādhavaḥ sphuṭam/
tāvac ca vāmahastena puraḥ kṛtvā 'rdhaphālakam//58//
bhikṣāpātraṃ samādāya dakṣiṇena kareṇa ca/
gṛhītvā naktam āhāraṃ kurudhvaṃ bhojanaṃ dine//59//
śrāvakāṇāṃ vacaḥ śrutvā tadānīṃ yatibhiḥ punaḥ/
taduktaṃ sakalaṃ śīghraṃ pratipannaṃ manaḥpriyam//60//

It would be of some interest to observe how the other versions narrate this part of the story. Both the Kannada *Vaḍḍārādhane* and the Apabhraṃśa *Kahā-Kosu* of Śrīcandra follow Hariṣeṇa's narrative regarding the manner of holding the *ardhaphālaka*. It is remarkable that all three later versions are unaware of the practice of holding the *ardhaphālaka* on the left arm as reported in these earlier versions, and as shown on the Mathura sculptures. Raidhū's narrative (see above n. 2) uses the expression *kaḍi-paḍi bandhivi*, which suggests that the monks tied a loincloth around their waists. Rāmacandra Mumukṣu's account places the cloth (*śvetaṃ kambalaṃ*=a white blanket) on the shoulder (*skandhe*) in such a way that the waist and private parts are covered (*liṅgaṃ kaṭipradeśaṃ ca jhampitaṃ yathā bhavati tathā skandhe nikṣipya gacchantu...tathā pravartamānā Ardhakarpaṭitīrthābhidhā jātāḥ*) (Jain, R.: 1982, 75). Ratnanandin's version merely says that those monks placed a blanket(?) on their head and put on the *ardhaphālaka: vinaṣṭo munayaḥ kālaḥ ' śrūyatāṃ no vacas tataḥ...dhṛtvā surallakaṃ śīrṣe paridhāyārdhaphālakam/ naktaṃ bhaktaṃ samānīya vāsare kurutāśanam//* (Jacobi, 1884: 32).

We may note here a few variations that may be of some significance in the manner of holding the begging bowl (*bhikṣā-pātra*). Both Haribhadra's version and the Kannada *Vaḍḍārādhane* state that these monks should hold the bowl in their right hand while they carry the *ardhaphālaka* on their left arm. The remaining versions introduce a new element in the story. Here the monks are told to carry a stick (*daṇḍa*) in their right hand (to ward off dogs). Śrīcandra's *Kahā-Kosu* states that the begging bowl should be covered by the *ardhaphālaka*, which at the same time covers the monk's nudity. The introduction of the stick at this point of the story points to the Digambara belief that the custom of carrying a special long walking stick—in addition to the bowl—by Śvetāmbara monks was also to be traced to the same time as that of the adoption of the *ardhaphālaka*. For an illustration of this, see Jaini (1979), 262, illustration no. 26. It may be observed further that all the monks standing in this group are holding the walking stick in their left hand and a small (wooden) pot tied to a sling in their right hand.

15. evam kṛte sati kṣipraṃ kāle susthatvam āgate/
sukhībhūtajanavrāte dainyabhāvaparicyute//61//
Rāmilla-Sthavira-Sthūlabhadrācāryāḥ svasādhubhiḥ/
āhūya sakalaṃ saṃgham ittham ūcuḥ parasparam//62//
hitvārdhaphālakaṃ tūrṇaṃ munayaḥ prītamānasāḥ/
nirgrantharūpatāṃ sārām āśrayadhvaṃ vimuktaye//63//
śrutvā tadvacanaṃ sāraṃ mokṣāvāptiphalapradam/
dadhur nirgranthatāṃ kecin muktilālasacetasaḥ//64//
Rāmillaḥ Sthaviraḥ Sthūlabhadrācāryas tryo 'py amī/
mahāvairāgyasampannā Viśākhācāryam āyayuḥ//65//
tyaktvārdhakarpaṭaṃ sadyaḥ saṃsārāt trastamānasāḥ/
nairgranthyaṃ hi tapaḥ kṛtvā munirūpaṃ dadhus trayaḥ//66//
iṣṭaṃ na yair guror vākyaṃ saṃsārārṇavatārakam/
Jina-Sthavirakalpaṃ ca vidhāya dvividhaṃ bhuvi//67//
Ardhaphālakasaṃyuktam ajñātaparamārthakaiḥ/
tair idaṃ kalpitaṃ tīrthaṃ kātaraiḥ śaktivarjitaiḥ//68//

16. The author of the *Bhadrabāhu-kathānaka* is asserting that prior to this time there was only one *kalpa* (mode of mendicancy) for all monks, namely, the Jina-kalpa, which entailed the practice of total nudity, and that the apostate monks of his narrative who had started wearing the *ardhaphālaka* separated from this main group and called themselves the Sthavira-kalpa. We should, however, be cautious in accepting such a claim: the distinction between the Jina-kalpa and Sthavira-kalpa based solely on nudity does not conform to the standard meanings of these terms in either the Digambara or Śvetāmbara tradition.

Regarding the Jina-kalpa, both agree that monks following this tradition were not subject to the supervision of a pontiff *ācārya* in such matters as confession and so forth and lived in isolation, as did the Jina Mahāvīra following his renunciation, rather than as part of an organized mendicant community. They both maintain that the Jina-kalpa came to an end with the death of the *ācārya* Jambu, 62 years after the death of Mahāvīra. After this time, the only mode of mendicancy available to monks was the Sthavira-kalpa, the mode of the elders, which required monks to live under the supervision of an *ācārya*. According to both traditions, therefore, the Jina-kalpa had ceased to exist in the fifth century B.C., several centuries prior to our story and the *ardhaphālaka* images found in Mathura.

In addition to this, neither the Digambaras nor the Śvetāmbaras agree with the designation of Jina-kalpa monks as naked and Sthavira-kalpa monks as clothed. According to the Digambaras, a monk, whether he was a follower of the Jina-kalpa or the Sthavira-kalpa, could not wear any clothes whatsoever. Upon assuming the five *mahāvratas*—including that of *aparigraha*—he renounced all possessions, even clothing.

The Śvetāmbaras, however, do not consider a monk's clothing as possession (*parigraha*) and therefore do not require their monks to renounce the use of clothes altogether. Even though it is now required that all Śvetāmbara monks wear clothing, this was apparently not always the case. According to their canonical texts (e.g. *Ācārāṅga-sūtra* and *Uttarādhyayana-sūtra*), their renunciation provided for the options of both the clothed (*sacelaka*) and unclothed (*acelaka*) modes of monkhood. Therefore, the terms Jina-kalpa and Sthavira-kalpa are not equated in their tradition with unclothed and clothed mendicancy respectively. This much seems certain: the Sthavira-kalpa monks were required to wear at a minimum two pieces of clothing. Jina-kalpa monks also kept two pieces of clothing, but if they so chose, they could keep just a single cloth (also called *śāṭaka*) not only for the purpose of modesty but for protection from the cold. If they were young and in good health, they had the further option of abandoning this cloth altogether and thereby becoming *acelaka* monks. Such an option of renouncing the use of clothing is reflected in the Śvetāmbara accounts of the life of the first and last Jinas of the current cycle, Ṛṣabha and Mahāvīra, while the other 22 Jinas are said to have continued to wear clothing throughout their lifetimes (see Jaini, 1979: 14).

For the mendicant status of *ardhaphālakas* in the Digambara tradition, see n. 31 below. For a further discussion of the terms Jina-kalpa and Sthavira-kalpa from the Śvetāmbara perspective, see Tatia and Kumar (1981). For the Digambara view, see Jacobi (1884: 37-8), and *Jinendra Varṇī* (1970-73).

17. Lāṭānāṃ prīticittānāṃ tatas taddivasaṃ prati/
babhūva Kāmbalaṃ tīrthaṃ Vapravādanṛpājñayā//80//
ataḥ Kambalikātīrthān nūnaṃ Sāvalipattane/
Dakṣiṇāpathadeśasthe jāto Yāpanasaṃghakaḥ//81//
iti śrīBhadrabāhukathānakam idam//131//

18. Jacobi (1884: 16): 'Whatever the Digambara tradition says about the origin of the *Ardhaphālaka* sect, must, since the Śvetāmbaras report nothing corresponding, be regarded with caution.'

19. For further references to the alleged migration of Jaina mendicants to the South under the leadership of *ācārya* Bhadrabāhu during the reign of Candragupta Maurya, see Jaini (1979: 5, n. 6).

20. The sixteenth-century Digambara author Śrutasāgara (in his *Ṭīkā* on the *Darśana-prābhṛta* of Kundakunda) quotes the following verse which lists five such groups:
kiṃ taj Jainābhāṣam? uktaṃ ca—Gopucchikaḥ Śvetavāsaḥ Drāviḍo Yāpanīyakaḥ/ Niṣpicchaś ceti paṃcaite Jainābhāṣāḥ prakīrtitāḥ//
Ṣaṭprābhṛtādisaṅgrahaḥ, 11. See n. 22 below.

21. In this connexion I should like to recall a talk that I had in 1951 at Ahmadabad with the eminent Śvetāmbara Jaina monk, the late Muni Śrī Puṇyavijayajī Mahārāj, on the topic of the veracity of the Digambara account of the origin of the clothed Jaina monks. He observed that although carrying pots by Digambara monks during a period of a drought might make some sense for collecting a small amount of alms from home to home, he could not see any reason for the naked monks' acceptance of clothes at the same time. To quote his own words as I remember them, 'What would be the connexion

between not getting food and wearing clothes?' I confronted a few Digambara pandits with his question and received only a brief comment to the effect that, 'Once you break one major rule, in this case collecting food in bowls, it would not be too difficult to break another, such as not wearing clothes.' The *Bhadrabāhu-kathānaka* seems to have been the first Digambara text to have anticipated such a question and provided a credible answer.

22. apavādaveṣaṃ dharann api mithyādṛṣṭir jñātavya ity arthaḥ. ko 'pavādaveṣaḥ? kalau kila mlecchādayo nagnaṃ dṛṣṭvopadravaṃ yatīnāṃ kurvanti tena Maṇḍapadurge śrīVasantakīrtinā svāminā caryādivelāyāṃ taṭṭīsādarādikena śarīram ācchādya caryādikaṃ kṛtvā punas tan muñcantīty upadeśaḥ kṛtaḥ saṃyaminām ity apavādaveṣaḥ (Śrutasāgara's *Ṭīkā* on the *Darśana-prābhṛta* of Kundakunda), (*Ṣaṭprābhṛtādisaṅgrahaḥ*, 21.) See Jaini (1991: 101). For an earlier view attributed to Kundakunda, see below, n. 31.

23. Premi (1956: 562): svasti....jayati bhagavān jinendraḥ... Kadambakulasatketoḥ...śrīŚāntivaravarmmeti... tatpriyajyeṣṭhatanayaḥ śrīMṛgeśanarādhipaḥ... kārayitvā jinālayaṃ śrīVijayapalāśikāyāṃ Yāpani(ī)ya-Nirgrantha-Kūrccakānāṃ ... dattavān bhagavadbhyo 'rhadbhyaḥ.

24. '*yathoktaṃ Yāpanīyatantre*...,' quoted by Haribhadra in his *Lalitavistarā* commentary on the *Caityavandana-sūtra*. For this text, see *Strīnirvāṇa-Kevalibhuktiprakaraṇe* of Śākaṭāyana (with *Svopajñavṛtti*), 58-60. See also Jaini (1991: 45).

25. Śvetabhikṣu-Jāpulisaṃghakke modaliganādaṃ. [*Vaḍḍārādhane*, 93]

26. Upadhye (1973: 1974: 12).

27. Cf. kacci, bhikkhu, khamanīyaṃ, kacci yāpanīyaṃ... khamanīyaṃ bhagavā, yāpanīyaṃ bhagavā. (*Vinaya Piṭaka*, I, 59.) The corresponding Prakrit form *javaṇa* occurring in the following passages seems to have escaped the notice of Upadhye: na rasaṭṭhāe bhuṃjejjā, jāvaṇaṭṭhā mahāmuṇī (*Uttarajjhayaṇāyiṃ*, viii, 12); jāvaṇaṭṭhā vā nisevae maṃthuṃ, (xxxv, 17). annāya uṃchaṃ caraī visuddhaṃ javaṇaṭṭhayā samuyāṇaṃ ca niccaṃ. [*Dasaveyāliya-suttaṃ*, ix, 3]

28. The later three texts of Rāmacandra Mumukṣu, Raidhū, and Ratnanandin extend the story further and probably in order to explain this phenomenon. According to them, these apostate Digambara monks, after coming to Valabhī, had taken to wearing white clothes (in addition to a blanket and a walking-stick, *kambala* and *daṇḍa*). The princess of that country became a great devotee of them. When she was married to the king of Karahāṭaka (modern Karhāḍ, south of Poona), she invited them to reside in their kingdom. But the king (apparently a follower of the Digambara order of monks) refused to welcome these white-clad monks. The princess then implored these monks to give up their clothes and adopt the mode of the Digambara monkhood, which they did. These stories conclude by saying that although outwardly these monks were Digambaras, they nevertheless professed their false doctrines (*kevali-bhukti, strī-mokṣa*, etc.) and hence their group came to be known as Yāpana-saṅgha. See also Premi (1956: 56, n. 1) and Upadhye (1974: 18).

29. Digambarāḥ punar nāgnyaliṅgāḥ pāṇipātrāś ca. te caturdhā Kāṣṭhāsaṅgha-Mūlasaṅgha-Māthurasaṅgha-Gopyasaṅghabhedāt....Gopyās tu... strīṇāṃ muktiṃ kevalināṃ bhuktiṃ ca manyante. Gopyā Yāpanīyā ity ucyante. *Ṣaḍdarśanasamuccaya* (*Tarkarahasyadīpikā-vṛtti*), 160-61; see Upadhye, 1974: 22, and Jaini, 1991, 149-50.

30. 'Yāpanīyās tu vesarā ivobhayam api manyante, ratnatrayaṃ pūjayanti, *Kalpaṃ* ca vācayanti, strīṇāṃ tadbhave mokṣaṃ, kevalijinānāṃ kavalāhāraṃ...ca kathayanti. [*Ṣaṭprābhṛtādisaṅgrahaḥ*,11]

31. The only term that seems to allude to the idea of *ardhaphālaka* would appear to be *celakhaṇḍa*. This is found in chapter 3, verse 21 of the *Pravacanasāra*, where the first-century Digambara author Kundakunda talks about the necessity of a monk to abandon attachment to external objects of support (*upadhis*). The tenth-century commentator on this text, Amṛtacandra, understands this verse as the renunciation of all *upadhis* but offers no enumeration of the intended objects. However, Jayasena's twelfth-century commentary follows a version of the text that contains three additional verses at this point. In the first verse, a claim has been made that the scripture allows the use of a *celakhaṇḍa*, 'piece of cloth', a begging bowl made from a gourd, and other such objects, to which Jayasena's commentary adds 'other objects such as a blanket, a soft mat for sleeping, etc.'

genhadi va celakhaṇḍaṃ bhāyaṇaṃ atthi tti bhaṇidaṃ iha sutte/
jadi so cattālambo havadi kahaṃ vā aṇārambho//III, *3//
vatthakkhaṇḍaṃ duddiyabhāyaṇaṃ aṇṇaṃ ca geṇhadi ṇiyadaṃ/
vijjadi pāṇarambho vikkhevo tassa cittammi//III, *4//
geṇhai vidhuṇai dhovai sosei jadaṃ tu ādave khittā/
patthaṃ ca celakhaṇḍaṃ bibhedi parado va pālayadi//III, *5//

Jayasena, aware that these verses did not appear in the older version of the text available to Amṛtacandra, is of the opinion that these are the words of Kundakunda and explains further that these verses were 'for the purpose of instructing the disciples who followed the opinion of the Śvetāmbaras' (*evaṃ Śvetāmbaramatānusāriśiṣyasambodhanārthaṃ*... (*Pravacanasāra*, 272). Given the available texts, it is not possible to determine whether these verses were actually Kundakunda's or not. However, Upadhye, in the introduction to his translation of this text, remarks, 'I do not find that there is any strong case against Kundakunda's authorship, as a composer or compiler, of these additional [a total of 36] *gāthās*, except one or two *gāthās* whose position I have detected to be dubious in that context' (*Pravacanasāra*, 49-50). If these verses were in fact part of the ealiest versions of the text, then it would be possible to argue that Kundakunda was indeed aware of a group of Jaina mendicants, whose sectarian identity is not disclosed, with a 'piece of cloth' who might have resembled the monks depicted on the Mathura sculptures.

For the occurrence of the term *celakhaṇḍa* in the sense of a loincloth (*kaupīna*) worn by the most advanced layman (prior to becoming a *muni*) in the Digambara tradition, see n. 41 below.

32. ekasmiṃ hi divase bhikkhū nigaṇṭhe disvā kathaṃ sanuṭṭhāpesuṃ: 'āvuso sabbaso apaṭicchannehi acelakehi ime nigaṇṭhā varatarā ye ekaṃ purimapassaṃ pi tāva paṭicchādenti, sahirikā maññe ete 'ti. taṃ sutvā nigaṇṭhā 'na mayaṃ etena kāraṇena paṭicchādema. paṃsurajādayo pi pana puggalā eva jīvitindriyapaṭibaddhā, evañ ca te no bhikkhābhājanesu mā patiṃsu iminā kāraṇena paṭicchādemā ti vatavā tehi saddhiṃ vādapaṭivādavasena bahuṃ kathaṃ kathesuṃ. (*Dhammapada-Aṭṭhakathā*, (xxii. 8. *Nigaṇṭhānaṃ vatthu*). III. 489: tr. by Burlingame, 1921, xxx, 196.)

33. The Ājīvikas (the followers of Makkhali Gosāla) have traditionally been

described in the Pali texts as *acelakas* (naked) (see Malalasekera, 1960: I. 238). Judging by the above passage in the *Dhammapada-Aṭṭhakathā,* they would have to have been without any clothes at all. However, there is a discrepancy between the textual description and the visual representation of Ājīvika monks found in Gandharan sculptures. Several depictions of the scene of the death (*mahāparinirvāṇa*) of the Buddha show a naked Ājīvika standing among the lamenting Buddhist monks and the seated young *paribbājaka* Subhadda. The Ājīvika is shown holding a *mandārava* flower (as narrated in the *Dīghanikāya,* II, 162-3) in his raised right hand and a piece of cloth—like a handkerchief—folded in his lowered left hand, as for example in Marshall: 1960, pl. 91. fig. 127; pl. 92, fig. 128; and pl. 93, fig. 129. It is noteworthy that he does not hide his nudity by that piece of cloth. In another frieze from Gandhara depicting the same scene (Craven, 1976: 91, pl. 54) he is shown clutching the folded cloth with his left hand in such a way as to partially cover his nudity, but without any contrivance at hiding it as is manifest in the Ardhaphālaka images of Mathura. Assuming then that the *acelakas* referred to in the Pali canon are neither the Ājīvikas depicted in Gandharan art nor the Nigaṇṭhas referred to above in the Aṭṭhakathās, the possibility remains that the term points to the existence of such Jaina monks who at no time allowed any piece of cloth whatsoever, as claimed by Kundakunda (see n. 31), and received the designation '*digambara*' (sky-clad) in the post-canonical period.

34. The idea of using a piece of cloth to cover the begging bowl is supported by the commentaries to the Śvetāmbara canon. According to Deo (1956: 270-71), one of the types of cloth used in association with the begging bowl, the *paḍala* (*paṭala*) was 'sufficient enough to cover not only the pot but even the shoulder of the monk. It means that the monk put it on in such a way as to cover a portion of the body and he kept the pot inside the *paṭala.*' He cites as his source the *Oghanijjutti* (679-702). He also mentions a passage from the *Bṛhatkalpa-bhāṣya* (213a) in which monks on begging rounds are to cover the shoulder and the pots with the *paṭalas* (p. 413). However, from the description found here and in paragraph 15 below, I do not believe it is possible to equate this cloth with that mentioned in either of the passages in the Buddhist texts.

35. Ekasāṭakāti. ekasāṭaka-nigaṇṭhā viya ekaṃ pilotika-khaṇḍaṃ hatthe bandhitvā eken' antena hi sarīrassa purima-bhāgaṃ paṭicchādetvā vicaraṇakā.
[*Udānaṭṭhakathā* (*Paramattha-Dīpanī*), 330-31]

36. See n. 31 above.

37. ahāsuyaṃ vaissāmi jahā se samaṇe bhagavaṃ uṭṭhāe/
saṃkhāe taṃsi hemante, ahuṇo pavvaie rīitthā//1//
ṇo cev 'imeṇa vattheṇa, pihissāmi taṃsi hemante/
so pārae āvakahāe, eyaṃ khu aṇudhammiyaṃ tassa//2//
saṃvaccharaṃ sāhiyaṃ māsaṃ, jaṃ ṇu rikkāsi vatthagaṃ bhagavaṃ /
acelage tao cāī, taṃ vosirijja vatthaṃ aṇagāre//4//
(*Ācārāṅga-sūtra,* I, viii, i.) see Jacobi 1884: part 1, 79.

38. tae ṇaṃ samaṇe bhagavaṃ Mahāvīre... egaṃ devadūsaṃ ādāya ege abīe muṇḍe bhavittā agārāo aṇagāriaṃ pavvaie, samaṇe bhagavaṃ Mahāvīre saṃvaccharaṃ sāhiamāsaṃ cīvaradhārī hotthā, teṇa paraṃ acelae pāṇipaḍiggahiye.

(*Kalpa-sūtra* §§ 114-15.) See Jacobi, 1884: part 1, 259-60.

39. komalaṃ dhavalaṃ sūkṣmaṃ syūtaṃ candrakarair iva/
devadūṣyaṃ devarājaḥ skandhadeśe nyadhād vibhoḥ//
[*Triśaṣṭiśalākāpuruṣacaritra*, I, iii, 64]

40. See a video entitled 'Tīrthaṅkara Bhagavān Śrī Mahāvīra', produced in 1992 by the Institute of Jainology, 31 Lancaster Gate, London, W2 3LP.

41. Samantabhadra gives the following description of an *ailaka* in his *Ratnakaraṇḍaśrāvakācāra:*
gṛhato munivanaṃ itvā gurūpakaṇṭhe vratāni parigṛhya/
bhaikṣāśanas tapasyann ukṛṣṭaś celakhaṇḍadharaḥ//
Commenting on the last word, Prabhācanda says:
celakhaṇḍadharaḥ kaupīnamātravastrakhaṇḍadhārakaḥ āryaliṅgadhārīty arthaḥ. [*Ratnakaraṇḍaśrāvakācāraḥ Saṭīkaḥ*, v, 26]
The fact that even a '*celakhaṇḍa*' would be unacceptable for a Jaina monk is demonstrated by Rāmacandra Mumukṣu's comment (see n. 14 above) that a Digambara monk may put a blanket on his shoulder in such a manner as to cover his nudity only in a calamity such as the one described in this story and must give it up when normal conditions have returned.

42. See Smith (1901) and Jaini (1979: 7 and pl. 5).

43. For further information on names of the *gaṇas* and *gacchas* found in Jaina Mathurā Inscriptions, see Deo (1956: 513-19) and Upadhye (1974: 9-10), where he cites A. Guerinot's Introduction to *Repertoire 'depigraphic jaina* (Paris, 1908). For a list of the Sthaviras in Śvetāmbara texts, see Jacobi (1884, part 1, 286-95).

BIBLIOGRAPHY

TEXTS AND TRANSLATIONS

Ācārāṅga-sūtra: *Āyāraṃgasuttaṃ*, ed. Muni Shri Puṇyavijayajī. (Jaina Āgama Series. no. 2.)Bombay: Shri Mahavira Jain Vidyalaya. Transl. by H. Jacobi in *Jaina-sūtras*, part 1, 1-213. (Sacred Books of the East, Vol. xxii.) London: Oxford University Press, 1884.

Bhadrabāhu-bhaṭṭārara-kathe. See *Vaḍḍārādhane.*

Bhadrabāhu-Cāṇakya-Candragupta-kathānaka [in *Apabhraṃśa*] of Raidhū. See Jain, Rajaram (1982).

Bhadrabāhucarita of Ratnanandin. See Jacobi, H. (1884).

Bhadrabāhukathānaka (Kathā no. 38 in the *Puṇyāsravakathākośa*) of Rāmacandra Mumukṣu. See Jain, Rajaram (1982).

Bhadrabāhukathānakaṁ of Hariṣeṇa. See *Bṛhatkathākośa.*

Bhagavatī-ārādhanā of Śivārya. Bombay: Anantakīrti Granthamālā, 1932.

Bṛhatkathākośa of Hariṣeṇa, ed. A. N. Upadhye. (Singhi Jain Series, no. 17) Bombay: Bhāratīya Vidyābhavana, 1943.

Dasaveyāliya-suttaṃ (*Daśavaikālika-sūtra*), ed. Muni Puṇyavijayajī and Pandit Amritlal M. Bhojak. (Jaina Āgama Series. no. 15.) Bombay: Shri Mahavira Jain Vidyalaya, 1977.

Dhammapada-Aṭṭhakathā [4 vols.], ed. H. C. Norman. London: Pali Text Society, 1906-15. Transl. by E. W. Burlingame: *The Buddhist Legends.* (Harvard Oriental Series. Vols. 28-30.) Cambridge, Mass.: Harvard University Press, 1921.

Kahā-Kosu of Muni Śrīcandra, ed. H. L. Jain. Ahmedabad: Prakrit Text Society,

1969.
Kalpa-sūtra (*Kappasuttaṃ*—includes *Therāvalī*), ed. Mahopādhyāya Vinayasāgara. Jaipur: Prakrit Bharati, 1977. Transl. by Hermann Jacobi as *The Kalpa-sūtra of Bhadrabāhu* (includes *List of the Sthaviras*, 286-95), in *Jaina-sūtras*, part 1.217-85. (Sacred Books of the East, Vol. xxii.) London: Oxford University Press, 1884.
Pariśiṣṭaparva of Hemacandra: Sanskrit text, ed. by H. Jacobi. (Bibliotheca Indica, no. 96.) Calcutta: 1932. (2nd ed.)
Pravacanasāra of Kundakunda with Amṛtacandra's *Tattvadīpikā* and Jayasena's *Tātparyavṛtti*, ed. A. N. Upadhye, Agas: Rājachandra Jaina Sāstramālā, 1964.
Ratnakaraṇḍaśrāvakācāra of Samantabhadra with Prabhācandra's *Ṭīkā*, ed. J. K. Mukhtar. Bombay: Māṇikachandra Digambara Jaina Granthamālā. 1925.
Ṣaḍdarśanasamuccaya of Haribhadra with Guṇaratna's *Tarkarahasyadīpikāvṛtti*. Sanskrit text, Hindi transl. by Mahendra Kumar Jain. Varanasi: Bhāratīya Jñānapīṭha, 1970.
Saṃyutta-Nikāya, ed. L. Feer. London: Pali Text Society, 1880. Transl. by F. L. Woodward and Mrs. Rhys Davids: *The Book of the kindred sayings*: London: Pali Text Society, 1924.
Saṃyutta-Nikāyaṭṭhakathā (=*Sāratthappakāsinī* of Buddhaghosa). ed. F. L. Woodward, London: Pali Text Society, 1929-32.
Ṣaṭprābhṛtādisaṅgrahaḥ of Kundakunda: Prakrit texts with Śrutasāgara's Sanskrit *Ṭīkā*, ed. Pannalal Soni. Bombay: Māṇikchandra Digambara Jaina Granthamālā, 1921.
Strīnirvāṇa-Kevalibhuktiprakaraṇe of Śākaṭāyana (with *Svopajñavṛtti*): Sanskrit text, ed. Muni Jambūvijaya. Bhavanagar, Gujarat: Jaina Ātmānanda Sabhā. 1974. Transl. of the *Strīnirvāṇa-prakaraṇa* by Padmanabh S. Jaini (1991).
Triṣaṣṭiśalākāpuruṣacaritra of Hemacandra, ed. Caraṇavijaya Muni. Bhavnagar: Jain Ātmānanda Sabhā, 1933. Transl. by Helen M. Johnson as *The lives of sixty-three illustrious persons*. 6 vols. Baroda: Oriental Institute, 1962.
Udāna, ed. P. Steinthal. London: Pali Text Society, 1948.
Udānaṭṭhakathā of Dhammapālācariya, ed. F. L. Woodward, London: Pali Text Society, 1926.
Uttarajjhayaṇāyiṃ (*Uttarādhyayana-sūtra*), ed. Muni Shri Puṇyavijayajī and Pandit Amritlal M. Bhojak. (Jaina Āgama Series, no. 15.) Bombay: Shri Mahavira Jain Vidyalaya, 1977. Transl. by H. Jacobi in *Jaina-sūtras*, part 2, 1-232. (Sacred Books of the East, Vol. XLV.) London: Oxford University Press, 1895.
Vaḍḍārādhane (*Śivakoṭyācārya-viracita*), Kannada text, ed. D. L. Narasimhacar. Mysore: Sharada Mandira, 1970. (4th ed.) [See also *Bhrājiṣṇu Viracita Vaḍḍārādhane*, ed. H. P. Nagarajaiah, Bangalore University, 1993, 80-81.]
Vinaya Piṭaka. 5 vols. London: Pali Text Society, 1879-83.

OTHER REFERENCES

Craven, Roy C. *Indian Art: A Concise History*, London: Thames and Hudson, 1976, (Repr. 1987).
Deo, Shantaram Bhalchandra. *History of Jaina Monachism*. (Deccan College Dissertation Series, no. 17.) Poona, 1956.
Jacobi, Hermann. 'Ueber die Entstehung der Śvetāmbara and Digambara Sekten', *ZDMG*, 38, 1884, 1-42.
Jain, Rajaram. *Story of Bhadrabāhu, Cāṇakya, Candragupta and Short Description of*

King Kalki of Mahākavi Raidhū (*GVD* Jaina Series, no. 29.) Varanasi: Shri Ganesha Varni Digambara Jaina Samsthana, 1982.

Jaini, Padmanabh S. *The Jaina Path of Purification*, Berkeley: University of California Press, 1979.

Jaini, Padmanabh S. *Gender and Salvation: Jaina Debates on the Spiritual Liberation of Women.* Berkeley: University of California Press, 1991.

Jinendra Varṇī. *Jainendra Siddhānta Kośa.* [4 vols.] Delhi: Bhāratīya Jñānapīṭha. 1970-73.

Joshi, N. P. 'Early Jaina icons from Mathura', in *Mathurā: The Cultural Heritage*, Doris Srinivasan (gen. ed.). New Delhi: American Institute of Indian Studies, 1989: 332-67.

Khadabadi, *B. K. Vaḍḍārādhane: A Study*, Dharwad: Karnataka University, 1979.

Malalasekera, G. P. *Dictionary of Pāli Proper Names*, London: Luzac and Co. 1960.

Marshall, Sir John. *The Buddhist Art of Gandhara.* Karachi: Ministry of Education. Govt. of Pakistan, 1973. (2nd ed.)

Ohira, Suzuko. *A Study of Tattvārthasūtra with Bhāṣya.* (L. D. Series, no. 86), Ahmedabad: L. D. Institute of Indology, 1982.

Premi, Nathuram. *Jaina Sāhityakā Itihāsa* [in Hindi]. Bombay: Hindi Grantha Ratnakara, 1956.

Rice. Lewis B. *Mysore and Coorg from the Inscriptions.* [First publ. 1909.] New Delhi: Asian Educational Services, 1986.

Schlingoff, Dieter. 'Jainas and other "heretics" in Buddhist art,' in N. N. Bhattacharya (ed.), *Jainism and Prakrit in Ancient and Medieval India.* New Delhi: Monohar, 1994, 71-82.

Shah, Umakant P. *Jaina-Rūpa-Maṇḍana* [Jaina iconography]. Vol. 1, New Delhi: Abhinav Publications, 1987.

Shah, Umakant P. 'Evolution of Jaina iconography and symbolism', in U. P. Shah and M. A. Dhaky (ed.). *Aspects of Jaina Art and Architecture.* Ahmedabad: L. D. Institute of Indology, 1975, 49-74.

Shah, Umakant P. *Studies in Jaina Art.* Banaras: Jaina Cultural Research Society, 1955.

Smith, Vincent A. *The Jain Stupa and Other Antiquities of Mathura.* Allahabad: Government Press, 1901.

Tatia, Nathmal, and Muni Mahendra Kumar. *Aspects of Jaina Monasticism.* Ladnu, Rajasthan: Jaina Viśva Bhāratī, 1981.

Upadhye, Adinath N. 'Yāpanīya Saṅgha: A Jaina sect' *Journal of the University of Bombay*, 1933, i. 6. 224-31.

Upadhye, Adinath N. 'On the meaning of Yāpanīya,' in *Śrīkaṇṭhikā—Dr. S. Srikantha Shastri Felicitation Volume*, Mysore, 1973: 197-8.

Upadhye, Adinath N. 'More light on the Yāpanīya Saṅgha,' *Annals of the Bhandarkar Oriental Research Institute*, LV, 1-4, 1974, 9-22.

Williams, R. *Jaina Yoga: A Survey of the Mediaeval Śrāvakācāras.* London: Oxford University Press, 1963.

VI

JAINA PURĀṆAS

CHAPTER 18

Jina Ṛṣabha as an *Avatāra* of Viṣṇu*

Avatāra, or the periodical incarnation of the deity, is a cardinal doctrine of the Vaiṣṇava sect of Brāhmaṇical Hinduism. The increasing number of the *avatāras* is an indication of the popularity of this doctrine both among the theologians and among the devout laity. The modest list of three (Varāha, Kūrma, and Matsya) of the Brāhmaṇa literature[1] grows into a list of 10 traditional *avatāras* (Matsya, Kūrma, Varāha, Nṛsiṃha, Vāmana, Paraśurāma, Rāma, Kṛṣṇa, Buddha, and Kalkin) in the *Mahābhārata*, and ends up in a still longer list of 22 in the *Bhāgavatapurāṇa*.[2] The latter has in its inflated list quite a few 'minor' (*aṃśa*) *avatāras*, mostly, consisting of names of great sages renowned for their austerities and learning, e.g. Nārada, Nara, Nārāyaṇa, Kapila, Dattātreya, Ṛṣabha, and Veda-Vyāsa.

The purpose of an *avatāra* is 'to serve the righteous, to destroy the wicked, and to establish the right', as proclaimed in the *Bhagavadgītā*.[3] As a result, an *avatāra* is associated with the task of forceful destruction of a demon (*asura*) (e.g. Rāvaṇa in the case of Rāma) or of the demonic (e.g. the *kṣatriyas* in the case of Paraśurāma). The *aṃśāvatāras* on the other hand are solely concerned with the revelation of the divine truth, and are therefore, more in the tradition of a *guru*, the propagators of the faith.

The declaration of the Lord of the *Gītā* (x, 41) that whatever being shows 'supernal manifestation' (*vibhūtimat*) or majesty or vigour is sprung from a fraction of his glory, may be taken as an

*This article was published originally in *Bulletin of the School of Oriental and African Studies*, Vol. XL, part 2, pp. 321-337, University of London, 1977. Reprinted with kind permission of Oxford University Press.

open sanction for conferring the status of an *avatāra* on any person of an exalted nature. Nevertheless, the inclusion of the Buddha in the list of the *avatāras* must sound incredible as he evidently is not only an adversary of Viṣṇu but is opposed to the very theistic conception of the Vaiṣṇava religion.[4] The full story of the 'avatarization' of this great *śramaṇa* is shrouded in mystery. More or less all major Purāṇas follow the lead of the *Mahābhārata*,[5] and confine their account of this great *avatāra* to only a couple of lines. The account invariably consists of the repetition of the fiction that the [anti-Vedic] preaching of the Buddha had [also] the divine purpose of destroying the *asuras*, who as a result of his teaching desisted from offering the sacrifices and thus ceased to be a danger to the gods! The credit for assigning this *avatāra* a more generous role goes probably to Jayadeva, the twelfth-century Vaiṣṇava poet who in his *Gītagovinda*[6] emphasized the great compassion of the Buddha [towards the animals slaughtered in the Vedic sacrifices].

The present paper proposes to examine yet another case of a *śramaṇa* turned into an *avatāra* of Viṣṇu. This pertains to Ṛṣabha, the first of the 24 *tīrthaṅkaras* of the Jains, who is cast into the role of a 'minor' or partial (*aṃśa*) *avatāra* by the author of the *Bhāgavatapurāṇa*.[7] According to the latter, Ṛṣabha is an incarnation of Viṣṇu who 'descended' to earth in order to establish the *śramaṇa-dharma* of the naked ascetics (*vāta-raśanānāṃ śramaṇānāṃ ṛṣiṇām...*).[8] The study enables us to observe the extraordinary manner in which a Vaiṣṇava apologist, while denouncing the Jain faith, appropriates the central figure of that religion by the device of the doctrine of *avatāra*.

The main sources for the Jain account of Ṛṣabha are the Jain canonical texts like the *Kalpasūtra*[9] and the *Jambudvīpa-prajñapti*,[10] and a large number of Jain Purāṇas of the classical period, notably the *Ādipurāṇa*[11] of the Digambara *ācārya* Jinasena (c. ninth century), and the *Triṣaṣṭi-śalākā-puruṣa-caritra*[12] of the Śvetāmbara *ācārya* Hemacandra (thirteenth century). Barring a few minor details, the Digambara and the Śvetāmbara accounts show a remarkable agreement on the main events in the legendary life of Ṛṣabha[13] as summarized below.

According to the Jaina tradition, 24 *tīrthaṅkaras* 'ford-makers' (i.e. saviours) appear in each time cycle which consists of six regressive (*avasarpiṇī*) and six progressive (*utsarpiṇī*) periods during which time there is a gradual decline and progress of civilization respectively. Ṛṣabha was the first of the 24 *tīrthaṅkaras* of the present time cycle, whereas Mahāvīra (the historical Nigaṇṭha Nātaputta of the Buddhist and Jain canons) was the last of them. Ṛṣabha thus flourished some billions of years ago in the regressive half of the present cycle towards the close of the third period. Prior to this there was the golden age during which time conditions similar to paradise (*bhogabhūmi*) prevailed upon the earth. There were, for instance, wish-fulfilling trees (*kalpavṛkṣas*) instead of orchards, and only the 'patriarch' (*kulakara*) in the place of kings. There was no organization like the caste system or the graduated system of four *āśramas* culminating in *mokṣa.* All marriages were happy for the simple reason that a couple gave birth only to a single pair of mixed twins who duly married each other. All this was fast disappearing towards the close of the third period when in Ayodhyā Ṛṣabha was born to Nābhi, the fourteenth *kulakara,* and his wife Marudevī.

In the course of time Ṛṣabha was married to his twin sister Sumaṅgalā who bore him a son called Bharata. The latter became the first *cakravartin* and gave his name to the subcontinent of India (Bhāratavarṣa). His twin sister Brāhmī was the first to learn the art of writing (hence the name *Brāhmī-lipi*) devised by her father. Ṛṣabha is said to have taken another wife by the name of Sunandā who had been 'widowed' by the death of her 'natural' husband,[14] the first infantile death which marked the end of the golden age (when premature death was unknown) and foreshadowed the beginning of the fourth period aptly named *duḥṣamāsuṣamā* 'more sorrow and less happiness'. Sunandā bore Ṛṣabha twins called Bāhubalī and Sundarī, who were followed by 94 sons. According to the age-old custom the two brothers would have taken their own twin sisters as their wives. But Ṛṣabha foresaw the beginning of the new age and got his eldest son Bharata married to Sundarī, the twin sister of Bāhubalī, and the latter to Brāhmī, the sister of Bharata. He is thus credited with having been the first to forbid matrimony between twins (a practice alluded to in the Ṛgvedic dialogue between Yama and Yamī), and thereby laying the foundations of a new marriage system.

The extinction of the *kalpavṛkṣas* forced the people to look for new sources of food. Ṛṣabha is credited with the discovery of fire (by friction) and also of tilling and such other activities connected with agriculture. For this the Jain *ācāryas* have given him the title of *prajā-pati*, the Lord of the beings. He was also responsible for the creation of various professions such as swordmanship (*asi*), writing (*maṣi*), commerce (*vāṇijya*), farming (*kṛṣi*), arts (*vidyā*), and crafts (*śilpa*).[15] From these developed the three castes, viz. the Kṣatriya, Vaiśya, and Śūdra. The institution of the Brahman caste is attributed by the Jain authors not to Ṛṣabha but to his son Bharata as will be seen below. These professions and the castes transformed the earth from a *bhogabhūmi* (place of enjoyment) into a *karmabhūmi* (place of action). With the decline in worldy goods and the increase in the greed of people, there arose the need of a ruler able to command obedience and dispense justice to all. In fulfilling yet another need of the time Ṛṣabha became the first king of mankind, comparable to King Mahāsammata of the Pali canon. As a king he laid down the laws and thus became the first lawgiver at the dawn of civilization. Ṛṣabha was also the first anchorite (*śramaṇa* or *muni*), the first omniscient being (*sarvajña* or *Jina*), and the first great teacher of the path of liberation (*tīrthaṅkara*). He totally renounced his wordly life while still young, and became a *digambara* (sky-clad=naked) mendicant. He lived in seclusion and silence, his hair growing long over his shoulders, oblivious of himself and of the world. Hundreds of images, some going back to the close of the Mauryan period, depict this ascetic Ṛṣabbha, showing his upright posture and dishevelled hair, engrossed in meditation and deep trance. His vow of fasting is said to have lasted for almost six months, at the close of which he went around begging for food. He walked the whole length of the Ganges, from Ayodhyā to Hastināpura, but failed to obtain alms proper for a *śramaṇa*. People came forward offering him all the worldly things, including their marriageable daughters, says one Purāṇa,[16] as no one had any experience of attending properly to the needs of a recluse, and the latter would beg his food only in silence. It was not until a whole year had passed that a king named Śreyāṃśa witnessed in his dream an act of charity he had performed in his previous life. Directed by this dream he offered the sage fresh juice of sugarcane (*ikṣu*) on the third day of the full moon of the month of Vaiśākha, a day sacred to the Jains and celebrated even to this day as *akṣaya-tṛtīyā* 'the Immortal Third.

Ṛṣabha continued in this ascetic life for over a thousand years, at the end of which he attained that enlightenment which the Jains identify with omniscience (*kevalajñāna*). He was now a *jina*, a spiritual victor, who had broken for ever the bonds of *saṃsāra*. But Ṛṣabha was not an ordinary *jina* content with his own liberation. He had in his previous births practised those virtues which distinguish a *jina* as a *tīrthaṅkara*, a supreme teacher who during his lifetime brings enlightenment to many, and whose teaching lasts for several millenniums guiding the aspirants on the path of liberation. The Jain canon claims that at the time of the *nirvāṇa* of Ṛṣabha on Mount Kailāśa in the Himālaya, the order of the Jains consisted of 84,000 monks (*śramaṇas*), 300,000 nuns (*śramaṇīs*), 305,000 laymen (*śrāvakas*), and as may as 554,000 laywomen (*śrāvikās*), and also that the number of his disciples who had realized omniscience had reached 20,000.[17]

As for the teachings of Ṛṣabha, the Jains maintain that these, being identical with the nature of reality (*vatthusāhavo dhammo*), do not originate from any single person. This *dharma* is eternal but needs to be revived from age to age, a task accomplished by the periodical appearance of the *tīrthaṅkaras*. The teachings of Ṛṣabha are therefore the same as those of his predecessors from bygone ages, and are identical with the preachings of Mahāvīra, the last *tīrthaṅkara* (527 B.C.). These doctrines can be summed up by the concepts of *anekāntavāda*, *ahiṃsā*, and *karmavāda* by which the Jains respectively reject the extremes of eternalism and annihilationism (found as they see it in all other doctrines), adopt the path of total non-violence consisting of the five *mahāvratas* (incompatible with religions advocating sacrifice to gods), and repudiate the theistic doctrines of a creator and his *avatāras* or his grace.

Although several Purāṇas mention Ṛṣabha (together with his illustrious son Bharata) in the genealogy of Manu,[18] the *Bhāgavatapurāṇa* appears to be the first and probably the only work to accord him the status of an *aṃśāvatāra* of Viṣṇu. The *Bhāgavata* account is therefore of singular interest as it provides, as nowhere else, the motive for conferring on the saint of a demonstrably heretic religion the high status of an *avatāra*. This account is set in a suitable context of the story of Priyavrata[19] (reminiscent of many a *śramaṇa*, including the Buddha and Mahāvīra) who, although young, had resolved to renounce the world and refused to rule the kingdom of his father, the great

Svāyambhuva Manu. Thereupon Brahmā himself, accompanied by the sage Nārada, approached Priyavrata and persuaded him to enjoy the pleasure conferred upon him by the Lord, and to lead the life of a householder (*gṛhastha*) practising devotion and the control of the senses. Priyavrata then agreed to rule the kingdom and took Varhiṣmatī the daughter of Viśvakarman as his wife, who bore him 10 sons. The eldest of these was Agnīdhra who succeeded him to the throne and begot nine sons on an *apsaras* named Pūrvacitti. Their eldest son Nābhi espoused the daughter of Meru named Merudevī (cf. Nābhi and Marudevī of the Jain tradition) and ruled the kingdom after the death of the King Agnīdhra.

Nābhi had no offspring for a long time from his queen Merudevī. He therefore propitiated the Lord (who is sacrifice incarnate) by various sacrificial rites. Pleased by his devotion the Lord Viṣṇu manifested himself in his auspicious form (of four arms adorned with conch, discus, club, and lotus) before the King Nābhi and his queen and the *ṛtviks* at the celebration of the *pravargya* ceremony. The *ṛtviks* duly worshipped the Lord for this extraordinary grace and prayed that 'a son like unto the Lord' be granted to Nābhi and his queen. Being thus implored by venerable *ṛtviks*, the compassionate Lord Viṣṇu addressed them as follows.

'O ye Sages, your words are never futile. Yet you have begged a boon that is not easy of granting inasmuch as, being Supreme, I alone am equal and like unto Myself. Nevertheless, the words of Brahmans must not be falsified as they are my mouth. Not finding anyone else comparable to me, I shall by a portion of My own divine essence descend in the house of King Nābhi.'

Accordingly, the Lord, desirous of pointing out the *dharma* unto the naked (wind-clad) and celibate *śramaṇa* sages, assuming a pure form descended into the womb of queen Merudevī as Ṛṣabha.[20]

All the divine marks were clearly visible on the person of the child Ṛṣabha. He grew to be a mighty prince endowed with effulgence and fame. Even Indra, the king of the gods, became envious of his fame and withdrew the seasonal rains from the land of Nābhi. Undaunted, Prince Ṛṣabha, the Lord of *yoga*, by the powers of his *yogamāyā*, caused heavy rain showers in his kingdom thus earning the love and gratitude of all his subjects. The king, gratified by the excellent virtues of his son, established him on the throne and retired to a penance grove with his Queen Merudevī, where he spent the remainder of his life in devotion to the Lord Vāsudeva.

The divine Ṛṣabha considered his own country to be a *karmakṣetra*[21] (the field of activity, cf. the Jain *karmabhūmi*) and in order to instruct his subjects in the duties of a householder lived himself for some time in a *gurukula*. Thereafter, having pleased his teachers with gifts he returned home and received a damsel named Jayantī as his queen from Indra. He begot on her 100 sons of great might, the eldest of whom was named Bharata. This Bharata was a great *yogin* and supremely virtuous, and it was after his name that the land of Ṛṣabha was named Bhāratavarṣa.[22] Of the 99 sons, the following nine, viz. Kuśāvarta, Ilāvarta, Brahmāvarta, Malaya, Ketu, Bhadrasena, Indraspṛh, Vidarbha, and Kīkaṭa became the foremost [warriors] serving Bharata. The following nine, viz. Kavi, Hari, Antarikṣa, Prabuddha, Pippalāyana, Āvirhotra, Draviḍa, Camasa, and Karabhājana became *Mahābhāgavatas* or the propagators of the Bhāgavata faith. The remaining 81 sons of Ṛṣabha were humble and fond of performing sacrifices; and as such they became Brahmans of pure actions.[23]

Although King Ṛṣabha was the master of himself and identified himself with the Lord, he undertook many activities like an ordinary mortal in order to instruct the ignorant householders in the time-honoured goals of *dharma, artha, kāma,* and *mokṣa*. He was fully conversant with the mystical teachings pertaining to the Brahman (or of the *Vedas*), yet he chose to govern his subjects according to the laws (such as *sāma, dāna,* etc.) laid down by the Brahmans.[24] He also performed 100 sacrifices complete in every respect according to their prescribed rites.

Once upon a time while wandering, Ṛṣabha arrived in the country of Brahmāvarta where he saw his own sons in the assembly of great Brāhmaṇical sages (*brahmarṣi*). Ṛṣabha instructed them on the value of the human body and how it can be used for austerities that lead one to the eternal bliss of the Brahman. He spoke to them of the knot (*granthi*) forged by the union of man and woman, and showed the path of cutting this knot by renouncing the attachment to one's ego. In what appears to be a summary of the teaching of the *Ṛṣabhāvatāra*, the author of the *Bhāgavatapurāṇa* gives in this context a whole chapter consisting of 27 verses[25] stressing the need of renunciation and devotion, the twin doctrines of the Bhāgavata cult. The entire section is remarkable for its non-sectarian preaching, unexceptionable on the whole to any person of an ascetic persuasion. Its effect however, is marred firstly by the admonition of Ṛṣabha to his sons not to renounce but to serve their eledest brother Bharata with 'mind free from afflictions' (*akliṣṭa-buddhyā*), and next by the following few verses which glorify the Brahmans and raise them even higher than the Lord.

'...human beings are superior to the animals..., devas are superior to men..., Indra is the foremost of the devas..., Brahmā's sons, Dakṣa, etc., are superior to Indra..., Śaṅkara is superior to Dakṣa, etc.,..., Brahmā is superior to Śaṅkara..., Brahmā has his being in Me; and therefore I am superior to Brahmā. I too worship the Brahmans. Thus the Brahmans, being superior to Me, are to be worshipped by all.

'O Brahmans! I do not find any being equal unto the Brahmans.... I do not find so much satisfaction in *agnihotra* sacrifice as in receiving what has been offered with faith in the mouth of the Brahmans...'[26]

Having thus admonished his worthy sons, he decided to impart instructions to the great sages (*mahāmunīnām*) in the exalted path (*dharma*) of a *parama-haṃsa* distinguished for their high order of devotion, knowledge, and asceticism (*bhaktijñānavairāgyalakṣaṇam*). Accordingly having installed Bharata on the throne, Lord Ṛṣabha, with only his naked body as his possession, with dishevelled hair and with the look of a maniac, renounced the world and went away from the country of the Brahmāvarta.[27] He took the vow of silence and assumed the guise of an *avadhūta*, and appeared like a *piśāca*, or like an imbecile, deaf and dumb. Wherever he would go, whether to a city or a village, or mountains or forests, wicked people, like flies assailing a wild elephant, would harass him with harsh words and inflict on him indignities, such as throwing at him stones and excreta. He did not, however, pay any attention to such torment for he had realized the unreality of this world. Thus he wandered unperturbed and alone, all over the earth. Having observed that the people were an obstruction to his practice of *yoga*, and that they could be warded off only by means of a hideous and loathsome way of life, he took up the vow of *ajagara* (residing in one place like a python?), whereby he would drink, eat, and pass excreta at the same place, and his body became covered therewith. He also followed the conduct of a cow, deer, or crow, eating, drinking, or passing urine and excreta, either while standing, sitting, or walking.[28] Thus did divine Ṛṣabha engage himself in austerities and yoga, and he considered himself at one with the Lord Vāsudeva.

He sojourned in this way in the guise of an *avadhūta*, concealing his divine nature, and wearing various dresses, observing diverse practices, and speaking various dialects. Then with a view to instructing the Yogins in the proper method of preparing themselves for death, the divine Ṛṣabha resolved to renounce his own body.[29] He desisted from all activities by realizing the identity of his individual self with the supreme self. Although he had thus renounced all actions, the body of Lord Ṛṣabha, like a potter's wheel moving of itself for some time, went of its own accord from place to place to the countries of southern Karṇāṭaka, namely Koṅka, Veṅka, and Kuṭaka. There, in the forest adjoining the Kuṭaka mountain, Lord Ṛṣabha wandered like a maniac with his body naked, his hair dishevelled, and his mouth filled with a stone. At that time a dreadful forest fire, kindled by the clashing of bamboos felled by a terrible wind, engulfed the entire forest and burnt down the body of the divine Ṛṣabha.[30]

The foregoing account has much in common with the Jain legend of Ṛṣabha. Both trace his lineage to Nābhi, the son of a *kulakara* in the Jain account and of a Manu in the *Bhāgavatapurāṇa*. The latter does not refer to the innovations introduced by Ṛṣabha as believed by the Jains, but uses the word *karamakṣetra* comparable to the Jain term *karmabhūmi*. Both accounts proclaim Bharata as the eldest of the 100 sons, and also as the originator of the name Bhāratavarṣa. The episodes of Ṛṣabha's sermon on renunciation and the subsequent admonition to his sons to serve Bharata seem to echo the more plausible Jain account.[31] In the latter, Bharata is bent upon the policy of conquest and demands submission of his brothers. Offended, they approach their father—now a Jina—for justice, who preaches the virtues of renunciation and receives them in his order of *śramaṇas*. The description of Ṛṣabha as an *avadhūta*, particularly the repeated references to his nakedness and the dishevelled hair, suggest some familiarity on the part of the author of the *Bhāgavatapurāṇa* with the images of this *tīrthaṅkara* referred to above. The accounts of the cruel indignities which Ṛṣabha is made to suffer in the *Bhāgavatapurāṇa* are no doubt missing in the Jain sources; yet they compare well with similar torments suffered by Mahāvīra, as described in the *Ācārāṅga*,[32] prior to his attainment of the *kevalajñāna*. The Jains will emphatically reject the various 'hideous' vows (e.g. the *ajagaravrata*) attributed to Ṛṣabha since they condemn these practices as *mithyāvratas*, unbecoming of a Jain *śramaṇa*. Even so, there is enough of the 'hideous' in the practices of a Jain monk (e.g. the prohibition against bathing and brushing one's teeth) to allow a non-Jain author to introduce those vows in the life of a recluse. The Jain will also not agree that Ṛṣabha (or any Jina for that matter on account of his exalted state) could meet his death in the manner described above. Yet, the Jain veneration for the practice of *sallekhanā* (voluntary death by fasting)[33] is so well-known that the author of the *Bhāgavatapurāṇa* might consider it legitimate to apply it to the life of so great a saint as Ṛṣabha.

What distinguished the *Bhāgavata* legend is the glorification of the Brahman caste through Ṛṣabha, conspicious by its absence in the Jain account. The Lord Viṣṇu agrees to be born as the son of Nābhi to make sure that the words of the *ṛtviks* are not made futile as they are his mouth. Ṛṣabha himself is cast in the mould of an ideal king following the *āśrama* order. It is emphasized that he rules according to the laws laid down by the Brahmans and even performs 100 sacrifices complete in all respects. Of his 100 sons who are all Kṣatriyas by birth, 81 'become' Brahmans and engage themselves in the activities of a *śrotriya*. Even when Ṛṣabha admonishes his sons to serve Bharata, or praises the ideal of renunciation, he must be made to glorify the Brahmans by declaring that they are higher even than the supreme spirit, and that feeding them is more pleasing to the Lord than the *agnihotra*.

The declared purpose of the Ṛṣabhāvatāra, viz. the teaching of the *dharma* to the naked and celibate *śramaṇas*, or teaching the Yogins the exalted path of the *paramahaṃsa*, is in no way served by this repeated glorification of the Brahmans. One cannot fail to suspect here a deliberate attempt on the part of the author of the *Bhāgavatapurāṇa* to demonstrate to the followers of Ṛṣabha that their traditional anti-Brahmanism was quite inconsistent with the extraordinary devotion of their great saint to the Brahmans, and also his lavish patronage of the Vedic sacrifices. The *śramaṇas* had persisted in making exclusive claims to the role of being omniscient saviours or *tīrthaṅkaras*, who alone showed the true path of renunciation. The *Ṛṣabhāvatāra* appears to be a challenge of the Brahmans to this *śramaṇa* claim. The teacherhood of Ṛṣabha was not denied; indeed it was reaffirmed as if by an offical sanction. But it was made abundantly clear that he was a teacher not because of his alleged omniscience, but because he was an *avatāra* of the Brāhmaṇical deity, the prime source of all knowledge, particularly that of salvation. The 'avatārization' of Ṛṣabha was facilitated by the undeniable fact that the *avadhūta* cult had always flourished among the ascetic order, irrespective of their Śramaṇite, Vaiṣṇavite, or Śaivite persuasion. The creed of the naked ascetics leading celibate lives engaged in Yogic trances was known even to the Vedas as is evidenced by the *Keśisūkta* of the tenth book of the *Ṛgveda* (x, 136). Indeed the words *vātaraśanānām munīnām* of the *Bhāgavatapurāṇa* are directly borrowed from the second verse of this *sūkta*:

múnayo vấtaraśanāḥ piśáṅgā vasate málā/
vấtasyánu dhrấjiṃ yanti yád deváso ấvikṣata//

It must, however, be noted that neither in this nor in any other Vedic hymn is the word *śramaṇa* linked with the *vātaraśana-munis*. As a matter of fact, the word *śramaṇa* is not encountered until the time of the *Śatapatha Brāhmaṇa* (14.7.1.22=*Bṛhadāraṇyaka Upaniṣad* 4.3.22) and the term *paramahaṃsa* is of still later date. As for the name Ṛṣabha, it is interesting to note that it is not included in the list of seven *ṛṣis* (viz. Jūti, Vātajūti, Viprajūti, Vṛṣāṇaka, Karikrata, Etasá, and Ṛṣyaśṛṅga) enumerated by Sāyaṇa as the respective authors of the seven verses of the *Keśisūkta*. The Ṛgveda has three hymns—III, 13 and 14 addressed to Agni, and IX, 71 to Pavamāna Soma—credited to a seer named Ṛṣabha; but he is a son of Viśvāmitra (*Ṛṣabho Vaiśvāmitraḥ*), a detail missing in the account of the *Bhāgavatapurāṇa*, and his hymns have no connexions whatsoever with asceticism. The word *ṛṣabha* is no doubt of common occurrence in the Vedic hymns; but contrary to the belief of many modern Jain apologists,[34] there is no conclusive evidence to show that it was ever used as a substantive or as a name of a person. It appears highly probable therefore that it was the author of the *Bhāgavatapurāṇa* who with great ingenuity brought the three terms (*Vātaraśanā munayaḥ, śramaṇa*, and *paramahaṃsa*) together and applied them with considerable advantage to the life of Ṛṣabha who was widely worshipped among the *śramaṇas* of his time.

It is not difficult to identify these *śramaṇas* of the *Bhāgavatapurāṇa*. They could not have been the Buddhists for the simple reason that Ṛṣabha (notwithstanding a stray reference to that name in the *Mahāvastu*, ed. Senart, I, p. 137, 1.2) was not one of their saints. The *Bhāgavata* version of Ṛṣabha's death with a stone in his mouth (an indulgence not allowed by the Jain monastic rules) might suggest that this one motif derives from the sect of the Ājīvikas whose leader Makkhali Gosāla while on his deathbed is reputed to have held a mango stone in his mouth.[35] But there is no evidence that the Ājīvikas ever worshipped Ṛṣabha as one of their teachers, and the sect was by this time moribund. This leaves only the Jains, the only *śramaṇa* school that survived in India, who worshipped Ṛṣabha even more than they worshipped their last *tīrthaṅkara* Mahāvīra, and whose lay devotees occupied seats of power in the Deccan and Karṇāṭaka at the time of the composition of the *Bhāgavatapurāṇa*.

Indeed, there is no great mystery hiding the identity of the Jains as the *śramaṇas* of the *Bhāgavatapurāṇa*. The latter makes it almost explicit in the following invectives presented as a prophecy with which it concludes the story of the *Ṛṣabhāvatāra*.

'When the King of Koṅka, Veṅka, and Kuṭaka, called Arhat, comes to hear of this conduct of the divine Ṛṣabhadeva, he too will give himself over to it. Indeed, since irreligion will thrive in the Kali age, the king, confounded by inevitable fate, will abandon the security of his religion and in consequence of his deluded understanding will promote the heretical and evil ways of the *Pākhaṇḍas*.

It is for this reason that villainous people, confounded by the illusion-provoking power of God, will forsake the duties of purity and good conduct that are enjoined upon them and take up at will wicked vows that mock the gods, such as not bathing, not rinsing their mouths, non-purity and pulling out their hair. With their understanding thus corrupted by the irreligion-rife Kali age, they will forever deride Brahman, the Brahmans, the Lord of the sacrifice, and other people. Then, having placed their trust in the blind man's leading a blind man that is the maintenance of one's own world by upstart non-vedic rites, they will themselves fall into the blind darkness of hell.

This incarnation has the purpose of helping those who abound in the quality of *rajas* to obtain salvation, and many verses are sung in its praise.'[36]

These imprecations confirm the astute observation made by the celebrated grammarian Patañjali (150 B.C.) that the *śramaṇas* and the Brahmans are 'eternal enemies' like the snake and mongoose.[37] The *Bhāgavatapurāṇa,* as noticed by Wilson,[38] is most probably following here the lead given by the *Viṣṇupurāṇa* which brackets all the heretic schools (viz. the Jains, the Buddhists, and the Cārvākas) and condemns them together for their cpposition to the Vedas, the Brahmans, and the sacrifices. However, the *Viṣṇupurāṇa* nowhere mentions the heretic teachers by their names, and certainly does not call them the *avatāras* of Viṣṇu. Instead it describes these anonymous teachers as 'fraudulent devices" employed by the Lord to misguide the *asuras* and wean them away from the Vedic path.[39] What distinguishes the *Bhāgavatapurāṇa* is that it persists in imprecating the *śramaṇas* (particularly the Jains) while it elevates one of their great teachers, viz. Ṛṣabha, to the status of an *avatāra.* An inquiry into the circumstances which might have led the proponents of the Bhāgavata cult to assert the 'divinity' of a *śramaṇa* teacher, particularly of Ṛṣabha, is of considerable interest for a study of the mutual borrowing of two distinct and rival faiths.

If the *Buddhāvatāra* was any precedent, then Mahāvīra, a contemporary of the Buddha and the last of the 24 *tīrthaṅkaras,* should have been the natural choice for a '*Jināvatāra*'. Yet the author of the *Bhāgavatapurāṇa* chose to give a prehistoric figure like Ṛṣabha precedence over Mahāvīra. The latter is hardly ever mentioned in any Brāhmaṇical scriptures including the Epics and the Purāṇas. Presumably Mahāvīra, on account of his adherence to the theory of the soul (*ātman*), was much less hostile to the Vedic tradition than the *anātmavādin* Buddha, and consequently less well-known. Even among his followers, there never was an exclusive cult of Mahāvīra, for it is well-known that even during his lifetime he was worshipped together with Pārśva (the twenty-third *tīrthaṅkara* according to the tradition) who preceded him by some 250 years. The same thing cannot be said of Gautama the Buddha. There is, no doubt, a Buddhist tradition, authenticated by the Niglīvā pillar edict of Aśoka (pertaining to the Buddha Koṇāgamana), which speaks of six and, at a later date, of even 24 Buddhas who preceded the historical Gautama, the Buddha. But unlike Mahāvīra Gautama was, and has always been, considered supreme in the hierarchy of the Buddhist pantheon of Buddhas and Bodhisattvas. On the other hand, the *tīrthaṅkara* Ṛṣabha of the Jains has much in common with the Buddha Dīpaṅkara, the first of the 25 Buddhas of the present age. The latter according to the *Buddhavaṃsa* also appeared at the beginning of the new age and was the first to renounce the world and to show the path of *nirvāṇa*. Both are credited with having been the first teachers of the last of the saints of their respective traditions. Thus Dīpaṅkara is said to have initiated into the *bodhisattva* path a young Brahman named Sumedha, the future Siddhārtha Gautama. Similarly, Ṛṣabha is said to have made the prophecy that Marīci (a son of Bharata) would become the last *tīrthaṅkara* and would be known as Mahāvīra.[40] In fact the legendary biographies of Gautama and Mahāvīra begin with the narration of their births as Sumedha and Marīci respectively.[41] In view of their relationship (of a *śāstṛ* and *śiṣya*), Dīpaṅkara would be expected to occupy a position higher than his (once) disciple Gautama. This is not, however, borne out by the Buddhist tradition where Dīpaṅkara remains a minor figure, and is practically unknown to the Brāhmaṇical world. By contrast, Ṛṣabha comes to be given a higher status among his equals (the remaining *tīrthaṅkaras*), a special kind of image is reserved for depicting him and his illustrious son Bāhubalī,[41] the younger brother of Bharata, and he is chosen by a rival faith for the distinction of an *avatāra*.

It must, however, be noted that the prominence given to Ṛṣabha even among the Jains is of a much later date than that of their canonical literature. The extant canonical texts (e.g. the *Kalpasūtra*) contain only the descriptions of the five traditionally auspicious occasions of his life (viz. the conception, birth, renunciation, enlightenment, and *nirvāṇa*) and a few significant statements to the effect that he was the first king, the first anchorite, the first omniscient being, and the first *tīrthaṅkara*. The other details of his life, as noted above, or of his son Bharata which will follow, are to be found only in the commentaries beginning with the *Āvaśyaka-niryukti* of Bhadrabāhu II, written in the sixth century A.D. It is therefore not surprising that Ṛṣabha should remain unnoticed in the ancient Brāhr aṇical literature, including the

Mahābhārata. Nor is it likely that Bhadrabāhu's narration would draw the attention of the Brahmans to the legend of Ṛṣabha. Firstly, the account is in Prakrit and appears in a commentary on a text called *Āvaśyaka,* used primarily by Jain monks in their daily ritual and hence not easily accessible to the public abroad. Secondly, there is nothing polemical in the whole account which could have offended a votary of the *Bhāgavata* cult.

The imprecations quoted above leave no doubt that the author of the *Bhāgavatapurāṇa* had before him a hostile community of the devotees of Ṛṣabha which had sought to usurp the traditional role of the Brahmans, under the patronage of a king of Karṇāṭaka, presumably a convert to the Jain faith. Of course there never was a king named Arhat as the author of the *Bhāgavatapurāṇa* would have us believe. The word *arhat* is a synonym for a Jain saint. But this does not preclude the possibility of a real king who was a Jain and who might have patronized the Jains much to the chagrin of the Brahmans of South India where the *Bhāgavatapurāṇa* is believed to have originated. The exact date of the *Bhāgavatapurāṇa* is not known, but it is now generally recognized as a work of the tenth or the early eleventh century A.D. Although the Jain inscriptions of this period claim a large number of patrons among the rulers of Karṇāṭaka, the only person that fits the description of the heretical King Arhat of the *Bhāgavatapurāṇa* is the Rāṣṭrakūṭa King Amoghavarṣa I who ruled from Mānyakheṭa in the ninth century (A.D. 814-77).[42] It was under the patronage of this Jain king, an apostate from his traditional Vaiṣṇava faith, that Ācārya Jinasena[43]—himself a Digambara *muni*—wrote his epoch-making *Ādipurāṇa* on the life of Ṛṣabha and his son Bharata. It is highly probable that this work was an important source of the *Bhāgavatapurāṇa.*

Through this voluminous Purāṇa, Jinasena not only criticized the Brāhmaṇical doctrine of the creator and his creation (*īśvarakartṛtvavāda*), but openly challenged the authority of the Vedic scriptures, rejected the divinity of the Vedic gods, repudiated the efficacy of the Brāhmaṇical rites and rituals, and above all ridiculed the claim of the Brahmans to a superior social rank. Exploiting fully the rich potentialities in the legend of Ṛṣabha, the first *sarvajña* (omniscient one), Jinasena sought, as it were, to write a new history of the world, presided over by a Jain Brahmā, who pronounced a set of Jain Vedas, instituted a Jain division of the castes and duties, and proclaimed a series of Jain *saṃskāras* complete with Jain rites and litany. Of course, this was not the Brāhmaṇical Brahmā who in the words of Jinasena 'had made an ass of himself by desiring his own daughter Sarasvatī'—an incest acknowledged by the Purāṇas—but the Lord Ṛṣabha who had attained the true Brahman, viz. Omniscience. Having thus asserted the 'divinity' of this exalted human being, Jinasena proceeds to appropriate for Ṛṣabha the choicest words of praise hitherto reserved for the Brahmā of Hindu mythology.[44] Ṛṣabha is *hiraṇya-garbha* as there was a shower of gold at the time of his conception. He is *prajāpati, vidhātṛ,* and *sraṣṭṛ* as he was the first king, the first to invent fire and the means of livelihood, and the first to devise the social structure suitable for *karmakṣetra.* He is *svayambhū* as his spiritual 'rebirth' did not depend upon the instruction of any teacher; he was self-taught. He is also the *purāṇapuruṣa* or the primordial man, as he was the first to realize perfection, and *sahasrākṣa* and *viśvataścakṣuḥ* as he perceived everything by his omniscience. In short, he was to be called the Ādideva or the First Lord, the founder of human civilization and the dispenser of the laws both secular and spiritual. As if he was anticipating the 'avatārization' of his hero, Jinasena further calls him Acyuta (a name of Viṣṇu) or immovable, a sign of being a *vītarāga.* He is also described as *trinetra, bhavāntaka,* and *yogīśvara,* titles especially applicable to Śiva. It is interesting to note in this connexion that Jinasena applies to the *digambara* Ṛṣabha the Vedic term *vātaraśana,* and characterizes his disciples as *munayo vātarśanāḥ,*[45] manifestly a quotation from the *Keśisūkta* of the *Ṛgveda,* which might have suggested the idea of a new *avatāra* to the author of the *Bhāgavatapurāṇa.* Having thus invested Ṛṣabha with the divinity of the Hindu trinity, without of course making him either the creator, the sustainer, or the destroyer, Jinasena claims that the Vedas are not what the Brahmans chant at the slaughter of the sacrificial animals, but the *Dvādaśāṅgapravacana* or the scripture of the Jains, pronouced by the *Ādideva.*[46] As for the castes, they had no divine origin at all. According to Jinasena there is only one *jāti* called the *manuṣyajāti* or the human caste, but divisions arise on account of their different professions.[47] The caste of the Kṣatriyas came to be established when Ṛṣabha assumed the powers of a king and held weapons in his arms. The Vaiśya and the Śudra castes arose subsequently as he invented different means of livelihood and people were trained in diverse arts and crafts.

The Jain accounts unanimously declare that the caste of the Brahmans was not instituted by Ṛṣabha but by his son Bharata, the first *cakravartin.*[48] This agrees well with the Jain scheme according to which only those members of the first three castes (*kṣatriya, vaiśya,* and *śūdra*) who were initiates in the five vows of a layman (*aṇuvratas*) were entitled to be called *dvijas* or the 'twice-born'. The formation of a class of such initiates would be possible only after the founding of the order (*saṅgha*) of the *śrāvakas* or the laity by the *tīrthaṅkara* Ṛṣabha. The Prakrit commentaries on the *Āvaśyaka* take recourse to a folk etymology to explain the origin of the word *māhaṇa* (Sanskrit *brāhmaṇa*). It is said that Bharata on his return from his world conquest wished to share his wealth with his brothers who had already become ascetics in the monastic order of Ṛṣabha. Bharata approached them with a cart load of food and other gifts, but was grieved to hear that Jain ascetics could not partake of food specially prepared for them (*uddiṣṭa-āhāratyāga*). Since it is wrong for householders to receive alms thus freely given, Indra the king of gods suggested to Bharata that the food might be offered to the virtuous initiates who had taken the *aṇuvratas* of a householder. Bharata gratefully fed them and invited them to have their meals for ever at his place. Henceforth they were to forsake other means of livelihood which involved *hiṃsā* (e.g. tilling, etc.) and engage themselves in activities like the study and teaching of the scriptures, worship of the Jina, etc. They kept vigil on the king's conduct by reminding him 'you are conquered (by the passions); fear increases, therefore do not kill, do not kill (*mā haṇa*). They thus came to be called the *māhaṇas* or the Brahmans.[49]

Fanciful as it is, the explanation is indicative of what the Jains expected of a Brahman and why they would support the widespread custom of feeding Brahman householders. Jinasena ignores the word *brāhmaṇa* and concentrates on the term *dvija* which affords him a chance to describe in great detail (XXXVIII-XLII, in all 1, 113 *ślokas*) the corpus of 98 *saṃskāras* (sanctifying ceremonies) together with their prescribed rites, the performance of one which, called the *upanīti* (initiation) conferred upon an ordinary man the status of a 'twice-born'. There is no mention of the feeding of the Brahmans in the account of the *Ādipurāṇa.*

Instead, Bharata wished to find out the true initiates and devised a way of testing their devotion. He deliberately had the courtyard of his palace strewn with fresh flowers and sprouting grain and invited the citizens for a feast on a sacred day. Those who were careless in the observance of their vows walked across the courtyard disregarding the life in the vegetable kingdom. Those who were virtuous did not enter the palace lest they should destroy the subtle life and thus infringe their vow of non-violence. Bharata had them invited by a suitable path, honoured them, and encouraged them to accept one or more of the 11 stages of spiritual progress (*pratimā*) which would bring them close to the discipline of a monk. In recognition of their new status (*varṇalābha*) he conferred upon them the title of *dvija* and confirmed it by investing them with sacred threads (*yajñopavīta*) which indicated the number of *pratimās* they had assumed.[50]

Speaking of such *dvijas*, Jinasena states that these indeed are the true children of Jina and deserve to be called *devabrāhmaṇas*, the divine Brahmans worthy of worship. Anticipating a hostile reaction from the traditional Brahmans to this creed of a 'Jain Brahman', Jinasena adds:

'Now should a so-called Brahman through his vanity of birth confront him [a Jain Brahman] and say: "Well sir, did you become a god today all of a sudden? Are you not the son of so-and-so, is not your mother the daughter of so-and-so, that you should put your nose in the air and dare to walk about disregarding a person like me? What great miracle happened to you by your initiation into the Jain order?—you still walk on the earth and not in the sky!". Let him be told: "Please listen, you so-called Brahman, to our divine origin. Lord Jina is our father, and his pure knowledge is our womb. We are therefore truly born as gods, but if you find others of similar description, be free to call them also by the same title"'.[51]

Returning to the narrative, we learn that after a long time had passed it occurred to Bharata that it was wrong of him to have instituted a caste of the 'twice-born' without first obtaining the advice of the Lord Ṛṣabha. He therefore approached him and said:

'Sir, I have created a class of twice-born, the best among the householders who follow the rules laid down by you for the laity. I have also invested them with sacred threads, the sign of their vows, according to the stages of their spiritual progress (*guṇa-karma-vibhāgaśaḥ*). It was indeed childish of me, O Lord, that I should have presumed to do this while the Lord was still present with us. May the Lord please tell me if it was opportune and also point out to me the virtues and vices of this caste'.[52]

The answer as given in the *Ādipurāṇa* can almost be anticipated. It is one more prophecy of the evil things to follow, not altogether different either in spirit or in letter from the one we have encountered above in the *Bhāgavatapurāṇa.*

'O Son, that which has been done is good indeed, and moreover, the worship of pious Brahmans is good too. However, there will be some harmful consequences about which you must be informed. You have created the Brahman class, who will be righteous teachers as long as the Kṛta age endures, but when the Kali age draws near there will be backsliding teachers who, out of arrogance of their high birth, will embrace the very opposite of the right path. These people, full of the arrogance of their rank, will claim to be most excellent among men and soon, hankering after wealth, will delude the world with their false scriptures. The favoured treatment which they will enjoy will increase their presumptuousness and make them puffed up with a false pride, so that they will lead men astray as they themselves fashion false religious treatises.

They will be so short-sighted in that they will promote changes for the worse at the end of the age, and, their minds clouded by evil, they will become foes of religion. As they delight in injury to life and relish eating of honey and meat these wicked people will, alas, promote the *dharma* of action, and full of evil hopes, corrupt the *dharma* of non-violence in favour of the *dharma* of injuctions (*codanā*). As the Yuga progresses there will be rogues blasphemously wearing the sacred thread and eagerly engaged in the killing of life, thereby obstructing the right path.

Therefore, although the creation of the Brahman class is not of itself harmful today, it does contain the seed of harm as yet buried in the future, because impious heretics will be ushered forth. Nevertheless, although this seed of harm is truly there for the end of the age, there is no cause for removing it at present for you have not transgressed against the nature of dharma'.[53]

The 'Jainization' of Brahmā in the person of Ṛṣabha and the consequent 'Vaiṣṇavization' of the Jina through the device of the *avatāra* is a fine example of a vain drive towards the syncretism of two rival faiths. The waves of the *bhakti* movement that had swept over the whole range of Indian life finally overtook the atheist Jains and forced them to deify, as it were, their human *tīrthaṅkaras* or face the peril of extinction. Probably the move brought to the surface the emotional hunger of the Jain laity for an object of worship more gracious and glamorous than merely the austere figure of an exalted human teacher. Jinasena very skilfully provided the Jain laity with a new identity of a specially honoured caste of 'neo-Brahmans', a new book of codes in the guise of his Purāṇa, and a new image of the Jina endowed with a grandeur and majesty that could easily compete with the Hindu trinity. To be sure, the *tīrthaṅkaras,* like the Buddha of the Pali canon, had always been surrounded by heavenly attendants like Indra and Kubera who made special appearances on the five great occasions like the *kalyāṇakas.* But the new Jina was to be endowed with additional miraculous powers (*prātihāryas*) attesting to his newly acquired 'divinity'. He sits immobilized, as it were, on a lotus seat in the middle of a circular assembly called *samavasaraṇa* specially designed by the gods and is miraculously visible on all four sides. He is free from hunger and thirst, fatigue and sleep, and remains totally engrossed in the bliss of his omniscience. There is no actual preaching of a sermon. Yet an involuntary resonant sound (*divyadhvani*) of the *Oṃ* proceeds from his mouth answering all questions simultaneously to the satisfaction of the audience.[54] Indeed the Jina of the *Ādipurāṇa* has much in common with the latter-day Buddha of the *Lalitavistara.* Yet, unlike the latter whose new image was a result of a new doctrine of the three bodies (*trikāya*), the 'divinity' of the Jina was purely adventitious, unwarranted by the doctrine, imposed externally by the devout. The informed Jains were as much impressed by this superfluous accretion as the *Bhāgavatas* were by the *Ṛṣabhāvatāra.* For the Jina Ṛṣabha remained essentially a 'sky-clad' human being, his glory consisting exclusively in omniscience,[55] a distinction denied by the Jains to Brahmā, Śiva, or Viṣṇu or to one of his manifold *avatāras* whose volatile careers clearly exhibited their subjection to passions and disqualified them as the teachers of truth. Akalaṅka, a celebrated tenth-century logician, sums up the Jain search for a true God in his famous *stotra*[56] to a Jina.

'They call him Brahmā,
Yet his mind was filled
with passion for Urvaśī the nymph.
Behold him move with a bowl for food,
and a gourd for water!
Himself a disciple,
What can he teach an ascetic like me?

My Brahmā is the one
devoid of the heat of passion
free from hunger and thirst,
pure and perfect.'[57]

'They call him Śiva (the auspicious) and say:
"He has burnt to ashes the three worlds
with blazing fire of anger kindled by the Lord of Love,
he dances like a maniac
on the burning grounds of cemeteries,
has a son—the great Guha,
the commander of the gods' armies".

What is he to me?
Śaṅkara for me is the one
who has extinguished all fear,
lust, delusion, sorrow and anger,
the all-knower, the bringer of peace to all'.[58]

'They call him Viṣṇu (the all-pervasive) and say:
"He is the one who with mere fingernails
forcefully tore the chest of the lord of the demons,
and wrought the destruction of the Kauravas
by charioteering for Arjuna in the Great War."

Not for me is he a Viṣṇu:
The great Viṣṇu is he alone, the omniscient one,
whose infinite knowledge
pervades the entire world of knowables,
unimpeded by time and space.'[59]

'Whoever knows all that is to be known,
And sees beyond the billowing ocean of births,
Whose words, not marred by inconsistencies,
Stand supreme in truthful purity,
Such a man do I revere, beholding in him
One worthy of exceeding reverence, vessel of virtues,
In whom the taint of hatred is effaced:
Whether Buddha or Mahāvīra, Brahmā, Viṣṇu, or Śiva.'[60]

NOTES

1. See J. Dowson, *A Classical Dictionary of Hindu Mythology*, eleventh ed. (repr.), London, 1968, 34-5.
2. *Śrīmad Bhāgavata* [henceforth *Bhāg.*] VI, viii, 13-19 (Gītā Press).
3. *Bhagavadgītā*, IV, 7-8.
4. See P. S. Jaini, 'Śramaṇas: Their Conflict with Brāhmaṇical Society', in J. W. Elder (ed.), *Chapters in Indian Civilization*, I, Dubuque, Iowa, Kendell/Hunt, 1970, 41-81.
5. XII, 46, 107.
6. I, 1, 9.
7. *Bhāg.* V, iii-vii.
8. ...dharmān darśayitukāmo vātaraśanānāṃ śramaṇānām ṛsīṇām ūrdhvamanthināṃ śuklayā tanuvāvatatāra. [*Bhāg.* V, iii, 20]
9. *Kalpasūtra*, tr. H. Jacobi, SBE, XXII, 1884, 281-5. Also W. Norman Brown, *A descriptive and illustrative catalogue of miniature paintings of the Jaina Kalpasūtra*, Washington, D. C., 1934.
10. Together with *Vṛtti* by Śānticandra, Bombay edition, 1920.
11. *Ādipurāṇa* (parts 1 and 2), Sanskrit text with Hindi tr. by Pannalal Jain, Kashi, Bhāratīya Jñānapīṭha, 1963-5.
12. Tr. by Helen M. Johnson, GOS, LI, 1931. (Henceforth called *Triṣaṣṭi.*)
13. C. R. Jain's *Ṛṣabha Deva* (in English), Delhi, 1929, and Devendra Muni's *Ṛṣabhadeva: Ek pariśīlan* (in Hindi), Agra, 1967, summarize respectively the Digambara and the Śvetāmbara traditions. I am indebted to Devendra's work for references to several commentaries on the *Āvaśyaka.*
14. This account is missing in the Digambara tradition. See Devendra, 69.
15. *Ādipurāṇa*, XVI, 179 ff.
16. *Triṣaṣṭi*, 178.
17. *Kalpasūtra*, 284.
18. E.g. H. H. Wilson, The *Viṣṇupurāṇa*, London, 1840, 133.
19. The story of Priyavrata is not found in the *Viṣṇupurāṇa.*
20. aho batāyam ṛṣayo bhavadbhir avitathagīrbhir varam asulabham abhiyācito yad amuṣyātamajo mayā sadṛśo bhūyād iti. mamāham evābhirūpaḥ kaivalyād athāpi brahmavādo na mṛsā bhavitum arhatīti mamaiva hi mukhaṃ yad dvijadevakulam. tata Āgnīdhrīye 'ṃśakalayā 'vatariṣyāmy ātmatulyam anupalabhamānaḥ. iti niśāmayantyā Merudevyāḥ patim abhidhāyāntardadhe Bhagavān. barhiṣi tasminn eva Viṣṇudatta Bhagavān paramarṣibhiḥ prasādito

Nābheḥ priyacikīrṣayā tad avarodhāyane Merudevyāṃ dharmān darśayitukāmo vātaraśanānāṃ śramaṇānām ṛṣīnām ūrdhvamanthināṃ śuklayā tanuvāvatatāra. [*Bhāg.*, V, iii 17-20]

21. atha ha bhagavān Ṛṣabhadevaḥ svavarṣaṃ karmakṣetram anumanyamānaḥ. [*Ibid.*, V, iv, 8]
22. yeṣāṃ khalu mahāyogī Bharato jyeṣṭaḥ śreṣṭhaguṇa āsīd yenedaṃ varṣaṃ Bhāratam iti vyapadiśanti. [*Ibid.*, V, iv, 9]
23. yavīyāṃśa ekāśītir Jāyanteyāḥ pitur ādeśakarā mahāśālīnā mahāśrotrīyā yajñaśīlāḥ karmaviśuddhā brāhmaṇā babhūvuḥ. [*Ibid.*, V, iv, 13]
24. yady api svaviditaṃ sakaladharmaṃ brahmaṃ guhyaṃ brāhmaṇair darśitamārgeṇa sāmādibhir upāyair janatām anuśaśāsa... upacitaiḥ sarvair api kratubhir yathopadeśaṃ śatakṛtva iyāja. [*Ibid.*, V, iv, 16-17]
25. *Bhāg.*, V, v, 1-27.
26. . . , Bhavaḥ paraḥ so 'tha Viriñcivīryaḥ
sa matparo 'haṃ dvijadevadevaḥ//
na brāhmaṇais tulaye bhūtam anyat
paśyāmi viprāḥ kim ataḥ paraṃ tu/
yasmin nṛbhiḥ prahutaṃ śraddhayāhaṃ
aśanāmi kāmaṃ na tathā 'gnihotre // [*Ibid.*, V, v, 22-3]
27. upaśamaśīlānām uparatakarmaṇāṃ mahāmunīnāṃ bhaktijñāna-vairāgyalakṣaṇaṃ pāramahaṃsyadharmaṃ upśikṣamāṇaḥ . . . urvaritaśarīramātraparigraha unmatta iva gaganaparidhānaḥ prakīrṇakeśa ātmany adhyāropitāhavanīyo Brahmāvartāt pravarāja. jaḍāndhamūka-baḍhirapiśāconmādakavad avadhūtaveśo 'bhibhāṣyamāṇo 'pi janānāṃ gṛhītamaunavratas tūṣṇīṃ babhūva. [*Ibid.*, V, v, 28-9]
28. anupatham avanicarāpasadaiḥ paribhūyamāno makṣikābhir iva vanagajas tarjanatāḍanāvamehanaṣṭhīvanagrāvaśakṛdrajaḥprakṣepapūtivātaduruktaiḥ ... kuṭilajaṭilakapiśakeśabhūribhāro 'vadhūtamalinanijaśarīreṇa grahagṛhīta ivādṛśyata. yena ha vāva sa bhagavān lokam imaṃ yogasyāddhā pratīpam ivācakṣāṇaḥ tatpratikriyākarma bībhatsitam iti vratam ajagaram āsthitaḥ śayāna evāśnāti khādaty avmehati hadati sma . . . evaṃ gomṛgakākacaryayā. . .. [*Ibid.*, V, v, 30-40]
29. athaivam akhilalokapālalalāmo 'pi vilakṣaṇair jaḍavad avadhūtaveṣabhāṣācaritair avilakṣitabhagavatprabhāvo yogināṃ sāmparāyavidhim anuśikṣyan svakalevaraṃ jihāsuḥ . . . uparatānuvṛttir upararāma. [*Ibid.*, V, vi, 6]
30. tasya ha vā evaṃ muktaliṅgasya bhagavata Ṛṣabhasya yogamāyāvāsanayā deha imāṃ jagatīm abhimānābhāsena saṃkramamāṇaḥ Koṅka-Veṅka-Kuṭakān dakṣiṇa-Karṇāṭakān deśān yadṛcchayopagatḥ Kuṭakācalopavana āsyakṛtāśmakavala unmāda iva muktamūrdhajo 'saṃvīta eva vicacāra. atha samīravegavidhūtaveṇuvikarṣanajātogradāvānalas tadvanam ālelihānaḥ saha tena dadāha. [*Ibid.*, V, vi, 7-8]
31. *Ādipurāṇa*, XXXIV, 93-156.
32. *Ācārāṅga*: Jacobi, SBE, XXII, 1884, 79-87.
33. *On sallekhanā* see R. Williams, *Jaina Yoga*, London, 1963, 166 ff.
34. E.g. Hiralal Jain, *Bhāratīya saṃskṛti mē Jainadharma kā yogadān*, Bhopal, 1962, 15 ff.
35. See A. L. Basham, *History and Doctrines of the Ājīvikas*, London, 1951, 63.
36. yasya kilānucaritam upākarṇya Koṅka-Veṅka-Kuṭakānāṃ rājā 'rahan

nāmopaśikṣya kalāv adharma utkṛṣyamāṇe bhavitavyena vimohitaḥ svadharmapatham akutobhayam apahāya kupathapākhaṇḍam asamañjasaṃ nijamanīṣayā mandaḥ sampravartayiṣyate. yena ha vāva kalau manujāpasadā devamāyāmohitāḥ svavidhiniyogaśaucacāritravihīnā devahelanāny apavratāni nijanijecchayā gṛhṇānā asnānānācamanāśaucakeśolluñcanādīni kalinā 'dharmabahulenopahatadhiyo brahmabrāhmaṇyayajñapuruṣalokavidūṣakāḥ prāyeṇa bhaviṣyanti. te ca hy arvāktanayā nijalokayātrayā 'ndhaparamparayā āśvastās tamasy andhe svayam eva prapatiṣyani. ayamavatāro rajasopaplutakaivalyopaśikṣaṇārthaḥ .... [*Bhāg.*, V, vi, 9-11]

37. F. Kielhorn, *Vyākaraṇa Mahābhaṣya of Patañjali,* Bombay, 1892, I, 476.
38. The *Viṣṇupurāṇa,* 133, n. 7.
39. *Ibid.*, XVIII.
40. *Triṣaṣti,* I, 353 ff.
41. Also called Gommaṭeśvara. See Fergusson, *History of Indian and Eastern Architecture,* London, 1891, 267 ff., and A. L. Basham, *The Wonder That was India,* London, 1954, plate LIX.
42. See A. S. Altekar, *Rāṣṭrakūṭas and Their Times,* second ed., Poona, 1967.
43. *Ibid.*, 88-9.
44. See the *stotra* of 1008 names of Ṛṣabha in *Ādipurāṇa,* XXV, 99-217.
45. munayo vātaraśanāḥ padam ūrdhvaṃ vidhitsavaḥ/
tvāṃ mūrdhavandino bhūtvā tad upāyam upāsate// [*Ādipurāṇa,* II, 64]
digvāsā vātaraśano nirgrantheśo digambaraḥ/ [*Ibid.*, XXV, 204]
46. śrutaṃ suvihitaṃ vedo dvādaśāṅgam akalmaṣam/
hiṃsopadeśi yad vākyaṃ na vedo 'sau kṛtāntavāk//.
purāṇaṃ dharmaśāstraṃ ca tat syād vadhaniṣedhi yat/
vadhopadeśi yat tat tu jñeyaṃ dhūrtapraṇetṛkam// [*Ibid.*, XXXIX, 22-3]
47. manuṣyajātir ekaiva jātināmodayodbhavā/
vṛttibhedāhitād bhedāc cāturvidhyam ihāśnute// [*Ibid.*, XXXVIII, 45]
48. utpāditās trayo varṇās tadā tenādivedhasā/ [*Ibid.*, XVI, 183]
See XXXVIII which deals with *dvijanmanām utpattiḥ.*
49. *Āvaśyaka-cūrṇi and Āvaśyaka-Maladhāri-vṛtti* quoted in Devendra's *Ṛṣabhadeva,* 87-8. Also *Triṣaṣṭi,* I, 343 ff.
50. teṣāṃ kṛtāni cihnāni sūtraiḥ padmāhvayān nidheḥ/
upāttair brahmasūtrāhvair ekād ekādaśāntakaiḥ//
guṇabhūmikṛtād bhedāt kḷptayajñopavītinām/
satkāraḥ kriyate smaiṣām avratāś ca bhaiḥ kṛtāḥ//
[*Ādipurāṇa,* XXXVIII, 21-2]
51. atha jātimadāveśāt kaścid enaṃ dvijabruvaḥ/
brūyād evaṃ kim adyaiva devabhūyaṃ gato bhavān//
tvam āmuṣyāyaṇaḥ kin na kiṃ te 'mbā 'muṣya putrikā/
yenaivam unnaso bhūtvā yāsy asatkṛtya madvidhān//
jātiḥ saiva kulaṃ tac ca so 'si yo 'si pragetanaḥ/
tathāpi devatātmānam ātmānaṃ manyate bhavān//
devatātithipitragnikāryeṣvaprayato bhavān/
gurudvijātidevānāṃ praṇāmāc ca parāṅmukhaḥ//
dīkṣāṃ jainīṃ prapannasya jātaḥ ko 'tiśayas tava/
yato 'dyāpi manuṣyas tvaṃ pādacārī mahīṃ spṛśan//
ity upārūḍhasaṃrambham upālabdhaḥ sa kenacit/
dadāty uttaram ity asmai vacobhir yuktipeśelaiḥ//
śrūyatāṃ bho dvijammanya tvayā 'smad divyasambhavaḥ/

jino janayitā 'smākaṃ jñānaṃ garbho 'tinirmalaḥ//
tatrārhatīṃ tridhā bhinnāṃ śaktiṃ traiguṇyasaṃśritāṃ/
svasātkṛtya samudbhūtā vayaṃ saṃskārajanmanā//
ayonisambhavās tena devā eva na mānuṣāḥ/
vayaṃ, vayam ivānye 'pi santi cet brūhi tadvidhān//
[*Ādipurāṇa*, XXXIX, 108-16]

52. mayā sraṣṭā dvijanmānaḥ śrāvakācāracuñcavaḥ/
tvadgītopāsakādhyāyasūtramārgānugāminaḥ//
dosaḥ ko 'tra guṇaḥ ko 'tra kim etat sāmpratam na vā/
dolāyamānam iti me manaḥ sthāpaya niścitau// [*Ibid.*, XLI, 30-3]

53. sādhu vatsa kṛtaṃ sādhu dhārmikadvijapūjanaṃ/
kintu doṣānuṣṅgo 'tra ko 'py asti sa niśaṃyatām// . . .
tataḥ kaliyuge 'bhyarṇe jātivādāvalepataḥ/
bhraṣṭācārāḥ prapatsyante sanmārgapratyanīkatām//
te 'mi jātimadāviṣṭā vayaṃ lokādhikā iti/
purā durāgamair lokaṃ mohayanti dhanāśayā//. . .
ahiṃsālakṣaṇaṃ dharmaṃ dūṣayitvā durāśayāḥ/
codanālakṣṇaṃ dharmaṃ poṣayiṣyanty amī bata//
pāpasūtradharā dhūrtāḥ prāṇimāraṇatatparāḥ/
vartsyadyuge pravartsyanti sanmārgaparipanthinaḥ//
dvijātisarjanaṃ tasmān nādya yady api doṣakṛt/
syād doṣabījam āyatyāṃ kupākhaṇḍapravartanāt// [*Ibid.*, XLI, 45-54]

54. *Ādipurāṇa*, XXIV, 80-5.

55. Samantabhadra, for instance, is explicit in his praise of the Jina as the teacher of truth:
devāgamanabhoyānacāmarādivibhūtayaḥ/
māyādiṣv api dṛṣyante nātas tvam asi no mahān//
sa tvam evāsi nirdoṣo yuktiśāstrāvirodhivāk/ . . ..
[*Devāgamastotra* of Samantabhadra, 1-6. Ed. J. K. Mukhtar, Varanasi, 1967].

56. *Akalaṅkastotra* (see *Nitya-namittika-pāṭhāvalī,* Mahāvīrāśrama, Karanja, 1956).

57. Urvaśyām udapādi rāgabahulaṃ ceto yadīyaṃ punaḥ/
pātrīdaṇḍakamandaluprabhṛtayo yasyākṛtārthasthitim//
āvirbhāvayituṃ bhavanti, sa kathaṃ Brahmā bhaven mādṛśāṃ/
kṣuttṛṣṇāśramarāgarogarahito Brahmā kṛtārtho 'stu naḥ// [*Ibid.*, 4]

58. dagdhaṃ yena puratrayaṃ śarabhavā tīvrārciṣā vahninā/
yo vā nṛtyati mattavat pitṛvane yasyātmajo vā Guhaḥ//
so 'yaṃ kiṃ mama Śaṅkaro bhayatṛṣāroṣārtimohakṣayam/
kṛtvā yaḥ sa tu sarvavit tanubhṛtāṃ kṣemaṅkaraḥ Śaṅkaraḥ// [*Ibid.*, 2]

59. yatnād yena vidāritaṃ kararuhair daityendravakṣasthalaṃ/
sārathyena Dhanañjayasya samare yo 'mārayat Kauravān//
nāsau Viṣṇur anekakālaviṣayaṃ yaj jñānam avyāhatam/
viśvaṃ vyāpya vijṛmbhate sa tu Mahāviṣṇuḥ sadeṣṭo mama// [*Ibid.*, 3]

60. yo viśvaṃ veda vedyaṃ jananajalanidher bhaṅginaḥ pāradraṣṭā/
paurvāparyāviruddhaṃ vacanam anupamaṃ niṣkalaṅkaṃ yadīyam//
taṃ vande sādhuvandyaṃ sakalaguṇanidhiṃ dhvastadoṣadviṣantam/
Buddhaṃ vā Vardhamānaṃ Śatadalanilayaṃ Keśavaṃ vā Śivaṃ vā//
[*Ibid.*, 9]

CHAPTER 19

Mahābhārata Motifs in the Jaina *Pāṇḍavapurāṇa**

Judged in the context of the 18 Purāṇas, or even the 18 Upa-, or subsidiary Purāṇas, the title, *Pāṇḍavapurāṇa,* must seem unusual, since the Pāṇḍavas are neither gods nor *avatāras,* nor sages; for it is the exploits of these divine or semi-divine figures that form the subject-matter of the traditional Purāṇas. The Jainas' choice of this title would therefore appear to be a deliberate effort to present a Jaina version of the *Mahābhārata* story, a version which would show how the virtuous Pāṇḍavas and the rather harmless Balarāma are reborn in heaven, whereas Kṛṣṇa, the 'nārāyaṇa', and Jarāsandha, the 'pratinārāyaṇa',[1] are consigned to hell.

The Jainas, very early in their literary history, composed several versions of the *Harivaṃśapurāṇa,*[2] ostensibly glorifying the life of their 22nd Tīrthaṅkara, Nemi, but actually recasting the story of his celebrated elder cousin, known to the Brāhmaṇical tradition as Kṛṣṇa, an *avatāra* of Viṣṇu. But the emergence of the *Pāṇḍavapurāṇa* is a relatively later phenomenon. There are several *Pāṇḍavapurāṇas* originating in Western India, mainly in the region near Abu in the present State of Rajasthan. The earliest of these, dated A.D. 1214, is called *Pāṇḍava-Carita,*[3] by Devaprabha, a mendicant of the Śvetāmbara sect, and is a work of 9788 *ślokas* divided into 18 cantos, following Ācārya Hemacandra's (1089-1172) version of the Pāṇḍava story, as narrated in the

*This article was published originally in *Bulletin of the School of Oriental and African Studies,* Vol. XLVII, Part 1, pp. 108-115, University of London, 1984. Reprinted with kind permission of Oxford University Press.

Triṣaṣṭi-śalākā-puruṣa-caritra.[4] Devaprabha's version conforms also, in many details, to the narratives found in the *Mahābhārata*. However, towards the end of the sixteenth century, we find two *Pāṇḍavapurāṇas*, both by the clerics (Bhaṭṭāraka) of the Digambara sect, one by Śubhacandra (1552), and another by Vādicandra (1600). The former recently has been published in the Jīvarāj Jain Granthamālā Series, with a Hindi translation.[5] This work consists of 5301 *ślokas*, divided into 25 cantos and makes a great many changes (to some extent suggested by the rather brief allusion to this story in the eighth-century *Harivaṃśapurāṇa* of Punnāṭa Jinasena)[6] in the original story of the Pāṇḍavas, especially as it pertains to the genealogy of the Pāṇḍava brothers. The author of this work must have found the traditional lineage extremely abhorrent, especially in the cases of the births of Dhṛtarāṣṭra and Pāṇḍu, who were begotten on their widowed mothers by the notorious Veda-Vyāsa, himself the illegitimate child of the sage Parāśara and the fisherman's daughter Satyavatī (the grandmother of Dhṛtarāṣṭra and Pāṇḍu).

Śubhacandra, with no scruples regarding the Śvetāmbara tradition, which had somehow followed the *Mahābhārata* genealogy (as is evident from the *Triṣaṣṭi-śalākā-puruṣa-caritra* of Hemacandra), sets out to correct this abomination, as he calls it, and presents the following strictly sanitized version. Here King Śāntanu, the progenitor of the Pāṇḍavas, is married to Sevakī, whose name is not attested elsewhere.[7] Their child is Parāśara, the sage's namesake but not the sage himself. He marries Gaṅgā, and they have a child, the famous Gāṅgeya, otherwise known as Bhīṣma. King Parāśara falls in love with Guṇavatī (elsewhere known by the name Satyavatī), an orphan raised by a fisherman. He marries her and promises her that her child will inherit the kingdom. Bhīṣma, the legitimate heir to the throne, as in the story of the *Mahābhārata*, declares that he will observe the vow of celibacy, and thus facilitates the union of his father and Guṇavatī. In the *Mahābhārata* story Citrāṅgada and Vicitravīrya are born to Satyavatī, and they die young, leaving their widows with no children, thus making it necessary for Vyāsa to beget children on them. Our author completely excises the sections on the birth of these two princes; instead he declares Vyāsa to be the legitimate son of King Parāśara and Guṇavatī. Vyāsa is married to Subhadrā (no connexion with Kṛṣṇa's sister in the *Mahābhārata* story). They have three sons, Dhṛtarāṣṭra, Pāṇḍu and Vidura. Pāṇḍu has a premarital affair with Kuntī and fathers Karṇa on her. He eventually marries her and her sister Mādrī and has five sons, the Pāṇḍavas, who in this story are conceived not by gods (as in the *Mahābhārata*) but by himself. Pāṇḍu, penitent over his killing of a deer, renounces the world to become a monk, as befits a Jaina king. Dhṛtarāṣṭra (who is not blind in the Jaina version) has one hundred sons, from Gāndhārī and seven other queens, the eldest of them being the villain Duryodhana. Dhṛtarāṣṭra, too, after hearing a prophecy about the destruction of his entire family, renounces the world, placing the kingdom in the hands of Bhīṣma. He very wisely divides the kingdom between the Pāṇḍavas and the Kauravas, the former ruling from Hastināpura and the latter from Indraprastha. Duryodhana, however, resents even this and, resorting to playing dice, succeeds in winning the Pāṇḍavas' kingdom and sending the sons of Pāṇḍu into exile for 12 years. The war that takes place when they return is identical to the war in the *Mahābhārata*, but is subsumed under a larger war, namely, that of Kṛṣṇa and Jarāsandha, in which the Kauravas side with the latter. The villainous Duryodhana and his brother die in this war, and the Pāṇḍava brothers emerge victorious. Eventually they too renounce the world and, after practising great austerities, are reborn in various heavens.

Kṛṣṇa's father, as in the *Mahābhārata* story, is the brother of Kuntī, the Pāṇḍavas' mother. He helps the Pāṇḍavas win the war, just as they help him defeat his arch-enemy Jarāsandha of Magadha. But the Jaina story reduces Kṛṣṇa to human stature by totally excising the battle scene of the *Bhagavad-Gītā*[8] and also by showing Kṛṣṇa to be scheming and selfish. Śubhacandra exploits the famous Jaina story of Nemi's renunciation of the world in discrediting Kṛṣṇa as no other Jaina author had done. It is said that at the time of Nemi's marriage to Rājimatī, Kṛṣṇa had gathered animals to be slaughtered for the marriage feast. When Nemi, on his ceremonial procession to the bride's house, saw this he was overcome by pity for the animals and instantly renounced the world to become a mendicant. Śubhacandra suggests that Kṛṣṇa had imprisoned the animals in order to eliminate Nemi as a rival to the kingdom, by provoking him to renunciation.[9] Śubhacandra's narrative thus smacks of a strong sectarian antipathy not only towards the Vaiṣṇava version of the Pāṇḍava story, but even to the long-assimilated Kṛṣṇa of the Jaina Purāṇas. The foremost reason for the Jaina attempt to write a new *Pāṇḍavapurāṇa* at this late date would appear to be the sectarian animosity between the two prominent communities of Western India, namely the Vaiṣṇavas and the Jainas.

This sectarian rivalry appears to have also led to the composition of a second *Pāṇḍavapurāṇa* by Bhaṭṭāraka Vādicandra (A.D. 1600), who victimizes the Śaivas. His work has not yet been published, but I am in the process of editing the Sanskrit text consisting of some 2800 verses.[10] The first chapter of this work is extraordinary in that the author gives here a genealogy of the Pāṇḍavas, which he alleges was to be found in the [Brāhmaṇical] *Śivapurāṇa* (*Śiva-Purāṇābhimata-Pāṇḍavotpatti-varṇano nāma prathamaḥ sargaḥ/*). He expresses his outrage at this rather ignoble genealogy and promises to correct it by presenting the truthful version (*Jaina-matābhimata-Dhṛtarāṣṭra-Pāṇḍu-Vidura-sambhava-varṇano nāma*) as it was originally narrated by Mahāvīra.[11]

This alleged genealogy, which Vādicandra found in his version of *Śivapurāṇa*, is of great interest to students of the Purāṇa literature. The following episodes demand special attention:

1. In the *Mahābhārata* story Matsyagandhā (or Satyavatī) is said to have been the daughter of a king named Vasu and his queen Girikā, a water spirit.[12] She was raised by a fisherman and became the unwed mother of Veda-Vyāsa [by Parāśara] and, eventually, the legitimate wife of King Śāntanu. In our author's version of the *Śivapurāṇa* Śāntanu himself is said to have fathered Matsyagandhā. The story, in brief, is as follows: Śāntanu was once in a distant part of the kingdom. His wife (name not given), perceiving an opportune moment for conceiving a child, sent a pigeon (*rājīva*) to fetch his semen from her lord. The king emitted his seed, which he collected in a pot, and, tying the pot to the neck of that pigeon, sent it home to his wife. On the way the pigeon was attacked by another bird, the pot fell in the river, and a fish was impregnated by its contents. The child born was found by a fisherman, and, since she smelled strongly of fish, she was called Matsyagandhā. When she became mature, she was purified of her smell by the sage Parāśara, who begat Veda-Vyāsa on her.[13] After several years King Śāntanu happened to pass by that fisherman's house, and, having fallen in love with her, he sought her hand in marriage.[14] Śāntanu's marrying his own daughter

and thus committing an incestuous act unbeknown to himself is the first occasion on which Vādicandra claims to find in the *Śivapurāṇa* a major departure from the traditional version of the *Mahābhārata.*

2. Bhīṣma's famous declaration that he would renounce all rights to his kingdom, as well as his lifelong vow of celibacy, in support of that declaration is common to both the *Mahābhārata* and the Śvetāmbara-Jaina versions. Vādicandra adds here a most remarkable detail, which he claims to have found in the *Śivapurāṇa.* According to this, Bhīṣma not only took such a vow but, out of love for his father, immediately cut off his own genitals (*pitur bhaktyā sa ciccheda svaliṅgakam/*) and thus earned his name, Bhīṣma, the Terrible.[15]

3. The *Mahābhārata* story tells of the two sons born to Satyavatī and Śantanu, namely Citrāṅgada and Vicitravīrya. There they are said to have died young (apparently due to debauchery) and without issue. The *Śivapurāṇa,* with which Vādicandra is familiar, gives a totally different account of their deaths. It is said that these two brothers, out of hatred of their step-brother, Bhīṣma, defamed him by linking him in a scandalous relationship with their mother (*svamātur mastake mudā kalaṅkaṃ vratino kārṣṭām*). A certain minister, however, took them to task and warned them of the evil consequences that would befall them unless they performed an act of purification. We are told that the two brothers entered fire in propitiation and were burned to death.[16]

4. The next episode concerns Gāndhārī, the wife of Dhṛtarāṣṭra and the mother of Duryodhana and 99 other (still-born) sons according to the *Mahābhārata.* According to Vādicandra's reading of the *Śivapurāṇa* she was frustrated by her blind husband's inability to give her children. She therefore copulated with a hundred goats, for, as the author observes, 'What will a woman desiring sons not do? (*śatacchāgaiś ca sā reme kiṃ kuryān na sutārthinī /*)?' However, those goats were slaughtered in a sacrifice (apparently for the birth of a son) by Dhṛtarāṣṭra, and they were all reborn in heaven. Recalling Gāndhārī's love for them, they visited her (in human form?), and begat a hundred sons, the eldest of whom was Duryodhana.[17]

The major female characters of the *Mahābhārata,* namely Satyavatī, Kuntī, Mādrī, and Draupadī, have been involved in sexual aberration of one form or another (premarital relationships, carnal contact with gods, or polyandry). Gāndhārī, alone appears to have been free from any such defilement. Only Vādicandra recounts this instance of Gāndhārī's alleged misconduct and claims that it appeared in the *Śivapurāṇa.*

These are some of the salient points raised by Vādicandra's account of the *Śivapurāṇa* version. One must wonder whether these aberrations from the original story of the *Mahābhārata,* involving such unsavoury acts as Śantanu's incestuous marriage to his daughter, Bhīṣma's self-castration, the unheard-of defamation of Bhīṣma's character, and Gāndhārī's acts of bestiality originate from the so-called *Śivapurāṇa* or merely from the vicious imagination of Vādicandra, influenced by his sectarian hatred of the Śaivas.

The veracity of Vādicandra's attribution of these infamous episodes to the *Śivapurāṇa* must be examined. At the outset one questions the very connexion of the story of the Pāṇḍavas, who are the blood-relations of Kṛṣṇa, and thus the original Vaiṣṇavas, with the god Śiva or *Śivapurāṇa,* which extols his divine acts. The only occasion in which Arjuna, a Pāṇḍava, meets Śiva, is to be found in the episode known as 'Kirātārjuna', where Arjuna fights Śiva, in the guise of a hunter, and obtains from him the invincible weapon called *Gāṇḍīva.* The genealogy of Śantanu has no place in this particular episode. This is confirmed by an examination of the extant *Śivapurāṇa,* a massive work consisting of some 20,000 verses.[18] In this text Arjuna appears only in the episode mentioned above,[19] and Vādicandra's other characters (notably, Bhīṣma, Kuntī, and Gāndhārī) are conspicuously absent. It is not likely that Vādicandra had access to any other version of the *Śivapurāṇa,* which might have contained the material which he condemns. We may safely conclude, therefore, that Vādicandra himself concocted these aberrations and knowingly attributed them to the *Śivapurāṇa.* Whether the Śaivas, in their sectarian feud with the Vaiṣṇavas, would have stooped so low must remain an open question. The author of the *Śivapurāṇa,* however, must be declared innocent of misrepresentation; if he had strayed from the *Mahābhārata* account his audience certainly would have noticed, and the variant version would have found its way into other Purāṇas as well.

Could there be any legitimate reason then for Vādicandra to ignore the other Purāṇas, especially the Vaiṣṇava Purāṇas, and single out the *Śivapurāṇa* for such calumny? Since the sectarian animosity towards Śaivism alone does not fully explain the Jaina attacks on *Śivapurāṇa*, one must look for remarks in the *Śivapurāṇa* offensive to the Jainas.

The *Śivapurāṇa* in fact contains several chapters in which the origins of the Jina and his mendicant followers are described in a most unsavoury form. According to this account Lord Viṣṇu (at the instigation of Lord Śiva) created a man, 'illusion personified' (*māyāmayaṃ puruṣaṃ*), specifically charged to teach *adharma*, or unlawful behaviour, to the demons, who would thereby depart from the path of righteousness and be consigned to lower worlds (*pātāla*). This man was Arhat, and he produced false scriptures in Apabhraṃśa, opposed to the Vedic teachings as well as the Smṛti. He preached practices contrary to the *varṇāśrama-dharma*, refuted the virtues inherent in the chastity of women devoted to their husbands (*strī-dharmaṃ khaṇḍayāmāsa pātivratyaparaṃ mahat/*), and, with the clever use of his magic powers of attraction (*abhyasyākarṣaṇīṃ vidyāṃ vaśīkṛtyamayīm api*), he led the females of the demons astray. He was able even to initiate many demons, notably Tripura into the mendicant order of the Jainas, and thus helped the divine mission of Viṣṇu in destroying the demons. In the Kaliyuga, however, says the author of *Śivapurāṇa*, he settled in the Marusthalī (the deserts of Rajasthan), where many people became disciples of this false mendicant, who is described as shaven-headed, wearing rags, holding a piece of cloth in front of his mouth, and constantly uttering the words 'dharma, dharma'.[20]

Before we draw any conclusions regarding the relevance of Vādicandra's work to the comparative study of the Purāṇas, we must stress that Vādicandra is an exception to the Jaina tradition of tolerance of other creeds. Many Jaina writers, including famous authors such as Jinasena, Hemacandra, Somadeva, and Devaprabha, have offered Jaina versions of the stories of the Brāhmaṇical heroes, especially those of the *Rāmāyaṇa* and *Mahābhārata*. They have not hesitated to describe the Brāhmaṇical gods, or their *avatāras*, as unworthy of worship because of their devotion to worldy activities, such as warfare and sex. They have been outspoken in their condemnation of animal sacrifice, approved by the Brāhmaṇical tradition. They have been alert in guarding their own Jinas from appropriation by the Brahmans, as is evident in the Jaina *Ādipurāna* of Jinasena (ninth century), who retaliates against the *Bhāgavatapurāṇa's* depiction of Ṛṣabha, the first Jaina Tīrthaṅkara, as an *avatāra* of Viṣṇu, by claiming that Ṛṣabha was the founder of the caste system and that the Jainas were the true Brahmans.[21] In all these Jaina efforts to keep their devotees within the Jaina fold, no other Jaina author has gone as far as Vādicandra, in depicting the non-Jaina traditions, whether Vaiṣṇava or Śaiva, in such slanderous terms.

We may nevertheless evaluate the importance of the Jaina *Pāṇḍavapurāṇas* as indications of the sectarian jealousies and feuds that were current during the fifteenth and sixteenth centuries. At least two of the traditional Purāṇas, most notably the *Śivapurāṇa* and to a lesser extent the *Bhāgavatapurāṇa*, contain long chapters depicting the Jainas as aberrant. The Purāṇas are, by definition, concerned with ancient, or pre-historical events such as the creation of the universe, the foundations of civilization, and the destruction of demons. The presence of passages in the *Bhāgavatapurāṇa* and the *Śivapurāṇa* hostile to the Jainas reflects the strifes of the contemporary sectarian scene and thus can be used as reliable documents for the study of Indian society at that time.

This should also help us to ascertain the chronological order of the Purāṇas. The depiction of the Jainas in the *Bhāgavatapurāṇa*, itself originating in South India, is that of the Digambara sect, who had settled in Karnataka on the coast of the Arabian Sea. The Jainas described in the *Śivapurāṇa*, however, belong to the Śvetāmbara sect, perhaps to the Sthānakavāsīs, the reformists who had become very influential by the beginning of the sixteenth century in Rajasthan and Marwar, and had even converted a large number of Śaivas to their faith.[22] The mention of the name 'Marusthalī' in the *Śivapurāṇa*, as the preferred abode of the Jaina mendicants, suggests that the author of the *Śivapurāṇa* came from that area and was a witness to the success of the Jainas in what was a stronghold of Śaivism. Probably the other Purāṇas and Upapurāṇas also contain similar materials. A comparative study of these would be of great value in ascertaining the relative chronology of the Purāṇas, in determining their geographical origin, and most importantly in understanding the society to which they were addressed.

NOTES

1. The Jaina Purāṇas describe Balarāma. Jarāsandha, and Kṛṣṇa, respectively, as a hero (*balabhadra*), leading an ideal Jaina life; a villain (*pratinārāyaṇa*), evil personified; the hero's companion or ally (*nārāyaṇa*), representing as it were the force of righteous indignation and carrying out the destruction of the villain. In the (Jaina) *Rāmāyaṇa* stories these roles are assigned respectively to Rāma (*balabhadra*), Rāvaṇa (*pratinārāyaṇa*) and Lakṣmaṇa (*nārāyaṇa*). The *balabhadra* is reborn in heaven (or may even attain *mokṣa*) but the *nārāyaṇa* and *pratinārāyaṇa* are fated to be reborn in a hell (*naraka*). Eventually they are reborn as humans and attain *mokṣa*. See P. S. Jaini, *The Jaina Path of Purification,* Berkeley, 1979, 305.
2. For a comprehensive bibliography of the Jaina Purāṇas, see Hiralal Jain, *Bhāratīya Saṃskriti mē Jaina-dharma kā Yogadān* (in Hindi), Bhopal, 1962, 412-16.
3. *Pāṇḍavacaritaṃ Mahākāvyam,* ed. Kedarnath and Panshikar, Kāvyamālā Series, 93, Bombay, 1911. (Henceforth referred to as *PM.)*
4. *Triṣaṣṭiśalākāpuruṣacaritra,* Vol. v, tr. into English by Helen M. Johnson, Oriental Institute, Baroda, 1962. (Gaekwad's Oriental Series, No. 139).
5. *Pāṇḍavapurāṇam,* ed. and tr. into Hindi by J. P. Shastri, Jivaraj Jain Granthamālā, No. 3. Sholapur, 1954. (Henceforth referred to as *PP.*)
6. *Harivaṃśapurāṇa* of Punnāṭa Jinasena, ed. tr. into Hindi by Pannalal Jain, Bhāratīya Jñānapīṭha, Varanasi, 1962.
7. Probably indentical with Śatakī mentioned in the *Uttarapurāṇa:*
   Śakti nāma mahīśasya Śatakyāś ca Parāśaraḥ/
   tasya matsyakulotpannarājaputryāṃ suto 'bhavat// 70-102
   Satyavatyāṃ sudhīr Vyāsaḥ punar Vyāsa-Subhadrayoḥ/
   Dhṛtarāṣṭro mahān Pāṇḍur Viduraś ca sutās trayaḥ// 70-103
   Uttarapurāṇa of Guṇabhadra, ed. and tr. into Hindi by Pannalal Jain, Bhāratīya Jñānapīṭha, Varanasi, 1954.
8. Devaprabha devotes only sixteen verses to what may be called the Jaina version of the *Bhagavadgītā*. See *PM,* xiii, 24-34. Śubhacandra, however, dismisses the entire episode of Arjuna's hesitation to fight but puts the following words in the mouth of Kṛṣṇa (consoling Arjuna lamenting the death of the young Abhimanyu):
   vidyate 'vasaro nātra śokasya śṛṇu vairiṇaḥ/
   saṃyuge jahi, dhīratvaṃ dhara dharmaviśārada//
   jahi putrasya hantāraṃ tatphalaṃ ca pradarśaya/ [*PP,* xx, 52-3]
9. rāyalobhena Vaikuṇṭho melayitvā bahūn paśūn/
   vāṭake bandhayāmāsa Nemivairāgyasiddhaye//
   vivāhārthaṃ jino gacchan vīkṣya baddhān bahūn paśūn/
   pṛṣtvā tadrakṣakān prāpa vairāgyaṃ rāgadūragaḥ// [*PP,* xxii, 42-3]
10. This edition of Vādicandra's *Pāṇḍavapurāṇa* (henceforth referred to as *VPP*) is based on two palm-leaf manuscripts, one from the Digambara Jaina Maṭha Mudabidre (Karnataka State), and the other from the Bibliothèque Nationale at the University of Strasbourg. For a description of these manuscripts, see C. B. Tripathi, *Catalogue of the Jaina Manuscripts at Strasbourg* (serial No. 199), Leiden, 1975.

11. At the beginning of the story, however, the author of the *VPP* refers to the *Bhārata* as the source for the Brāhmaṇical version: King Śreṇika of Magadha asks Mahāvīra's disciple Indrabhūti:
Kuru-Pāṇḍavayoḥ svāmin kathaṃ vairam abhūd iha/
yuddhena kulanāśaś ca kathaṃ jaya-parājayau//
yathākathañcic chrīnātha mithyādṛṣṭimukhān mayā/
śrūyate tena me cetaḥ satataṃ saṃśayāyate//
Bhārataṃ yan mayā'śrāyi . . . vijiñātam apy alam// [*VPP*, i, 72-3]
12. The *Mahābhārata,* ed. V. S. Sukthankar, I, *adhyāya* 57, 1-55, Poona, 1933.
13. Births of Matsyagandhā and Veda-Vyāsa:
babhūva nṛpatiḥ khyātaḥ Śantanuḥ Puru-vaṃśabhūḥ/
ekadā vasudhāṃ so 'pi sādhanārthaṃ viniryayau//
ṛtukālaṃ samālabhya gṛhasthā tasya bhāminī/
vīryaṃ sā bhartur ānetuṃ rājīvaṃ prāhiṇod drutam//
...tat smṛtes tasya saṃjāto vīryadrāvo madotkaṭaḥ// ...
tāmre pātre svavīryaṃ ca nidhāya nṛpatis tadā//
pārāpatagale tadd hi pātreṇāmā babandha saḥ//
...Gaṅgāyām apatad reto mīnī tatrāgalac ca tat/
ādhatta mīnī tadyogād garbhabhāram anākulam//
prayāti kāle tāṃ mīnīm avadhīd dhīvaro Dharaḥ/
apaśyat kanyakāṃ tatra Matsyagandhābhidhāṃ manaḥ//
...atha tāṃ yauvanonmattāṃ vīkṣya Pārāśaro muniḥ/...
garbhas tadyogato jātaḥ Śaivaśāstreṣv idaṃ vacaḥ//
kutra vīryaṃ kva vā mīnī kathaṃ vā garbhadhāriṇī/
kva kanyā kva munir nātha kathaṃ saṃyogapaddhatiḥ//
pūrṇe garbhe hi sā kanyā Veda-Vyāsābhidhaṃ sutam/
asūtaṃ tāpasākāraṃ śaiśave vedavādinam// [*VPP*, i, 72-93]
14. King Śantanu marries his own daughter Matsyagandhā:
saṃsādhya vasudhāṃ sarvāṃ parāvṛtya nadīṃ itaḥ/
śrīŚantano 'tha tat kanyām apaśyan nijavīryajām//
sugandhāṃ rūpasampannāṃ prekṣya so 'pi smarāśayaḥ/
nikaṣā nāvikaṃ gatvā yācate sma ca tat sutām// [*VPP*, i, 95-6]
The Jaina authors probably confuse the *Mahābhārata* story of the King Vasu-Uparicara who also impregnates a fish in the manner narrated above with that of Śantanu; it is not unlikely, however, that the confusion was deliberate. No other version makes Śantanu the father of Satyavatī.
15. nāṅgahīno jano rājā naivam antaḥsutodbhavaḥ/
vitarkyeti pitur bhaktyā sa ciccheda svaliṅgakam//
bhīṣmaṃ karma kṛtaṃ tena tato Bhīṣmo janair mataḥ/
yādṛk karma kṛtaṃ tādṛk prāpat khyātiṃ jane 'khile// [*VPP*, i, 105-6]
16. Death of Citra and Vicitra (step-brothers of Bhīṣma):
yāti kāle tayor jātau sutau Citra-Vicitrakau/
...sapatnījanito yasmāt tasmād dveṣavidūṣitau//
purvodāntam ajānantau svamātur mastake mudā//
kalaṅkaṃ vratino kārṣṭāṃ tāvan mantrī vaco 'vadat/...
yuvayos tena bhavitā pāpabandho niraṅkuśaḥ//
ittham ākarṇya tad vākyaṃ tat pāpavinivṛttaye/
praveśaṃ cakratur vahnau niryadbhūri sphuliṅgake//
aputrau tau dharādhīśau mṛtim āpatur āpadā/
arājakaṃ tato rājyaṃ samabhūc Śāntanīyakam// [*VPP*, i, 113-18]

17. Gāndhārī copulates with 100 goats:
...paścāt sthirāyuṣaṃ cāndhaṃ samprāpyā 'py asutā tarām/
śatacchāgaiś ca sā reme, kiṃ kuryān na sutārthinī//
yāti kāle hi te chāgā Dhṛtarāṣṭreṇa bhūbhujā/
sarve ca yajñasamaye māritā svargavāñchayā//
yajñakuṇḍe hatā chāgāḥ svargavāsam agus tataḥ/
saṃsmṛtvā prāktanaṃ snehaṃ te smarārtā ajāmarāḥ//
Gāndhāryā gṛham āgatya bhajante tām anāratam/
tebhyas tasyāṃ samutpannāḥ ṣaṇmāseṣu ca nandanāḥ//
Duryodhanādināmānaḥ iti ke 'pi jagur vidaḥ/...
kva chāgāḥ krīḍanaṃ rājñyā kva vā svarganivāsabhūḥ/
āgamo hi kathaṃ teṣāṃ kutas tebhyaḥ sutodbhavaḥ//
kathaṃ te kudhiyaḥ Śaivāḥ satyəm etat bruvanti ca/
dṛḍhamithyātvam āpannāḥ kiṃ kiṃ jalpanti no narāḥ//[*VPP*, i, 137-45]
18. *Śivapurāṇa*, ed. by Ramateja Shastri Pandeya, Paṇḍita Pustakālaya, Varanasi.
19. *Śivapurāṇa, Saṃhitā* II, *Adhyāyas* 37-41 (pp. 654-68).
20. The editor of the *Śivapurāṇa* introduces this section under the following heading:
Tripuradānavamohanārthaṃ Viṣṇunā Jinasyotpādanaṃ tad dvārā
Ārhatyadīkṣayā Tripurasya Arhaddharmāṅgīkaraṇam;
Jinadharmakathanaprasaṅge devānāṃ
grāmyadharmādyaniyamavarṇanam.
Sanatkumāra uvāca:
asṛjac ca mahātejāḥ puruṣaṃ svātmasambhavam/
ekaṃ māyāmayaṃ teṣāṃ dharmavighnārtham Acyutaḥ//
muṇḍinaṃ mlānavastraṃ ca gumphipātrasamanvitam/
dadhānaṃ puñjikāṃ haste cālayantaṃ pade pade//
vastrayuktaṃ tathā hastaṃ kṣīyamāṇaṃ mukhe sadā/
dharmeti vyāharantaṃ hi vācā viklavayā munim//
. . . Viṣṇuḥ . . . vacanaṃ cedam abravit/
yad arthaṃ nirmito 'si tvaṃ nibodha kathayāmi te/
Arihaṃ nāma te syāt tu hy anyāni śubhāni ca/ . . .
Apabhraṃśamayaṃ śāstraṃ karmavādamayaṃ tathā/
śrautasmārtaviruddhaṃ ca varṇāśramavivarjitam//
gantum arhasi nāśārthaṃ muṇḍas Tripuravāsinam/
tamodharmaṃ saṃprakāśya nāśayasva puratrayam//
tataś caiva punar gantvā Marusthalyāṃ tvayā vibho/
sthātavyam ca svadharmeṇa kalir yāvat samāvrajet//
tataḥ sa muṇḍī paripālayan Harer, ājñāṃ tathā nirmitavāṃś ca śiṣyān/
yathāsvarūpaṃ caturas tadānīṃ māyāmayaṃ śāstram apāṭhayat svayam//
[*Śivapurāṇa*, II (*Rudrasaṃhitā*), v, Yuddhakāṇḍa), 4th *Adhyāya*, 1.24]
21. *Ādipurāṇa* (Parts 1-2), ed. and tr. in Hindi by Pannalal Jain, Bhāratīya Jñānapīṭha, Varanasi, 1963-5, Parvas 38-40. *Bhāgavatapurāṇa*, V, iii-vii, Gītā Press. See also P. S. Jaini, 'Jina Ṛṣabha as an *avatāra* of Viṣṇu', *BSOAS*, XL, 2, 1977, 321-37.
22. For a description of the missionary activities of Jaina monks and the conversion of a large number of the Rajasthani and the Marwadi clans to Jainism, see Agarchand Nahta and Bhavarmal Nahta, *Kharatara Gaccha ke Pratibodhita Gotra aur Jātiyāṃ* (in Hindi), Shri Jinadattasuri Sevasaṅgha, Calcutta, 1973.

ADDITIONAL NOTE

See Padmanabh S. Jaini, "*Pāṇḍava-Purāṇa* of Vādicandra: Text and Translation." *Journal of Indian Philosophy,* (Cantos I and II) Vol. 25, 1997, pp. 1-3; (Cantos III and IV) Vol. 25, 1997, pp. 91-127; (Cantos V and VI), Vol. 26, 1998, pp. 1-63, Kluver Academic Publishers, Dordrecht, Netherlands.

CHAPTER 20

Bhaṭṭāraka Śrībhūṣaṇa's *Pāṇḍavapurāṇa:* A Case of Jaina Sectarian Plagiarism*

Although the term plagiarist (*kāvya-caura,* literally robber of others' poems) is not unknown to Sanskrit Lexicons,[1] no illustration of such an act of plagiarism has been attested to in the works on Sanskrit poetics. This is not surprising given the ancient and medieval Indians' well-known indifference toward preserving the names, places or dates of their authors. The superabundance of the anonymous verses found in the numerous Sanskrit anthologies could have served as an open treasure for a scheming verse-maker to appropriate any number of these verses without fear of easy detection. But the general tendency seems to be the reverse, namely, to attribute one's own compositions to famous authors, such as Bhartṛhari of the *nīti-śataka* fame for Sanskrit verses, or Kabīr and Mīrā for the vernacular compositions called *bhajanas.* It is therefore a matter of some interest for a student of Sanskrit literature when a major Sanskrit work amounting to several thousand *ślokas* can be proved, beyond doubt, to be the product of skilful plagiarism. The purpose of this paper is to show that a seventeenth-century Jaina bhaṭṭāraka (cleric) called Śrībhūṣaṇa did indeed plagiarize a major work entitled *Pāṇḍavapurāṇa* by stealing it from the work of an earlier Jaina author of a rival sect.

*This article was published originally in *Middle Indo-Aryan and Jaina Studies: Proceedings of the VIIth World Sanskrit Conference,* eds. Bronkhorst and Caillat (Leiden: E. J. Brill, 1991), pp. 59-68. Reprinted with kind permission of E. J. Brill.

The name Śrībhūṣaṇa is not altogether unknown to scholars acquainted with the history of Jaina literature of Western India. In his pioneering work on the history of the medieval Jaina authors, Nathuram Premi[2] has a chapter on Śrībhūṣaṇa which contains the following information on the literary achievements of this author. Śrībhūṣaṇa was a bhaṭṭāraka of the Digambara sect known as Kāṣṭhāsaṅgha of the Nandītaṭa branch (*gaccha*). He belonged to the lineage of Rāmasena and was an immediate successor to Vidyābhūṣaṇa, whose seat of authority (*maṭha* or *gaddī*) was at Sojitrā in Gujarat. In addition to several small works dealing mostly with Jaina rituals, he was the author of three major Purāṇas in Sanskrit, namely the *Pāṇḍavapurāṇa* (A.D. 1600), the *Śāntināthapurāṇa* (1602) and the *Harivaṃśapurāṇa* (1618). The manuscripts of all three of these works are extant but none have been published. Premi reproduces portions from their colophons which give important information on the lineage of the Kāṣṭhāsaṅgha and the dates and places of his encounter in Bombay in 1905 with the then occupant of the Sojitrā seat, a bhaṭṭāraka named Ratnakīrti, from whom he borrowed for a short period a Sanskrit manuscript entitled *Pratibodha-cintāmaṇi* attributed to bhaṭṭāraka Śrībhūṣaṇa. This work, Premi reports, was full of sectarian animosity toward the members of the Mūlasaṅgha,[3] who claimed their descent from the Ācārya Padmanandi, also known as Kundakunda, the celebrated author of such works as the *Samayasāra* and the *Pravacanasāra,* etc.[4] Premi also found in the possession of bhaṭṭāraka Ratnakīrti another manuscript of an ancient chronicle of the Mūlasaṅgha called *Darśanasāra*[5] by Devasena, the original readings of which had been arbitrarily changed by Śrībhūṣaṇa, obviously in retaliation for Devasena's uncomplimentary account of the origins of the Kāṣṭhāsaṅgha. We have thus, an already established record of Śrībhūṣaṇa's unscrupulous habit of altering works of historical importance to serve his sectarian purposes. The present paper will demonstrate that Śrībhūṣaṇa went much further than this—that he actually committed an act of plagiarism by stealing a complete work of an author called Śubhacandra, a bhaṭṭāraka of the Mūlasaṅgha, who flourished in Rajasthan only some fifty years earlier.

In my recent article "*Mahābhārata* motifs in the Jaina *Pāṇḍavapurāṇa,*"[6] I have discussed at some length the Jaina version of the *Mahābhārata* story, appearing for the first time as a separate text in the eighth-century *Harivaṃśapurāṇa*[7] of the Digambara poet Punnāṭa Jinasena and later under the title of *Pāṇḍava-Carita*[8] (A.D. 1214) by the Śvetāmbara author Devaprabha, and subsequently under the title of *Pāṇḍavapurāṇa* by the Digambara bhaṭṭāraka Śubhacandra (A.D. 1552). This latter work of Śubhacandra was published in 1954 with a Hindi translation.[9] This Purāṇa consists of 5301 *ślokas* and is divided into twenty-five cantos (*sargas*), and follows in the main the *Harivaṃśapurāṇa* of Punnāṭa Jinasena, albeit with a great many changes of its own. We learn from the colophon of this work that Śubhacandra belonged to the Mūlasaṅgha and had composed this work in the city of Śakavāṭa (modern Sāgavāḍ) in Vāgura (Bāgaḍa), in Rajasthan. He was the author of some twenty-five works, including four *caritras* and a commentary on the *Anagāradharmāmṛta* of the thirteenth-century lay scholar Āśādhara. Śubhacandra, as is the custom with Jaina authors of this genre, pays homage at the outset to his most famous predecessors in the Mūlasaṅgha, notably Kundakunda, Samantabhadra, Pūjyapāda and Akalaṅka, and acknowledges his debt to the authors Jinasena and Guṇabhadra whose Purāṇa works had been the major source of his new composition. But what is noteworthy about Śubhacandra is that at the end of each *sarga* he acknowledges the assistance he received from his disciple Brahma Śrīpāla, an advanced lay disciple (*varṇī*). At the end of the work, while concluding his own *praśasti,* he lavishes high praise on this Brahma Śrīpāla, calling him a great holy man, a brilliant scholar and a logician, who had revised the entire text of the *Pāṇḍavapurāṇa,* and had transcribed it in the form of a book.[10] The modesty of the Jaina mendicant authors is well-known even to this day—their names appear at the end of a long list of the teachers in their lineage, but Śubhacandra's case seems to be unique, for he chose to acknowledge publicly and repeatedly the assistance received from his junior, a lay disciple.

Śrībūṣaṇa, the subject of our research, would seem to offer a conspicuous contrast to this example of integrity set by the bhaṭṭāraka Śubhacandra. I became aware of this fact in the summer of 1985, when I happened to read the original manuscript of Śrībhūṣaṇa's *Pāṇḍavapurāṇa,* apparently the only surviving copy of this work, in the Jaina temple library at Karanja,[11] a prominent Jaina town in the state of Maharashtra. As I began reading this manuscript, I was constantly reminded of Śubhacandra's

Pāṇḍavapurāṇa and wondered if the two texts might not have been identical. A close comparison of this unpublished manuscript with the printed text of Śubhacandra revealed that the works were not identical, but the resemblance of their readings left no doubt that one of them must have been a plagiarized version of the other. Both texts are divided into twenty-five *sargas*, and their *sarga* titles are identical. A verse by verse correspondence does not exist, since the unpublished manuscript has 6,080 *ślokas*, as against the 5,301 *ślokas* in the printed text of Śubhacandra. Notwithstanding the originality (or otherwise) of the 779 additional *ślokas* in Śrībhūṣaṇa's version, a close scrutiny revealed that the remainder of this work owed its origin to the verses composed by Śubhacandra some fifty years earlier. After making several sample comparisons from each chapter, I was convinced that Śrībhūṣaṇa had in front of him Śubhacandra's *Pāṇḍavapurāṇa* which he had very cleverly recast almost verse for verse and had passed it off under his own name, without making any acknowledgement whatsoever of Śubhacandra's work.

I have for this aricle chosen one chapter—the only chapter in both versions consisting of an identical number of verses—which narrates the five auspicious occasions (*pañcakalyāṇas*)[12] in the life of Kunthunātha, the seventeenth Tīrthaṅkara. The verses from Śubhacandra's *Pāṇḍavapurāṇa* appear in bold-face type and are immediately followed by the version found in Śrībhūṣaṇa's *Pāṇḍavapurāṇa* in plain type. The underlined portions indicate the parallel passages found between the two. The correspondence both in the narrative and vocabulary is so manifest that no further argument is necessary to prove our point that Śrībhūṣaṇa had committed a flagrant act of plagiarism.

// Ṣaṣṭhaṃ parva //

Kunthuṃ kunthvādijīvānāṃ kunthanān muktamānasam /
supathyaṃ bhavyajīvānāṃ vande satpathapātinām //1//
Padmaprabham ahaṃ vande padmābhaṃ padmalāñchitam /
puṇyatīrthapraṇetāraṃ s(ś)ās(ś)vaṭaṃ sambhavaṃ śivam //1//
atha Śāntisutaḥ śrīmān <u>Nārāyaṇasamāhvayaḥ</u> /
Śāntivardhana<u>saṃjñas tu Śānticandras tato 'bhavat</u> //2//
atha Śāntisuto khyātaḥ <u>Nārāyaṇasmāhvayaḥ</u>/
Śāntivardhana<u>nāmā ca Śānticandras tato 'bhavat</u> //2//

Candracihnaḥ Kuruś ceti Kuruvaṃśasamudbhavāḥ /
evaṃ bahusv atīteṣu Śūraseno nṛpo 'bhavat //3//
Candracihnaḥ Kuruḥ śuddhaḥ Kuruvaṃśodbhavāḥ nṛpāḥ /
evaṃ bahuṣv atīteṣu S(Ś)ūraseno 'bhavan nṛpah //3//
yasmin rājyaṃ prakurvāṇe 'bhūvan nānāsunītayaḥ /
ītayaḥ kvāpi saṃnaṣṭā ghasre tārāgaṇā iva //4//
yasmin rājñi mahī[ṃ] pāti babhūvur nā[nā] tapodhanāḥ /
ītayaḥ kvāpi no lakṣyāḥ divi tārāgaṇo yathā //4//
yaḥ śūraḥ śūratādhīśaḥ śūrasahasrasaṃyutaḥ /
sūrābhaḥ kevalo yasya raso 'bhūc chūrasaṃśritaḥ //5//
śūrasaṃsevyapādābjo śūrālaṅkṛtagātrakaḥ /
śūre raso bhaved yasya kevalṃ tasya bhūbhṛtaḥ //5//
yatpratāpāt pare bhūpā hitvā pattanasajjanān /
darīṣu darasaṃdīptāḥ śerate śayanātigāḥ //6//...
yasya pratāpato bhūpā tyaktvā pattanasajjanān /
sevante sma vanāny uccair bhayabhrāmitagātrakāḥ //6// ...
yadvaktracandram āvīkṣya padmā sadmātigā sadā /
jaleṣu śerate yasmād virodhaś candrapadmayoḥ //9//
yadāsyaṃ śaśi(?) saṃvīkṣya padbhyāṃ padmātigā bhṛśam /
vasante sma jale yasmād virodhaḥ śaśipadmayoh //9//
yadvakṣojamahākumbhau sevate hi nidhīcchayā /
sphuran manoharo hāro nāgavan nāgamārthinau //10//
yadvakṣojodbhavau kumbhau sevate 'sya nidhīcchayā /
caṃca(cala?)ccārutaraudārau veṇināgena santatam //10//
yastsevāvadhisambaddhāḥ Śryādayo 'marayositaḥ /
kurvanti sarvakāryāṇi puṇyāt kiṃ hi durāsadam //11//
yasyāḥ sevāṃ paraṃ prāptāḥ pādayoḥ surayoṣitaḥ /
kurvanti viśvakarmāṇi puṇyāt kiṃ kiṃ na labhyate //11//
dhanadhārādharo dhīro Dhanado hi yadaṅgane /
jalavad ratnadhārāṃ ca varṣatīti mahādbhutam //12//
Dhanado dhanadhārāṃ vai saṃvavarṣa tadaṅgaṇe /
meghadāreva saṃlakṣyāvacchinnā nabhaso 'malā //12//
ratnadhārādharatvena vasudhākhyāṃ gatā dharā /
yatra garbhotsave tat kiṃ yan nābhūt pramadāvaham //13//
ratnadhārādharatvāc ca dharā jātā jagattraye /
yasya garbhāvatāre 'pi kiṃ na syāt saukhyadāyakam //13//

I

saikadā ṣoḍaśasvapnān niśāpaścimayāmake /
suptā 'tha śayane 'drākṣīn nṛpapatnī nṛpālikā //14//

niśāyāḥ paścime yāme sā 'drākṣīt svapnaṣoḍaśān /
suptā śayyāsane rājñī viś(b)uddhā śuddhacetasā //14//
viditvā vādyanādena prātaḥ sāntaḥsukhāvahā /
kṛtanityakriyā snātvā milanmaṅgalamaṇḍanā //15//
jñātvā prātaḥ suvādyenājāgarit sā sukhāvahā /
kṛtvā prābhātikaṃ karma sanepathyā samaṅgalā //15//
svasevāparasaṃsaktā dyotayantā sadonabhaḥ /
vidyullateva sā 'drākṣīt bhūpaṃ jīmūtavat sthitam //16//
bhūpaṃ sadogataṃ matvā vidyu[lla]teva samāgamat /
meghābham iva rājendraṃ dhanadhārāvivarṣan(ṇ)am //16//
nṛpāsanārdham āsīnā natvā tatpādapaṅkajam /
vyajñāsīt svapnasaṃghātam aghavighnaughaghātakam //17//
bhūpasyārdhāsane devī upaviśva vyajījñapat /
svapnān s(ś)āntasvabhāvena viśvamāṅgalyasūcakān //17//
viditvā tatphalaṃ bhūpo 'vadhivīkṣaṇataḥ kṣaṇāt /
kramataḥ kramasaṃbhāvi phalaṃ teṣām avarṇayat //18//
jñātvā avadhibodhena bhūpena viditātmanā /
teṣāṃ phalaṃ ca tasyāgre 'varṇayad vibudhāgraṇī //18//
śrutvā vaco 'ṃśunā spṛṣṭā tatsphuradvadanāmbujā /
abjinīvāsrasaṃsparśād atuṣac coṣṇadīdhiteḥ //19//
śrutvā vaco 'ṃśunā spṛṣṭā sā sphuradvaktrapaṃkajā /
nalinīva yathā saṅgāt pataṅgasya prabhāvataḥ //19//
Śrāvaṇe bahule pakṣe daśamyāṃ saṃdadhe cyutam /
Sarvārthasiddhito devaṃ devīgarbhe suśodhite //20//
Śrāvaṇe bahule pakṣe daśamyāṃ garbham uttamam /
Sarvārthasiddhitaś cyutvā devaṃ devī dadhe tadā //20//
biḍaujā jaḍatāmukto jñātvā tadgarbhasaṃbhvam /
samāgatya ghaṭanāniṣṭhas tatkalyāṇaṃ tadā 'karot //21//
maghonāgatya vegena jñātvā garbhāgataṃ jinam /
kalyāṇakam akarot tatra devavrajāvṛtena vai //21//

II

sā muktāphalavad garbhaṃ śuktikeva samujjvalā /
dadhatī dhāma saṃdīptā dyotate sma smayāvahā //22//
sā śuktivad dadhe garbhaṃ yathā muktāphalaṃ varam /
tathā devī jinaṃ dhatte garbhabādhāpahaṃ sadā //22//
dīptadevīgaṇaiḥ sevyā sevyārthaphaladāyinī /
praśnitā gūḍhakāvyādyai reje sā ratnakhānivat //23//
dī(i)vyadevīvrajaiḥ sevyā sā sevāphaladāyinī /
viditā gūḍhasatkāvyaiḥ s(ś)us(ś)ubhe ratnakhānivat //23//

sārah kah saṃsṛtau devī sukhaṃ kiṃ cābhidhīyate /
śarmāśarmakaraṃ kiṃ hi vadādyākṣaratah pṛthak //24//...
ko'tra sārataro loke sātaṃ kiṃ śarmadāyakam /
vada tvaṃ ca mahādevī ādyavarṇaiḥ pṛthak pṛthak //24//...
sūryāt kā jāyate loke kā sthitā vidusāṃ mukhe /
Arjunah kīdṛśaḥ kā syād Gaṅgā Bhāgīrathīti ca //26//
kotpadyate raver yogāt vidusāṃ vadane 'sti kā /
jiṣṇuś ca kīdṛśaḥ kā syād Gaṅgā Bhāgīrathīti ca //26//
evaṃ praśnottare 'sūtā sā sutaṃ prāg yathā ravim /
navame māsi Vaiśākhe śuklapakṣādime dine //27//
iti praśnottarair devī rañjayan vacanottaraiḥ /
nākanārīvrajo nityaṃ gadyakāvyāvilair varaiḥ //27//
navamāseṣv atīteṣu sā sūta sutam uttamam /
Vaiśākhaśuklapakṣasya ādime divase tathā //28//
Meghavāhanamukhyās te samāgatya surāsurāḥ /
nayanti sma jinaṃ merumūrdhānam cordhvagāminaḥ //28//
pīṭhe saṃsthāpya sampaṭhya satpāṭhaṃ paṭhanodyatāḥ /
kṣīrābdhivāribhir devā abhyasiñcañ jinottam //29//
surāsurāḥ samāgatya jinaṃ nītvā mahotsavaiḥ /
asnāpayan suragirau devendrā dānadāyinaḥ //29//
saṃjñayā Kunthum ājñāya samānīya pure surāḥ /
pitroḥ samarpayāmāsur Maghavapramukhāḥ surāḥ //30//
saṃjñayā Kunthunāmānaṃ punar nītvā nṛpālayam /
pitroḥ samarpayāmāsur jagmus te suranāyakāḥ //30//

III

yauvane vardhamānaḥ sa vardhamānaguṇodayaḥ /
pañcatriṃśaddhanuḥkāyo niṣṭaptāṣṭāpadadyutiḥ //31//
yauvanaṃ prāpa devendro vardhamānaguṇodayaḥ /
pañcatriṃśaddhanūtsedho sadaṣṭāpadasannibhaḥ //31//
sphurat pañcasahasronalakṣasaṃvatsarasthitiḥ /
prāptarājyapado bhogān bhuñjan bhadrabharāvahaḥ //32//
sphurat pañcasahasronalakṣasaṃvatsarasthitiḥ /
rājyālaṃkṛtagātro saḥ bhogān bhuñjan yathepsitān //32//
cakralakṣmīṃ samāsādya samabhūc cakralāñchanaḥ /
smṛtapūrvabhavajñāno vyaraṃsīd bhavataḥ sa ca //33
cakritvaṃ ca samāsādya nidhānaratnasaṃyutaḥ /
kiñciddhetuṃ samālokya virakto 'bhūj jinādhipaḥ //33//
jñātvā Laukāntikā devās tādṛśaṃ taṃ stavastavaiḥ /
stutvā dīkṣodyataṃ natvā samaguḥ pañcamīṃ divam //34//

devā Laukāntikās tāvad etya stutvā jineśvaram /
punar devāḥ samāyātāḥ natvā cakrur mahotsavam //34//
putre niyuktarājyo 'sau Vijayāśibikāṃ śritāḥ /
devendraiḥ saha samprāpat Sahetukavanaṃ varam //35//
rājyaṃ nyasya nije putre Vijayāṃ śibikāṃ śritaḥ /
devendraiḥ saha samprāpat Sahetukavanaṃ varam //35//
janmano divase ṣaṣṭhopavāsī tatra bhūmipaiḥ /
sahasrair luñcanodyuktair ayāsīt saṃyamaṃ vibhuḥ //36//
janmano divase svāmī ṣaṣṭhopavāsasaṃyutaḥ /
sahasrair bhūmipaiḥ sākaṃ saṃyamaṃ prāpa tīrtharāṭ //36//

IV

tatpure Dharmamitrākhyaḥ pāraṇāhni dadau mudā /
tasmai ca pāyasaṃ so 'taḥ prāpad āścaryapañcakam //37//
tatpure Dharmamitrākhyas tasmai dānaṃ dadau mudā /
pāyasaṃ prāpa devendrāt pañcāścaryam anuttaram //37//
nītvā soḍaśa varsāṇi chādmasthyena Sahetuke /
vane ṣaṣṭhopavāsī sa Tilakadrumamūlagaḥ //38//
chādmasthyena tato nītvā kālo ṣoḍaṣavārṣikaḥ /
ṣaṣṭhopavāsabhṛt svāmi vane sthitvā jineśvaraḥ //38//
Caitrajyotsnā 'parāhṇe ca tṛtīyāyāṃ samudyamī /
ghātikarmakṣayaṃ kṛtvā kaivalyam udapādayat //39//...
ghātikarmakṣayaṃ kṛtvā Tilakādhaḥ sthito jinaḥ /
Caitrajyotsnā parāhṇe ca tṛtīyāyāṃ kṛtodyamī //39//
sa prāpa kevalaṃ bodhaṃ lokālokāvabhāsakam //40ab//...

V

māsamuktakriyaḥ prāpa Sammedādriṃ sahasrakaiḥ /
munibhiḥ samagān muktiṃ kṣīṇakarmā yatīśvaraḥ //47//...
ityādividhaiḥ saṅghaiḥ vijahāra mahītalaṃ /
māsam āvas(ś)esāyuḥ Sammedādrim agāj jinaḥ //47//...

āsīd yaḥ prāg Videhe nṛpamukuṭataṭighṛṣṭapādāravindo
dakṣo vai Siṃhapūrvo ratha iti nṛpatiḥ siddhaSarvārthasiddhiḥ /
Kunthuḥ kunthvākhyajīvapramukhasukhadayādāyako nāyakas tāt
cakrī tīrthaṅkaro 'sau varaguṇamataye kāmadevo varo vaḥ //50//
yo āsīt prāg Videhe suramukuṭataṭāghṛṣṭapādāravindo
ramyo vai Siṃhapūrvo rathaprathitabhuvi sarvaSarvārthasiddhiḥ /
Kuṃthuṃ kuṃthvākhyasaṃjñāṃ naravaramahitāṃ saṃsṛtau nirmalāṃ vai

cakreśo tīrthanātho suravaramahito devadevo jinendraḥ //50//
puṣyat pāpāri kuṃthur varamathanamito mīnaketoḥ suketo dhartā dharme dharitrīṃ tribhuvanamahitaḥ Kunthunāthaḥ sunāthaḥ/ kunthvādīnāṃ dayāḍhyo varapathapathikas tīrtharāṭ cakrarājaḥ śumbhat saubhāgyabhartā bhavavanadahanaḥ pātu pāpāt sa yuṣmān //51//

pātu Kunthujinapo janatānām
pāpataḥ prathitapuṇyas(ś)āsanaḥ /
kāmadevapadavīpadadhāro
karmapaṅkarahito munimukhyaḥ //51//

iti śrībhaṭṭārakaŚubhacandrapraṇīte BrahmaŚrīpālasāhāyyasāpekṣe śrī *Pāṇḍavapurāṇe Mahābhāratanāmni* śrīKunthunāthapurāṇaprarūpaṇaṃ nāma ṣaṣṭhaṃ parva //6//

iti śrī bhaṭṭāraka Vidyābhūṣaṇasatpaṭṭābharaṇasūriśrī Śrībhūṣaṇaviracite *Pāṇḍavapurāṇe Bhāratanāmni* śrīKunthunāthapurāṇaprarūpaṇaṃ nāma ṣaṣṭhaṃ parva //6//

It is clear that the two texts of the sixth *sarga* are almost identical, with the exception of the first and the last verse. Śubhacandra begins with an invocation of Kunthunātha, becasue he is narrating the legend of this Jina in this *sarga*. Śrībhūṣaṇa's version begins with a homage to Padmaprabha, the sixth Jina. Śubhacandra adheres throughout to the practice of invoking the person who features dominantly in a given *sarga*, whereas Śrībhūṣaṇa chooses to invoke the twenty-four Tīrthaṅkaras, one each for each of the twenty-four *sargas*, respectively, repeating the name of Mahāvīra the last Jina, for the twenty-fifth *sarga*. He also chooses to have the last verse of each *sarga* in a different metre than found in his original model, namely, Śubhacandra's version. This would appear to be the extent of Śrībhūṣaṇa's originally; he probably thought that by changing the first and last verses of each *sarga* and by adding here and there several verses of his own, he could cover up his act of plagiarism. The several hundred additional verses in his recast probably suggest a strategy to convey his superior skill in verse-making by the sheer bulk of his work over his rival Śubhacandra, the author of the original text. It should also be remembered that the *Pāṇḍavapurāṇa* was his first major composition which gave him enough experience to embark upon two more works, namely, the *Śāntināthapurāṇa* finished in 1602 (within a short period of only two years after the recast of the *Pāṇḍavapurāṇa*) and the *Harivaṃśapurāṇa*, completed after a much longer interval, in 1618. Whether these two Purāṇas are also recasts of some earlier works by other authors is a question that can be determined only after a careful scrutiny of their as yet unedited manuscripts.

Despite the fact that we have witnessed here an open act of plagiarism it cannot be denied that Śrībhūṣaṇa is a skilful verse-maker, able to recast the entire work of such a magnitude within the constraints of its metrical form. Jaina authors have occasionally cultivated an interest in the art called *pādapūraṇa*, a favourite pastime of Sanskrit poets. This was a healthy exercise in composing new lines of a verse and completing it with one or more lines from some well-known work of a famous poet. The composition called *Pārśvābhyudaya* of the eighth-century Jinasena is an excellent example of such an art.[13] Each of the 364 verses of this *kāvya* has one line drawn from the *Meghadūta* of the great poet Kālidāsa, but narrating the spiritual progress of the twenty-third Jina, Pārśva. Another example would be of a less known work called *Nemicarita* (or *Nemidūta*),[14] based on the legend of the twenty-second Jina Nemi and his abandoned bride Rājimati, by the fifteenth-century poet Vikrama from Khambhat in Gujarat. This poem contains 126 verses with the last line of each being identical with last line of the corresponding verse in the *Meghadūta*. These are not the products of plagiarism, but rather examples of the skilfulness of the poets, and were undertaken out of admiration for the original work. In the case of Śrībhūṣaṇa one must ask the question if he was inspired more by a personal ambition to exhibit his skilfulness as a poet, or by a sectarian spirit (as had been revealed by Premi's earlier researches) to match his Kāṣṭhāsaṅgha lineage with that of the rival sect of the Mūlasaṅgha, which had a *Pāṇḍavapurāṇa* of its own, composed by a recent author who also happened to be a bhaṭṭāraka in a neighbouring state, and thus a rival for the patronage of the Jaina laity. The latter would appear to be the real reason for this rather fruitless endeavour, for the only occasion where his recast version differs significantly from the original text is suggestive of a sectarian bias, and that appears in the beginning portion of the first *sarga*. Here the omission of the name of the venerable Ācārya Kundakunda, the founder of the Mūlasaṅgha is conspicuous by its absence. Instead, we have a long list of lesser known celebrities of the Kāṣṭhāsaṅgha, so unceremoniously ignored by the authors of the Mūlasaṅgha, e.g. Rāmasena, Dharmasena, Vimalasena, Viśvasena, Viśālakīrti, and last but not least, Vidyābhūṣaṇa, the preceptor and immediate predecessor of bhaṭṭāraka Śrībhūṣaṇa himself.[15]

NOTES

1. See Böhthlingk and Roth, *Sanskrit-Wörterbuch,* p. 266, St. Petersburg, 1855.
2. Nathuram Premi, *Jaina Sāhitya aur Itihāsa* (in Hindi), pp. 389-394, Hindī Grantha-Ratnākara, Bombay, 1956.
3. On the bhaṭṭāraka lineages of the Mūlasaṅgha and the Kāṣṭhāsaṅgha, see V. P. Johrapurkar, *Bhaṭṭāraka Sampradāya* (in Hindi), Jīvarāja Jaina Granthamālā, Sholapur, 1958.
4. On Kundakunda and his place in the Jaina monastic tradition, see A. N. Upadhye (ed.), *Pravacanasāra,* (Intro. pp. 1-45), Śrīmad Rājachandra Aśrama, Agas, 1964.
5. On the authenticity of this work, see A. N. Upadhye, "*Darśanasāra* of Devasena: Critical Text", in *Annals of the Bhandarkar Oriental Research Institute,* XV, nos. 3-4, pp. 198-206.
6. P. S. Jaini, "*Mahābhārata* motifs in the Jaina *Pāṇḍavapurāṇa*", in the *Bulletin of the School of Oriental and African Studies,* University of London, Vol. XLVII, Part 1, pp. 108-115, 1984. It may be noted here that this article dealt with one more version of [the unpublished] *Pāṇḍavapurāṇa* of bhaṭṭāraka Vādicandra (A.D. 1600) of the Mūlasaṅgha lineage. Vādicandra does not show any acquaintance with the works of either Śubhacandra or Śrībhūṣaṇa.
7. *Harivaṃśapurāṇa* of Punnāṭa Jinasena, ed. and tr. into Hindi by Pannalal Jain, Bhāratīya Jñānapītha, Varanasi, 1962.
8. *Pāṇḍavacaritaṃ Mahākāvyam,* ed. Kedarnath and Panshikar, Kāvyamālā Series, 93, Bombay, 1962.
9. *Pāṇḍavapurāṇam* of Śubhacandra, ed. and tr. into Hindi by J. P. Shastri, Jīvarāja Jaina Granthamālā, No. 3, Sholapur, 1954.
10. śiṣyas tasya samṛddhibuddhiviśado yas tarkavedī varo
vairāgyādiviśuddhivṛndajanakaḥ Śrīpālavarṇī mahān /
saṃśodhyākhilapustakaṃ varaguṇaṃ satPāṇḍavānām idam
tenālekhi purāṇam arthanikaraṃ pūrvaṃ varaṃ pustake //
Śrīpālavarṇinā yenākāri śastrārthasaṅgrahe /
sāhāyyaṃ sa ciraṃ jīyād varavidyāvibhūṣaṇaḥ //XXV, 182-183.
11. I am grateful to the trustees of the Balātkāragaṇa Jaina Mandira of Karanja for their kindness in providing me a xerox copy of this manuscript. It is written on paper and consists of 358 pages with eleven lines on each side. According to the colophon it was copied in 1803 (Vikrama Saṃvat 1860) in Karanja at the Candranātha temple by Ācārya Ratnakīrti (*saṃvat 1860 varṣe...Kāraṃjāgrāme...Candranāthamandire...Ratnakīrtyācāryen(ṇ)a...svahastena likhitaṃ pūrṇakṛtam...*, page 358b).
12. For a description of the five *kalyāṇas,* see P. S. Jaini, *The Jaina Path of Purification,* Ch. I, University of California Press, 1979.

13. *Pārśvābhyudaya* together with *Bālabodhinī-ṭikā,* ed. and tr. into English, by M. G. Kothari, Nirṇayasāgara Press, Bombay, 1909.
14. *Nemicarita,* ed. and tr. into Hindi, by Udayalalji Kashlival, Śrī Jaina Grantharatnākara Kāryālaya, Bombay, 1914. This work is also known by the title *Nemidūta.* For a detailed description of the *Pārśvābhyudaya* and the *Nemidūta,* see Gulabchandra Chaudhari, *Jaina Sāhitya kā Bṛhad Itihāsa* (in Hindi) Part 6: *kāvya-sāhitya,* pp. 546-548. Pārśvanātha Vidyāśrama Śodha Saṃsthāna, Varanasi, 1973.
15. Nemicandraś ciraṃ jīyād viyaccāriḥ bhaved balāt /...
Ratnakīrttiḥ bhaved ratnarohan(ṇ)ācalavat sadā /...
aṇvartho dharmaseno 'bhūd Dharmaseno guṇāgraṇīḥ /...
Vimalasenako sūri ravir iva virājate /...
Viśvasenasūri jīyād Viśālo sarvakīrtikaḥ /...
Vidyābhūṣaṇasūrīndro granthānāṃ grathane kṣamaḥ //I, 21-26.

CHAPTER 21

Jaina Purāṇas: A Purāṇic Counter Tradition*

When discussing the Jaina Purāṇas and their relationship to the Brahminic Purāṇas, one is immediately struck by a metaphor that is readily understood by readers of Indological studies published in the early twentieth century. With rare exceptions, these works contain a large number of additions and corrections, which in turn need further additions and corrections, ad infinitum. Even a cursory glance at the Jaina Purāṇas makes it clear that the Jaina authors who composed them knew the Hindu Epics and Purāṇas well, studied them with the attention worthy of a board of censors examining the offensive portions of a story, and finally decided to rewrite the script in conformity with their own doctrines and sensibilities. To the credit of the Jainas, it must be said that they did not accomplish this project by any surreptitious means but instead, as will be seen below, achieved their goal by declaring openly that they were setting the record straight. For they alleged that certain narratives of these texts had been deliberately falsified by their adversaries, the Brahmins, proponents of the Vedic rituals and worshippers of such divinities as Brahmā, Viṣṇu, and Śiva. For the Jainas, who did not believe in a creator God, who rejected the efficacy of the Vedic and Tantric rituals, and who questioned the power of the Deity to grant salvation, the Purāṇic descriptions of the sport of these divinities was of no value whatsoever. Indeed,

---

*This article was published originally in *Purāṇa Perennis*, ed. Wendy Doniger, (Albany: State University of New York Press, 1993) pp. 209-249 and 284-293 (notes). Reprinted with kind permission of State University of New York Press.

one might surmise that if the Purāṇas had been content only to extol the virtues of these gods, the Jainas probably would have ignored them as literature unfit for study by devout followers of the Jina, and of little consequence for their own creed. For the Jainas too had their own texts, called the Jinacaritas (biographies of their celebrated Tīrthaṅkaras), which could be expanded into popular narratives that could compete with the heretical Purāṇas.

What made the Jaina writers view these Hindu Purāṇas with hostility was the Brahminic attempt to appropriate such worldly heroes as Rāma and Kṛṣṇa, sanctify their secular lives, and set them up as divine incarnations of their god Viṣṇu. The devotional movements that grew up around these so-called *avatāras* threatened to overwhelm the Jaina laity, who mostly belonged to the affluent merchant castes, and there was the increasing danger that they might return to the Brahminic fold from which they had earlier been converted. Rāma and Kṛṣṇa originally figured as human heroes even in the Brahminic Epics, which extolled their righteous rulership or heroic victories and thus were acceptable to all Indians, regardless of religion or creed. But once the proponents of Vedic religion identified them with the Vedic god Viṣṇu, the Jaina teachers seemed to have been faced with a difficult choice: either to accept the Brahminic version of history and forego their own identity as upholders of a different faith or to set forth a new version of these tales in which these two heroes would be integrated into the Jaina tradition and their magnificent lives would be made subservient to the holy careers of the Tīrthaṅkaras, the last of whom, namely, Vardhamāna, was appropriately hailed as Mahāvīra the Great Hero!

The legends of the Tīrthaṅkaras are as foreign to the Brahminic traditions as are stories of the Vedic and Purāṇic divinities to the Jainas. But both traditions must have found something that could be profitably exploited to present their own world-views and ethical teachings in the historical accounts of Rāma and Kṛṣṇa, their mildly virtuous brothers Lakṣmaṇa and Balarāma, and their valorous adversaries, Rāvaṇa and Jarāsandha, respectively. The Jaina authors, who may well have preserved a different recension of these accounts than the one handed down in the Brahminic tradition, might have then decided to portray these heroes in such a manner as would be consistent with their peculiar doctrines of *karma* and salvation. This probably explains both the complete absence of the category known as *itihāsa* (Epic) in the Jaina literature and the presence of such unusual narrative texts as *Paümacariya* and *Pāṇḍavapurāṇa,* names conspicuously absent from the traditional list of Brahminic Purāṇas. The Jaina Purāṇas are thus distinguished from their Brahminic counterparts by their integration of the pan-Indian *itihāsas* with the exclusively Jaina legends of the Tīrthaṅkaras, which span more than an entire eon (*kalpa*).

How and when this process of Jainizing the accounts of the Epic heroes began is a question that, strangely enough, has not yet been raised. But a glance at the beginnings of the Jaina Purāṇic literature[1] indicates that this trend towards assimilation could have begun only after the elevation of Kṛṣṇa as an *avatāra* of Viṣṇu in the Brahminic Epics and Purāṇa. This hypothesis is based on the fact that in the Jaina texts the names Baladeva and Vāsudeva are not restricted to the brothers otherwise known as Balarāma and Kṛṣṇa, the two Purāṇic *avatāras* of Viṣṇu; instead, they serve as names of two distinct classes of mighty brothers, who appear nine times in each half of the time cycles of the Jaina cosmology and jointly rule half the earth as half-Cakrins! The texts give us no clue as to how the Jainas arrived at such an extraordinary class of beings, conspicuously absent from the Brahminic mythology as well as the earlier strata of the Jaina canonical literature. But it is possible to trace their origin to certain earlier lists of *śalākā puruṣas,* "Illustrious Beings," appearing in the *Jinacarita* of the pontiff Bhadrabāhu, who is said to have been a contemporary (and teacher) of Candragupta, the Mauryan emperor (ca. 330 B.C.E.). Incorporated in the famous *Kalpa Sūtra*[2] since very ancient times, this text contains a list of twenty-four Tīrthaṅkaras, beginning with Ṛṣabha and ending with Vardhamāna Mahāvīra, and contains a skeletal biography of these Supreme Teachers, with special emphasis on the five *kalyāṇas* or auspicious moments of their holy career, namely, conception (*garbha*), birth (*janma*), renunciation (*dīkṣā*), enlightenment (*kevalajñāna*) and death (*nirvāṇa*).

The Theravāda list of the twenty-five Buddhas (with Siddhārtha Gautama as the last), given in the *Buddhavaṃsa,*[3] was also probably formulated in the post-Mauryan period. Both of these Śramaṇic lists predate the lists of the Daśāvatāras and the still larger lists of the Aṃśāvatāras found in the later Purāṇas.[4] At some time soon after the compilation of the *Jinacarita,* the Jaina teachers seem to have drawn up a similar list of Cakravartins, next only to their Tīrthaṅkaras in glory, as is suggested by the example of Bharata, the eldest son of the first Tīrthaṅkara, Ṛṣabha. Bharata appears in the Jaina canon as an ideal layman and a king, upholder of the Jaina law of nonviolence or noninjury (*ahiṃsā*), the first Cakravartin of this eon, from whom was derived the name *Bhāratavarṣa*, the continent of India. The list contained the following names of twelve such Cakravartins, appropriately, half the number of the Tīrthaṅkaras, who claimed to be the Lords of Six Continents (*ṣaṭkhaṇḍa-adhipati*),[5] of which only the first two can be traced to the Brahminic Purāṇas: (1) Bharata, (2) Sagara, (3) Maghavan, (4) Sanatkumāra, (5) Śānti, (6) Kunthu, (7) Ara, (8) Subhauma, (9) Mahāpadma, (10) Hariṣeṇa, (11) Jayasena, and (12) Brahmadatta.

It is said that three of these twelve Cakravartins, namely, Śānti, Kunthu and Ara, played the role of a Cakravartin as well as that of a Tīrthaṅkara, thus effectively reducing the number of Cakravartins to nine, a figure that will serve as a model in preparing other categories of the Illustrious Beings as well. Of the remaining nine, six Cakravartins, following the example of Bharata, renounced the world to become Jaina mendicants and attained release (*mokṣa*) after their death. Two, however, Subhauma and Brahmadatta, ruled unrighteously and were reborn in hell. It is evident that the Jaina list of Cakravartins made provision for bringing into the Jaina fold both virtuous heroes and villainous tyrants, in order to illustrate the Jaina doctrine of karmic justice as well as the path of salvation.

The hero as a spiritual victor, or Jina (an epithet claimed in ancient times for both the Buddha and Mahāvīra), and as a supreme ruler, or Cakravartin, were categories that originated in the Śramaṇic traditions of the Gangetic valley. In compiling the lists of these two kinds of "heroes", therefore, the Jainas were not influenced by Brahminic mythology or literary models. But the categories of Baladevas and Vāsudevas are unknown to the Buddhist tradition and, as noted earlier, cannot be traced to the earlier strata of the Jaina canon. The introduction of these novel categories in the Jaina tradition, therefore, cannot be explained without reference to the myths surrounding the two popular cultic figures of the Vaiṣṇava tradition, namely, Balarāma and his younger brother, Kṛṣṇa of Mathura.

Archaeological remains found in the region of Mathura and literary references appearing in such works as that of the grammarian Patañjali support the fact that the popularity of these two cultic figures had reached its zenith in the Mauryan and the Śuṅga period and that the Bhāgavata religion had become widespread in Mathura and the Western India. This period coincides with the large scale migration of Jainas from Magadha to Mathura, where they flourished for several centuries, and their subsequent journeys to Punjab, Rajasthan, and Gujarat, and thence to the Deccan. It seems probable that close contact of their laypeople with the votaries of these cultic figures might have induced the Jaina *ācāryas* to devise means of integrating them with the Jaina tradition. There probably existed a canonical tradition that their twenty-second Tīrthaṅkara, Nemi, was a prince of the Yādava clan and that he was a cousin of Balarāma and Kṛṣṇa.[6] By accepting the Brahminic myths associated with these two heroes, albeit modified to suit the Jaina sensibilities, and by making them subservient to the Tīrthaṅkara Nemi, the Jainas could claim that these two popular heroes had actually once been members of the Jaina community and had, in these degenerate times, been falsely claimed by the Brahmins as incarnations of their god Viṣṇu. Several ancient (probably Kuśāṇa) images depicting the Tīrthaṅkara Nemi on a high pedestal flanked by the figures of Balarāma and Kṛṣṇa, now preserved in the Mathura Museum, attest to the credibility of our hypotheses.[7]

But Balarāma and Kṛṣṇa were not the only human *avatāras* of Viṣṇu: long before them another pair of illustrious brothers had flourished; these brothers, Rāma and Lakṣmaṇa, also had been appropriated by the Brahmins as incarnations of the same deity appearing on earth to vanquish the demon Rāvaṇa. The coincidence of finding two such pairs of brothers, deeply attached to each other and fighting the same enemy, must have played some part in suggesting to the Jaina authors the possibility of devising newer categories of Illustrious Beings as a supplement to their lists of the Tīrthaṅkaras and Cakravartins.

The designations of these new categories of heroes, the Baladevas and Vāsudevas, are clearly adaptations of the personal names of the two Yādava brothers, Balarāma and Kṛṣṇa, respectively. The Jaina texts are ambiguous in defining their precise roles, but the intention of the *ācāryas* seems to be to depict the one (the Baladeva) as leading the life of an ideal Jaina layman, subsequently renouncing the world to become a Jaina monk, and to portray the other (the Vāsudeva) as the hero's companion, who is capable of carrying out terrible destruction regardless of the evil consequences that may ensue. They are often described as the joint sovereigns of half the earth (half-Cakrins), who play out their respective roles only during those long intervals when a Cakravartin, the ruler of the whole earth, may not appear. They are nine pairs of brothers born of the same father but different mothers; the elder brothers are the Baladevas and the younger are the Vāsudevas. All of the Baladevas fit the stereotype of Balarāma: like him they are white in complexion and can be recognized because they carry the weapon that characterized him, the plough (*aparājita-hala*). Because of this, they are also known as "Halabhṛts".[8] The following names appear in the list of Baladevas: Vijaya, Acala, Dharma, Suprabha, Sudarśana, Nandiṣeṇa, Nandimitra, Rāma (also called Padma), and Balarāma. It should be noted here that Rāma, the hero of the *Rāmāyaṇa,* is reckoned as a Baladeva and, hence, is referred to by the Jaina Purāṇas as Halabhṛt, although no Brahminic account designates him as such.

All of the Vāsudevas are modelled after the descriptions of Kṛṣṇa found in the Brahminic Purāṇas. They are blue-black (*nīla*) in complexion and are designated by several names applied exclusively to Kṛṣṇa in the Brahminic tradition, for example, Keśava, Mādhava, Govinda, Viṣṇu, Janārdana, and, most importantly, Nārāyaṇa which is used regularly as a synonym for the generic name Vāsudeva. The Vāsudevas are said to remain young forever, without growing facial hair, and come to possess the following seven gems (*ratnas*): the wheel (*sudarśana-cakra*), the mace (*kaumudī-gadā*), the sword (*saunandaka-asi*), the missile (*amogha-śakti*) the bow (*śārañga-dhanu*), the conch (*pañcajanya-śaṅkha*), and the diamond (*kaustubha-maṇi*).[9] The following names appear in the list of Vāsudevas: Tripṛṣṭha, Dvipṛṣṭha, Svayambhū, Puruṣottama, Puruṣasiṃha, Puruṣapuṇḍarīka, Datta, Lakṣmaṇa, and Kṛṣṇa. The noteworthy feature of this list is that it includes Lakṣmaṇa; the son of Daśaratha thus gets the appellation Vāsudeva (literally, "son of Vasudeva"), a title never applied to him in the Brahminic texts.

The two lists above are accompanied by a complementary list of the Prati-vāsudevas, or Prati-nārāyaṇas, the deadly adversaries of the Vāsudevas.[10] This list includes: Aśvagrīva, Tāraka, Madhu, Madhusūdana, Madhukrīḍa, Niśumbha, Bali, Rāvaṇa, and Jarāsandha. Rāvaṇa and Jarāsandha are, of course, immediately recognizable; and the other Prati-vāsudevas, unlike the members of the other two categories of heroes, are not altogether unfamiliar. Some of them are names of demons (*asuras*) destroyed by Viṣṇu in his various *avatāras*. In the Jaina Purāṇas, however, they are presented as *vidyādharas*, men possessing great magic powers but given to excessive forms of greed, lust (as in the case of Rāvaṇa), or envy (as in the case of Jarāsandha). It is said that a Prati-vāsudeva has nursed a deep enmity against a Vāsudeva in previous lives and that the accumulated hatred culminates in a tremendous battle of cosmic proportions during his present incarnation. Further, it is believed that the wheel-gem called "*sudarśana*" first appears miraculously in the armory of the Prati-vāsudeva, tempting him to challenge the Vāsudeva, his predestined enemy, to battle. However, partly because of the Baladeva's power of merit, but mainly because of the invincible valor of the Vāsudeva, the wheel-gem fails to kill him when hurled by the Prati-vāsudeva in his direction. Instead, it comes of its own accord into the hands of the Vāsudeva, who throws it at the Prati-vāsudeva and beheads him; thereupon the Vāsudeva is hailed by gods and men as a half-Cakrin, the Lord of the Three Continents (Trikhaṇḍādhipati). Pursued by his evil *karma*, the Prati-vāsudeva is reborn in hell but, in due course, becomes a human being, follows the Jaina path, and attains *mokṣa*.

As was also the case with the Prati-vāsudevas, the class names Baladeva and Vāsudeva, the epithets used in describing the gods, and their personal names leave no room for doubting that the Jaina authors had deliberately embarked upon a project of producing grand narratives that would run parallel to those popularized by the Vaiṣṇavites. However, in retelling their versions the Jaina authors shrewdly made a major change that was to accomplish at a single stroke both the elevation of Rāma to the status of a Jaina saint and the consignment of Kṛṣṇa to hell. Both of these incarnations of Viṣṇu should have been accorded equal status, since both had successfully vanquished demonic forces and thereby had accomplished the avowed purpose of an *avatāra*. Yet, employing their discriminatory wisdom, the Jainas raised Rāma to the benevolent category of a Baladeva by freeing him from the dreadful task of killing Rāvaṇa. Instead, the Jainas chose to have this destruction occur at the hands of Lakṣmaṇa and thus cast him, together with Kṛṣṇa, in the role of the brave but malevolent Vāsudeva. They were then free to declare quite candidly that in accordance with the inscrutable laws of *karma,* all Baladevas had attained *mokṣa* (with the exception of Balarāma, who had been reborn in heaven), while their brothers the Vāsudevas were condemned to hell for having violently killed their archenemies, the Prati-vāsudevas, in fulfilment of a long-cherished evil aspiration (*nidāna*) from past lives.[11]

This would appear to be the process by which the "corrections" introduced by the Jainas into the Brahminic accounts of the Epic heroes occurred. In the course of time, even these Jainized versions would receive further modifications at the hands of zealous sectarian authors. Additional lists, such as that of the nine Nāradas[12] (Jaina counterparts of the Brahminic sage of that name, they were the instigators of strife between the Vāsudevas and the Prati-vāsudevas) and that of the eleven Rudras[13] (apostate Jaina mendicants who would misuse their occult powers) appeared, making the narratives as edifying and entertaining as those of their rivals. Thus is explained the origin of the sixty-three Illustrious Beings[14] (*śalākāpuruṣas*: twenty-four Tīrthaṅkaras, twelve Cakravartins, nine Baladevas, nine Vāsudevas, and nine Prati-vāsudevas), who comprised the subject-matter of the Jaina versions of the *itihāsas* and Purāṇas, an amalgamation of narratives pertaining to both the Spiritual Victors (Jinas) and the worldly heroes of the land of Bhāratavarṣa.

Just as the traditional eighteen Purāṇas, together with the Epics, are considered *smṛtis,* which were subservient in their authority to the *śrutis,* or Vedic literature, the Jaina Purāṇic literature is also relegated to a position secondary to that of the Jaina canon, known as the Pūrvas and Aṅgas. These latter two are said to have proceeded from the mouth of the Tīrthaṅkara Mahāvīra and to have been handed down in the oral tradition through the lineage of the Gaṇadharas, the immediate mendicant disciples of Mahāvīra, and, in a subsequent period, the *ācāryas.* According to Jaina tradition, the subject-matter of the Purāṇas, namely, the sixty-three Illustrious Beings, was included in the section called the "Pūrvas" (Ancient Ones), which seems to be a Jaina synonym for the Purāṇa itself. However, the Pūrva became extinct soon after the death of Mahāvīra; according to unanimous Jaina tradition, the last person to retain the memory of a portion of it was the mendicant Bhadrabāhu, the chief pontiff of the Jaina mendicant community prior to the emegence of the Digambaras and the Śvetāmbaras, two rival sects. Both traditions agree that he was a contemporary of Candragupta, the first Mauryan king, who flourished around 330 B.C.E.

After the death of Bhadrabāhu the split between the two sects was so severe that each of them refused to acknowledge the authenticity of the scriptures that had been received in the other's tradition; and each eventually set up its own canonical, commentarial, and narrative literature in conformity with its own sectarian beliefs. Therefore, despite the fact that the contents of the Jaina Purāṇas are traced to the now extinct Pūrvas, the literature that has grown through the ages is a development that began several centuries after the death of Mahāvīra and was imbued with a sectarian spirit from its very inception. Both the Digambaras, who claimed that the entire Aṅga canon was also lost, and the Śvetāmbaras, who asserted that a great deal of it was preserved in their tradition, devised a new category of scripture, *anuyoga* (literally, "Additional Questions" [asked of Mahāvīra]), which was in four parts. The first of these, simply called the *prathamānuyoga,* was devoted to the biographies of the twenty-four Jinas of the present half of the Jaina time cycle (the Avasarpiṇī or "Descending" half), to which were added, as we saw above, the narratives of the remaining *śalākā puruṣas,* forming the present-day Purāṇas of the Jaina community. Thus what we have available under the rubric of the Jaina Purāṇas are two sets of sectarian narratives, each purporting to describe accurately a single set of the lives of the sixty-three Illustrious Beings.

Unlike the Brahminic Purāṇas, most of which are of unknown authorship and in Sanskrit, all of the Jaina Purāṇas have well-known authors and are available in Sanskrit, Prakrit, and Apabhraṃśa as well. As a matter of fact, the earliest extant Jaina Purāṇa is in Maharashtri Prakrit, composed probably in conformity with the Jaina belief that Prakrit was the sacred language in which the words of Mahāvīra were preserved. However, this earliest narrative work is neither labelled as a "Purāṇa" nor named after a Tīrthaṅkara. Instead, as the title *Paümacariya*[15] would indicate, it is a *cariya* (Sanskrit *carita*), a "biography," a term rather close to the designation *itihāsa,* and celebrates the life of Padma, a Jaina name of Rāma, the eighth Vāsudeva of Jaina mythology, who was none other than the hero of Vālmīki's *Rāmāyaṇa.* The author of this work, Vimalasūri, is said to have been a mendicant of the Digambara sect. According to the colophon preserved in the text, the work was completed in the year 530 after the death of Mahāvīra; this corresponds to the fourth year of the common era. However, the linguistic study of the text has led scholars such as Hermann Jacobi and K. R. Chandra to place it in the third or fourth century C.E. The entire work is divided into 118 sections and consists of 8,651, *gāthās,* which can be considered equivalent to about twelve thousand *ślokas* in extent; it is probably the earliest and longest poetical work extant in Prakrit.

There is probably no connection between the title *Paümacariya,* and the *Padma Purāṇa,* one of the eighteen Brahminic Purāṇas. The word *padma* in the title of latter work does not refer to Rāma, as it does in the Jaina work, but rather to the lotus shape of the earth after its recreation at the beginning of a new evolutionary cycle (*sarga*).[16] Vimalasūri's choice of the names *Padma* over the more familiar *Rāma* and *Rāghava* (names that were not unknown to him) may be considered an attempt to assert a Jaina identity for a work on the hero of the *Rāmāyaṇa.* This should not, however, mislead us into believing that *Paümacariya* is merely a Jaina story of Rāma, for the work essentially covers all of the *śalākā puruṣas,* who flourished from the time of Ṛṣabha, the first Tīrthaṅkara, up to that of the twentieth Tīrthaṅkara, Munisuvrata, in whose regime (*tīrtha* or *śāsana*), roughly corresponding to the second Brahminic *yuga,* the actual story of Rāma took place. This becomes evident when we analyze the contents of the book's 118 chapters. The first 24 describe the Illustrious Beings who flourished before the time of Rāma; the next 61 chapters are devoted to the exploits of the brothers Rāma and Lakṣmaṇa, the eighth Baladeva and Vāsudeva, respectively, and end the account with their coronation in Ayodhyā after the destruction of Rāvaṇa, the eighth Prativāsudeva. In the remaining 33 chapters the poet describes the events following the banishment of Sītā; these events lead up to the death of Lakṣmaṇa and Rāma's renunciation and attainment of *mokṣa.*

The introductory portions of the *Paümacariya* reveal quite openly the purpose of writing the story: the presentation of a Jaina account of the tale of Rāma that should be seen as a deliberate rejection of the Brahminic version of the same story. The *Cariya* opens with a scene depicting Śreṇika, the king of Magadha, approaching Lord Mahāvīra in the holy assembly and asking him questions about the veracity of the accounts of Rāma and Rāvaṇa that he has heard from "*kuśāstra-vādins*" (expounders of false scriptures), a reference undoubtedly to the Brahminic version of that story. It should be remembered that Śreṇika was a recent convert to Jainism through his wife Cellanā, an aunt of Mahāvīra. The king is therefore an excellent instrument for the Jainas to use as an interlocutor, especially where there was an occasion to point out the beliefs of the heretics that needed to be examined. It is not surprising, therefore, that the king reaffirms his faith in Jainism by showing his disbelief in accounts he heard formerly, in which Rāvaṇa and his brothers were demons (*rākṣasas*) or given to the eating of flesh or in which Rāvaṇa defeated Indra, the king of gods, and yet had his powerful armies defeated by a bunch of monkeys (*vānaras*)! Śreṇika is specific in pointing his finger at the source of this travesty as he sees it: "The poets have composed the *Rāmāyaṇa* with perverse contents, like the killing of a lion by a deer or like the destruction of an elephant by a dog . . . All this appears to me to be lies, contrary to reasoning, and not worthy of belief by wise men."[17]

These and other similar questions raised by Śreṇika provide an opportunity for the Jaina author to put forth a new story of Rāma as it was originally narrated by the Omniscient Jina to the king, and as the author had received it in the tradition of the *ācāryas*. But the story proper will not begin until the king is given a detailed account of the lineage (*vaṃśa*) in which the hero Rāma was born, and that tale is closely connected with the origin of civilization at the start of a new time cycle. Thus a full discourse on the Jaina concept of time and space or the universe, known as *saṃsāra*, is required to be unfolded for the king to appreciate properly the place of Rāma in the Jaina history of the world. It is by this circuitous method that Vimalasūri introduces the Purāṇa topics known to us as creation, destruction, ancient dynasties, epochs of the Manus, and later dynasties. These *pañcalakṣaṇas*, the five characteristics of the Brahminic Purāṇas, thus become guidelines for the Jaina Purāṇas as well, albeit under different headings. They provide the Jainas with a new opportunity to expound their worldview, especially in the contexts of their independent cosmology, the beginning of civilization in our epoch, and the founding of the Jaina order of monks, from which would rise the most holy of the Illustrious Beings, the Tīrthaṅkaras and their eminent lay devotees.

Having thus provided a brief but essential outline of the Jaina doctrine pertaining to time, space, and the movement of souls therein, and having narrated in brief form the narratives of the twenty Tīrthaṅkaras, the nine Cakravartins, and the seven previous sets of the Baladevas, Vāsudevas, and Prati-vāsudevas, Vimalasūri launches the story Padma, the Jaina version of Rāma, the son of Daśaratha. The story itself does not differ significantly from the version given in the Vālmīki *Rāmāyaṇa*;[18] the changes are more in the details of the plot or in the incredible descriptions of the secondary characters that had so confused the king (and, no doubt, many others who had heard it)! Rāvaṇa, in the Jaina version, is not a demon but a Jaina layman who has mastered certain magic powers (*vidyās*), is hailed as a *vidyādhara,* and has at his command a large host of other such beings to help him in his ambition to rule the world. Even the monkeys of the *Rāmāyaṇa* namely, Bali and Sugrīva, are here declared to be *vidyādharas,* with Hanumān enjoying the additional distinction of being a God of Love (Kāmadeva), possessing a large harem of most beautiful women, yet destined to become a Jaina monk and attain *mokṣa* in that very life.

Vimalasūri also very cleverly employs the Jaina motif of renunciation in order to rectify some of the wrongs done to certain eminent heroines of the Epic. Kaikeyī, for example, has been portrayed by Vālmīki as a selfish woman wantonly demanding the kingdom for her son Bharata; in the Jaina version she is made to appear rather more like a concerned mother anxious to keep her son with her. In the Jaina story, Daśaratha seriously contemplates renouncing the world to become a Jaina monk; when the young Bharata hears of this, he becomes determined to follow his father into the forest and to assume the vows of a Jaina mendicant. Kaikeyī cannot bear the loss of both husband and son and believes that Bharata could be lured back to household life if he were offered the kingdom. Daśaratha readily agrees to this—in payment of the boon he has previously promised her—and informs Rāma of his decision, whereupon the noble Rāma obeys his father's will and proceeds to the forest of his own accord, accompanied by

Sītā and Lakṣmaṇa.

The motif of renunciation becomes even more appropriate in the treatment of Sītā: in the Brahminic version, Sītā ends her life by what is euphemistically called "entering the earth," that is, committing suicide by falling into a pit. In Jainism, retribution for such a death is instantaneous rebirth in hell. The Jainas probably were determined not to make her suffer beyond what she had already undergone; in the Jaina version she renounces the world to become a Jaina nun as soon as her sons have been united with their estranged father. We have already alluded to the story of the death of Rāvaṇa, the Prati-vāsudeva, at the hands of Lakṣmaṇa the Vāsudeva, and their rebirth in hell as a consequence of their violent activities. We are told that Sītā, after performing great austerities, is reborn in heaven as a male god; having discovered by means of her supernatural knowledge the fallen state of these two heroes, she visits them in their hell and admonishes them to give up their long-cherished enmity. As for Rāma, the supreme hero of the *Paümacariya,* he transcends both heaven and hell by renouncing worldly life to become a Jaina mendicant and becomes a Siddha, a Perfected and Omniscient Being, at the end of his mortal life.

It may be pertinent to ask whether indeed Vimalasūri was influenced in his depiction of the story of Rāma and Lakṣmaṇa by the Purāṇic narratives of Balarāma and Kṛṣṇa, who, as we have suggested, were the models for the Jaina categories of Baladeva and Vāsudeva, respectively. Since the story of Rāma ends long before the advent of the twenty-second Tīrthaṅkara, Nemi (a cousin of Balarāma and Kṛṣṇa in the Jaina tradition), Vimalasūri's story does not include these latter heroes, but there is a rather insignificant detail in the *Paümacariya* that does betray such an influence. It is well-known that in the Purāṇic texts Kṛṣṇa is said to have had sixteen thousand wives; this tradition is very much a part of the folklore surrounding the Kṛṣṇa myth even to this day. As we have seen earlier, Kṛṣṇa and Lakṣmaṇa are both called "Vāsudevas" (or "Nārāyaṇas") in Jaina mythology. Since the descriptions of these two heroes have been almost identical in many respects, one would expect that Lakṣmaṇa in the Jaina tradition would be found to have had a similar number of wives. One is therefore not surprised to find that the *Paümacariya* and the subsequent Jaina narratives about Lakṣmaṇa do indeed describe him as having sixteen thousand wives, with Rāma and Balarāma having only half as many wives as their younger brothers, the Vāsudevas![19]

Obviously the Jaina authors did not think much of Rāma's alleged virtue of monogamy as extolled in the Brahminic *Rāmāyaṇa.* Or, most probably, they found it expedient to make this change in order to establish uniformity with regard to the descriptions of these two pairs of Baladevas and Vāsudevas; this principle would be extended later to all of the remaining pairs of these two classes of heroes. Rāma's single wife certainly would have looked extraordinary in contrast to his brother's thousands of spouses. The excessive number of wives attributed to Rāma might also serve better to emphasize the greater degree of his detachment when the time of his renunciation would arrive. In the case of Lakṣmaṇa, however, as a Vāsudeva he was destined to be reborn in hell; hence his excessive indulgence in carnal pleasures would only contribute to his inevitable fate.

Vimala's Prakrit *Paümacariya* became the standard text for a great many Jaina compositions on the life of Rāma. Most noteworthy of these is the Sanskrit *Padma-Carita* in eighteen thousand *ślokas,* completed in 676 C.E. by the Digambara mendicant Raviṣeṇa.[20] Raviṣeṇa's Sanskrit rendering with added embellishments inspired the composition of Sanskrit Purāṇa works by a large number of Jaina poets, in both the Digambara and Śvetāmbara sects, as well as two Purāṇas in Apabhraṃśa by two Digambara laymen, one the eighth-century Svayambhū[21] and another the eleventh-century Puṣpadanta.[22]

The *Paümacariya* bore the name of Padma, that is, Rāma, because this hero flourished at a time when there was no living Tīrthaṅkara; hence a Baladeva, a *śalākā puruṣa* of a lesser order, could be elevated to the position of the supreme hero of this text. In the case of Kṛṣṇa and Balarāma, however, a similar elevation could not be effected, because the Yādava brothers were contemporaries, indeed, cousins of the twenty-second Tīrthaṅkara, Nemi (also called Ariṣṭanemi or Neminātha). The second stage in the development of the Jaina Purāṇas, therefore, begins ostensibly as a description of the advent of this Jina Nemi and only secondarily as that of the Epic heroes Balarāma and Kṛṣṇa. Since all three of these heroes were born in the great Hari dynasty (of which the Yadus were a prominent branch), a Purāṇa named after that lineage could readily encompass the narratives of a Tīrthaṅkara and of the two lesser Epic heroes as well. It is therefore fitting that the Prakrit *Paümacariya* should be succeeded by a text entitled *Harivaṃśapurāṇa,* composed in 783 C.E., in Saurashtra—a Vaiṣṇavite stronghold—by a Digambara mendicant, [Punnāṭa] Jinasena.[23]

Whether the Jaina author owed his title to the *Harivaṃśa Parva,*[24] an appendix to the *Mahābhārata,* is a question that cannot be answered with certainty. There is no doubt, however, that both narratives share a great many common episodes, especially ones that concern the life of Kṛṣṇa and that of his sister Ekanāsā. Even so, there are a great many other characters in the Hari lineage who do not come under the purview of the *Harivaṃśa Parva.* One notable example is Kṛṣṇa's father, Vasudeva, whom the Jainas consider to be one of the twenty-four Kāmadevas of our time cycle.[25] For reasons that are not clear to us, the Jainas of Jinasena's time were more fascinated by this old character than by his more charismatic adolescent son, who wandered the pastures of Mathura! A great work called *Vasudeva-hiṇḍī* (Travels of Vasudeva), in two parts of eleven thousand and eighteen thousand verses, respectively, was composed as early as the fifth century C.E. in Maharashtri Prakrit by the two Śvetāmbara mendicant authors Saṅghadāsagaṇi and Dharmadāsagaṇi.[26] The entire work was devoted to narratives concerning the amorous exploits of its hero, Vasudeva, who wandered all over India for a hundred years and won the hands of numerous women in marriage. Such a work, however, could not qualify as a Purāṇa, since Vasudeva was only a Kāmadeva and, as such, could not be a part of the traditional list of the *śalāka puruṣas.* Jinasena's *Harivaṃśapurāṇa,* therefore, affords him a fresh opportunity to bring together a great many such related episodes (*ākhyānas*) and to weave them into the more prominent narratives of the officially accepted heroes. In this manner, the *Harivaṃśapurāṇa* grew to be a treasure-house of information on such miscellaneous items as music (*Saṅgīta-śāstra*), dance (*Sāmudrika-śāstra*), and art (*Śilpa-śāstra*), to mention only a few—a Jaina encyclopedia, as it were, in the manner of the Brahminic Purāṇas.

With regard to form, however, Jinasena closely follows the pattern established earlier by Vimalasūri. His work also begins with King Śreṇika's visit to the assembly of Mahāvīra, where the king asks a question about a contemporary, King Jitaśatru, a scion of Hari's clan who had recently died as a Jaina saint. In response, Mahāvīra, through his interlocutor Gautama, narrates the origin of the Hari dynasty, preceded by a description of other illustrious dynasties, notably the Ikṣvāku and the Kuru, in which had been born a great many Tīrthaṅkaras and other *śalākā puruṣas*. The first seventeen chapters of the *Harivaṃśapurāṇa* are thus devoted to the description of the notable events that took place during the regimes of the first twenty-one Tīrthaṅkaras, culminating with that of Nemi, during whose time the Yādava branch of the Hari dynasty came into being.

In the eighteenth chapter the author sets forth the family tree of the ten Yādava brothers, the Vṛṣṇis, of whom King Samudravijaya, the father of Tīrthaṅkara Nemi, was the oldest, and Vasudeva, the father of Balarāma and Kṛṣṇa, the youngest. One might expect the Purāṇa to proceed at this point with the narrative of the Jina Nemi, yet the author finds it necessary to devote a full twelve chapters to describing the amorous pursuits of Vasudeva. The poetic accounts of Kṛṣṇa's rapturous amorous activities with the *gopīs* and other women is well known to us through the *Harivaṃśa Parva* and the *Bhāgavatapurāṇa*. One wonders if the Jainas, in portraying the father rather than the son in this manner, were not attempting to deflect attention away from Kṛṣṇa, the popular god of medieval India. Perhaps freeing Kṛṣṇa from the debaucheries otherwise attributed to him in the Brahminic Purāṇas made it possible for the Jainas to accept him as one of their own heroes, dignified enough to share the company of other *śalākā puruṣas*! Be that as it may, the actual story of Nemi, Kṛṣṇa and Balarāma thus begins only in the thirty-third chapter, almost exactly at the midpoint of the *Harivaṃśapurāṇa*.

The narrative pertaining to Kṛṣṇa gives the Jaina authors an excellent opportunity to introduce the episode of the *Mahābhārata* war between the Pāṇḍavas and their cousins, the Kauravas. The Pāṇḍavas were maternal cousins of Kṛṣṇa (sons of his aunts Kuntī and Mādrī), and their family strife made Kṛṣṇa's participation necessary for their victory in the war against the faction of Duryodhana. Here, too, the Jainas have effected a great many changes in the *Mahābhārata* story: excising entirely those parts that were offensive to them (such as Vyāsa's begetting children by Levirate appointment [*niyoga*] on the widows Ambikā and Ambālikā) or modifying other stories, such as that of Kuntī's obtaining children by the help of gods or the polyandry of Draupadī.[27] Nor did the Jainas have Kṛṣṇa appear in the great war as a charioteer for Arjuna preaching his Divine Song, the *Bhagavad Gītā*, but instead only as an instigator and an advocate of bravery in warfare.

The narrative pertaining to the untimely renunciation of Nemi (on the eve of his marriage) and his attainment of Jinahood dominates the rest of the work. The Purāṇa concludes with the description of Kṛṣṇa's death at the hands of his step-brother Jarākumāra (as in the *Bhāgavata* story); the renunciation of Balarāma and the five Pāṇḍava brothers, together with their innumerable spouses, including Satyabhāmā and Draupadī; their rigorous austerities; and the attainment of heaven by everyone except Kṛṣṇa, who, alas, being a Vāsudeva, was born in the same hell where his archenemy Jarāsandha, the last Prati-vāsudeva, had been dispatched by him earlier in the great war!

There are five principal characters who stand out in Jinasena's rendering of the Kṛṣṇa narrative. Of these, Nemi is an entirely Jaina character and does not figure in the Brahminic accounts. We have already remarked on the relatively excessive amount of attention paid by the Jainas to Vasudeva, the father of Kṛṣṇa and Balarāma. Before we turn to further modifications made by the Jainas in the stories of the latter two heroes, we may pause here to take into account a very important Jaina narrative pertaining to Kṛṣṇa's sister. She does not play a major role in the Brahminic narratives, either in the *Harivaṃśa Parva* or in the *Bhāgavata-purāṇa*. But Jinasena's version, for reasons that will become evident, devotes an entire chapter to the unfolding of her rather tragic life. This sister of Kṛṣṇa, Ekānaṃśā, who is worshipped as a personification of Durgā, appears probably for the first time in the *Harivaṃśa Parva* in connection with the birth of Kṛṣṇa.[28]

According to this account, Lord Viṣṇu asked his Yogamāyā to be born as a daughter to the cowherd couple Nanda and Yaśodā at the time when he himself was to be born to Devakī as Kṛṣṇa. It was foreseen that this daughter of Yaśodā would be exchanged for Devakī's son, Kṛṣṇa. Accordingly, she was brought home to Mathura by Vasudeva and placed by the side of Devakī, who did not know of the exchange and believed that she had given birth to a daughter. Kaṃsa, expecting the birth of Kṛṣṇa as foretold by the sage Nārada, went to Devakī's side; when he realized that the baby was a female, he grabbed it and, out of spite, smashed it to pieces by hurling it against a rock. Of course, this was no ordinary infant; she rose immediately into the sky, appeared in the fully divine form of a goddess and warned Kaṃsa of his impending doom. She made her abode in the Vindhya mountains and was known as Devī Ekānaṃśā, an epiphany of Durgā, a guardian deity of hunters and other hill-dwelling tribals, from whom she received offerings of flesh and blood.[29] The author of the *Harivaṃśa Parva* does not explain explicitly why she had to be the chosen deity of hunters, but probably it was not considered an inappropriate role for a woman who had, after all, been born into a lower-caste cowherd family.

The Jainas probably could have chosen to ignore this story entirely or could have dismissed it with only a brief account of her death at the hands of Kaṃsa similar to the earlier accounts of Kaṃsa killing Kṛṣṇa's six brothers, born to Devakī before him. But the Jainas must have seen here an excellent opportunity to educate at least their own devotees, if not also the Vaiṣṇavites (who believed this story to be literally true), about the error of the Brahminic accounts of her becoming a bloodthirsty goddess. The name Ekānaṃśā is rarely used elsewhere but is attested for the first time in the *Harivaṃśa Parva*, where it is used as a synonym for such epithets of Durgā as Kātyāyanī, Pārvatī, Nārāyaṇī, Vindhyavāsinī, and so on, and where she is depicted as favouring devotees who propitiate her with flesh and blood. Yet in this same text she is also called an "Āryā,"[30] a term that is used among the Jainas for a nun (*sādhvī*), a circumstance that probably explains the peculiarly Jaina ending of her story.

The word Ekānaṃśā, literally meaning "the single portionless one," itself does not appear in Jinasena's work, but there can be no doubt that this obscure name must have inspired the Jaina story of Kṛṣṇa's sister called, instead, "Ekanāsā." Ekanāsā literally means "one having a single nose," (that is, nostril) and sounds a great deal like Ekānaṃśā; and it is not unlikely that by the time of Jinasena this goddess had come to be known by that name, at least among the lower classes of her worshippers, and was not therefore a purely Jaina invention. Jinasena very ingeniously utilizes this name to construct a counter story to that of the *Harivaṃśa Parva*.

According to his version, adopted by all succeeding Jaina writers,

Ekanāsā was not a goddess but the daughter of the herdsman Nanda and his wife Yaśodā. As in the Brahminic story she was brought to Mathura in exchange for Kṛṣṇa. In the Jaina story, however, Kaṃsa does not kill the female infant. At first, Kaṃsa thinks that a woman could be no threat to him, but later he reflects that her future husband might well become his enemy; therefore he disfigures her face by pounding on her nose. As a result of this she came to be known as Ekanāsā, "one with a single nostril," or Cippiṭa-nāsikā, "one with a crushed nose". This girl grew to become a voluptuous maiden, but because of her hideously deformed nose she was mocked by all and remained without a suitor. It is said that in the full prime of her youth, as she was admiring herself in a mirror, the young sons of Balarāma passed by her and ridiculed her nose, called her by the hated epithet Cippiṭa-nāsikā and ran away, laughing derisively at her.[31] Stung by this ridicule, Ekanāsā (whose real name is not given anywhere by Jinasena or other authors) went crying to a Jaina mendicant and begged him to reveal the past *karma* that had brought this misfortune upon her. Perceiving her past life, the monk told her that in a previous birth she had been a very handsome man, proud of his looks and heedless and cruel. Feeling disgust for a Jaina monk seated in meditation, he drove his cart against him and caused him to fall and break his nose. The misfortunes in her present life were retributions for her act of wilful mischief against a holy man.

Moved deeply by this story of her past life, Ekanāsā, full of remorse, renounced the world while still a maiden and became a Jaina nun under the guidance of Suvratā, a nun superior. Wandering from place to place with her teacher, she traveled far from Mathura and entered the forests of Vindhya. There she dedicated herself entirely to the most extreme forms of austerities and sat day and night in meditation in isolated forests and on mountaintops. One day, while she was seated rapt in meditation, an army of hunters from that forest who were marching forth together to rob a caravan happened to see her in that position under a tree. Thinking her to be the deity of the forest (*vanadevatā*), they greeted her, asked a boon of protection from her, and pledged to be her slaves and devotees if they were to be successful in their venture. While they were gone, a lion attacked her; the nun Ekanāsā quietly suffered the terrible violence, died peacefully, and was reborn in heaven. When the hunters returned to the site after their successful expedition, they found only a great deal of blood on the place where she had been seated and not a trace of her body, other than three pieces of her fingers. The hunters, who were not instructed in the true religion of nonviolence (*ahiṃsā*), believed that the goddess had disappeared but that she must take delight in blood, since it was in evidence everywhere. Worshipping the three pieces of fingers as emblems of the goddess, they offered her sacrifices of their domestic animals, such as goats and buffaloes.

Thus began, according to the Jaina *Harivaṃśapurāṇa,* the horrible worship of this goddess Vindhyavāsinī, the cruel "guardian deity" of the heretics! Having narrated this account, entitled "Durgotpatti-varṇana," Jinasena warns the Jaina laymen of the dangers of listening to false scriptures, worshipping the wrong gods, and indulging in the manifold stupidities of the world (*lokamūḍhatā*) practiced in the name of *dharma!*[32] Ekanāsā does not appear again in Jinasena's narrative, but her depiction here as a cruelly deformed woman sitting in unshakable meditation even at the moment of her death makes her probably a unique example of a heroine among the many Purāṇic accounts of male heroes.

Returning to the main hero of the *Harivaṃśapurāṇa,* the "Vāsudeva" Kṛṣṇa, one finds that Jinasena retains a great many of the accounts of his childhood as narrated in the *Harivaṃśa Parva,* the only major modification being that his numerous enemies are not demons (*asuras*), but animals or human beings endowed with magical powers. For the Jainas these stories had no great religious significance. What distinguishes the Jaina account from the Brahminic narrative is Kṛṣṇa's relationship to his cousin Nemi, the Tīrthaṅkara, on the one hand, and to his elder brother Balarāma, the "Baladeva," on the other.

Jinasena's narrative of Kṛṣṇa does not begin with his present life but looks back to several of his former lives and extends for at least two lives beyond his death as a "Vāsudeva". It is customary for Jaina authors to begin the life story of a major character with a significant event in one of his or her past lives that may hold the seed that bears fruit in the events of the present life of that person. The story of Kṛṣṇa thus begins in the seventh life prior to his current incarnation.[33] During that lifetime, the person now known as Kṛṣṇa was employed as a cook in the household of a king and gained a great reputation for preparing the most delicious meat dishes; he earned the title of Amṛta-rasāyana, as well as the lordship of ten villages. When the king died and his son succeeded to the throne, the new king came under the influence of a Jaina monk and gave up eating meat altogether. The cook was thus left without a job and also lost the revenue of nine of his ten villages. Realizing that a Jaina monk, the preceptor of the new king, was the cause of his loss, he fed the monk a poisonous bitter gourd; as a result the monk died. Because of this evil act, this cook was reborn in hell; eventually he emerged from that abode and, after various travails in succeeding births as a human being and once as a heavenly being, he was born as Kṛṣṇa, the ninth Vāsudeva. The significance of Jinasena's narration of this story of Kṛṣṇa's past life as a cook of meat dishes does not become clear until we examine his relationship to Jina Nemi, his cousin.

As noted above, Nemi was the youngest son of Samudravijaya, the eldest brother of Vasudeva, the father of Kṛṣṇa and Balarāma. Nemi must have been quite young, probably an adolescent, during Kṛṣṇa's war with Jarāsandha. He enters the Kṛṣṇa narrative when the latter was already married to several of his wives, including Satyabhāmā, Rukmiṇī and Jāmbavatī. To these ladies Nemi was a younger brother-in-law (*devara*). It is well-known even to this day in Rajasthan and Gujarat that a platonic romantic relationship often takes place between younger brothers and their elder brothers' wives. All of the Jaina accounts are unanimous in depicting Nemi as a very handsome but shy young man, one having little inclination towards the amorous sports in which the wives of Kṛṣṇa and Balarāma constantly tried to engage him. One day, the story goes, they all enticed Nemi to sport with them in a pond; and when he left to dry himself he playfully asked Satyabhāmā, Kṛṣṇa's chief queen, to wash his wet clothes, a request that only a husband should properly make. Satyabhāmā pretended to be offended by this slight and taunted Nemi by asking if by making such a request he meant to set himself equal to her husband, the Lord of the Pāñcajanya conch. His pride hurt, Nemi walked away in anger and entered the armory of Kṛṣṇa, in which the conch, Pāñcajanya, was in safekeeping. It was believed that no one but Kṛṣṇa could lift this "jewel" of a conch, let alone blow it. Nemi marched inside and amazed the guardians of the conch by lifting it up and blowing it; the reverberations of the sound of the conch reached all over the city and even caused elephants to break their chains in agitation.

When Kṛṣṇa discovered that Nemi had ventured to blow the Pāñcajanya, he realized that his younger cousin was a serious potential rival for his wives' affections as well as for his kingdom, and he resolved to test Nemi's strength. Therefore, in a friendly manner, he asked Nemi to engage in an arm-wrestling contest. Nemi simply extended his arm for Kṛṣṇa to bend it down, but his arm stood like an iron crossbar and Kṛṣṇa was unable to shake it by even a hair's breadth. Several Jaina manuscripts illustrating this scene in the life of Nemi show Kṛṣṇa swinging like a monkey from Nemi's arm, unable to bend it.[34] Kṛṣṇa took the defeat gracefully and embraced Nemi; suggesting that it was time for him to get settled as a married man, he arranged for Nemi's alliance with princess Rājimati.

However, the threat of Nemi's superior might haunted Kṛṣṇa, and he was determined to remove this thorn in his side. He devised a plan for creating a situation that would result in Nemi's going to the forest as a monk. The fateful subconscious impression of his past life as a cook of meat dishes must have in some way led him to forge a plan to gather in the public park of Dvārakā a large herd of animals made ready for the butcher's knife, apparently for the wedding feast of Nemi and Rājimati.[35] Thus as the bridegroom's procession made the rounds of the city on the day of the wedding, heading towards the home of the bride, Nemi's chariot passed by this park, and he was moved by the pitiable sight of these miserable animals bleating and crying. When Nemi learned from his charioteer that the animals had been brought there for those of his guests who ate meat, his heart was overcome with remorse, and he immediately left the wedding procession and turned toward the forest, with the determination to become a monk. Neither the wailings of Rājimati nor the pleas of Kṛṣṇa and Balarāma were able to dissuade him from his purpose.

It is well known that even in the most ancient times the Jainas have been—as attested by the evidence of Buddhist texts[36]—very scrupulous in the observance of a vegetarian diet for both laymen and monks and have never been known to serve any meat dishes under any circumstances whatsoever. In the entire narrative literature of the Jainas, there is no parallel to this story of a Jaina household, especially one so distinguished as to have given birth to a Tīrthaṅkara, preparing to slaughter animals to feed their guests. One might not be off the mark in suggesting that the purpose of this Jaina story was to defame Kṛṣṇa by making him capable of so heinous an act, calculated to sabotage his cousin's marriage and royal career. That the Jaina authors felt compelled even to allow such a story in their narrative of Kṛṣṇa is a sure indication of the fact that they had very serious problems in assimilating into their fold this divinity of a heretic faith, who was notorious for his unethical conduct. As noted above, Kṛṣṇa was to be reborn in hell—it would be his second time in that dismal abode since we began to trace his past lives—as a consequence, at least in Jaina minds, not so much of his acts of violence against his enemies in the great war as of his perpetration of this particular act of intended animal slaughter. Nevertheless, once Nemi had become a mendicant, Kṛṣṇa seems to have been a fervent devotee of the Jina Nemi and engaged in such pious acts as the occasional fasting required of a devout Jaina layman.

The Jaina account of the succeeding events in the lives of Kṛṣṇa and Balarāma, culminating in the destruction of Dvārakā by the curse of the sage Dvaipāyana, are related in much the same manner in the Jaina Purāṇas as they appear in the Brahminic texts, but they make a sudden departure from these texts when they come to describe the scene of the deaths of these two brothers. In the *Bhāgavatapurāṇa*, for example, the Yādavas killed each other under the influence of liquor, and even Balarāma and Kṛṣṇa got into a fistfight. When all of the remaining members of the Yādava clan perished in this manner, Balarāma, it is said, approached a rock beside the sea, sat down upon it, and peacefully breathed his last. Kṛṣṇa, we are told, lay resting all alone under a tree with one leg raised across his knee. A hunter named Jarā (old age), thinking it was a deer, shot an arrow at Kṛṣṇa and pierced his heel, wounding him mortally. As the hunter approached the body he realized his terrible mistake, but Kṛṣṇa reassured him and asked him to convey the news of the destruction of Dvārakā to the Pāṇḍavas. Then, by his yogic power Kṛṣṇa ascended to his divine abode, leaving behind no mortal remains.[37]

The Jaina account of this concluding event in the lives of these two brothers is markedly different, calculated to remove once and for all any doubt about their being anything but ordinary human beings! According to Jinasena, the sage Dvaipāyana was not a heretical ascetic but a Jaina monk given to extreme austerities, one who had amassed great Yogic powers, which, if misused, were capable of burning anything at will. It is said that while drunk with liquor, some of the young Yādava princes, notably some of the sons of Balarāma and Kṛṣṇa, insulted the haughty sage and then assaulted him, thereby provoking his anger and the resulting destruction of Dvārakā by fire. Kṛṣṇa and Balarāma begged the sage to spare the lives of their children but were barely able to escape from the city themselves. The two brothers then wandered all alone, shorn of their royal insignia, barefoot in the sands of the desert of Kutch.

There Kṛṣṇa, suffering from great thirst and unable to walk even one step further, begged Balarāma to fetch water. While Balarāma was away, Jarākumāra, an older step-brother of Kṛṣṇa who had left his parental home in his youth and had somehow survived in the desert by hunting, saw him from a distance; thinking him to be an animal, he shot an arrow at him and wounded him fatally. He realized his mistake as he approached Kṛṣṇa, and, full of remorse, confessed to him that he left his home precisely to avoid such an occurrence, which had been predicted for him by a soothsayer, and that the inevitable had at last happened. Kṛṣṇa recognized him and asked him to go to tell the Pāṇḍavas about the destruction of Dvārakā and also of his death, and, seeing no sign of Balarāma, gave his Kaustubha jewel as a token for him to reclaim the Yādava kingdom. As Jarākumāra departed, Kṛṣṇa covered himself completely with his upper garment and lay there thinking of all those among his relatives who had renounced the world, following the noble example of Nemi. He lamented the fact that he was not able to engage in any such holy act due to the heavy burden of his karmic deeds. Yet he reaffirmed his faith in the teaching of the Jina, chanted Pañcanamaskāra-*mantra* (a holy Jaina litany) and greeted Lord Nemi as he breathed his last. He was reborn instantaneously in [the third] hell.[38]

As in the case of Lakṣmaṇa, Kṛṣṇa's descent to hell as a result of his being a Vāsudeva need not come as a surprise to those who know the Jaina laws of *karma*. Yet what is greatly astonishing is that simultaneously with his statement of Kṛṣṇa's rebirth in hell, Jinasena declares that Kṛṣṇa was destined to be a future Tīrthaṅkara.[39] It should be remembered that, although it is required for a Vāsudeva to be reborn in hell, it is certainly not a Jaina rule that a Vāsudeva must become a Tīrthaṅkara. Jinasena must have had some scriptural authority for making such a claim for Kṛṣṇa, but he does not reveal any specific actions of Kṛṣṇa that might have earned for him such a unique status, either before or during his life as a Vāsudeva. Nor does Jinasena indicate how distant this future will be; but subsequent Jaina writers agree that Kṛṣṇa will be the sixteenth Tīrthaṅkara in the next time cycle,[40] which gives him a fairly long period of time to spend in his present abode. There is also unanimous agreement that Kṛṣṇa's birth as a human being will take place immediately as he emerges from hell and that it will be his last birth, the birth as a Tīrthaṅkara. If this were the case, then one must wonder when Kṛṣṇa could have accumulated those sixteen meritorious acts that are considered prerequisites for birth as a Tīrthaṅkara.[41] It seems that Kṛṣṇa's destination to become so exalted a person as a Tīrthaṅkara was the result of an exceptional concession made by the Jaina *ācāryas* in an effort to rehabilitate Kṛṣṇa and make this assimilation irrevocable.

Returning to the scene of Kṛṣṇa's death, we find that Balarāma returned after a long time and did not realize that Kṛṣṇa was dead but thought that he was asleep and let him rest. After several hours without seeing any sign of movement, Balarāma suspected that Kṛṣṇa might have died, but so deep was his attachment to Kṛṣṇa that he refused to believe it. For six months, we are told, he carried Kṛṣṇa around, bathing his body and taking care of it and crying over his silent brother. Eventually the Pāṇḍavas, accompanied by Jarākumāra, arrived in the desert and found him in that miserable condition. Even they could not persuade Balarāma to believe that Kṛṣṇa indeed was dead. A god named Siddhārtha, the soul of Kṛṣṇa's former charioteer, saw Balarāma in this state and by magical means created in front of him a scene in which someone was planting a lotus on a rock. When Balarāma laughed at the foolishness of the god's act, the celestial being in turn pointed out the stupidity of Balarāma in carrying a dead body around with the hope of reviving it! That finally opened his eyes, and the Pāṇḍavas brought the corpse of Kṛṣṇa to Tungi, a hill top, where it was cremated.[42] Both Balarāma and the Pāṇḍavas handed over their kingdoms to Jarākumāra and renounced the world to become Jaina monks. Then, leading the holy life of Yogis, they one by one died peacefully in meditation. Of the five Pāṇḍavas, Yudhiṣṭhira, Bhīma and Arjuna attained *mokṣa*[43] at the end of their lives, while Nakula and Sahadeva were reborn in heaven.

Balarāma could not overcome his attachment to Kṛṣṇa and hence was not yet ready to attain *mokṣa.*[44] He therefore was reborn in heaven and started immediately to seek his lamented brother. His grief knew no bounds when, with his extrasensory perception, he saw that Kṛṣṇa was nowhere to be found in heaven but had been consigned to hell. Using his supernatural powers, Balarāma then descended into hell and approached Kṛṣṇa and asked him to ascend to heaven with him. But as soon as Kṛṣṇa made an effort to rise, his limbs began to drip as if they were made of butter. Kṛṣṇa then realized the force of the inexorable laws of *karma,* and asked his brother to return to heaven. He then resolved to be reborn as a human being and to strive to attain *mokṣa.*[45]

This Jaina account of the deaths of the two *śalākā puruṣas* and their passing into the destinies of heaven and hell, respectively, are truly remarkable. The Jaina tradition that Kṛṣṇa died before Balarāma and that Balarāma carried Kṛṣṇa's dead body around for six months was probably intended to counter the Vaiṣṇavite belief that Kṛṣṇa, being an *avatāra,* was transported to his divine abode in his physical body (*sadehamukti*). As for Balarāma, who also was considered a minor *avatāra* in the Brahminic stories, his lack of fortitude in the face of his brother's death belied any such claim of a divine portion in him. It should be remembered that Balarāma's counterpart in the Jaina *Rāmāyaṇa,* namely Rāma, also survived his younger brother Lakṣmaṇa and mourned over his death for a long time; and yet Rāma, unlike Balarāma, was deemed virtuous enough to attain *mokṣa* in that very life.

Balarāma's visit to hell to raise Kṛṣṇa follows the example of Sītā, who, after having been born in heaven, visited Lakṣmaṇa in hell to admonish him to abide by the Jaina faith. The Jainas probably saw in these visits merely an affection for a former brother and brother-in-law and hence considered them fitting conclusion to their stories. Jinasena's *Harivaṃśapurāṇa,* however, goes a step further and describes an extraordinary scene showing the weakness of the brothers Kṛṣṇa and Balarāma, a weakness that appears inappropriate in a soul who was, as noted earlier, destined to become a Tīrthaṅkara upon his immediate rebirth as a human being. Incredible as it may seem, Jinasena's account tells us that when the god Balarāma took leave of Kṛṣṇa in hell, the latter implored him to popularize the cult of Viṣṇu by uttering the following words:

> O Brother, return to heaven, and enjoy the fruits of your meritorious deeds. I, too, at the end of my life here, shall attain human birth for the sake of *mokṣa*. We shall together then perform austerities by taking refuge in the teaching of the Jina and will together destroy the bonds of *karma* and attain the bliss of *mokṣa*. But in the meantime, please, for the sake of increasing my glory, fill the whole land of Bharata with temples containing images of me bearing the conch and the wheel and the mace in my hands. Fill the minds of the people of Bhāratavarṣa with astonishment by displaying [scenes depicting] the two of us, accompanied by our sons, and so forth [that is, spouses], and endowed with great riches.[46]

Jinasena's account concludes with the following words:

> Hearing these words of Kṛṣṇa, Balarāma, that King of Gods, came to the land of the Bharatas and, constrained by love for his brother, did as he was enjoined by Viṣṇu. He created representations of Kṛṣṇa and Balarāma holding the wheel and the ploughshare, respectively, standing in celestial mansions [*vimānas,* that is *rathas*?], and had their images enshrined in a great many temples dedicated to Lord Vāsudeva, which were located in large cities. He thus made the entire world fall under the spell of Viṣṇu and returned to his abode in heaven.[47]

Having narrated this extraordinary story, which probably had no other purpose than to explain to the Jainas how a pair of Jaina heroes, one of whom was a would-be Tīrthaṅkara at that, came to be worshipped as the deities of the heretics, Jinasena closes his narration by drily observing: "Alas! What will not be done by those who are given to such [foolish] affection!"[48]

Vimalasūri's *Paümacariya* took us up to the twentieth Tīrthaṅkara and Punnāṭa Jinasena's *Harivaṃśapurāṇa* brought us to the narrative of the twenty-second Tīrthaṅkara Nemi. In both texts the emphasis was more on the Baladeva-Vāsudeva pairs of heroes than on the Tīrthaṅkaras themselves. It is for this reason that these two narrative works, although commonly considered to be Purāṇas, do not qualify as *Mahāpurāṇas*, the characteristic Jaina designation for the comprehensive biographies of all the sixty-three *śalākā puruṣas*. This honor truly belongs to the ninth-century narrative work *Triṣaṣṭi-lakṣaṇa-śrī mahāpurāṇa-saṅgraha*, or, in brief, *Mahāpurāṇa*. This monumental work of some twenty thousand *ślokas*, written in two parts (*Ādipurāṇa*[49] and *Uttarapurāṇa*,[50] respectively), was initiated by the Digambara mendicant Jinasena, who is said to have been a teacher of the Rāṣṭrakūṭa King Amoghavarṣa I, who ruled from Mānyakheṭa in the ninth century (814-77 C.E.). This Jinasena was probably unaware of the *Harivaṃsapurāṇa* written by his predecessor of the same name, who is, hence, differentiated by his ecclesiastical lineage name, Punnāṭa. It is stated in the text that (the second) Jinasena died after having completed the first section, *Ādipurāṇa*, comprising forty-six chapters and dedicated entirely to the story of the first Tīrthaṅkara, Ṛṣabha, and the first two chapters of the second section. The remainder of the work, extending to the seventy-sixth chapter and containing the biographies of all the remaining Tīrthaṅkaras and the other Illustrious Beings, was completed by Jinasena's immediate disciple, Guṇabhadra.

Hitherto Jaina authors appeared to have been preoccupied with the narratives of "historical" figures, the Epic heroes of the *itihāsa* literature. Jinasena was to arrest this trend and to concentrate attention not only on the Tīrthaṅkaras, the true heroes of the Jainas, but especially on the life stories of the first Tīrthaṅkara Ṛṣabha and his son, Bharata, the first Cakravartin. Although adopted at some stage by the Brahminic Purāṇas as their own minor characters, as will be seen below, both Ṛṣabha and Bharata were truly Jaina characters, and their assimilation required no special effort. Since their advent in the Jaina mythology took place at the very beginning of the present cycle of time, they could be hailed by the Jainas as the founding fathers of our civilization, lawgivers for secular welfare as well as for the spiritual path of salvation.

In his introductory chapter of the *Ādipurāṇa*, Jinasena rightly claims that his work is a *Mahāpurāṇa* because it deals with all the sixty-three *śalākā puruṣas*, but it can also be considered an *itihāsa*, as well as a *dharmaśāstra*. Although he makes specific references to creation and the other *pañcalakṣaṇas*, he chooses a novel characterization for his Purāṇa consisting of such items as space (*kṣetra*, that is, Jaina cosmology), time (*kāla*, that is, the infinite cycles of time divided into ascending and descending halves), the fourfold organization of community as monks, nun, laymen, and laywomen (*tīrtha*), the Great Beings (*sat-puruṣas,* that is, the *śalākā puruṣas*), and finally their conduct (*carita*).[51]

The narrative of the first Tīrthaṅkara Ṛṣabha thus begins with a description of the present half of the Jaina time cycle, the *avasarpiṇī* (Descending). It is said that this period began billions of years ago when human beings lived in the paradise that was earth and were sustained by wish-fulfilling trees (*kalpavṛkṣas*) and had no form of government whatsoever. As time passed, the magic trees disappeared, the population increased, and there arose a need to organize a society with leaders able to teach farming and other means of producing food, preserving it for storage and distribution, and protecting it from the depredations of greedy people. Thus began the first social structure, the heads of which were called "Kulakaras" or "Manus". The first of these was Pratiśruti, in whose line was born Nābhi, the fourteenth Kulakara. Ṛṣabha, the first Tīrthaṅkara and the fifteenth Kulakara, was born to Nābhi's wife, Marudevī. Jinasena devotes a great many verses to the conception and birth of this first *śalākā puruṣa,* the founder of Jainism in our epoch.

According to Jinasena's narrative, gods appeared on earth to celebrate these two auspicious events in the career of the new Tīrthaṅkara, calling him the "first lord", the "Ādideva". At this time all men were equal, and as yet society was not divided into the four classes (*varṇas*). Indeed, it may be said that such a division came into existence quite inadvertently, when Ṛṣabha, as he grew to be a young man, bore arms and assumed the role of a king and gave the title of Kṣatriya to those who were assigned the duty of protecting the people and enforcing the law. Eventually, as he discovered different means of livelihood, such as the sword (*asi,* that is, government), ink (*masi,* that is, reading and writing), agriculture (*kṛṣi*) the arts (*vidyā*), crafts (*śilpa*), and commerce (*vāṇijya),* there came into existence groups of people engaging in one or another of these occupations, who came to be called "Kṣatriyas", "Vaiśyas", and "Śūdras". The Brahmin class had not yet come into being, and the path of renunciation also was as yet unknown.

Kulakara Ṛṣabha led a fruitful life as a householder and fathered one hundred sons and two daughters. The eldest of his sons,

Bharata, became the first of the twelve Cakravartins of the Jaina Purāṇic tradition. Eventually, Ṛṣabha renounced the world to become a Jaina mendicant; divested of all his possessions including his clothing, the wandered about "sky-clad", a fact agreed upon both by Digambara and Śvetāmbara traditions alike. Thus he had the distinction of being the first renouncer of our epoch. It is said that a great many of his friends, sons, and even grandsons, at first joined him in assuming the holy vows of homelessness and celibacy but soon left him due to their inability to withstand the rigours of his discipline. Ashamed to return to their homes, these proud men became wanderers, calling themselves *parivrājakas,* the founders of what the Jainas consider to be heretical schools of mendicants, such as the Ājīvikas, Ekadaṇḍins, Tridaṇḍins, Vaikhānasas, and so forth.[52]

Ṛṣabha, however, remained firm in his austerities and became the omniscient Jina, the first initiator of a new Tīrtha, an institution that had been extinct for countless years. A great many of his former subjects, including many of his sons and two daughters, called "Brāhmī" and "Sundarī", became members of the order of monks and nuns. The Jina Ṛṣabha then laid down rules for the guidance of laypeople also, whereby they could progressively refrain from worldly activities and gradually reach the stage of mendicancy. Thus there came into being an ideal society predominantly consisting of these four sections, collectively called the "Tīrtha", with groups of apostates subsisting on its fringes and professing their heresies.

One would expect that the Lord of this Tīrtha would be described merely as a saint rapt in meditation and living for the most part in seclusion in a forest. But such is not the case; the Ādi, that is, the First Tīrthaṅkara, after whom Jinasena's Purāṇa is named, is portrayed as possessing such majesty and gradeur that it would surpass any description of the great Trinity of Purāṇic mythology: Brahmā, Viṣṇu, and Śiva. Jina Ṛṣabha is a sky-clad (*digambara*) mendicant, and yet in Jinasena's account we find him seated in the midst of a palatial assembly especially prepared for his sermons by Indra the king of gods and flanked by gods who hold raised parasols and proclaim his lordship over the three worlds. He has a human body, and yet it is so pure that its luster can outshine the divine bodies of the heavenly beings assembled there. By an extraordinary miraculous power he can be seen facing all four directions at once, a feature claimed by the Brahminic Purāṇas for Brahmā, the creator.

The Jainization of Rāma and Kṛṣṇa having been completed by his predecessors, Jinasena seems to have set his sights on claiming the functions of the Purāṇic holy trinity for the founder of Jainism. He employs the most characteristic adjectives traditionally reserved for Brahmā to describe his chosen Deity, Lord Ṛṣabha.[53] Thus Ṛṣabha is called "womb of gold" (*hiraṇyagarbha*), as there was a shower of gold when he was born! He is hailed as "lord of creatures" (Prajāpati) and "ordainer" (*vidhātṛ*), for he was the first king and the first to invent fire and other means of livelihood. He is called "self-existent" (*svayambhū*) because he was self-taught and hence had a spiritual rebirth independent of a teacher. Being the first to realize perfection in our epoch he is called "primordial man" (*purāṇa-puruṣa*), and because of his omniscience he can be described by the [*Puruṣa-sūkta*] term "all-seeing" (*viśvataścakṣuḥ*)! In short, he is to be called the "first lord," the "Ādideva", the "very Brahmā himself".

Ṛṣabha may be called "Viṣṇu" as well, since his knowledge is all pervasive. And he is truly "unfallen" (*acyuta*), as he has reached the most sublime state, which is unshakable and eternal. Being the most auspicious, he deserves to be called "Śiva", and he is "the end of being" (*bhavāntaka*), for he has freed himself from the bonds of *saṃsāra*. And above all he is lord of Yogis (*yogīśvara*), for he has reached *kaivalya* solely by the path of meditation (that is, without the aid of an external agency). Such investment of Ṛṣabha with the divinity of the Purāṇic trinity without, of course, making him the creator, sustainer or destroyer, allows Jinasena to deify his human Jina and to claim for him both the antiquity and the spiritual authority that will be required to challenge the validity of the Vedic and Purāṇic teachings on creation and dissolution, the false claim of divinity for their gods and *avatāras*, and, above all, their doctrine of the divine origin of the caste system and alleged supremacy of the Brahmin within it.

The examination of the Brahminic doctrines of creation and secondary creation provides Jinasena with an excellent opportunity to enage in a debate on the validity of a theistic creation, and to propound the Jaina doctrines of the plurality of souls and their transmigration and possible release from the regions of Jaina cosmology, all without the benefit of a superior being—the Creator

God. As for the epochs of the Manus, Ṛṣabha himself was a Manu and himself laid down the duties of the various sections of society; these can never be found in the false scripures that enjoin animal sacrifices in the name of *dharma* but only in the Jaina scriptures. The same holds true for the knowledge of royal dynasties (*vaṃśas*), for the best of these lineages, such as the Ikṣvāku, Kuru, and Hari lineages, also originated from Ṛṣabha and his son Bharata, the first Cakravartin. Having thus contested the right of the Brahminic Purāṇas to instruct on the proposed goals of a scripture, Jinasena expounds the Jaina teachings pertaining to all those areas considered to be essential for the true realization of the four goals of human life (*puruṣārthas*).

The differences between the Brahminic and Jaina cosmologies as expounded by Jinasena need not detain us here, but the Jaina challenge to the alleged superiority of the Brahminic class, a major theme of the *Ādipurāṇa,* surely merits discussion. As has been pointed out earlier, there were no caste distinctions at the beginning of our epoch, since all mankind was a single caste (*manuṣyajātir ekaiva*), according to Jinasena.[54] Divisions arose, however, not because of any premeditated design, but as a result of the discovery of new means of livelihood. It is also significant that Ṛṣabha was portrayed as a householder, and not as the holy Jina, at the time when the Kṣatriya, Vaiśya, and the Śūdra classes evolved; this would deny any sacredness to their origins through a holy injunction, as in the case of the Vedic *Puruṣa-sūkta* in the Brahminic tradition. What is, however, far more significant is the fact that in the Jaina narrative the class of the Brahmins was promulgated, not by the omniscient Jina, but by his householder son Bharata; this deprives that class of any sanctity whatsoever.

There are two Jaina narratives that explain the origin of the Brahminic class, one appearing in the commentarial and Purāṇic literature of the Śvetāmbaras and the other in the *Ādipurāṇa* of Jinasena. A fanciful derivation of the Sanskrit word *brāhmaṇa* from the Prakrit form *māhaṇa* provides the context for the Śvetāmbara story. It is said that Bharata, after his conquest of the world, returned with a large amount of booty and wanted to share it with his ninety-nine brothers, who had become Jaina monks in the monastic order established by Jina Ṛṣabha. He approached them with a cartload of food and other gifts, but this was rejected on the grounds that Jaina monks may not accept food specially prepared for them (*uddiṣṭa*). Indra, the king of gods, then suggested to Bharata that the food might be offered to those laypeople who had assumed the minor vows (*aṇuvratas*) prescribed by Ṛṣabha for householders and had thus been initiated as laypeople (*upāsakas*). Bharata offered them food and other gifts and invited them to have their meals at his palace forever. Not only were they to be permanent guests of his household but also to forsake all means of livelihood that involved violence (*hiṃsā*) and devote their lives to the study and teaching of the scriptures and the worship of the Jina. Their most important task, however, was to keep a vigil over the Cakravartin's conduct by admonishing him, "Do not kill, do not kill" (*mā hana, mā hana*): thus they came to be called *māhaṇas,* that is, Brahmins! Fanciful as this derivation of the word *brāhmaṇa* through its Prakrit form might be, it was endorsed by the great Jaina grammarian Hemacandra.[55] It is the Jaina way of explaining not only the origin of the Brahmin class but also the beginning of the pan-Indian rite of feeding Brahmins, a practice not unknown even to the orthodox Jainas of our day; it is claimed that the Jainas started this good practice in order to promote *ahiṃsā,* but, alas, it has now degenerated into an adjunct to the common household rituals!

Jinasena ignores both the Prakrit *māhaṇa* and the Sanskrit *brāhmaṇa* and concentrates on the the word *dvija* (twice-born) for his explanation of the origin of the Brahmin class under the patronage of Bharata. According to his narrative, a large number of laymen, headed by Bharata himself, had been initiated into the vows (*aṇuvratas*), which had been enunciated by Jina Ṛṣabha for householders. Bharata wished to reward the true initiates and devised a way of testing their adherence to the vows. He had the courtyard of his residence strewn with fresh flowers and sprouting grain and invited the citizens to a feast on a sacred day. Those who were careless crossed the courtyard without regard for the vegetable life, but those who were virtuous did not enter lest they trample on it and thus break their vows against harming living beings. Bharata then invited those virtuous people to enter by a suitable path, and he honored them. He also encouraged them to assume futher restraints on their conduct so as to make progress on one or more of the eleven stages of spiritual progress (*śrāvaka-pratimā*)[56] as laid down by the Jina Ṛṣabha, which would prepare them for mendicant life. Those who accepted this new status (*varṇa-lābha*) he designated as the "Twice-born" (*dvijas*) in the discipline of the Jina. He confirmed their advancement by investing them with sacred threads (*yajñopavīta*), the number of which indicated the number of stages (*pratimās*) they had assumed. Thus began the ritual known as initiation (*upanayana*) and the practice of wearing sacred threads, as well as the formation of a special class of people (*dvijas*), the first "divine Brahmins" (*deva-brāhmaṇas*) of our epoch.[57]

A long time was to elapse before Bharata began to have doubts about the wisdom of his instituting a class of "Twice-born" without first obtaining the permission of Lord Ṛṣabha. He therefore approached Ṛṣabha and described the manner in which he had established the "Twice-born" and begged the Lord to declare to him both the consequence of his presumptuous act as well as the virtues and vices of this class.

Jinasena's strictures concerining this class, as will be seen presently, match in spirit and letter the invective and prophecies that appear in the Brahminic Purāṇas against the followers of Ṛṣabha. This portion of the *Ādipurāṇa* therefore deserves to be reproduced fully here:

> O son, that which has been done is good indeed, and moreover, the worship of pious Brahmins is good, too. However, there will be some harmful consequences about which you must be informed. You have created the Brahmin class, who will be righteous teachers as long as the Kṛta Age endures, but when the Kali Age draws near there will be backsliding teachers who, out of pride in their high birth, will embrace the very opposite of the right path. These people, full of the arrogance of their rank, will claim to be most excellent among men, and soon, greedy for wealth, they will delude the world with their false scriptures. The favored treatment that they will enjoy will increase their presumptuousness and make them puffed up with a false pride, so that they will lead men astray as they themselves fashion false religious treatises.
>
> They will be so short sighted that they will promote changes for the worse at the end of the Age, and, their minds clouded by evil, they will become the enemies of religion. As they delight in injury to life and relish eating honey and meat,

> these wicked people will, alas, promote the *dharma* of action and, full of evil hopes, corrupt the *dharma* of nonviolence in favor of the *dharma* of injuctions (*codanā*). As the Age progresses, rogues will blasphemously wear the sacred thread and engage eagerly in the killing of life, thereby obstructing the right path.
>
> Therefore, although the creation of the Brahmin class is not of itself harmful today, it does contain the seed of harm as yet buried in the future, because impious heretics will come forth. Nevertheless, although this seed of harm is truly there for the end of the Age, there is no cause for removing it at present, for you have not transgressed against the nature of *dharma*.[58]

Jinasena was apparently not content with his suggestion that the present-day Brahmins were descendants of apostates from the original groups of devout Jaina laymen, the first to be designated as "Twice-born" by Cakravarti Bharata. His prophecy that in degenerate times these so-called Brahmins would compose their own scriptures disregarding the doctrine of *ahiṃisā* had come true; the Jaina authors had studied them with great care and had noted several portions that openly enjoined animal sacrifices. Still, these texts by themselves did not explain how the Brahmins came to adopt as their means of livelihood the performances of sacrifices and other rituals. In his zeal to establish a community of Jainas parallel to that of Brahminic society, Jinasena put forth a new lawbook (*dharmaśāstra*), a Jaina lawbook, as it were, to serve both as a manual of ritual, complete with litany, and as a code of civil law as well. In this manner the third distinguishing mark of the Jaina Purāṇas namely, reigns (*tīrtha*), corresponding to the epochs of the Manus of the Brahminic Purāṇas, would be fulfilled for the first time by a Jaina Purāṇa.

The ritual of initiation, for example, as described above, was carried out by Bharata himself and needed neither a priest nor the sacred fire. Indeed, the notion that fire is sacred is alien to Jaina doctrine, since for them the four basic elements, earth, water, air, and fire, belong to the species of life that has only the tactile sense and therefore ranks lowest in the classification of sentient beings. For the Brahminic tradition, fire was sacred because it was the embodiment of both Agni the fire god and Agni the domestic priest (*purohita*) of the gods. Jinasena therefore shows great courage of conviction when he declares that fire by itself has no inherent sacredness or divinity (*na svato 'gneḥ pavitratvaṃ devatārūpam eva vā*). Anticipating a question about the propriety of Jaina laymen lighting fires on such occasions as marriages and other rites of passage, Jinasena replies that fire can nevertheless be considered pure, on account of its contact with the body of the Tīrthaṅkara Ṛṣabha at the time of his cremation. Lest this association between the holy Jina and fire be taken as granting absolute sacredness to fire, Jinasena hastens to add that fire is to be considered suitable for worship only on a conventional level (*vyavahāranaya*); it is comparable to the worship of holy places and pilgrimage sites that become worthy of worship only because a Jina has attained death (*nirvāṇa*) in those places.[59]

Jinasena's explanation of the sacredness of fire seems to have gained acceptance by the learned sections of both the Digambara and the Śvetāmbara sects, as can be witnessed from similar explanations found in the works of the twelfth-century author Hemacandra. In his monumental work, the *Triṣaṣṭiśalākā-puruṣacaritra,* the *Mahāpurāṇa* of the Śvetāmbara tradition, Hemacandra goes even further and suggests that the ritual of the fire (*agnihotra*), the hallmark of the Brahmin class, is to be traced to the cremation ceremony of the Jina Ṛṣabha. The three different fires that came to be held sacred by the Vedic Brāhmins had truly originated from those fires in which the bodies of the Jina Ṛṣabha, the sages born of the noble Ikṣvāku lineage, and those of the remaining saints (Arhats), had been respectively cremated.[60]

What was originally an act of piety, namely, keeping the holy flame alive, turned gradually into a means of livelihood in the hands of the Brahmins of degenerate times. They employed it even in the worship of demigods and goddesses who were given not only to false views, but also to the most unholy practice of receiving offerings of flesh and blood. It is clear from reading the *Ādipurāṇa* that during the time of Jinasena a large number of the Jaina laity had come to accept the worship of these heretic gods and goddesses as a legitimate part of their worship of the Jinas and had probably installed their images in their own temples as well. Jinasena was waging an open war against the worship of these non-Jaina divinities and had to combat their influence by installing a new set of Jaina "guardian deities" somehow associated with the lives of the Tīrthaṅkaras and thus worthy of occupying a place of honor near the pedestal of the Jina and sharing in the devotions offered by the laity. Through his Purāṇa, which he characterized as a *dharmaśāstra,* Jinasena demanded that a true Jaina should remove the images of the heretic gods (*mithyā-devatā*) from his residence, and added: "He should in a public manner (*prakāśam*) take them away somewhere else and abandon them, saying: 'until now, out of ignorance we have worshipped you with respect. However, now the time has come for us to worship our own guardian deities (*śāsana-devatā*). Pray do not be angry; you may go wherever you please.'"[61]

Jinasena's *Ādipurāṇa* thus discharged the function of a lawbook containing recommendations and prohibitions addressed to the followers of a Jina. Prior to his time, the Jaina books of discipline concerned themselves with the conduct of monks and nuns alone. There were guide books (*Śrāvakācāras*) to instruct the laity in keeping the vows prescribed and to set forth the procedures for their observation. But the Jainas lacked the type of lawbook comparable to the *Manusmṛti,* for example, in the Brahminic tradition. Jinasena's *Ādipurāṇa* fills this need and carries with it the kind of authority one associates with *dharmaśāstra* literature pertaining to the duties of the castes, rites of passage, and so forth. In writing the *Ādipurāṇa,* Jinasena thus introduced a new function for the Jaina Purāṇas, namely, educating the Jaina community to preserve its identity as a community separate from that of the Brahmins, a task that they perceived was necessary in the face of the Brahminic attempts to absorb them.

Jinasena did not live to complete his work; the lives of the remaining sixty-one *śalākā puruṣas* were therefore compressed into a single volume, the *Uttarapurāṇa,* by his disciple Guṇabhadra. The reader is immediately aware of his stereotyped descriptions of the warfare conducted by the Cakravartins and other heroes. Once again Guṇabhadra returns to the narratives of Rāma and Lakṣmaṇa or of Kṛṣṇa and Balarāma. These show further modifications of the versions of Vimala or of Punnāṭa Jinasena, modifications that strive even futher to remove certain aspects of these stories that the medieval Jainas found offensive to their moral sensibilities. In Guṇabhadra's narrative of the *Rāmāyaṇa,* for example, Rāma is not asked to abdicate in favour of Bharata, as he is in Vimalasūri's *Paümacariya,* but instead leaves Ayodhyā of his own volition, together with Sītā and Lakṣmaṇa and sets out to found a kingdom of his own. Similar changes in the stories of the Kṛṣṇa legend also appear in other Purāṇas by subsequent authors, most notably in the writings of the Śvetāmbara *ācāryas,* especially in Hemacandra's work referred to above. The works hitherto examined in some detail all happen to be the works of Digambara writers, for whom the Purāṇas were the only surviving scriptures. The Śvetāmbaras, however, had such canonical narratives as the *Nāyādhammakahāo*[62] or the *Uvāsagadasāo,*[63] which relate the stories of some of the *śalākā puruṣas,* including Kṛṣṇa. Their narratives, therfore, often differ from those found in the Digambara tradition.

A fine example of this is provided by the story of Draupadī as narrated in the literature of these two sects. No Jaina writer has been comfortable with the *Mahābhārata* account of Draupadī's polyandrous marriage to all five Pāṇḍava brothers. Digambara writers have tended to treat this as a slander of the Brahmins against the character of Draupadī and the Pāṇḍavas, and have devised means of explaining the event away as a gross misrepresentation of an accidental falling of the garland, thrown by Draupadī to Arjuna, on the heads of all five brothers at the time of her self-choice (*svayaṃvara*) marriage.[64] The author of the *Harivaṃśapurāṇa,* who explains this event in the above manner, takes the heretical Brahmins to task for suggesting that she had actually married all five brothers and wonders why their tongues do not split into a hundred pieces for uttering such slanderous words against so pure a woman and against the brothers of Arjuna, who treated her as their sister![65]

Hemacandra, on the other hand, in his *Triṣaṣṭi,* allows the polyandrous marriage to stand as something that had indeed happened, but he explains it by recourse to a story of Draupadī's past as given in the Śvetāmbara scripture *Nāyādhammakahāo* and its ancient commentaries. According to this story, Draupadī in one of her former lives was a beautiful woman called Nāgaśrī, who out of disgust towards a Jaina monk had fed him poisonous food that caused great burning in his body. As a result she suffered for long periods in hell and in animal existences and eventually was reborn as a beautiful woman—but one with peculiar defect: anyone who touched her carnally would experience the great pain of being burned by fire. Although she attracted a large number of suitors, no one dared to approach her; when finally she was married to a man of her liking he screamed in anguish at her first touch and ran away from the bridal chamber. Nāgaśrī was then abandoned by her husband's hosehold as well as by her own parents and wandered alone from place to place for several years. Eventually she became a Jaina nun and threw herself wholeheartedly into severe austerities hoping thereby to get rid of her ailment. One day, it is said, she saw five handsome young men pursuing a beautiful courtesan, and Nāgaśrī, having been deprived of her conjugal happiness, felt a forceful longing (*nidāna*) that as a result of her severe penances she might enjoy similar pleasure in her next life. She died instantly at that moment and in the course of time was reborn as Draupadī. Her polyandrous marriage to the Pāṇḍavas was therefore predestined by her *nidāna*,[66] a theme all too familiar to us from the stories of Kṛṣṇa, Ekanāsā, and others; it had to be endured and could be overcome only by an act of renunciation demanding an equal force of will by her and all of her husbands, which did eventually occur.

The brief survey of the major trends in the Jaina Purāṇic literature given above supports our contention that the Jaina writers, in addition to their primary purpose of expounding Jaina doctrine, used this medium to combat Brahminic influences emanating from their Epics and Purāṇas. One must ask here whether the Jainas in fact had any reason to believe that they were under attack from their perceived adversaries, and also whether indeed the authors of the Brahminic Purāṇas were even aware of these Jaina appropriations of their heroes, the two *avatāras* of Viṣṇu, as well as their attempt to Jainize, as it were, the god Brahmā-Prajāpati through the character of Jina Ṛṣabha.

An answer to these questions cannot be truly given without first establishing the chronological order in which the Brahminic Purāṇas were committed to writing. No Jaina Purāṇa has ever been mentioned in any of the traditional eighteen Mahāpurāṇas or the Upapurāṇas, and, with the exception of Ṛṣabha and his son Bharata, no other character of the Jaina Purāṇas has figured in their narratives. The Jainas, on the other hand, show a remarkable familiarity with the Brahminic Purāṇas, although only one late Jaina Purāṇa, namely, the seventeenth-century *Pāṇḍavapurāṇa*, explicitly mentions the *Śivapurāṇa* in criticizing the latter's alleged misrepresentation of the Pāṇḍava story.[67] But such a lack of cross-references does not tell us the whole story of the mutual impact between these two literary traditions, which were probably competing for the patronage of a common audience, namely, the mostly urban and affluent sections of the Indian community.

Nothing for example is known about the process by which Gautama, the Buddha, came to be assimilated into the Vaiṣṇava tradition to make him worthy of being declared a full *avatāra* of Viṣṇu. One would expect the Brahminic authors to devote at least an episode or an entire chapter, if not an independent Purāṇa, to explain this momentous event in the history of the Vaiṣṇava religion. Yet all that one finds are a few lines here and there, often copies of what are probably the original verses of the *Viṣṇupurāṇa,* which tell us nothing more than that Lord Viṣṇu employed his power called "Yogamāyā" and was thereby born as Buddha, the son of Śuddhodana in the land of Kīkaṭas (district of Gayā), to delude the demons, lead them astray into non-Vedic creeds, and thus bring about their destruction.[68] The Buddhist records are even more silent on this fateful co-option of their supreme teacher by a heretical cult. We do not know if the Buddhists were even aware that he was hailed as an *avatāra* of a god, a truly blasphemous act against one whose atheistic doctrines were not secret to anyone. Indeed, it has been suggested that the Buddhists lost ground in the land of their birth precisely because they remained oblivious to the dangers inherent in such assimilation: first, that of the Buddha being represented as an *avatāra* of Viṣṇu, and second, that of their heavenly Bodhisattvas (such as Mañjuśrī and Avalokiteśvara) being regarded as emanations of Śiva.[69]

Only two short Jākata tales about Rāma and Kṛṣṇa[70] are known to have been written in the Buddhist tradition, in marked contrast to the Jaina's voluminous Purāṇic and other narratives devoted entirely to these Epic characters, which survive to this day. It is very much to the credit of the Jainas, therefore, that they were vigilant about what was being said in the "heretic" Purāṇas and took vigorous steps not only to correct the "errors" perpetrated by their adversaries but even to confound them by producing revised versions of the events that claimed to be the authentic ones! We will never know the reasons why the Brahminic authors chose to favour the Buddha over his contemporary Jaina teacher Mahāvīra for the role of the *avatāra* of Viṣṇu, especially when it is realized that there are far more numerous, albeit oblique, references in their Purāṇas to Jaina heroes and their religion than to Buddhism and its heroes. Two examples of such references can be noted here, an earlier one from the *Bhāgavatapurāṇa* and a later one from the *Śivapurāṇa.*

The *Bhāgavatapurāṇa* betrays its knowledge of Jainism by its use of the word *Arhat,* a characteristic epithet of the Jina, in connection with its narrative pertaining to one of Viṣṇu's twenty-two minor (*aṃśa*) *avatāras,* namely, Ṛṣabha, who appears there in the company of such Brahminic sages as Kapila, Nārada, and Veda-Vyāsa. According to the author of the *Bhāgavatapurāṇa,* the purpose of the Ṛṣabha-*avatāra* was to establish the *śramaṇa dharma* of the naked ascetics (*vātaraśanānāṃ śramaṇānām ṛṣīṇām*).[71] As in the Jaina tradition, Ṛṣabha of the *Bhāgavatapurāṇa* was also born to Marudevī Nābhi, one of the Manus; his story in the *Bhāgavatapurāṇa* is different in that Nābhi is said to have performed a great Vedic sacrifice that so pleased Viṣṇu that he himself consented to be born as his son Ṛṣabha. This Ṛṣabha too begot a hundred sons, the eldest of whom was Bharata, the first Cakravartin, after whom the land of Ṛṣabha was named Bhāratavarṣa. Unlike his counterpart in the Jaina accounts, this Ṛṣabha himself as well as his sons became great devotees of the Brahmins and propitiated Viṣṇu with many sacrifices. In fulfilment of his function as an *avatāra,* this Ṛṣabha then renounced the world to become a naked ascetic, a celibate *avadhūta;* after spending a great many years in severe austerities, he died in a forest fire while fasting to death and became one with Vāsudeva.

Although the Jainas would strongly repudiate of the details that appear in the *Bhāgavatapurāṇa* account of Ṛṣabha, most importantly the claims that he was associated with Vedic sacrifices and devoted to the Brahmins and to Viṣṇu, as well as the account of the manner of his death, there could be no objection to his being described as someone who taught the Yogis the ascetic path of nudity. What is most offensive to them, however, is the great hostility to their religion shown openly in the following invective, which is presented as prophecy by the *Bhāgavatapurāṇa* in its conclusion of the story of the Ṛṣabha-*avatāra*:

> When Arhat, the king of Koṅka, Veṅka, and Kuṭaka, comes to hear of this conduct of the divine Ṛṣabhadeva, he too will give

himself over to it. Indeed, since irreligion will thrive in the Kali Age, the king, confounded by inevitable fate, will abandon the security of his own religion and in consequence of his deluded understanding will promote the heretical and evil ways of the heretics (*pākhaṇḍas*).

It is for this reason that villainous people, confounded by the illusion-provoking powers of God (*devamāyāmohitāḥ*), will forsake the duties of purity and good conduct that are enjoined upon them and take up at will wicked vows that mock the gods, such as not bathing, not rinsing their mouths, not maintaining purity, and pulling out their hair. With their understanding thus corrupted by the irreligious Kali Age, they will forever deride *brahman*, the Brahmins, the Lord of the sacrifice, and other people. Then, trusting in the maintenance of their own world by upstart non-Vedic rites, like a blind man leading the blind, they will themselves fall into the blind darkness of hell.[72]

I have examined elsewhere[73] the many allusions to the practices of Jaina monks and the historical significance of the references made to "King Arhat" in the above quotation: it must be taken as referring to a king of the Deccan newly converted to the Jaina faith, and could well refer to Amoghavarṣa I (814–77 C.E.), the Rāṣṭrakūṭa king who was claimed as a patron of the Jaina *ācārya* Jinasena, the author of the *Ādipurāṇa*. The old idea found in the *Viṣṇupurāṇa* that Viṣṇu became incarnate as the Buddha through the power of his Yogamāyā in order to delude the demons is now applied instead to the Jaina Tīrthaṅkara Ṛṣabha and to the contemporary royal houses whose members had once been staunch followers of the Vedic religion but had since embraced the heretical religion.

The account in the *Śivapurāṇa* also contains the word *Arhat,* although no Jaina character such as Ṛṣabha is mentioned there by name. According to this account, Lord Śiva instigated Lord Viṣṇu to create a man, "illusion personified" (*māyāmayaṃ puruṣam*), with the sole purpose of teaching *dharma* to the demons, who by adhering to his false teaching would be consigned to the lower worlds (Pātāla). Viṣṇu then created such a man, Arhat, who became a mendicant and produced false scriptures in Apabhraṃśa that were opposed to the teachings of the *śruti* and *smṛti* and contrary to the *dharma* of class and stage of life. He was able to initiate the demon Tripura and others into the mendicant order of the Jainas, and brought about their destruction as desired by the gods Viṣṇu and Śiva. While this story agrees substantially with the *Viṣṇupurāṇa* account of the Buddha *avatāra* of Viṣṇu, the author of the *Śivapurāṇa* goes a step further and brings the narrative of this Arhat up to date by placing him in the Rajasthan desert, a stronghold of the Jaina community. In the Kali Age, he says, this Arhat (the *māyāmaya puruṣa*) will settle in Marusthalī and initiate into the Jaina mendicancy a large number of men who will go about wearing rags, holding pieces of cloth in front of their mouths, and constantly uttering the words, "*Dharma, dharma!*" The description is certainly meant to be a mockery of the Jaina monks of Rajasthan called "Sthānakavāsis," an offshoot of the Śvetāmbara sect, who are recognized even to this day by their *muhpatti* (a piece of white cloth held like a surgical mask over the mouth).[74]

The specific reference to place names like Koṅka, Veṅka, and Kuṭaka in the *Bhāgavtapurāṇa,* and to Marusthalī in the *Śivapurāṇa,* in connection with the depiction of the "heresy" called "Jainism" proves abundantly that the Brahminic authors of the Purāṇas were well-acquainted with the Digambara and the Śvetāmbara mendicant communities of Karnataka/Maharashtra and Gujarat / Rajasthan, respectively, where they floursihed during medieval times.

The passages from the *Bhāgavatapurāṇa* and the *Śivapurāṇa* quoted above, which openly use invective against Jaina holy men and their teachings, were probably a response of the Brahminic tradition to the persistent and sustained attack on their gods and teachings made in the Jaina Purāṇas. Yet the converse is also not impossible: should it be proved that these Brahminic imprecations predate the works of Vimalasūri or even of the two Jinasenas, which seems unlikely, it is conceivable that the Jainas decided to play the same game as the Brahmins and went them one better by undertaking a wholesale appropriation not only of the most popular *avatāras* of the god Viṣṇu, but even of the god Brahmā-Prajāpati, the creator god of the Brahminic Purāṇas. Whereas we have enough evidence to show that the Jainas had indeed studied the Brahminic Purāṇas, there is very little indication that their works were studied by the authors of the Brahminic Purāṇas, for had the Brahmins indeed seen what the author of the

Harivaṃśapurāṇa or the *Paṇḍavapurāṇa* had said about them, they would certainly have made some angry rejoinders. Unfortunately, no record of such literary retaliation has become available to us. In view of the kind of religious and sectarian segregation that exists between various communities of India, it is more than likely that non-Jainas ceased to have any contact with the Jaina material; and hence Jaina works enjoyed a very limited readership, probably confined only to a few Jaina monks and still fewer members of the learned laity.

Fortunately for us, a single piece of literary evidence from the time of Hemacandra, the twelfth-century *ācārya,* has survived, and it sheds unprecedented light on the way in which those of the Brahminic tradition did indeed react when confronted publicly with Jaina stories about their Purāṇic heroes. It is well-known that Hemecandra, the renowned author of the *Triṣaṣṭi,* had been the celebrated teacher of Kumārapāla, the Śaivite king who had converted to the Jaina faith. Hemacandra was on many occasions hailed as a court pandit, an upholder of the Jaina faith in what was once a fortress of Śaivism and Vaiṣṇavism. Prabhācandra, the author of the *Prabhāvakacarita,* who made a compilation of the biographies of several Śvetāmbara *ācāryas,* has given the following account of one of Hemacandra's sermons on the life of the Pāṇḍavas, and how it led to a great scuffle between the Brahmins and the Jainas that was finally resolved by the royal preceptor Hemacandra himself:[75]

> One day during the rainy season, when Ācārya Hemacandra was in residence at a Jaina temple called "Caturmukha," he narrated the life of the Tīrthaṅkara Nemi in front of the fourfold assembly. The whole city, attracted by his most excellent speech, came there to listen to him and to have his *darśana.* Now, one day, in the course of this narration of Lord Nemi's life, he described in detail the episode pertaining to the renunciation of the Pāṇḍava brothers and their becoming Jaina monks.
>
> The Brahmins who heard it were extremely jealous of his growing popularity and went to the king and complained to him, saying, "Lord, in the far distant past the great sage Vyāsa Kṛṣṇadvaipāyana had narrated the extraordinary life of Yudhiṣṭhira and his brothers, having known it by means of his

supernatural knowledge of future events. There in his work [the *Mahābhārata*] it is said that towards the end of their lives the sons of Pāṇḍu went wandering among the snow-filled Himālayas and, having performed there the ritual bathing and the proper rites, they propitiated Lord Śiva [that is, the *śivaliṅga*] established at the holy Kedāra. Their minds thus filled with devotion to Lord Śiva, they then met their death. But these Śvetāmbaras, who are actually Śūdras since they have abandoned the true words of the Purāṇas, babble things about the Pāṇḍavas in their own assemblies, things which are contrary to the *smṛtis.* Because of this conduct, which is absolutely inappropriate, there is great calamity in store for you in the future. It is only proper that when your subjects are given to wrong conduct they must be restrained by the king. Therefore, O king, think deeply in your heart about what should be done in this matter, and do it." Having spoken thus, the group of Brahmins, who had been so extremely bold in their speech fell silent.

The king replied, "The protectors of the earth do not act without contemplation and must not show disrespect to any particular faith without due consideration. Therefore these Śvetāmbara monks should be questioned further [on this matter]. If they give us a truthful answer, then they are to be honored by us, for that is just. For our friend here, the venerable Ācārya Hemacandra, is a great sage who has renounced all attachment and is free from all possessions. How could he ever speak anything untruthful? This matter therefore needs much contemplation."

The learned Brahmins also agreed and said, "So be it." Then the king had Hemacandra, the lord of the sages, summoned and questioned him, saying, "A king belongs to all and is impartial in this matter. Is it true that, according to the scriptures, the Pāṇḍavas renounced the world according to Jaina rules [that is, they became Jaina monks]?". The venerable *ācārya* said, "This has been said by our ancient *ācāryas* in our scriptures, and it is [equally] true that their sojourn in the Himālayas is described in the *Mahābhārata.* But we do not know whether those [Pāṇḍavas] who are described in our scriptures, are the same as those who are described in the work [*Mahābhārata*] of sage Vyāsa, or yet by still other authors in different works."

To this the king said, "But then, O sage, were there more

than one of these persons, and were they all born in ancient times?" Then the teacher said, "O king, listen to my answer. In the narrative of Vyāsa itself there is the following episode about Bhīṣma the grandfather, who is also known as the descendant of the Ganges. At the time of entering the battlefield he told his attendants, 'At my death cremate my body only on a piece of earth which has always been pure, a place where no one has ever been cremated.' After acquitting himself justly in the war, Bhīṣma died. His attendants remembered his words and, lifting his body, took it to a hill. There on its top, which had never been visited by any man, they readied it [for cremation]. At that time a divine voice spoke:

> A hundred Bhīṣmas have been cremated here,
> and three-hundred Pāṇḍavas,
> and a thousand Droṇācāryas;
> As for Karṇas (cremated here),
> their number is beyond counting1"[76]

[Having quoted this verse from the *Mahābhārata*] Hemacandra said: "Hearing this [verse], in our minds we believe that among the hundreds of Pāṇḍavas mentioned here it is possible that some may have been Jainas. Moreover, on the Śatruñjaya hilltop their images can be seen, and also in the temple dedicated to Jina Candraprabha in the city of Nāsika, as well as in the great pilgrimage spot of Kedāra. We have gained our knowledge of *dharma* from various sources. Let the Brahmins who are experts in the Vedas and who believe in the *smṛtis* [that is, the *Mahābhārata*] also be questioned now about this matter [namely, the plurality of the Pāṇḍavas]. Knowledge can be obtained from any source. Like the River Ganges it cannot be claimed by anybody as his paternal property!"

Having heard this speech, the king addressed the Brahmins, "Is what the Jaina sage says true? Give me your reply, if indeed there is truth on your side. Surely in this matter you should give only a truthful answer, since the lord of the earth must act only after due consideration. In settling this matter, mine will be the last word, since I am impartial regarding all schools of philosophy, and also because I have erected temples in honor of gods of all faiths." Not knowing what to answer, the Brahmins remained silent. The king too honored the *ācārya* and said, "No fault attaches to you, not even the slightest, while you speak the truth."[77] Honored thus by the king, the teacher Hemacandra shone in the sky of Jaina teaching like the light of the midday sun.

The Brahmins lost their case precisely because they did not have a complete edition of the *Mahābhārata,* one with a verse-index! I assumed that the verse quoted by Hemacandra must be found in the modern critical edition of the great Epic, and took the trouble to look it up on behalf of the defeated Brahmins. But, to my utter surprise, there was no trace of it anywhere, not even in a marginal note. Is it possible that Hemacandra composed this verse on the spot and confounded the Brahmins? If so, then he himself played, as it were, the final role of that Arhat of the Brahminic Purāṇas, the strange emanation of Viṣṇu!

NOTES

1. For a brief survey of the Jaina Purāṇic literature, see M. Winternitz, *A History of Indian Literature,* vol. 2, trans. S. Ketkar and H. Kohn (University of Calcutta, 1933), section 4.479-520; Hiralal Jain, *Bhāratīya Saṃskriti meñ Jain Dharma kā Yogadān* (in Hindi) (Bhopal: Madhya Pradesha Shasana Sahitya Parishad, 1962); Gulabchandra Chaudhari, *Jain Sahitya kā Bṛhad Itihās,* pt. 6, (in Hindi), Parshvanatha Vidyashrama Granthamala, vol. 20, (Varanasi, 1973), 35-128.
2. *Jaina Sūtras,* translated from Prakrit by Hermann Jacobi, pt. 1, (*Kalpa-Sūtra,* pp. 217-311 [*Jinacarita,* pp. 217-85]), The Sacred Books of the East, vol. 22, 1884.
3. *Buddhavaṃsa and Cariyāpiṭaka,* ed. N. A. Jayawickrama (London: Pali Text Society, 1968).
4. For a list of twenty-two *aṃśāvatāras,* see *Śrīmad-Bhāgavata,* Gītā Press Edition, vi, viii, 13-19.
5. For a scriptural description of the Cakravartins, see Jinendra Varni, *Jainendra-Siddhānta-Kośa,* 4 (Varanasi: Bhāratīya Jñānapīṭha, 1944): 10-16.
6. See *Uttarādhyayana,* lecture 22, translated by Hermann Jacobi, in *Jaina Sūtras,* pt. 2, the Sacred Books of the East, vol. 45 (1895).
7. See R. C. Sharma, "Jaina Sculptures of the Gupta Age in the State Museum, Lucknow," in *Śrī Mahāvīra Jaina Vidyālaya Golden Jubilee Volume,* (Bombay, 1968), 142-53; U. P. Shah, "Evolution of Jaina Iconography and Symbolism," *Aspects of Jaina Art and Architecture,* ed. U. P. Shah and M. A. Dhaky, (Ahmedabad, 1975), 49-74.
8. See *Jainendra-Siddhānta-Kośa,* 4, pp. 16-17.
9. See *Jainendra-Siddhānta-Kośa,* 4, pp. 18-20.

10. See *Jainendra-Siddhānta-Kośa*, 4, pp. 20-21.
11. aṇidāṇagadā savve Baladevā Kesavā ṇidāṇagadā /
uddhaṃgāmī savve Baladevā Kesavā adhogāmī //
Tiloya-paṇṇatti 4.1436, quoted in the *Jainendra-Siddhānta-Kośa* 4, p. 18.
12. kalahappiyā kadāyiṃ dhammaradā Vāsudevasamakālā /
bhavvā nirayagadiṃ te hiṃsādoseṇa gacchaṃti //
Trilokasāra 835, quoted in the *Jainendra-Siddhānta-Kośa* 4, p. 22.
13. savve dasame puvve Ruddā bhaṭṭā tavāu visayatthaṃ /
sammattarayaṇarahidā buḍḍā ghoresu ṇirayesuṃ //
Tiloya-paṇṇatti 4.1442, quoted in the *Jainendra-Siddhānta-Kośa* 4, p. 22.
14. The inclusion of the Prati-vāsudevas in the list of the *śalākā puruṣas* has not escaped controversy. Śīlāṅka's (ca. 868) *Mahāpurāṇa*, for example, omits them for this list and hence is entitled *Caupaṇṇamahāpurisa-cariya*. see Winternitz, *History of Indian Literature*, vol. 2, 506 n. 1.
15. *Paümacariya* of Vimalasūri, (Varanasi: Prakrit Grantha Parishad, 1962).
16. padmākārā samutpannā pṛthivī saghanadrumā /
tad asya lokapadmasya vistareṇa prakāśitam //
Vāyupurāṇa, Adhyāya 45, quoted in Baladeva Upadhyaya, *Purāṇa-vimarsha* (in Hindi), (Varanasi, 1960).
17. sīho maeṇa nihao sāṇeṇa ya kuṃjaro jahā bhaggo /
taha vivarīyapayatthaṃ kaīhi Rāmāyaṇaṃ rahiyaṃ //
aliyaṃ pi savvaṃ eyaṃ uvavattiviruddhapaccayaguṇehiṃ /
na ya saddahaṃti purisā havaṃti je paṃḍiyā loe //
evaṃ ciṃtaṃto cciya saṃsayaparihārakāraṇaṃ rāyā /
jinadarisaṇussūyamaṇo gamaṇucchāho tao jāo // [*Paümacariya* 2.116-18]
18. For the Jaina versions of the Rāma story, see Camille Bulche, *Ramakathā* (in Hindi) (Prayag, 1950).
19. Cf. Pṛthivīsundarīmukhyāḥ Keśavasya [i.e., Lakṣmaṇasya] manoramāḥ /
dviguṇāṣṭasahasrāṇi devyaḥ satyo 'bhavan śriyaḥ //
Sītādyaṣṭasahasrāṇi Rāmasya prāṇavallabhāḥ /...
halāyudhaṃ mahāratnam Aparājitanāmakam //
Uttarapurāṇa 68.666-67, quoted in the *Jainendra-Siddhānta-Kośa*, 4, pp. 18-19.
20. *Padma-Carita* of Raviṣeṇa, 3 pts., (Varanasi: Bhāratīya Jñānapīṭha, 1958-59.
21. *Paümacariu* of Svayambhū, ed. H. C. Bhayani, 3 pts., (Bombay: Bhāratīya Vidyābhavana, 1953 and 1960).
22. *Mahāpurāṇa* of Puṣpadanta, ed. P. L. Vaidya, 3 parts, (Bombay: Manikchandra Digambara Jaina Granthamala, 1937-47). See also sections 81-92 (pt. 3), entitled *Harivaṃśapurāṇa*, in a German translation by L. Alsdorf, (Hamburg, 1936).
23. *Harivaṃśapurāṇa* of [Punnāṭa] Jinasena, edited with Hindi translation by Pannalal Jain (Varanasi: Bhāratīya Jñānapīṭha, 1962).
24. *The Harivaṃśa*, ed. P. L. Vaidya (Poona: Bhandarkar Oriental Research Institute, 1969), vol. 1.
25. kālesu jinavarāṇaṃ cauvīsānaṃ havaṃti cauvīsā /
te Bāhubalippamuhā kaṃdappā niruvamāyārā //
Tiloya-paṇṇatti 4.1472, quoted in the *Jainendra-Siddhānta-Kośa* 4, p. 22.
26. *Vasudevahiṇḍī* ed. Muni Caturavijaya and Muni Punyavijaya, 2 pts. (Bhavanagara: Jaina Atmananda Sabha, 1930-31); J. C. Jain, *Vasudeva-Hiṇḍī: Authentic Jaina Version of Bṛhatkathā:* (Ahmedabad: L. D. Institute of

Indology, 1977).

27. For a brief survey, see Padmanabh S. Jaini, "*Mahabhārata* Motifs in the Jaina *Pāṇḍavapurāṇa*," *Bulletin of the School of Oriental and African Studies*, 47, no. 1 (1984), 108-15; Padmanabh S. Jaini, "Bhaṭṭāraka Śrībhūṣaṇa's *Pāṇḍavapurāṇa:* a case of Jaina sectarian plagiarism?," *Panels of the* VIIIth *World Sanskrit Conference*, vol. VI and VII (Leiden: E. J. Brill, 1991), pp. 59-68.

28. For a discussion on the goddess Ekānaṃśā in the Purāṇas, see Vinapani Pande, *Harivaṃśapurāṇa kā Saṃskritika Vivecana* (in Hindi) (Uttar Pradesh: Hindi Samiti Granthamala, Publication Division, 1960). On the possible identity of Ekānaṃśā with the Tamil goddess Pinnai (a sister as well as a lover of Kṛṣṇa), see Dennis Hudson, "Pinnai, Krishna's Cowherd Wife," in *The Divine Consort*, ed. J. S. Hawley and D. M. Wulff (Berkeley: Berkeley Religious Studies Series, 1982), 256. Both accounts appear to be unfamiliar with the Jaina tradition discussed here.

29. tatas tvāṃ gṛhya caraṇe śilāyāṃ nirasiṣyati /
nirasyamānā gagane sthānaṃ prāpsyasi śāśvatam // ...
kīrṇā bhūtagaṇair ghorair man nideśānuvarttinī /
kaumāraṃ vratam āsthāya tridivaṃ tvaṃ gamiṣyasi // ...
tatraiva tvaṃ bhaginyarthe gṛhīṣyati sa Vāsavaḥ /
Kuśikasya tu gotreṇa Kauśikī tvaṃ bhaviṣyasi //...
sa te Vindhyanagaśreṣṭhe shānaṃ dāsyati śāśvatam /
tataḥ sthānasahasrais tvaṃ pṛthivīṃ śobhayiṣyasi //...
kṛtānuyātrā bhūtais tvaṃ nityaṃ māṃsabalipriyā /
tithau navamyāṃ pūjāṃ tvaṃ prāpsyase sapaśukriyām // ...
[*Harivaṃśa, Viṣṇuparva, Adhyāya* 58]

30. Āryāstavaṃ pravakṣyāmi yathoktaṃ ṛṣibhiḥ purā /
Nārāyaṇīṃ namasyāmi devīṃ tribhuvaneśvarīm // ...
[*Harivaṃśa, Viṣṇuparva, Adhyāya* 59.1]

31. (a) svasuḥ prasūtiṃ pratividya Kaṃsaḥ prasūtyagāraṃ vighṛṇaḥ praviśya/
vilokya bālām amalām amuṣyāḥ patiḥ kadācit prabhaved arir me //
vicintya śaṅkākulitas tadeti nirastakopo 'pi sa dīrghadarśī/
svayaṃ samādāya kareṇa tasyāḥ praṇudya nāsāṃ cipiṭīcakāra //
[*Harivaṃśapurāṇa* 35.31-32]

(b) vasunibha Vasudevo Devakī cātmajasya
praśamitaripuvahner vīkṣya viśrabdham āsyam /
sukham atulam agātām Ekanāsā ca kanyā
bhuvi sutasahajānāṃ samprayogaḥ sukhāya //
[*Harivaṃśapurāṇa* 36.50]

(c) iti samaye prayāti tu kadācid asau praṇatair
upahasitā prayādbhir avaśād Balarājautaiḥ /
Vicipiṭanāsikaṃ rahasi darpaṇake svamukhaṃ
sphuṭam avalokya. tadbhavavirāgam agāt trapitā //
[*Harivaṃśapurāṇa* 49.13]

32. avitaham ity amī vitatham eva śaṭhā kavayaḥ
svaparamahārayo vidadhate vikathākathanam /
paravadhakāpatheṣu bhuvi teṣu tatheti janaḥ
suraravamūḍhadhīḥ patati gaḍḍarikākaṭavat // ...
atinicitāgnivāyujalabhūmilatātarubhiḥ
kṣitir apacetanaiś ca gṛhakalpitadaivatakaiḥ /

ravividhutārakāgrahagaṇair jananetrapathair
gaganam ato 'stu muḍhir iha kasya janasya na vā //
[*Harivaṃśapurāṇa* 49.37, 47]

33. See *Harivaṃśapurāṇa* 33.150-73.
34. Cf. ākuñcya caraṇau paścāt sārasarvābhisārataḥ /
lalambe Nemidoḥstambhe Kṛṣṇaḥ kapir iva drume //
na ca Nemibhujastambhaḥ sūtramātram api kvacit /
sthanāc cacāla kiṃ Meroś cūli calati vātyayā //
Pāṇḍava-Caritam of Maladhāri Devaprabha, Kāvyamālā Series no. 93 (Bombay, 1911), 16.54-55.
35. Cf. paredyuḥsamaye pāṇijalasekasya Mādhavaḥ /
yiyāsur durgatiṃ lobhasutīvrānubhavodayāt //
durāśayaḥ surādhīśapūjyasyāpi mahātmanaḥ /
svarājyādānam āśaṅkya Nemer māyāvidāṃ varaḥ //
nirvedakarṇaṃ kiñcin nirīkṣyaiṣa viraṃsyati /
bhogebhya iti saṃcintya tadupāyavidhitsayā // ...
vyādhādhipair dhṛtānītaṃ nānāmṛgakadambakam /
vidhāyaikatra saṃkīrṇaṃ vṛtiṃ tatparito vyadhāt //
Uttarapurāṇa of Guṇabhadra [Varanasi: Bhāratīya Jñānapīṭha, 1954], 71.152-55.
36. See, for example, the story of Sīha Senāpati, *Vinaya-Piṭaka*, vol. 1 (London: Pali Text Society, 1879-83), 233 ff.
37. atha tāv api saṃkruddhāv udyamya Kurunandana /
erakāmuṣṭiparighau carantau jaghnatur yudhi // ...
Rāmaḥ samudravelāyāṃ yogam āsthāya pauruṣam /
tatyāja lokaṃ mānuṣyaṃ saṃyojyātmānam ātmani //
Rāmaniryāṇam ālokya bhagavān Devakīsutaḥ /
niṣasāda dharospasthe tūṣṇīm āsādya pippalam // ...
musalāvaśeṣāyaḥkhaṇḍakṛteṣur lubdhako Jarā /
mṛgasyākāraṃ tac caraṇaṃ vivyādha mṛgaśaṅkayā //
[*Śrimad Bhāgavata* 11.30.23-33]
bhagavān pitāmahaṃ vīkṣya vibhūtīr ātmano vibhuḥ /
saṃyojyātmani cātmānaṃ padmanetre nyamīlayat //
lokābhirāmāṃ svatanuṃ dhāraṇādhyānamaṅgalam /
yogadhāraṇayā "gneyyā 'dagdhvā dhāmāviśat svakam //
[*Śrimad Bhāgavata* 11.31.5-6]
38. puṇyodayāt purā prāptāv unnatiṃ yau janātigām /
cakrādiratnasampannau balinau BalaKeśavau //
puṇyakṣayāt tu tāv eva ratnabandhuvivarjitau /
prāṇamātraparīvārau śokabhāravaśīkṛtau //
prasthitau dakṣiṇām āśāṃ jīvitāśāvalambinau /
kṣutpipāsāpariśrāntau yātau satkāṃkṣiṇau pathi // ...
tasmin gate Haris tīvravraṇavedanayārditaḥ /
uttarābhimukho bhūtvā kṛtapañcanamaskṛtiḥ // ...
karmagauravadoṣeṇa mayā 'pi na kṛtaṃ tapaḥ /
ityādiśubhacintātmā bhaviṣyat tīrthakṛdd Hariḥ /
baddhāyuṣkatayā mṛtvā tṛtīyāṃ pṛthivīm itaḥ //
[*Harivaṃśapurāṇa* 62.1-3, 58-63]
39. bhaviṣyat tīrthakṛdd Hariḥ. [*Harivaṃśapurāṇa* 62.62]

40. For a chart of the twenty-four future Tīrthaṅkaras, see *Jainendra-Siddhānta-Kośa*, 2, p. 376.
41. See "Tīrthaṅkara," *Jainendra-Siddhānta-Kośa* 2, p. 372; P. S. Jaini, "Tīrthaṅkara-prakṛti and the Bodhisattva Path," *Journal of the Pali Text Society* (London) 9 (1981): 96-104.
42. Pāṇḍavaiḥ saha Jarāsutānvitais Tuṅgyabhikhyagirimastake tataḥ /
saṃvidhāya Haridehasaṃskriyāṃ Jāraseyasuvitīrṇarājyakaḥ //
[*Harivaṃśapurāṇa* 63.72]
43. jñātvā bhagavataḥ siddhiṃ pañca Pāṇḍavasādhavaḥ /
Śatruñjayagirau dhīrāḥ pratimáyoginaḥ sthitāḥ //
śukladhyānasamāviṣṭā BhīmĀrjunaYudhiṣṭhirāḥ /
kṛtvā 'ṣṭavidhakarmāntaṃ mokṣaṃ jagmus trayo 'kṣayam //
[*Harivaṃśapurāṇa* 65.18-22]
44. ekaṃ varṣaśataṃ kṛtvā tapo Haladharo muniḥ /
samārādhya pariprāpto brahmaloke sureśatām //
[*Harivaṃśapurāṇa* 65.33]
45. avadhijñātaKṛṣṇaś ca gatvā 'sau Vālukāprabhām /
dṛṣṭvā 'nujaṃ nijaṃ devo duḥkhitaṃ duḥkhito 'bhavat //
ehy ehi Kṛṣṇa yo 'haṃ te bhrātā jyeṣṭho Halāyudhaḥ /
brahmalokādhipo bhūtvā tvatsamīpam ihāgataḥ //
ity uktvā taṃ samuddhṛtya svarlokaṃ netum udyate /
deve tasya vyalīyanta gātrāṇi navanītavat //
tataḥ Kṛṣṇo jagau deva bhrātaḥ kiṃ vyarthaceṣṭitaiḥ / ...
bhrātar yāhi tataḥ svargaṃ bhuṅkṣva puṇyaphalaṃ nijam /
āyuṣo 'nte 'ham apy emi mokṣahetuṃ manuṣyatām //
āvāṃ tatra tapaḥ kṛtvā jinaśāsanasevayā /
mokṣasaukhyam avāpsyāvaḥ kṛtvā karmaparikṣayam //
[*Harivaṃśapurāṇa* 65.43-51]
46. āvāṃ putrādisaṃyuktau mahāvibhavasaṅgatu /
Bhārate darśayānyeṣāṃ vismayavyāptacetasām //
śaṅkhacakragadāpāṇir madīyapratimāgṛhaiḥ /
Bhārataṃ vyāpaya kṣetraṃ matkīrtiparivṛddhaye //
[*Harivaṃśapurāṇa* 65.52-53]
47. ityādi vacanaṃ tasya pratipadya sureśvaraḥ /
samyaktve śuddhim ākhyāpya Bhārataṃ kṣetram āgataḥ //
bhrātṛsnehavaśo devo yathoddiṣṭaṃ sa Viṣṇunā /
cakre divyavimānasthacakrilāṅgaladarśanam //
Vāsudevagṛhaiś cakre nagarādiniveśitaiḥ /
Viṣṇumohamayaṃ lokaṃ snehāt kiṃ vā na ceṣṭyate //
[*Harivaṃśapurāṇa* 65.54-56]
48. Also: dhik dhik svarmokṣasaukhyapratigham
atighanasnehamohaṃ janānām // [*Harivaṃśapurāṇa* 65.58d]
49. *Ādipurāṇa* of Jinasena, edited with Hindi translation by Pannalal Jain, 2 pts. Varanasi: Bhāratīya Jñānapīṭha, 1944.
50. *Uttarapurāṇa* of Jinasena and Guṇabhadra, edited with Hindi translation by Pannalal Jain (Varanasi: Bhāratīya Jñānapīṭha, 1944).
51. sa ca dharmaḥ purāṇārthaḥ purāṇaṃ pañcadhāḥ viduḥ /
kṣetraṃ kālaś ca tīrthaṃ ca satpuṃsas tadviceṣṭitam // [*Ādipurāṇa* 2.38]
52. See *Ādipurāṇa* 18. 51-60.
53. See the stotra of 1008 names of Ṛṣabha in *Ādipurāṇa* 25.99-217.

54. manuṣyajātir ekaiva jātinamodayodbhavā /
vṛttibhedāhitād bhedāc cāturvidhyam ihāśnute // [*Ādipurāṇa* 38.45]
55. *Triṣaṣṭiśalākāpuruṣacaritra* of Hemacandrasūri, trans. Helen M. Johnson, vol. 1, Gaekwad Oriental Series vol. 51, (1962), 343 ff.
56. See P. S. Jaini, *The Jaina Path of Purification* (Berkeley and Los Angeles: University of California Press, 1979), chap. 4.
57. teṣāṃ kṛtāni cihnāni sutraiḥ padmāvhayān nidheḥ /
upāttair brahmasūtrāhvair ekād ekādaśāntakaiḥ //
guṇabhūmikṛtād bhedāt kḷptayajñopavītinām /
satkāraḥ kriyate smaiṣām avratāś ca bahiḥ kṛtāḥ // [*Ādipurāṇa* 38.21-2]
58. sādhu vatsa kṛtam sādhu dhārmikadvijapūjanam /
kintu doṣānuṣaṅgo 'tra ko 'py asti sa niśamyatām // ...
tataḥ kaliyuge 'bhyarṇe jātivādāvalepataḥ /
bhraṣṭācārāḥ prapatsyante sanmārgapratyanīkatām //
te 'mi jātimadāviṣṭā vayam lokādhikā iti /
purā durāgamair lokaṃ mohayanti dhanāśayā //
ahiṃsālakṣaṇaṃ dharmaṃ dūsāyitvā durāśayāḥ //
codanālakṣaṇaṃ dharmaṃ poṣayiṣyanty amī bata //
pāpasūtradharā dhūrtāḥ prāṇimāraṇatatparāḥ /
vartsyadyuge pravartsyanti sanmārgaparipanthinaḥ //
dvijātisarjanaṃ tasmān nādya yady api doṣakṛt /
syād doṣabījam āyatyāṃ kupākhaṇḍapravartanāt // [*Ādipurāṇa* 39.45-54]
59. na svato 'gneḥ pavitratvaṃ devatārūpam eva vā /
kintv arhaddivyamūrtījyāsambandhi pāvano 'nalaḥ //
tataḥ pūjāṅgatām asya matvā 'rcanti dvijottamāḥ /
nirvāṇakṣetrapūjāvat tatpūjā 'to na duṣyati //
vyavahāranayāpekṣā tasyeṣṭā pūjyatā dvijaiḥ /
Jainair adhyavahāryo 'yaṃ nayo 'dyatve 'grajanmanaḥ //
[*Ādipurāṇa* 40.88-90]
60. *Triṣaṣṭiśalākāpuruṣacaritra* 1.6.546-56. See P. S. Jaini, "The Pure and the Auspicious in the Jaina Tradition," *Journal of Asian Perspectives* (Leiden) 1, no. 1 (1985): 69-76.
61. nirdiṣṭasthānalābhasya punar asya gaṇagrahaḥ /
syān mithyādevatāḥ svasmād viniḥsārayato gṛhāt //
iyantaṃ kālam ajñānāt pūjitāḥ sma kṛtādaram /
pūjyās tv idānīm asmābhir asmatsamayadevatāḥ //
tato 'pamṛṣitenālam anyatra svairam āsyatām /
iti prakāśam evaitān nītvā 'nyatra kvacit tyajet // [*Ādipurāṇa* 39.45-47]
62. See M. Winternitz, *A History of Indian Literature*, vol. 2, 445-49.
63. *Uvāsagadasāo* [i.e., *Upāsakadaśāḥ*], published in English as *The Religious Profession of an Uvāsaga*, trans. A. F. R. Hoernle, 2 vols., Calcutta: Bibliotheca Indica, 1888-90.
64. Draupadī ca drutaṃ mālāṃ kandhare 'bhyetya bandhure /
akarot karapadmābhyām Arjunasya varecchayā //
viprakīrṇā tadā mālā sahasā sahavartinām /
pañcānām api gātreṣu capalena nabhasvatā //
tataś capalalokasya tattvamūḍhasya kasyacit /
vāco vicerur ity uccair vṛtāḥ pañcānayety api //
[*Harivaṃśapurāṇa* 45.135-37]

65. atyantaśuddhavṛtteṣu ye 'bhyākhyānaparāyaṇāḥ /
tesāṃ tatprabhavaṃ pāpaṃ ko nivārayituṃ kṣamaḥ //
sadbhūtasyāpi doṣasya parakīyasya bhāṣaṇam /
pāpahetur amoghaḥ syād asadbhūtasya kim punaḥ //
prākṛtānām api prītyā samānadhanatā dhane /
na strīṣu triṣu lokeṣu prasiddhānāṃ kim ucyate //
mahāpuruṣakoṭīsthakūṭadoṣavibhāṣiṇām /
asatāṃ katham āyāti na jivhā śatakhaṇḍatām //
[*Harivaṃśapurāṇa* 45.152-35]

66. See *Triṣaṣṭiśalākāpuruṣacaritra*, vol. 5, G.O.S. vol. 139, 198-202.

67. Bhaṭṭāraka Vādicandra (ca. 1600) in his *Pāṇḍavapurāṇa* devotes the first *sarga* to describe the geneology of the Pāṇḍavas as allegedly found in the *Śivapurāṇa:* Śivapurāṇābhimata-Pāṇḍavotapattivarṇano nāma prathamaḥ sargaḥ. See my article "The *Mahābhārta* Motifs in the Jaina *Pāṇḍavapurāṇa*", referred to above in note 27.

68. For the Purāṇic passages dealing with the Buddhāvatāra, see R. C. Hazra, *Studies in the Upapurāṇas*, vol. 1, (Calcutta: Sanskrit College, 1958), 144 ff.; Ramshankara Bhattacharya, *Itihāsa-Purāṇa kā Anushīlan* (in Hindi) (Varanasi, 1963.), 280-86.

69. See P. S. Jaini, "The Disappearance of Buddhism and the Survival of Jainism: A Study in Contrast," *Studies in the History of Buddhism*, ed. A. K. Narain, (Delhi, 1980), 81-91.

70. The Daśaratha-Jātaka (Jātaka no. 461) and the Ghaṭa-Jātaka (Jātaka no. 454), respectively, refer to Rāma and Kaṇha. See *The Jātaka*, ed. V. Fausboll, (reprint; London: Pali Text Society, 1963).

71. ... bhagavān paramarṣibhiḥ prasādito Nābheḥ priyacikīrṣayā tadavarodhāyane Merudevyāṃ dharmān darśayitukāmo vātaraśanānāṃ śramaṇānām ṛṣīṇām ūrdhvamanthināṃ śuklayā tanuvāvatatāra. [*Śrīmad Bhāgavata* 5.3.20]

72. yasya kilānucaritam upākarṇya Koṅka-Veṅka-Kuṭakānāṃ rājā 'rhan nāmopaśikṣya kalāv adharma utkṛṣyamāṇe bhavitavyena vimohitaḥ svadharmapatham akutobhayam apahāya kupathapākhaṇḍam asamañjasaṃ nijamanīṣayā mandaḥ sampravartayiṣyate. yena ha vāva kalau manujāpasadā devamāyāmohitāḥ svavidhiniyogaśaucacāritravihīnā devahelanāny apavratāni nijanijecchayā gṛhṇānā asnānācamanāśuacakeśolluñcanādīni kalinā 'dharmabahulenopahatadhiyo brahmabrāhmaṇayajñapuruṣalokavidūṣakāḥ prāyeṇa bhaviṣyanti. te ca hy arvāktanayā nijalokayātrayā 'ndhaparamparayā āśvastās tamasy andhe svayam eva prapatiṣyanti. [*Śrīmad-Bhagavata* 5.6.9-11]

73. P. S. Jaini, "Jina Ṛṣabha as an *Avatāra* of Viṣṇu", *Bulletin of the School of Oriental and African Studies* 40, no. 2, (1977): 321-337.

74. Sanatkumāra uvāca:
asṛjac ca mahātejāḥ purusaṃ svātmasambhavam /
ekaṃ māyāmayaṃ teṣāṃ dharmavighnārtham Acyutaḥ //
muṇḍinaṃ mlānavastraṃ ca gumphipātrasamanvitam /
dadhānam puñjikāṃ haste cālayantaṃ pade pade //
vastrayuktaṃ tathā hastaṃ kṣīyamāṇaṃ mukhe sadā /
dharmeti vyāharantaṃ hi vācā viklavayā muniṃ //
... Viṣṇuḥ ... vacanaṃ cedam abravīt /
yad artham nirmito 'si tvaṃ nibodha kathayāmi te /
Arihaṃ nāma te syāt tu hy anyāni śubhāni ca / ...
Apabhraṃśamayaṃ śāstraṃ karmavādamayaṃ tathā /

śrautasmārtaviruddhaṃ ca varṇāśramavivarjitam //
gantum arhasi nāśārthaṃ muṇḍas Tripuravāsinām /
tamodharmaṃ samprakāśya nāśayasva puratrayam //
tataś caiva punar gantvā Marusthalayāṃ tvayā vibho /
sthātavyaṃ ca svadharmeṇa kalir yāvat samāvrajet //
tataḥ sa muṇḍī paripālayan Harer
ājñāṃ tathā nirmitavāṃś ca śiṣyān /
yathāsvarūpaṃ caturas tadānīṃ
māyāmayaṃ śāstram apāṭhayat svayam //
Śivapurāṇa ed. Ramateja Shastri Pandeya (Varanasi, Pandit Pustakālaya), 2 (Rudrasaṃhitā), 5 (Yuddhakāṇḍa), fourth *Adhyāya,* 1-24.

75. See *Prabhāvakacarita* of Prabhācandra, ed. Jinavijaya Muni, Singhi Jain Series, no. 13 (1940), 187-88.

76. Vyāsasandarbhitākhyāne śrīGaṅgeyaḥ pitāmahaḥ /
yuddhapraveśakāle 'sāv uvāca svaṃ paricchadam //
mama prāṇaparityāge tatra saṃskriyatāṃ tanuḥ /
na yatra ko 'pi dagdhaḥ prāg bhūmikhaṇḍe sadā śucau //
vidhāya nyāyyasaṅgrāmaṃ muktaprāṇe Pitāmahe /
vimṛṣya tadvacas te 'ṅgam utpāṭyāsaya yayur girau //
amuñcan devatāvāṇī kvāpi tatrodyayau tadā //
tathā hi—
atra Bhīṣmaśataṃ dagdhaṃ Pāṇḍavānāṃ śatatrayam /
Droṇācāryyasahasraṃ tu Karṇasaṃkhyā na vidyate //
[*Prabhāvakacarita* 188, 159-62]

77. rājā śrutvāha tatsatyaṃ vakti Jainarṣir eṣa yat /
atra brūtottaraṃ tathyaṃ yady asti bhavatāṃ mate //...
uttarānudayāt tatra maunam āśiśriyāṃs tadā / ...
rājñā satkṛtya Sūriś cābhāsyata svāgamoditam /
vyākhyānaṃ kurvatāṃ samyag dūṣaṇaṃ nāsti vo 'ṇv api //
[*Prabhāvakacarita* 188, 167-71]